DATE DUE

APR 2 6 2016	
MAY 1 0 2016	
MAR 2 2 2018	
APR 0 5 2018	

BRODART, CO.   Cat. No. 23-221

THE SECOND AMENDMENT

IN LAW AND HISTORY

*Historians and Constitutional Scholars
on the Right to Bear Arms*

EDITED BY CARL T. BOGUS

With contributions by
Michael A. Bellesiles, Carl T. Bogus, Michael C. Dorf, Daniel A. Farber,
Paul Finkelman, Steven J. Heyman, William G. Merkel, Jack N. Rakove,
Lois G. Schwoerer, Robert J. Spitzer, H. Richard Uviller

THE NEW PRESS   NEW YORK

Published in the United States by The New Press, New York, 2002
Distributed by W. W. Norton & Company, Inc., New York

LIBRARY OF CONGRESS CATALOGING-IN-PUBLICATION DATA

The Second Amendment in law and history : historians and constitutional scholars
on the right to bear arms / edited by Carl T. Bogus.
p.   cm.
Includes bibliographical references and index.
ISBN 1-56584-699-0 (hc.)
1. Firearms—Law and legislation—United States.   2. Firearms—Law and
legislation—United States—History.   3. United States.   Constitution.
2nd Amendment.   I. Bogus, Carl T.
KF3941 .S43 2001
344.73'0533—dc 21   2001034255

The New Press was established in 1990 as a not-for-profit alternative to the large, commercial
publishing houses currently dominating the book publishing industry. The New Press operates in
the public interest rather than for private gain, and is committed to publishing, in innovative ways,
works of educational, cultural, and community value that are often deemed insufficiently profitable.

The New Press, 450 West 41st Street, 6th floor, New York, NY 10036
www.thenewpress.com

Printed in the United States of America

2 4 6 8 10 9 7 5 3 1

Contents

Acknowledgments

This book grows out of a symposium that was held at the Chicago-Kent College of Law in April of 2000. Two institutions and two individuals deserve particular recognition. First, everyone who reads and benefits from the papers in this volume is indebted to the Joyce Foundation for providing major support. We are especially grateful to Roseanna Ander of the Joyce Foundation, who appreciated the importance of a symposium on the Second Amendment among the nation's very best scholars in constitutional law and history. It was Ms. Ander's vision, as well as her foundation's financial support, that made this project possible. Second, we are grateful to the Institute for Law and the Humanities at the Chicago-Kent College of Law and the *Chicago-Kent Law Review* for co-sponsoring the conference and publishing the papers in their original form. Special thanks is owed to Professor Steven J. Heyman of the Chicago-Kent College of Law for his valuable counsel and hard work in all aspects of this project.

—CARL T. BOGUS
September 2001
Bristol, Rhode Island

THE SECOND AMENDMENT

IN LAW AND HISTORY

1. The History and Politics of Second Amendment Scholarship: A Primer

Carl T. Bogus*

I f there is such a thing as settled constitutional law, the Second Amendment may have been its quintessential example. The United States Supreme Court addressed the amendment three[1] times—in 1876,[2] 1886,[3] and 1939[4]—and on each occasion held that it granted the people a right to bear arms only within the militia. Although in some circles today there is much discussion about what the word "militia" means, the Supreme Court had no trouble with the term. It held that the amendment referred to the militia defined in Article I, section 8, of the Constitution, that is, the militia organized by Congress and subject to joint federal and state control.[5] This is generally referred to as the "collective rights" model because it holds that the Second Amendment grants the people a collective right to an armed militia as opposed to an individual right to keep and bear arms for one's own purposes outside of, even notwithstanding, governmental regulation.

For nearly a century, the collective rights model remained not only widely accepted but uncontroversial. While from time to time Second Amendment challenges were raised to ordinances or court orders restricting possession of firearms, the courts—relying on the Supreme Court's three opinions—steadfastly adhered to the collective rights position.[6] As Robert J. Spitzer has discovered, from the time law review articles first began to be indexed, in 1887, until 1960, all such articles dealing with the Second Amendment endorsed the collective rights model.[7]

The first article advocating the individual rights interpretation appeared in 1960. Titled "The Right to Bear Arms: A Study in Judicial Misinterpretation," it was a student article, published in the *William and Mary Law Review*,[8] and, as Spitzer shows, it was marred by errors.[9] There is nothing in the article that suggests what motivated the author to write it, though the first source cited was the National Rifle Association's magazine *American Rifleman*.[10] The author conceded that courts adhered to the collective rights view. He wrote:

> The majority of the jurisdictions have concluded that both the United States Constitution and the various state constitutions, having a similar provision relating to the right to bear arms, refer to the militia as a whole composed and reg-

ulated by the state as it desires. The individual does not have the right to own or bear individual arms, such being a privilege not a right.[11]

However, arguing that "society has recognized that man has the right to preserve his own species," the author argued for a dual right, that is, both a collective right of the people to an armed, government-regulated militia and an individual right to own arms for self-defense.

Five years later the American Bar Foundation made the Second Amendment the topic of its annual essay contest in constitutional law. Contestants were asked to address the question: "What does the Second Amendment, guaranteeing the 'right of the people to keep and bear arms' mean? Does the guarantee extend to the keeping and bearing of arms for private purposes not connected with a militia?"[12] I do not know what prompted the foundation to make the right to bear arms the subject of its essay contest, but I can guess. On November 22, 1963, President John F. Kennedy was assassinated in Dallas, Texas. America was shaken. Two days later, Lee Harvey Oswald was gunned down by Jack Ruby, who had carried a concealed handgun into Dallas police headquarters. In response to these events, Senator Dodd of Connecticut introduced legislation to ban the interstate sale of firearms to anyone under eighteen years of age.[13] Publicly, the NRA supported the bill. Opposing it would have presented the NRA with a serious public relations problem; Oswald had bought the rifle used to kill Kennedy by mail order from an advertisement in *American Rifleman*,[14] and the NRA could not afford to be perceived as siding with assassins and criminals. Nevertheless, while officially supporting the bill the NRA spent $144,000 to alert its members about the proposed "anti-gun" legislation, suggesting they act individually to defeat "threats" to "loyal Americans."[15] The bill never came out of committee.

The Kennedy assassination awoke America to gun violence and to the existence of the gun lobby. A furious Senator Dodd called for an investigation "to identify and expose the activities of the powerful lobbyists who have successfully stopped gun legislation from being passed in every Congress."[16] NRA president Bartlett Rummel wound up testifying before Congress, whom he told: "We have not drummed up people from all over the country to contact you . . . these communications to you have more or less arisen spontaneously."[17] The NRA won the battle (and, indeed, many subsequent battles), but demands for gun control would continue to grow, and increasingly the gun lobby would employ the Second Amendment as a defense against those efforts.

This, then, was the context in which the American Bar Foundation made the Second Amendment the subject of its 1965 essay contest. The winning essay was written by a Chicago lawyer named Robert A. Sprecher and published by the *American Bar Association Journal* in two installments.[18] Sprecher's article is important because it was the first nonstudent article urging an individual right interpretation of the Second Amendment; it received a major award and was published in the journal with the widest circulation in the legal profession.

Sprecher argued that "We should find the lost Second Amendment, broaden its scope, and determine that it affords the right to arm a state militia and also the right of the individual to keep and bear arms."[19] Sprecher's article, skillfully written, employed a form of argument that was to be emulated by many of his successors. In support of his proposition, Sprecher cited Plato, Aristotle, Rousseau, Machiavelli, Adam Smith, Blackstone, Toynbee, the Magna Carta, the English Bill of Rights, the laws of Solon, the Declaration of Independence, Tom Paine, Alexander Hamilton, James Madison, Joseph Story, John Marshall, Hugo Black, Earl Warren, the Universal Declaration of Human Rights, and other authorities—all within nine pages. Needless to say, little effort was made to place quotations in context, within either the times and circumstances in which they were made nor the documents from which they were snipped. This was an argument based not on a careful reading of history or on legal analysis but on *Bartlett's Familiar Quotations.*

Sprecher's article had another problem as well. Claiming that the "few modern writers on the subject of the right to keep and bear arms are sharply divided as to whether the right is personal or relates solely to the militia," Sprecher cited a total of four articles, two for each side of the debate. For the individual rights side, Sprecher cited the student article in the *William and Mary Law Review* and another student article, published fifteen years earlier in the *University of Pennsylvania Law Review.*[20] This second article, however, was badly misused. The author did not write to endorse the individual rights interpretation of the Second Amendment but to advocate uniform firearm laws, including a national licensing system for sportsmen and others carrying firearms. He argued that the Second Amendment did not bar such regulation; moreover, he suggested that if the amendment were designed to provide a means to rebel against an oppressive government it had become an anachronism in the age of modern warfare.[21]

Sprecher had manufactured out of whole cloth the so-called sharp division over the Second Amendment. In fact, he himself was only the second author to endorse the individual rights position. Sprecher's article, with its thoughtless stream of quotes masquerading as scholarship, was to become the forerunner of an entire genre of Second Amendment writings, though not immediately. By the end of the decade only one other article, a ten-page, state bar journal article, had endorsed the individual rights model. At this juncture, a total of three articles endorsed the individual rights model while twenty-two subscribed to the collective rights view.[22]

Over the next two decades things changed. From 1970 to 1989, twenty-five articles adhering to the collective rights view were published (nothing unusual there), but so were twenty-seven articles endorsing the individual rights model.[23] However, at least sixteen of these articles—about 60 percent—were written by lawyers who had been directly employed by or represented the NRA or other gun rights organizations, although they did not always so identify themselves in the author's footnote.[24] Two of these authors, Stephen P. Halbrook and Don B. Kates, Jr., deserve special mention. Each has turned himself into something of a cottage industry. Though, in a sense, they have become competitors, Halbrook and Kates have had strikingly similar careers. Both were briefly academics—Kates taught in a law school for three years and Halbrook in university philosophy departments for nine years—who then left the academy to open law practices in which they represent gun rights organizations and firearm manufacturers, among others. Each has become a celebrity within the gun rights community, maintaining his prominence with a stream of books and articles. Between them they have, to date, written or edited at least eight books,[25] twenty-three law review articles,[26] and countless op-ed pieces and other writings about the right to bear arms and the evils of gun control.[27] Kates writes a monthly column titled "Gun Rights" for *Handguns* magazine.[28] Books by both men can be purchased via the NRA Web site.[29] Halbrook and Kates have their own Web sites as well, promoting themselves to potential clients and fans (Kates's site includes pictures of his son and his favorite works of art, featuring *Liberty Leading the People* by Eugène Delacroix, picturing Liberty leading the charge against the government while clasping a banner in one hand and a musket in the other).[30] One difference between them is intramural within the gun rights community: Halbrook was allied with the NRA and Kates with competing organizations, such as the Second Amendment Foundation.

Halbrook, especially, advocated an insurrectionist theory of the Second Amendment. That is, he argues that the amendment is designed to ensure that citizens are armed and ready to fight against their own government should it become tyrannical. Halbrook believes the framers wanted "a force of the whole armed populace . . . to counter inroads on freedom by government,"[31] and "to guarantee the right of the people to have 'their private arms' to prevent tyranny and to overpower an abusive standing army or select militia."[32]

In 1994 Harvard University Press published *To Keep and Bear Arms: The*

Origins of an Anglo-American Right,[33] by Joyce Lee Malcolm. Praised by in-surrectionists as "the definitive historical treatise on the right to bear arms,"[34] and ballyhooed in *American Rifleman,*[35] Malcolm's book went into a third printing within a year of its initial publication. The book received attention outside the gun rights community as well. Justice Antonin Scalia pronounced the book "excellent" and noted he was impressed that Malcolm was not a "member of the Michigan Militia, but an Englishwoman."[36] It was an amusing assumption. Malcolm's name may sound British, and Bentley College, where Malcolm teaches history, may sound like a college at Oxford, but in fact Malcolm was born and raised in Utica, New York, and Bentley is a business college in Massachusetts.

The Second Amendment was derived from the English Declaration of Rights of 1689, which included a provision that "Subjects which are Protes-tants may have Arms for their Defence suitable to their Conditions and as allowed by Law."[37] Malcolm's thesis is that this provision created an individ-ual, English right to have arms—that it gave individuals the right to keep and bear arms notwithstanding the enactment of any laws to the contrary—and that the American founders accepted this legacy in the Second Amendment. Al-though this thesis may sound plausible to those uninitiated in English history, it has been severely criticized.[38] The provision was not meant to address *whether* the government could regulate the possession of arms (everyone ac-cepted that it could) but rather *who* could do so, King or Parliament. This is what the phrase "as allowed by law" was all about. Parliament passed laws al-lowing certain subjects to have specified weapons, and the king was obliged to respect Parliament's law-making authority in this, as well as other, areas. Criti-cisms notwithstanding, Malcolm's work remains one of the foundational texts of the individual rights school.

A new chapter in the history of Second Amendment scholarship began in 1989 when Sanford Levinson published an article titled "The Embarrassing Second Amendment" in the *Yale Law Journal.*[39] What was significant was not so much the content of the article—it was a twenty-three-page essay saying lit-tle more than what had been said before by Halbrook and Kates (both of whom it cited)—but the pedigree of the author. Levinson, who holds an endowed chair in one of the nation's elite law schools, is a prominent constitutional scholar as well as a liberal Democrat. Though on the one hand Levinson de-nied he was taking a position at all—"[i]t is not my style to offer 'correct' or 'in-correct' interpretations of the Constitution," he wrote[40]—the tone and tenor of the essay made clear Levinson's affinity not only for the individual rights model but for insurrectionist theory as well. The implications of what he viewed as a proper reading of history, Levinson wrote, "might push us in un-expected, even embarrassing, directions: just as ordinary citizens should participate actively in governmental decision-making through offering their own deliberative insights, rather than be confined to casting ballots once every two or three years for those very few individuals who will actually make decisions, so should ordinary citizens participate in the process of law enforcement and defense of liberty rather than rely on professional peacekeepers, whether we call them standing armies or police." [41]

It is one thing for gun zealots to believe it is acceptable that disgruntled citizens take up arms, whether against the elected government or as vigilantes; it is quite another for a prominent, constitutional law professor to do so. And that was precisely Levinson's point. He suggested constitutional scholars had not taken the Second Amendment seriously simply because they did not like it. They did not like guns; and they did not like people who liked guns. [42] Here was the true liberal—educated at Harvard Law School, writing in the *Yale Law Journal,* a member not of the NRA but of the ACLU—willing to seek truth even if it offended his personal, political, or class prejudices and predilections.

Levinson did not say this directly, and it was not quite true. "I have no personal interest in possessing or using a firearm," Levinson declared in a more obscure piece, noting his membership in the ACLU. [43] In fact, Levinson's commitment to insurrectionist theory stems as much from political and policy preferences as it does from constitutional fidelity. Levinson is a New Deal Democrat who wants his party to stop supporting gun control because he believes it needs gun owners in its coalition. [44] Moreover, he says he has "learned to treat with respect the views of those who view a general prohibition of firearm ownership as an important step toward tyranny. We should learn to take seriously the bumper sticker that states, 'If guns are outlawed, only the government will have guns.' " [45] Levinson's genuine insurrectionist bent comes through in his version of the slogan, which traditionally reads, "If guns are outlawed, only outlaws will have guns." [46]

Contrarian positions get play. Clarence Thomas got attention from the Reagan administration because he was a black man and an affirmative action recipient who opposed affirmative action. Law professors writing articles that say the courts are right and have always been right, or liberal Democrats supporting gun control, draw yawns. Levinson's "Embarrassing Second Amendment" piece got attention, both in the popular press [47] and in the law reviews. [48] It remains perhaps the best-known law review article on the subject.

Buoyed by the number of articles supporting its position, and the big catch in Sanford Levinson, the NRA launched a concerted effort to promote more writing supporting the individual rights position. Through a related foundation, the NRA began distributing large sums to friendly scholars. In 1991 and 1992 it dispensed grants totaling $38,369.45 to Halbrook alone. [49] In 1992 the NRA helped fund a new organization called Academics for the Second

Amendment (A2A) headed by Professor Joseph E. Olson of the Hamline University School of Law, who had recently been elected to the NRA's National Board of Directors.[50] Though its published advertisements said A2A sought to "foster intellectually honest discourse" on the Second Amendment,[51] only the like-minded were invited to participate.[52] In 1994 the NRA launched an annual "Stand Up for the Second Amendment" essay contest, offering a first prize of $25,000.[53]

The NRA effort would turn out to be a great success. At least fifty-eight law review articles endorsing the individual rights view would be published during the 1990s (as opposed to twenty-nine favoring the collective rights position).[54] The NRA and its allies would make much of this count. More important, other prominent scholars would join the NRA camp.

In 1991 and 1992, Akhil Reed Amar of the Yale Law School published two articles about the Bill of Rights in which he addressed the Second Amendment, among other provisions.[55] Amar saw the Second Amendment as a right belonging to the people collectively, yet he embraced insurrectionist theory nevertheless. "[T]o see the Amendment as primarily concerned with an individual right to hunt, or protect one's home, is like viewing the heart of speech and assembly clauses as the right of persons to meet to play bridge, or to have sex," he wrote.[56] "In the event of central tyranny," he continued, "state governments could do what colonial governments had done in 1776: organize and mobilize their citizens into an effective fighting force capable of beating even a large standing army."[57]

Yet in Amar's view this does not mean that the Second Amendment pertains to the government militia. "A good many scholars have read the Amendment as protecting only arms-bearing in organized 'state militias,' such as SWAT teams and National Guard units. If this reading were accepted the Second Amendment would be at base a right of state governments rather than citizens," which, as Amar saw it, is not the case because the right is given not to the states but to the people.[58] Citing Halbrook, Amar concluded that "militia" means "all Citizens capable of bearing arms," because that is how the term was then understood.[59]

What Amar seemed not to recognize, or at least did not acknowledge, is that "militia" is defined in the Constitution itself.[60] The founders disagreed about how the militia ought to be organized. For example, Madison favored a universal militia while Hamilton argued for a select militia.[61] However, they agreed as a constitutional matter to leave this up to Congress; and the Constitution expressly gives Congress the power to organize the militia. Thus, the militia is what Congress decides it is, regardless of whether it differs from an eighteenth-century model. Currently, the militia is indisputably the National Guard because Congress has so decided[62] (and, Amar's suggestion notwithstanding, no one reasonably contends the militia includes SWAT teams). If Amar wrestled directly with Congress' power to define the militia, he might be forced to reconsider his insurrectionist view. How can the armed militia be a bulwark against governmental tyranny if it is organized and regulated by the government itself?

In 1994 William Van Alstyne of the Duke University School of Law—citing Halbrook, Kates, and Levinson, among others—published a nineteen-page essay endorsing the individual rights position.[63] Van Alstyne rather ambiguously suggested that the founders' purpose was to allow the people to keep and bear arms against government tyranny.[64] If this is indeed what Van Alstyne meant to argue, he undercut his argument by stating (without explanation) that the right to keep and bear arms extends to handguns but not howitzers. If the right is designed to allow the people to resist government tyranny, it would have a greater application to weapons needed to combat the government's military forces than to those designed for self-protection, and would apply to howitzers before it would to handguns.

Before the decade drew to an end, two other prominent scholars endorsed an individual rights view, though neither did so in a way that could fully please the NRA. Leonard W. Levy, winner of the Pulitzer Prize in history in 1969, devoted a short chapter to the Second Amendment in a book about the Bill of Rights.[65] "Believing that the amendment does not authorize an individual right is wrong," Levy declared. "The right to bear arms is an individual right."[66] Moreover, wrote Levy, "the right is an independent one, altogether separate from maintenance of a militia."[67] At first blush that seems like a strange conclusion, since Levy begins his discussion by making much of the specific mention of the militia in the amendment's preamble,[68] and states that the amendment was, at least in part, designed to prevent the federal government from destroying the state militias.[69] But Levy attempted to resolve the contradiction by explaining that the militia had become an anachronism because we no longer depend on it for national defense. Levy flatly rejected the insurrectionist view. "An armed public is not the means of keeping a democratic government responsible and sensitive to the needs of the people," and allowing preparation for revolution leads to anarchy.[70] As Levy saw it, although the militia purpose of the right has evaporated over time, a remaining residue "still enables citizens to protect themselves against law breakers."[71] In Levy's view this is not only a right subject to governmental regulation but, indeed, "a right that must be regulated."[72]

The most celebrated new member of the individual rights view is Laurence H. Tribe of Harvard Law School, one of the best-known law professors in America. In 1999 Tribe released the long-awaited third edition of his famous treatise, *American Constitutional Law.*[73] Tribe and his publisher promoted the book by broadcasting the fact that Tribe, for the first time, had addressed the Second Amendment, and that this most prominent of liberal constitutional scholars had concluded that the amendment guarantees an individual right. "I've gotten an avalanche of angry mail from apparent liberals who said, 'How could you?,'" Tribe told one interviewer. "But as someone who takes the Constitution seriously, I thought I had a responsibility to see what the Second Amendment says, and how it fits."[74] This got attention. Tribe's view was widely reported in the press[75]; and Charlton Heston invoked Tribe's name in his president's column in the NRA's magazine.[76]

Tribe wanted to transcend what he perceived to be a petty and partisan debate. He wrote in his treatise that Second Amendment scholarship was "radically underdeveloped" because of an insistence on seeing the right in "binary terms," that is, scholars subscribed either to the individual rights school and argued that all forms of gun control were unconstitutional, or to the collective rights school and argued the Second Amendment was irrelevant.[77] Tribe was going to rise above this and occupy a sensible middle position. Relying heavily on Amar, Tribe seemed to argue that because the militia included all able-bodied, adult, white males in the eighteenth century, a right given to militia members would, after the Thirteenth and Nineteenth Amendments, belong to everyone.[78] Tribe tried not to follow Amar into the insurrectionist thicket, but did not clearly define where this left him. Tribe wrote that "the core meaning of the Second Amendment is a populist/republican/federalism one."[79]

It is, of course, impossible to delineate the boundaries of a right, to decide what regulations are constitutionally permissible, without first clearly articulating the fundamental purposes of that right. Only then can one judge whether a restriction impinges on a fundamental purpose of the right. Tribe's formulation of a core purpose fulfilling "populist/republican/federalism" objectives is too vague to be useful.[80]

Tribe also wrote that "gun ownership today has little political significance and . . . might well be thought to destroy rather than promote the kinds of values with which civic republicanism is associated."[81] The essence of what he seemed to be saying was: the Second Amendment grants individuals a constitutional right; all constitutional rights must be taken seriously; no rights are absolute; and gun control measures that "seek only to prohibit a narrow type of weaponry (such as assault rifles) or to regulate ownership by means of waiting periods, registration, mandatory safety devises, or the like . . . are plainly constitutional."[82] But why are bans on assault weapons clearly constitutional?

Tribe writes that "it is clear that Congress may not, consistent with the Second Amendment, prohibit state militias from equipping their members with *appropriate* weaponry, just as Congress may not enact a general ban on membership in a state militia."[83] But what is appropriate weaponry? Appropriate for what purpose? Tribe says bans on assault rifles are clearly constitutional, even though National Guardsmen are armed with assault weapons. Presumably, Tribe means that it is constitutionally permissible to ban assault weapons in private hands, outside National Guard regulation, but that depriving a state of an armed National Guard would be problematic. At bottom, however, this means there is no individual right, only a collective right, to an armed state militia.

Perhaps what Tribe was saying is that the Second Amendment gives states the right to have armed militia so that they will be able to play an active role in preserving their own security. The states have the principal obligation of protecting public safety within their borders, and the federal structure would be upset if the states were entirely beholden to the federal government for whatever armed force is necessary to protect public safety and welfare. Thus, while the main body of the Constitution gives Congress the authority to arm and organize the militia, the Second Amendment forbids Congress from either insisting upon unarmed militia or organizing the militia out of existence. But if this indeed is Tribe's position then, once again, his protestations notwithstanding, Tribe essentially embraces the collective rights model, the sum and substance of which is that the Second Amendment protects the right of the states to have armed militia.

Following the horrific event in Littleton, Colorado, on April 20, 1999, Tribe and Amar seemed to have second thoughts about the Second Amendment, or at least about the political ramifications of their work. Amar published an article in the *New Republic*,[84] and Amar and Tribe together wrote an op-ed article for the *New York Times*.[85] The theme of both pieces was the same: no right is absolute so (whatever the Second Amendment may mean) "reasonable"[86] and "[r]ealistic"[87] gun controls are constitutionally permissible.

Tribe and Amar also joined a group of more than forty historians and law professors in signing a letter to NRA president Charlton Heston, publicized in an advertisement in the *New York Times*, that stated "the law is well-settled that the Second Amendment permits broad and intensive regulation of firearms."[88] Unfortunately, little was clear beyond Tribe's and Amar's desire to dissociate themselves and their work from the gun lobby. Writing together, Tribe and Amar stated that the core of the right to bear arms is "self-protection."[89] That was an interesting term, for it straddled both self-defense and collective defense without definitely including or excluding either. Amar's *New Republic* piece, published less than three months after the event at Littleton, was even more obfuscatory. Amar connected the right to bear arms with the militia and military affairs, and then continued:

Statists are right to see the amendment as localist and to note that law and government help bring the militia together. So, too, with the jury. Twelve private citizens who simply get together on their own to announce the guilt of a fellow citizen are not a lawful jury but a lynch mob. Similarly, private citizens who choose to own guns today are not a well-regulated militia of the people; they are gun clubs. But what the statist reading misses is that, when the law summons the citizenry together, these citizens act as the people *outside* the government, rather than as a professional and permanent government bureaucracy. A lynch mob is not a jury, but neither is the Occupational Safety and Health Administration. Likewise, the NRA and other gun clubs are not the militia, but neither is the National Guard.[90]

Unfortunately, while Amar tells us many things that the militia is not, he fails to say what it *is*. Worse, Amar's thesis is self-contradictory. A militia is like a jury in that it embodies collective action; juries are not lynch mobs because they act under lawful authority (and, more than that, act only under close supervision and control by the court); however, people in the militia would be acting outside the government. A body of citizens acting under lawful authority, closely regulated by the state and acting outside of government is an oxymoron. Finally, Amar never explains why he wants to define militia instead of allowing Congress to do so, as provided in Article I, section 8, of the Constitution.[91] Why is the militia not the National Guard when Congress says it is, and when the Constitution gives Congress the authority to organize the militia as it sees fit?

Levinson, Amar, Van Alstyne, Levy, and Tribe's endorsement of the individual rights position was politically important because of who they were, not what they said. Along with Cass R. Sunstein of the University of Chicago Law School, Harvard's Larry Tribe and Yale's Akhil Amar may be two of the three most prominent constitutional law scholars currently teaching in American law schools. According to recent surveys of the legal literature, Tribe's book, *American Constitutional Law,* is the most-cited legal treatise of all time; Amar was, at the time of the survey, the most-cited legal scholar under age forty; Van Alstyne and Levy are among the most-cited legal scholars in America; and Levinson's articles are among those most frequently published by the nation's top ten law reviews.[92] People who are neither lawyers nor academics may be amazed that there are studies collecting such data; but, of course, the fact that there are speaks volumes. In this status-obsessed profession, the individual rights model had achieved status by association. "This was a frivolous, crazy position, and it is no more," remarked Sunstein, who has not studied the issue and was a neutral in the debate.[93]

It was, however, status more than new facts, ideas, or analysis that these five scholars brought to the individual rights model. These writings comprised something of an academic chain letter. Levinson's endorsement of the individual rights position in the august pages of the *Yale Law Journal* made it easier for Amar to follow suit, which in turn made it easier for Van Alstyne, and so on. Undoubtedly, each scholar took comfort from those preceding him.

If it seems that I have rather cursorily dismissed the work of these five serious, highly regarded scholars, it is because their work on this topic is itself rather cursory. None of the five rolled up his sleeves and gave the Second Amendment the kind of thorough treatment that often characterizes their other work. Levinson's twenty-three-page essay represents the longest and most carefully considered treatment of the subject among the group, but Levinson himself made it clear that his principal purpose in writing was to stimulate thinking and writing by others rather than to provide a definitive statement on the subject. And, as discussed, the work by the other four are all plagued by internal inconsistencies.

Much has also been made out of the sheer volume of articles supporting the individual rights position. In a brief asking the Supreme Court to reconsider the right to bear arms, Academics for the Second Amendment told the Court (somewhat misleadingly) that thirty-seven of the forty-one most recent law review articles addressing the amendment endorsed the individual rights model.[94] A2A was disdainful of the opposing articles. "Their quality does not exceed their quantity," A2A told the Court. "Three of the four articles were written by employees of anti-gun lobbying groups, the fourth by a politician; all appear in minor reviews and none were published on their merits—each being in a symposium in which anti-gun groups and/or individuals were invited to submit articles dealing with their position."[95] Indeed, others wrote, so great is the new "consensus" about the Second Amendment that "much as physicists and cosmologists speak of a 'Standard Model' in terms of the creation and evolution of the universe," the individual rights model could now be renamed the "standard model."[96] The term "standard model" has caught on, used by both those who accept and reject its thesis.

These three elements—the mass of individual rights literature, the endorsement of the five prominent scholars, and use of the term "standard model"—combined to lead many to believe that new scholarship has reached a new consensus. Two Supreme Court justices have taken note of these events and have suggested that the Court should reconsider the Second Amendment. Citing Amar, Levinson, Van Alstyne, Halbrook, and Kates, among others, Justice Thomas wrote: "Marshaling an impressive array of historical evidence, a growing body of scholarly commentary indicates that the 'right to keep and bear arms' is, as the Amendment text suggests, a personal right." Thomas went on to express the hope that the Court would be able to reconsider the Second Amendment at a future date.[97] And citing Van Alstyne and standard modeler Joyce Lee Malcolm, Justice Antonin Scalia has noted that he would find it "strange" if the Second Amendment does not grant an individual right.[98]

Until recently, there was little reason for scholars agreeing with the collective rights model to address the topic. There is, after all, no panache in scholars writing articles that proclaim that the courts have always been right on a particular topic. But the writings of the five prominent endorsers of the individual rights position stimulated scholars on the other side of the debate as well. Several are of special significance.

In a lengthy article published in the *New York Review of Books,* which he later expanded and incorporated into his book *A Necessary Evil: A History of American Distrust of Government,* Garry Wills not only severely critiqued the conclusions of Halbrook, Kates, and Malcolm, but questioned their competence.[99]

Wills argued that the group often took quotes out of context and failed to understand their eighteenth-century meanings. Wills noted, for example, that Kates and Halbrook both argued that the Second Amendment was clearly intended to guarantee a personal right to carry personal weapons since it gave people the right to bear arms. This meant, claimed Kates and Halbrook, that people had a right to weapons they could carry rather than, say, howitzers or missiles. Halbrook supported this argument with an entry from Noah Webster's original dictionary, which referred to bearing arms in a coat. Thus, argued Halbrook, the Second Amendment guaranteed people a right to possess the kind of weapons they could carry in a coat pocket. One could almost hear Wills laughing as he showed that "bear arms" was a term of art meaning participating in military affairs. "One does not bear arms against a rabbit," he observed. And as for the business about bearing arms in a coat, Wills explained that this had to do with heraldry, not haberdashery. Webster was referring to a coat of arms.

Wills criticized Amar and Levinson for their insurrectionist views as well, which he related to their other work. His weighing in so forcefully on the collective rights side was, of course, significant in itself. As a recipient of the Pulitzer Prize in history and one of the most respected public intellectuals in America, Wills provided a counterbalance of authority. But the greatest significance of Wills's work in this area was his devastating critique of the standard modelers. By drawing effectively on his own background in the classics, Wills showed how badly standard modelers were reading eighteenth-century language. He showed, as well, how these errors came to permeate the literature as the standard modelers cited one another in a revolving circle of concurrence and purported validation.

Three historians—Michael A. Bellesiles of Emory University (who is a contributor to this volume), Saul Cornell of Ohio State University, and Don Higginbotham of the University of North Carolina—have made significant contributions to the debate. Bellesiles showed that, contrary to myth, there were relatively few guns but rigorous firearms regulation in eighteenth-century America.[100] Cornell compared the rhetoric of eighteenth-century anti-Federalists in Pennsylvania—whom standard modelers often quote to show that the founders believed in an individual right to have guns—with their actual practice of firearm regulation. Much as Wills had explained how standard modelers did not understand eighteenth-century terms of art, Cornell showed that standard modelers were not sensitive to the realities of the times and the agendas and beliefs of the people they were quoting. He accused standard modelers of practicing "law office history," that is, failing to adequately understand the relevant period. Cornell went on to persuasively argue that, contrary to how their words are often portrayed today, many anti-Federalists "understood liberty in terms rather different than those of modern liberal rights–based constitutional theories" and considered the right to keep and bear arms to be connected with service in the government-regulated militia.[101]

Higginbotham, who is probably the foremost authority on early American military affairs, has shown that it is dangerous to give too much weight to anti-Federalist rhetoric about the right to bear arms or the composition of the militia.[102] "Congress, composed largely of Federalists, showed no inclination whatsoever to mollify Antifederalists on the subject of the militia," he wrote. Indeed, Higginbotham argued, rhetoric alone, Federalist or anti-Federalist, will never get us very far in understanding the founders' intent regarding the Second Amendment. Higginbotham called the amendment "heavy in emotional content but thin in substance" and offered his best guess that Madison intended it to mean that the states could arm and equip the militia if the federal government failed to do so, and, perhaps, to imply that the states could use the militia as they saw fit when they were not in federal service.

Finally, among the significant works prior to the publication of this volume, I immodestly include one of my own, in which I argued that Madison wrote the Second Amendment to assure his constituents in Virginia and the South generally that Congress could not undermine the slavery system by disarming the militia, on which the South relied for slave control.[103] It is my increasingly firm belief that this explains the mystery as to why Madison would write a provision that gives Congress the authority to organize the militia as it sees fit, which includes the right to who serves in the militia, and yet gives the people a right to keep and bear arms within the militia. In essence, Madison's provision states that Congress cannot use its power to organize and arm the militia to wholly deprive the states of an armed militia. Put another way, in order to ensure that they have a degree of control over their own security, the states have some minimum right to an armed militia.

With the publication of this volume, the debate over the Second Amendment moves to a new plane. When in 1989 Sanford Levinson wrote "The Embarrassing Second Amendment," he lamented that Second Amendment scholarship represented something of a backwater, that scholars of the first rank were not taking the amendment seriously. That is no longer the case. The reader holds in his or her hands an anthology by some of the keenest minds working today in the fields of constitutional law and history. This is a group whose work has been recognized with a host of prestigious awards, up to and including the Pulitzer Prize. They do not disappoint, and have produced a collection of highly original work. No one will accuse them of treating the subject cursorily. And they know how to write; the reader will find their work not only provocative but a pleasure to read. Everyone who believes this topic deserves to be taken seriously will be grateful.

2. Lost and Found: Researching the Second Amendment

Robert J. Spitzer*

THE MEANING OF THE SECOND AMENDMENT

Few parts of the Constitution are so often invoked, yet so misunderstood, as the Second Amendment. Polemic aside, the meaning of the Second Amendment is relatively clear. As the text itself says, "A well regulated Militia, being necessary to the security of a free State, the right of the people to keep and bear Arms, shall not be infringed." Supreme Court Chief Justice Warren Burger wrote that the Second Amendment "must be read as though the word 'because' was the opening word,"[1] as in "[Because] a well regulated Militia [is] necessary to the security of a free State . . ." As debate concerning the Second Amendment preceding and during the First Congress made clear, the amendment was added to allay the concerns of anti-Federalists and others who feared that state sovereignty, and more specifically the ability of states to meet military emergencies on their own, would be impinged or neglected by the new federal government, which had been given vast new powers, particularly and alarmingly over the use of military force. In other words, the inclusion of the Second Amendment embodied the Federalist assurance that the state militias would be allowed to continue as a viable military and political supplement to the national army at a time when military tensions within and between the states ran high, suspicions of a national standing army ran even higher, and military takeovers were the norm in world affairs. Debate concerning what became the Second Amendment during the First Congress dealt with the narrow military questions of the need to maintain civilian government control over the military; the military unreliability of militias as compared with professional armies; possible threats to liberties from armies versus militias; and whether to codify the right of conscientious objectors to opt out of military service (an early version of the amendment included such language).[2]

As four Supreme Court cases and more than twenty lower federal court rulings have made clear, the Second Amendment pertains only to citizen service in a government-organized and -regulated militia (remembering that militiamen were expected to bring their own firearms), the regulation of which specifically appertains to Congress in Article I, section 8.[3] The abysmal performance of civilian (also referred to as unorganized or general) militias in the

War of 1812 essentially ended the government's use of such forces to meet military emergencies. Millett and Maslowski noted that "After the War of 1812 military planners realized that no matter how often politicians glorified citizen-soldiers . . . reliance on the common militia to reinforce the regular Army was chimerical."[4] As Ehrman and Henigan observed, the "history of the state militias between 1800 and the 1870s is one of total abandonment, disorganization, and degeneration."[5] Instead, the government came to rely on professional military forces that were expanded in times of emergency by the military draft. The select or volunteer militias used in the Civil War (which also date to colonial times) were institutionalized and brought under federal military authority as the National Guard early in the twentieth century.[6] Further, even if the Second Amendment did pertain to personal weapons ownership or use outside of militia service, the court has refused to incorporate it via the Fourteenth Amendment, unlike most of the rest of the Bill of Rights, thereby limiting its relevance only to federal action. In any case, the Second Amendment provides no protection for personal weapons use, including hunting, sporting, collecting, or even personal self-protection (this latter is covered under criminal law and the common law tradition).

Despite the definitive nature of constitutional reading, historical lessons, and court rulings, some legal writers, publishing primarily in law journals, have sought to spin out other interpretations of the Second Amendment.[7] These authors have succeeded via these journals in finding legitimacy for a variety of erroneous and even nonsensical arguments concerning the meaning of the Second Amendment. Arguments advanced in these publications have, in turn, seeped into the public press. When this happens, it may easily magnify what might otherwise be a minor distortion.

To take one example, an article in *The Wall Street Journal* reported late in 1999 that one of the key factors leading to new academic interest in the Second Amendment was "a recently unearthed series of clues to the Framers' intentions." Two examples are cited in the article. One is an allegedly recently discovered "early draft" of the Second Amendment authored by James Madison where "he made 'The right of the people' the first clause [of the Second Amendment]. . . ." The second is a letter written by Thomas Jefferson to an English scholar, named John Cartwright, in which "Jefferson wrote that 'the constitutions of most of our states assert, that all power is inherent in the people; . . . that it is their right and duty to be at all times armed.' "[8] No citations or attributions are provided in the article as to who made these "discoveries," or who claimed that they are new or significant. In fact, despite the article's claim to the contrary, neither of these quotes is "recently unearthed," nor are they "clues" to the meaning of the Second Amendment. The first of these quotes has been known to scholars of the Constitution for decades, as it was part of Madison's original Bill of Rights resolution, offered in the House of Representatives on June 7, 1789, and has been a part of publicly available congressional records from that day to this. It has also been cited in past writings on the Second Amendment and the Bill of Rights.[9] It is thus no new discovery, nor does it alter what is already known about the Second Amendment.[10]

The Jefferson letter to Cartwright was reprinted in *The Writings of Thomas Jefferson*, published in 1904. Leaving aside the facts that Jefferson did not attend the Constitutional Convention of 1787, was not a member of the First Congress, and penned the letter in question in 1824, the full quotation from which the brief excerpt above was drawn makes clear what Jefferson was writing about.

> The constitutions of most of our States assert, that all power is inherent in the people; that they may exercise it by themselves, in all cases to which they think themselves competent (as in electing functionaries executive and legislative, and deciding by a jury of themselves, in all judiciary cases in which any fact is involved,) or they may act by representatives, freely and equally chosen; that it is their right and duty to be at all times armed; that they are entitled to freedom of person, freedom of religion, freedom of property, and freedom of the press.[11]

Jefferson was referring to state constitutions, and offering a seat-of-the-pants listing of Bill of Rights freedoms, therefore including the reference to being armed as a right and duty (remembering that federal and state laws then required men of militia age to be so armed for militia service). Nothing Jefferson said in this letter amounts to a new contribution to the understanding of the Second Amendment, nor does it contradict existing meaning. Yet a reader of *The Wall Street Journal* might reasonably conclude that these so-called new clues to the Second Amendment are both, when in fact they are neither.

LIBERAL, LIBERAL, LIBERAL

Two particular claims have surfaced with increasing regularity in the media pertaining to new interpretations of the Second Amendment in what is generally described as the "individualist" view. One is the claim, offered with considerable rhetorical flourish, that the individualist view has been embraced recently by liberals. Thus, for example, the *New York Times* noted with much ballyhoo that "the influential liberal constitutional law expert" Laurence Tribe now believed that the Second Amendment might protect an individual right to own firearms.[12] Columnist William Safire also noted that some liberals seemed to be shifting positions on the issue, an observation made as well by newspaper columnist Walter Shapiro and writer Daniel Lazare.[13] A recent headline in the *Wall Street Journal* summed up this alleged tidal shift in liberal thought this way: "Liberals Have Second Thoughts On the Second Amendment."[14] The effort to assert that the individualist view (as well as generalized opposition to gun control) is not limited to political conservatives is not a new phenomenon, as it has percolated up from the arguments of several legal and academic writers who oppose stronger gun laws.[15] But the personal ideological leanings of those who write on the Second Amendment offer no insight into the debate itself.

This recent debate over whether some liberals have now agreed upon the individualist view is a red herring, precisely because the focus on ideological pedigree becomes a substitute for a substantive debate of the actual merits of the individualist claims. Indeed, the merits of the claims concerning the meaning of the Second Amendment are not even raised in most of the press articles just cited. If the debate over this, or any, legal or public policy issue comes to be about the ideological pedigree of those on each side rather than about the facts of the case, then the facts of the case become irrelevant. As a political tactic, there may be some gain in trying to legitimate an argument by extolling the people who hold it, or by noting that the position is held by people of multiple ideological stripes (assuming, of course, that one can accept such claims at face value). Such claims are, at best, an irrelevant distraction to determining what the Second Amendment actually means[16]; at worst, they represent a shoddy effort to offer legitimacy to an argument that cannot stand well purely on its merits.

"We Win"

The second rhetorical device raised in recent media accounts—one that also percolates up from academic writings[17]—is the unilateral declaration that the individualist view represents a new academic consensus. So, for example, Lazare asserts that the debate over the Second Amendment is simply at an end: "The amendment *does* confer an individual right to bear arms. . . . "[18] Historian Joyce Lee Malcolm is quoted as saying that "[i]t is very hard . . . to find a historian who now believes that it is only a collective right . . . [t]here is no one for me to argue against anymore."[19] *USA Today* reports that "Most constitutional scholars agree with"[20] the individualist view.

While one of the purposes of this article is to examine the extent to which this claim is actually grounded in the academic literature, this unilateralist claim is, on its face, roughly akin to a participant in a contest who suddenly stops competing, declares victory, and leaves, in the hope that the declaration may become the fact. Media acceptance of this claim to victory for the individualist view belies the fact that this debate continues. This claim also draws attention away from the facts of the case. It is to those facts that we now turn.

THE "INDIVIDUALIST" CRITIQUE

The central critique of the collective or court view of the Second Amendment is that this amendment conferred an "individual" right to bear arms, aside or apart from any government-based militia activity. That is, some argue that the ownership of firearms is a constitutionally based protection that applies to all individuals, without any attachment to militias or the government, just as free speech and the right to counsel apply to all individuals. Although many variations of the individualist critique have been spun out, the core argument is usually supported by plucking key phrases from court cases and colonial or federal debate that refer to a right of Americans to own and carry guns.[21]

This line of analysis has three problems. First, as a matter of constitutional law, the issue of the bearing of arms as it pertains to the Constitution and the Bill of Rights always comes back to service in a government-organized and -regulated military unit[22] and the balance of power between the states and the federal government, as reflected in the two most important historical sources: the records of the constitutional convention and those of the First Congress when the Bill of Rights was formulated. Gun ownership was undeniably an important component of colonial and early federal life, but practical necessity did and does not equal constitutional protection. Moreover, as historian Michael Bellesiles has found, actual firearms ownership in America has been greatly exaggerated and mythologized. He reports that, from colonial times to 1850, gun ownership never exceeded 10 percent of the population, owing in large measure to the scarcity of guns, which were difficult and expensive to produce, and the considerable difficulty involved in maintaining in working condition those that existed.[23] Even though state and federal laws required men of militia age to keep and maintain firearms, these laws were simply not followed or enforced.[24]

Second, the definition of the citizen militias at the center of this debate has always been limited to men roughly between the ages of eighteen and forty-five.[25] That is, it has always excluded a majority of the country's adult citizens—men over age forty-five, the infirm of all ages, and women (who of course did not enjoy political rights comparable to men's until the twentieth century). Even among those males who were eligible to serve, actual service in the militias was significantly less than universal. As historian John Shy notes, the composition and organization of American militias fluctuated according to military necessity of place and time,[26] underscoring the fact that a militia's raison d'être was collective defense or internal security,[27] and not individual protection (while understanding that individuals might, and surely did, obtain protection through militia action) or other private purposes. Moreover, those who actually served "were not the men who bore a military obligation as part of their freedom."[28] That is, freedmen and property owners could and would opt out of militia service,[29] while vagrants, vagabonds, and the unemployed more often filled the ranks. Even African Americans served in early militias, as in the case of the Yamasee War, waged in South Carolina from 1715–16, when a militia force of six hundred white men and four hundred black men defeated a force of Native Americans. By the 1730s, escalating fears of slave revolts ended the practice.[30] Therefore, "universal" citizen militia service and the right to bear arms is not, and never has been, a right enjoyed by all citizens, unlike other Bill of Rights protections such as free speech, religious freedom, or right to counsel. This also puts to rest the idea that the phrase "the people" in the Second Amendment somehow means *all* of the people.[31]

The third problem with the individualist argument is that the matter of personal or individual self-defense, whether from wild animals or modern-day predators, does not fall within, nor is it dependent on, the Second Amendment rubric. Nothing in the history, construction, or interpretation of the amendment applies or infers such a protection. Rather, legal protection for personal self-defense arises from the British common law tradition and modern criminal law, not from constitutional law.[32]

The "Right of Revolution"

Some take the individualist view even further by arguing that the Second Amendment does or should protect the ownership of arms for everyone because of an innate "right of revolution," or as a mechanism to keep the country's rulers responsive to the citizens. While this theory, whether emphasizing revolutionary overthrow of a regime or an "insurrectionist" use of violence to change personnel within a regime, poses interesting intellectual questions about natural law and the relationship between citizens and the state, it does not find support anywhere in the text, background, or court interpretation of the Second Amendment.

The Constitution clearly and forcefully disdains anything resembling a right of revolution, as it gives Congress the powers "To provide for calling forth the Militia to execute the Laws of the Union, suppress Insurrections and repel Invasions" in Article I, section 8; to suspend habeas corpus "in Cases of Rebellion or Invasion" in section 9; and to protect individual states "against domestic Violence" if requested to do so by a state legislature or governor in Article IV, section 4. Further, the Constitution defines treason in Article III, section 3, this way: "Treason against the United States, shall consist only in levying War against them [the United States was originally referred to in the plural], or in adhering to their Enemies." Finally, those suspected of treason may not avoid prosecution by fleeing to another state; the Constitution states in Article IV, section 2, that "A Person charged in any State with Treason . . . and be found in another State, shall on Demand of the executive Authority of the State from which he fled, be delivered up." In other words, the Constitution specifically and explicitly gives the government the power to forcefully suppress anything even vaguely resembling revolution. Such revolt or revolution is by constitutional definition an act of treason against the United States. The militias are thus to be used to *suppress,* not *cause,* revolution or insurrection.

These powers were further detailed and expanded in the Calling Forth Act of 1792,[33] which gave the president broad powers to use state militias to enforce both state and federal laws in instances where the law is ignored or in cases of open insurrection. This act was passed by the Second Congress shortly after the passage of the Bill of Rights. In current law, these powers are further elaborated in the *U.S. Code* sections on "Insurrection."[34] As Roscoe Pound noted, a "legal right of the citizen to wage war on the government is something that cannot be admitted. . . . In the urban industrial society of today a general right to bear efficient arms so as to be enabled to resist oppression by the government would mean that gangs could exercise an extra-legal rule which would defeat the whole Bill of Rights."[35] Donald Beschle observed: "History and logic do not permit one to take the right of armed revolution as a serious proposition of positive constitutional law. Only the legal revolutions provided by the political process are recognized by the Constitution."[36] Cornell elaborates on the relationship between the American revolution and subsequent American governance by noting that "Americans did accept a right of revolution. Such a right, however, was not a constitutional check, but a natural right that one could not exercise under a functional constitutional government."[37] Any so-called right of insurrection or revolution is carried out against the government, which means against that government's constitution as well, including, in the United States, the Bill of Rights and the Second Amendment. One cannot carry out a right of revolution against a government while at the same time claiming protections within it.[38]

One of the most startling qualities of the individualist law-review literature is the rapidity and enthusiasm with which some teachers of law embrace the virtues of armed American insurrection.[39] Sanford Levinson, for example, states in a widely cited article published in the *Yale Law Journal* that "It is not my style to offer 'correct' or 'incorrect' interpretations of the Constitution." Yet he then proceeds to do just that, calling into question the conventional (court) understanding of the Second Amendment. In the process, he asserts that the Second Amendment is an expression of republicanism that does and should take citizen participation beyond peaceful, constitutional means:

Just as ordinary citizens should participate actively in governmental decision-making through offering their own deliberative insights, rather than be confined to casting ballots once every two or four years for those very few individuals who will actually make decisions, *so should ordinary citizens participate in the process of law enforcement and defense of liberty rather than rely on professionalized peacekeepers, whether we call them standing armies or police* [emphasis added].[40]

In short, Levinson offers as a bona fide constitutional argument the proposition that vigilantism and citizen violence, including armed insurrection, against the government are legal, proper, and even beneficial activities within the Second Amendment umbrella. The idea that vigilantism and armed insurrection are as constitutionally sanctioned as voting is a proposition of such absurdity that one is struck more by its boldness than by its pretensions to seriousness. Yet it appears repeatedly in the individualist literature.[41]

Finally, in none of this writing is there any substantive consideration of what real revolution entails.[42] Groups and individuals in modern America who most closely adhere to a violence-based revolutionary ethos—for instance, the Silver Shirts, the Branch Davidians, the Ku Klux Klan, Lee Harvey Oswald, rioters in Los Angeles—win no admirers from the Second Amendment writers discussed here. As Carl Bogus aptly observes, "Timothy McVeigh understands insurrectionist theory."[43] Academics who toy with any serious notions about revolutions would be well advised to consult the voluminous scholarly literature on the subject found in political science and related fields, which details and underscores the extent to which violence (especially including, but not limited to, the murder of top governmental leaders), societal dislocation, and disruption of a nation's economic, social, and political fabric make revolution or armed insurrection anything but a simple, reasoned, desirable, or commensurate alternative to peaceful methods of societal change.[44] The great truism of the American political system has been precisely its ability to effect political change through nonviolent, routinized, and orderly means.

Collateral Claims and the Research Record

The law journal articles that advance these arguments make a series of related, supporting claims. They assert that 1) little to nothing of any consequential scholarly nature has been published on the Second Amendment, especially before the 1980s[45]; 2) the individual view was or is the prevalent one until recent critics started saying otherwise (i.e., what I have identified here as the "court" view)[46]; 3) the courts have committed a kind of dereliction of duty insofar as they have been all but silent or indifferent on the matter, to the point of neglect or willful avoidance[47]; and 4) alternately, that since three of the four

Supreme Court rulings on the Second Amendment were handed down in the nineteenth century, court doctrine is somehow defective, irrelevant, outdated, unclear, emaciated, or "embarrassing," in particular because the three are preincorporation.[48] Each of these claims is false.

Table 1

LAW JOURNAL ARTICLES TAKING "COURT" AND "INDIVIDUALIST" VIEWS OF THE SECOND AMENDMENT*

	Court	*Individualist*
1912–1959	11	0
1960–1969	11	3
1970–1979	8	6
1980–1989	17	21
1990–1999	29	58
Total	76	88

* Data compiled from articles listed in the Appendix (pages 36–47). Coded and compiled by the author. Articles cited in the *Index to Legal Periodicals,* 1888–October 1999 (vol. 93, #1).

In order to assess these claims and, simultaneously, to understand the provenance of Second Amendment writings as they have unfolded in the law literature, I examined nearly three hundred law journal articles dealing with gun control and the Second Amendment, published from 1912 to 1999, as cited in, and culled from, the *Index to Legal Periodicals.* I began my search of the *Index* from its beginning, with the first volume, published in 1888,[49] through the October 1999 index (vol. 93, #1), under the subject headings "weapons" and "right to bear arms." (This latter heading appeared in the *Index* starting only in volume 31, 1991.) Book reviews were omitted, as were articles that discussed, but did not take any clear position on, the meaning of the Second Amendment. Of the nearly three hundred cited articles examined, 164 offered significant comment or assessment concerning interpretation of the Second Amendment. All of these articles are listed chronologically in the Appendix to this article (pages 36–47), and are categorized according to whether they argue for the court or individualist view.

The first article was published in 1912 in the *American Law Review.* It discusses a case arising from the Supreme Court of Georgia involving a challenge to a state law that required persons wishing to carry a handgun to first obtain a license to do so from the state. Challenged as a violation of the Constitution's Second Amendment, and as a violation of a comparable provision in the Georgia State Constitution, the court ruled in favor of the restriction. Discussing the broader principle of the meaning of the Second Amendment, the article said that "The many decisions which have already been made as to statutes against carrying concealed weapons or weapons of a certain character show two general lines of reasoning; first, that such provisions should be construed in the light of the origin of the constitutional declarations and the necessity for an efficient militia or for the common defense; second, that they should be construed in connection with the general police power of the state and as subject to legislative regulation thereunder."[50] A second, brief article appeared in *Law Notes* in 1913, speculating on a legal challenge to a New York state gun law and citing *Presser v. Illinois*.[51]

Two years later, the first full-blown treatment of the Second Amendment appeared in the *Harvard Law Review*. Authored by noted constitutional scholar Lucilius Emery, the article discusses the British tradition behind the Second Amendment, pertinent American history, and various comparable state constitutional provisions. Emery quotes *Presser*, and concludes that "Only persons of military capacity to bear arms in military organizations are within the spirit of the guaranty [i.e., the Second Amendment]."[52] Emery ends by saying that "the carrying of weapons by individuals may be regulated, restricted, and even prohibited according as conditions and circumstances may make it necessary for the protection of the people."[53] Emery's article was widely reprinted (these reprints were cited in the *Index to Legal Periodicals*, but are not included in the Appendix).

Including these three early articles, a total of eleven articles on the Second Amendment appeared in law journals from 1912 to 1959. All of them reflected what is here labeled the "court" view of the Second Amendment—namely, that the Second Amendment affects citizens only in connection with citizen service in a government-organized and -regulated militia. Then, in 1960, an article published by Stuart R. Hays raised two new Second Amendment arguments that would appear often in subsequent articles. One argument asserted that the Second Amendment supported an individual or personal right to possess firearms (notably for personal self-defense), separate and apart from citizen service in a government militia. The second novel argument was that the Second Amendment created a citizen "right of revolution," one which, in Hays's opinion, was properly exercised by the American South during the Civil War. In Hays's words, "The Southern States . . . were engaged in a lawful revolution."[54] Hays rested these two arguments primarily on his assertion that the English tradition defined the "right to bear arms" as incorporating both a right of revolution and a right of personal self-defense.

The Hays article incorporated an array of errors and omissions. First and foremost, his analysis of Second Amendment meaning failed to consider key primary evidence on the meaning of the Bill of Rights, namely the debate at the First Congress; Hays's article based much of its analysis on a misreading of prior British history[55]; it incorrectly cited *Dred Scott v. Sandford* (1857) as applicable to Second Amendment interpretation (the case dealt with whether a slave living in a free state was entitled to citizenship rights, but in any case was overturned by the passage of the Thirteenth and Fourteenth Amendments), and misspelled Chief Justice Roger Taney as "Tanney"[56]; it incorrectly labeled the court's opinion in *Presser v. Illinois* (1886), written by Justice Woods, as a "dissent" (there was no dissent in *Presser*)[57]; it mis-cited and misspelled the case of *U.S. v. Cruikshank* as *Cruickshank v. U.S.*[58]; and it cited the wrong years for the cases of *Miller v. Texas* (1894; not 1893), *Presser* (1886; not 1885), and *Robertson v. Baldwin* (1897; not 1899).[59] While some of these errors are minor, when taken together they summarize an article whose scholarship, produced by the author while he was a student,[60] was less than reliable. On this broken reed was subsequent individualist analysis built.

To return to Table 1 and the light it sheds on the various collateral claims arising from individualist writings, pertaining to the first claim that little or nothing of a scholarly nature has been published on the meaning of the Second Amendment, thirty-nine law journal articles, all referenced in the *Index to Legal Periodicals,* were published on the Second Amendment from 1912 to 1980. Interestingly, only nine of these took the individualist position. If any criticism can be leveled at these thirty-nine articles, it is that they cover the ground too well, to the point of redundancy. This assertion of little scholarly writing also carries within it a second, implicit, assertion—that any relative handful of articles, by virtue of their small number, ipso facto, cannot have adequately examined and discussed the issue in question. Obviously, this judgment is false, absent a content analysis of the articles, since a single, careful article might indeed examine with adequate depth and care any given subject. Beyond this, to say that few articles have been written on this subject is, in and of itself, false. In any case, the focus simply on the numbers of articles says nothing about whether this, or any, subject has received adequate, proper, or appropriate treatment.

The second assertion, claiming that the individualist view was the dominant one, is also contradicted by the numbers given in Table 1, citing the existence of twenty-two articles taking the court view published over a span of fifty-eight years (from 1912 to 1970), compared with just three articles taking the individualist view, with all three published in the 1960s. In fact, the table reveals that the individualist position has proliferated only since the 1980s, with twenty-one individualist articles published from 1980–89, as compared to seventeen taking the court view.[61] The numbers jumped again in the 1990s, with fifty-eight articles taking the individualist view, and twenty-nine taking the court view. The assertion that the individualist view has been the dominant one is also contradicted by standard reference works. For example, in his standard work on the Constitution, Jack Peltason states that the Second Amendment "was designed to prevent Congress from disarming the state militias, not to prevent it from regulating private ownership of firearms."[62] In his classic book on the Bill of Rights, Irving Brant writes: "The Second Amendment, popularly misread, comes to life chiefly on the parade floats of rifle associations and in the propaganda of mail-order houses selling pistols to teenage gangsters."[63] Similar, if less sarcastic, sentiments are found in other standard works.[64]

The third assertion—that the courts have committed a kind of dereliction of duty with respect to the Second Amendment—is also false, given the existence of four Supreme Court cases—*U.S. v. Cruikshank* (1876); *Presser v. Illinois* (1886); *Miller v. Texas* (1894); and *U.S. v. Miller* (1939), including a brief acknowledgment of this line of cases in *Lewis v. U.S.* (1980)—all of which explicate and support the aforementioned court interpretation that the Second Amendment comes into play only in connection with citizen service in a government-organized and -regulated militia, and that this amendment has not been incorporated under the Fourteenth Amendment, despite the opportunity to do so afforded by numerous lower-court appeals spanning the previous sixty years. Further, these recent lower federal court opinions have been even more emphatic and detailed in asserting that, as the Ninth Circuit noted in 1996, "We follow our sister circuits in holding that the Second Amendment is a right held by the states, and does not protect the possession of a weapon by a private citizen."[65] The inescapable conclusion is that the Supreme Court, especially as amplified by lower federal courts, has settled this matter and has no interest in crowding its docket with cases that merely repeat what has already been decided. The high court may, of course, change its mind on the matter, and there is reason to believe that two current justices are interested in revisiting the subject. Justice Clarence Thomas noted in his concurring opinion in *Printz v. U.S.* that:

> The Court has not had recent occasion to consider the nature of the substantive right safeguarded by the Second Amendment. If, however, the Second Amendment is read to confer a *personal* right to "keep and bear arms," a colorable argument exists that the Federal Government's regulatory scheme . . . runs afoul of that Amendment's protection. As the parties did not raise this argument, however, we need not consider it here.[66]

Justice Antonin Scalia raised similar suggestions.[67] Be that as it may, federal court rulings up until the present are uniform in their interpretation. The one exception to this is the recent case *U.S. v. Emerson* (46 F.Supp.2d 598 [N.D. Tex. 1999]), in which a federal district court judge ruled that a man who was charged with violating a restraining order that included a gun ownership restriction (after the man had brandished a handgun in the presence of his estranged wife and child) did in fact have a Second Amendment right to own the gun. As of this writing, the case is on appeal.[68]

The fourth assertion—that three of the four key Supreme Court cases on the Second Amendment came in the nineteenth century and are therefore somehow irrelevant or deficient—is transparently false, since no legal doctrine imposes a statute of limitations or expiration date on binding court precedent, unless the precedent is ignored or overturned, neither of which has occurred for Second Amendment law.[69] While it is true that the three earlier cases that came before the Supreme Court began the piecemeal incorporation of the Bill of Rights in 1897, the process has never been extended by the court to the entire Bill of Rights.[70] The last incorporation case came in 1969, and the process is generally considered to be at an end, with the possible exception of the excessive fines and bails clause of the Eighth Amendment.[71] Since then, the Third Amendment, the grand jury clause of the Fifth Amendment, the Seventh Amendment, the fines and bails clause, as well as the Ninth and Tenth Amendments, have not been incorporated. The preincorporation Second Amendment cases thus continue to stand as good law.[72]

SEEKING SHELTER UNDER THE FOURTEENTH AMENDMENT

This discussion of incorporation raises an additional, related argument, namely, that the Fourteenth Amendment somehow created, enhanced, or validated a constitutionally based individual right to bear arms aside or apart from citizen militia service. To support this claim, advocates generally cite post–Civil War debate in Congress that referenced the Second Amendment or the bearing of arms. Typical of these claims is that of Stephen Halbrook, who quotes Senator Jacob M. Howard's (R-MI) comments during debate in 1866 over the Fourteenth Amendment. "When he introduced the Fourteenth Amendment in Congress, Senator Jacob M. Howard . . . referred to 'the personal rights guaranteed and secured by the first eight amendments of the Constitution; such as freedom of speech and of the press; . . . *the right to keep and bear arms*. . . . [emphasis added by Halbrook]' "[73] Halbrook makes two claims from this and related quotes. One is that the reference to "personal rights," apparently offered in the same context as mention of the right to bear arms, means that this "personal right" is an "individual right." The second claim is to argue for total incorporation, i.e., application of all of the rights included in the Bill of Rights to the states. While even this abbreviated quote suggests that Senator Howard was merely listing the parts of the Bill of Rights, the full quote from Senate debate clarifies the point further.

> To these privileges and immunities [spoken of in Article IV of the Constitution], whatever they may be—for they are not and cannot be fully defined in their entire extent and precise nature—to these should be added the personal rights guarantied and secured by the first eight amendments of the Constitution; such as the freedom of speech and of the press [First Amendment]; the right of the people peaceably to assemble and petition the Government for redress of grievances, a right appertaining to each and all the people [First Amendment]; the right to keep and bear arms [Second Amendment]; the right to be exempted from the quartering of soldiers in a house without the consent of the owner [Third Amendment]; the right to be exempt from unreasonable searches and seizures, and from any search or seizure except by virtue of a warrant issued upon formal oath or affidavit [Fourth Amendment]; the right of an accused person to be informed of the nature of the accusation against him, and his right to be tried by an impartial jury of the vicinage [Sixth Amendment]; and also the right to be secure against excessive bail and against cruel and unusual punishments [Eighth Amendment].[74]

It is clear from the full quotation that the senator's reference to "personal rights" was simply a synonym for all of the rights of the Bill of Rights. There is no reason to believe that this reference articulates, or implies, an individual right to bear arms aside or apart from the conventional understanding of citizen participation in a government-organized and -regulated militia. As for the question of full incorporation of the Bill of Rights under the Fourteenth Amendment, one may argue that this quote supports the contention. While the argument that the Fourteenth Amendment was designed to provide for total incorporation is a minority viewpoint among constitutional scholars (and it has been rejected by the courts), it is at least a bona fide argument. The claim that the Fourteenth Amendment somehow created, elevated, or ratified an individual right to bear arms, as part of either the Second or Fourteenth Amendments, is not.[75] In any case, to make such an argument about the Fourteenth Amendment is also to argue implicitly that the Second Amendment, as originally drafted, did not create such an individual right in the first place (otherwise, there would be no reason to resort to the Fourteenth Amendment to support such a line of reasoning). Akhil Amar, in fact, makes this argument explicitly when he says that "Creation-era arms bearing was collective. . . . Reconstruction gun-toting was individualistic."[76]

M. J. Quinlan offers the same kind of analysis when, for example, he quotes Rep. Roswell Hart (R-NY) during House debate in 1866, who said:

> "citizens shall be entitled to all privileges and immunities of other citizens"; where "no law shall be made prohibiting the free exercise of religion"; where "the right of the people to keep and bear arms shall not be infringed"; where "the right of the people to be secure in their persons, houses, papers, and effects, against unreasonable searches and seizures, shall not be violated," . . . [quote marks in original] [77]

Quinlan concludes that "Apparently, several commentators in the Reconstruction Congress considered the Second Amendment's right to keep and bear arms an individual right." [78] Once again, the speaker is simply reciting Bill of Rights protections, as demarcated by the use of quote marks. The quotation does nothing to support the individualist view, as even Quinlan's use of the modifier "apparently" suggests.

Halbrook expands this Fourteenth Amendment analysis when he attempts to link the Fourteenth Amendment with the Freedman's Bureau Act of 1866 and the Civil Rights Act of 1866; thus he can draw on the debate and text of these bills to argue that, when taken together, they provide "the rights of personal security and personal liberty [and] include the 'constitutional right to bear arms.' " [79] Again, Halbrook culls congressional and state debate for any and all references to firearms, the bearing of arms, and the like. Not only is Halbrook seeking to argue that "the Fourteenth Amendment was intended to incorporate the Second Amendment," but, further, to argue that the "Fourteenth Amendment protects the rights to personal security and personal liberty, which its authors declared in the Freedmen's Bureau Act to include 'the constitutional right to bear arms.' To the members of the Thirty-Ninth Congress, possession of arms was a fundamental, individual right worthy of protection from both federal and state violation." [80] In other words, beyond arguing for total incorporation, Halbrook argues that the Fourteenth Amendment itself protects the bearing of arms.

This line of reasoning has several obvious problems. First and foremost, while it is true that the same Congress sought to extend similar, basic rights through the trio of enactments, including the Fourteenth Amendment, the Fourteenth Amendment simply does not stipulate anything like a right to bear arms. No court has ever found, or suggested, that the Second Amendment was somehow repeated, amplified, or elevated by the Fourteenth. While similar, each of these three enactments is, as a matter of law, different, and to attempt to draw out legislative intent behind one enactment (the Fourteenth Amendment) by bringing in others (the Civil Rights Act and the Freedmen's Bureau Act) is both desperate and erroneous. [81]

Second, the discussion of arms, personal security, and militias in Congress during this time is by no means a discussion that revolves solely around the Second Amendment. Remember that the American South was in a state of near total destruction and utter chaos, a fact heightened by the race hatred prevalent in the region in the aftermath of the freeing of millions of former slaves, and the presence of thousands of former Confederate soldiers who were allowed to keep their arms. Little wonder that there was so much discussion in Congress of security and safety issues.

Third, as an interpretation of the Second Amendment, the congressional debates of the 1860s deserve no special, if any, consideration. These debates were not debates over the meaning of that amendment per se, occurring as they did more than seventy years after adoption of the Bill of Rights. They were political debates over how best to extend hard-won rights, restore order, and reconfigure governance in the American South.

A fourth problem is that the yearning for total incorporation, or any kind of elevation of the Second Amendment, was rejected by political contemporaries. Eight years after adoption of the Fourteenth Amendment, the Supreme Court explicitly rejected the idea in *U.S. v. Cruikshank*. Speaking for the court, Chief Justice Waite wrote:

> The second and tenth counts are equally defective. The right there specified is that of "bearing arms for a lawful purpose." This is not a right granted by the Constitution. Neither is it in any manner dependent upon that instrument for its existence. The Second Amendment declares that it shall not be infringed; but this, as has been seen, means no more than that it shall not be infringed by Congress. This is one of the Amendments that has no other effect than to restrict the powers of the National Government.[82]

In 1873 the Supreme Court dealt total incorporation what constitutional scholar Henry J. Abraham called "a crushing defeat"[83] in *The Slaughterhouse Cases* (16 Wallace 36; 1873). The thinking of most constitutional scholars on this subject is summarized by Andrea L. Bonnicksen this way: "A look at the debates surrounding the framing of the Fourteenth Amendment reveals some evidence that the members of Congress did intend the Amendment's due process clause to incorporate the Bill of Rights, but the more compelling evidence shows otherwise."[84] As discussed earlier, the Court did not incorporate any part of the Bill of Rights until 1897. This fact alone puts to rest Halbrooks's assertions.

The research tactic applied to attempting to find a connection between the Fourteenth and Second Amendments follows that described by Garry Wills in characterizing individualist research on the Second Amendment. "The tactic . . . is to ransack any document, no matter how distant from the . . . debates, in the hope that someone, somewhere, ever used 'bear arms' in a non-military way."[85] In the case of incorporation, this search extends, fruitlessly, to eight decades after the writing of the Second Amendment.

Despite this array of chimerical claims, the law journal article count in Table 1 shows an explosion of individualist articles, such that a recent article has dubbed its individualist view as "The New Consensus on the Second Amendment."[86] The key prop of the claim is the sheer number of such articles, as though the weight of numbers creates a kind of intellectual precedent. Yet given the parade of bad analysis these articles represent, how can this phenomenon be explained? Three considerations help explain the presence of this body of analysis: the law journal breeding ground; the presence of the state in law; and partisan support.

The Law Journal Breeding Ground

The discipline of law is unique among academic disciplines in that its professional journals are governed mostly by student-run law review boards, and, with a few exceptions, submissions are not subject to the process of peer review, or even faculty oversight.[87] The consequences of these facts for law review content have been extensively discussed and debated within the law school community, and have at least two particular effects pertinent to this analysis. First, while the peer-review process found in every other discipline is subject to legitimate criticisms, including cronyism and institutional conservatism, law review student editors simply do not possess, and cannot be expected to possess, the knowledge and expertise of those who have researched and published in a field. Second, law reviews seek and reward through publication articles that are, by the field's own admission, highly duplicative and unnecessarily packed with footnotes. This occurs in a contemporary atmosphere where there is a proliferation, even a glut of law reviews—more than eight hundred by one count.[88] Given such a huge publishing field, these characteristics have increasingly produced a contrary editorial drive to publish articles for their distinctiveness rather than for their scholarly soundness.

These and other criticisms emerge from the legal profession itself.[89] In the words of one member of the legal community, law reviews are "dominated by rather exotic offerings."[90] Another critic notes the simultaneous drives that produce both duplication and distinctiveness: "Student editors prefer pieces that recite prior developments at great length, contain voluminous and largely meaningless citations for every proposition, and deal with topics that are either safe and standard on the one hand, or currently faddish on the other."[91] The matter of redundancy also sets legal publications apart from the scholarly literature of virtually every other discipline. It is almost unimaginable that so many repetitive publications would find their way into print in political science or other disciplines, because redundancy is an obvious and typical ground for rejection. These unique publishing conditions help explain the trends described in this article.[92] In addition, the sheer volume of publishing possibilities provides a uniquely wide opportunity for the cultivation and propagation of particular legal theories, since even a tiny percentage of law review articles devoted to a particular argument could easily amount to dozens of published articles.

Much modern constitutional and legal analysis has fallen primarily, if not entirely, to the legal community, and to its scholarly mouthpiece, law reviews. This fact is not offered as a criticism of the legal community, which indisputably produces a great deal of fine scholarship, including in the realm of the Second Amendment. While law reviews do produce important and valuable scholarship, the unique review and publishing characteristics of these journals, as they reflect their discipline, have opened the door to highly suspect bodies of analysis. As Garry Wills has noted in his analysis of the individualist school of Second Amendment writing, "It seems as if our law journals were being composed by Lewis Carroll using various other pseudonyms."[93]

The case of the new interpretations of the Second Amendment discussed here supports the proposition that law reviews can be a breeding ground for defective analysis and wayward public policy.[94]

The State in Law

A second explanation for the proliferation of Second Amendment articles is predicated by political scientist Theodore J. Lowi, who notes of his discipline that "U.S. political science is itself a political phenomenon and, as such, is a product of the state."[95] It should come as little surprise that the same concept applies to political science's sister discipline, law. Almost without exception, the very earliest articles on the Second Amendment paralleled, and discussed, changes in state public policy concerning gun laws, beginning with the enactment of New York's strict gun law, the so-called Sullivan law, in 1911, to early federal enactments in 1919, 1927, 1934, 1938, and the Supreme Court's 1939 ruling in *U.S. v. Miller*. Second Amendment publications lapsed, along with federal regulatory efforts, until the mid-1960s, when renewed focus on gun issues culminated in passage of the Gun Control Act of 1968.

The next important wave of gun legislation emerged during the Reagan administration, culminating with the enactment of the Firearm Owners Protection Act of 1986. Coinciding with these legislative changes was the country's turn to the right, and the National Rifle Association's (NRA) hard right and more politicized turn of the late 1970s and '80s. In the wake of this anti–gun control tide, it is logical that supporting writings appeared in law journals and other publications. In the 1990s, unprecedented focus on the 1993 Brady Law and the 1994 assault weapons ban and other gun policy controversies further fanned law review writing.[96]

That these political phenomena helped drive gun scholarship is clearly seen in the text of these writings, a phenomenon of particular predictive significance in the legal community, where law journal writings are extremely sensitive to breaking legislative and judicial decisions.

Partisan Support

A third explanation for the expanding body of individualist scholarship pertaining to the Second Amendment is more predictably and strictly political, in that gun advocacy groups have a vested interest in promoting academic writing to buttress and legitimize their political agendas. A group formed in 1992 by individuals seeking to promote other interpretations of the Second Amendment, called Academics for the Second Amendment (A2A), asserted in an open letter[97] that "The Second Amendment does not guarantee merely a 'right of the states,' but rather a 'right of the people,' a term which . . . is widely understood to encompass a personal right of citizens." The organization further stated that "Our primary goal is to give the 'right to bear arms' enshrined in the Bill of Rights its proper, prominent place in Constitutional discourse and analysis." This group received $6,000 from the NRA, out of a total of $90,000 raised by the group. The A2A's president, Joseph Olson, has served on the NRA's governing board. In 1992 the NRA's Firearms Civil Rights Legal Defense Fund contributed $5,000 to cover the expenses for academics who attended the A2A conference that year. In 1993 the NRA's Legal Defense Fund contributed $99,000 "for undisclosed 'right to bear arms research and education.' "[98] Further, the NRA offered a first prize of $25,000 (a considerable amount of money in academic circles for academic work) for its 1994–95 essay contest, titled "Stand Up for the Second Amendment." The annual contest "seeks publication-quality law review pieces on gun-rights issues."[99] Another group, formed in 1994 and called the Lawyer's Second Amendment Society, similarly seeks to advance the individualist view through its activities and publications.[100] Finally, a notable number of individualist writers have ties to gun groups.[101]

According to one critic, these activities have a very specific public policy purpose—namely, they are "part of a concerted campaign to persuade the courts to reconsider the Second Amendment, to reject what has long been a judicial consensus, and to adopt a different interpretation—one that would give the Amendment judicial as well as political vitality and would erect constitutional barriers to gun control legislation."[102] Aside from the now large number of individualist articles, there is reason to believe that these efforts have borne other fruit, given the 1999 Texas case *U.S. v. Emerson* mentioned earlier, and given the fact that Justice Thomas raised the individualist perspective (as *dicta*) in his concurring opinion in *Printz v. U.S.* Although the constitutional challenge to the background-check requirement of the Brady Law (a law passed by Congress in 1993 that imposed a five-business-day waiting period on the purchase of a handgun) in *Printz* was based on the Tenth Amendment, not the Second Amendment, in a footnote Thomas cited individualist law review articles by Halbrook, Van Alstyne, Amar, Cottrol and Diamond, Levinson, and Kates.[103]

This is certainly not the first time that interest groups have sought to push particular arguments in law journals as a preparatory move to advance litigation. In 1959, political scientist Clement E. Vose chronicled the efforts of the NAACP and sympathetic legal scholars to "blast the constitutional log jam" that thwarted efforts to end racial segregation (in particular, the restrictive covenant cases) by generating sympathetic and supportive law journal articles.[104] Efforts to dovetail academic writing with public policy advocacy are legitimate; sacrificing academic standards of sound research in the name of policy advocacy is not.

Conclusion

In the mad scramble to win legitimacy for their arguments, individualist authors have produced an ever-growing stack of articles. A near-obsessive emphasis on numbers of publications has allowed them to turn the focus of the debate away from the merits of the arguments themselves and toward the number of articles as well as the pedigrees of the articles' authors. This essay plays the numbers game as well—but not to declare a winner by virtue of who publishes more. Rather, its aim is to point out that many of the basic claims made about the Second Amendment literature by individualist writers are simply and demonstrably wrong. Contrary to individualist claims, an extensive body of writing on the Second Amendment has been published well before 1980, extending back more than seven decades; prior to 1990, the individualist view of the Second Amendment was never the dominant view, regardless of how one measures this; the Supreme Court has committed no dereliction of duty for not accepting recent appeals based on the Second Amendment, although the Court may well do so at some point in the future; and Supreme Court rulings do not somehow expire or lapse into nonexistence simply because they predate the twentieth century.

Some may admire the individualists' beautifully stitched intellectual finery—the careful seamwork, the gorgeous brocade, the workers' craftsmanship. This is one emperor, however, that has no clothes.

APPENDIX

Chronological Coding of "Court" (C) and "Individualist" (I)
Law Journal Articles

1912

C "The Constitutional Right to Keep and Bear Arms and Statutes Against Carrying Weapons." *American Law Review* 46 (September–October 1912): 777–79.

1913

C "Right to Bear Arms." *Law Notes* 16 (February 1913): 207–8.

1915

C Emery, L. A. "The Constitutional Right to Keep and Bear Arms." *Harvard Law Review* 28 (March 1915): 473–77.

1928

C McKenna, D. J. "The Right to Keep and Bear Arms." *Marquette Law Review* 12 (Fall 1928): 138–49.

1934

C Brabner-Smith, J. "Firearm Regulation." *Law and Contemporary Problems* 1 (October 1934): 400–14.

1939

C Montague, W. "Second Amendment, National Firearms Act." *Southern California Law Review* 13 (November 1939): 129–30.

C "Second Amendment." *St. John's Law Review* 14 (November 1939): 167–69.

1940

C Breen, V., et al. "Federal Revenue as Limitation on State Police Power and the Right to Bear Arms—Purpose of Legislation as Affecting its Validity." *Journal of the Bar Association of Kansas* 9 (November 1940): 178–82.

C Weiner, F. B. "The Militia Clause of the Constitution." *Harvard Law Review* 54 (December 1940): 181–220.

1941

C Haight, G. I. "The Right to Keep and Bear Arms." *Bill of Rights Review* 2 (Fall 1941): 31–42.

1950

C "Restrictions on the Right to Bear Arms: State and Federal Firearms Legislation." *University of Pennsylvania Law Review* 98 (May 1950): 905–19.

1960

I Hays, S. R. "The Right to Bear Arms, A Study in Judicial Misinterpretation." *William and Mary Law Review* 2 (1960): 381–406.

1965

C Fletcher, J. G. "The Corresponding Duty to the Right of Bearing Arms." *Florida Bar Journal* 39 (March 1965): 167–70.

I Sprecher, Robert A. "The Lost Amendment." *American Bar Association Journal* 51 (June/July 1965): 554–57, 665–69.

1966

C Feller, P. B., and K. L. Gotting. "The Second Amendment: A Second Look." *Northwestern University Law Review* 61 (March/April 1966): 46–70.

C Rohner, R. J. "The Right to Bear Arms: A Phenomenon of Constitutional History." *Catholic University Law Review* 16 (September 1966): 53–84.

1967

C "Firearms: Problems of Control." *Harvard Law Review* 80 (April 1967): 1328–46.

C Mann, J. L., II. "The Right to Bar Arms." *South Carolina Law Review* 19 (1967): 402–13.

I Olds, N. V. "Second Amendment and the Right to Keep and Bear Arms." *Michigan State Bar Journal* 46 (October 1967): 15–25.

C Riseley, R. F., Jr. "The Right to Keep and Bear Arms: A Necessary Constitutional Guarantee or an Outmoded Provision of the Bill of Rights." *Albany Law Review* 31 (January 1967): 74–87.

1968

C Mosk, S. "Gun Control Legislation: Valid and Necessary." *New York Law Forum* 14 (Winter 1968): 694–717.

1969

C "Constitutional Limitations on Firearms Regulation." *Duke Law Journal* 18 (August 1969): 773–801.

C Grundeman, A. "Constitutional Limitations on Federal Firearms Control." *Washburn Law Journal* 8 (Winter 1969): 238–47.

C Levine, R. B., and D. B. Saxe. "The Second Amendment: The Right to Bear Arms." *Houston Law Review* 7 (September 1969): 1–19.

C Sheppard, E. H. "Control of Firearms." *Missouri Law Review* 34 (Summer 1969): 376–96.

1970

I   McClure, J. A. "Firearms and Federalism." *Idaho Law Review* 7 (Fall 1970): 197–215.

1971

C   Levin, J. "Right to Bear Arms: The Development of the American Experience." *Chicago-Kent Law Review* 48 (Fall–Winter 1971): 148–67.

C   McCabe, M. K. "To Bear or to Ban—Firearms Control and the 'Right to Bear Arms.'" *Journal of the Missouri Bar* 27 (July 1971): 313–28.

1972

C   Edwards, G. "Commentary: Murder and Gun Control." *Wayne Law Review* 18 (July–August 1972): 1335–42.

1973

C   Wallitsch, T. A. "Right to Bear Arms in Pennsylvania: The Regulation of Possession." *Duquesne Law Review* 11 (Summer 1973): 557–75.

1974

I   Hardy, D. T., and J. Stompoly. "Of Arms and the Law." *Chicago-Kent Law Review* 51 (Summer 1974): 62–114.

C   Riley, R. J. "Shooting to Kill the Handgun: Time to Martyr Another American 'Hero.'" *Journal of Urban Law* 51 (1974): 491–524.

I   Weiss, J. A. "A Reply to Advocates of Gun-Control Law." *Journal of Urban Law* 52 (1974): 577–89.

1975

C   Weatherup, R. G. "Standing Armies and Armed Citizens: An Historical Analysis of the Second Amendment." *Hastings Constitutional Law Quarterly* 2 (Fall 1975): 961–1001.

1976

I   Caplan, D. I. "Restoring the Balance: The Second Amendment Revisited." *Fordham Urban Law Journal* 5 (Fall 1976): 31–53.

I   Whisker, J. B. "Historical Development and Subsequent Erosion of the Right to Keep and Bear Arms." *West Virginia Law Review* 78 (Fall 1976): 171–90.

1977

C   Jackson, M. H. "Handgun Control: Constitutional and Critically Needed." *North Carolina Central Law Journal* 8 (Spring 1977): 189–98.

C   Santee, J. C. "Right to Keep and Bear Arms." *Drake Law Review* 26 (1976–77): 423–44.

1978
I   Caplan, D. I. "Handgun Control: Constitutional or Unconstitutional?—A Reply to Mayor Jackson." *North Carolina Central Law Journal* 10 (Fall 1978): 53–58.

1980
I   Cantrell, C. L. "The Right to Bear Arms: A Reply." *Wisconsin Bar Bulletin* 53 (October 1980): 21–26.
C   Elliott, R. L. "Right to Keep and Bear Arms." *Wisconsin Bar Bulletin* 53 (May 1980): 34–36.

1981
I   Halbrook, S. A. "Jurisprudence of the Second and Fourteenth Amendments." *George Mason University Law Review* 4 (Spring 1981): 1–69.

1982
C   Ashman, M. C. "Handgun Control by Local Government." *Northern Kentucky Law Review* 10 (1982): 97–112.
C   Benedict, M. "Constitutional Law—Second Amendment Right to Bear Arms—Quilici v. Village of Morton Grove." *Akron Law Review* 16 (Fall 1982): 293–301.
C   Bernardy, P., and M. E. Burns. "Of Lawyers, Guns, and Money: Preemption and Handgun Control." *University of California at Davis Law Review* 16 (Fall 1982): 137–66.
I   Caplan, D. I. "The Right of the Individual to Bear Arms: A Recent Judicial Trend." *Detroit College Law Review* (Winter 1982): 789–823.
I   Dowlut, R., and J. A. Knoop. "State Constitutions and the Right to Keep and Bear Arms." *Oklahoma City University Law Review* 7 (Summer 1982): 177–241.
C   Freibrun, E. S. "Banning Handguns: Quilici v. Village of Morton Grove and the Second Amendment." *Washington University Law Quarterly* 60 (Fall 1982): 1087–1118.
I   Gardiner, R. E. "To Preserve Liberty—A Look at the Right to Keep and Bear Arms." *Northern Kentucky Law Review* 10 (1982): 63–96.
I   Gottleib, A. M. "Gun Ownership: A Constitutional Right." *Northern Kentucky Law Review* 10 (1982): 138–54.
I   Halbrook, S. P. "To Keep and Bear Their Private Arms: The Adoption of the Second Amendment, 1787–1791." *Northern Kentucky Law Review* 10 (1982): 13–39.
C   Klunin, K. F. "Gun Control: Is it a Legal and Effective Means of Controlling Firearms in the United States?" *Washburn Law Journal* 21 (Winter 1982): 244–65.

C Pierce, D. R. "Second Amendment Survey." *Northern Kentucky Law Review* 10 (1982): 155–62.

1983

C Barrett, S. R., Jr. "The Right to Bear Arms and Handgun Prohibition: A Fundamental Rights Analysis." *North Carolina Central Law Journal* 14 (1983): 296–311.

C Bass, H. I. "Quilici v. Village of Morton Grove: Ammunition for a National Handgun Ban." *DePaul Law Review* 32 (Winter 1983): 371–97.

I Dowlut, R. "The Right to Arms: Does the Constitution or the Predilection of Judges Reign?" *Oklahoma Law Review* 36 (Winter 1983): 65–105.

I Halbrook, S. A. "Tort Liability for the Manufacture, Sale, and Ownership of Handguns?" *Hamline Law Review* 6 (July 1983): 351–82.

I Kates, D. B. "Handgun Prohibition and the Original Meaning of the Second Amendment." *Michigan Law Review* 82 (November 1983): 204–73.

I Malcolm, J. L. "The Right of the People to Keep and Bear Arms: The Common Law Tradition." *Hastings Constitutional Law Quarterly* 10 (Winter 1983): 285–314.

C Spannaus, W. "State Firearms Regulation and the Second Amendment." *Hamline Law Review* 6 (July 1983): 383–90.

1985

I Halbrook, S. P. "The Right to Bear Arms in the First State Bills of Rights: Pennsylvania, North Carolina, Vermont, and Massachusetts." *Vermont Law Review* 10 (Fall 1985): 255–320.

1986

C Beschle, D. L. "Reconsidering the Second Amendment: Constitutional Protection for a Right of Security." *Hamline Law Review* 9 (February 1986): 69–104.

I Halbrook, S. P. "What the Framers Intended: A Linguistic Analysis of the Right to 'Bear Arms.' " *Law and Contemporary Problems* 49 (Winter 1986): 151–62.

I Hardy, D. T. "Armed Citizens, Citizen Armies: Toward a Jurisprudence of the Second Amendment." *Harvard Journal of Law and Public Policy* 9 (Summer 1986): 559–638.

C Hunt, M. T. "The Individual Right to Bear Arms: An Illusory Public Pacifier?" *Utah Law Review* (1986): 751–79.

I Kates, D. B. "The Second Amendment: A Dialogue." *Law and Contemporary Problems* 49 (Winter 1986): 143–62.

I Shalhope, R. E. "The Armed Citizen in the Early Republic." *Law and Contemporary Problems* 49 (Winter 1986): 125–41.

1987

C Carlson, P. E. "Quilici and Sklar: Alternative Models for Handgun Control Ordinances." *Washington University Journal of Urban and Contemporary Law* 31 (Winter 1987): 341–72.

I Hardy, D. T. "The Second Amendment and the Historiography of the Bill of Rights." *The Journal of Law & Politics* 4 (Summer 1987): 1–62.

I Lund, N. "The Second Amendment, Political Liberty, and the Right to Self-Preservation." *Alabama Law Review* 39 (Fall 1987): 103–30.

1989

C Brown, W. "Guns, Cowboys, Philadelphia Mayors, and Civic Republicanism: On Sanford Levinson's 'The Embarrassing Second Amendment.' " *The Yale Law Journal* 99 (December 1989): 661–67.

C Callaghan, M. O. "State v. Buckner and the Right to Keep and Bear Arms in West Virginia." *West Virginia Law Review* 91 (Winter 1988–89): 425–49.

I Dowlut, R. "Federal and State Constitutional Guarantees to Arms." *University of Dayton Law Review* 15 (Fall 1989): 59–90.

C Ehrman, K. A., and D. A. Henigan. "The Second Amendment in the Twentieth Century: Have You Seen Your Militia Lately?" *University of Dayton Law Review* 15 (Fall 1989): 5–58.

I Halbrook, S. P. "Encroachments of the Crown on the Liberty of the Subject: Pre-Revolutionary Origins of the Second Amendment." *University of Dayton Law Review* 15 (Fall 1989): 91–124.

I Levinson, S. "The Embarrassing Second Amendment." *The Yale Law Journal* 99 (December 1989): 637–59.

C Udulutch, M. "The Constitutional Implications of Gun Control and Several Realistic Gun Control Proposals." *American Journal of Criminal Law* 17 (Fall 1989): 19–54.

1990

I Bordenet, B. J. "The Right to Possess Arms: The Intent of the Framers of the Second Amendment." *University of West Los Angeles Law Review* 21 (1990): 1–30.

I Moncure, T. M. "Who Is the Militia—the Virginia Ratifying Convention and the Right to Bear Arms." *Lincoln Law Review* 19 (1990): 1–25.

I Morgan, E. C. "Assault Rifle Legislation: Unwise and Unconstitutional." *American Journal of Criminal Law* 17 (Winter 1990): 143–74.

I Tahmassebi, S. B. "Gun Control and Racism." *George Mason University Civil Rights Law Journal* 2 (Winter 1990): 67–99.

1991

I Amar, A. R. "The Bill of Rights as a Constitution." *The Yale Law Journal* 100 (March 1991): 1131–1210.

C Calhoun, C. "Constitutional Law—Eleventh Circuit Interprets Firearms Owners' Protection Act to Prohibit Private Possession of Machine Guns." *Suffolk University Law Review* 25 (Fall 1991): 797–804.

I Cottrol, R. J., and R. T. Diamond. "The Second Amendment: Toward an Afro-Americanist Reconsideration." *The Georgetown Law Journal* 80 (December 1991): 309–61.

C Dobray, D., and A. J. Waldrop. "Regulating Handgun Advertising Directed at Women." *Whittier Law Review* 12 (1991): 113–30.

I Halbrook, S. P. "The Right of the People or the Power of the State: Bearing Arms, Arming Militias, and the Second Amendment." *Valparaiso University Law Review* 26 (Fall 1991): 131–207.

C Henigan, D. A. "Arms, Anarchy and the Second Amendment." *Valparaiso University Law Review* 26 (Fall 1991): 107–29.

I Moncure, T. M., Jr. "The Second Amendment Ain't About Hunting." *Howard Law Journal* 34 (1991): 589–97.

C O'Donnell, M. T. "The Second Amendment: A Study of Recent Trends." *University of Richmond Law Review* 25 (Spring 1991): 501–18.

C Scarry, E. "War and the Social Contract: Nuclear Policy, Distribution, and the Right to Bear Arms." *University of Pennsylvania Law Review* 139 (May 1991): 1257–1316.

C Williams, D. C. "Civic Republicanism and the Citizen Militia: The Terrifying Second Amendment." *The Yale Law Journal* 101 (December 1991): 551–615.

1992

I Amar, A. R. "The Bill of Rights and the Fourteenth Amendment." *Yale Law Journal* 101 (April 1992): 1193–1284.

I Johnson, N. J. "Beyond the Second Amendment: An Individual Right to Arms Viewed Through the Ninth Amendment." *Rutgers Law Journal* 24 (Fall 1992): 1–81.

I Kates, D. B. "The Second Amendment and the Ideology of Self-Protection." *Constitutional Commentary* 9 (Winter 1992): 87–104.

C O'Hare, R. A., Jr., and J. Pedreira. "An Uncertain Right: The Second Amendment and the Assault Weapon Legislation Controversy." *St. John's Law Review* 66 (Winter 1992): 179–206.

I Wagner, J. R. "Gun Control Legislation and the Intent of the Second Amendment: To What Extent Is There an Individual Right to Keep and Bear Arms?" *Villanova Law Review* 37 (1992): 1407–59.

1993

C Blodgett-Ford, S. "Do Battered Women Have a Right to Bear Arms?" *Yale Law and Policy Review* 11 (1993): 509–60.

C Bogus, C. T. "Race, Riots, and Guns." *Southern California Law Review* 66 (May 1993): 1365–88.

I Halbrook, S. A. "Rationing Firearms Purchases and the Right to Keep Arms: Reflections on the Bills of Rights of Virginia, West Virginia, and the United States." *West Virginia Law Review* 96 (Fall 1993): 1–83.

I Martire, P. V. "In Defense of the Second Amendment: Constitutional & Historical Perspectives." *Lincoln Law Review* 21 (1993): 23–37.

I Quinlan, M. J. "Is There a Neutral Justification for Refusing to Implement the Second Amendment or Is the Supreme Court Just 'Gun Shy'?" *Capital University Law Review* 22 (Summer 1993): 641–92.

1994

C Fox, K. A., and N. C. Shah. "Natural Born Killers: The Assault Weapon Ban of the Crime Bill—Legitimate Exercise of Congressional Authority to Control Violent Crime or Infringement of a Constitutional Guarantee?" *St. John's Journal of Legal Commentary* 10 (Fall 1994): 123–50.

I Kates, D. B. "Gun Control: Separating Reality From Symbolism." *Journal of Contemporary Law* 20 (1994): 353–79.

I Reynolds, G. H. "The Right to Keep and Bear Arms Under the Tennessee Constitution: A Case Study in Civic Republican Thought." *Tennessee Law Review* 61 (Winter 1994): 647–73.

I Van Alstyne, W. "The Second Amendment and the Personal Right to Arms." *Duke Law Journal* 43 (April 1994): 1236–55.

I Vandercoy, D. E. "The History of the Second Amendment." *Valparaiso University Law Review* 28 (Spring 1994): 1007–39.

C Walsh, T. J. "The Limits and Possibilities of Gun Control." *Capital University Law Review* 23 (1994): 639–66.

1995

C Aborn, R. M. "The Battle Over the Brady Bill and the Future of Gun Control Advocacy." *Fordham Urban Law Journal* 22 (Winter 1995): 417–39.

C Ballinger, J. "Torts: Torts and Gun Control: Sealing Up the Cracks and Helping Licensed Dealers Avoid Sales to Unqualified Buyers." *Oklahoma Law Review* 48 (Fall 1995): 593–625.

C Blodgett-Ford, S. "The Changing Meaning of the Right to Bear Arms." *Seton Hall Constitutional Law Journal* 6 (Fall 1995): 101–88.

I Capezza, M. "Controlling Guns: A Call for Consistency in Judicial Review of Challenges to Gun Control Legislation." *Seton Hall Law Review* 25 (1995): 1467–95.

I Cottrol, R. J., and R. T. Diamond. " 'Never Intended to be Applied to the White Population': Firearms Regulation and Racial Disparity—The Redeemed South's Legacy to a National Jurisprudence?" *Chicago-Kent Law Review* 70 (1995): 1307–35.

I Denning, B. P. "Can the Simple Cite Be Trusted?: Lower Court Interpretations of United States v. Miller and the Second Amendment." *Cumberland Law Review* 26 (1995–96): 961–1004.

I Dennis, A. J. "Clearing the Smoke From the Right to Bear Arms and the Second Amendment." *Akron Law Review* 29 (Summer 1995): 57–92.

I Dennis, W. G. "A Right to Keep and Bear Arms? The State of the Debate." *Washington State Bar News* 49 (July 1995): 47–54.

C Dougherty, C. "The Minutemen, The National Guard, and the Private Militia Movement: Will the Real Militia Please Stand Up?" *John Marshall Law Review* 28 (Summer 1995): 959–85.

C Dunlap, C. J., Jr. "Revolt of the Masses: Armed Civilians and the Insurrectionary Theory of the Second Amendment." *Tennessee Law Review* 62 (Spring 1995): 643–77.

I Funk, T. M. "Gun Control and Economic Discrimination: The Melting-Point Case-in-Point." *The Journal of Criminal Law & Criminology* 85 (Winter 1995): 764–806.

I Garcia, M. I. "The 'Assault Weapons' Ban, the Second Amendment, and the Security of a Free State." *Regent University Law Review* 6 (Fall 1995): 261–98.

I Halbrook, S. P. "Congress Interprets the Second Amendment: Declarations By a Co-Equal Branch on the Individual Right to Keep and Bear Arms." *Tennessee Law Review* 62 (Spring 1995): 597–641.

I Halbrook, S. P. "Personal Security, Personal Liberty, and 'the Constitutional Right to Bear Arms': Visions of the Framers for the Fourteenth Amendment." *Seton Hall Constitutional Law Journal* 5 (Spring 1995): 341–434.

I Halbrook, S. P. "Second-Class Citizenship and the Second Amendment in the District of Columbia." *George Mason University Civil Rights Law Journal* 5 (Summer 1995): 105–78.

C Herz, A. D. "Gun Crazy: Constitutional False Consciousness and Dereliction of Dialogic Responsibility. *Boston University Law Review* 75 (January 1995): 57–153.

I Johnson, N. J. "Shots Across No Man's Land: A Response to Handgun Control, Inc.'s Richard Aborn." *Fordham Urban Law Journal* 22 (Winter 1995): 441–51.

I Kopel, D. B., and R. E. Gardner. "The Sullivan Principles: Protecting the Second Amendment from Civil Abuse." *Seton Hall Legislative Journal* 19 (1995): 737–75.

C Littman, R. J. "Gun-Free Schools: Constitutional Powers, Limitations, and Social Policy Concerns Surrounding Federal Regulation of Firearms in Schools." *Seton Hall Constitutional Law Journal* 5 (Spring 1995): 723–70.

I Reynolds, G. H. "A Critical Guide to the Second Amendment." *Tennessee Law Review* 62 (Spring 1995): 461–512.

I Reynolds, G. H., and D. B. Kates. "The Second Amendment and States' Rights: A Thought Experiment." *William and Mary Law Review* 36 (August 1995): 1737–68.

C Romano, T. E. "Firing Back: Legislative Attempts to Combat Assault Weapons." *Seton Hall Legislative Journal* 19 (1995): 857–93.

I Shelton, G. L. "In Search of the Lost Amendment: Challenging Federal Firearms Regulation Through the 'State's Right' Interpretation of the Second Amendment." *Florida State University Law Review* 23 (Summer 1995): 105–39.

C Tobia, J. S. "The Brady Handgun Violence Prevention Act: Does It Have a Shot At Success?" *Seton Hall Legislative Journal* 19 (1995): 894–920.

1996

I Barnett, R. E., and D. B. Kates. "Under Fire: The New Consensus on the Second Amendment." *Emory Law Journal* 45 (Fall 1996): 1139–1259.

I Bursor, S. "Toward a Functional Framework for Interpreting the Second Amendment." *Texas Law Review* 74 (April 1996): 1125–51.

I Denning, B. P., "Palladium of Liberty? Causes and Consequences of the Federalization of State Militias in the Twentieth Century." *Oklahoma City University Law Review* 21 (Summer/Fall, 1996): 191–245.

I Denning, B. P., and G. H. Reynolds. "It Takes a Militia: A Communitarian Case for Compulsory Arms Bearing." *William and Mary Bill of Rights Journal* 5 (Winter 1996): 185–214.

I Docal, R. "The Second, Fifth, and Ninth Amendments—The Precarious Protectors of the American Gun Collector." *Florida State University Law Review* 23 (Spring 1996): 1101–43.

I Larish, I. A. "Why Annie Can't Get Her Gun: A Feminist Perspective on the Second Amendment." *University of Illinois Law Review* (1996): 467–508.

I Larizza, R. J. "Paranoia, Patriotism, and the Citizen Militia Movement: Constitutional Right or Criminal Conduct?" *Mercer Law Review* 47 (Winter 1996): 581–636.

I Lund, N. "The Past and Future of the Individual's Right to Arms." *Georgia Law Review* 31 (Fall 1996): 1–76.

C   Polesky, J. E. "The Rise of Private Militia: A First and Second Amendment Analysis of the Right to Organize and the Right to Train." *University of Pennsylvania Law Review* 144 (April 1996): 1593–1642.

I   Szczepanski, K. D. "Searching for the Plain Meaning of the Second Amendment." *Buffalo Law Review* 44 (Winter 1996): 197–247.

1997

C   Dowd, D. W. "The Relevance of the Second Amendment to Gun Control Legislation." *Montana Law Review* 58 (Winter 1997): 79–114.

I   Espohl, F. "The Right to Carry Concealed Weapons For Self-Defense." *Southern Illinois University Law Journal* 22 (Fall 1997): 151–80.

C   Harman, R. "The People's Right to Bear Arms—What the Second Amendment Protects: An Analysis of the Current Debate Regarding What the Second Amendment Really Protects." *Whittier Law Review* 18 (Winter 1997): 411–44.

C   Ingram, J. D. "The Right (?) to Keep and Bear Arms." *New Mexico Law Review* 27 (Summer 1997): 491–516.

I   Johnson, D. E. "Taking a Second Look at the Second Amendment and Modern Gun Control Laws." *Kentucky Law Journal* 86 (Fall 1997/98): 197–222.

I   Kopel, D. B., and C. C. Little. "Communitarians, Neorepublicans, and Guns." *Maryland Law Review* 56 (1997): 438–554.

I   McAffee, T. B. "Constitutional Limits on Regulating Private Militia Groups." *Montana Law Review* 58 (Winter 1997): 45–78.

I   McAffee, T. B., and M. J. Quinlan. "Bringing Forward the Right to Keep and Bear Arms." *North Carolina Law Review* 75 (March 1997): 781–899.

I   Murley, D. E. "Private Enforcement of the Social Contract." *Duquesne Law Review* 36 (Fall 1997): 15–48.

I   Powe, L. A., Jr. "Guns, Words, and Constitutional Interpretation." *William and Mary Law Review* 38 (May 1997): 1311–1403.

1998

I   Barnet, T. "Gun 'Control' Laws Violate the Second Amendment and May Lead to Higher Crime Rates." *Missouri Law Review* 63 (Winter 1998): 155–93.

C   Bogus, Carl T. "The Hidden History of the Second Amendment." *U.C. Davis Law Review* 31 (Winter 1998): 309–408.

I   Denning, B. P. "Gun Shy: The Second Amendment as an 'Underenforced Constitutional Norm,' " *Harvard Journal of Law and Public Policy* 21 (Summer 1998): 719–91.

C   Gunn, S. H. "A Lawyer's Guide to the Second Amendment." *Brigham Young University Law Review* (1998): 35–54.

I   Harmer, D. "Securing a Free State: Why the Second Amendment Matters."
    Brigham Young University Law Review (1998): 55–101.
C   Healey, B. J. "Plugging the Bullet Holes in U.S. Gun Law." *John Marshall
    Law Review* 32 (Fall 1998): 1–34.
I   Kopel, D. B. "The Second Amendment in the Nineteenth Century."
    Brigham Young University Law Review (1998): 1359–1545.
I   Volokh, E. "The Commonplace Second Amendment." *New York Univer-
    sity Law Review* 73 (June 1998): 793–821.
C   Williams, D. C. "The Unitary Second Amendment." *New York University
    Law Review* 73 (June 1998): 822–30.
I   Worthen, K. J. "The Right to Keep and Bear Arms in Light of Thornton."
    Brigham Young University Law Review (1998): 137–75.

1999
I   Beason, R. H. "*Printz* Punts on the Palladium of Rights." *Alabama Law
    Quarterly* 50 (Winter 1999): 561–84.
I   Halbrook, S. P., and D. B. Kopel. "Tench Coxe and the Right to Keep and
    Bear Arms." *William and Mary Bill of Rights Journal* 7 (Fall 1999):
    347–400.
C   Streit, K. T. "Can Congress Regulate Firearms?" *William and Mary Bill of
    Rights Journal* 7 (Fall 1999): 645–70.

3. The Second Amendment in Action

MICHAEL A. BELLESILES*

W hat follows may be entirely irrelevant. There are those who argue that historical inquiry offers nothing to our understanding of the Second Amendment. This postmodernist position is well represented by Charlton Heston, who has dismissed historical scholarship as not in the least bit relevant and has called for historians to stop wasting their time in the archives.[1] Akhil Amar recently stated that current understandings of the original meaning of the Second Amendment "might be false as a matter of historical fact but [are] nonetheless true as a matter of constitutional law."[2] William Van Alstyne insists that historical research into the context of the Second Amendment "doesn't seem to me to make a very great deal of difference against the background of Bunker Hill, and the minutemen, and the imagery that this is the nature of things."[3] Postmodernism denies the value and even the validity of historical context, emphasizing instead language and image; truth itself is a rhetorical social construct, it is the critic's representation of the past that matters. The adversarial approach to the past, such as is demonstrated by the self-proclaimed "standard model" of the Second Amendment, usually takes a nonhistorical perspective, preferring to hunt for supportive quotations while subjecting well-known statements to excruciating linguistic deconstruction rather than undertaking the difficult and time-consuming task of archival research. Another feature of postmodern scholarship that is evident in the supposed standard model is an assertion of an intellectual monopoly. Thus Don Kates and Randy Barnett declare "virtual unanimity" among scholars "that there is no tenable textual or historical argument against a broad individual right view of the Second Amendment,"[4] and Joyce Lee Malcolm insists "there is no one for me to argue against anymore."[5] Not only have they proclaimed themselves victorious in a match without competitors, they also insist that they are better than the 1927 New York Yankees.

The postmodernist perspective is, of course, blasphemy to a historian. We tend to lose our senses of humor when people say that facts neither matter nor exist, look very stern, and warn that the next stop is Holocaust denial. However, this paper is not concerned with the recent debate over the meaning of the Second Amendment, which has been well and hotly discussed elsewhere.[6]

This paper is concerned with capturing the social, legal, and military context of the Second Amendment.

The continuing efforts of states to control access to and use of guns once the Second Amendment was part of the Constitution seemingly indicates a lack of concern for an individual "right" to own a gun. The absence of notable opposition to such state action, even when it extended to disarming a portion of the population, speaks to popular attitudes that failed to see gun ownership as a protected individual right. At the same time, the federal government came to see public indifference to firearms ownership as a major threat to national security, and responded by slowly building a standing army and beginning a program to provide guns directly to members of the militia at no cost. But popular disinterest undermined both efforts, with government censuses repeatedly revealing a surprising dearth of firearms. In brief, those responsible for its ratification saw the Second Amendment as a hindrance neither to governmental regulation of firearms nor to efforts by the federal government to arm specific groups of citizens.

THE CONSTITUTIONAL BACKGROUND

There were more guns in North America in 1783 than at any time in its history to that date. Lacking any gun manufactories, the United States had been lucky to acquire thousands of arms from Europe; 85 percent of the firearms used by American troops during the American Revolution came from France and the Netherlands.[7] Those who led the Continental Army to victory understood that the United States put itself in a precarious diplomatic and defensive position by depending on European sources for firearms. They also appreciated that the thousands of French, Dutch, and British guns in American hands would quickly decay and rot if not collected and maintained in government arsenals. They knew full well that no reliance could be placed on the militia to provide for the new nation's security, internal or external. The efforts of these nationalists to find and then create a stable source of firearms for the United States began a long process on the part of the federal government to arm its white male citizens.[8] On the other hand, many in the elite held that more guns equaled more to fear. Poor whites might put such weapons to an incorrect, class-based use that could disrupt or destroy the new nation. Senator Rufus King warned his colleagues in 1790 that "it was dangerous to put Arms into the hands of the Frontier People for their defense, lest they should Use them against the United States."[9] Nationalists found ample justification for their fears in Shays's Rebellion.

The uprising in western Massachusetts in 1786 and '87 presented an obvious indication of the dangers facing the country. The Shaysites themselves kept insisting that their political protest followed Revolutionary traditions. Facing serious economic adversity and an unresponsive state government that used the courts to pursue aggressively those who could not meet their debts, hundreds of poor farmers acted, as crowds often had in the colonial period, to close the courts and harass tax collectors. These insurgents considered their protests legitimate, presenting petitions to the General Court and holding county conventions when these petitions failed to receive a response.[10]

The Massachusetts government felt differently, acting with energy in crushing what they saw as a rebellion, a challenge to legitimate authority. As during many colonial conflicts, the Shaysite crowd was the militia, limiting the state's ability to call on those forces for support. Uninterested in compromise or negotiation, the legislature declared the uprising an "open, unnatural, unprovoked, and wicked rebellion." In order to "establish the just authority and dignity" of government, the General Court suspended habeas corpus, granted the governor emergency powers, and raised what amounted to a private army through contributions from Boston's merchants. The first clash came at the Springfield arsenal, where Daniel Shays's followers, many of them veterans, hoped to acquire the guns they needed to resist effectively the state's army. The state's forces were well armed from the arsenal's stores, which included cannon. The only shots fired were fifteen rounds of grape from that artillery, which killed four of the farmers and sent Shays's forces fleeing in terror. A week later, General Benjamin Lincoln routed the remaining insurgents without firing a shot, effectively ending Shays's Rebellion.[11]

Though the rebels had not exactly distinguished themselves in the martial arts, their uprising had far-reaching consequences. George Washington wrote to James Madison that "We are fast verging to anarchy and confusion." The crisis in Massachusetts was but a local variant of a national problem requiring a federal solution.[12] The political elite unified around the notion that there was no room for such insurrections in the new nation. George Washington wrote Benjamin Lincoln that the insurgents "had by their repeated outrages forfeited all right to Citizenship."[13] Even Samuel Adams, one of America's leading democrats, rejected pardon for the Shaysites: "The man who dares to rebel against the laws of a republic ought to die."[14] It would be very difficult to find an American political leader who favored a right to insurrection against duly elected governments.

To those favoring a stronger national government, the Revolution had clearly demonstrated the flaws in the militia when faced with a foreign invader, while the rebellion in Massachusetts indicated the unreliability of the militia when confronted with internal disorder. From Edmund Randolph's opening speech, the Constitutional Convention of 1787 returned often to militia reform. The majority of those present hoped that the constitution they were writing would prevent further disorder by bringing the militia under more direct federal control. In justifying writing an entirely new government compact to supercede the Articles of Confederation, Randolph gave as his first reason: "1. that the Confederation produced no security agai[nst] foreign invasion; . . . and that neither militia nor draughts being fit for defence on such occasions, enlistments only could be successful." The "common defence" required some sort of national army. The Revolution demonstrated that *"Volunteers* [are] not to be depended on" in case of war; while *"Militia* [are] difficult to be collected and almost impossible to be kept in the field. . . . Nothing short of a regular military force will answer." Randolph did not seek to terminate the militia; rather, in Alexander Hamilton's words, "the Militia of all the States [are] to be under the sole and exclusive direction of the United States." [15]

A few delegates worried that the states would lose their sovereignty if the militia came under federal control, while Rufus King and Gouverneur Morris feared that northern militia would be called upon to put down slave insurrections. General Charles Pinckney, who held that "Uniformity was essential" in the militia as "the States would never keep up a proper discipline of their militia," dismissed all these objections as pointless "distrust of the Genl Govt." John Langdon agreed, finding "no more reason to be afraid of the Genl. Govt than of the State Govts." The overriding sense of the convention was that the militia could not be expected to, as Randolph put it, "suppress domestic commotions" and thus required federal supervision. The alternative was disorder. [16]

Historians have amply demonstrated the difficulty of ascribing to the framers of the Constitution a consensus on their original intention. The Constitutional Convention hammered out a document full of compromises and barely obtained concessions. [17] One point at least won complete agreement: Congress should arm the militia. Some delegates called for the states to organize and discipline the militia, but no one stated that any state could keep its militia well armed; everyone agreed with the need for federal guidance. Luther Martin, a member of the Philadelphia convention who turned anti-Federalist, told the Maryland Assembly that "As to *giving such a power* [to regulate the militia], there was no objection; but it was thought by some, that this power *ought* to be given with certain *restrictions.*" Martin had hoped for a limitation on the president's power to order a militia beyond the borders of its home state. [18] The convention brushed aside this proposal and agreed with James Madison that the whole purpose of federal regulation "is to secure an effectual discipline of the Militia." The states had repeatedly proven their inability to arm, discipline, and deliver their militia when called upon. "The States neglect their Militia now," Madison went on, "and the more they are consolidated into one nation, the less each will rely on its own interior provisions for its safety. . . . The Discipline of the Militia is evidently a *National* concern, and ought to be provided for in the *National* Constitution." [19]

Madison had his way, as Article 1, section 8, of the Constitution made Congress responsible for "organizing, arming, and disciplining, the Militia." Some modern observers argue that the framers perceived the militia as a check on governmental power; yet the Constitution accomplishes the exact opposite, making the militia a potential tool of the central government for the repression of any challenge to federal authority. Congress had the authority to call "forth the Militia to execute the Laws of the Union, suppress Insurrections and repel Invasions." [20]

Under the Constitution, the new federal government held the traditional political power of controlling the supply of and access to firearms. [21] Colonial American governments had followed the British precedent in maintaining authority over firearms. [22] Guns were used and owned at sufferance, the state reserving the right to limit, regulate, or impress those arms at its discretion. Under common law this "reserved right of the sovereign" differed from eminent domain, lacking a requirement for just compensation. Since firearms were always seen as in the service of the monarch, impressing guns did not require a special act of Parliament. The American Revolution did not change that English heritage, as the loyalists discovered when their firearms were confiscated. [23] State legislatures needed no further argument than public safety, or, in Constitutional terms, the state's police powers, to justify gun regulation. In this regard they adhered to the English common law heritage and the practice of every European nation. Gun regulation in the Revolutionary period, and afterward, aroused amazingly little debate beyond accusations that they were not stringent enough or rigorously enforced. The authority of the state to regulate gun ownership was repeatedly framed by the need to arm the militia. [24]

The Constitution's treatment of the militia was in keeping with the Articles of Confederation and the several state constitutions that aimed to craft a workable militia structure. The Articles, passed by Congress in 1777 though not approved by the states until 1781, made the states responsible for the arming and regulation of the militia. Article 6 stated that "every state shall always keep up a well regulated and disciplined militia, sufficiently armed and accoutered, and shall provide and constantly have ready for use, in public stores, a due number of field pieces and tents, and a proper quantity of arms, ammunition and camp equipage." [25] The first state constitutions included a range of militia and gun-related articles. The Virginia Declaration of Rights of 1776 stated that "a well-regulated militia, composed of the body of the people trained to arms, is the proper, natural and safe defence of a free state . . . and that in all cases, the military should be under strict subordination to, and governed by, the civil power." It is hard to miss those opening words, in which Virginia declared the necessity of a state-directed militia, trained in the use of firearms.[26]

The Massachusetts Constitution of 1780 proclaimed that "The people have a right to keep and to bear arms for the common defence." That right did not place the individual beyond the discipline of the state, for the next sentence stated that "And as in time of peace armies are dangerous to liberty, they ought not to be maintained without the consent of the Legislature; and the military power shall always be held in exact subordination to the civil authority, and be governed by it." Article 4, section 1, of the Massachusetts Constitution granted the legislature authority to pass laws for the support and regulation of the state's militia, while Article 12 required all militia officers to report to the governor every three months on the number of arms and other military equipment held in his unit.[27] Even privately owned guns were held at state sufferance. The notion that an individual should be allowed to use a firearm without regard to state regulation appeared ludicrous to Massachusetts' political leadership. John Adams clarified that such an unhindered right to gun ownership would "demolish every institution and lay the laws prostrate, so that liberty can be enjoyed by no man."[28]

The most seemingly individualist renderings of gun rights must be matched against the actions of those responsible for these statements. For instance, the 1776 Pennsylvania Constitution declared that "The people have a right to bear arms for the defense [of] themselves and the State; and as standing armies in time of peace are dangerous to liberty, they ought not to be kept up. And the military should be kept under strict subordination to, and governed by the civil power." Again, it is the state's authority that stands out in this declaration; and the state of Pennsylvania did not hesitate to exercise that authority, disarming loyalists and anyone else who refused to take an oath of allegiance to the government. Gun ownership in Pennsylvania, as in every other state, was premised on the notion that the individual would use that weapon in the state's defense when called upon to do so; and to make the point completely clear, the state required an oath to that effect. The Test Act mandated the disarming of those who would not take the oath of allegiance.[29] As Don Higginbotham points out, "In all the discussions and debates from the Revolution to the eve of the Civil War, there is precious little evidence that advocates of local control of the militia showed an equal or even a secondary concern for gun ownership as a personal right."[30]

The militia provisions of the Constitution outraged the anti-Federalists, who insisted on state control. The anti-Federalists sought limits on the powers of the central government rather than an enhancement of individual rights. After the Philadelphia Convention, Luther Martin and other anti-Federalists imagined every possible scenario of federal tyranny rendering the states impotent. Under the Constitution, Martin charged, Congress could decide not to arm the militia, with the result that the militia would have few, if any, guns. Patrick Henry pursued this reasoning, suggesting that Congress could render the states defenseless. A militia abandoned by the federal government registered as a substantial threat to states that actively repressed and enslaved a large minority, or, in South Carolina, a majority of their population. "Of what service would militia be to you," Henry asked, "when most probably you will not have a single musket in the State; for as arms are to be provided by Congress, they may or may not furnish them?" Apparently Martin and Henry believed the people incapable of acquiring their own firearms. As Henry explained, if the federal government "neglect or refuse to discipline or arm our militia, they will be useless; the states can do neither." To not arm the militia was to leave them unarmed. Henry feared what Congress would not do; others suspected that the federal government would use its control over the militia to oppress the states.[31]

Not surprisingly, Federalists found it absurd that anyone would think that the central government would either send the militia into one state at a time to attain supremacy or disarm the militia through inaction. After all, it was Congress, with representatives drawn from those very states, that would pass the necessary legislation. In his reply to Martin, Oliver Ellsworth charged that "one hour you sported the opinion that Congress, afraid of the militia resisting their measures, would neither arm nor organize them, and the next, as if men required no time to breathe between such contradictions, that they would harass them by long and unnecessary marches." It seemed to Ellsworth that the anti-Federalists wanted both sides of the argument, fearing that the federal government would both arm and fail to arm the militia.[32]

Federalists found an additional logical flaw in anti-Federalist logic: the Constitution left the militia under the direct control of the states when not in national service. As Edmund Randolph observed, militia officers were all appointed by the state governments and were therefore hardly likely to act contrary to their own state's interests.[33] For the Federalists, the Constitution's militia clauses operated within their understanding of concurrent power. State and federal governments shared authority over the militia. The Constitution made Congress responsible for organizing and arming the militia, but nothing in that wording contradicted the states' ability to use the militia as they saw fit when not in active federal service. Any state could act to correct flaws in its militia, for example, a paucity of firearms. The militia, Federalists argued, would be neither so strong as to become a standing army nor so weak as to be ineffectual against domestic insurrection.[34] Most Federalists followed the lead of Madison and Randolph at the Virginia ratifying convention in maintaining that a federally regulated militia was the best way of avoiding a standing army.[35]

However, the Federalists were a bit disingenuous in insisting that a well-regulated militia would allow the United States to avoid a standing army. They had every expectation that the new constitutional government would build a more powerful army. Certainly most Federalists would have agreed with Gouverneur Morris's later assessment that "An overweening vanity leads the many, each man against the conviction of his own heart, to believe or affect to believe, that militia can beat veteran troops in the open field." At the Constitutional Convention, Morris wrote, "this idle notion, fed by vaunting demagogues, alarmed us" into giving support to the militia. They should have recalled better the Revolution, which taught that "to rely on militia was to lean on a broken reed." Alexander Hamilton was more succinct in *Federalist* 25: "I expect to be told that the militia of the country is its natural bulwark, and would be at all times equal to the national defence. This doctrine, in substance, had like to have lost us our independence. . . . The facts which, from our own experience, forbid a reliance of this kind, are too recent to permit us to be dupes of such a suggestion."[36] The only politically rational alternative was to bring the militia under federal control while also building a real American army.

THE SECOND AMENDMENT

James Madison had promised during the ratification process to consider amendments to the Constitution. Madison kept his word, a remarkable political action. Several of the recommended amendments addressed the structure of the militia, including limitations on the number of militia under federal control, specifics of their training, the nature and duration of martial law, the use of militia beyond a state's borders, the status of conscientious objectors, and the degree of state control over the militia. None became part of the Second Amendment, as Madison preferred simplicity and clarity in all the amendments he put before Congress.[37]

Madison rejected all changes to the Constitution that he thought would weaken the federal government, including its control over the militia. Rhetorically he asked, "For whose benefit is the militia organized, armed and disciplined? For the benefit of the United States."[38] He was willing to respond to the fears of the anti-Federalists by granting the states, in Carl Bogus's words, "a concurrent authority to arm their militia."[39] The result was a single sentence with a clarifying preamble: "A well regulated Militia, being necessary to the security of a free State, the right of the people to keep and bear Arms, shall not be infringed."

Madison stated his own understanding of the Second Amendment when he presented it to the House of Representatives. "In our government it is, perhaps, less necessary to guard against the abuse in the executive department than any other; because it is not the stronger branch of the system, but the weaker." The people had no need to fear their national government, for it had few means by which it could exert its authority. The real danger lay closer to home, in a tyrannical majority lacking checks on its democratic power. "In a government modified like this of the United States," Madison continued, "the great danger lies rather in the abuse of the community than in the legislative body. The prescriptions in favor of liberty, ought to be levelled against that quarter where the greatest danger lies, namely, that which possesses the highest prerogative of power: But this [is] not found in either the executive or legislative departments of government, but in the body of the people, operating by the majority against the minority." Madison feared an unrestrained citizenry, and the Bill of Rights, he thought, should protect the minority against the majority's transgressions.[40]

The Second Amendment's purpose may be fairly indicated by the ensuing debate and legislation. The House debate focused on two issues: the "use of the militia" in preventing "the establishment of a standing army," and the wisdom of allowing religious exemptions for service in the militia.[41] The congressional legislation that followed uniformly sought to regulate the militia, starting with the first national militia act of 1792. Meanwhile, legislatures in every state further revealed their understanding of gun rights in the limitations they imposed on gun ownership, whether in denying that right to blacks, Catholics, Indians, or to the foreign born.[42] The leaders of the new nation followed Washington's lead in calling for a standing army backed by a smaller, organized, and better-armed militia. The Constitution provided the framework for such a structure. The first Congress set about giving it shape.[43]

GUN OWNERSHIP UNDER THE SECOND AMENDMENT

The Second Amendment was part of the Constitution in 1794 when the Whiskey Rebellion broke out in western Pennsylvania. As Saul Cornell has shown, even leading anti-Federalists supported suppressing this threat to internal security. With congressional support, President Washington moved quickly to exercise his constitutional authority to call out the militia to put down a domestic insurrection. In the process he became more convinced than ever that little or no reliance was to be placed on the militia.[44]

Washington issued a call for 13,000 militia from Pennsylvania, Maryland, Virginia, and New Jersey. Ironically, one of the prime demands of the Whiskey rebels was a stronger standing army. While Pennsylvania's governor, Thomas

Mifflin, successfully kept firearms out of the hands of the western militia, Washington opened the federal repositories to arm the troops he led into the field against the Whiskey rebels.[45] The rebellion simply evaporated before Washington's show of force; the only deaths came from a pistol going off accidentally and a drunken brawl that ended with a fatal bayonet wound.[46] One can only speculate whether the Whiskey rebels would have behaved differently had they known just how ignorant of firearms were most of Washington's troops. Hardly a disciplined force, the militia looted, drank heavily, and beat civilians randomly. It was neither well trained nor well armed. General Samuel Smith, commander of the Maryland militia, reported to the House of Representatives that the majority of the Virginia and Maryland troops were ignorant of the use of arms. Many did not know how to load a musket, and others had never carried one in their lives.[47] Even young gentlemen like Meriwether Lewis reported for duty without a gun.[48] Secretary of War Henry Knox reported that only one-third of the militia called up to respond to the rebellion bore arms. The rest had to be supplied from federal stockpiles.[49]

Such reports on the inadequacies of the militia during the Whiskey Rebellion led to renewed calls for a select militia and a stronger standing army. "The militia," Lawrence Delbert Cress has written, "had only reluctantly taken up arms, and then only after the infusion of a large number of substitutes and volunteers." Even many of the administration's opponents, soon to be known as Democratic Republicans, now doubted the worth of the militia; and former anti-Federalists joined in supporting the disarming of the Whiskey rebels, despite the Second Amendment.[50] One of these men, William Findley, who had sympathized with the rebels, was appalled by the militias' conduct. The first necessity of any republic had to be public order; if the militia could not handle it, Findley stated, then a standing army would. Federalists and Republicans agreed that the task of the militia was to enforce social order; they also agreed that there was a great deal of room for improvement.[51]

Washington and Knox used the example of the Whiskey Rebellion to keep the army fully supplied. The army, however, had to content itself with weapons from the Revolution, cleaned and repaired at West Point, an inadequate situation in Washington's eyes.[52] Two problems, therefore, faced the American defensive establishment in the 1790s: the unorganized and untrained condition of the militia, and the impending shortage of usable firearms. The Federalists proposed two obvious solutions: a select militia and federal support for a domestic firearms industry.

Debates over the militia dominated the first federal Congress. These carefully considered discussions even addressed the exact bore of the muskets to be used by the militia. The representatives returned repeatedly to just how much authority the federal government should have in exercising its constitutional mandate of regulating the militia. Several representatives noted that every increase in federal power came at the expense of the states while others doubted the value of the militia. Thomas Fitzsimmons rejected the need for militia training as "a great tax on the community, productive of little instruction or edification, either in regard to military tactics, or the morals of a civilized nation." Most members, however, agreed with Roger Sherman of Connecticut that "the different states had certainly an inherent right to arm and protect the lives and property of the citizens." But to "more effectively . . . exercise this right" the states needed "to give up to the general government the power of fixing what arms the militia should use, by what discipline they should be regulated," and various other forms of ordering the nature of the militia. The only power left to the states in this formulation was "the right to say what descriptions of persons should compose the militia, and to appoint the officers that were to command it." Joshua Seney of Maryland thought that even this latter qualification granted the states power that they could easily abuse.[53]

While Congress was quite willing to grant the president control over the militia, it did not support his pet plan for a select militia. Washington agreed completely with Friedrich von Steuben's dismissal of the "flattering but . . . mistaken idea—that every Citizen should be a Soldier." The Revolution had made clear that "the use of arms is as [much] a trade as shoe or boot making."[54] Secretary of War Knox proposed to Congress that they create an active, highly trained (ten to thirty days per year), and well-armed reserve, which could be called into service by a state or the federal government. As in all of the militia proposals of the antebellum years, the federal government would supply guns to those serving in the select militia. The "universal militia" would become nothing more than a way of registering all those eligible to carry arms in time of war.[55]

Knox's proposal was logical, legal, and necessary, and would have aided the nation enormously in a range of future crises. Congress would have nothing to do with it. The people's representatives may have shared the view of former anti-Federalist John Smilie of Pennsylvania, who warned that "when a select militia is formed; the people in general may be disarmed."[56] But Smilie, like most anti-Federalists, had no problem granting the state the authority to decide who should be allowed to serve in the militia or to limit those ineligible from owning guns. Nor did most anti-Federalists want to see the propertyless carrying arms in or out of the militia.[57]

The debate over the future of the militia demonstrated an ideological fissure in America. Federalists looked to Europe and saw that warfare was changing fast, with massive armies and well-trained corps of light infantry sweeping away the last remnants of medieval warfare. Harrison Gray Otis was not alone in thinking that in the United States the "art of war is least understood." He insisted that at least a few men must be trained in modern methods of warfare, if only to advise the militia when war came. To prevent disaster, the country needed a larger army staffed by professional soldiers and a centralized select militia subject to extended training. Federalist support for volunteer militia companies appeared to Republicans an obvious assault on the ideal of a universal militia. The fact that the universal militia had never existed and that the current militia showed no signs of life remained irrelevant to this ideological absolute.[58]

A curious side effect of these heated debates over the militia was a brief militia revival—a resurgence born of political fears. In 1798 and 1799, faced with the threat of war with France, Federalists called for a stronger army and more centralized militia. Wild rumors circulated widely, including that Republicans were hoarding arms and that Hamilton was going to lead the army against domestic opponents. Federalist John Nicholas published a letter accusing the Virginia legislature of storing arms in the capitol for use in a rebellion against the federal government. He found evidence in the legislature's recent reorganization of the militia and its appropriation of funds to buy arms for the militia and to build an armory in Richmond.[59] Federalists in Richmond and Petersburg responded by organizing the first private militia companies.[60] Shortly thereafter, Republicans in Philadelphia organized their first private militia company, the Republican Blues, "in order to defend the country against foreign and domestic enemies and [to] support the laws."[61] Pressured by the states, Congress passed a new militia act, but Governor Stone of Maryland refused to cooperate until the federal government reimbursed the state for the arms it lost during the Whiskey Rebellion. Along with the threat, he sent a request for new arms for the militia, reporting that the state was dangerously underequipped. The next governor repeated these entreaties and was also ignored.[62]

The private, volunteer companies were generally better armed and far more enthusiastic than their state-sponsored counterparts. For instance, the Washington Artillery of Washington, D.C., which was founded during this crisis, maintained its exclusivity by requiring the election of new members. Recruits were expected to supply their complete uniform as a sign of seriousness, but guns came from the company's private supply, which was sufficient for the entire troop. A new member of the company did not have to own a gun, but he did need a tailor.[63] In comparison, during the war scare of 1798, the nearby Alexandria militia regiment, only 18 percent of whom bore arms, frantically turned to the Virginia government for an additional 500 muskets. The governor offered 250, noting that requests for arms were coming in from militia companies all over Virginia. The Fairfax County militia was in slightly better shape, needing only 250 guns to finish arming their 563-member militia.[64] The regular militia seemed a lost cause to many. In 1800 Secretary of War James McHenry wrote the chair of the House Committee on Defense that "Even in times of the greatest danger, we cannot give to our militia that degree of discipline . . . upon which a nation may safely hazard its fate."[65]

In the midst of these military preparations, the Fries Rebellion temporarily disrupted southeast Pennsylvania. Outraged by the new direct federal tax on houses, lands, and slaves, as well as by the Alien and Sedition acts, groups of citizens defied federal authority. In the first months of 1799, the rebels, most members of the militia, threatened tax assessors, forcing one to "dance around" a liberty pole, while another was "committed to an old stable and . . . fed rotten corn." But the insurgents' greatest crime came when John Fries, a local militia commander, led more than one hundred men armed with swords, clubs, and muskets to free some prisoners. No shots were fired in this traditional effort to protest corrupt authority in what Fries's attorney Alexander Dallas called a "system of intimidation." To President John Adams, this system was treasonous, and he ordered five hundred federal troops under General William MacPherson to put down the uprising. There was no resistance and no violence as this little army disarmed the rebels and rounded up their leaders. Fries and two others were arrested, tried, convicted, and then pardoned, and that was the end of it.[66] As with the Whiskey Rebellion, the insurgents found little support once the government acted. Even ardent Jeffersonians, while objecting to the use of federal troops instead of the state militia, agreed that "anyone challenging federal authority should be brought to justice."[67] There was no reference to the Second Amendment when Fries's supporters were disarmed by the state.

Following on the heels of the war scare and "rebellion" in Pennsylvania came the closely contested national election of 1800. It looked briefly as though the "Revolution of 1800" would be just that. But the poorly prepared state of the participants indicate that it would have been a relatively bloodless affair. As rumors spread that the Federalists might prevent Thomas Jefferson from taking office in 1801, Republican John Beckley of Pennsylvania charged that Federalists had removed "several hundred stand of arms and 18 pieces of cannon, heretofor in the hands of the Militia, . . . into the public arsenals of the U.S."[68] Fearing a showdown, Governor Monroe of Virginia planned for the Virginia militia to block any effort by federal troops to remove the federal arms stored in Virginia by seizing them for state use.[69] Monroe even sent a spy to check the quality of these arms. Major T. M. Randolph reported that these "4000 excellent muskets and bayonets" had been captured from the British at Yorktown.[70] Governor Thomas McKean of Pennsylvania was even more emphatic in his preparations, informing Jefferson that "arms for upwards to twenty thousand were secured" by his government for the militia in case their service was required. He did not expect them to bring their own arms, but planned to supply the militia with state and federal arms.[71] Yet with the temporary resolution of the conflict with France and the peaceful inauguration of Thomas Jefferson, the crisis passed and military enthusiasm waned, and militia companies throughout the country died a peaceful death.[72]

THE SEARCH FOR GUNS

In some ways the militia debates of the 1790s skirted a far more important issue. Real political independence required military independence, which in turn necessitated a domestic arms industry. Every state saw it as the government's responsibility to, in the words of Georgia's militia law, "Arm and Array" the militia "for suppressing all such insurrections, as may happen."[73] But no state was able to meet this goal on its own, even when faced with insurrection. At such times of crisis the states turned to the federal government, which would frantically attempt to find sufficient guns for the militia. But most national leaders agreed that such an approach posed dangers to the nation. Washington raised this question in his first annual message to Congress in 1790, clearly stating the lessons he had learned in the war. "A free people ought not only be armed, but disciplined; . . . and their safety and interest require that they should promote such manufactories as tend to rend them independent of others for essential, particularly military, supplies."[74] Over the ensuing seventy years, the federal government worked to make the United States self-sufficient in arms production.

Washington, Secretary of War Knox, Treasury Secretary Alexander Hamilton, and every member of Congress who had participated in the American Revolution knew that most Americans did not own guns and had no interest in buying them. As Hamilton said, guns were not "objects of ordinary and indispensable private consumption or use."[75] It was evident to Hamilton that private demand for firearms would never lead to a sufficient supply for the military. And since guns were most important as military weapons, domestic production should be encouraged by the government. Eighteenth- and twentieth-century experts both agree that firearms used by professionals—soldiers and hunters—had a life expectancy of five years. At that point they needed serious maintenance and repair, or to be replaced. The British army, which required the regular cleaning and inspection of all its guns, replaced roughly one-tenth of its well-made Brown Besses every year before the Napoleonic Wars. Applying this replacement rate, and taking no account of population growth, means that Americans, if indeed every adult white male used a gun regularly to hunt, needed to purchase some 50,000 guns a year by 1800. Where were they to find this many guns?

The first militia act in 1792 amply demonstrated the problems inherent in any effort to arm the militia or army. Congress, in trying to keep the militia alive, passed "An Act More effectually to provide for the National Defence." This act declared that "every free able bodied white male citizen" between the ages of eighteen and forty-five should be enrolled in the militia and must appear "when called out to exercise." Further, "every citizen so enrolled, shall . . . be constantly provided with a good musket or firelock" and other accoutrements. Congress took upon itself the responsibility of providing those guns, and specified that within five years all muskets "shall be of bores sufficient for balls of the eighteenth part of a pound." All arms and ammunition intended for militia use remained exempt from attachment in any civil suit.[76] To keep track of its arms, each company was to make regular returns of arms and ammunition to each state's adjutant general, who in turn reported directly to the president.[77] To begin this process, Congress ordered the purchase of 7,000 muskets. Over the next two years the government was able to purchase only 480 "rifle guns."[78]

The experience of individual states matched warnings from the executive branch.[79] Late in 1792, during a brief conflict with the Creeks, Charles Pickney reported to the South Carolina assembly that the frontier militia was dangerously underarmed. The western counties "if properly supplied by Government with the means, [are] well disposed to exert themselves in defence of their possessions," but the state lacked sufficient stores to arm them. Governor Moultrie added his voice in alarm over "the defenceless Situation of the Frontier Inhabitants for want of Arms and Ammunition."[80] The legislature ordered that the two hundred stands of arms stored in the state house should be sent west and authorized the governor to purchase six hundred more muskets for public use. It took a year to acquire these guns, by which time the state government determined that it needed even more guns, which it attempted to acquire in Philadelphia. To ensure that these state guns were better cared for, the legislature ordered the building of an arsenal capable of holding arms for 5,000 men at Abbeville. This arsenal was finished in December 1793, and the state then tried, unsuccessfully, to get the national government to pay for it. Whenever even a limited frontier war broke out, state governments had to request the aid of other states and the federal government, empty the public storehouses of guns for the frontier, and seek to purchase ever more arms.[81]

Such experiences persuaded the state governments that they could not possibly arm their militia without federal help. The 1792 national militia act had not clarified the most important questions: Where would the states acquire

guns, and who would pay for them? Maryland took the unique path of allowing its militia system to collapse in hopes of forcing the federal government to
do something.[82]

Henry Knox thought he had the solution in his effort to federalize arms production. In 1794 Knox reported to Congress on the condition of the American
militia. By Knox's estimate, the nation could field 450,000 militia, of whom no
more than 100,000 owned nor could be supplied with guns. The remaining
350,000 muskets, plus replacements for unusable weapons among the remaining 100,000, could not be bought in Europe, given the war there, even if the
United States could afford such a purchase. Nor could American gunmakers
hope to supply more than some 3,000 guns per year. Knox saw only one
choice: government arsenals. "The only solid resource to obtain a supply, is
the establishment of manufactories within each state."[83]

Despite initial fears of granting the central government too much power,
Congress agreed with Washington, Knox, and Hamilton on the importance of
arming the militia and army. If war broke out against a European power, the
United States would be in no position to offer an adequate defense, and it
could no longer expect to receive arms from France, as it had during the Revolution. America had to create domestic sources of firearms. Congress therefore
appropriated the funds to purchase 14,000 muskets and to build three armories to make firearms. The first of these national armories was built at
Springfield, Massachusetts, the second at Harpers Ferry, Virginia—the third
was never built. The United States government was now in the gun-making
business, an enterprise it would dominate and direct through the 1860s.[84]

Congress knew that American gun manufacturers could not collectively
produce the 14,000 arms they hoped to buy. They did seek to confine the market by forbidding the export of American-made arms, the idea being that the
government needed all the guns produced in the United States—not that there
was any market for the more expensive and inferior American-made guns outside the United States. In return for that limitation on production, Congress
indicated its willingness to buy whatever American gunsmiths could make.
Based on Hamilton's and Knox's estimates of maximum production, they expected that production level to be seven thousand muskets in two years. To
meet the shortfall, Congress appropriated $100,000 to buy British firearms
and awarded the British firm Ketland a contract to make the locks for the
American-made muskets and rifles, a trade they maintained until 1812. Thus
the United States' first large purchase of firearms after the winning of independence came from England, and American gun manufacturers could hope
to reach the modest target of 3,500 guns per year only by being supplied with
English-made locks.[85]

Nonetheless, American gunsmiths did not reach their target of 3,500 firearms per year. As delays persisted, the new secretary of war, Timothy Pickering, admitted that buying American-made guns was not only more expensive but also less efficient. Regardless, he insisted to the Senate that the long-term advantages of patronizing American gunsmiths far outweighed the disadvantages, especially as these manufactories would certainly go out of business without government contracts. On Washington's orders, Pickering subsidized domestic production by ordering an additional nine thousand muskets "after the model of the French arms, which compose, by far, the greatest part of those in our magazines." He issued further interest-free advances and distributed English gunlocks even though the previous orders had not yet been met. They were all in serious denial.[86]

The government had better luck with its own armories. Nonetheless, high levels of government support did not translate into satisfactory production levels. Springfield Armory, which aimed to produce 4,200 muskets per year between 1795 and 1799, manufactured 7,750 in its first five years, 37 percent of its goal. In the first decade of the nineteenth century, Springfield Armory averaged just over five thousand guns of all kinds per year. Harpers Ferry could not meet that standard. As Merrit Roe Smith has written, "Productivity at Harpers Ferry between 1801 and 1806 revealed few signs of growth," with an annual output of 1,700 arms a year.[87]

President Thomas Jefferson, driven by his agrarian ideals, initially hoped to find evidence that he could avoid the expense of supporting arms production. In 1803 he instructed Secretary of War Henry Dearborn to conduct a careful census of firearms in America, with the intention of demonstrating that the American militia owned sufficient firearms. The results disappointed Jefferson. In a country with 524,086 official militia, Dearborn found 183,070 muskets, 39,648 rifles, and 13,113 other firearms, for a total of 235,831 guns (there were also 11,882 sabers). That was enough guns for 45 percent of the militia, a quarter of the white male population, and just 4.9 percent of the nation's total population. Half of all these guns were in the hands of the federal government, with about one-quarter in state arsenals.[88] Dearborn's study was much more thorough than Henry Knox's 1793 effort, and was disturbing enough for him to make an additional meticulous count of all federal firearms in 1806 that validated his earlier findings.[89] Dearborn concluded that if the United States continued to rely on the militia for its defense, and if the people would not arm themselves, then the federal government would have to do so.

On this point, at least, Jeffersonians and Federalists agreed. Though they disputed who in the militia should get the arms—the Federalists calling for a select militia—they did not question that the militia needed guns. Dearborn's numbers convinced a unified Congress to pass the 1808 Militia Act, the single most important piece of legislation promoting the development of a domestic gun industry.[90] This act appropriated $200,000 a year "for the purpose of providing arms and military equipment for the whole body of the militia of the United States, either by purchase or manufacture." The act further authorized the president to erect arsenals and arms manufactories "as he may deem expedient." "All the arms procured in virtue of this act, shall be transmitted to the several states . . . in proportion to the number of the effective militia in each state and territory."[91]

Over the next thirty years the federal government supervised several more censuses of firearms, an enterprise in keeping with the traditional English assize of arms. In addition, most states conducted similar surveys into the 1840s. Collectively these censuses reveal a slow increase in the total number of arms available in the United States, though it would take the Civil War to finally provide arms sufficient for those men expected to serve in the militia.[92] What is most intriguing about this process is that there is no evidence of any objection to these censuses in any newspaper, journal, or legislative record. It would appear that the people of the United States did not question the right of their government to determine the number, condition, and location of firearms, even in private households. In the South in light of the constant fear of slave uprisings, this governmental power bordered on a necessity.

Even Thomas Jefferson, that supposed champion of individual and states' rights, sought during his presidency to increase federal control over the militia and arms production. Seven of Jefferson's eight annual messages to Congress called for greater federal regulation of the militia.[93] His Republican colleagues in Congress shared his concern. The government armories at Springfield and Harpers Ferry were doing fairly well, producing between five and ten thousand guns every year between them. But that was barely enough to keep the army in working firearms. Congress hoped that a concerted effort by the federal government to arm the militia would encourage gunsmiths to expand their operations. Jefferson appointed Tench Coxe, purveyor of public supplies, to handle the procurements.

In June 1808, Coxe took the unusual step of placing advertisements in most of the major newspapers in the country, calling for bids. Over the next five months Coxe signed contracts with all but one of the gunsmiths who replied to his advertisement (because his shop was too small).[94] These nineteen agreed to deliver a total of 85,000 muskets over the next five years. The single largest contract was for 10,000 muskets with Pennsylvania's Henry family, in its third generation of gun making. The government advanced nearly $100,000 to aid these gun manufacturers, not a single one of whom met their schedules. After two years, by which time 17,000 muskets were due, only 3,000 had been delivered. By the end of 1813, the government was required to spend one million dollars and acquired at least 85,000 muskets; they had spent half that amount and received 34,477 guns (40 percent). Several manufactories wanted to give up and get out of their contracts; even the Henry family bailed out after delivering 4,246 guns. The new Commissary General of Purchases, Callender Irvine, willingly agreed to terminate all these contracts, especially after his inspection convinced him that the guns delivered had little value beyond what they would fetch as scrap.[95]

In short, gun production outside of the two national armories continued to be a matter of small-scale operations. Tench Coxe's report of American gun manufactures in June 1813 listed a total of 154 gunsmiths in eleven states, 115 of them in Pennsylvania. He placed the total value of these enterprises at $593,993; an average capitalization of $5,165, but a mean of just over $1,000. Coxe did not discuss the manufacturing capabilities of America's gunsmiths, even though there was a war on. Instead the poor quality of these guns captured his attention, leading him to suggest that it was about time for the government to establish adequate testing facilities.[96]

At the very time that many Jeffersonians began questioning the capacity and ability of American gun manufacture, others started wondering whether Washington had not in fact been right about the militia. In 1809, Connecticut's Benjamin Tallmadge, a member of the House of Representative's Committee on the Militia, issued the usual insistence on the value of the militia. In response, General Ebenezar Huntington, Revolutionary War veteran and past commander of the Connecticut militia, stated roughly that "as soldiers [the militia] are not worth their rations." He did not believe that the government should waste its time arming the militia, as they did not take care of their arms, which were soon "destroyed with rust," and, he concluded, "I have no doubt might be considered a total loss in five years." Huntington returned to Knox's older idea of volunteer units, smaller and better trained and committed to taking care of their arms. Without such reform, the militia would be little better than "food for powder on the day of battle."[97]

Republicans came to realize that their ideology of a well-armed universal militia had no relation to reality. Prominent Republicans like Joseph Priestly and John Taylor of Caroline, wrote in favor of a professional army, dismissing traditional fears of a standing army as irrelevant. National survival had to take precedence over ideological purity. Maximillian Godefroy, a French veteran living in Maryland, published a pamphlet in 1807 arguing that the American resistance to all military skills, from shooting to marching, left the country no alternative but to turn to a professional army. In America, Godefroy wrote, "military talents are repulsed, and military ideas rejected as useless." While

Europe was developing a whole range of new military techniques, the United States clung to vain hopes that the militia would somehow save the nation. Many in Congress agreed with representative Harmanus Bleeker of New York, who stated that "the militiaman is best employed at his plough." [98]

David Humphreys had stated the case plainly in 1803 when he observed that military skills are "not so simple and easy as to come instinctively without practice." [99] The most ardent Republicans came to understand that the militia needed guns in order to learn how to use them. In state after state, officials complained that they were not yet receiving the free arms promised under the 1808 Militia Act. In 1809 Joseph Bloomfield of New Jersey began an angry letter to Congress by quoting the Constitution as requiring Congress to arm the militia. He then added pointedly, "They have not done it. The National Legislature have neglected what they ought have done the moment it was in their power," to arm the militia. He lambasted the idiocy of expecting individuals to arm themselves, a highly unlikely prospect. In no state, Bloomfield declared, had even one-sixth of the militia succeeded in arming itself appropriately. He lay the responsibility for the nation's undefended condition squarely on Congress, which shirked its most fundamental duty. [100]

The federal government could do only so much to overcome two centuries of reliance on Europe for firearms. In 1810 Secretary of the Treasury Albert Gallatin issued a report on gun manufactures. After fifteen years of government support, Gallatin listed guns under "manufactures of iron," which "consist principally of agricultural implements," adding that "all of the finer species" of such work are imported from Britain. The two government arsenals reached a peak of 19,000 muskets that year, with another 20,000 guns made by private manufacturers nationwide—39,000 guns for a population of 7,202,014, more than a million of whom were supposed to be in the militia (enough guns for less than 4 percent of the militia). [101] The government still had a long way to go if it hoped to meet the Constitution's mandate in Article 1, section 8, "To provide for organizing, arming, and disciplining, the Militia."

GUNS AND SLAVERY

No contemporary can be found to argue that the Second Amendment hindered the state's authority to regulate firearms. Nor were similar passages in state constitutions perceived as blocking such legislation. As Carl Bogus has reminded us, slavery played a key role in the South's understanding of the Second Amendment. [102] The Southern militia's primary purpose was the preservation of white supremacy. The slave patrols, whose members were drawn from the militia rosters, handled routine policing. [103] But slave insurrections pushed the militia to its limits, demonstrating that not even the fear of slave uprisings sufficed to motivate the majority of whites to own guns and practice their use.[104]

The first great test of the Southern militia under the Constitution came in Virginia in 1800. In that first year of the new century, an African American named Gabriel rattled the South to its core with a vivid example of the danger posed to the whites. Gabriel's Rebellion also revealed a core paradox in the question of arms in the South: the need of the State to hold guns that would be easily accessible to the militia, but not so to the slaves. These stored arms became the most tempting target for any revolutionary force. Thus Gabriel's first goal was to capture the militia arms stored in the state capitol, for his forces would be armed only with swords, knives, pikes, and what few muskets he could seize from white planters.[105]

As soon as Governor James Monroe heard the rumors of the planned uprising, he ordered all the "publick arms" moved from the capitol to the penitentiary under a guard of thirteen armed militia—a surprisingly small force but all that was available at the time. The problem then became to issue some of these arms to the militia units called up by Monroe.[106] A general panic spread through much of Virginia at the start of Gabriel's uprising, and whites demanded immediate militia protection. The Suffolk militia, short of guns, appealed to the governor for aid. Monroe promised to supply arms, but then discovered that the state had insufficient guns even for the five hundred militia so far ordered into action. The militia officers appealed repeatedly for aid, without success, finally arming their troops with whatever they could lay their hands on, primarily bladed weapons.[107]

Most observers felt that only heavy rains and the early discovery of the uprising prevented a successful slave rebellion. As James Callender wrote Thomas Jefferson, the insurrection "could hardly have failed of success, . . . for after all, we could only muster four or five hundred men of whom no more than thirty had Muskets."[108] Norfolk mayor Thomas Newton was delighted to hear that the militia had been called out, but complained that "they have not arms, and are on that account only equal to the slaves except in numbers." Mayor Newton insisted that it was the state's job to see that the militia was properly armed.[109]

During the slave insurrection scare of 1802, Monroe reserved most of the state's arms for the 19th Regiment of Richmond, charged with protecting the capital. That unit was fully armed with "four hundred and twelve stands of public Arms." Monroe felt that he had learned his lesson from Gabriel's Rebellion, and that with the vast majority of his citizens "unarmed . . . they may become a prey to a very small force." He therefore sought to ensure that the slave patrols were better armed and far more intrusive.[110] The terror aroused in the white breast by this slave rebellion saw an increase in interest in the militia across the South.[111]

The Southern governments responded to their fear of slave insurrection by shifting more funds to arming their militia, and by ensuring that there was no individual right to bear arms. It seems almost too obvious to point out that the Second Amendment did nothing to prevent the various states from disarming those perceived as dangerous to public safety and passing laws forbidding the possession of guns by these people. Thus every Southern state not only forbade slaves from carrying firearms, but they also outlawed the ownership of guns by free blacks.[112] The only challenge to this legislation came in 1844. The North Carolina Supreme Court ruled unanimously that laws restricting the use of firearms by free blacks did not violate the Second Amendment.[113]

MADISON'S LESSON

Under the leadership of James Madison, the United States entered the War of 1812 grotesquely unprepared for a sustained conflict. Jefferson had allowed the army's total strength to fall to 2,400 men in 1807. As the war approached, Congress authorized an army of 10,000; but recruiters had little luck finding that many men in America willing to serve. When Congress declared war in June, the U.S. Army consisted of 6,750 men. Wellington commanded 46,000 men at the Battle of Salamanca the next month, while Napoleon led an army of 450,000 into Poland.[114]

William King, the assistant inspector general of the U.S. Army, found the vast majority of federal arms "in infamously bad order."[115] Matters were much worse among the militia. In his preliminary war message, President Madison called upon "the several states, to take effectual measures to organize, arm, and equip, according to law" their militia. They were in desperate need of help, with nearly every militia in the country appealing for arms and ammunition.[116] Pennsylvania's adjutant general reported that his state's 99,414 men could take the field with 30,366 guns, both publicly and privately owned. In July 1813, the House Committee of Military Affairs stated a transparent truth: "The war found the militia badly armed."

General William Lenoir informed North Carolina's governor that "a considerable part of" the seven thousand militiamen who reported for service were "unarmed." He had no idea "how they are to be furnished with arms." The situation was worse in Vermont, Rhode Island, and New York. The latter state's Senator Obadiah German felt that "the evils attending upon calling a large portion of the militia into actual service for any considerable time, is almost incalculable." He correctly prophesized that the event "will teach you the impropriety of relying on them for carrying on the war."[117] The historian

Lawrence Delbert Cress has offered a more biting conclusion: "Ironically, the ideological tenets that had informed Republican critiques of Federalist policy over the previous decade would render the republic in the years preceding the War of 1812 virtually defenseless—this despite a clearly discernible sense that the nation's peacetime forces required significant reform."[118]

The federal government did its best to make up for its previous complacency, rushing to supply modern, usable muskets to the army, and any kind of guns to the militia. The War Department gave priority to those militia it thought most likely to see battle, sending 5,000 muskets to Connecticut, 2,000 to New York, and 1,500 to Louisiana in the first year of the war. The secretary of war was particularly concerned with the militia in the area of Washington itself, which would be called upon should the British attack the nation's capital. The Maryland militia therefore received 1,500 guns and the D.C. militia 2,200 as an indefinite loan; old arms in their possession were recalled for repair. Each militia member who received a gun took it into his personal possession on promising to care for it and to return it when required. Repeatedly militia officers reported that many of those receiving firearms appeared to have never handled one before.[119]

The concerns of the War Department were well founded, for when the British did attack Washington, D.C., in August 1814, the militia crumbled. The British expeditionary force was tiny by European standards, a mixed force of 4,370 infantry, marines, and sailors, with just three artillery pieces. In theory they faced an aroused populace able to field some 50,000 militia within a day's march of the capital. There were certainly enough registered members of the militia, but they had rarely mustered, let alone trained, and most were unarmed. The Virginia militia had no supply of flints, a necessity for actually firing a gun, while the governor of Pennsylvania could not call out the militia to protect Washington because the legislature had failed to pass a new militia law. Those who did show up did everything wrong, even reversing the famous mythology by forming themselves into neat ranks in open fields while the British fired at them from behind the cover of trees. Admiral Alexander Cochrane's forces easily defeated the nearly 12,000 U.S. regulars and militia he encountered, including General John Stricker's beautifully uniformed Baltimore regiment of 3,000 men. Thousands of Americans quietly slipped away for home without ever firing a shot in defense of their nation's liberty. It was a sorry show, as smoke rose from the burning White House and British sailors cavorted in the Capitol.[120]

Many contemporaries thought the local militia units simply cowardly, but at least one regiment had a sound reason for not acting in defense of the capital city: they had almost no guns. Colonel George Minor testified before Richard M. Johnson's House committee investigating the fall of Washington, D.C., in

October 1814. Minor, in command of Virginia's 60th Regiment, arrived at Washington, D.C., with six hundred infantry and one hundred cavalry. He found his troops grievously short of arms, reporting personally to President Madison "as to the want of arms, ammunition &c." Madison sent him to General Armstrong, who told him that "arms, &c. could not be had that night, and directed me to report myself next morning to Colonel Carbery, who would furnish me with arms, &c.; which gentleman, From early next morning, I diligently sought for, until a late hour in the forenoon, without being able to find him, and then went in search of General Winder." He found Winder and was told to wait. As a consequence, this regiment, described by General Widner as "wholly unarmed," never saw battle.[121] As his capital burned, President Madison may have reflected on the failure of the federal government to successfully arm its citizens.

But few people in this first generation of constitutional government questioned the federal government's inherent authority to regulate and arm the militia. The Supreme Court cast aside the old anti-Federalist position in *Houston v. Moore* (1820) and *Martin v. Mott* (1827). Both decisions upheld the clearest reading of Article 1, section 8, on the Constitution as granting the federal government complete control over the militia. Justice Joseph Story quoted the Second Amendment in *Houston v. Moore*[122] to demonstrate the need for Congress to regulate the militia. "A rational interpretation," Story wrote, "must construe this power as exclusive in its own nature and belonging solely to Congress." Any other reading granting the states more authority over the militia would be disruptive and "repugnant to the constitutional laws" already passed by Congress.[123] In *Martin v. Mott* Story held that Congress, as representative of the people, could be counted on to "guard against usurpation or wanton tyranny."[124] The Second Amendment was read entirely within this context of the government's need to regulate the militia. There was no dissent in either case.

CONCLUSION

Legislatures, whether local or national, worked on the assumption that they had a legitimate interest in passing acts to secure the public safety. As a consequence, measures that placed precise limitations on the use and possession of firearms passed largely unchallenged. On the one occasion when such legislation was overturned, in *Bliss v. Commonwealth* (1822), the Kentucky Supreme Court ruled that state regulation of firearms violated the state's militia amendment, which granted an explicitly individual right to bear arms. In response, the legislature immediately amended the state constitution to allow such legislation, rewriting the militia amendment to more closely match the federal Constitution's Second Amendment. Otherwise, court after court agreed with the logic of Tennessee's high court, in *Aymette v. State* (1840), that "The object then, for which the right of keeping and bearing arms is secured, is the defence of the *public*," and that nothing in the Constitution limits the legislature "from passing laws regulating the manner in which these arms may be employed."[125]

Such decisions validated a wide variety of gun regulations at the state and federal levels. Congress retained tight control over the sale of firearms and ammunition to the Indians, again needing no further justification than public safety. The Indian Intercourse Act of 1834 placed strict limitations on those selling any kind of arms to Indians, and required a federal license in order to enter into the Indian trade.[126] States worked to keep firearms out of the hands of those persons marked as unsafe. As in the past, blacks—slave or free—were included, and those states that elected nativist governments in the 1840s and '50s disarmed Catholics and the foreign born.[127] As always, political enemies had no right to bear arms. The new U.S. government and several state governments made that abundantly clear during a number of uprisings in the early national period, from the Whiskey Rebellion in 1794 through Dorr's Rebellion in 1842, as well as anything approximating a slave uprising.[128]

Throughout the country, states responded to the threat of concealed weapons. Not only pistols, but a variety of small, well-made bladed weapons like dirks and Bowie knives, as well as sword canes, could too easily be concealed and produced in the midst of an argument to lethal effect. As the early American political scholar Benjamin Oliver wrote in 1832, the "cowardly and disgraceful" act of carrying concealed weapons transformed what might have been a barroom brawl into a deadly encounter. The Second Amendment, which Oliver held relevant only to the militia system, offered nothing "to prevent congress or the legislatures of the different states from enacting laws to prevent citizens from always going armed."[129] Most state legislators agreed with Oliver's interpretation. As early as 1801 the Tennessee legislature made it illegal for anyone to "publicly ride or go armed to the terror of the people, or privately carry any dirk, large knife, pistol, or any other dangerous weapon, to the fear or terror of any person."[130] Louisiana's 1813 act outlawing the carrying of concealed firearms allowed police officers to stop and search anyone suspected of carrying a concealed weapon.[131] Several state constitutions forbade noncitizens from possessing firearms.[132] This fear of concealed weapons accelerated in the 1830s as pistols became smaller. In 1832 Illinois instituted a $100 fine for anyone caught carrying "upon him any pistol, gun, knife, bludgeon, or other offensive weapon"; Ohio's fine was $200.[133] In 1837 Georgia's legislature forbade shopkeepers from selling or even keeping in stock pistols and concealable bladed weapons.[134] The Georgia supreme court later declared this statute unconstitutional in that it prohibited the carrying of weapons, but constitutional in its prescription of how they were carried.[135]

Repeatedly, individuals directly involved in the ratification of the Second Amendment voted unhesitatingly to limit the rights of gun ownership. If one believes that actions reveal more of intentions than does abstract language, then it is difficult to mistake the initial legal and political understanding of the Second Amendment. But maybe this is all irrelevant. Perhaps—and here is the second reason for ignoring this research—the original intention of the framers of the Constitution and the Bill of Rights should not enter into our civic deliberations. After all, as Jack Ravoke convincingly established, the original meaning of the framers was that future generations should not be guided by eighteenth-century events and ideas.[136]

This is not to negate the value of historical knowledge, however. I offer the modest suggestion that the historical context of a constitutional amendment is relevant to, though not determinative of, its meaning. Any study of the historical context of the Constitution and Bill of Rights cannot escape the fact that they were drafted in the midst of a long-term perceived militia crisis. In the absence of police, the militia was expected to maintain internal order, responding to insurrections, whether by slaves or political radicals. With a feeble standing army, the leadership of the United States hoped that the militia could protect the nation's security. But the militia could do neither. In a time of insecurity and uncertainty, the political leadership throughout the United States turned to the federal government to, as Article 1, section 8, of the Constitution states, "provide for organizing, arming, and disciplining the Militia." The Second Amendment confirmed that commitment to organize and arm the militia. When the framers said that a well-regulated militia is necessary to the security of a free state, they meant it.

4. The Second Amendment: The Highest Stage of Originalism

JACK N. RAKOVE*

In the annals of contemporary scholarship, the ongoing debate over the Second Amendment seems exceptional in several respects.[1] Where else, for example, does one encounter a school of interpretation that imitates modern physics by calling itself the "standard model," which is the presumptuous label appropriated by those who argue that the Second Amendment protects an individual right to keep and bear arms?[2] The reader who seeks to test this brazen claim against the slim evidentiary foundation on which it rests often finds himself wandering in a maze of footnotes where one secondary source cites another with nary a document in sight. The casual errors of fact that one routinely encounters in this maze suggest that many of the participants in the debate about the origins of the Second Amendment are not quite as familiar with the periods and events they are studying as their rhetorical posture might imply. Indeed, something about the passions that swirl around this debate engenders rhetorical excesses that would seem completely out of place in any other realm of scholarship.[3]

But perhaps the most distinctive aspect of the Second Amendment debate is the extent to which the individual rights interpretation rests upon an explicit commitment to the theory of constitutional interpretation known as originalism. Two statements culled from the preface to a leading work on the subject clearly make the point. "Yet if the Bill of Rights has any meaning at all, it must be based on the linguistic usage of those who wrote it," Stephen Halbrook notes. And, again, in predicting some ultimate definitive review of existing precedent by the Supreme Court: "The highest court is bound not by judicial precedent but by the intent of the framers of the Constitution"—who embrace not only the authors of the Second Amendment but the Fourteenth as well.[4] To be sure, full deployment of the individual rights interpretation relies on another doctrine that some originalists are loath to endorse, for converting the Second Amendment into an effective shield against firearms regulations that would emanate primarily from state and local governments requires invoking the incorporation doctrine of the Fourteenth Amendment.[5] It would nevertheless be difficult to identify any other constitutional controversy in which originalist modes of analysis figure quite so prominently.

With apologies (not that any are due) to Lenin, the Second Amendment thus represents the highest stage of originalism, because the advocates for its most expansive interpretation place their greatest reliance on its framers and adopters for arguments about its meaning. They do this, too, in order to counter the seemingly commonsense notion that this is the one clause of the Constitution for which contemporary evidence about the actual consequences of having a well-armed people should weigh most strongly in our thinking. For at bottom, the case for the regulation of the sale, use, and possession of firearms rests on the simple conviction that the high number of casualties incurred annually by the deliberate and accidental use of firearms provides a sufficient, not to say compelling justification for state regulation. It is doubtless important to establish as well that this regulation is made legitimate by a long history of prior legislation, judicial doctrines permitting such legislation, and a reading of the Constitution that says that the Second Amendment really was about supporting a militia that remained subject to the legislative regulation of Congress and the states, while the states were never divested of the fundamental responsibility for regulating "internal police" in the interest of public health and welfare.[6] At the same time, it is reasonable to conclude that the most compelling arguments for regulation presuppose that this is one realm of behavior where the concerns of the present have every right to supersede the obsolescent understandings of generations long past.

Yet originalism remains a legitimate mode of constitutional analysis, and even those who doubt its capacity and authority need to respect its claims. By the same token, however, avowed originalists can be held accountable for the quality of the analyses they offer, and the criticisms to which this theory of interpretation is vulnerable. It is not a self-evident truth that originalism is the sole authoritative mode of constitutional interpretation, nor do many who dabble in originalist analyses always reflect on the logic of what they are doing. It is one thing to ransack the sources for a set of useful quotations, and another to weigh their interpretative authority. Originalism is first and foremost a theory of law and constitutional interpretation, but its viability depends upon its approach to history and its use of historical evidence.

As a venture in originalism, the individual rights interpretation depends upon two essential propositions, one concerned with the definition of militia and the other with its function. Where a plain-text reading of the Second Amendment in the light of the militia clause of Article I, section 8, might suggest that the institutional character of the militia is subject to legislative definition by Congress, the individual rights interpretation insists that the militia must be identified with the whole body of the people. In this view, the concept of the militia had a fixed and consensually accepted meaning in ordinary eighteenth-century usage, so that it was essentially coterminous with the free adult male population physically capable of bearing arms; and if the language of the

Constitution is not to be rendered completely plastic, modern interpretation has to preserve that meaning. Such a militia cannot be equated with our modern conception of the National Guard, which is only a latter-day incarnation of the so-called select militia that eighteenth-century republicans regarded as a surrogate of the dreaded standing army—an institution too closely tied to government to be counted upon as a defender of the people's liberties. This definition in turns illuminates the key *functional* argument on which the individual rights interpretation depends. This argument insists that the ultimate purpose of a general militia is to serve as a deterrent against the danger of tyranny, and that only a well-armed people, possessing privately held weapons, can discourage would-be oppressors from executing their nefarious schemes. This interpretation cannot afford to limit the functions of the militia to those described in Article I, section 8, which clearly treat the militia as a public institution whose duties extend to the suppression of armed resistance against government; it must instead insist upon its pre-, extra-, and even anti-constitutional functions of resistance against tyranny to the point of revolution.

These complementary arguments are originalist for two reasons. First, the definition of the membership of the militia cannot be left to legislative determination, as the Militia Clause and the Necessary and Proper Clause might otherwise suggest. It instead depends on the common usage of the time, and this steers us past the four corners of the constitutional text into the political discourse of the eighteenth century. Second, the rationale for maintaining a broad definition of militia further depends upon the political understandings of that era, in particular the belief that an armed citizenry is a necessary deterrent against tyranny. A plain-text reading of the Constitution, which treats the militia as an institution for suppressing armed insurrection, and which nowhere endorses a right to revolution against republican government, would not by itself be conducive to that interpretation.

In assessing the merits of these originalist claims, we must recognize three further difficulties that color any attempt to provide a historically grounded account of the original meaning of the Second Amendment.

First, notwithstanding all the evidence that individual rights proponents profess to invoke in support of their views, in fact only a handful of sources from the period of constitutional formation bear directly on the questions that lie at the heart of our current controversies about the regulation of private firearms. If Americans had indeed been concerned with the impact of the Constitution on this right, and had addressed the subject directly, the proponents of the individual rights theory would not have to recycle the same handful of references to the dissenters in the Pennsylvania ratification convention and the protests of several Massachusetts towns against their state's proposed constitution, or to rip promising snippets of quotations from the texts and speeches in which they are embedded. Because the private ownership and use of weapons were not at issue in the late 1780s, we are compelled to draw inferences from observations that turn out, in most cases, to be concerned with the militia and its public functions, not with the individual ownership and use of firearms.[7]

Second, because eighteenth-century firearms were not nearly as lethal as those available today, we similarly cannot expect the discussants of the late 1780s to have cast their comments about keeping and bearing arms in the same terms that we would. Theirs was a rhetoric of public liberty, not public health; of the danger from standing armies, not that of casual strangers, embittered family members, violent youth gangs, freeway snipers, and careless weapons-keepers. Guns were so difficult to fire in the eighteenth century that the very idea of being accidentally killed by one was itself hard to conceive. Indeed, anyone wanting either to murder his family or protect his home in the eighteenth century would have been better advised (and much more likely) to grab an ax or knife than to load, prime, and discharge a firearm. And even had guns been more effective as personal weapons, it is nearly inconceivable that eighteenth-century notions of the police power of state and local governments would have precluded their regulation in the name of some vague threat of tyranny. The American colonies and states were not a libertarian utopia; their traditions of governance permitted legislatures and institutions of local government to act vigorously in the pursuit of public health and safety.

The third difficulty lies in the fact that our reading of the Second Amendment is conditioned by our living in an era that naturally assumes that bills of rights exist to create legally enforceable immunities against the coercive power of the state. Whether this efflorescence of rights talk and the litigation that accompanies it are healthy features of the American polity is a subject of ongoing debate[8]; but the consequences for our conception of constitutional rights is clear. In the eighteenth century, however, bills of rights were often regarded as statements of principle, meant to inform and shape the political behavior of both officials and citizens; whether they established legally enforceable claims was far from certain.[9] Many clauses in the first eight amendments to the Constitution certainly aspired to have and eventually acquired that character, but the Second Amendment is arguably the one provision that partook most of the principle-enunciating attributes of the early state declarations of rights. Our quest to discover a perfect syntax and vocabulary for its twenty-seven words thus risks ascribing to a general statement of principle a measure of legal exactitude it was never conceived to carry.

It might be worth stating, as precisely as possible, the rival propositions upon which an evaluation of the originalist approach to the Second Amendment should depend. In its most succinct form, the individual rights interpretation equates the people whose right to arms the amendment protects with the entire body of the citizenry, who are members of a general militia that exists, to some significant extent, independently of legislative provision. The purpose and function of that right rest, in part, on the individual's natural right of self-protection, but they depend more fundamentally on the value of preserving an armed citizenry as a deterrent to oppression, in the (latent) exercise of a natural right of resistance that would be abrogated if citizens lacked access to the arms required to challenge tyranny emanating from either national or state governments.[10] These concerns were so deeply embedded in eighteenth-century American political culture as to trump the two countervailing propositions upon which the collective rights interpretation in turn rests.

First, the extant records of deliberation (as well as the plain text) of the Constitution strongly suggest that the only issue its adopters were consciously considering was the militia, which would henceforth exist as an institution defined by law. No coherent understanding of the existence and scope of a private, individual right to keep and bear arms could accordingly be derived, because that question did not present itself for public debate in the form in which we now know it. Second, and arguably more important, the attachment that some currents of eighteenth-century political thinking did place on the deterrent value of an armed citizenry should be counterposed to the orthodox understanding of the extent of the police powers of the state (or, in the American case, the states), which authorized government to legislate broadly for the public health and welfare.[11] This belief was no less a matter of constitutional orthodoxy in 1789 than the general principle that standing armies posed a danger to liberty, and it therefore casts the originalist dimensions of the Second Amendment debate in the most critical light.

To ask whether contemporaries would have allowed the individual rights interpretation of the Second Amendment to trump this orthodox conception of the regulatory police power of the states identifies, I believe, the true conundrum or desideratum. In effect, the individual rights interpretation elevates the speculative danger of tyranny, rooted in potent historic memories of the turmoil of seventeenth-century England, above the observed costs and casualties that the modern cry for firearms regulation seeks to address. Conversely, the collective rights interpretation inverts these concerns. It presumes that the manifest dangers of the present outweigh the memories of the past, and indeed that the living generation has a right to seek security against the wanton abuse of firearms, consistent with the principles that have long enabled states and localities to legislate on behalf of public health and welfare.

For the record, then, I believe that the current controversy over the meaning of the Second Amendment, if treated primarily as a problem of originalism, should be cast in these terms: Would the presumed preexisting equation of the militia with an armed mass of the citizenry, justified by the need to preserve a natural right of revolution, outweigh (1) the evidence that the principal concern of the late 1780s lay with allocating legislative power over the militia between national and state governments, and (2) the traditional understanding of the police power that the Tenth Amendment (truism that it may be) would have reserved to the states?

ORIGINALISM: SOME METHODOLOGICAL REFLECTIONS

All exercises in constitutional interpretation begin with a text, but originalism cannot be reduced to mere textualism. A merely textualist approach can stipulate that the word "people" has the same meaning in the Second Amendment as it has in the Fourth Amendment or the Petition and Assembly Clause of the First Amendment or the unenumerated rights and reserved powers of the Ninth and Tenth Amendments.[12] This assumption, though not unreasonable, is itself an arbitrary one, for reasons that James Madison well explained in *Federalist* 37 when he observed that "No language is so copious as to supply words and phrases for every complex idea, or so correct as not to include many equivocally denoting different ideas."[13] But if the meaning of a disputed term could be determined simply by analyzing its usage within the four corners of the constitutional text, originalism in any substantive sense would be superfluous. True originalism begins where textualism alone fails. It assumes that the meaning of a provision cannot be ascertained by staring at it long enough, or by juxtaposing it with other relevant clauses, but must instead be derived from usage, or elaborated in terms of some contemporary context of thought and debate, thus requiring the intrepid interpreter to initiate an inquiry into sources extrinsic to the text.

If we were dealing with the text of the original, unamended Constitution, we could bring four main sets of sources to bear on our interpretative quest. Two of these consist of the records of debate from the constitutional deliberations of the late 1780s: the journal and notes of debates from the Federal Constitutional Convention of 1787, which offer the best evidence of the "original intentions" of the authorial framers; and the records of the ratification campaign that ensued, which illuminate the "original understanding(s)" of the public and the delegates in the state conventions. The two other sets of sources, necessarily defined more broadly, might be labeled contextual. One consists of the variety of inherited intellectual traditions, discourses, and languages that collectively constituted the underlying political grammar and conceptual vocabulary of debate. The second, rather more elusive category comprises what might be called the lessons of recent experience: issues and concerns, perceptions and preferences shaped in the crucible of revolution.[14]

This classification of the different categories of evidence relevant to originalist forays leads to two further observations. First, all originalist inquiries are necessarily historical in nature, and therefore should be conducted with some attention to the problems that historians encounter in weighing the uses and limits of different forms of evidence. Better to be conscious about the nature of the evidence, and its particular properties, than to lump all of its morsels into one hotchpot of tasty quotations. Second, and rather more problematically, the task of distinguishing different forms of evidence exposes critical differences in the ways in which historians and legal analysts might evaluate the probative value of the sources. Historians attempting to divine the original meaning of the Constitution would prefer the intentions of the framers to the understandings of the ratifiers, because while the latter were only deciding whether to accept or reject the completed document, the former were making the actual decisions that gave it form and content. But the normative principles on which the robust form of originalism rests place greater weight on ratifier understanding, and treat the framers' expressed intentions as probative only insofar as they illuminate what the ratifiers were also thinking.[15]

Several additional qualifications deserve consideration when we turn our attention from the main text of the Constitution to the original meaning of its amendments. First, the conditions under which the First Congress assembled in the early spring of 1789 differed significantly from those surrounding the Federal Constitutional Convention two years earlier. When the framers of the Constitution straggled into Philadelphia in May 1787, public discussion of their potential agenda of action remained diffused and unfocused—which in turn explains why James Madison's efforts to shape that agenda loom so large in understanding why the convention took the course it did. Madison admittedly played something of the same role in forcing the First Congress to pursue "the nauseous project" of amendments, but the proposals he placed before the House of Representatives in his speech of June 8, 1789, had been culled from the extensive corpus of amendments recommended by the state ratification conventions in response to the wide-ranging public discussion of the Constitution.[16]

Second (and conversely), the amendments that Congress proposed to the states in August 1789 received nothing like the sustained public discussion that greeted the original Constitution. Scholars who go hunting for evidence of the *reception* of the Bill of Rights typically return disappointed. There are scattered traces of popular responses to the substance of the amendments—including a few items relating to the Second Amendment—but, in comparison to the mass of materials from the prior discussions, the pickings are slim.[17]

Third, it is important to note that the drafting of the amendments was controlled by Federalists who remained skeptical, like Madison himself, of the value or necessity of a national bill of rights. The concessions extracted from Federalists in closely contested state conventions to join in *recommending* amendments to the consideration of Congress amounted to something less than a firm agreement. The Federalists were decisive victors in the first national elections of 1788–89, and the difficulty Madison encountered in convincing his congressional colleagues to take up the issue of amendments suggests that few of them thought that prompt action was required to fulfill the ostensible bargain struck the year before. Madison felt otherwise. During his difficult campaign against James Monroe for election to the House, Madison had publicly committed himself to support amendments; once elected, he was the most likely member to undertake the initiative of actually drafting amendments. Equally important, Madison hoped to make prompt action a fitting capstone to the entire ratification process by conciliating those moderate anti-Federalists who sincerely if misguidedly believed that a Constitution lacking a bill of rights was defective. But as his speech of June 8, 1789, makes clear, his motives were far more political than jurisprudential, and his colleagues' indifference suggests that they remained skeptical about the value of the exercise.[18] Conversely, to those anti-Federalists who had been elected to Congress, the cause of amendments had lost its luster because they now knew that all the structural changes to the Constitution they desired had no chance of acceptance.

Understanding this aspect of the politics behind the Bill of Rights is critical to an originalist inquiry because it indicates that the final decisions about Madison's proposals fell not to those who were most ardent for the cause of amendments but to those who doubted that such amendments were even useful, much less necessary. To put the point more directly: Federalists did not cave in to their opponents' demands, or modify the Constitution to meet their substantive criticisms; nor, conversely, were anti-Federalists able to impose their understandings on the party that carried the first national elections. The claim that the best or most representative reading of the amendments would conform to the understanding and concerns of the Constitution's original opponents is therefore highly problematic. Comments from across the political spectrum remain relevant to capturing the range of meanings that Americans ascribed to the protections incorporated in the first ten amendments, but to claim that an ordinal anti-Federalist understanding would be dispositive is simply wrong.[19]

Finally, the decision to frame the amendments as supplemental articles, rather than follow Madison's proposal to insert them directly into the original constitutional text, arguably had the effect of preserving a modicum of the juridical ambiguity that had previously made it difficult to ascertain the exact constitutional status of declarations of rights. Did such documents establish legally enforceable claims, or were they better construed as statements of principle, meant to guide officials in the exercise of their duties and to enable the people at large to monitor and judge the conduct of their rulers by laying down standards whose violation would expose a deeper threat to liberty? A bill of rights, in this view, was more a political than a legal text. It was precisely because declarations of rights, of the kind that accompanied many of the early state constitutions, could so be read that Madison originally proposed to "interweave" his amendments with the text of the Constitution. Adopted in that way, they would act as explicit restrictions affecting particular institutions of government; their legal authority would become more precise and explicit, thereby enhancing the security afforded to rights. Conversely, framing the amendments as supplemental articles, Madison warned, would make it "difficult to ascertain to what parts of the instrument [the Constitution] the amendments particularly refer."[20] But that was exactly what Congress, ultimately, preferred to do. In taking that course, however, the majority arguably still shared the dominant conception of 1776, which viewed a bill of rights as a statement of principles affirming the existence of particular rights but not clearly delegating responsibility for their enforcement or protection to any institution.

One final consideration arguably differentiates originalist interpretations of the Bill of Rights from those relating to the main text of the Constitution. The latter is essentially a closely integrated bundle of provisions organizing institutions of government, defining their respective powers, and establishing rules for the appointment and tenure of their members. Though concepts derived from English constitutional history exerted important lingering influences over these matters, it was the experience of American republican constitutionalism since 1776, coupled with the inherently federal structure of the Union and the divided sovereignty to which it led, that defined the parameters of deliberation and decision making at Philadelphia.[21]

On matters of practical constitutional design, Hobbes and Locke, potent political thinkers that they were, had little to teach Americans, and American constitutionalism was formed, in any case, in reaction against many facets of the eighteenth-century British constitution. But in the realm of rights, where the legacy of the common-law mind operated so powerfully, a stronger case can be made for some continuities in understanding between prior Anglo-American thinking and the formulations of the 1770s and '80s. Particular rights had an independent history of their own, and Leonard Levy and other scholars have indeed demonstrated the possibility of tracing changing notions of particular rights in a way that pays close attention to existing and evolving legal doctrine. The right to bear arms is clearly susceptible to the same kind of examination. But we can never forget that it is a *history*—that is, a process of change over time—we are tracing, and that the ways in which Americans conceived of and formulated rights were a product not just of what they had inherited but of what they had experienced. American "rights talk," as Richard Primus has recently argued, is a contingent "social practice" that always reflects immediate political commitments and struggles.[22]

All of these strictures about the practice of originalism may seem to demand more precision and nuance than the subject really requires. Perhaps the original meaning of the Constitution, like pornography, is something we can just recognize as a matter of common sense: James Madison and his colleagues, of course, never imagined that the Constitution could mean X [insert your least favorite interpretation of a particular provision or some other controversial doctrine]. But if originalism is to be taken seriously—and not invoked simply as a rhetorical club in the cause of legal or political argument—the analytical problems it poses require reflection. The dispute over the meaning of the Second Amendment cannot be immune to such scrutiny.

TEXT

All constitutional inquiry begins with the authoritative text, which may be imagined as a scriptural statement surrounded by columns of commentaries that consist of evidence to be derived from the deliberations that produced the actual language, popular discussions during the ratification campaign, intellectual traditions, and what I have called lessons of experience. As everyone knows, the essential textualist controversy over the Second Amendment revolves around the relation, if any, between the introductory formula ("A well regulated militia being necessary to the security of a free state") and the operative statement that "the right of the people to keep and bear arms, shall not be infringed." Staring at the sentence or reading it aloud will not help one decide whether the preamble is superfluous or deeply informative of the end the right is meant to attain. Instead, a textual analysis can take at least these forms: correlating the meaning of "people" with other uses in the Constitution; doing the same for "militia"; and asking what light the evolution of the specific textual formula finally adopted might shed on the intentions of its framers.[23] Defenders of the individual rights interpretation emphasize the harmony between the "people" of the Second Amendment and the putatively identical entity of the

First, Fourth, Ninth, and Tenth amendments. If the use of "people" in these other provisions clearly covers rights exercised by individuals, the argument goes, then it follows that the right protected by the Second Amendment is also held by individual citizens.[24] But defenders of the individual rights theory are rather more reluctant to link the "militia" of the preamble to the institution provided for in Article I of the Constitution; here, they prefer a preexisting definition not dependent on the specific provision made for its future organization.

What can we infer about the meaning of the Second Amendment, as finally approved, by tracing its textual evolution? The changes made as the amendment worked its way through Congress support two main inferences. One concerns the omission of a significant qualifier evoking a particular definition of the militia; the other reveals a potentially important alteration in syntax.

As first introduced by Madison on June 8, the clause read:

> The right of the people to keep and bear arms shall not be infringed; a well armed, and well regulated militia being the best security of a free country: but no person religiously scrupulous of bearing arms, shall be compelled to render military service in person.[25]

Here Madison departed from the corresponding recommendation of the Virginia ratification convention (item seventeen in its proposed list of enumerated rights), and the formulation to which he was likely to be most sensitive. The Virginia resolution began:

> That the people have a right to keep and bear arms; that a well-regulated militia, composed of the body of the people trained to arms, is the proper, natural, and safe defence of a free state. . . .

Both Madison's and the Virginia convention's versions arguably recognized two rights, not just one: a right to bear arms, not explicitly tied to membership in the militia; and a right to enjoy the superior form of defense afforded by a well-regulated militia, which would obviate the need for the standing army that the original Virginia resolution had then denounced, though with a warning rather than with a flat prohibition.[26] Madison had omitted the clause defining the militia as "the body of the people," but he preserved the duality of rights. Moreover, his respective use of the semi-colon and colon in this article suggested that the concept of a "well regulated militia" served to justify the exclusion of the "religiously scrupulous" from military service, and not the importance of the people keeping and bearing arms.[27]

The committee of the House to which Madison's amendments were referred made two changes in his draft.[28] First, it transposed the syntax, placing the reference to the militia first and replacing the semi-colon separating the two parts of the clause with a comma. Second, it offered a more specific definition of the militia. The clause now read:

> A well regulated militia, composed of the body of the people, being the best security of a free state, the right of the people to keep and bear arms, shall not be infringed; but no person religiously scrupulous of bearing arms, shall be compelled to render military service in person.[29]

This new definition of the militia was in turn eliminated in the Senate, where the amendment received its final form. On September 4, the Senate first entertained, then rejected, a motion to add the elements of the Virginia recommendation that Madison had omitted. Five days later, it rejected a motion to insert "for the common defense" after "arms," and then proceeded to replace "the best Security" with "necessary to the Security." In its final form, the amendment went to the House, which accepted it without apparent objection.[30]

None of this legislative history of the drafting of the Second Amendment conclusively resolves the vexing question that lies at the heart of the entire controversy: whether "the people" is best interpreted as the entire citizenry, as the individual rights interpretation insists; or refers instead simply to whatever form a militia composed of soldiers who retain a significant measure of their civilian identity might take, as the collective rights interpretation and prevailing law hold. Defenders of the individual rights interpretation like to point to the outline for Madison's speech of June 8, 1789, which contains a note seemingly stating that his proposed amendments "relate 1st to private rights," as evidence that Madison so regarded the right to bear arms. But that terse inscription stands alone, and is not explicitly linked to the right to bear arms; Madison's sole reference to arms alludes to the parliamentary Bill of Rights of 1689, and there is no corresponding passage in the recorded version of his speech that develops this point.[31] Nor does Madison's proposed placement of this right in Article I, section 9, conclusively demonstrate its fundamentally private nature, as individual rights theorists like to contend, because the original version of the petition and assembly clause would have immediately preceded it, and that clause is also susceptible to a collective rights interpretation. The controlling theme of Article I, section 9, is neither the definition of individual rights nor restrictions on the powers of the states (the subject of section 10); it refers to limitations on the powers of Congress.

The most striking defect in the textualist component of the individual rights interpretation lies elsewhere, however: in the disparity in the ways in which the key words "people" and "militia" are defined. However one gauges the relative authority of the two sections of the Second Amendment, a reading that assumes the primacy of text would insist that every word be given due weight; indeed, textualism, as practiced by someone like Akhil Amar, presupposes that each word has been carefully chosen to fit a completely consistent constitutional vision. But in this case, textualist practice proves curiously inconsistent. "People" is routinely defined intratextually, by reference to its use in other amendments; and "militia" leaps beyond the proverbial four corners of the document, and is parsed in terms of a historically contingent definition of what the militia has been and must presumably evermore be.

Amar himself provides a case in point. He first tells us that "when used without any qualifying adjective"—such as the notorious "select"—" 'the militia' referred to all citizens capable of bearing arms," making the "militia" of the dependent clause of the amendment identical with the "people" of the main clause. The House would have made that equation explicit when it added the qualifying phrase "composed of the body of the people" to its draft; when the Senate "stylistically shortened" the clause by deleting that phrase, it presumably restored only that assumed definition.[32] But how do we know that this senatorial editing was stylistic and not substantive? Any effort to define "militia" intratextually must begin with Article I, section 8, clause 16, which treats the militia as an entity that Congress has the legislative responsibility for "organizing, arming, and disciplining." The effect of the Senate's editing was to leave the extent of the militia open to congressional discretion. It might well remain plausible to assume that Americans hoped and even expected that the militia would continue to resemble the body of the people, but any plain-text reading would suggest that Congress retained all the authority it needed to determine whether a select militia would or would not prove more desirable than a massed array of the whole of the male population. Rather than accept this strictly or merely textual reading of the relevant language, Amar has to reach beyond the text to suggest that "Anti-Federalist and republican ideology" offer the best clues to the fixed meaning of militia. The meaning of militia in the original Constitution now depends on its meaning in the Second Amendment, even though the final version of that amendment eliminated the qualifying phrase that exponents of "Anti-Federalist and republican ideology" would have preferred. Unfortunately, there were only two anti-Federalists in the Senate, both from Virginia, and it is simply counterintuitive to suppose that they would have favored eliminating the qualifying phrase that their own state's ratification convention had originally proposed.[33]

A textualist reading of the evolution of the amendment could plausibly support at least these inferences. First, if Congress was intent on preserving the traditional image of the militia as the collective body of the people, as the individual rights interpretation suggests, its elimination of the appropriate language to that effect is surprising. Congress had open to it the option of engrafting a more expansive definition of the militia onto the Constitution; it rejected that option. Second, if the semi-colon in Madison's original resolution could be read as stating two distinct rights, and not one, its replacement by a comma would seem to connect the two parts of the amendment more closely; that is, it would link the preamble and the right more intimately than had been the case before, and thereby tie the right of arms-bearing to the institution of the militia. Third, if it is conceded that the reference to militia in the preamble to the amendment has some relevance to its meaning—which, of course, a textualist must, because textualism presumes that every word is there with a purpose— then a textual approach requires us to ask how other provisions of the Constitution use the same term; and any reader of Article I, section 8, would find it hard to deny that the text there considers the militia not as an unorganized mass of the citizenry but as an institution subject to close legislative regulation. Fourth, acceptance of language restricting the people's right to bear arms to matters relating to the "common defense" would have had the effect of curtailing the capacity of the militia to be deployed for the other purposes assigned in Article I, section 8: "to execute the Laws of the Union" and to "suppress Insurrections." But Congress rejected that limitation, and the "militia" of the Second Amendment thus remained an entity to be mobilized to preserve, not subvert, the Constitution. One might presumably argue that the militia could spontaneously mobilize to protect the Constitution against a government staging an anti-constitutional coup de main, coup de marche, or coup d'état, but nothing in the text of the Constitution supports that conception of its role.

FRAMERS' INTENTIONS

One striking aspect of the standard statements of the individual rights interpretation is how little attention its advocates pay to the debates of either the Federal Constitutional Convention or the First Congress.[34] This is unsurprising. Although many concerns, assumptions, and beliefs are *imputed* to the framers of both the Constitution and the Second Amendment, there is virtually nothing in the extant record of the in camera debates of 1787 and 1789 that directly addresses the issues that lie at the core of our contemporary controversy. Neither at Philadelphia nor New York would it have occurred to anyone to ask whether adoption or amendment of the Constitution would diminish the capacity of state and local governments, in the exercise of their conventional police powers, to impose legislative restrictions on the use or ownership of firearms. That was a concept that would have been difficult to formulate in either 1787 or 1789. Had the convention wished to do so, it might, in theory, have considered restricting the power of the state governments to limit the fun-

damental right of arms-bearing and -keeping in conjunction with the limitations on state authority found in Article I, section 10, of the Constitution. But
the framers had no plausible, much less compelling, reason to even ask
whether there should be any change in the traditional legislative competence
of the states.

Similarly, the structure of debate in 1789 did not oblige the members of the
First Congress to consider the authority of the state legislatures to regulate private use and ownership of weapons. The entire thrust of that debate was directed at identifying powers of the national government requiring moderation
in the interest of protecting the rights of either the people or the states. But any
prospect that the adoption of amendments would be used to protect the people against both the national government *and* the states evaporated when the
Senate rejected James Madison's favorite proposal to impose limitations on
the states in the realms of freedom of speech, religion, and trial by jury.[35] The
entire debate over the amendment in the House of Representatives is concerned with the propriety of exempting religiously scrupulous persons from
the obligation to bear arms if summoned to do so—an issue completely irrelevant to the current controversy over gun control, yet strongly supportive of the
idea that the amendment was indeed about the militia. Tenuous inferences
about private rights may be drawn, perhaps, from remarks made by a handful
of representatives, but, again, none of these confront the central issue directly.

Nevertheless, insofar as interpretation of the Second Amendment is inter-
twined with the question of the status of the militia under the Constitution,
some guidance might be found in the relevant debates on that subject at the
Federal Constitutional Convention, principally the discussions of August 18
and 23, 1787. These debates bear directly on one of the central assumptions
undergirding the individual rights interpretation, which is that the word "militia" cannot be narrowly defined as a "select militia," itself dangerous because
subject to the control of government, but must instead be read broadly to embrace the entire adult male population. In the most expansive reading, this
militia forms independently and spontaneously; it does not owe its existence
to state law; and it must therefore mean that "all of the people all of the time
(not just when called for organized militia duty) have a right to keep arms."[36]
The clear implication must be that the militia (in this sense) has always existed,
and will ever exist, as a popular institution that precedes, and is immune to,
both state and national law; it is, in effect, a pre- and extra-constitutional body
whose existence, even if latent, is not constrained by law. Otherwise it could be
reduced to the dreaded modern incarnation of a select militia: a National
Guard composed of weekend warriors whose two weeks plus twelve weekends
of annual training efface their apparent status as citizen soldiers.

Whatever else might be said of this problematic definition of the militia, it does not comport with the actual discussion of the subject at Philadelphia. For as Madison's notes of debates conclusively demonstrate, that entire discussion explicitly recognized that the militia was to be the joint object of congressional and state legislation. What was at issue was where the boundary between national and state responsibilities would lie. Nothing that was said during the principal discussions of August 18 and 23 supports the contention that the militia would henceforth exist as a spontaneous manifestation of the community at large.

In the draft constitution submitted by the committee of detail on August 6, the sole clause relating to the militia would have authorized the national legislature "To call forth the aid of the militia, in order to execute the laws of the Union, enforce treaties, suppress insurrections, and repel invasions."[37] When the convention reached this clause on August 18, George Mason "moved as an additional power 'to make laws for the regulation and discipline of the Militia of the several States reserving to the States the appointment of the officers,' " which Mason justified on the grounds of the value of "uniformity." His motion was challenged by the Connecticut delegate Oliver Ellsworth, who offered a substitute motion requiring the militia to "have the same arms & exercise and be under rules established by the Genl Govt. when in actual service of the U. States and when States neglect to provide regulations for militia, it shd. be regulated & established" by Congress. Ellsworth argued that the states should not be deprived of their authority over the militia because they "would pine away to nothing after such a sacrifice of power." By this, of course, he clearly meant that the state governments would atrophy. That view was supported by John Dickinson, who proposed a scheme whereby the national power to discipline the militia would be limited to "one fourth part at a time, which by rotation would discipline the whole militia." Mason took this objection seriously enough to modify his original motion by inserting the phrase, "not exceeding one tenth part in any one year," noting by way of introduction that this "suggested the idea of a select militia."[38] But this amendment was in turn criticized by General Charles Pinckney, John Langdon, and Madison, all arguing that there were compelling reasons not to divide responsibility for the militia between the national government and the states. In response, Ellsworth dismissed "the idea of a select militia as impracticable." After several further exchanges, the convention referred both versions of Mason's motion to a "grand committee" (one delegate from each state) it had just appointed.[39]

The committee's recommendation, delivered three days later, was taken up on August 23. In revived form, the clause now read:

To make laws for organizing, arming & disciplining the Militia, and for governing such parts of them as may be employed in the service of the U.S. reserving to the states respectively, the appointment of the officers, and authority of training the militia according to the discipline prescribed.[40]

The ensuing debate is noteworthy in two respects. First, although three separate motions were introduced during this debate to modify the committee's proposal, all in the interest of confining the authority vested in Congress while enhancing the authority reserved to the states, in the end the convention rejected all three, thereby preserving the original language.[41] Second, in the course of this debate several delegates made remarks that offer revealing insight into the framers' deeper understanding of militia-related issues. When, for example, Rufus King, speaking for the committee, first explained that the national authority over "*arming*" the militia meant "specifying the kind, size and caliber of arms," Madison worried that this explanation "did not extend to furnishing arms"; and King thereupon explained that "*arming* meant not only to provide for uniformity of arms, but included authority to regulate the modes of furnishing, either by the militia themselves, the State Governments, or the National Treasury."[42] While the first of these alternatives suggests a private duty to obtain arms, as specified by legal regulations, the latter obviously envisioned either the states or the Union providing arms of their own lawful authority.

Whether any institution other than the national government could be relied upon to keep the militia armed and disciplined, however, was something that Madison and his colleague Edmund Randolph very much doubted. "The States neglect their Militia now," Madison observed, "and the more they are consolidated into one nation, the less each will rely on its own interior provisions for its safety & the less prepare its militia for that purpose; in like manner as the Militia of a State would have been still more neglected." Randolph endorsed this judgment a few minutes later, "observing that the Militia were every where neglected by the State Legislatures, the members of which courted popularity too much to enforce a proper discipline."[43] So ardent was Madison for strong national supervision of the militia that he subsequently moved, without success, that the appointment of officers by the states should be confined to those "*under the rank of General officers*," but the main motion was ultimately approved without dissent.

Why is it necessary to call attention to this debate or, conversely, why do individual rights writers say so little about it? Its significance would seem so obvious as to require no notice. But in the strange world of Second Amendment discourse, what is most obvious sometimes requires the greatest emphasis.

For the framers of the Constitution, whose usage does have some relevance to ascertaining the original intent underlying the document they wrote, the word "militia" could no longer be unthinkingly or automatically equated with the entire male population capable of bearing arms. That definition certainly remained one of the options from which they could choose, and some of their comments indicate that some delegates still thought of the state militia in just these terms. When Dickinson and Mason, for example, contemplated rotating portions of the militia under federal discipline, they were presumably imagining drawing on that larger pool. But that is not the point. What matters is that the framers, clearly reasoning on the basis of hard-earned experience, saw the militia as an institution that would henceforth be regulated through a combination of national and state legislation firmly anchored in the text of the Constitution, rather than some preexisting, pre-constitutional understanding. Wherever the exact balance between national and state responsibility would be struck, the militia would always be subject to legislative regulation. When the framers referred to the "states" in these debates, they were always alluding to their governments, not to the people at large. The "authority of training the militia according to the discipline prescribed by Congress" that the Constitution reserved to the states was a power and responsibility of the state governments to implement national law. Americans were still entitled to believe that, as a matter of principle and policy, a militia "composed of the body of the people" offered the safest alternative to a standing army, tyranny, or any number of other evils, but that does not alter the fundamental delegation of legal authority to the new Congress that the framers understood they were proposing. The Militia Clause itself, buttressed by the Necessary and Proper Clause, empowered Congress, acting conjointly with the state legislatures, to decide what form the American militia would henceforth take.

None of this carried any threat to existing private rights of gun ownership, save, perhaps, in the eventuality that a crisis found the nation poorly armed and legislation was required, as it had been in the past, to bring firearms in all states of repair and disrepair out of private hands so that they could be returned to active and effective public service. Yet this history does call into question the idea, seemingly central to the individual rights argument, that the very concept of the militia had an irrevocable, unalterable populist meaning immune to lawful revision by Congress and the state legislatures.

RATIFIER UNDERSTANDING

As is well known, anti-Federalist criticisms of the Constitution emphasized the danger that American liberties would face from a consolidated national government that would not only possess both the purse and the sword but itself face the daunting task of executing its law across the broad and diverse expanses of an extended republic. Nor is there any mystery as to where the fear of standing armies originated: it was a legacy of the Radical or Real Whig tradition, which so shaped eighteenth-century American political ideology,[44] and it could be well documented by familiar references both to the military rule that Cromwell had imposed on England in the 1650s and to the later efforts of James II to use an army increasingly officered by local Catholics as a domestic police force. Federalists answered the charge that the new Constitution would both permit and require government by a standing army in various ways. On prudential grounds, they argued from experience and a priori principles both that national security would mean nothing if the new government was not fully empowered to raise regular military forces. Nor would these forces constitute a standing army in the rigorous sense of the term, because the two-year limit on appropriations meant that a fresh election of the people's immediate representatives would provide an effective constitutional and political check.

Federalists tended to treat this charge with the same disdain with which they dismissed many Anti-Federalist criticisms. Hamilton's refutation of the standing army allegation in *Federalist* 24, for example, is a sustained sortie in sarcasm. So, too, is his dismissal, in *Federalist* 29, of the idea that it would be dangerous to rely upon a "select" militia—the same institution that proponents of the individual rights interpretation insist Americans generally deemed to be nearly as threatening as a standing army. As far as Hamilton (framer, ratifier, and distinguished commentator on the Constitution, and leading member of its first cabinet) was concerned, the only good militia was a select militia. Indeed, Hamilton's discussion in this essay, cast in the form of the advice he would give to a future Congress, captures nicely the tension in Federalist thinking between the received definition of the militia, on the one hand, and the institution the new government should regulate, on the other. Hamilton opens this passage by declaring that "The project of disciplining all the militia of the United States is as futile as it would be injurious, if it were capable of being carried into execution." As used here, the phrase "all the militia" connotes the body of the people; but Hamilton immediately proceeds to explain why the inconvenience, cost, and sheer impracticality of training the entire population make it desirable to form "a select corps of moderate extent" who could provide the "well regulated militia" (a phrase Hamilton uses) that the mass of the citizenry could never constitute.[45] A Hamiltonian gloss on the Second Amendment would presumably equate the people whose arms-bearing right must be protected with the militia that could be "well regulated" only if it was select.[46]

To examine Federalist rhetoric on the militia is to enter a conceptual world wherein the attitudes and concerns that characterized their opponents' mode of thought no longer unthinkingly apply. Equally obviously, these differences also go far toward explaining why the members of the First Congress felt compelled to include some provision—however vaguely worded—relating to the militia in their proposed amendments. Yet it is no less obvious that the ratification debates of 1787–88 did not directly implicate the critical issues at stake today—the extent of national and state authority to regulate the private use and ownership of firearms. Again, we are left to draw inferences from scattered remarks that were principally concerned with the respective powers of the national and state governments in the regulation of the militia.

There is one conspicuous exception to this judgment: the oft-quoted amendments published by the anti-Federalist minority in the Pennsylvania ratification convention, which met at Harrisburg in November 1787. Soundly outnumbered by a two-to-one ratio in the convention, this minority had struggled to have its concerns taken seriously by a Federalist majority anxious to promote the cause of ratification elsewhere by gaining a quick and unequivocal decision in favor of the Constitution.[47] Federalists grudgingly listened to the amendments their antagonists wished to propose, but refused not only to consider them but even to allow them to be entered on the convention's journals, forcing the minority to publish their proposals in the form of a dissent. Two of the minority's fifteen proposed amendments bear on the arms and militia issues:

7. That the people have a right to bear arms for the defense of themselves and their own state, or the United States, or for the purpose of killing game; and no law shall be passed for disarming the people or any of them, unless for crimes committed, or real danger of injury from individuals; and as standing armies in time of peace are dangerous to liberty, they ought not to be kept up; and that the military shall be kept under strict subordination to and be governed by the civil power.
8. The inhabitants of the several states shall have liberty to fowl and hunt in seasonable times, on the lands they hold, and on all other lands in the United States not enclosed, and in like manner to fish in all navigable waters, and others not private property, without being restrained therein by any laws to be passed by the legislature of the United States.[48]

These statements appear to be by far the strongest affirmations of a belief in a private right to own and use arms, to be rendered immune to federal regulation; they also appear to be the only statements to frame and affirm the right in this way. They therefore are vulnerable to the charge, among others, that these resolutions are the exceptions that prove a different rule.

A number of qualifications make the probative value of these resolutions doubtful. They were the work of a distinct minority within the Pennsylvania convention, and ensuing tests of strength in the first federal elections held a year later saw Federalists sweeping the delegation that Pennsylvania sent to the new Congress. The resolutions say nothing at all (because there was no reason that they should do so) about the *state's* power to regulate ownership and use of firearms—a power that the state had in fact already exercised.[49] While the resolutions articulate a fear of national power, they do not identify the provisions of the Constitution that threatened private rights of ownership, much less the fowling and hunting practices of residents of a state in which the federal government could have no valid title to any land.[50] Nor did the minority members offer any further explanation of the source of their fear when they published their explanatory "Address and Reasons of Dissent" two weeks after the convention adjourned.[51] Interestingly, that "Address" overlooked the right to bear arms when it turned to discussing the most important rights to be secured by "the emission of a BILL of RIGHTS."[52] When the dissenters addressed the militia issue at the very close of their protest, they framed their challenge in terms not of private rights of ownership but rather of the danger that Congress would abuse its power over the militia by subjecting its members to martial law, trampling on the rights of those "conscientiously scrupulous of bearing arms," and marching its members near and far in the cause of "riveting the chains of despotism on their fellow citizens, and on one another."[53] Finally, it was exactly these resolutions that inspired the Federalist writer Noah Webster to propose, jestingly, a further restriction: "That Congress shall never restrain any inhabitant of America from eating and drinking, *at seasonable times,* or prevent his lying on his *left side,* in a long winter's night, or even on his back, when he is fatigued by lying on his *right.*"[54] Was this really the kind of right, Webster insinuated, deserving national constitutional protection?

Had anti-Federalists elsewhere rallied around this early expression of the extent of the right to bear arms, our current debate would, arguably, not have to rely on far less direct or salient data. Instead, we are left to wrestle with the implications of statements that are far more concerned with the familiar juxtaposition of standing army and militia than with the nature, source, and extent of private rights or the limitations upon state legal regulation. Prominent among these more direct comments is a remark made by George Mason during the Virginia ratification convention, which advocates of the individual rights interpretation often cite as a succinct endorsement of the equation permanently identifying the militia with the people. "Who are the Militia?" Mason asked on June 14, 1788. "They consist now of the whole people, except a few public officers."[55]

One is not surprised that Mason's very next sentences disappear from the citations of writers like Kates and Halbrook:

> But I cannot say who will be the militia of the future day. If that paper on the table [the Constitution] gets no alteration, the militia of the future day may not consist of all classes, high and low, and rich and poor; but may be confined to the lower and middle classes of the people, granting exclusion to the higher classes of the people.[56]

As far as Mason was concerned, amendments that did not reach the power of Congress to regulate the militia would be unavailing, because the composition of the militia would be subject to legislative revision. Nor does this crucial point exhaust the importance of Mason's observation, because once his speech is firmly located in the context in which it was made, it supports conclusions rather at odds with the self-reaffirming pronouncements that individual rights advocates customarily make.

When Mason spoke, he was not, of course, anticipating our controversy but participating in a debate of his own day, and if we are to understand the force of his remarks, we have to know what was under discussion in that debate. Mason was speaking near the end of a two-day debate on the militia clauses of the Constitution (though here, as on other occasions at Richmond, the pyrotechnics of Patrick Henry were occasionally responsible for discussions veering in strange directions). Given that both Federalists and anti-Federalists discussed the conditions under which the militia could be disarmed, it might seem surprising that the scholarly literature has slighted this debate.[57] But the surprise quickly dissipates when one understands the assumptions that united speakers from both sides.

When debate began on Saturday, June 14, the first point discussed was the role the militia might be asked to play in enforcing law and suppressing insurrections. In the midst of his lengthy first speech on this subject, which quickly reached the danger of a standing army, Mason warned about the danger that the militia might be abolished. Should the national government ever "attempt to harass and abuse the militia," Mason warned,

> they may easily abolish them, and raise a standing army in their stead. There are various ways of destroying the militia. A standing army may be perpetually established in their stead. . . . The militia may be here destroyed by that method which has been practised in other parts of the world before. That is, by rendering them useless, by disarming them. Under various pretences, Congress may neglect to provide for arming and disciplining the militia, and the State Governments cannot do it, for Congress has an exclusive right to arm them, &c. . . . Should the national Government wish to render the militia useless, they may neglect them, and let them perish, in order to have a pretence of establishing a standing army.

Mason reminded the delegates that, forty years earlier, just such a sinister scheme had been proposed by Governor Keith of Pennsylvania, "to disarm the people" in order to "enslave them," but not to "do it openly"—presumably by confiscating their weapons—"but to weaken them and let them sink gradually, by totally disusing and neglecting the militia." Mason's wish, therefore, was to obtain "an express declaration that the State Governments might arm and discipline" the militia should Congress fail to do so.[58] He further warned that the national government might destroy the militia by using its disciplinary power to make service in the militia so "odious to the people themselves . . . as to make them cry out, *Give us a standing army.*"[59]

Mason was answered by Madison, who argued that the power to arm the militia would in fact remain a "concurrent" one, shared between the national government and the states. National responsibility was essential, Madison suggested, because experience demonstrated "that while the power of arming and governing of the militia had been solely vested in the State Legislatures, they were neglected and rendered unfit for general service."[60] Madison's notion of concurrent powers in turn drew a strong rebuttal from Patrick Henry, who asserted that congressional power over the militia was exclusive, not concurrent. If it were in fact concurrent, Henry reasoned, the militia would wind up "doubly armed." This would impose a double set of costs on the militia, Henry warned; yet he also reasoned from experience in terms that strongly echoed Madison. "Every one who is able may have a gun," Henry observed. "But have we not learned by experience, that necessary as it is to have arms, and though our Assembly has, by a succession of laws for many years, endeavoured to have the militia completely armed, it is still far from being the case." In his view, the proper remedy was to empower Congress to arm the militia only after "the States shall have refused or neglected to do it."[61]

Subsequent speakers returned to the question of determining how the militia had actually been armed in the past or might best be armed in the future. "But it is said, the militia are to be disarmed," the Federalist delegate George Nicholas observed. "Will they be worse armed than they are now?" Madison was correct to argue for a concurrent power, Nicholas continued.

> For the power of arming them rested in the State Governments before, and although the power be given to the General Government, yet it is not given exclusively. For, in every instance, where the Constitution intends that the General Government shall exercise any power exclusively of the State Governments, words of exclusion are particularly inserted.[62]

Following this speech, the debate took one of its periodic flights away from the specific clause ostensibly under discussion. When the militia came back into view some time later, Mason repeated his charge that Congress would use its disciplinary power to impose "such severities . . . on the militia, as would make them wish the use of militia to be utterly abolished; and assent to the establishment of a standing army."[63] But then Mason, too, veered off to other issues, even surviving a call to order to keep him on point.

We should not be surprised that advocates of the individual rights interpretation pay so little attention to these exchanges, because they demonstrate, first and foremost, that leading Federalists and anti-Federalists alike assumed that the real problem was to determine which level of government should be made responsible for making sure that the militia was properly armed. George Mason's notion of how the citizenry might be disarmed did not presuppose that federal agents would come gently rapping on farmhouse doors, confiscating weapons and leaving the people evermore unable to thwart the tyrannical designs of their ambitious masters. Rather, the national government would disarm the citizenry simply by failing to provide them with the arms that in fact they rarely possessed or managed to maintain. The preferred anti-Federalist alternative was not to allow citizens to acquire weapons on their own; it was, rather, to shift the burden of supporting the militia to the state governments. But in either case, the militia would clearly remain an institution created and regulated by government. And its effectiveness would depend not on a citizenry already well armed with their own weapons, but on the capacity of government to provide and maintain weapons that the people evidently lacked.

Had this debate been confined to this issue alone, it would already suggest some serious deficiencies in the individual rights account. But the discussion, which resumed on Monday, June 16, is also revealing in another respect closely related to our modern controversy. For now, with Henry palpably struggling to stick to his subject, discussion turned to the role of the militia in suppressing insurrection and the matter of concurrent national and state powers. In Henry's curious view, seconded by William Grayson, that power "was *exclusively* given to Congress. If it remained in the states, it was by implication." [64] Habituated as they were to his distortions, Federalist speakers found this point hard to swallow: John Marshall even "asked if Gentlemen were serious" in these assertions, when "the least attention" would demonstrate their errors. The state governments had always possessed these powers, and nothing in the Constitution deprived them of their original authority to use the militia for their own purposes, except in those specified cases when Congress could legally call the militia into federal service. [65] State governments would have every right to call out their militia to suppress insurrections, whether emanating from the enslaved element of their populations (who would certainly have enjoyed a natural right to obtain arms for their self-preservation, but whose access to arms was carefully restricted by law) or any other source of disaffection.

Again, what was at stake in this debate was the question of which level of government should be empowered to use the militia to suppress insurrections, not the specter that the Constitution would make it impossible for a privately armed people to rise up against either national or state oppressors. It was in this context that Mason asked whether a militia that consisted "now of the whole people" would preserve that character in future. But here his express concern was not with the danger of the people disarmed, much less of federal confiscation of private weapons, but rather to exempt the militia from the "ignominious punishments and heavy fines" that he expected would be imposed by a Congress too "small, and inadequate" in number to have any "fellow-feeling for the people."[66]

Locating Mason's remark in the context in which it was uttered, then, brings us into a world of assumptions very different from the selective and anachronistic ones that polemicists now choose to impose upon it. In this world, disarming the militia meant that the government would fail to supply its members with firearms they had little private reason to keep, not sending the lackeys of power out to haul in rusty fowling pieces that would probably not fire in any case, and that one would not bear into combat against better-armed regular troops. In this world, every male citizen might well be eligible for militia service, but the militia was an institution legally created by government, not some pre- or extra-constitutional entity immune to legal regulation. In this world, what was under debate was not the need to protect a right to revolution but a debate about federalism—that is, a debate about the respective competence and authority of the national and state governments. And in this world, too, the suspicions that anti-Federalists like Mason and Henry voiced only illustrated the deeper deficiencies in their case against the Constitution.

One encounters similar misrepresentations of context in other treatments of leading statements from the ratification period. Among these, the most important is the use made of James Madison's paean to the militia in *Federalist* 46. Rare is the individual rights exposition that does not cite Madison's prediction that any attempt by a standing army to impose tyranny "would be opposed [by] a militia amounting to nearly half a million of citizens with arms in their hands." It was to "be doubted," Madison continued, "whether a militia thus circumstanced could ever be conquered by such a proportion of regular troops" as the national government could plausibly acquire. Then Madison went on to remind his readers of "the advantage of being armed, which the Americans possess over the people of almost every other nation," and which stood them in sharp contrast to the monarchies of Europe, "which are afraid to trust the people with arms."[67]

We should not be surprised to discover that these vintage snippets are often presented independently of the larger argument they are meant to support and indeed of the very sentences in which they are embedded. Madison's purpose in this essay (and the preceding *Federalist* 45) was to compare the relative advantages that the national and state *governments* would enjoy in the zero-sum competition for power that anti-Federalists believed the Constitution would launch, and that they further predicted would end in the consolidation of all real authority in the Union while the states withered away as effective jurisdictions of governance.[68] Nowhere in these essays did Madison address, much less defend, the idea that the armed citizenry consisting of the body of the population would be called upon to resist the oppression emanating from the national and state governments in collusion. Instead, his concern throughout was to explain why the political affections and institutional resources that the state governments would command would render any real danger of the erosion of their authority unlikely—including the worst-case scenario of military despotism that he then deemed improbable to the point of absurdity.[69]

The militia was one of those resources that would rally to the support of state government, as (surprise!) the sentences from which his most frequently quoted phrases are extracted (or wrenched) make clear. Thus the sentence in which the reference to half a million armed citizens appears continues: "officered by men chosen from among themselves, fighting for their common liberties"—which are presumably invested in the autonomy of their state governments—and, most important, "united and conducted by governments possessing their affections and confidence," the political ingredients that Madison understood would best determine the outcome of whatever rivalry existed between the two levels of American federalism.

Similarly, the sentence distinguishing Americans from other peoples begins with the phrase "Besides the advantage of being armed," and then concludes by noting that "the existence of subordinate governments [that is, the states] to which the people are attached, and by which the militia officers are appointed, forms a barrier against the enterprizes of ambition, more insurmountable than any which a simple government of any form [that is, a unified nation-state, whether absolutist like France or parliamentary like Britain] can admit of." So, too, the thought that other peoples might be less tyrannized if they were possessed of arms is a prelude to a further comment on the advantages of federalism:

> But were the people to possess the additional advantages of local governments chosen by themselves, who could collect the national will, and direct the national force; and of officers appointed out of the militia, by these governments and attached both to them and to the militia, it may be affirmed with the greatest assurance, that the throne of every tyranny in Europe would be speedily overturned, in spite of the legions which surround it.

Nowhere does Madison treat the idea of an armed citizenry existing independently of any government as the best deterrent against despotism; rather, his argument throughout rests on the supposition that the militia is an institution of government, subject to its legal regulation, and the greater likelihood that the members of this militia will commit their affections and loyalty to repel any "projects of ambition" that the national government might undertake to pursue the "downfal[l] of the State Governments."[70] Tyranny in the compound republic of the United States would not take the form of a joint national-state assault on the liberties of the people. Rather, it would necessarily involve an effort by the national government to encroach upon the rights and powers of the states; and should this encroachment take place without the approval of the people's representatives, the state governments would serve as the rallying point for resistance.

For a final example, consider the treatment of the militia question by the writer known as the Federal Farmer, usually identified in the current historical literature as Melancton Smith, the moderate anti-Federalist who eventually co-operated in securing ratification by the New York convention in which Federalists were a distinct minority. In his eighteenth and final letter, the Farmer included the Mason-like statement that "A militia, when properly formed are in fact the people themselves, and render regular troops in a great measure un-necessary."[71] Halbrook, though mistakenly identifying the Farmer with Richard Henry Lee, quotes at length from this essay, which includes an impor-tant discussion of the difference between a general militia composed of the body of the people and the select militia, which might turn into a tool of power.[72] But again, the omissions are revealing. Like Madison in *Federalist* 46, the Farmer posed the problem as one of allocating powers over the militia be-tween two levels of government. His definition of the militia is preceded by this statement of the problem: "In a federal republic, where the people meet in dif-ferent assemblies, many stipulations are necessary to keep a part from trans-gressing, which would be unnecessary checks against the whole met in one entire legislature, in one entire government." The issue, again, was a matter of allocating powers within a structure of federalism, not of defining private rights. Moreover, in discussing the advantages of a general militia over a select militia, the Farmer actually winds up arguing against the idea that the militia should consist of the entire population. His own idea, the Farmer wrote, was that "the federal head may prescribe a general uniform plan, on which the re-spective states shall form and train the militia, appoint their officers, and solely manage them, except when called into the service of the union." Such an "arrangement," he continued,

> places the sword in the hands of the solid interest of the community, and not in the hands of men destitute of property, of principle, or of attachment to the soci-ety and government, who often form the select corps of peace or ordinary estab-lishments: by it, the militia are the people, immediately under the management of the state governments, but on a uniform federal plan . . . [73]

In this analysis, it turns out, there are two kinds of select militia, neither of which comprises the whole body of the people. A nationally organized select militia would likely draw upon the worst elements of society, the dregs who formed the feared regular troops of European monarchies; while a state-based select militia (here equated with "the people") would consist of the solid citizens, to the exclusion of the same untrustworthy elements who could not be counted upon to maintain the social order. In both cases, the Federal Farmer constructs his argument within a matrix of federalism; he never posits the distinction between government (whether national or state) and population on which the individual rights interpretation relies.

Beyond illustrating the propensity of individual rights writers to truncate quotations mercilessly, the considerations of these debates and texts demonstrate that the discussions of 1787–88 were preoccupied with the question of the militia, and that this question was addressed almost exclusively under the rubric of federalism. Whether there was, or should be, a private, constitutionally sanctioned right to own and use firearms was simply not at issue. The rhetoric of ratification certainly included many statements from both sides on the advantages of a well-regulated militia as a valuable alternative to a standing army, but such statements did not require either side to reach the question of the nature and extent of a private right of ownership and use, much less the question of the power of the states to legislate should the use of firearms prove inimical to the health and welfare of society. No one on either side would have denied that individuals had a private legal right to the ownership of weapons, but the structure of debate neither encouraged nor required anyone to ask whether a constitutional right or duty linked to service in the militia could prevail over matters concerning the internal police of the states—a responsibility that would clearly fall under the reserved powers of the states soon to be recognized in the Tenth Amendment. Both Federalists and anti-Federalists, however, did appear to agree on one crucial point: the militia was an institution subject to the legislative control of one level of government or another.

INTELLECTUAL LEGACIES

Once one understands how little substantive support the individual rights theory derives from the records of debate in 1787–89, it becomes easier to understand why its advocates spend so little time reconstructing these debates and instead rely on that mode of originalist reasoning that emphasizes the influence of preexisting intellectual traditions. Because those debates did not directly ask whether the new government would be empowered to regulate private ownership of firearms, proponents of the individual rights interpretation necessarily turn to those sources that suggest that a general belief in the liberty-securing advantages of private ownership was so deeply grounded in eighteenth-century Anglo-American political and legal culture as to undergird and inform all discussion of the question. As Joyce Malcolm suggests, the key clues to unlocking the meaning of the Second Amendment lie in "the English legacy," as it was absorbed and elaborated by the American colonists and revolutionaries. "The English model was constantly before the framers of the American Constitution," Malcolm observes. The Americans faced daunting challenges, but

> Happily, English strategies for prudent control of the sword were ready to hand. When delegates copied English policies the public was reassured. When they departed from them there was grave concern, which was not allayed until the passage of the Second Amendment brought the American system more into line with English practice. Here, then, is the key to the meaning and intent of the much-misunderstood Second Amendment.[74]

One is only left to wonder how Americans coped with the other departures from English practice that the Constitution embodied. Presumably anti-Federalists would have been even more assured had the framers of the Constitution restored monarchy and created an American nobility.

There is, of course, nothing unique about this effort to locate the ideas, great and small, of American constitutionalism within larger intellectual contexts. An enormous literature describes the influence on American thinking of a host of traditions, ranging from knowledge of the writings of antiquity, in which all learned men were versed, to the latest discoveries of Newtonian physics and Lockean psychology, with ample room for other political, religious, historical, economic, and even literary modes of thought. Yet even if we concede that different facets of American constitutionalism reflected one or more or all of these legacies, traditions, and discourses, the formidable task remains of explaining exactly how these background beliefs attained dispositive constitutional authority under the conditions of debate and decision prevailing between 1787 and 1791.

It is one thing, after all, to say that a particular belief or opinion or attitude was part of the zeitgeist, but another matter entirely to assay its interpretative authority. Nor is this a problem unique in any way to the Second Amendment. It is in fact a fundamental problem, in writing the intellectual history of the Constitution, to know how to correlate the received wisdom that shaped the general parameters of political thinking with the particular decisions on numerous provisions that had to be taken as American constitutionalism embarked on its inventive, radically textual course. One can posit, for example, that Locke exerted a pervasive influence over American ideas about the right of resistance, education, and epistemology—but, with the exception of the Religion Clause and the Just Compensation Clause, one would be hard-pressed to fashion a Lockean interpretation of any provision of the Constitution. Montesquieu's theory of the separation of powers exerted enormous influence over American thinking, as evidenced by the formulaic restatement of the theory found in the early state constitutions and declarations of rights. Yet as any reader of *Federalist* 47 knows, one can understand the sense that Americans made of this theory—in either 1776 or 1787—only by reconstructing the varied ways in which the framers of their constitutions tried to apply his "doctrine" (if that is even the right term for it).[75]

Consider the problems that Malcolm encounters in the concluding chapter of her recent book on the subject, which is devoted primarily to examining the English background to American practice. Taking Malcolm seriously requires an immediate suspension of disbelief, for neither the language of the Bill of Rights of 1689 nor the doctrine of parliamentary supremacy readily supports the idea that the subject's right to have arms lay beyond the sphere of legislative regulation.[76] Malcolm suggests that the reported popularity of Blackstone's *Commentaries* in the colonial market means that the colonists also accepted (lock, stock, and barrel, so to speak) his passing comment on the value of the "auxiliary right" of subjects having "arms for their defence." But one cannot implicitly assume that Blackstone's general popularity made his position authoritative on every point; if it had, the colonists would have had to fold their constitutional tents in the face of Blackstone's assertion of parliamentary supremacy. Moreover, Blackstone's own language can be read just as easily—arguably more so—to support the power of legislative regulation. The subjects' right must be "suitable to their condition and degree, and such as are allowed by law," and it is further characterized as "a public allowance, under due restriction, of the natural right of resistance and self-protection." Nothing in this language could plausibly be read to establish a private right immune to legislative regulation. Nor does the allusion to natural right operate as a similar prohibition. It was, after all, one of the great commonplaces of eighteenth-century rights talk to observe that natural rights are always modified by the terms of the social compact. Anglo-Americans operated in a political and legal culture that was deeply respectful of the natural right of property, but that did not prevent legislatures on both sides of the Atlantic from imposing taxes and other regulations of the rights of property in the normal exercise of their power.[77]

Once Malcolm reaches American shores, the problematic nature of her argument becomes even more evident. Legislation requiring various groups of colonists (primarily in the seventeenth century) to carry arms does not establish the existence of a late-eighteenth-century right lying beyond legislative regulation; and, in any case, a legislature that can require arms to be carried in the interest of intimidating slaves and Indians can also prohibit the same act in the name of public security.[78] Nor does repetition of the hackneyed point that the colonists freely shared an English fear of standing armies even begin to identify the limits on legislative regulation. Only one of the state declarations of rights (Pennsylvania) adopted in the early years of independence asserted a right to bear arms for self-defense, as well as the common defense; and only the Virginia declaration qualified its reference to the militia with the apposite phrase, "composed of the body of the people." [79]

Not to worry, however, Malcolm assures us. Even those states that "failed to mention a right to have arms for individual defence" must have intended to endorse a general militia. And how do we know this? "Because of their long-standing prejudice against a select militia as constituting a form of standing army liable to be skewed politically and dangerous to liberty, every state had created a general militia." Moreover, "the individual's right to be armed, where not specifically mentioned, is unmistakably assumed." And how do we know this? Because the broad statement of the usual trinity of natural rights, including the right "of enjoying and defending life and liberty" or "obtaining happiness and safety" would be meaningless "if citizens were deprived of the right to be armed." [80]

This is less an argument from ample historical evidence than a faulty syllogism resting on questionable premises and circular reasoning. At crucial junctures in her argument—when one has to ask just how was the English legacy translated into American practice—Malcolm resorts to such vaguely asserted forms of evidence as "long-standing prejudice," things that are "unmistakably assumed," and the abiding influence of Blackstone's statement about the danger of "oppression," typically omitting his qualifications subjecting possession and use of arms to legal restriction. These are assertions rather than demonstrations; they establish only that such familiar themes as the fear of standing armies and the belief in a natural right of self-defense were part of the universe of political attitudes shared by eighteenth-century Americans. They do not explain, however, how much interpretative weight these preexisting "attitudes, prejudices, and policies" [81] can bear when we try to determine what the adopters of the Second Amendment thought they were doing, much less why the principles so loosely stated there should trump either existing understandings of the legislative powers of the states or the relevant textual provisions of the federal Constitution.

What the individual rights interpretation establishes, then, is something less than meets the eye. Did Americans in general believe or affirm the value of an armed citizenry? Of course they did, and in doing so they freely invoked images made familiar by the common radical whig reading of history. Was this belief part of the intellectual currency that shaped the general discussion of issues relating to the standing army, the militia, and the respective authority of the national and state governments? Of course it was. But did Federalists and anti-Federalists agree about the relative importance of an armed citizenry in promoting the future welfare of the United States? No they did not. For anti-Federalists, the appeal to the armed citizenry was meant as an alternative to the substantive provisions of the Constitution, which threatened the creation of a standing army that would command obedience at the point of a bayonet.[82] For Federalists, by contrast, the presumed existence of an armed citizenry offered yet another reason to dismiss anti-Federalist predictions of tyranny as so many phantasms of their opponents' overheated imaginations.

Yet even if one recognizes that this belief remained part of the political culture of the late 1780s, a critical problem persists: How would the legal authority of the states to regulate the use and ownership of firearms be affected or altered by a constitutional provision understood as a restriction on the authority of the national government? If the colonies and states had previously exercised jurisdiction in this area, as they demonstrably had, and if the logic of the anti-Federalist position was to enhance the authority of the state governments vis-à-vis that of the new national government, what difference would the adoption of the Second Amendment make to the reserved powers of the states? A belief in the value of an armed citizenry is consistent with a view of the Second Amendment as an injunction to the federal government not to rely solely on its own army, but to continue to keep the militia well armed and disciplined. It could similarly be read as a reminder to the state governments of their responsibility not to depend solely on federal largesse (funded mandates, in effect) to perform their duty to maintain their militia, especially to counteract the danger of domestic insurrection. But there is no evidence that the generalized belief in the armed citizenry distilled in the Second Amendment was understood to be the equivalent of an Article I, section 10, restriction on the legislative authority of the states.

Lessons of Experience

This reliance on intellectual sources of American attitudes is the more striking when it is set against a final category of evidence that the individual rights interpretation seems reluctant to embrace: the lessons learned by the experience of the Revolutionary War, or, more generally, from the departures in constitutional thinking and practice to which the Revolution gave rise. Put simply, the individual rights interpretation is an argument against change, and is in that sense fundamentally ahistorical. It assumes that a body of writings absorbed by Americans prior to 1776 was completely formative of how they thought after 1776; the principles ostensibly laid down in *Cato's Letters* and the other supposed sources remained determinative of American thinking through 1789 (and beyond). Nothing that intervened in the form of experience and experiment could alter or diminish the weight of that received authority.

By contrast, the interpretation of the Second Amendment that anchors its meaning in the immediate debates of the late 1780s, and especially in the specific issue of the militia, presupposes that fundamental changes in American thinking had begun to develop since 1776. The rhetorical deference that Federalist writers sometimes paid to traditional concepts (like the value of an armed citizenry) could not disguise the self-consciously empirical and experimental qualities of mind that distinguished the proponents of constitutional reform from its antagonists. Anti-Federalists may have been men of little faith in the Constitution because they remained all too faithful to ideas that may have carried them into revolution in 1776, but which experience had since rendered problematic if not obsolete.[83] In this view, the debate over the militia cannot be explained merely by reference to Machiavelli, or Trenchard and Gordon, or Blackstone. Authority unconfirmed or actively challenged by events was no longer binding; it could be weighed only in the light of events and experience. To put the point more directly: Their ideas (like ours) were shaped not only by what they read but also (and arguably more powerfully) by what they did or had done to them. Thinking of the origins of the Second Amendment within this context yields two major challenges to the individual rights interpretation, one of which (the more familiar) can be labeled political, the other (and more recently explored) behavioral.

The political context, which is principally identified with the writings of the historians Lawrence Cress and Don Higginbotham,[84] has already been implicated throughout this essay: it suggests, quite simply, that the true object of debate in the late 1780s was the militia, and that thinking about the militia was now driven primarily by lessons derived from the crucible of revolutionary conflict. That the militia had served important functions in that war is not to be denied, and recent historical scholarship has confirmed the point.[85] But to say that the militia had been useful was not to say that national defense could henceforth be allowed to rely upon it. Projects of militia reform were supported by the retired commander in chief, George Washington, and the new secretary of war, Henry Knox, in the mid-1780s, but they fell victim to the desuetude of the Continental Congress. The calling of the Federal Constitutional Convention, however, gave Washington and other like-minded men a new opportunity to lay the necessary groundwork for the desired reforms, and the resulting provisions of the Constitution reflected their desire. Henceforth the militia would be an institution subject to substantial national regulation, with the state governments sharing responsibility for appointment of officers and the actual conduct of training and having concurrent power to use these units, when not called into national service, for their own lawful purposes (including, of course, the suppression of insurrections by disaffected citizens presumably exercising their natural right of revolution).

Nothing in the ensuing discussions of these proposals required or even encouraged either Federalists or anti-Federalists to consider the matter of state or national regulation of the private ownership and use of firearms. It follows that no coherent intentions or understandings can be confidently ascribed to a problem that was never cogently formulated in its own right. Whether or not individuals had a right to own firearms free of regulation by the states was a matter of complete indifference in 1787–89.

The behavioral context is most clearly associated with the work of Michael Bellesiles, which will doubtless attract substantial notice and scrutiny upon its imminent publication. Probing beyond the hackneyed paeans to American sharpshooting that occur both in the primary sources (some of them clearly contrived for European eyes[86]) and in later writings, Bellesiles is evidently the first historian to examine the actual use of firearms in the colonial, revolutionary, and postrevolutionary eras. What he discovers, among other things, is that many, perhaps the majority of, American households did not possess firearms; that Americans imported virtually all of their firearms; that the weapons they had were likely to deteriorate rapidly, firearms being delicate mechanisms, prone to rust and disrepair; that gunsmiths were few, far between, and not especially skilled; that the militia were poorly armed and trained, their occasional drilling days an occasion for carousing rather than acquiring the military art; that Americans had little use for hunting, it being much more efficient to slaughter your favorite mammal grazing in the neighboring pasture or foraging in nearby woods than to take the time to track some attractive haunch of venison with a weapon that would be difficult to load, aim, and fire before the fleshy object of your desire went bounding off for greener pastures. (Trapping was much more efficient than hunting; hunting was then primarily a leisure activity for the elite.) All of these considerations make plausible and explicable the concerns we have already noted in describing the Virginia ratification debate of mid-June 1788: that without a national government firmly committed to the support of the militia, the institution would wither away from inefficiency, indifference, and neglect (which is pretty much what happened in any case, for reasons both Federalists and anti-Federalists readily foresaw). Americans of all political persuasions could pay rhetorical lip service to the value of an armed citizenry because that sentiment was embedded in the traditions that the individual rights interpretation celebrates; the reality, however, was quite otherwise.[87]

Bellesiles's findings, coupled with the evidence that militia reform was indeed the object of debate, thus illustrate a fundamental problem that all originalist inquiries must address. Once we move beyond the immediate records of debate to reconstruct the deeper assumptions and concerns upon which they rested, originalists need to assess the relative importance of two quite different sets of sources, one consisting of intellectual traditions that doubtless shaped a grammar of discussion, the other of a set of experiences that fashioned an agenda for action. The tension between these two ways of thinking contextually would presumably operate at any period, but we have good reason to think that it was felt more acutely during the revolutionary era, when Americans were deeply aware of the fundamental break that their experiment in republican constitutionalism was making with the received wisdom of the past. This claim appears repeatedly in Federalist literature—including, most notably, *The Federalist*—and it renders problematic the naive, not to say ahistorical, claim that underlies the approach taken by Malcolm and other writers of the individual rights school: that transposition of the English experience or the authority of received tradition fills in the silences in the evidentiary record. It may or it may not; but the argument cannot stand on assertion alone. It requires some comparison of received ideas and the lessons of experience, but one searches the individual rights literature in vain for any sustained mention, much less discussion, of the immediate concerns on which Americans were acting. In their account, the prior conception of the militia rooted in tradition somehow trumps the newer notions that the experience of the Revolution made more urgent. That is an arguable conclusion but, if so, it must be argued, and historical argument requires weighing conflicting evidence, not simply accepting one source and discounting another.

A DECLARATORY RIGHT

Modern thinking about constitutional rights is powerfully and indelibly shaped by the legacy of the Fourteenth Amendment, the gradual development of the incorporation doctrine, the civil rights revolution of the 1950s and '60s, and the broader controversies that followed the landmark, rights-enlarging decisions of the Warren and Burger courts. The logic of the individual rights interpretation of the Second Amendment is deeply indebted to these developments in three ways, two of which are fairly obvious while the third is rather more subtle, even deceptive.

First, the rights revolution established the protection of individual rights as the dominant paradigm governing our underlying conception of the problem of rights in general, for it is the "no person" who claims recognition under the Due Process and Equal Protection clauses of the Fourteenth Amendment who has evolved into the image of the "lone rights bearer" lamented by Mary Ann Glendon.[88] It is the individual gun owner whose right is perceived to be the endangered object of legislative restriction.

Second, the incorporation doctrine makes the actions of state and local legislative bodies restricting the exercise of federally sanctioned rights subject to judicial review, and its incomplete application accordingly leads to the question: Why has the constitutional right seemingly affirmed by the Second Amendment not enjoyed the benefit of incorporation? Indeed, ending the exile of the Second Amendment to the district of unincorporated rights is as much the object of the individual rights interpretation as insisting upon a particular account of the original understanding of 1787–91. It would do no good to demonstrate conclusively that the framers and ratifiers of those years really did regard a fundamental right to own weapons as a necessary security against the danger of tyranny, if one could not at the same time produce a compelling rationale for its incorporation today.

There is, however, a third legacy of incorporation that also shapes—or perhaps distorts—our historical understanding of the nature of the right that the Second Amendment asserts. Given the broad application of the incorporation doctrine to remedy injustice and secure relief in decision after landmark decision, it is only natural that we now regard the Bill of Rights as a set of legally enforceable claims and commands. If a right is asserted, there must be a remedy when its exercise is infringed, and a remedy requires recourse to law. To have a right without a legally efficacious remedy is arguably to have no right at all, and, if that is so, it would seem rather naive and pointless to think that a bill of rights (any bill of rights) is merely a set of hollow principles. As invested as we are (legally) in the jurisprudence of the Bill of Rights and (culturally) in veneration of the wisdom of the constitutional fathers, it is difficult to suggest that they could have been so naive as to enumerate rights for which they did not intend remedies.

Yet at the time when the Second Amendment was adopted, it was still possible to conceive of statements of rights in quite different terms, as assertions or confirmations of vital principles rather than the codification of legally enforceable restrictions or commands. The state declarations of rights of 1776 were filled with statements of this nature, and many of these statements—and, arguably, the bills of rights in toto—lacked legal authority. A statement endorsing the principle of rotation in office did not impose term limits on legislators; it simply reminded voters that they would be well advised, from time to time, to send the bumpkins back to the country. To be sure, it was precisely because such statements had demonstrated their "inefficacy" that Madison first dismissed bills of rights as so many "parchment barriers,"[89] and then proposed interweaving his amendments in the most salient places in the Constitution, rather than see them appended as supplemental articles. The movement away from the norms of 1776 was also reflected in his congressional colleagues' rejection of the formulaic restatement of natural rights that Madison had originally proposed as a sort of second preamble to the Constitution, and which he revealingly classified as "a bill of rights," in apparent contradistinction to his remaining, interwoven amendments.[90] Any comparison of the amendments of 1787 with the state declarations will reveal how far American thinking had moved since 1776.

Yet among all the provisions of the federal Bill of Rights, the Second Amendment is the one that most clearly echoes the earlier tradition. That is the most obvious explanation for the mysterious presence of the distinctive preamble that is the object of so much analysis, from the syntactical to the metaphysical. As Eugene Volokh has recently noted, the preamble is not quite so esoteric or exceptional a statement as it is often made to appear. Set in the larger context of Revolutionary era pronouncements, it is almost "commonplace."[91] But intent as Volokh is on parsing the relation of the preamble to the operative provision, he misses a more obvious point that better captures or represents the context in which the Second Amendment was formulated. What was still a commonplace was the idea that a declaration of rights could contain statements of republican principles as well as provisions confirming or specifying natural rights (freedom of conscience), political safeguards (freedom of speech, press, assembly, and petition), common law procedural rights (Fourth, Fifth, Sixth, and Eight amendments), or superfluous remedies against idiosyncratic grievances (such as quartering of soldiers in peacetime).

Under this interpretation, the Second Amendment can be read as a simple, elegant, distilled version of the comparable statements found in the state declarations of rights and the amendments recommended by several ratification conventions. It affirmed the essential proposition—or commonplace—that liberty fared better when republican polities relied upon a militia of citizen-soldiers for their defense, rather than risk the dire consequences of sustaining a permanent military establishment. It therefore served as a principled reminder to the federal government (or, more particularly, to Congress) to act to ensure that the militia would indeed remain well organized, armed, and disciplined—not least by guaranteeing that arms be provided to state governments and citizen soldiers who might otherwise lack the resources and desire to obtain and maintain costly firearms prone to disrepair.

The Second Amendment, however, also omitted more restrictive provisions that anti-Federalists would have liked or expected to find there, because the dominant Federalist majority in Congress saw no need to make the text more explicit. There was no need, for example, to repeat the ritual mantra against standing armies, for Federalists had repeatedly insisted that the constitutional restriction of appropriations to two years meant that a true standing army—that is, a permanent military force existing independently of control by the people's representatives—could literally not be created. One can speculate, too, that the Senate deleted the substantive phrase, "composed of the body of the people," for sheer redundancy, in an act (Amar suggests) of "stylistic shortening." But a Congress that wanted to affirm a general principle without compromising its own capacity (or that of future congresses) to decide what form the militia should take would have had more potent reasons to eliminate that phrase. By the same token, while the Second Amendment generally endorsed the value of a well-regulated militia, as a mere statement of principle it made no alteration of any kind in the delegation and allocation of legislative authority as delineated in Article I.

It goes almost without saying that the statement of a general principle may fall well short of the provision of adequate remedies for its infringement. But that deficiency would have mattered to the framers of the Second Amendment only insofar as they believed that the Constitution posed a real threat requiring a remedy. They lacked any incentive to move beyond the vague generalities of the language they finally adopted, and good reason not to do so if greater precision could be read as imposing a meaningful restriction on the ability of Congress to develop whatever form of militia the consideration of national security seemed to require.

Yet the brevity and ambiguity of the Second Amendment may illuminate a deeper problem with the very conception of a bill of rights. We may be reluctant to admit it, but the task of reducing the statement of a right to a concise textual formula, in the style of the national Constitution, suggests that the concept of a right may be far more difficult to cabin successfully than other kinds of statements we expect to find in a constitutional text. Stating a theory of freedom of speech or conscience, for example, is not quite equivalent to specifying modes of election or terms of office or even the respective powers of institutions. The very concept of a right remains a source of philosophical perplexity, and so, on occasion, does the identification of the rights bearer, including the keeper and bearer of arms. Is that right a duty we owe to the state or a manifestation of a natural right of resistance and self-protection? Is the individual who can claim to exercise a right to protect his home the same individual who forms part of the people mobilized in the militia? Does it make sense to speak of an individual right to arms in the context of a right of revolution, which must be a collective act of mass resistance if it is not to devolve into an expression of anarcho-terrorism? [92]

In his letter discussing the problem of bills of rights as "parchment barriers," Madison casually mentioned the problem that would arise if "a positive declaration of some of the most essential rights could not be obtained in the requisite latitude." [93] His particular example involved a right to which he was far more attached than the right to bear arms: freedom of conscience. Madison worried that this cherished right might have to be textually tailored more narrowly than it should be in principle if it was to acquire the requisite political support. But Madison's concern with the difficulty of stating a right in a textually satisfactory way may illuminate a deeper problem. What textual formula, expressed in the succinct style that the American constitutional tradition initially favored, could possibly capture and distill the matrix of principles and concerns that underlie any conception of a right, while simultaneously identifying the rights bearer, the interest to be protected, and the point where that protection yields to legitimate demands for regulation? Given the circumstances of 1789, when we cannot be certain how seriously the framers of the Bill of Rights were taking their assignment, it takes a high degree of confidence in their desire to achieve "perspicuity" to conclude that the authors of the amendments were acting with as much textual exactitude as we seek to extract in our own labored readings of these twenty-seven words.

CONCLUSION

Beneath their huzzas of conquest delivered on a field supposedly cleared of beaten opponents, cowed into retreat by the exemplary scholarship of the victors, the proponents of the individual rights interpretation betray the reason for the peculiar emphases and distortions that mark their writings. Had there been any reason for the constitutional disputants of the late 1780s to discuss, directly and consciously, the extent of private rights of the ownership and use of firearms, advocates of the individual rights interpretation would certainly have filled their articles with the apposite remarks. They would not have had to pepper their quotations with the telltale ellipses that invite critical readers to check what has been omitted (as, for instance, in the use made of *Federalist* 46); or make preposterous claims that are easily refuted (such as James Madison's supposed endorsement of Tench Coxe's description of the right to bear arms as a private right); or suggest that the deletion of a substantive qualification of the nature of the militia ("composed of the body of the people") was an inconsequential exercise in editorial concision; or use one textual rule for defining "people" and another for "militia." Had the framers and ratifiers of the Constitution really perceived the problem in terms of a private right detached from service in the public institution of the militia, we would know it, and the writings of Halbrook, Kates, Malcolm, and others would take a different form. For ceteris paribus, direct expressions of framers' intentions and ratifiers' understandings would always provide the best evidence of the original meaning of a disputed constitutional clause.

But the structure of the debates of the late 1780s did not conduce to pose the problem in the form that proponents of the individual rights interpretation would prefer to exploit. As the records from the Federal Constitutional Convention, the ensuing ratification campaign, and the debates in the First Congress of 1789 all demonstrate, the issue under discussion was always the militia, and that issue was posed primarily as a matter of defining the respective powers of two levels of government. It was the inertial condition of American federalism—the existence of states with some intractable measure of autonomy, including the militia, yet bound for collective security in a federal union coeval with their independence—that ineluctably gave the debate this form. This controlling circumstance, to be sure, did not prevent odd expressions of concern about the private ownership and use of weapons from being *voiced,* but it did prevent such concerns from reaching the threshold required for focused discussion, much less becoming the true object of debate. Nor was there then any reason to think of the ownership and use of firearms as a problem of public health and welfare. Under conceptions prevailing then and even now, such concerns fell completely under the conventional police powers of the states, and nothing in the structure of debate between 1787 and 1789 invited inquiry into the effect the Constitution would have in this realm. The debate over a bill of rights, as everyone knows, was about limiting the powers of the proposed national government, not trenching further on the traditional police responsibilities of the states. Similarly, because firearms had little practical use in private life, and were hardly dangerous except in warfare, it is completely anachronistic to expect the disputants of the eighteenth century to have comprehended, much less addressed, the problem of firearms regulation in its modern form. For much the same reason, the framers and ratifiers of the Fifth Amendment did not consider the problem of wiretapping or more sophisticated forms of electronic surveillance; nor did they ask whether a Constitution that allowed the national government to raise land and naval forces would be embarrassed by the establishment of the United States Air Force.

Given these difficulties, it is not surprising that the individual rights interpretation relies so much on the weight of received tradition, in the form of warnings about the danger of standing armies, the virtues of an armed citizenry, and what Joyce Malcolm disarmingly calls "long-standing prejudice" or things that are "unmistakably assumed." Sir William Blackstone never visited America, nor was he a member of the Federal Constitutional Convention, but his works were widely read, so it naturally follows that his speculative claim that an armed people would be able "to restrain the violence of oppression" provides the proverbial smoking pistol to solve the mystery of the Second Amendment.[94]

All that this emphasis on received wisdom can establish or confirm, however, is the familiar point that Americans feared standing armies and hoped that the maintenance of a well-regulated militia would obviate the need for a substantial national military establishment. This was, indeed, to borrow Malcolm's phrase, a long-standing prejudice, and it certainly left its mark on the grammar of eighteenth-century republicanism. But the authority of such prior sentiments was exactly what the revolutionaries and constitutionalists of the 1770s and '80s were prepared to, and did, challenge. Long-standing prejudice suggested that the British constitution was the embodiment of the best political science of the era, but Americans not only departed freely from its form and structure, they also invented a new definition of what a constitution itself was in order to replace the one they had inherited. The exercises of constitution writing in 1776 and, especially, in 1787 were shaped within the crucible, the hothouse experience, of revolution and revolutionary war, and some of the lessons that experience taught bore directly on the subject at hand: the role and value of either the militia as an organized institution or of an armed citizenry whose private weapons proved to be inadequate in number, quality, and repair. Not surprisingly, the individual rights interpretation passes in nearly complete silence over the obvious question: Were Americans in the late 1780s thinking about the militia in exactly the same unchanged terms as they had in 1776? Some of them admittedly were, but they were far more likely to be numbered among the losers in the constitutional debates of 1787–89 than among its victors. And that is why we can fairly conclude that Madison had substantive reasons for omitting the phrase "composed of the body of the people" from his original draft of the amendment; why a Senate that included Rufus King, one of the committee members who framed the militia clause at the Federal Constitutional Convention, would have deleted this phrase after the House had added it; and why a conference committee that included Madison for the House left that deletion unchallenged.

Finally, the complete omission from the individual rights interpretation of any discussion of the police power of the states constitutes potentially its most telling flaw, while simultaneously exposing a deeper dilemma in its dependence on originalism. If we read the Constitution intratextually, how do we triangulate the echoes between the "people" of the Second and Ninth Amendments, on the one hand and, on the other, the reserved powers of the states under the Tenth Amendment? Like the Second Amendment, the Tenth Amendment takes the form of an ambiguously stated injunction, which arguably adds little if anything to the positive content of the Constitution. Yet it is impossible to conceive how the Tenth Amendment could have excluded the traditional power of government to legislate broadly for public health and safety from the reserved powers of the states. It is precisely because this traditional function was (and remains) so essential to our concept of governance that the individual rights interpretation has to insist that the principal purpose of the Second Amendment is to provide a powerful deterrent against tyranny. Only by evoking that speculative threat to the Republic itself can the individual rights interpretation identify a danger more ominous than the actual costs annually incurred through the casual and deliberate use of firearms.

If, then, one wished to adjudicate the Second Amendment dispute on originalist grounds, it would not be enough to adduce a historically delimited meaning of the word "militia" and the existence of a right of resistance and revolution that would be rendered meaningless if the population were disarmed. One would also have to ask whether the adopters of the Second Amendment thought or understood that they were seriously restricting the normal police powers of the state in order to preserve that revolutionary option. Even putting aside the formidable problems that this essay has emphasized in the individual rights interpreters' use of originalist evidence, their arguments would still need to confront a completely different line of originalist argument—anchored in the Tenth Amendment—that they have so far largely ignored. One originalist argument holds that the danger of tyranny still warrants a broad construction of the Second Amendment, and that the right to be armed must therefore vest in the population as a whole, because the modern militia (the National Guard) is already too closely tied to the potential source of despotism to act the part that Madison and others of his generation accorded to the state-based militia of their era. The other argument holds that the Constitution, amended or unamended, did not diminish the capacity of the states to legislate in pursuit of the public health and safety. What has changed over time is not our basic understanding of the responsibility of state governance in this respect, other shifts in the balance of state and federal activity notwithstanding, but rather our appreciation of the danger that casual use of firearms poses.

The true way, then, in which the Second Amendment problem (as an exercise in originalism) should be cast is this: If its adopters had the same evidence available to them that we possess today, would they place greater weight on the speculative danger of tyranny, rooted in their reconstruction of the history of early modern Europe and their fear of consolidated power? Or would they agree that pressing problems of the present warrant placing greater emphasis on the police powers of the states? Either position can be argued on originalist grounds, but posing the problem in this way identifies a deeper irony in the larger debate. For, at bottom, the individual rights interpretation insists that fears rooted in the historical memories of the eighteenth century should still take priority over the judgments we are entitled to reach after two centuries of constitutional self-government. Those fears were certainly legitimate then, for the founders of American constitutionalism had good reason and historical evidence aplenty to wonder whether their experiment would work. That is what makes their leap of constitutional faith so compelling, and their fears of standing armies and national despotism so understandable.

Is it true, however, that the success of American constitutionalism two centuries and more later is due to the existence of a well-armed citizenry? We have been told that the decline of bowling leagues may be an index of the well-being of democratic civil society, but does it follow that the welfare of constitutional governance is directly correlated with the distribution of portable weapons, up to and including the automatic weapons that occasionally figure in school-yard shootings? Somehow I have labored under the impression that the strength of our constitutional culture lies elsewhere, in the commitment of our citizenry to principles of representative government, equality, and (increasingly) tolerance. Yet after this disconcerting journey into the Second Amendment theater of scholarship, my confidence has been shaken.

5. "A Well Regulated Militia": The Second Amendment in Historical Perspective

PAUL FINKELMAN*

"A well regulated Militia, composed of gentlemen freeholders, and other freemen, is the natural strength and only stable security of a free Government."
—George Mason, the Fairfax County Committee of Safety,
January 17, 1775[1]

The history of the drafting and adoption of the Second Amendment emerges out of the historical events surrounding the failure of the national government under the Articles of Confederation. This failure led to a call for a convention to revise the Articles. While American leaders were contemplating calling the convention to revise the Articles, violent resistance to traditional law enforcement—most notably Shays's Rebellion in Massachusetts—underscored the sense of crisis that many Americans felt. Farmers led by Captain Daniel Shays marched on the local courthouses in western Massachusetts, shutting down the courts and intimidating judges and others. Eventually militia companies from eastern Massachusetts dispersed Shays and his followers.

The delegates to the Philadelphia Convention met with this event fresh in their memory, and the knowledge that the government under the Articles of Confederation was helpless in the face of lawless violence and rebellion. The delegates, fearful of a weak government unable to defend itself, wanted to create a strong government, capable of repelling foreign invasions and suppressing domestic insurrections. Such a government needed a standing army, which could be supplemented by a trained, well-regulated militia. The delegates anticipated that the army, and the militias, might someday have to disarm the rabble, the mob, the next collection of disappointed, lawless rioters, led by the next Shays to come along.

The same men who wrote the Constitution, creating a strong central government, also wrote the bill of rights that amended the Constitution. Contrary to popular myth, the amendments were not a radical revolutionary response to the conservative constitution. The Congress of 1789, which wrote the Bill of Rights, was totally and completely dominated by Federalists, supporters of the Constitution, who had no desire to undermine the stability of the new government or to diminish its power. Thus, when they added amendments to the Constitution, they did so carefully, for the most part avoiding any amendments that might have subverted the powers of the new government. James Madison proudly noted that "the structure & stamina of the Govt are as little touched as possible" by the amendments he proposed.[2] It is in this context that the Second Amendment was written, and it is in this context that is must be understood.

As Madison and the Federalists who controlled the First Congress well understood, the Second Amendment was designed to preserve the power of the national government in maintaining order, while at the same time reaffirming that the states would always have the power to organize, train, and if necessary arm their militias, so long as they were "well regulated." The framers of the Bill of Rights emphatically did not seek to undermine the power of the national government to govern, to maintain peace and "domestic tranquility," and, if necessary, to disarm the mob and suppress insurrections.

We see this history from the beginning of the Constitutional Convention through the ratification of the Bill of Rights. Thus when he introduced the Virginia Plan at the Philadelphia Convention, Governor Edmund Randolph "commented on the difficulty of the crisis," facing the nation and spoke of "the necessity of preventing the fulfilment of the prophecies of the American downfall." Randolph "then proceeded to enumerate the defects" in the present government, noting that "the confederation produced no security agai[nst] foreign invasion; congress not being permitted to prevent a war nor to support it by th[eir] own authority" and that "neither militia nor draughts being fit for defense on such occasions, enlistments only could be successful, and these could not be executed without money." He pointed out that "the federal government could not check the quarrels between states, nor a rebellion." He expressed his admiration for those who had written the Articles of Confederation, but noted that they had produced that document "when the inefficiency of requisitions was unknown—no commercial discord had arisen among any states—no rebellion had appeared as in Massts.—foreign debts had not become urgent—the havoc of paper money had not been foreseen—treaties had not been violated—and perhaps nothing better could be obtained from the jealousy of the states with regard to their sovereignty."[3]

Most of the convention delegates agreed with Randolph's analysis and quickly moved from revising the Articles of Confederation to writing a wholly new constitution. In the end they produced a document that strengthened the national government and provided a framework for a viable national defense. Opponents of the new form of government—anti-Federalists who feared a strong national government—proposed numerous amendments in the state conventions called to ratify the Constitution. The anti-Federalists also expressed their fears of the new Constitution in an enormous amount of public commentary.[4]

The public commentary and proposed amendments fall into two general classes. The bulk of the proposed amendments were designed to remake the Constitution by severely limiting the power of the national government. If the anti-Federalists had had their way, the United States would have reverted to a decentralized collection of sovereign states with a weak national Congress, an almost invisible federal judiciary, and a powerless military with virtually no standing army.

Not surprisingly, the Federalists who dominated the First Congress rejected all of these structural changes and did little to alter the power of the national government under the new Constitution. What the Federalists did do was offer a series of amendments that, for the most part, recognized existing limitations on the national government under the new Constitution.

The Bill of Rights confirmed that the national government would not trample on the rights of conscience, deny people due process of law, or impose cruel and unusual punishments on convicted criminals. While some of its provisions actually created new rights—such as the Sixth Amendment's right to counsel—most of the amendments simply confirmed what the national government could not do under the Constitution. The Second and Tenth Amendments reconfirmed existing relations between the states and the national government, but they did not create any new rights or structural relationships. Specifically, the Second Amendment reconfirmed that though the national Congress would have the primary responsibility for arming and organizing the state militias, if Congress failed to do its job the states could maintain their own militias.

I
The Anti-Federalists' Goals

During the debates over ratification Governor Patrick Henry of Virginia and many other anti-Federalists used the absence of a bill of rights in the Constitution to galvanize opposition to ratification. They persisted, from beginning to end, in claiming that the Constitution would create a tyranny and that the failure to insert a bill of rights was an indication of the desire of the framers to take away the liberties of the American people.

However, for the most dedicated opponents of the Constitution, the demand for a bill of rights was fundamentally a ruse. What they truly hoped to do was defeat the Constitution and thus either leave the Articles of Confederation in place or force a second convention, which would have created a substantially weaker national government than the Philadelphia Convention had proposed.

Their plan for stopping ratification ended in July 1788, when the anti-Federalists were outmaneuvered in their two most important strongholds, Virginia and New York. New Hampshire's ratification had supplied the necessary ninth state resulting in the Constitution going into effect. Ratification in Virginia and New York not only put the Federalists well over the top but, more important, brought the most populous state (Virginia) and the state with the nation's most important seaport (New York) into the government.

As they met with defeat in one state after another, the anti-Federalists fell back to their secondary position of demanding amendments to alter the nature of the government. Thus, in a number of the states, the defeated anti-Federalists proposed amendments that they hoped would be added after ratification. They did not like this strategy, but it was the best they could hope for. Some of these amendments contained proposals that would have created a bill of rights, but most of the anti-Federalist proposals were crippling amendments that would have resulted in a weaker Constitution. Indeed, Saul Cornell has noted in his careful study of the anti-Federalists, "interestingly, the amendments that were most widely proposed were, not those that sought explicit safeguards for individual rights, but those that attempted to shift the balance of power within the federal system: prohibitions of federal oversight of elections and direct taxation and explicit restriction of the power of the federal government to those powers expressly delegated by the Constitution."[5]

The anti-Federalists wanted the state ratifying conventions to endorse their proposed amendments. But this was not always possible because the anti-Federalists usually negotiated from a position of weakness with the Federalist majorities in the state conventions. In Pennsylvania, for example, the Federalist majority completely ignored the anti-Federalists, who then issued their "reasons of dissent" as a pamphlet.[6] In Maryland the anti-Federalists met with the same fate and had to resort to a newspaper publication of their proposed amendments. As Herbert Storing notes, the Maryland anti-Federalists tried to get the convention to endorse their amendments in return for a promise that they, the anti-Federalists, would support the Constitution. Having successfully ratified the Constitution, however, the Maryland Federalists "brushed aside" the deal offered by the anti-Federalists, who had just been soundly defeated.[7]

On the other hand, in Massachusetts, New Hampshire, and Virginia the Federalist majority, to placate large anti-Federalist minorities, included the proposed amendments as part of the official proceedings of the ratifying convention. This was also the case in New York. In that state the anti-Federalists were in the majority, but in the end a substantial minority of anti-Federalists voted to ratify the Constitution because ten states had already done so. In addition, growing support for the Constitution in and around New York City convinced many anti-Federalist delegates at the New York Convention that their constituents now wanted ratification.

John Jay, a leader of the Federalists, helped bring this about by a preemptive strike: he proposed that the convention attach a list of recommended amendments to its ratification. This "embarrassed the Antifederalists," by compelling them to admit the weakness of their position and, in a sense, forcing them to cut the best deal they could with the Federalists. In the end, however, Jay's move led to a compromise with the more moderate anti-Federalists, who agreed to vote for ratification in exchange for Federalist endorsement of recommended amendments. To sweeten the deal, Jay also offered to support a circular letter calling for a second convention, but this was, in reality, a "sham compromise that was in fact a total surrender" of the anti-Federalists. In the end enough anti-Federalists voted for ratification to get the document through the New York convention. Appended to the ratification was an absurdly long list of proposed changes that included some thirty-two amendments plus twenty-five statements of principles.[8]

By the end of the ratification process, the conventions in Massachusetts, South Carolina, New Hampshire, Virginia, and New York had appended various proposed amendments to the Constitution[9] to their ratification documents. In addition, the anti-Federalists in Pennsylvania and Maryland had published their own recommended amendments.[10] The officially endorsed amendments numbered more than a hundred, but many of the separate amendments actually covered many topics. Thus, the total number of proposed amendments was at least two hundred. Many went to what we normally think of as Bill of Rights protections. However, the majority of the anti-Federalist demands were structural in nature, designed to remake the Constitution by weakening the national government. By eliminating duplications, "[a]bout 100 separate proposals can be distinguished." A "clear majority" of these called for structural changes.[11]

When Madison proposed what became the Bill of Rights in Congress, he ignored virtually all of the structural proposals, which not surprisingly infuriated the hard-core anti-Federalists. Indeed, the refusal of Madison and his committee to even consider the long list of structural changes proposed by the Virginia ratifying convention led Virginia's two senators, William Grayson and Richard Henry Lee, two of the three anti-Federalists in the U.S. Senate, to publicly denounce the proposed amendments. They did not like Madison's amendments because they believed these amendments would undermine their cause, prevent the calling of a second convention, and yet leave the structure of the Constitution intact. As Madison explained to Jefferson, even before the Constitution was ratified, the anti-Federalists wanted to "strike at the essence of the System," and either return to the government of the old Confederation, "or to a partition of the Union into several Confederacies." [12]

A good example of what the anti-Federalists really wanted can be seen in the Virginia Convention's list of forty proposed amendments. The first twenty proposals formed "a Declaration or Bill of Rights asserting and securing from encroachment the essential and unalienable Rights of the People." Some of these, such as a requirement for rotation in office and a prohibition on hereditary offices, were structural in nature, but most were not. They dealt with the civil liberties that are today protected by the Bill of Rights subsequently adopted in 1791. [13]

Following this initial list of twenty amendments, which would form a "Bill or Declaration of Rights," the Virginia convention wrote twenty more proposed changes, which were called "Amendments to the Body of the Constitution." [14] With the exception of one proposal dealing with juries, this list contained proposals that would have remade the powers of the government and revamped the political process. Many of the proposals would have hamstrung the operations of the national government, weakened all three branches of the government, and made the system more cumbersome.

This second list, which for anti-Federalists like Patrick Henry was by far the more important one, proposed a wholesale remaking of the system of government. The Virginia anti-Federalists wanted super majorities in Congress for many important government functions, including: a three-fourths majority of both houses for all noncommercial treaties; two-thirds majority of the Senate for the adoption of all commercial treaties; a two-thirds majority in each house of Congress for all regulations of commerce (which the anti-Federalists called navigation laws); a two-thirds majority in Congress to maintain a peacetime army; mandatory term limits (rotation in office, as they called it) for presidents; and severely limited federal jurisdiction over what became the District of Columbia. Aside from the Supreme Court, these anti-Federalists would have allowed only "courts of Admiralty." They would have had impeachment trials of senators by "some Tribunal other than the Senate," and limited the power of the national government to collect taxes in the states. [15]

Anti-Federalists in other states wanted similar changes that would have cut the heart out of the new Constitution. Virtually all the anti-Federalists would have rewritten the judiciary article to prevent the creation of a system of national courts. New York's ratifying convention, which was dominated by anti-Federalists, proposed structural changes similar to those Virginia wanted. In addition, a Constitution amended to satisfy New York would have limited federal jurisdiction in controversies between states only to cases involving land grants; prohibited any federal treaty from operating against a state constitution, thus undermining the supremacy clause; prohibited Congress from granting monopolies; required a two-thirds majority in both houses of Congress to borrow money or to declare war; provided strict temporal limitations on the suspension of habeas corpus; required rotation in office for United States senators; prohibited federal capitation taxes; limited the president's power to grant pardons; limited federal power to adopt bankruptcy laws; limited federal diversity jurisdiction in cases involving land; and prohibited the creation of intermediate appellate federal courts. Anti-Federalists in Massachusetts and New Hampshire would have limited federal court jurisdiction, prohibited the federal government from granting monopolies, and cut back on the federal government's power to tax.[16]

The fact that the majority of anti-Federalist proposals were structural, rather than libertarian, underscores the fact that the most prominent anti-Federalists were only marginally interested in a bill of rights. Indeed, among the hard-core anti-Federalists it is clear that the argument about a bill of rights was, for the most part, a stalking horse for their larger goal, which was to undermine the strength of the new central government.

Anti-Federalist leaders like Henry and Lee really wanted to defeat the Constitution and either go back to the old system or force a second convention, where they could rewrite the document along the states' rights lines that interested them. But, having failed to defeat the Constitution, they strove for crippling amendments that went to the very structure of that document. James Madison believed that the anti-Federalist leaders were involved in a "conspiracy against direct taxes" and that this was the "real object of all their zeal in opposing the system." Madison believed their ultimate goal was to destroy the power of the national government to levy any taxes and thus "re-establish the supremacy of the State Legislatures."[17] As a result, they vociferously demanded a bill of rights before the Constitution was ratified in hopes that the purported lack of libertarian protections would persuade more moderate Americans to help them defeat ratification. Once the Constitution was ratified, however, they were no longer interested in a bill of rights and instead wanted a wholesale restructing of the Constitution.

This brief overview of the major anti-Federalists demands illustrates how out of step they were with the Federalist majorities in the ratifying conventions, and how decisively they were defeated in 1787–88 when the Constitution was ratified. Similarly, they were even more out of step with the massive Federalist majority in Congress in 1789, which proposed the Bill of Rights. In 1789–91 the hard-core anti-Federalists suffered their third defeat, as Federalists and moderate anti-Federalists accepted the Bill of Rights, and, with it, the victory of the Constitution itself.

The Second Amendment arose out of the conflict between Federalists and anti-Federalists over those portions of the Constitution that dealt with the militia and the national army. But it was ultimately tied to the larger Federalist–anti-Federalist conflict over the nature of the new government itself.

II
THE CONSTITUTION, THE MILITIA, AND THE NATIONAL ARMY

The framers in Philadelphia gave Congress and the president shared responsibility for the ultimate control of the militia. They also gave state governments important responsibilities and powers in organizing and training militias, while at the same time taking ultimate authority from the states.

Article I of the Constitution gives Congress power to "declare War," "to raise and support Armies," to "maintain a Navy," to make "Rules for the Government and Regulation of land and naval Forces," to "provide for calling forth the Militia to execute the Laws of the Union, suppress Insurrections, and repel Invasions," and "to provide for organizing, arming, and disciplining, the Militia." Furthermore, Article I declares that the states may not "keep Troops, or Ships of War in time of Peace." Article II makes the president of the United States the "Commander in Chief of the Army and Navy" and "of the Militia for the several States, when called into actual Service of the United States." These provisions also contain two important limitations. Congress can appropriate money for the military for only two years, and the states retain the power to appoint all militia officers and to train the militia, provided this training complies with "the discipline prescribed by Congress."[18]

Taken together, these provisions contemplated two levels of military protection for the new nation: a national army created and governed solely by Congress and ultimately under the authority of the president in his capacity as commander in chief; and a system of state militias, essentially organized and under control of the states but subject to regulation by Congress and to "federalization" at the command of the president. Part of that regulation includes the idea that the national government has the power—and the obligation—to provide arms for the local militias. To that end the U.S. Constitution provided that "The Congress shall have Power . . . To provide for organizing, arming, and disciplining the Militia."[19] At the convention Rufus King explained the meaning of this clause: "*arming* meant not only to provide for uniformity of arms, but included authority to regulate the modes of furnishing, either by the militia themselves, the State Governments, or the National Treasury."[20] In other words, the defense of the United States would rely on both the state militias and the standing army.

For a variety of reasons, most anti-Federalists feared these arrangements.

They were most concerned about the standing army. According to the traditional Whig and Republican ideology of the period, a "standing army" threatened the liberties of a free people. This argument was rooted in English history, where the army was traditionally a remote mercenary force, disconnected from the people, and under the direct control of a hereditary monarch. The experience of the Revolution also led to hostility to a standing army. In 1770, after Lord Hillsborough sent British troops to American soil, Benjamin Franklin observed that "Instead of *preventing* complaints by removing the causes," the British government "thought best that Soldiers should be sent to *silence* them."[21] The Declaration of Independence, which Franklin later helped write, polemically, but accurately, included the standing army in its laundry list of complaints against the King:

> HE has kept among us, in Times of Peace, Standing Armies, without the consent of our Legislatures.
> HE has affected to render the Military independent of and superior to the Civil Power.
> HE has [given] . . . his Assent to . . . Acts of pretended Legislation:
> FOR quartering large Bodies of Armed Troops among us.

Madison and other Federalists believed that the Constitution directly responded to these issues in several ways. According to the Constitution the military was triply under civilian control: Congress regulated all branches of the military; the president was the ultimate commander in chief of all the military; the governors controlled the state militias when not under federal authority. Meanwhile, appropriations for the military were limited to two years, thus preventing a true standing army from taking control. The only "military" provision of the declaration not directly addressed by the Constitution was the fear of the "quartering of large Bodies of Troops among us." Wisely, the framers left that problem to the political process. Given the close proximity to the British in Canada, the Spanish in the West, and native Americans everywhere, it would have been foolish indeed to prohibit the placement of troops close to population centers.[22] Ironically, of course, modern civic leaders across the nation avidly compete for the location of forts and bases in communities. The complaint of many communities—like that in Fort Dix, New Jersey—is that Congress, the president, or some faceless base-closing commission has refused to continue to "quarter . . . large Bodies of Troops among us."

The anti-Federalists proposed amendments that would have altered these provisions of the Constitution. Had they succeeded, the United States would have become a fundamentally different, and weaker, nation. However, Madison and his colleagues in Congress soundly rejected the anti-Federalists' proposals.

III
ANTI-FEDERALIST HOPES: THE CASE OF THE PENNSYLVANIA MINORITY

By the end of the Pennsylvania ratifying convention, the anti-Federalists had been soundly defeated. After the convention they published their "Reasons of Dissent." [23] Part of this document contained a list of fourteen proposed amendments to the Constitution. Some of these proposals—those dealing with the protection of individual libertarian rights and legal due process—were later incorporated, almost word for word, into the Bill of Rights. The essence, and in some places the exact language, of the Free Exercise clause [24] and the free press and speech clauses [25] of the First Amendment are found in these fourteen proposals, as is the essence and language of the Fourth,[26] Fifth,[27] Sixth,[28] Seventh,[29] and Eighth [30] amendments. Elements of the Tenth Amendment are also found there.[31] The Congress ignored a number of other proposed amendments on taxation, the size of the House of Representatives, the power of the federal courts, and the treaty-making power.

The Pennsylvania anti-Federalists also proposed amendments concerning the army, the militia, the right to bear arms, and the right to hunt. These proposed amendments, which are found in three of the fourteen offered by the Pennsylvania minority, help us understand the intentions of the framers of the Second Amendment. This understanding, however, is a negative one. By seeing what the framers of the Second Amendment *did not do,* we can better understand what they *did* do.

Had the proposals of the Pennsylvania anti-Federalists on this issue been written into the Bill of Rights, the Second Amendment might be the most easily understood of the first ten amendments. It is of utmost significance, however, that unlike other aspects of the Pennsylvania proposals that had been incorporated into the Bill of Rights, on these issues Madison and his colleagues in the First Congress emphatically rejected the goals and the language of the Pennsylvania anti-Federalists.

Thus, it is useful to consider what Congress might have written, but did not. Number Seven of the amendments listed in the "Reasons of Dissent" provided:

> That the people have a right to bear arms for the defense of themselves and their own state, or the United States, or for the purpose of killing game; and no law shall be passed for disarming the people or any of them, unless for crimes committed, or real danger of public injury from individuals; and as standing armies in the time of peace are dangerous to liberty, they ought not to be kept up; and that the military shall be kept under strict subordination to and be governed by the civil powers.[32]

Number Eight, an entirely separate provision, asserted that:

> The inhabitants of the several states shall have liberty to fowl and hunt in sea-
> sonable times, on the lands they hold, and on all other lands in the United States
> not enclosed, and in like manner to fish in all navigable waters, and others not
> private property, without being restrained therein by the laws to be passed by
> the legislature of the United States.[33]

Number Eleven of the dissent was the only one that contained two separate
paragraphs. At first glance the paragraphs seem entirely separate and oddly
juxtaposed. Careful examination suggests a connection. The first paragraph
declared:

> That the power of organizing, arming, and disciplining the militia (the manner
> of disciplining the militia to be prescribed by Congress) remain with the indi-
> vidual states, and that Congress shall not have authority to call or march any of
> the militia out of their own state, without the consent of such state, and for such
> length of time only as such state shall agree.[34]

The second paragraph of Number Eleven asserted:

> That the sovereignty, freedom, and independency of the several states shall be
> retained, and every power, jurisdiction, and right which is not by this constitu-
> tion expressly delegated to the United States in Congress assembled.[35]

This second paragraph, when tied to the previous one, underscores the connection many anti-Federalists saw between state sovereignty and the control of
the state militia.

These proposed amendments to the Constitution relate to at least six separate issues: the right of self-protection through the ownership of weapons; the
right to serve in the militia; the right to hunt and fish; the prevention of a standing army; the power of Congress over the states; and the power of the states to
control their own armies or militias.

If Congress in 1789 had accepted these proposals of the Pennsylvania minority then one might persuasively argue that the Constitution, as amended,
guaranteed a personal and individual right of Americans to own weapons "for
the defense of themselves and their own state, or the United States, or for the
purpose of killing game." Both the self-defense interests and the "American
sportsman" interests of gun owners would then have been explicitly protected
by the Bill of Rights. We might today argue about what sorts of weapons were
protected. It is not clear that such provisions would protect the private ownership of Saturday night specials, assault rifles (however Congress might define
them), submachine guns, sawed-off shotguns, bazookas, or flamethrowers.
Whatever fell in or out of the protected arena, however, the constitutional principle of private ownership of weapons would have been clear.

Had Congress added these provisions to the Bill of Rights we would live in a very different country than we do today, assuming, of course, that we still had a country. It is entirely possible that the provisions limiting both a standing army and the power of the national government to call up the militia would have long ago led to a destruction of the nation from either outside forces or internal disruptions.

If we contemplate the implications of the Pennsylvania proposals—especially in light of subsequent developments in American history—we immediately see why Congress completely rejected the Pennsylvanians' demands for state control of the militia and for personal ownership of guns.

Such provisions might have prevented the Washington administration from effectively suppressing the Whiskey Rebellion or the Madison administration from calling out troops to face down the British in 1812. Without the ability to call up the militia President Andrew Jackson might not have successfully stood up to the nullificationists in South Carolina. In responding to the Nullification Proclamation in 1832, President Jackson reminded the citizens of South Carolina that "Disunion by armed force is *treason*,"[36] and made it clear that this behavior would be met by military force equal to the task of crushing the rebellion.[37] This would not have been possible if the states had had full control of the militias, or if the national government had been precluded from disarming rebellious citizens. Similarly, had the Pennsylvania anti-Federalists had their way, it is unlikely that the Pierce administration could have successfully utilized the Massachusetts militia to help return the fugitive slave Anthony Burns from Boston in 1854.[38]

Then, of course, there is the war of 1861–65—called variously the Civil War, the War Between the States, and the War for Southern Independence, but rarely anymore by its only official name, the War of the Rebellion. Had the restrictive provisions of the Pennsylvania minority been in place, President Lincoln might have been unable to call out the state militias to suppress the rebellion.

Madison and his colleagues could not have predicted the Whiskey Rebellion, the Nullification crisis, or the Civil War. But they were shrewd enough to know that the lack of national military power—and with it the power to disarm those who are in rebellion or might be in rebellion—would undermine any national state. Having just created a stronger national state in the wake of Shays's Rebellion and similar rebellions in other states,[39] the Federalists in Congress, many of whom had been at the Philadelphia Convention, the state ratifying conventions, or both, took no steps to undermine the ability of the national government to protect itself from enemies without or rebels and traitors within.

If the Second Amendment had responded to the demands of the Pennsylvania minority, and similar demands from other anti-Federalists, the national government would have been severely, perhaps fatally, weakened from the beginning. Congress would have been unable to regulate the use, ownership, or display of firearms in those places where it has plenary jurisdiction, such as the District of Columbia, the federal territories, or overseas possessions, including such present-day lands as Puerto Rico and the Virgin Islands.

At the time of the drafting of the Constitution "every state had gun control legislation on its books." [40] But an amendment along the lines of the Pennsylvania anti-Federalists would have prevented such a law in the federal district. It also might have prevented preemptive strikes against pirates, illegal slave traders (after 1808), filibusters preparing for the illegal invasion of Latin American countries,[41] or others gathering weapons for illegal purposes.

As previously discussed, one of the primary reasons for calling the Constitutional Convention was the fear that without a stronger central government the new nation would be unstable, militarily weak, and might not survive. In 1786 disgruntled farmers in western Massachusetts had shut down courts and threatened a full-scale civil war in the Bay State. Some militia units had joined the rebels before Shays and his followers were finally dispersed by militiamen from eastern Massachusetts. Shays's Rebellion had deeply frightened the elected political leaders who governed the nation after the Revolution. As Edmund Randolph had noted when he introduced the Virginia Plan at the Philadelphia convention, the "rebellion [that] had appeared as in Massts" underscored the need for a stronger government.[42]

The Federalists at the Philadelphia Convention wanted a government that would have the prestige, organizational apparatus, tax revenue, and, if necessary, the military power to suppress such rebellions in the future. Indeed, Shays's Rebellion helped convince many of the need for a new Constitution with a strong national military.

The kind of amendments the Pennsylvania minority wanted would have undermined these powers and the new government itself. Such amendments would have crippled the national government's ability to suppress insurrections, regulate trade with the Indians,[43] fight piracy, even prevent crime in the federal district (now Washington, D.C.), in the federal territories, and wherever else there was federal jurisdiction. Thus, in drafting the Bill of Rights James Madison and his congressional colleagues emphatically rejected the sweeping provisions of the Pennsylvania minority and other anti-Federalists relating to the military, the militia, and firearms, as well other structural changes and limitations on the national government, and instead adopted a much more limited amendment—directed at only one issue: the preservation of the organized state militias as a military force.

The congressmen of 1789 were not interested in protecting the rights to "killing game," "to fowl and hunt in seasonable times," "to fish in all navigable waters," or even to guarantee that people should be able to "bear arms for the defense of themselves." Congress was certainly on notice that demands for explicit protections of such rights were on the table and could easily have put such language into the Bill of Rights. Madison and the rest of the Congress were well aware of the "Reasons of Dissent," which was printed in numerous Pennsylvania papers, including the important *Pennsylvania Packet,* and also published as a broadside. That Madison and the Congress did not propose amendments along the lines demanded by the Pennsylvania minority leads to a prima facie conclusion that they did not intend to incorporate such protections into the Bill of Rights.

IV
THE BILL OF RIGHTS: PRESERVING THE CONSTITUTION

Why is it that Madison and his colleagues rejected the demands of the Pennsylvania anti-Federalists on the issues of guns, the militia, and the national military? The Second Amendment, like the others among the Bill of Rights, was designed to preserve the Constitution as written in 1787 by adding to it rights that did not fundamentally alter the nature of the national government or significantly limit its powers.

In examining what became the Second Amendment it is also critical to remember that Madison, who proposed the amendments, had in fact little enthusiasm for them. His paternity as the father of the Bill of Rights was truly reluctant. When Madison introduced the amendments to the House of Representatives, he did not argue with passion or conviction for his proposal. He told the Congress that he had "never considered" a bill of rights "so essential to the federal constitution" that the lack of one should have been allowed to impede ratification. But with the Constitution ratified, Madison was willing to concede "that in a certain form and to a certain extent," a bill of rights "was neither improper nor altogether useless." While proposing amendments that were neither "improper" nor "useless" Madison was careful, as he noted in a private letter to Edmund Randolph, to make sure that "the structure & stamina of the Govt. are as little touched as possible." It is this goal of Madison—to protect the "structure & stamina" of the new government—that most illuminates the very limited nature of what became the Second Amendment.[44]

In general, Madison saw the Bill of Rights as clarifying the meaning of the Constitution and not fundamentally changing its nature. He had no problem expressly protecting freedom of religion, for example, because he did not think that the purpose of the Constitution was to allow Congress to regulate religion, even where Congress had plenary jurisdiction. Similarly, he had no desire to deny the right of a jury trial in federal prosecutions, so he had no problem explicitly protecting that right in the Sixth Amendment. In the same way, Madison did not think that the purpose of the Constitution was to allow the national government to dismantle or disarm the state militias. Since some people feared the Federalists might do this, Madison was willing to put a provision in the Bill of Rights explicitly stating that Congress would not disarm the state militias. At the same time, he had no interest in preventing Congress from regulating weapons in the places where Congress had clear legislative power. Thusly, Madison did not accept the sweeping proposed amendments of the Pennsylvania anti-Federalists on this issue. Madison had worked for a strong government—with its national army and power to federalize state militias—at the Philadelphia Convention. He had no interest in undermining this in the Bill of Rights either by prohibiting a standing army, removing the power of the national government to control the state militias, or by permitting individual citizens or groups of them to have unfettered access to weapons.

Indeed, given what was accomplished in 1787, it would have been out of character for the Congress, dominated as it was by supporters of the new Constitution, to cripple the new government's ability to control dangerous, musket-toting elements of the population like Daniel Shays. Similarly, it would have been out of character to take the citizens' army—the militia—and turn it over to the complete control of state governors, who might not be sympathetic to the policies of the national regime. Not surprisingly, in their Bill of Rights—including what became the Second Amendment—the Congress did not authorize these things.

V
The Bill of Rights: A Great Federalist Victory

It is a commonplace among some scholars to view the struggle for the Bill of Rights as a victory for the anti-Federalists, the original opponents of the Constitution. At first glance, this makes a certain sense. Many anti-Federalists argued that they feared a strong central government because the Constitution lacked a bill of rights. If the Constitution had a bill of rights, these anti-Federalists claimed, they could then support the system of government created in Philadelphia. Because the anti-Federalists asked for a bill of rights, some scholars incorrectly see the adoption of the Constitution's Bill of Rights as a successful counterattack of the anti-Federalists.

This argument is at best only half true. Certainly it is unlikely that the Federalists, who completely dominated the new government, would have proposed and passed a bill of rights if anti-Federalists had not called for one. But it is clear that the Bill of Rights adopted by Congress, and sent on to the states, contained only a tiny portion of what the anti-Federalists wanted. Moreover, these changes were in many ways the least important in the minds of those among the anti-Federalist leadership, such as Patrick Henry and Richard Henry Lee. Hard-core anti-Federalists considered the Bill of Rights to be a "tub to the whale,"[45] designed to distract the people from calling a second convention to substantially rewrite the Constitution.

One insight into the anti-Federalist disappointment over the amendments comes from a cursory glance at the order of the states that ratified them. Five of the first six states to ratify the Bill of Rights were Federalist strongholds.[46] Virginia, the state most often associated with the call for a bill of rights, was actually the last state to ratify the ten amendments that became the Bill of Rights.

The story of ratification of the Bill of Rights in Virginia illustrates just how much the anti-Federalist amendments were a defeat for their cause. Patrick Henry, the most powerful political figure in this anti-Federalist stronghold, disliked the proposed amendments. He had campaigned against the Constitution because he wanted to defeat it and start all over. He used the lack of a bill of rights as an argument against the Constitution, but when offered the Bill of Rights in 1789 he balked. Henry fully understood that a bill of rights would destroy the possibility of achieving his real goal, which was to destroy or completely undermine and remake the new Constitution. Henry and his cohorts correctly realized that if the lack of a bill of rights was no longer an issue, many of the softer anti-Federalists would be satisfied with the Constitution and accept the new government. Thus, in October 1789, Virginia's two U.S. senators, William Grayson and Richard Henry Lee, urged their state to defeat the Bill of Rights and hold out for more sweeping amendments. Following this plan for more than two years Patrick Henry prevented the Virginia legislature, which he dominated, from ratifying the new amendments. Henry was hoping that in these two years Americans would come to accept his view that the stronger national government was dangerous to the liberty of the people. But in Virginia the opposite happened. Two intervening elections sapped much of Henry's strength in the assembly, which finally ratified the Bill of Rights in December 1791.[47]

Ultimately the anti-Federalists were triple losers.[48] They failed to prevent ratification of the Constitution; they failed to make ratification conditional on the adoption of a whole series of amendments; and, in the end, they failed to gain acceptance of what they considered to be their most important amendments. The Virginia anti-Federalists, as discussed, proposed forty separate amendments to the Constitution, including twenty to the "Body of the Constitution." Congress ignored these twenty and a good number of the other twenty that would have made up a "Declaration or Bill of Rights."[49] New York's proposed amendments take up seven printed pages, with fifty-nine separate paragraphs and scores of proposed changes. New Hampshire modestly proposed only twelve changes, and Massachusetts a paltry eight. But had Congress accepted all, or most, of the proposals of just these four states, along with the demands of the minority of Pennsylvania, the amendments would have effectively rewritten the Constitution, creating an altogether different kind of government.

Again, we should not be surprised that this did not happen. Most Federalists wanted no changes in the Constitution. They believed a bill of rights was unnecessary because, as a government of limited and enumerated powers, they felt the new national government could not threaten fundamental rights and individual liberties. Nevertheless, Federalists in the First Congress were willing to accept amendments that enumerated basic civil liberties and procedural rights or explicitly reaffirmed limitations on the national government that the Federalists believed were already within the Constitution of 1787. These amendments were not designed to affect, nor did they affect, the structure of the Constitution or the new national government formed under it. In presenting them to Congress, Madison was unequivocally "unwilling to see a door opened for a re-consideration of the whole structure of the government, for a re-consideration of the principles and the substance of the powers given."[50] The Bill of Rights was emphatically not a Constitution,[51] nor was it designed to alter in any significant way the political relationships created by the Constitution. The Bill of Rights did not shift any political power from the national government to either the states or "the people." In Madison's mind it merely clarified the constitutional powers, rights, and responsibilities of the national government.

The hard-core anti-Federalists, of course, did not like Madison's proposed amendments precisely because they believed the amendments would undermine their cause, while leaving the structure of the Constitution intact. They wanted to "strike at the essence of the System," and either return to the government of the old Confederation, "or to a partition of the Union into several Confederacies."[52]

As the "loyal opposition" in the ratification process,[53] the anti-Federalists are responsible for putting the demand for a bill of rights on the national agenda. Moreover, their demands forced the Federalists to respond. The accomplishment of the anti-Federalists was to pressure the Federalists to add a bill of rights to the Constitution. In a sense, however, this "accomplishment" was their failure. The anti-Federalists, especially the hard-core opponents of the Constitution led by Patrick Henry, did not want to modify the Constitution with a bill of rights so that it would be more palatable to the people; they wanted to totally undermine the Constitution or replace it with something else. This they failed to achieve.

VI
FEDERAL POWER TO SUPPRESS VIOLENCE

In addition to creating national military powers, the Constitution contains a series of clauses that empowered Congress to suppress the activities of people who threatened the public order. Certainly the framers anticipated that most law enforcement would be at the local level, but they also knew that some would come at the national level.

Congress had the power to punish counterfeiting, to "punish Piracies and Felonies committed on the high Seas, and Offences against the Law of Nations," to "suppress Insurrections and repel Invasions," by employing the militias, and to suppress the African slave trade after January 1, 1808. Congress also had the power to "regulate Commerce with foreign Nations, and among the several States, and with the Indian tribes." In addition, the United States government was obligated to "protect" each state from "Invasion" and "domestic Violence."[54]

As previously noted, some of the impetus for the Constitution was the violence of Shays's Rebellion and the general fear of anarchy. This was clear during the convention, as Randolph's first speech suggests. Even before the delegates met in Philadelphia, those who would emerge as Federalists argued for a strong and vigorous government to defeat anarchy. In the months before the convention, Alexander Hamilton declared, "It might be said that too little power is as dangerous as too much, that it leads to anarchy, and from anarchy to despotism."[55] And just as the convention began to get down to business, General Henry Knox, who was not a delegate, wrote "we are verging fast to anarchy and that the present convention is the only means to avoid the most flagitious evils that ever afflicted three millions of freemen."[56]

Delegates at the Convention picked up on this theme, and tied it to the military. Charles Pinckney argued that a strong national government was necessary to create "a real military force." He noted that "The United States had been making an experiment without" a strong military "and we see the consequence in their rapid approaches toward anarchy." James Wilson believed that the nation needed to be strong to avoid "wars" and to make "treaties." Wilson argued that a weak government would be "liable to anarchy & tyranny."[57] Hugh Williamson feared that "the probable consequences of anarchy in the U.S." would be military force against the states, which in turn would lead to tyranny. Thus, the framers wrote a Constitution that made the state militias subordinate to the national government and guaranteed that the national government would have the power to enforce its law.

After the convention, Federalists hammered home this theme. Writing as "Publius," Alexander Hamilton argued that "A Firm Union will be the utmost moment to the peace and liberty of the States" and would prevent "domestic faction and insurrection." The alternative was a society "kept in a state of perpetual vibration, between the extremes of tyranny and anarchy." Only the Constitution could prevent the recurring "tempestuous waves of sedition and party-rage."[58] With the Constitution ratified, George Washington could only hope the new system would work as planned:

> The business of this convention is as yet too much in embryo to form any opinion of the conclusion. Much is expected from it by some; not much by others; and nothing by a few. That something is necessary, none will deny; for the situation of the general government, if it can be called a government, is shaken to its foundation, and liable to be overturned by every blast. In a word, it is at an end; and, unless a remedy is soon applied, anarchy and confusion will inevitably ensue.[59]

Madison was not as hopeful as the great man from Mount Vernon. In private correspondence he argued that the government created by the Constitution was still too weak. Shortly before the convention ended he wrote in secret code to Jefferson, who was still in France, that the plan of government "will neither effectually answer its national object nor prevent the local mischiefs which every where excite disgusts against the state governments." In late October he still bemoaned that the convention had not adopted his proposal to give Congress a "constitutional negative on the laws of the States."[60]

Clearly, supporters of the Constitution, who thoroughly dominated Congress in 1789 when the Bill of Rights was written, had no intention of undoing their handiwork with a series of debilitating amendments that would weaken the national government. They emphatically rejected attempts to undermine the power of the government to control weapons of war and to suppress a revolution. For example, they rejected New Hampshire's suggestion for an amendment to prohibit the creation of a standing army "in time of Peace unless with consent of three fourths of the Members of each branch of Congress." The New York anti-Federalists would have banned standing armies altogether. But the First Congress would have none of this. It was not about to compel the nation to wait until the rebellion had actually started before it could organize an army and step in to disarm another Daniel Shays.[61]

Not surprisingly, then, when Madison reluctantly and unenthusiastically proposed his amendments, he wanted to be certain that "the structure & stamina of the Govt. are as little touched as possible." He also "limited" his proposed amendments "to points which are important in the eyes of many and can be objectionable in those of none." Thus, Madison tried to avoid controversial political issues affecting the structure of the government and concentrated on alterations that would preserve individual liberty. He thought that "nothing of a controvertible nature ought to he hazarded" because that might defeat the amendments and lead to renewed support for a second convention. He told Edmund Randolph that he had avoided anything of a "controversial nature" because of the "caprice & discord of opinions" in the House and Senate, which had to approve the amendments by a two-thirds vote, and in the state legislatures, three-fourths of which had to approve the amendments. The amendments had a "twofold object of removing the fears of the discontented and of avoiding all such alterations as would either displease the adverse side, or endanger the success of the measure." [62]

Finally, we must remember that those who created the United States understood the nature of a revolution; they had participated in one. In their Declaration of Independence they certainly asserted the right to "alter or abolish" any government. [63] But with a democratic republic created by the Constitution the need for a violent revolution disappeared. Every two years there would be an opportunity to participate in an orderly process to replace the existing government. Some of the very early state constitutions, written during the Revolution itself, not surprisingly endorsed the right of revolution. But the framers of 1787 did not endorse such a right. The Constitution does not have a "suicide" clause in it, and no one intended that it should have such a clause. Indeed, as John Marshall said, even before the convention finished its deliberations: "Nothing but the adoption of some efficient plan from the Convention can prevent Anarchy first, & civil Convulsions afterwards." [64] After the convention, Oliver Ellsworth, who would precede Marshall as chief justice, summed up this position: "Anarchy, or a want of such government as can protect the interests of the subjects against foreign and domestic injustice, is the worst of all conditions." [65] The goal was to prevent anarchy, violence, and rebellions. This was done by controlling the militias and the army, and retaining the right to limit weapons to those who formed "a well regulated militia."

President Jackson made this point clear during the Nullification Crisis, when warning South Carolina to step back from the brink of secession and constitutional disaster. Responding to the Palmetto State's claim to a Revolutionary-era heritage, Jackson reminded the nullifiers that they were "free members of a flourishing and happy Union. There is no settled design to oppress you." [66] Jackson's point, which Lincoln would reiterate to the South in 1861, was that the Constitution contemplated numerous ways for unhappy citizens, or even states, to protest federal legislation, but that this did not include nullification, secession, or any other sort of rebellion.

The Constitution provided for a standing army and for the national government to arm and provide rules and regulations for state militias, which could be federalized when necessary. The Second Amendment allows these state militias, which were "well regulated" by statutes passed by Congress, but the amendment was clearly not designed to ensure some sort of permanent revolutionary potential. Indeed, allowing for armed, unregulated citizens, who could threatem the public order and the national state, was unnecessary, unwise, and utterly in conflict with the "more perfect Union" the framers had created in Philadelphia. The "father of the Constitution," as Madison is often called, did not draft the Bill of Rights in order to undo his hard work at Philadelphia.

VII
ANTI-FEDERALIST FEARS OF FEDERAL MILITARY POWER

Anti-Federalists, of course, thought the Constitution created a government that was *too* strong. Hostile to a strong central government, they feared the concentration of power, including military power, in the hands of the president and the Congress. Among their many fears, they worried that the military clauses in the Constitution might threaten the states in one of two quite contradictory ways.

Some anti-Federalists feared that the ability of the new government to nationalize the state militias was the first step toward a military dictatorship. As early as 1783 George Washington had argued for stronger national control over the militias. In his "Sentiments on a Peace Establishment," Washington argued for drawing from the state militias a select group of men, either as volunteers or draftees, who would serve in a national army.[67] As many scholars have noted, and as his own letters show, Washington had little use for the militias, and would probably have happily seen them wither away while a trained professional army maintained the defense of the nation. Henry Knox, the secretary of war under the Articles of Confederation, proposed a less drastic form of nationalized training for the state militias, and their removal from the states, when necessary, for no more than a year at a time. However, such reforms went nowhere on the national level. Virginia tried to institute Washington's modest proposal that militia officers be chosen on the basis of ability, rather than social class and connections, but that reform fell flat on its face.[68]

The Constitution offered a remedy for these proposals, by allowing for the nationalization of militia training and rules, and by allowing the federalization of the militias under the president's control when necessary "to execute the Laws of the Union, suppress Insurrections, and repel Invasions."[69] But such powers truly frightened the anti-Federalists.

"Philadelphians" feared that the "president general" would be able to "order . . . the militia to exercise, and to march when and where he pleased." In Maryland an anti-Federalist, writing as "A Farmer and Planter," worried that with such a provision the national government would levy oppressive taxes and, when the people refused to pay them, "your great Lords and Masters . . . [can] send the militia of Pennsylvania, Boston, or any other state or place, to cut your throats, ravage and destroy your plantations, drive away your cattle and horses, abuse your wife, kill your infants, ravish your daughters, and live in free quarters, until you get into a good humor, and pay all that they may think proper to ask of you, and you become good and faithful servants and slaves."[70] The new government would, in effect, be able to federalize the militia of one state and use it against another. The national government might also be able to use a local militia, under federal officers, to attack their neighbors. This, the opponents of the Constitution feared, would be the first step to tyranny.

The next step would be to actually take over the state militias, ordering them here and there, and suppressing liberty. Mercy Otis Warren, writing as "A Columbian Patriot," echoed this fear, complaining that under the Constitution "the militia of the country, the bulwark of defense, and the security of national liberty is no longer under the control of civil authority" but instead would be under the control of the president and the Senate. Warren, carried away by her own rhetoric, referred to the president and Senate as the "Monarch" and the "aristocracy."[71]

While some anti-Federalists feared the federalization of the militia, others feared that the national government would simply destroy the militia. John De-Witt, writing in Massachusetts, complained that the organizers of the new government "do not mean to depend upon the citizens of the States alone to enforce their powers." DeWitt argued that the only protection of a free state against tyranny was "a well regulated militia, composed of the yeomanry of the country," which had always "been considered as the bulwark of a free people." He worried that the national government would "neglect to arm, organize and discipline the men" in the state militias, thus making them weak and ineffective. Then a standing army could easily defeat the state militias and take over the nation. Similarly "Brutus," writing in New York, predicted that men would be "impressed from the militia" and forced into the national army.[72]

Other anti-Federalists tied the taxing power to the creation of a national army. "Brutus" devoted an entire essay to the combined power of the United States "to borrow money . . . and to raise and support armies."[73] Indeed, a common theme among many anti-Federalists was the fear of national taxes that would be collected by military force. One way of avoiding this was to cripple the military and thus prevent the national government from having the force to suppress tax rebellions. The anti-Federalists could not figure out whether this force would be the federalized militia that "A Farmer and a Planter" feared, or a standing army that could easily defeat a demoralized and untrained state militia, as DeWitt feared. But, either way, the strong national government, with its strong military, was the enemy. The plans of Washington outlined in his "Sentiments on a Peace Establishment," or the less drastic suggestions of Secretary of War Knox, only confirmed the dangers imposed by the military clauses of the new constitution. By 1787–88 both men had become ardent Federalists, and everyone assumed that if the Constitution were ratified Washington would be elected president. The anti-Federalists had strong reasons to fear that the new government might indeed destroy the state militias.

Thus, the opponents of the Constitution proposed amendments to limit the national government, including many changes in the military structure. As we know, these proposals failed to gain any substantial support in Congress.

VIII
THE DEBATE IN CONGRESS AND THE LANGUAGE
OF THE AMENDMENT

There is frustratingly little of the congressional debates over the Bill of Rights available to modern scholars. The Senate kept no records of its debates for this period, only records of bills, motions, and votes. The House spent little time on what became the second constitutional amendment. The debate began with Madison's first draft of the proposed amendment, which read as follows:

> A well regulated militia, composed of the body of the people, being the best security of a free state, the right of the people to keep and bear arms shall not be infringed; but no person religiously scrupulous shall be compelled to bear arms.[74]

The draft language suggests that the framers saw this essentially as an amendment about the militia; any right to own weapons was a collective right, derived from the right of each state to maintain a "well regulated militia." Thus, the amendment spoke of "the body of the people." In drafting the amendment, Madison was careful to let the anti-Federalists know that the militias were secure, but he also in warned the states not to persecute people on account of their religious beliefs.

Congressional debate over the amendment centered almost entirely on the last clause, providing an exemption from militia service for the "religiously scrupulous." In the end Congress scrapped this clause.

Most of the House debate came from two anti-Federalists, Elbridge Gerry and Aedanus Burke. Burke wanted amendments, but not Madison's, which he asserted in this debate were "frothy and full of wind, formed only to please the palate; or they are like a tub thrown out to a whale, to secure the freight of the ship and its peaceable voyage." In addition to their concern over conscientious objectors, the anti-Federalists in the debate made the usual, almost pro forma, attack on a standing army.[75] Burke, for example, made a futile attempt to require a two-thirds vote in Congress to create a peacetime standing army. In general the anti-Federalists showed their deep fear of the national government. The Federalists, with the votes to back them up, said little more than necessary.

The debaters never sought to clarify the meaning of the words "to keep and bear arms shall not be infringed." But the overwhelming tenor of the debate is that the congressmen saw this as a discussion about the militia. The last clause, providing an exemption for pacifists, fits with this understanding. Nowhere in the debate is there the slightest hint about a private or individual right to own a weapon. This should not surprise us, for, as one of the leading military historians of the period notes, "In all the discussion and debates" over the Second Amendment, "from the Revolution to the eve of the Civil War, there is precious little evidence that advocates of local control of the militia, showed an equal or even a secondary concern for gun ownership as a personal right."[76] The records of the state courts and legislatures for this period reflect this conclusion, as numerous courts accepted the notion that to "bear arms" was a term connected solely to the militia and the military. As the Tennessee Supreme Court noted in 1840, reflecting years of experience in the American colonies and states, "The object, then, for which the right of keeping and bearing arms is secured is the defense of the public." The term "bear arms" had a "reference to their military use." "A man in the pursuit of deer, elk, and buffaloes might carry his rifle every day for forty years, and yet it would never be said of him that he had borne arms; much less could it be said that a private citizen bears arms because he has a dirk or pistol concealed under his clothes, or a spear in a cane."[77]

Despite the failure of the House to explore the meaning of "bear arms," this first draft does give us an important insight into the meaning of the term. Some modern commentators try to separate it from the first clause of the Second Amendment—"A well regulated Militia, being necessary to the security of a free State"—and argue for an independent federal right to carry (bear) guns. But the text of the initial draft shows that this is not what the term "bear arms" meant at the time. Rather, the term can have meaning only if it is connected to "militia" service. Otherwise, the last clause of the proposed amendment—"but no person religiously scrupulous shall be compelled to bear arms"—would have had no meaning at all. Since no states at the time required people to carry weapons for personal use, it would have been absurd to declare that "religiously scrupulous" people could not be "compelled to bear arms," if "bear arms" meant only carrying weapons. No state at the time, nor any state before, had ever compelled people to carry weapons in their private capacity. Rather, state governments had compelled people to carry weapons—to bear arms— only as part of their militia duty. Thus, the term "bear arms" in the final amendment, if understood as it was presumed to be at the time of the drafting, could *only* have been seen in the context of military service.[78]

Another insight to this comes from the New Hampshire Convention. In order to placate the anti-Federalist minority, the Federalists in the New Hampshire convention endorsed twelve proposed amendments. Two of these amendments dealt with military issues. The Tenth provided "That no standing Army shall be Kept up in time of Peace unless with the consent of three fourths of the Members of each branch of Congress; nor shall Soldiers in Time of Peace be Quartered upon private Houses without the consent of the Owners." [79] The Congress ignored the first clause, which would have led to a significant diminution of national power. On the other hand, they endorsed the second clause, and incorporated it into what became the Third Amendment.

The other military amendment proposed by New Hampshire is more interesting. The Twelfth, and last, on the New Hampshire list declared: "Congress shall never disarm any Citizen unless such as are or have been in Actual Rebellion." [80] There are two ways we might interpret "disarm," which of course is the opposite of "keep and bear arms." If we took this to be an individual right, it would mean that Congress would have been unable to pass a federal law to disarm convicted felons, or indeed people in the process of committing a crime. The Constitution gave Congress full legislative power over the national capital, the territories, and other property owned by the United States. Now, it would seem preposterous to believe that the New Hampshire Federalists, who, as "cautious supporters of the Constitution," [81] had just voted to ratify the Constitution, wanted to strip Congress of all power to prevent crime in its jurisdiction, and all power to remove guns from criminals, pirates, or others threatening the public order, unless they were in rebellion. But if we see the language of "disarm any Citizen" as part of the notion of "bearing arms" for the militia, then the clause is suddenly reasonable and sensible. The New Hampshire Federalists are saying, in effect, that Congress cannot disarm the militias—the civilian-based armies of the states—unless they "are or have been in Actual Rebellion." On another linguistic level this is the only interpretation that makes any sense. Surely New Hampshire could not imagine a single citizen, or even a handful of malcontents, being "in Actual Rebellion." But the citizens in the militia could be. Indeed, during Shays's Rebellion, "[s]ome militia units in the insurgent counties supported the rebels." Similarly, in New Hampshire "[a] less publicized confrontation had occurred" in which "angry debtors led by militia officers surrounded the building in Exeter where the legislature was in session." A day later militia units from eastern New Hampshire "dispersed the insurgents." [82]

Thus the people in New Hampshire understood, from their own recent history, that the militia could turn on the government and might have to be disarmed. Yet surely they did not fear any government that could take weapons out of the hands of criminals, pirates, and the like. Thus, the only plausible understanding of New Hampshire's use of the term "disarm" is in the context of the militia.

In this context, to "keep and bear arms" is a right that is intrinsically collective: it is the right of the community to "keep and bear arms" for the purposes of maintaining a "well regulated" militia. The final insight to the meaning of the language of the amendment comes from its structure. No other amendment explains its purpose. The First Amendment, for example, prohibits Congress from "abridging the freedom of speech," but does not contain an explanation, such as "in order to secure open political debate." Nor in the free exercise clause did Congress feel the need to say something like, "in order to prevent religious intolerance, Congress shall make no law . . . prohibiting the free exercise thereof." But the Second Amendmemt is different. There were calls, such as those from the Pennsylvania minority, for protection of a personal right to own weapons, for hunting and other nonmilitary reasons. Congress clearly rejected this concept, limiting the right "to bear arms"—traditionally a phrase tied to military service—to collective service in the "well regualated militia."

IX
TO BEAR ARMS: A COLLECTIVE OR INDIVIDUAL RIGHT?

Sanford Levinson, in a provocative article, dismisses the collective rights interpretation of the language in the Second Amendment with the clever argument that the term "people" must refer to individuals because that is how the term is used in the Fourth Amendment.[83] This analysis, in the end, may not be terribly persuasive. He notes that the Fourth Amendment uses the term "people" but that "[i]t is difficult to know how one might plausibly read the Fourth Amendment as other than a protection of individual rights."[84] This surely makes sense. But does it prove that the term "people" in the Second Amendment must also refer to individual rights? We certainly understand that words in the Constitution can have multiple meanings.

Consider, for example, the term "people" in the First Amendment—"Congress shall make no law . . . prohibiting . . . the right of the people peaceably to assemble." If it is hard to construe the word "people" in the Fourth Amendment to be anything but a reference to individuals, it is equally difficult to construe the term in the First Amendment as anything but a collective right. Clearly, the idea of the people assembling contemplates a large number of people and not a single person assembling.

Linguistically, then, the term "people" in the Second Amendment might be understood either way. Standing alone, the phrase "the right of the people to keep and bear arms" could apply to individuals or, collectively, to "the people." But unlike the use of the word in the Fourth Amendment, the Second Amendment ties the term "people" to a collective entity, the "well regulated Militia," which is "necessary to the security of a free State." This understanding is also supported by the original wording of the amendment, which referred to the "body" of the people. Linguistically the amendment can easily be read to be about the "body" of the people. The amendment does not say, "individually armed citizens, being necessary to the security of a free state." The Amendment explicitly refers to the "militia"—a collective organization—and a specific kind of militia at that, one that is "well regulated." It is hard to imagine individuals being "well regulated" by the government. They are only "regulated" as a group.

Levinson also poses the clever query: "One might ask why the Framers did not simply say something like 'Congress shall have no power to prohibit state-organized and directed militias.' " [85] We might just as cleverly turn Levinson's question around. One might ask, if they had intended to protect the individual right to own weapons, why didn't the framers simply say something like, "Congress shall have no power to prohibit the private ownership of guns." Indeed, that was what the anti-Federalists in much of the country had asked for in their proposed amendments and truly *wanted* Congress to say. The fact that Madison refused to adopt such language—and that Congress did not amend the proposal to add such language—suggests that the Federalists who were in control of the Congress in 1789 did not intend to create an individual right. Indeed, they added the explanatory clause at the beginning of the amendment— "A well regulated Militia being necessary to the security of a free State"—to make certain that no one would misunderstand their intent.

The internal language of the clause also makes Levinson's reading, and that of other individual rights proponents, seem absurd. If the right to keep and bear arms "shall not be infringed," then the national government presumably has no power, in any of its many jurisdictions, to disarm anyone. A comparison with the Pennsylvania state constitution of 1776 illustrates this. That constitution says "That the people have a right to bear arms for the defense of themselves and the state; and as standing armies in the time of peace are dangerous to liberty, they should not be kept up. And that the military should be kept under strict subordination to, and governed by, the civil power." [86]

Under the Pennsylvania state constitution, the right to bear arms "for defense of themselves" can be seen as an individual right, but it is strictly limited to self-defense. [87] It does not give one the right to use arms to commit crimes, to intimidate others, [88] to hunt, [89] or even for recreational target practice. Presumably, as with most other "rights," the legislature could impose reasonable limitations on what constitutes a weapon of "defense."

Unlike the Pennsylvania constitution, the language of the Second Amendment is absolute: "shall not be infringed." If read as an individual right, criminals, convicted felons, pirates, or revolutionaries could all stand armed in the District of Columbia or in the federal territories. Pirates could load up their ships on the Potomac River and sail out to sea. Hunters could trample through Yellowstone or any other national park, guns in hand. Anyone might board a plane, gun in hand, or carry a weapon into Congress, the White House, or any other federal building. After all, what better place to exercise your Second Amendment rights than in front of your representatives or even in the courts of justice. Absurd as this would be, such people could not be "disarmed," at least until they began to commit a crime, if the Second Amendment creates an individual right to bear arms. Taken to its logical extreme, we might argue that, just as a federal felon, serving time, has some First Amendment rights to press, petition, and religion, or Eighth Amendment rights not to be subjected to cruel punishment, so too, a prisoner might claim some Second Amendment right. The Fifth Amendment allows the taking of liberty under some circumstances, while the Second, if read as an individual right, does not.

As we have seen, however, Madison and the great Federalist majority in the First Congress rejected any amendments that undermined the power of the national government. Is it conceivable that they failed to follow this philosophy with the Second Amendment? That they meant to implement the demands of the Pennsylvania anti-Federalists and, in effect, eviscerate the power of the national government? Such an argument goes against the entire history of the period.

Hence, the Second Amendment prevents Congress from abolishing the organized or "well regulated" state militias. Today such an argument may seem almost silly. Why, modern Americans might ask, would Madison bother to promise not to abolish the state militias, and why would the anti-Federalists think this was some sort of victory, or even a "tub" thrown at them?

Madison and his colleagues provided for an amendment dealing with the militia because most of the states that proposed amendments wanted some guarantee that Congress would not destroy their militias. The states understood that the power to regulate might imply the power to destroy. John DeWitt, Luther Martin, and other anti-Federalists certainly feared that the national government would indeed abolish the state militias. Washington's 1783 "Sentiments on a Peace Establishment" did not call for the outright abolition of the militias, but it did call for them to take a clearly secondary role in the defense of the nation. Moreover, Washington proposed skimming the best militiamen for national service and leaving to the state militias only those "who from domestic Circumstances, bodily defects, natural awkwardness or disinclination, can never acquire the habits of Soldiers."[90]

None of the Federalist framers saw it that way; they had no desire to destroy the state militias, just as they had no desire to impose a national church on the people, institute cruel and unusual punishments, or deny people the right against self-incrimination. A militia-protecting amendment was completely within the scope of Madison's desire to add amendments that would not affect "the structure & stamina of the Govt." He "limited" his proposed amendments "to points which are important in the eyes of many and can be objectionable in those of none."[91] A guarantee that the states could maintain well-regulated militias—militias that remained subject to congressional control and federal deployment—did not conflict with this goal.

Significantly, Madison also limited his "tub" to the anti-Federalists by having the national government promise not to dismantle the organized, "well regulated" state militias. This phrase, "well regulated" further shows that the amendment does not apply to just anyone. It does not apply to the "unorganized" militia, because that militia is certainly not "well regulated." Nor can it apply to individual citizens who might choose to keep and bear arms "for the defense of themselves." The Pennsylvania dissenters had wanted this, but they did not get it. A new mob, led by another Daniel Shays, could be disarmed by the national government. Nor does it apply to the hunter and sportsman. The majority in the First Congress intended to reassure the anti-Federalists that the national government would not disarm those who are trained by the state militia and in that body—the "well regulated militia."

Supporters of an individual rights interpretation of the amendment place great emphasis on the term "keep and bear arms." However, this is clearly a term of art, applied to militias in England and America, just as criminal cases at the time used the term of art "with force and arms." Beyond that, Madison wanted to reassure the states that their militias would be armed at all times. Without such a clause, Congress might allow the militias to continue, but nevertheless disarm them, thus making them impotent. This is what Great Britain had sought in 1775. The British government did not ban the colonial militias—after all, they were necessary in case of an invasion, Indian war, or rebellion. But if the militias were disarmed, as the lobster backs tried to do at Concord, they would be unable to resist British policy but could, nevertheless, be called out, and armed, to protect the empire. The battle on Lexington Green was fought to prevent the *disarming* of the local militias, not over their elimination.

The phrase "keep and bear arms" may also reflect the contemporary disputes over who would provide arms for the state militias. As noted above, at the convention, Federalists like Rufus King argued that Congress had the power to prescribe the kind of weapons the militia might use and even to buy the weapons for the militia. As Michael Bellesiles has shown, the militias at this time were often poorly armed, most white American men did not own arms, and there was great resistance among the people to having to arm themselves. Bellesiles has exposed and undermined the myth that most Americans owned a firearm. Another indication of the lack of arms in private hands was a law adopted by Virginia, as the Revolution was winding down, to require that those mustered out of service return their weapons to the state.[92]

During the ratification debates, the proponents of the Constitution reiterated the point that Congress would become the supplier of weapons for the states. Noah Webster, for example, pointed out that Congress had the "power to provide for the organizing, arming, and disciplining the militia," although he also noted that Congress could call out the militia only under certain well-defined circumstances.[93] Presumably, the power to "arm" the militia may also have included the power *not* to "arm" the militia. Thus, the Second Amendment guaranteed that the militias would be armed to head off the exaggerated fears of some anti-Federalists, who believed the Constitution was the prelude to a military takeover by a standing army led by the Senate and the president. Not only did the Congress lack the power to disarm the "well regulated" state militias, but if Congress failed to provide arms for them, presumably the states could appropriate money for their own arms or even order militia members to provide their own weapons.

X
MODERN POLICY AND THE SECOND AMENDMENT

Neither in 1787 nor in 1789 did Madison and the Federalists have any interest in disarming the state militias, just as they had no interest in imposing a national religion on the American people or in denying accused criminals the right to a jury trial. Thus, when the anti-Federalists demanded explicit protections on these and other points, Madison was willing to comply. He was not interested, however, in changing the power relations created at the Philadelphia Convention, or in undermining the nation's ability to defend itself from enemies and criminals, foreign or domestic.

The Second Amendment protected the right of the states to maintain and arm their own militias, as long was they were "well regulated" and ultimately under federal control. The Amendment was not a suicide clause allowing revolutionaries to create private militias with which to otherthrow the national government or even to impede the faithful execution of the law; it prevented Congress from abolishing the organized, well-regulated militias of the states.

The Second Amendment does not protect the individual right to hunt deer, collect antique weapons, go to the firing range, or even own a licensed pistol. Proponents of the private ownership of hunting rifles, fishing rods, skinning knives, or pistols need not fear this analysis of the Second Amendment. Such a constitutional protection was not needed then, and it is not needed today.

Oliver Ellsworth, who would later be chief justice of the United States, found the whole notion of specific protections of liberties silly. He answered the complaint that *"There is no declaration of any kind to preserve the liberty of the press, etc."* by noting: "Nor is liberty of conscience, or of matrimony, or of burial of the dead; it is enough that Congress have no power to prohibit either, and can have no temptation. This objection is answered in that the states have all the power originally, and Congress have only what the states grant them."[94]

Could Congress ban hunting rifles? It would be politically impossible and constitutionally absurd, although it would be possible and reasonable to ban hunting, and hunting rifles, in national parks. May Congress regulate the ownership, sale, use, and interstate transportation of firearms? Surely it can, within the constitutional limits of general federal police and commerce powers, just as the states, or the national government (where it has regulatory or police power), can regulate burial, marriage, or child custody. But just as regulations of marriage or burial must be reasonable, so, too, would regulation of firearms.

6. Muting the Second Amendment: The Disappearance of the Constitutional Militia

H. RICHARD UVILLER* AND
WILLIAM G. MERKEL**

Many have been baffled by the language of the single sentence that is the Second Amendment. Just what should we make of the odd—indeed unique—preamble, the language that precedes (but otherwise seems to have no connection to) the ringing declaration of the right to keep and bear arms?[1] Some emphasize the textual primacy of the militia, and insist that the right to arms belongs exclusively to this constitutionally sanctioned military organization. To these readers, the use of the word "people" in the main clause only restates the prerogatives held collectively by the militia.[2] Others, just as vehemently, regard the preamble as nothing but introduction, of no more substantive significance than an indrawn breath before the delivery of the message.[3] And the message, like others in the First, Fourth, Fifth, and Sixth amendments, is unequivocal: now and forever, in military pursuits and all others, guns are an individual entitlement immune from government curtailment.[4]

Fair consideration of the ample historical record, however, discloses that to the framers, the ratifiers, and indeed to the polity of newly fledged Americans generally, the language of the provision could hardly have been a more felicitous expression of its scope, intent, and purpose.[5] There seems to us little doubt that the provision protected as an individual right (and in more democratically generous form)[6] the ancient custom of free, adult citizens to keep and to carry arms,[7] but only in the context and for the advancement of the organized, communal military units generally believed to be indispensable to the preservation of political liberty.[8] During the ratification debate, some radical anti-Federalists did call for a wider, purely private right to own weapons, but, at least outside of New Hampshire, theirs remained marginal voices.[9] On the other hand, innumerable contemporary utterances, cutting a wide swath across the political spectrum and spanning the full breadth of the nation, support our militia-linked reading.[10] For the moment, we choose but one such expression from the ratifying Virginia Convention. Virginia's recommended constitutional amendments, drafted principally by George Mason and appended to its vote of ratification, include language that is virtually identical to the Second Amendment, but more illuminating:

Seventeenth, That the people have the right to keep and bear arms; that a well regulated Militia composed of the body of the people trained to arms is the proper, natural and safe defence of a free State. That standing armies in time of peace are dangerous to liberty, and therefore ought to be avoided, as far as the circumstances and protection of the Community will admit; and that in all cases the military should be under strict subordination to and governed by the Civil power.[11]

Like the framers of the Second Amendment two years later, Virginians at the ratifying convention embedded the right to keep and bear arms in a web of related military principles. As Robert E. Shalhope writes, "More often than not [Americans of the Revolutionary generation] considered these rights inseparable."[12] "Bearing" implied making muster, equipped and ready for service; "keeping" entailed steady readiness to serve when called upon to perform one's duty.[13] For the founding generation and for near contemporaries, then, the right to bear arms, far more than others enshrined in the Bill of Rights, brooked, tolerated, invited, and even demanded regulation because of its communal and military context.[14]

As the Virginia Convention's conjunction makes plain, the right of arms was not therefore an *individual right* in the same sense as the rights expressed in the Fourth, Fifth, Sixth, and even the First amendments to the United States Constitution. These are rights the exercise of which protected *personal integrity,* often at the expense of common interests. They reflect distinctly post-classical ideals, rooted in the principles of the common law, but accorded a basis in larger political theory only by the individual rights philosophers of the eighteenth century who forged the first modern conceptions of liberal democracy. They owe as much to the Enlightenment as to the Renaissance.[15] In contrast, the *personal right* expressed in the neoclassical language of the Second Amendment was understood by principal draftsman James Madison to serve the interests of the commonweal by buttressing *community security* and reducing the sway of a dangerous, potentially usurpatory standing army.[16]

The extent that we are today bound by the understanding of our foreparents, how far the running sands erode or reshape the governing intent of ancient text is, of course, an endless and perhaps fruitless debate.[17] But we think the significance of dramatically altered context two centuries later is especially loud and clear in the case of the Second Amendment, because the framers stated explicitly their social and ideological premise in the same breath as the right they enunciated.[18]

From the Militia to the National Guard

The text of the Second Amendment and the historical context in which that text was articulated point decisively to the conclusion that, to the framers, the Second Amendment right to keep and bear arms depended on maintenance of a viable militia.* To understand the twenty-first-century meaning of this eighteenth-century guarantee, we turn to the history of the American militia during the two-plus centuries following ratification. Our objective is to ascertain whether the militia contemplated by the framers has changed so fundamentally as to alter the contemporary legal significance of the constitutional provision designed to protect that militia from undue federal encroachment. We should emphasize that we do not say the change—change in the meaning of referents of words or in the social context of their utterance—necessarily undermines meaning or saps an expressed precept of force or effect in the altered circumstances. We mean to say only that when the purpose of a constitutional right is expressed directly in the Constitution in terms of an institution, there may come a point in the evolution of that institution where the original edict can no longer be applied without fundamental rewriting and unacceptable divergence from the contemplated purpose.[19] Our mission here is to examine the institution of "the militia" to determine whether it has evolved so far that the eighteenth-century term can no longer be applied to the modern version without a fatal distortion of meaning. Crucial to our understanding of this evolution of the militia is a comparison of the context in which the militia functioned at the framing and that in which it operates now.

The Decay of the Old Militia, 1789–1840

FEDERALISM AND THE MILITIA: ATTEMPTS AT NATIONAL REVIVAL
UNDER FEDERALISTS AND JEFFERSONIANS

In the years 1789–91, the operational role of the militia reflected the military dualism of the founders, who envisioned both a smallish standing army and a serviceably effective militia, each held in check by the federal structure. Writing for a unanimous Court in *Perpich v. Department of Defense*,[20] Justice Stevens aptly summarized the ideological and pragmatic bipolarity at the heart of the nation's early constitutional and statutory military law:

> Two conflicting themes, developed at the Constitutional Convention and repeated in debates over military policy during the next century, led to a compro-

---

* See our detailed treatment in Uviller & Merkel, *The Second Amendment in Context: The Case of the Vanishing Predicate,* 76 Chi.-Kent L. Rev 403 passim (2000), from which this essay is excerpted and refined.

mise in the text of the Constitution and in later statutory enactments. On the one hand, there was a widespread fear that a national standing Army posed an intolerable threat to individual liberty and to the sovereignty of the separate States, while, on the other hand, there was a recognition of the danger of relying on inadequately trained soldiers as the primary means of providing for the common defense.[21]

The constitutional compromise described by Justice Stevens authorized a federal army under executive command but dependent on Congress for biannual appropriations, and simultaneously established federal authority to prescribe militia training and equipment and to call the militia into federal service for limited purposes.[22] Two years later, the Second Amendment reflected its framers' aspirations that the nation rely on militia for the national defense, and made clear that the federal government lacked the power to disarm the state militia.[23] In deference to the passion of the anti-Federalists, the Second Amendment, like other elements of the Bill of Rights, prohibited the federal government from exercising a power never expressed or delegated in the original seven articles of 1787.

The dualistic military theory embodied in the Constitution proved harder to implement than to expound. As Justice Stevens noted, "Congress was authorized both to raise and support a national Army and also to organize 'the Militia' . . . [but] [i]n the early years of the Republic, Congress did neither."[24] The failure to organize either citizen or regular soldiery resulted not from inattention or dereliction, but from unbridgeable differences of principle between the administration and Congress, and from culturally entrenched antimilitarism within the public at large.

The Washington administration inherited a regular establishment of 672 officers and men from the Confederation.[25] With such a small regular force available, the western frontier appeared highly vulnerable to native attack and to British incursion from forts along the Great Lakes, which remained in royal hands despite clear provisions of the Treaty of Paris demanding their prompt evacuation.[26] But even with strengthened federal powers in place under the new Constitution, the nation's Revolutionary-era republicanism lived on to speak loudly for reliance on the common militia. In a climate of pervasive suspicion toward all aspects of potential central military power, the Congress of 1789 confronted the dual tasks of providing for the standing army Washington desired (if on a much smaller scale than the chief executive thought wise) and, at the same time, organizing the nation's militia pursuant to the Militia Clauses of the Constitution and the historic expectations of the states.[27]

The first president and the First Congress were not writing military policy on a clean slate, however. Throughout the Confederation period, Washington had vainly pressed the old Congress to increase the size of the army.[28] The

Confederation Congress lacked the authority to impose the general's desires on the states, but it had resisted Washington's suggestions for reasons of ideology as well as impotence.[29] Given the scope of antifederal hostility to a potentially vigorous federal military establishment, Washington understood that the new Congress was not likely to legislate a substantially larger army, even if the legislature was now endowed with authority to do more than merely ask the states for troops as its predecessor had done. Beyond the new powers to establish and maintain an army directly, Congress now also had the novel authority to organize the state militia for national purposes. Here Washington hoped to encounter less congressional resistance, and he personally urged Congress to act to organize the militia in August 1789.[30]

Congress was preoccupied during its first session with establishing the revenue system and the basic administrative and judicial machinery.[31] When Congress did take up systematization of the militia at the opening of its second session in January 1790, members became embroiled in controversy over "selection" or "classification."[32] On behalf of the administration, Secretary of War Knox presented to Congress a bill to establish a select, classified national militia, grouping the eligible population by age and requiring substantial service and training from the youngest cadre.[33] The administration hoped to effect benefits equivalent to those of a sizable standing army without arousing antifederal suspicions, but Knox's proposal quickly spawned resistance focused on the very issues that had generated the standing army dispute during the ratification struggle and animated the debates over the future Second Amendment in the previous congressional session.

A select—as opposed to a common or general—militia had been a favorite notion of Washington, Knox, and Secretary of the Treasury Hamilton since they'd first addressed the permanent organization of the nation's military immediately after independence.[34] All three were dissatisfied with the performance of amateur soldiers during the war, and favored the creation of a substantial professional army, but they had come to realize that this goal was not politically attainable. They therefore embraced the select militia as the next best option. To create an effective militia, Washington and his cabinet urged, militia soldiers required more training and discipline than could possibly be instilled by the states mustering their entire adult male population for a single day or, at best, a few days each year. To bring a better-trained militia into existence, the administration favored classifying the nation's male population into three age-based groups subject to differing levels of service and preparation. Under the militia plan that Knox proposed to Congress,[35] young men aged eighteen to twenty were to form an "advanced corps" and train up to thirty days a year under regular army supervision. Men from twenty-one to forty-five would form the "main corps" and train four days a year; and men from forty-six to sixty would form a "reserved corps." [36]

Knox hoped to fashion a federal defense system capable of meeting all crises, "whether arising from internal or external causes." [37] This severe federal implement was needed, according to Knox, because "convulsive events, generated by the inordinate pursuit of riches or ambition, require[d] that the government should possess a strong corrective arm." [38] Knox could not have chosen more incendiary language. If classifying men according to age and selecting only the youngest group for training and active service made sense in military and economic terms, it also entailed formation of fighting bands less firmly rooted in their communities by family and property than the historic common militia.[39] While this scheme would have mitigated the economic disruption associated with sending heads of families and proprietors of farms on extended training assignments or campaigns, it also would have vested each state's military power in the group of citizens most susceptible to demagoguery and most likely to support a Caesarist conspiracy. Thus, classification may not have implied that the nation would rely on a regular military establishment, but it did imply that the militia would be less than optimally republican.

For more than two years Congress wrestled with the Knox bill and its successors,[40] but the Militia Act that finally passed into law on May 8, 1792,[41] embodied no meaningful resolution of the selection issue, lacked any mechanism for federal enforcement, and therefore relied on the states to implement a largely hortatory organizational scheme. The act also abandoned provisions for separation of the militia-of-the-whole into age groups, for federally standardized training, and for federally supervised exercises. Instead, Congress simply laid out the organizational form of the nation's militia, dividing the force into divisions and battalions that were in turn subdivided into regiments and companies to match the structure of the regular force, and left to the states the problem of compelling citizens to fill out these units. The act required that states carry their "able-bodied white male citizen[s]" between the ages of eighteen and forty-four on the rolls, and exempted various federal officials from duty. But Congress also implicitly left the states free to continue the practice of exempting various additional categories of citizens, such as teachers, clergymen, and conscientious objectors. Indeed, Congress also seemingly left open the question of states including additional categories of persons—principally, free black males—in their state militia rosters, even though no federal service requirement attached to them by virtue of the act. In addition, the act limited the president's power to call forth the militia so that no one man would be called to serve for more than a maximum of three months in any one year, and no single individual would be burdened any more "than in due rotation with every other able-bodied man of the same rank."[42]

More important for our purposes, the act provided that citizens from whom militia service was required furnish their own standard arms and equipment. The command that citizens appear for militia duty fully armed and equipped could scarcely have been more explicit. The act stated

> That every citizen so enrolled and notified, shall, within six months thereafter, provide himself[43] with a good musket or firelock, a sufficient bayonet and belt, two spare flints, and a knapsack, a pouch with a box therein to contain not less than twenty-four cartridges, suited to the bore of the musket or firelock, each cartridge to contain a proper quantity of powder and ball: or with a good rifle, knapsack, shot-pouch and powder-horn, twenty balls suited to the bore of his rifle, and a quarter of a pound of powder; and shall appear, so armed, accoutred and provided, when called out to exercise, or into service, except, that when called out on company days to exercise only, he may appear without a knapsack.[44]

Similar clauses set forth standards by which officers should arm themselves.[45]

Thus the Second Congress amplified the vision of the militia as the time-honored *"constitutional army"*[46] that had informed the First Congress's drafting of the Second Amendment less than three years before. The Second Amendment guaranteed the right to keep and bear arms in the militia; the Militia Act laid down a detailed description of the weapons militiamen must keep and bear when called to serve. These were pointedly and unequivocally military arms ("a sufficient bayonet and belt, . . . a pouch with a box therein to contain not less than twenty-four cartridges, . . . each cartridge to contain a proper quantity of powder and ball"). Within five years of the act's passage, muskets held under the act were to have "bores sufficient for balls of the eighteenth part of a pound." Thus, the militia members were expected to keep and bear arms necessary for meeting the security needs of the nation, arms falling within certain standards and regular limits defined by Congress, arms that did not necessarily correspond to each individual's sense of convenience or perceived need to defend himself and family independent of military obligation.[47] Moreover, under the terms of the Militia Act, enrolled citizens were not simply required to furnish themselves regulation weapons, they were required to "hold [the stipulated arms] exempted from all suits, distresses, executions or sales, for debt or for the payment of taxes." The militiaman's musket was not therefore an unfettered article of personal property that he might dispense with according to his sense of whim or interest. Rather, the privately held guns of the militia were tokens of social, civic responsibility, with a legal status defined in very large measure by the legislative organ of the central state.

The Militia Act of 1792 was preceptive in form. But in operation it remained little more than a catalogue of congressional exhortations to the states. While some of the states enacted early measures seeking to bring into effect the act's provisions, all states had abandoned any pretense of compliance long before the Civil War.[48] The act stayed on the books until 1903.[49] For 111 years it represented not simply the cornerstone but virtually the entire edifice of federal militia law,[50] long outlasting the military utility of the muskets, firelocks, and spare flints it called on citizens to hold ready for the service of their states and country. Throughout that long period, all efforts of presidents, secretaries of war, and congressional leaders to flesh out the federal government's regulatory oversight of the myriad state militias stalled short of legislative fruition. Ultimately, from Knox's proposed classification scheme, through Secretary John C. Calhoun's attempt at centralizing reform after the repeated debacles of the War of 1812,[51] down to the ambitious and highly controversial selection plan proposed by Secretary Joel R. Poinsett during Martin Van Buren's administration,[52] the same intractable dilemma thwarted every effort to make the historic militia into a serviceable defender of American national security: although a disorganized, undifferentiated militia that made few financial or personal demands on the people was militarily useless, anything more was unpalatable to voters. While some voters remained committed to republican rhetoric, for many the value of a republican militia now took second place to the value of private pursuits.[53] By the time the federal government finally assumed meaningful and effective supervision of the militia in 1903,[54] the ancient War Department dream of achieving effective national security through reform or reorganization of the common militia had long been abandoned by even the most zealous critics of a robust military establishment.[55]

Notwithstanding these subsequent developments, loyalty to the common militia ideal behind the Second Amendment—and, concomitantly, aversion to the establishment of an effective military, whether professional or "selectively" amateur—remained powerful during the early national period. Militarism seemed in those early days anything but a chimerical danger. Numerous episodes between 1783 and 1798 highlight the stark reality behind classically republican-inspired fears that a military coup could be directed to the subversion of the infant republic. These incidents serve to highlight the pivotal stabilizing function of the legitimate militia envisioned by the framers of the Second Amendment.

By late winter of 1783 the war was over. But no peace had been ratified, and the Continental army had neither disbanded nor received its pay. This presented a situation all too similar to that existing at the close of the (first) English Civil War.[56] A group of disgruntled officers circulated the so-called Newburgh Addresses through the Continental camps, threatening that the army would take matters into its own hands if Congress did not act to rectify pressing back pay and pension demands. Only Washington's timely address to the officers on March 15 of that year (this was the famous "I have not only grown gray, but almost blind in the service of my country," or "spectacles," speech) diffused the situation short of a march on Philadelphia.[57] Later that spring, Hamilton openly suggested that the army intervene in government, and, much to the alarm of a then ultra-Whiggish nation, General von Steuben chose the same juncture to announce the founding of the Society of Cincinnati, a secretive and hereditary association of veteran officers of the Revolution that appeared to republicans a conspiratorial first step toward the establishment of a titled, privileged military aristocracy on the European model.[58] In June, after news of the Treaty of Paris reached America, new recruits in Philadelphia deserted, then barricaded Congress in the State House demanding pay and bonuses. Happily, this mob simply dispersed when Congress bravely adjourned for the night without acting on the soldiers' threats.[59] But before it disbanded, the Continental army had seemed poised on the brink of intervention in civil politics and a ready tool for any aspirant dictator desiring to cow the legislature. For precisely these reasons, newly independent Americans feared armies and preferred entrusting their security to the less dangerous hands of the citizen militia.

Three years after the Continental army finally decamped, Shays's Rebellion was put down (haltingly) by Massachusetts militia. But the progress of that insurrection was facilitated when discontented members of western county militia crossed over to the rebels and assisted in the seizure of the Continental arsenal at Springfield.[60] This evidence of the militia's unreliability sparked the Federalist movement that led to the Constitutional Convention and, ultimately, to the rise of the Federalist Party.[61] But if suspicions of the archdemocratic militia gave rise to Hamiltonian federalism in the 1780s, so too suspicions of a Caesarist federal military helped usher in Jeffersonian Republicanism in the 1790s.[62] Washington himself led the federalized militia that put down the Whiskey Rebellion in 1794, but he was visibly worn and aged, and the prospect of his lieutenant, Alexander Hamilton, marching through Pennsylvania at the head of the 13,000-strong "constitutional army"[63] alarmed even moderates.[64]

In 1798 President Adams called on Pennsylvania militia and five hundred regulars to put down another tax revolt, this time instigated by Revolutionary veteran John Fries who led western Pennsylvania's resistance to revenue officers' attempts to collect a "window tax" designed to finance an enormous army to fight the quasi-war with France. Adams showed great and characteristic moderation in pardoning Fries.[65] While he is rightly celebrated as the father of the navy, the second president remained at heart a Whiggish and historicist common lawyer, distrustful of overlarge standing armies and committed to constitutional rule, no matter how much he resented the principles and tactics of the opposition. We cannot say the same of his erstwhile colleague Hamilton. The former treasury secretary had been disgraced by sex scandal and had departed from government, but as the leader of the "High Federalists" he was the moving force behind the proposed army.[66] Indeed, it was Hamilton's plans for an ideologically purged army of 60,000 to fight a nonexistent war that most agitated the republican opposition. Rumors abounded that Hamilton intended to use the army to prevent Jefferson from taking power as the election of 1800 approached,[67] and republican governors in Pennsylvania and Virginia made secret plans to countermarch their militias on Washington.[68] Happily—although fully funded by Congress—the enormous phantom army never assembled, and when Adams was defeated and the electoral college convened, Hamilton showed his better nature by endorsing the republican leader Jefferson as a lesser evil than the "Cataline" Burr.[69] As Richard Hofstadter pointed out, this marked the first time in modern history that power passed peacefully from one elected party to another,[70] but it was perhaps a much closer call between civil war and peaceful transition than is generally acknowledged.

THE LAST YEARS OF THE MILITIA-OF-THE-WHOLE:
POPULAR DISCONTENT AND GOVERNMENT INERTIA

Notwithstanding the prominence of real and imaginary regular armies in the political crises of the 1780s and '90s, and the related persistence of republican rhetoric focusing on the constitutional importance of the militia, and despite the hortatory intentions embodied in the Militia Act of 1792, compulsory universal militia service disintegrated during the early years of the Republic. In state after state, the militia-of-the-whole fell into disfavor and disrepute.[71] In the years after the Revolution, fewer and fewer men made muster on militia days.[72] One reason was the increasing number of exceptions to the universal service obligation enacted by various state legislatures, who by the early nineteenth century had excused from military obligation not only clergy and conscientious objectors, but such citizens as school and university teachers, students, jurors, mariners, and ferrymen.[73] While the rest of the military-aged, white male population generally remained obligated to serve, in practice more and more people simply could not or did not wish to interrupt their everyday economic activities in an increasingly bustling, productive, and differentiated society in order to appear armed and accoutred on the appointed muster day. In general, nonattendees not entitled to an exemption were subject to fines on the order of ten dollars.[74] These penalties were enforced sporadically and selectively.[75] Adding to the growing resentment many felt at the seemingly irrelevant and obsolete service obligation was the fact that those better off could readily afford to pay the fine for nonattendance as a sort of tax, while for the average farmer or farmer's son, ten dollars remained a formidable burden.[76] Class antagonism grew stronger still as the Northeast industrialized in the first decades of the nineteenth century, and state legislatures added factory owners and foremen to the list of exempted citizens.[77]

Several developments during the War of 1812 contributed to the demise of the old militia. In the first place, many New Englanders resented war with Britain and Canada. New Englanders did not hasten to make muster with a view to invading Canada, as indeed they had hesitated to bear arms for the purpose of enforcing first Jefferson's embargo and then Madison's Non-Importation Order against British trade. The unpopularity of service in "Mr. Madison's War" helped sap the vitality of the militia in its New England heartland, where the institution remained more vigorous than in other parts of the nation.[78] Then, too, the governors of Massachusetts, Connecticut, Rhode Island, New Hampshire, and Vermont, who had been reluctant to order their militia to enforce the Embargo and Non-Importation Acts against Britain prior to the war, now refused to muster their troops for an invasion of Canada as commanded by the president.[79] To be sure, the Constitution did not contemplate the president ordering the militia to serve outside U.S. borders,[80] and the president lacked clear statutory authorization for so doing[81]; but in disobeying the commander in chief instead of seeking judicial relief, New England's chief executives flirted with treason.[82] The constitutional crisis over gubernatorial consent to presidential call-ups was not resolved in favor of the federal executive until the Supreme Court's decision in *Martin v. Mott*[83] twelve years after the war's end, and the narrower question concerning withholding of gubernatorial consent to militia service in foreign countries was not finally settled until the *Perpich* case in 1990.[84] More generally, the issue of the constitutionality of militia service outside U.S. borders remained a thorn in the side of presidents during the Mexican War, Spanish-American War, and World War I as well, and continues to inform National Guard policy to this day.[85] Over the course of the nineteenth century, uncertainty regarding the president's ability to rely on the militia for extraterritorial service became yet another factor contributing to the old militia's demise.

With a few exceptions, the common militia acquitted itself dishonorably during the War of 1812. Militia serving in a mixed federal/state command under General Dearborn refused to cross the international border at Lake Champlain preparatory to an attack against Montreal, forcing abandonment of the American offensive in the first year of the war.[86] Militia ineptitude was also a key factor in the August 1814 sacking of Washington, as British regulars marched through a patchwork army of seamen, handfuls of organized militia, and multitudes of untrained common militia arrayed across the Bladensburg Road, and straight into the capital. This spectacle, marking the low point of national humiliation, unfolded within eyesight of a hapless and helpless commanding general of the army and president of the United States, while Secretary of State James Monroe rode about frantically giving confusing orders.[87] Admiral Morison offers the following revealing account of the Bladensburg debacle:

> For five days the British army marched along the banks of the Patuxent, approaching the capital of the United States without seeing an enemy or firing a shot. In the meantime, Washington was in a feverish state of preparation. About 7000 militia, all that turned out of 95,000 summoned, were placed under an unusually incompetent general [Brigadier John Armstrong, Jr.] and hurried to a strong position behind the village of Bladensburg, athwart the road over which the invaders must advance. President Madison and some of the cabinet came out to see the fight. After the militia had suffered only 66 casualties they broke and ran, and [General Robert] Ross [commander of the British land forces], delayed a few hours by the bravery of marines and naval gunners, pressed on to Washington that evening (24 August 1814). Some officers arrived in time to eat a dinner at the White House that had been prepared for the President and Mrs. Madison.[88]

One must wonder whether Madison took this occasion to reflect on his famous comment in *The Federalist* about the invincibility of a nation boasting a militia of 500,000.[89]

While the British expeditionary force was ravaging American militia up and down the Chesapeake, American fortunes were beginning to turn in the far north. Ultimately, no development of the second war with Britain bode less well for the old militia than the emergence of the regulars. Along the Niagara Falls, Winfield Scott's heavily drilled U.S. infantry regiments fought the British to a standstill at Chippewa on July 5, and again at Lundy's Lane on July 25. With Scott's success, America finally appeared capable of defending itself on the ground, even of mounting a ground-based offensive. "By God, those are Regulars!" an astounded British Commander Riall reportedly exclaimed of Scott's stalwarts at Chippewa.[90] According to Henry Adams, "[t]he battle of Chippewa was the only occasion during the war when equal bodies of regular troops met face to face, in extended lines on an open plain in broad daylight, without advantage of position; and never again after that combat was an Army of American regulars beaten by British troops."[91] Crucially for our purposes, the regular infantry's valor in the Great Lakes campaigns of 1814 "contributed ... much to the prestige of the Regular Army and its acceptance as the necessary axis of American defense."[92] Thereafter, no prominent statesman would argue seriously, as Jefferson and Knox had once done, that a classified militia could wholly replace the U.S. Army. Throughout the nineteenth century, the regular army remained small, numbering between 6,000 and 27,000 in peace-time, slightly more during war.[93] But it, and not the militia, was henceforth ac-knowledged as the backbone of the nation's security.

As enthusiasm for militia service continued to decline after the War of 1812, so too did the ability of the average citizen to appear armed in compliance with the Militia Act of 1792 or applicable state regulations. In the early years of the nineteenth century, it was commonplace for militia captains to complain that more and more members of their companies appeared with no weapon at all, or with such poor makeshifts for guns as umbrellas, broomsticks, farm tools, and garden implements.[94] And as citizens came to lack the desire and equip-ment needed for militia service, so too they began to ridicule and burlesque the very concept of the citizen army. Abraham Lincoln's recollections of his youth-ful experiences of "militia trainings" in the West, where the militia lacked even that fading status that its deep historical roots and the nostalgic memories of aging Revolutionary-era veterans had preserved far to the eastward, are illus-trative:

> We remember one of these parades ourselves here, at the head of which, on horse-back, figured our old friend Gordon Adams, with a pine wood sword, about nine feet long, and a paste-board cocked hat, from front to rear about the length of an ox yoke, and very much the shape of one turned bottom upwards; and with spurs having rowels as large as the bottom of a teacup, and shanks a foot and a half long. That was the last militia muster here. Among the rules and regulations, no man is to wear more that five pounds of cod-fish for epaulets, or more than thirty yards of bologna sausages for a sash; and no two men are to dress alike, and if any two should dress alike the one that dresses most alike is to be fined (I forget how much). Flags they had too, with devices and mottoes, one of which latter is, "We'll fight till we run, and we'll run till we die."[95]

The Era of the Volunteers, 1840–1903

THE RISE OF THE VOLUNTEER GUARDS

In Jacksonian America, citizens retained little interest in compelled service in the old universal militia codified by the Militia Act of 1792 and extolled in the Second Amendment. Neither was service with the small regular army widely esteemed by citizenry or Congress, and the regulars continued to bear the brunt of all the familiar republican critiques, notwithstanding the grudging ac-ceptance accorded the army by the nation and the legislature following its vin-dication during the War of 1812. But even as an increasingly democratic and individualistic nation turned away from the common militia, and even as anti-militarism burgeoned into standard fare for the democratic press during the 1830s and '40s, a new generation of citizen-soldiers embraced the part-time

martial ideal by joining volunteer militia companies. These volunteer companies differed fundamentally from the common militia. As the name implies, the
units comprised willing volunteers, not coerced members of the public. The
volunteer units were selective and even elite in their membership, and consciously distanced themselves from the contemptible militia-of-the-whole.
Volunteers trained more frequently and more regularly than had the common
militia, and many units took pride in staging target shoots, military displays,
and parades. They wore showy, ornate uniforms fashioned after famous European units of the day. And while volunteer units were increasingly licensed and
recognized by the states in which they were based, and incorporated into their
states' military organizations,[96] the units were not typically (at least in peacetime) formed under state auspices, but instead through private initiative.

   As the cities grew and the economy boomed, busted, and boomed again in
the Jacksonian years, volunteer militia companies became commonplace in
urban areas. Typically, these new militias served as social clubs as well as military organizations, putting on balls and exhibitions in addition to engaging in
military exercises.[97] Many of the companies were affiliated with, or even coex-
tensive with, urban volunteer fire brigades. Rivalries between companies in the
same cities were not uncommon, and brawling between native Protestant
and Irish Catholic militia units was common sport at midcentury.[98] While
some volunteer companies specialized in socializing and preening in fine
uniforms, a number of elite units aspired to a genuine measure of military skill.
Jefferson Davis's own Mississippi Rifles distinguished themselves in the Mexican War, and generally the organized volunteer units fought far better in Mexico than the bands of unorganized Southwestern militia who hastened across
the border notwithstanding the constitutional prohibition against foreign service. When the Civil War came, it was the presence of established volunteer
companies—often fantastically uniformed like Elmer Ellsworth's New York
Zouaves—that enabled Winfield Scott to put an army in the field to defend
Washington while the government organized recruitment and gathered the
regulars.[99]

   Before the Civil War, volunteers acquired their arms, equipment, and elaborate uniforms wholly by their own means.[100] In this respect, too, they differed
from the common militia. The Militia Act required that citizens enrolled in
their states' militia provide themselves with standard arms and equipment, but
soon after the act's passage, states not already budgeting for militia arms typically set aside money for muskets for citizens unable to afford their own arms,
or even contracted to purchase muskets directly.[101] In 1798 Congress had provided for the purchase of 30,000 stands of arms to be requisitioned by the state
militia.[102] A decade later, in hopes of counteracting the increasingly lax approach of many states to military affairs, Congress established regular federal

appropriations for militia armaments, passing legislation to set aside $200,000 annually for states to claim to purchase arms.[103] Thus Congress took its first steps down a long road leading, in the early twentieth century, to the federal government's full-scale assumption of the responsibility for arming the militia that the Militia Act of 1792 had lodged with the individual, able-bodied man.[104] For many years, most of the money set aside annually under the 1808 law went unclaimed, attesting to the growing apathy with which state governments and citizens alike viewed service in the "constitutional army."[105] Not until blood-letting in Kansas and the *Dred Scott* decision heightened sectional tensions in 1857 did some of the Southern states begin to tap the federal well for militia moneys with a view to replenishing armories, which, like those of their sister states throughout the country, had been neglected for many years.[106]

A NATION OF VOLUNTEERS: THE GRAND ARMY OF THE REPUBLIC

Secession brought an end to Southern claims for federal funds, and Congress did not raise the militia appropriation during the Civil War. Instead, the War Department quickly assumed the task of arming directly the vastly expanded forces required to suppress the Southern insurrection.[107] The War of Secession marked the first time the nation confronted the need for mass mobilization under the Constitution, and the war was fought largely by citizen-soldiers, not by the common militia. Rather, the Union army was made up overwhelmingly of Volunteers (capitalized in Civil War parlance) who rallied to the federal flag. They arrived chiefly in units raised by the states in response to calls by Congress or the president, and enlisted directly into the service of the United States before embarkation to the front.[108] After considerable initial confusion regarding the bounds of state and federal authority, all arms used by the 2,666,999 soldiers who served in the Union armies[109] were procured and issued by the federal government.[110]

More than 90 percent of the Union Army was made up of Volunteers. These citizen-soldiers assumed a role more closely akin to that of federalized National Guard units in the twentieth-century world wars than that of early-nineteenth-century, part-time volunteer regiments. They served under federal command, wore standard-issue federal uniforms, and received federal pay (supplemented by state and federal enlistment bounties). Civil War recruitment amounted to a Napoleonic *levée en masse,* and while the overwhelming majority of Union soldiers were enlistees rather than draftees, the Grand Army of the Republic partook of the universality of the old common militia, even as it acquired the training and professionalism characteristic of the regulars.

A detailed look at the gradual, piecemeal construction of the Union Army highlights a crucial, intermediate phase of the transition from the militia norm envisioned by the Second Amendment's framers to the standing army model accepted nearly universally by Americans today. The constitutional consensus on the eve of war reflected the plain meaning and historic understanding of Army and Militia Clauses ratified in 1788: Congress had the power to raise and support armies, but what this meant is that Congress could recruit volunteer soldiers into the regular army by offering pay, bonuses, and other incentives. The sovereign power to compel military service rested exclusively with the states. The states, however, were debarred from keeping up regular troops in time of peace without Congressional consent by Article I, section 10, clause 3. The only military duty they could compel was service in the militia. Congress, meanwhile, was authorized to call up the state militia into national service "to execute the laws of the Union, suppress insurrections, and repel invasions" as specified in Article I, section 8, clause 15, and this power was partially delegated to the president by the Calling Forth Act of 1795.[111]

When Lincoln took office on March 4, 1861, he inherited intact the regular army of some 15,000 men from James Buchanan, who had done virtually nothing to counter the rising insurrection during the lame duck phase of his administration.[112] Although 30 percent of the army's officers defected to the Confederacy during the secession-winter, Lincoln later boasted that not one enlisted man abandoned his post.[113] The new commander in chief proceeded initially with caution. But on April 12 shore batteries fired on the federal garrison at Fort Sumter, Charleston Harbor, South Carolina, and three days later Lincoln called on the states to summon 75,000 volunteers for three months' service under the Militia Acts of 1792 and 1795 for the purpose of putting down rebellious combinations in the seven states that had left the Union and proclaimed a separate Confederacy at Montgomery; 91,816 men answered the call. A few weeks later, following the secession of Virginia and with further secession of slave-holding states deemed imminent, Lincoln, acting without congressional authorization, increased the size of the regular army by some 22,000, and called on the states to supply 40,000 three-year Volunteers. Within two months, more than 200,000 had enlisted.

The Thirty-seventh Congress convened two months early on July 4, 1861, and immediately voted to raise 1,000,000 Volunteers, half to serve as three-year men, and half for the duration of the war. (The latter ended up serving three-year terms as well.) By December 3, a federal recruiting service had replaced the separate state recruiters, and, with one extended interruption in early 1862, it handled all recruitment for the rest of the war. But on both sides the death tolls mounted, and visions of swift, easy victory dissipated in the smoky battlefields of Second Bull Run, Antietam, Perryville, Corinth, Fredericksburg, and Stones River during the summer and fall of 1862. No longer did Volunteers hasten to the call of arms as quickly as they had during the war's first heady months. The South had already adopted a system of national conscription to meet its growing manpower needs in April 1862, and now the North, reluctantly and incrementally, followed suit.[114] On July 17, 1862, Congress amended the Militia Act of 1792, delegating to the president the authority to specify a period of service of up to nine months whenever he called up the state militia, and granting him plenary power to make all necessary rules and regulations for states lacking adequate laws to govern their militia. In other words, Congress (acting seemingly without direct constitutional authorization) empowered the president to step in when states failed to compel the militia service the federal government required. But states did not make haste to implement a draft prescribed by the War Department pursuant to this framework. A restless populace chaffed in the face of danger, compulsion, commutation, and substitution, and recruitment continued almost wholly according to the volunteer principle for the next year of war.[115]

For the North, the war went badly. Manpower demands continued unabated, and Congress, the War Department, and Army Command anticipated gloomily the election year of 1864, when the three-year terms of the early Volunteers—the bulk of the Federal Army—were scheduled to expire. Since Confederate soldiers had largely mustered in for the duration, Union collapse loomed as a real possibility—barring reform and a change of fortune on the battlefields. On March 3, 1863, Congress acted decisively to forestall this eventuality. The Enrollment Act bypassed the militia powers altogether, and, for the first time in American history, resorted to the "power to raise and support armies" to legislate a federal draft. The act imposed military duty on all able-bodied male citizens and applicants between the ages of twenty and forty-five, and required their enrollment on two lists from which the conscripts were to be chosen.[116] Controversially, the act retained social class–based legacies of the old state militia systems, permitting substitution, and commutation upon payment of a fee of $300.

In preparation for the draft, federal agents spent the spring of 1863 going door to door collecting names for the enrollment register. Implementation of the actual draft—that is, selection of names and numbers from the enrollment lists—engendered resentment throughout the loyal states. In early July, tens of thousands of irate, chiefly Irish, Democratic-voting New Yorkers took to the streets, burning, looting, and lynching to protest the class aspects of the draft law. The riots were not controlled until federal troops arrived via train from the battlefields of Gettysburg.[117]

Resistance and riots notwithstanding—or, perhaps, because of those very factors—only 6 percent of soldiers to serve in the Union Army were draftees. One reason the Union was able to meet its recruiting needs short of full-scale coercion was the willingness of African Americans to enlist in the U.S. Army.

Nearly 200,000 black Volunteers—most of them Southerners living in Union-occupied areas, or former slaves who fled to the Union lines—had signed up by the war's end. With such notable exceptions as the 54th and 55th Massachusetts Regiments (commemorated in the film *Glory*), these soldiers usually by-passed state service altogether, and enrolled directly in the United States Colored Volunteers (later the U.S. Colored Troops.)[118]

REVITALIZATION AND PROFESSIONALISM

At the end of the Civil War, the two-million-plus wartime Volunteers were swiftly demobilized, the regulars dispatched to police the occupied South and the Indian frontier, and the few prewar volunteer companies that survived the war as fighting units decamped and went home. Prewar-style volunteer companies, old and new, remained part of the Northern social scene, but for a time, as the nation tried to heal its wounds, the volunteers' passion for martial exercises seemed to wane. However, the outpouring of patriotism that accompanied the nation's centennial sparked renewed interest in volunteer soldiering, and when industrial turmoil swept the nation in 1877, state governors called on organized state volunteers to put down riots. Indeed, labor unrest prompted state legislatures to renew interest in their state forces. Legislators made no pretense of reviving the long-defunct militia-of-the-whole, but they did all they could to foster the respectable part of society's interest in joining organized and newly forming volunteer units, which pointedly kept their distance from the unorganized militias memorialized in the ancient laws.[119]

In part to distinguish themselves from the disreputable unorganized militia, organized volunteer companies styled themselves guards or national guards. The revitalization of state national guards coincided with a passion for reform and improvement then sweeping all the professions, and national guard officers aggressively pursued recognition and accreditation for themselves and their organizations.[120] Organized militia officers from across the country joined forces in 1878 to form the National Guard Association (NGA) with the objective of obtaining funding and recognition from state legislatures and Congress.[121] During this period, legislative and judicial organs made crucial decisions on both the state and national fronts. While state legislatures were proclaiming the organized national guard units their only lawfully established militia,[122] the Supreme Court rejected a claim to individual entitlement to arms outside the context of militia service. In *Presser v. Illinois,* the Court rejected Second and Fourteenth Amendment challenges to state prohibitions on private parades of armed individuals, and held that the Constitution protected carrying arms only in lawfully established, organized militia units.[123]

Formation of the NGA reflected the professional aspirations of many late-nineteenth-century militia officers to keep pace with the increasing technical complexity of officership in an industrial age. The National Rifle Association also dates from these years, and it had its origins in some of the same concerns that animated the new NGA.[124] The NRA aimed not at aspiring officers, but at young men (particularly the wholesome, rural, native-born, nonunionized type) who might be called upon to fill out the rank and file of a rapidly mobilized, mass army of citizen-soldiers. Civilian America, according to both the NGA and the NRA, would benefit from acquiring a modicum of military knowledge, not simply because this fostered such Victorian values as self-improvement, sport, and outdoorsmanship but because military preparedness was a patriotic duty.

National respectability and national security appeared to depend on the volunteer martial spirit, as America seemed less and less isolated on an increasingly imperialistic and competitive world stage. No one doubted that a war with a major power would require mobilization on a scale surpassing even the Civil War. However, compared with the millions of full-time soldiers and trained reserves assembled by the powers of continental Europe, America's tiny Indian constabulary army of some 30,000 seemed insignificant indeed.[125] Only eccentric military reformers like Emory Upton urged America to keep pace with the Europeans, and the overwhelming majority of voters remained antimilitarist in outlook. If America were to avoid humiliation in any future conflict, it must therefore depend, at least initially, on civilian soldiery. And if these prospective citizen-soldiers were to have any hope of success, they must have prior training. To this end, the NRA saw itself as fulfilling a vital purpose by fostering marksmanship and firearms skill in the population eligible for military duty.[126]

While the NRA staged target shoots and formed rifle clubs, the NGA organized seminars and retreats, circulated periodicals, and lobbied state and federal officials. As the nineteenth century drew to a close, Congress began to take notice of the state guards and the NGA alike. Washington increased the annual militia appropriation for the first time in 1887, doubling funding under the 1808 law to $400,000 per annum. Congress acted again in 1900, increasing appropriations to $1,000,000 annually.[127] When Congress next increased federal militia funding in 1903, it simultaneously replaced the minimalist and hopelessly obsolete federal militia rules laid down in the acts of 1792 and 1795 with comprehensive National Guard legislation embodied in the Militia Act of 1903 (the "Dick Act"). From that time onward, increases in federal funding for the guard entailed ever greater army and War/Defense Department supervision of the constitutionally recognized militia.

The United States Army and the United States Army National Guard in the Twentieth Century

BIRTH OF THE MODERN NATIONAL GUARD

At the close of the nineteenth century, mobilization of state guard units to fight in the Spanish-American War was characterized by scandal and disorder. The disastrous preparation for war was duly recorded by the busy yellow press, who made the most of the stupidity of politicians, brass, and high command, as well as of the misfortunes experienced by regulars and civilian-soldiers alike. Prior to the invasion of Cuba, regular army and volunteers spent months awaiting transport out of Tampa, or stranded on sidings stretching back to South Carolina hoping for passage along the single rail line leading into the west Florida port. The soldiers' equipment was neither standardized nor serviceable and up to date. Guardsmen in particular went into combat wearing woolen uniforms too sweaty for the Tropics, and carrying smoky, single-shot rifles far inferior to the models borne by their Spanish adversaries. The most notorious reports of organizational ineptitude dwelled on servicemen suffering through spoiled canned beef and succumbing to epidemics at a time when advances in technology had made refrigeration readily available and inoculation against typhoid fever practicable. Few observers doubted that a more formidable adversary than Spain would have bested the logistically challenged Americans.[128]

In 1903, following further debacles involving mobilization of state guard units to police the newly won empire and put down the Philippine insurrection, Congress finally acted under pressure from President Roosevelt to subdivide the militia-of-the-whole—by then entirely fictitious—into an active militia (the National Guard) and an unorganized militia (the nonenrolled male population aged between eighteen and forty-five).[129] At the same time, the federal government standardized state units and equipment, and, in return for massive increases in federal funding, the states accepted vastly enhanced federal supervision of militia training.[130]

Congress acted again in 1908 to make the National Guard the country's first-line reserve, providing that as the Organized Militia, the National Guard would be called forth before the raising of new federal volunteers.[131] More fundamentally, Congress waived existing territorial limitations on National Guard call-ups, thereby attempting to bypass the issue of the constitutionality of militia service outside the United States, which had plagued the president and War Department in the wars of 1812–15, 1846–48, and 1898–1901. Within a few years, however, both the attorney general and the judge advocate general of the army had written reports finding this use of the militia to be unconstitutional,[132] presenting Congress anew with the problem of legally deploying American reservists overseas.[133]

This controversy came to a head during the preparedness movement that preceded America's entry into World War I. With war raging in Europe, American pacifists, socialists, and isolationists opposed any military expansion at all, while states-rights-conscious Southern Democrats (and many midwestern Republicans) typically favored no more than incremental augmentation of the National Guard (notwithstanding the constitutional problems associated with foreign deployment). Meanwhile, the newly minted general staff and many pro-British eastern progressives pushed for conscription, establishment of a reserve component wholly independent of the states, and the aggressive expansion of the regular army.[134] The bitterly contested National Defense Act of 1916 "federalized" the Organized Militia, thenceforth known only as the National Guard, and integrated it into the command structure of the War Department and the regular army.[135] The act specified the guard units the states were to maintain, set standards for guard officers, and made provision for federal drill pay to guardsmen.[136] New enlistees swore an oath to obey the president and uphold the U.S. Constitution.[137] Upon congressional authorization, the president was empowered to draft guard members into federal service for the duration of the emergency specified in the authorization bill. In the years before American entry into World War I, then, the state militias were integrated into a federally supervised U.S. Army National Guard and supplied with standardized, congressionally prescribed arms purchased with federal funds and kept in state arsenals, which were themselves increasingly financed by the national government. During the same period, the states acknowledged delegation of the provision of security against invasion to the U.S. Army and the Organized Reserves, laying the framework of state-federal relations that allowed the massive mobilization of citizens into soldiers in both World War I and World War II.[138]

CONTINUED EVOLUTION OF THE GUARD AND RESERVES DURING THE AGE OF STATISM

Expansion of the armed forces to wartime strength during World War I departed markedly from the systems of recruitment and mobilization established during either the Civil War or the Spanish-American conflict, when militia entered federal service in response to presidential calls to the states. Spanish-American War policy allowed individual guard members to volunteer for duty overseas and maintained intact each state unit from which three-quarters of personnel enlisted for federal service. By 1917 organized state volunteer units had been federalized and standardized under the rubric of the National Guard, and many guard members had been training regularly with their regiments since the beginning of the preparedness campaign during the early years of the European war. But General Pershing was convinced, perhaps rightly, that engagement against battle-hardened German veterans required not only further training of guard members under the auspices of the U.S. Army, but breakup of the guard units and integration of the state soldiers into components of the U.S. Army.[139] Fully 67 percent of the 3.68 million Americans serving with the army by Armistice Day were drafted directly into the U.S. Army under the Selective Service Act of 1917.[140] Still, hundreds of thousands of guard members saw active duty during the Great War. Their units, however, did not, as state components disappeared from War Department organizational charts and entered into virtual suspension as Americans prepared to fight in the war in Europe.[141]

Guard officers resented not only the disappearance of their units, but also the time-honored hauteur regular officers displayed toward their civilian-soldier colleagues.[142] In the aftermath of demobilization, the NGA was determined to resurrect the old state units and to preserve the guard's role as the nation's primary reserve in the face of heavy opposition from reform-minded centrists in the War Department, who favored development of a purely federal reserve component of the army.[143] The guard's aims coincided perfectly with the popular rejection of reform and centralization that marked postwar reaction and the return to normalcy and isolationism. The NGA had not yet built up the Capitol Hill lobbying machine that Generals John McAuley Palmer and Milton A. Reckord commanded during and after World War II, but thanks to the anticentrist leanings of many rural representatives, the NGA managed to stave off a War Department campaign to oust the guard in favor of federal reserves and even secured, at least initially, an increased level of federal funding.[144]

Under the National Defense Act of 1920, the National Guard was confirmed as the nation's first-line reserve, but the president was authorized to call out the guard only when greater troop strength than that provided by the regulars was required.[145] Still, Congress relied forthrightly on citizen-soldiers to provide the bulk of the nation's resources in the event of war and called for 435,000 guard members to be maintained in federally funded state units.[146] At the same time, the Defense Act restored to the guard a greater degree of control over its own affairs, with the Militia Bureau in the War Department coming under the direction of a guard general. Training the guard was to be part of the army's responsibility, but as more ROTC graduates became available, citizen-soldiers were expected to take a larger role in instructing their own brigades. For all of the National Guard's success on the Hill during the waning days of Wilson's presidency, during the Harding, Coolidge, and Hoover administrations the guard suffered from the same fiscal austerity that then plagued other federally supported programs, and rarely were guard formations recruited to their full strength during these years of retrenchment.[147]

The course toward federal integration and consolidation of America's citizen-soldiery resumed with vigor during the Hundred Days of the New Deal. But the NGA was able to ensure that rationalization and reform preserved more than merely a dignitary role for the states and the state adjutant generals' offices in the nation's federally supervised citizen reserve. Steering a compromise course between the claims of the War Department and the guard, Congress amended the Defense Act of 1916 to ensure that state units would continue intact when mobilized for overseas wars. More fundamentally, Congress gave express recognition to the dual status of the guard. Henceforth, guard units were to have twinned identities, being at once the militia of the states and a permanent reserve component of the U.S. Army. As a result of the 1933 amendments, the states accepted the dual enlistment system that continues to this day, whereby guard members, upon initiation, take simultaneous oaths to serve in their state units and in the regular army when called up to national duty.[148] For the first time, the National Guard became part of the army structure during peacetime as well as war, and the guard's federal administration was justified not under the Militia Clauses but under the Army Clause of the Constitution.[149] In the process, lawmakers "eliminated the word 'Militia' from the War Department organization by changing the name of the supervisory agency to National Guard Bureau."[150]

Notwithstanding a heightened level of army–guard integration, regulars retained their suspicions of guard members as America poised for entry into World War II. But the progress the guard had achieved during the interwar years of army-supervised training left the nation far better prepared in 1941 than it had been in 1917. By the time Nazi divisions swept across the Polish frontier, 200,000 American guard members were on active-duty status under six-year enlistments, training forty nights a year and performing an additional two weeks of field exercises each summer.[151] This citizen army seemed paltry when compared to the German, Japanese, Soviet, or French establishments, but the availability of semiexperienced guard components was of vital importance in freeing up regulars for the important job of training draftees and recruits as the army expanded to wartime strength.[152]

Guard units remained together under their familiar regimental designations during World War II and contributed much to the overall success of America's civilian army against the more thoroughly professional and regimented German and Japanese forces. As the War Department anticipated victory and partial demobilization, it envisioned a continued role for the guard. The government's commitment to allow civilian soldiers to return home was now tempered by an appreciation for the demands of America's much expanded military role abroad.[153] Doctrinaire hostility to nonprofessional soldiers was finally fading among top defense strategists, but some regular officers retained concerns over the guard's joint state–federal loyalties,[154] concerns partially borne out by Southern governors' mobilization of guard units to resist federally mandated racial integration in the 1950s and '60s.[155]

From the earliest days of the Republic, the preoccupation of the army's thought in peacetime has been the question of manpower, that is, how to muster from a historically civilian people adequate numbers of competent soldiers in the event of a major war.[156] For much of our history, good fortune and isolation rendered this an abstract question. During the two wars with Britain, the enemy lacked both the political will and a coherent strategy for bringing its superior military resources to bear effectively against what was then still a highly diffuse country.[157] In 1846, Mexico's military establishment was no larger than our own and outclassed by the professionalism, gunnery, and engineering skills of the tiny cadre of West Pointers at the head of the invading army.[158] During the Civil War, the South was, pretensions at chivalry notwithstanding, no more militaristic or war-ready than the North, and the Union's lack of military preparedness placed it at no disadvantage.[159] In 1898, Spain was an exhausted imperial power, utterly lacking in the industrial and manpower resources required to repel invasions of Cuba, Puerto Rico, and the Philippines by a top-flight naval and industrial power, no matter how disorganized the attacker's military planning.[160]

More than good luck, economic might, and optimism were required to fight and win the twentieth-century world wars. Victory over the Central Powers and the Axis required mobilization of the manpower of the entire nation. In both instances, millions of American civilians were organized and trained into armies capable of standing up to the most professional soldiers from the most militaristic countries, and far more quickly than conservative strategists in the regular establishment thought prudent or possible. Success in the world wars therefore weakened the case for the old general staff/War Department argument that American security required permanent militarization of the population on the Prussian model.[161] Yet no strategist could underestimate the value of training or preparedness, and no one failed to credit the professional officer and noncommissioned corps for their remarkable ability to impart knowledge, system, and skill to millions of their compatriots as the army set itself on a wartime footing. Thus, rejection of Continental-style militarism did not amount to a rejection of professionalism, or augur a reversion to the inchoate amateurism of the colonial militias. Quite the contrary, the wartime experience pointed to the necessity of maintaining a thoroughly professional, if not overlarge, regular army, but with sufficient links to civilian society to prevent both debilitating hostility of the general populace toward the army and dangerous contempt for the people by the soldiers. The National Guard was ideally suited to play a prominent role in this system of security.[162]

Military strategists, of course, have a pronounced tendency to plan to fight the last war rather than the next one. The vision just described was in fact a vision premised on preparedness for mass mobilization of the civilian population to fight a prolonged ground war on several foreign fronts against formidable military adversaries similarly arrayed. It was therefore premised in part on the ideal of universal military training (UMT), which was to enable the democratic/civilian societies, led by the United States, to mobilize their civilian populations with maximum speed and efficiency, while the regular army responded to the initial aggressions of a hostile, totalitarian coalition.[163] This vision was also obsolete before it was reduced to statute. On August 6, 1945, the U.S. Army Air Forces dropped an atomic bomb on Hiroshima, Japan, all but ending the war and ushering in a radically different strategic age. The advent of the American nuclear monopoly changed military planning almost overnight.[164]

At the dawn of the atomic age, the air force, newly separated from the army, became the glamour wing of the armed services and the favorite of strategists and planners in the Defense Department and on Capitol Hill. Army and NGA lobbyists struggled to justify continued funding for the oldest and most traditional military arm, for it was widely assumed that no potential antagonist would be possessed of sufficient folly to challenge American nuclear might. Ground forces retained a constabulary-style function in the occupied Axis countries, and as the cold war developed, forward positioning of troops provided a visible check against communist expansion. But a showdown, if it came, was expected to be quick, nuclear, and dispositive. No one seriously considered the possibility that America might ever again be compelled to mobilize the entire nation in the manner characteristic of the major wars from Napoleon's day to Hitler's. The historic role of the guard, as the strategic, trained personnel reserve of the nation, seemed relegated to irrelevancy, and plans for UMT were left to gather dust in Pentagon archives.

As it turns out, advance notice of the guard's impending demise was greatly exaggerated. When the Soviet Union shocked the world by testing atomic and then hydrogen bombs years before the intelligence community thought feasible, America's first response was the doctrine of massive retaliation, or mutual assured destruction.[165] Nuclear attack against America or its allies would be met by an overwhelming nuclear counterstrike, calculated to destroy the Soviet Union and likely to bring an end to life on earth. But the nuclear brinkmanship of the Dulles era soon wore thin, and more flexible, less apocalyptic policies were fashioned for the benefit of frazzled nerves on both sides of the Iron Curtain. Neither of the principal regional wars of the cold war era—the Korean War nor the Vietnam War—led to nuclear confrontation or escalated into worldwide conflict. In both instances, America's global commitments—and, principally, the forward positioning of NATO troops in Germany—so burdened the regular army that military expansion proved necessary to meet the requirements of war raging in Asia.[166] At the same time, conventional preparedness strategy dictated that trained reserves be maintained to facilitate further, rapid expansion in the event open hostilities should erupt in Europe or elsewhere around the globe while substantial American strength was committed to fighting on the Pacific Rim.[167] Vastly exaggerated reports of Soviet army strength militated in favor of a sizable, professionally trained reserve.[168] All this said, fighting substantial but limited Asian wars, even in a global security context, did not require mobilization of the entire nation.[169] Short of feeding and paying them, the army would not have known what to do with ten or twenty million soldiers. This need for one or two million more personnel than during peacetime—but no more than that—presented grave ethical and political difficulties for the Selective Service, the Defense Department, and the government.[170] Compelling wartime service of some—but not all—Americans generated bitter anger and resentment as the U.S. death tolls climbed to fifty and fifty-eight thousand in the respective Asian wars.[171]

All of these factors combined to redefine and solidify a mission for the National Guard in the later years of the twentieth century. The Vietnam War proved, in myriad ways, a political disaster, and neither the defense community nor the larger nation was ever quite the same after America suffered its first military defeat. Perhaps the least popular aspect of the war was the draft, and in 1972 Congress repealed the Selective Service Act in favor of the volunteer principle.[172] The army's reversion to the recruitment system redoubled its reliance on the guard and, by now, a substantial separate army reserve arm to meet future requirements for expansion and mobilization. This had the effect of cementing the mutual dependency and linkage between army and guard. With mutual assured destruction and the draft both discredited, the guard's future in the closing decades of the twentieth century seemed far more certain than in the immediate postwar years. But the ever more federal, wholly army-trained, all-volunteer National Guard of the Reagan years bore no familial resemblance to the old, independent, universal state militia.[173]

As far removed as the cold war National Guard was from the militia described in the Second Amendment and the Militia Act of 1792, twentieth-century America never completely forgot the civic republican fears that had once animated anti-Federalist advocates of a constitutional right to keep and bear arms. In his farewell broadcast of January 17, 1961, President Eisenhower warned of the growing power of the military-industrial complex.[174] The bloated defense budgets, procurement scandals, and defense-industry lobbyists that left the former commanding general of the army so uneasy had their counterparts in the standing (i.e., inactive and useless) armies, salaried place-

men, and overburdened exchequers of Elbridge Gerry's or James Harrington's day.[175] True, by Eisenhower's time, few Americans feared a military coup.
But there had always been more to the republican anti-army ideology than the
worry that janissaries might seize the palace or oust legislators from their seats.
Much more insidious was the threat that the imperial army would burden the
body politic with enervating debt and burden policymakers with improper
dependencies and obligations. In this respect, republican misgivings hardly
seem relics of a forgotten time.

Happily, however, the republicans' most gothic fears of a polity corrupted
by an army have not materialized in the democratic republic they helped to
found. Civilian control of the military has never been challenged—a remarkable fact in a constitutional system now more than two hundred years old.
Most of our great generals who became presidents—Washington, Grant,
Eisenhower—proved decidedly anti-Caesarist in the Executive Mansion (perhaps this is somewhat less true of Jackson). Indeed, throughout our history,
professional military officers have demonstrated a notable commitment to
civic values and respect for the democratic process. The anti-army prejudices
of the nineteenth century have steadily faded, and today the army is truly perceived as an instrument of the people, and not as a threatening alien organ. Lo-
calism endures in and on behalf of the National Guard, but as a species of
provincial politicking and state-level patronage rather than as a genuine military counterweight to federal power. Away from the peripheral fringe, even the
nation's most ardent anticentrists are now devotees of the army. More often
than not, the military is the only aspect of federal power for which our modern
anti-Federalists have any affection at all.

Quite apart from reflecting on the contemporary relevance or irrelevance
(or persistence or disappearance) of the ancient republican paradigm, our thesis ultimately turns on the evolution of the militia. And by the late twentieth
century, that institution had developed into a creature all but unrecognizable
from the perspective of the Second Amendment. In the years since World War
II, the role of a mass reserve in assuring national security has seriously diminished in consideration of the technical complexity of equipment and tasks
required of a thoroughly professional modern army, and because nuclear deterrence has made a mass war drawing all the personnel reserve of the country
unlikely. The need for a whole nation in arms has—in all likelihood, permanently—disappeared. At the same time, conscription has become so unpopular as to border on being politically unfeasible.[176] In this climate, the volunteer
principle has again supplanted the draft as the recruiting mechanism for fighting the limited wars that characterize the nuclear age, leaving no shadow of the
old militia's universality or compulsion about today's National Guard.[177]

It is not only the volunteer recruitment principle that distinguishes the early-twenty-first-century organized militia from the common militia of 1789. The issue of the militia's necessity to the security of the states and nation has been fundamentally recast. In 1789, the regular army numbered 672 men; the common militia, Madison boasted, numbered nearly half a million. Today, the regular United States military establishment numbers some 1.4 million soldiers, sailors, air personnel, and officers, while the U.S. Army National Guard (i.e., the statutorily defined organized militia) accounts for fewer than 361,000.[178] With the help of lobbying by the NGA, Congress has judged and continues to judge the National Guard necessary to the nation's security and funds it handsomely in every federal budget ($6.4 billion in fiscal year 1999— 10 percent of the army budget and 2.4 percent of the defense budget). In the most recent budget, Congress adjudged the guard worthy of 2.3 percent of the total of $282 billion it deemed necessary to secure the defense of the United States.[179] The states, too, fund their guards—or at least some of them do— albeit very much less generously than the federal government. In fact, according to Justice Stevens, "[t]he Federal Government provides virtually all of the funding, the materiel, and the leadership for the State Guard units."[180] In contrast to the National Guard, the unorganized militia—the shadow of the common militia so extolled by the framers of the Second Amendment—has not been funded by Congress since at least 1903. It is unclear that any state appropriated any of the funds Congress set aside for the common militia after Reconstruction, or that any state provided funds for the unorganized militia after 1877, or even after 1850. And by walking away from the muster points and parade grounds en masse during the first half of the nineteenth century, the American people themselves voted in the most direct way they could that their security, whether national or state, had nothing to do with the common militia. The old militia had died a natural death long before anyone now living was born. Indeed, it would be difficult to conceive of any institution *less* necessary to the security of the fifty free states in the year 2000 than the vanished common militia.

One more vital difference remains between the organized militia of today and the militia of 1789–91, and it is the most striking of all. The Militia Act of 1792 required citizens to acquire specified arms and keep them in their homes, ready to bear on muster day and when called up in emergencies. No matter that noncompliance was (or soon became) the rule, that many (or most?) households actually contained no functioning, regulation firearms at all.[181] The Militia Act embodied the norms envisioned in the Second Amendment. And those were that militiamen keep their required, regulation arms in their own homes. This was then the most practical approach. Armories contained some small arms as well as field pieces and powder, but the delays and inefficiencies occasioned by first reporting to a state armory, perhaps many miles distant, and then rallying to meet one's fellows where public danger loomed, would have been intolerable given the limits of eighteenth-century transportation and communication. Moreover, arms then required constant oiling and repair, meaning that they could be better maintained in the home, assuming house-holders were diligent in their charge.[182] Perhaps more fundamentally still, balls, cartridges, and shot did not begin to be standardized until Eli Whitney, after long delays, delivered on his 1798 contract to furnish the War Department with ten thousand mass-production muskets assembled on the interchange-able-parts principle.[183] Prior to the rise of standard-issue arms, each gun was an individual tool, almost a piece of art, cartridges for which were best assem-bled by the hands of the proprietor rather than in a factory under government contract.

Today, standard, mass-produced U.S. Army automatic rifles are issued to the National Guard by the army and kept safe in armories. The very same pieces are used by both the army and the guard, maintained according to the same manuals, and sometimes returned to the same armories, where they are stored under lock and guard until next issued to reservists, regulars, or guard members for exercise or duty. If repairs are necessary, army specialists perform them. Ammunition and firing pins are the subjects of meticulous record keep-ing and are issued separately from the weapon at the beginning of exercises.[184] Congress, the Department of Defense, the secretary of the army, and the state adjutants general have decided national and state security is best served by this system, under which identical, interchangeable equipment centrally stored can be issued to guard members and soldiers as training and military necessity demand. For reasons of efficiency and public safety, it is implausible that any member of Congress or official in the Department of Defense, army, or state adjutant general's office should advocate a return to the policy of keeping the arms used by the organized militia in guard members' homes. Most fundamen-tally of all, the arms once purchased by the militiamen themselves[185] are now government property and require the safekeeping accorded any other U.S. property—and especially dangerous property at that. In the year 2000, the militia world contemplated by the Second Amendment no longer exists, and no plausible analogy to that nexus can be reconstructed.

The concept of the militia embedded in the Second Amendment has so radi-cally changed over the centuries since its adoption that the right to arms, con-structed to serve it, is fundamentally deactivated. Changes in the concept expressed by the word "militia" have been gradual, and their impact on the meaning of the arms clause has been progressive. Certainly, the word contin-ues to connote a trained and organized military force. At the same time, it is difficult for twenty-first-century ears to discern the echoes of the overtones that two centuries previously were characteristic of the term.[186] More critically, the social context of the present—the society served by the militia and the nature of the militia's service to society—no longer resembles the social context of the militia in 1789. As a result, although the word "militia" retains meaning, the word "militia" as written in the Second Amendment has no referent and hence no application in the United States today.

As we have recounted—and as all scholars agree—the founding generation of Americans conceived of a militia as a group composed of all free, white males between the ages eighteen and forty-four[187] (except for the conscientious objectors and others entitled to an exemption), responding as needed for the common defense, at the call of local authority, and, above all, as a viable alternative to the feared standing army. This renaissance republican conception was soon recognized as the romance of revived classicism, and the militia gradually lost their characteristic charisma. By the early twentieth century, they were called by, trained by (1903), commanded by, armed by, and deployed by federal authority (1916). Losing all distinction from the regular army (1933), they were, by the middle of the twentieth century, nothing but a shadow of the founders' dream. Even their image as the personification of civic virtue had been fouled by disgraceful episodes and disastrous campaigns dating back to the days when the sainted George Washington was commanding general.[188]

This seems to us such a drastic change in the context of the term that we are led to conclude that there is no contemporary, evolved descendant of the eighteenth-century "militia" on today's landscape. Although the present-day National Guard units (successors to the militia) still receive a sizable chunk of the federal defense budget[189] and generally take their training and patriotism seriously, they are hardly of the same genus as the militia as understood in the eighteenth century. To cite only the most glaring distinction, they are part of the standing army rather than an alternative to it. And if today's National Guard fails to fit the concept of a militia, the notion is little short of ludicrous that the constitutional term applies to the scattered, small, unregulated bands of fatigue-clad, gun-loving, self-appointed libertarians taking secret target practice in the woods.[190]

In modern usage, then, the word "militia"—insofar as it is heard at all—describes no organization genetically related to the ennobled assembly identified by the term as originally written in the Constitution. Therefore, the introductory clause of the Second Amendment is today devoid of meaning, an empty vessel from which time and history have sucked every trace of the considerable substance it once had. And the right standing upon it—as the right memorialized in the second clause does—collapses for lack of footing.

What this means is that on the pressing issue of gun control the Constitution is neutral. The Second Amendment would take no notice if Congress, appalled by the prevalence of gun-assisted crimes, outlawed all handguns and assault rifles in private hands. By the same token, Congress could vacate the field, and, with a similar retreat by the states, the NRA would realize its fondest wish, and every competent adult would be allowed free purchase and proud ownership of firepower of every description. Thus, we conclude: let the great debate continue to rage—in the democratic branch where it belongs. But let us understand at last that the Second Amendment has no voice in the matter.

7. Natural Rights and the Second Amendment

STEVEN J. HEYMAN*

Men uniting into politick societies, have resigned up to the publick the disposing of all their Force, so that they cannot employ it against any Fellow-Citizen, any farther than the Law of the Country directs.

—John Locke[1]

The Second Amendment is an enigma. Although many aspects of the Bill of Rights are controversial, disputes usually focus on such questions as how far particular rights should extend and how they should apply under modern circumstances. By contrast, there is no consensus on even the most basic meaning of the Second Amendment, which reads, "A well regulated Militia, being necessary to the security of a free State, the right of the people to keep and bear Arms, shall not be infringed." Instead, the scholarly literature is sharply divided between two opposing views. One position asserts that the Second Amendment was intended to guarantee an individual right to keep and bear arms.[2] The other holds that the right is one that belongs to the people collectively, and that the right is essentially connected with the establishment of "[a] well regulated Militia."[3]

In resolving this debate, the most common methods of constitutional interpretation are of limited use. At least to modern readers, the amendment's language is ambiguous. The subject of the constitutional right, "the people," can be understood either in a collective sense, to refer to the community as a whole, or in an aggregate sense, to refer to all of its members. The reference to the "militia" points in a collective direction but is not conclusive on its own. As to the broader context of usage within the Constitution and the Bill of Rights, those documents use "the people" in both senses: sometimes collectively, sometimes individually.[4] Contemporary debates over the amendment were sparse and generally unilluminating. And, in contrast to most other provisions of the Bill of Rights, the Supreme Court has rarely addressed the meaning of the Second Amendment.[5]

Faced with these difficulties, constitutional scholars and historians often seek to understand the Second Amendment by situating it within a larger tradition or body of thought. Some scholars, on both sides of the debate, have discussed the amendment's background in the English legal and constitutional tradition.[6] Others have connected the right to arms with civic republican thought.[7] And still others, especially on the individual rights side, have argued that the amendment reflects natural rights philosophy.[8]

This argument—which has been advanced in varying forms by Randy Barnett, Stephen Halbrook, Don Kates, Nelson Lund, Joyce Lee Malcolm, and others—runs as follows. According to the natural rights tradition, which deeply influenced the American founders, individuals had an inalienable right to defend themselves against violence. It was to protect this right, among others, that society and government were formed. Within society, citizens had a right to defend themselves, not only against private violence but also against tyranny and oppression by the government itself. But this right could not be effectively exercised without arms. According to this view, the Second Amendment was intended, at least in part, to enable individuals to exercise their natural right to self-defense.

On its face, this view is a powerful one. Indeed, even Garry Wills, one of the most forceful critics of the individualist interpretation, concedes that arguments for "a natural right to own guns . . . might be sound or strong," though he denies that the Second Amendment was meant to secure such a right.[9]

The object of this essay is to challenge this understanding of the natural rights tradition. While this tradition does hold that individuals in a state of nature have a broad right to use force for self-preservation, the right is not an inalienable one. Instead, when individuals entered into society, they largely gave up this right in return for the protection they obtained under the law. And although the people retained the right to resist tyranny, this was a right that belonged to the community as a whole rather than to individuals. For these reasons, the natural rights tradition provides more support for a collective right than for an individualist interpretation of the Second Amendment.

After exploring John Locke's classic statement of natural rights theory, I shall focus on Sir William Blackstone's account of the right to arms, which provides the strongest textual evidence for a natural rights reading of the Second Amendment. Next, I shall discuss the right to arms in post-Revolutionary American thought and in the debates surrounding the Constitution and the Bill of Rights. The essay concludes with some reflections on what this history means for how we should interpret the Second Amendment today.

LOCKE AND THE NATURAL RIGHTS TRADITION

Is There a Right to Arms for Personal Self-defense?

John Locke's writings laid the foundations for natural rights theory in eighteenth-century England and America. Locke never mentions a right to arms for personal self-defense. At first glance, however, his theory would appear to strongly support such a right. Locke begins by envisioning individuals in a state of nature, before the formation of civil society and government. In that state, individuals are not only entitled to life, liberty, and property but also have a right to do anything necessary to preserve them, within the bounds of the law of nature. In particular, everyone has a natural right to judge for himself whether others are invading his rights, and to vindicate those rights by force if necessary. Indeed, the right to use force is not limited to self-defense. According to Locke, the fundamental law of nature enjoins the preservation not only of oneself but of mankind in general. In a state of nature, everyone is entitled to enforce this law by punishing those who injure other human beings.[10]

Thus, Locke recognizes a broad natural right to use force for the protection of oneself and others. If one assumes that weapons are useful for this purpose, then Locke's theory seems to provide a powerful justification for an individual right to have them. And if the purpose of government is to protect natural rights, it seems to follow that the law should recognize and secure this right. Of course, that is the conclusion that advocates of the individual rights interpretation of the Second Amendment draw from Locke's work.[11] But this conclusion is mistaken. The thrust of Locke's discussion is not to endorse a broad private right to use force, but exactly the opposite: to show why such a right must be radically restricted.

According to Locke, it is precisely the unrestrained use of force that makes the state of nature intolerable. The problem is that when every individual is judge in his own case, he is likely to act out of passion and self-interest, pursuing his own advantage at the expense of the rights of others. The lack of a clear, settled law to govern interactions between individuals aggravates the situation. Moreover, even when an individual is in the right, he may lack sufficient power to protect himself and his rights. For all these reasons, individuals live a most precarious existence in the state of nature, which is constantly in danger of degenerating into a war of all against all.[12]

The remedy for these evils lies in the social contract, in which individuals agree to form a society for the preservation of their life, liberty, and property. The terms of this contract have a crucial bearing on our problem. According to Locke, when an individual enters civil society, *"he gives up"* his

> Power . . . *of doing whatsoever he thought fit for the Preservation of himself,* and the rest of Mankind, . . . to be regulated by Laws made by the Society, so far forth as the preservation of himself and the rest of that Society shall require; which Laws of the Society in many things confine the liberty he had by the Law of Nature.

In return, the individual obtains all the benefits of society, including the right to be protected by the "whole strength" of the community. To make this protection possible, individuals "engage [their] natural force" to assist the community in enforcing the law, as well as defending the society from external danger.[13]

In short, while there is a broad natural right to use force for self-preservation, this is not an *inalienable* right, that is, a right that individuals can never part with. Indeed, according to Locke, it is only by surrendering this right that human beings are able to form a society at all. For the very notion of political society is that rights should be determined and disputes resolved not through the "private judgement" of each individual, backed by private force, but rather by the public judgment of the community, as expressed in general laws enacted by the legislature, administered by impartial judges, and enforced by the power of the community as a whole. For these reasons, Locke holds that the right to use force is an *alienable* right—a right that individuals give up when they form the social contract.[14]

This point emerges clearly when we compare this right with the liberty of conscience, which Locke regards as the paradigmatic inalienable right. In his *Letter Concerning Toleration,* he argues that the capacity to form one's own beliefs is inherent in and inseparable from the human mind—in a strict sense, it is impossible to part with this freedom. Holding one's own religious beliefs does no injury to others. Nor is there anything to be gained by relinquishing this right, for salvation can be attained only through sincere belief and worship.[15] For these reasons, freedom of belief is an inalienable right. And these arguments can be generalized to apply to freedom of thought more broadly.[16] By contrast, the liberty to use force against others, particularly with weapons, is not inseparable from individuals, and does impact on the rights of others. And there is a great deal to be gained by surrendering this right, for as a rule individuals are much more likely to attain security and preservation when the private use of force is excluded. It follows that the right to use force, unlike liberty of thought and belief, is an alienable right. This point is summed up in Locke's remark that "though Men uniting into politick societies, have resigned up to the publick the disposing of all their Force, so that they cannot employ it against any Fellow-Citizen, any farther than the Law of the Country directs; yet they still retain the power of Thinking" as they like, since that right is an inalienable one.[17]

The implications of our discussion for a right to arms should be clear. If individuals had an inalienable right to use force for self-preservation, they might also have a right to possess and use weapons for that purpose. But this argument fails if the right to use force is one that individuals surrender when they enter into society.

There is, however, an important exception to the general rule that the right to use force is an alienable one. Individuals give up this right only in those cases in which they are able to appeal to the law for protection. For this reason, Locke holds that when an individual faces an imminent attack on his life or person, he has a right to use all necessary force to defend himself.[18] To this extent, the right to self-defense is an inalienable one, which is retained within civil society. If this is true, however, does it not follow that individuals also have an inalienable right to own arms for self-defense?

There is no way to know what Locke would have thought of this argument, for he never addressed the issue. The logic of this view, however, is hardly compelling from a Lockean perspective. The difficulty with the argument is that it confuses two different questions: what an individual may rightfully do when he is subject to imminent attack, and what measures the legislature may properly take *ex ante* to protect the lives and safety of citizens. When a person is assaulted, he may do anything reasonably necessary to defend himself. This includes not only using his own natural force, but also using anything else in his possession, such as a deadly weapon. It does not follow, however, that the legislature cannot properly make a prospective judgment that citizens would enjoy a higher level of security if the possession of such weapons were restricted or even banned. To be sure, such a law would not be justified if weapons could be employed only for lawful self-defense. But that obviously is not the case, since they can also be used to wrongfully assault others. Under these circumstances, it is an empirical question whether the community would be safer with or without restrictions on guns. That would seem to be a question for the legislature to decide.

To summarize, Lockean theory holds that when individuals establish a society, they give up the right to use force against others in return for the protection they receive from the community. Immediate self-defense is an exception to this principle, for in that case there is no opportunity to appeal for protection. But one way in which the government can protect its citizens is by regulating the possession and use of weapons. For this reason, such regulation appears to fall on the alienable, not the inalienable, side of the line.

To put the point another way, Locke does not regard the ability of individuals to use force in their own defense as an end in itself. Instead, it is a means to the fundamental end of natural law—the preservation of oneself and of mankind in general. Indeed, as Locke's account of the state of nature demonstrates, the unrestrained right to use force according to one's own private judgment actually undermines, rather than furthers, the goal of self-preservation by leading to a war of all against all. Rational individuals would therefore choose to give up this right and to form a society for mutual preservation. Just as preservation is the reason why human beings institute government in the first place, so it also constitutes the "end or measure" of the government's power.[19] It follows that if the legislature reasonably determines that restrictions on weapons would advance this end, such restrictions would not violate the Lockean conception of natural rights.

That is not to say, of course, that Locke can be counted as a supporter of gun control laws, for he never addressed the issue. Instead, the point is simply that it is a mistake to assume, as many adherents of the individual rights interpretation do, that the issue can be resolved through an appeal to the notion of inalienable rights. Instead, from a Lockean perspective, the matter is one that appears to fall within the legislature's power to regulate for the common good.

The Lockean Rights of Resistance and Revolution

Thus far the question has been whether, in the Lockean view, individuals have a right to arms in order to defend themselves against private violence. Now let us consider whether they have such a right in order to defend themselves against the government itself.

Locke holds that, under the social contract, all political power is initially vested in the community as a whole. This includes the authority not only to make laws but also to direct the force of all the members of the community in order to execute those laws, as well as to defend against external dangers. In turn, the community usually delegates this political power to a particular government. The power is given with the trust that it be used only for the public good. Yet it is the nature of rulers, no less than other human beings, to pursue their own self-interests. For this reason, there is a danger that the rulers may come to perceive themselves as having "a distinct interest from the rest of the community." The government may then become tyrannical and seek to assert "absolute Arbitrary Power" over the people.[20]

In this situation, Locke argues that the people have a right to resist tyranny and to overthrow the government. Indeed, the immediate polemical purpose of the *Two Treatises* was to justify the Glorious Revolution of 1688, in which the absolutist King James II was driven out of England and replaced by William and Mary of Orange.[21] In this section, I will briefly explore Locke's account of resistance and revolution, and then discuss whether, as some scholars contend, his theory supports an individual right to keep and bear arms to oppose tyranny.[22]

This portion of the *Second Treatise*, which was written in the midst of a revolutionary upheaval, is far from a model of clarity, nor is it free from a certain degree of conflict and inconsistency. I believe, however, that Locke's position can fairly be described as follows.

The right of the people to resist oppression is a major theme of the *Second Treatise*. When rulers become tyrannical, they exercise force beyond the bounds of their rightful authority and thereby place themselves in a state of war with their subjects, who are entitled to defend themselves under the fundamental natural law of self-preservation.[23] The question then arises as to whether Locke conceives of this right to resistance as an individual or a collective one.

In principle, Locke holds that this right to resistance may be exercised not only by the community but also by private individuals. For several reasons, however, he puts little stock in a private right of resistance. First, such resistance is almost certain to be futile, for it is unreasonable to believe that a few individuals will be able to prevail against the force of the government. Second, Locke recognizes that his position is vulnerable to the objection that it would promote unjustified uprisings and rebellions, which, by plunging a country into civil war, are among "the greatest Crime[s] . . . a Man is capable of." Locke's response to both of these concerns is the same: resistance is unlikely to occur unless a majority of the people come to regard the government as tyrannical and oppressive. Thus for Locke resistance turns out to be collective in nature. This is certainly true as a practical matter, and it may well reflect considerations of principle as well. After all, the purpose of the social contract is to avoid a state of war by excluding "all private judgement" and private force, and ensuring that disputes are resolved as far as possible by the public judgment of the community. A private right to determine that the government is tyrannical and should be resisted is, of course, in some tension with this purpose. But a right of the community to make this judgment is entirely consonant with it.[24]

For all of these reasons, Locke's account strongly focuses on the right of *the people as a whole* to resist tyranny. Indeed, the right of resistance is almost inextricably connected with the right of revolution—the right to determine that the government has forfeited its authority and ought to be replaced with a new one. And that is clearly a right that belongs only to "the *Community*" or "*the People*" as a whole. As Locke expresses it, although the legislative is the supreme power within

> a Constituted Commonwealth, . . . there remains still *in the People a Supream Power* to remove or *alter the Legislative,* when they find the *Legislative* act contrary to the trust reposed in them. For all *Power given with trust* for the attaining an *end,* being limited by that end, whenever that *end* is manifestly neglected, or opposed, the *trust* must necessarily be *forfeited,* and the Power devolve into the hands of those that gave it, who may place it anew where they shall think best for their safety and security.

Locke concludes by connecting this right to revolution with the "Fundamental, Sacred, and unalterable Law of *Self-Preservation,*" which empowers the community to preserve itself and its members against oppression.[25]

Now let us consider the implications for a right to arms. Locke's views on a private right to resistance are highly ambivalent and hardly provide a strong basis for an individual right to arms to resist the government. Instead, he generally presents resistance as a collective rather than an individual activity. When the community determines that the government has become oppressive, it has a collective right to resist this oppression by force, to overthrow the government, and to institute a new one. Implicit in the rights to resistance and revolution is the right to take up arms against a tyrannical government. This, too, is a right that belongs to the people as a whole, not to individuals as such.

In asserting these rights under revolutionary conditions, the people can appeal to the natural law of self-preservation, a law that is "antecedent and paramount to all positive Laws" and constitutions.[26] Do the people also have a right to have arms within a "Constituted Commonwealth," to use for self-defense in the event that the government becomes tyrannical? Once again, this is a question that Locke himself does not address. Presumably, the people would insist on retaining such a right if it would be to their advantage to do so. It is unclear, however, whether this would be to their advantage. Arms involve dangers as well as benefits, since they can be used not only for legitimate self-defense and revolution but also for unlawful violence and rebellion. Whether the path of greater safety lies in retaining a right to arms or not cannot be determined by natural rights theory, i.e., by reason alone, but only by the people themselves when they establish a positive constitution. For this reason, it is necessary to look to the constitution itself to determine the existence and bounds of any such right.

Suppose, however, that there were a way to ensure that weapons could not be used for improper or factional purposes, but were strictly subject to the collective control of the people. In that event, a right to arms would seem clearly to the people's advantage, for there would be no danger that the arms would be used for unlawful violence or illegitimate rebellion. Under these circumstances, insisting on a right to arms would enhance the people's capacity for self-preservation without any corresponding disadvantages—assuming, that is, that citizens were willing to undergo the discipline and burdens incident to bearing arms within this collective context. I shall suggest below that this notion throws light on the meaning of the Second Amendment. That provision can be understood to protect the collective right of the people to have arms, subject to collective discipline and control within the context of "[a] well regulated Militia." A right of this sort makes sense within a Lockean analysis, and also makes sense of the language of the Constitution itself.

————————

Locke holds that individuals have a natural right to self-preservation, yet his thought provides little support for an individual right to arms. The community as a whole, however, may have such a right. Although these conclusions may appear paradoxical, they actually reflect some of the deepest themes of the natural rights tradition. Individuals have a right to protect themselves and their rights, yet they cannot effectively do so on their own. If they are to live in peace and security, disputes must be resolved not by private force but by the public judgment of an organized community. To make such a community possible, individuals must largely give up the right to use force against others. In return, the community undertakes to protect all of its members, not only against private violence, but also against governmental oppression. For the natural rights tradition, then, the locus of legitimate force lies not in private individuals but in the community as a whole. This is why the tradition provides more support for a collective than for an individual right to arms.

Finally, it is crucial to see such a right in proper perspective. Locke does not regard the revolutionary use of force as the only, or even as a particularly desirable, means of preventing tyranny. On the contrary, he regards the dissolution of government and the need for violent revolution as among the worst calamities that can befall a nation. A major purpose of Lockean political theory is to outline the features of a liberal constitutional state that are capable of preserving liberty without resort to revolution. For Locke, such a state must rest on the consent of the people, and must not transgress the limits established by the constitution and the fundamental principles of natural law. To prevent an undue concentration of authority, there should be a separation between the legislative, executive, and judicial powers. The legislative power should be entrusted to a collective body of persons who are subject to the laws that they themselves make. The legislature should be at least in some degree representative of the people and should be shielded from coercion or undue influence by the executive. Elections should be free. The legislature should govern through "settled standing Laws" that apply to all citizens equally. Although the legislature may regulate property rights, it may not take private property, even through taxation, without the consent of the people or their representatives. The executive should be subject to the law, and safeguards should be adopted to prevent abuse of power. When individuals suffer injury at the hands of the government, they should have legal avenues of redress. The laws should be administered by independent judges.[27] Finally, there must be room for dissent—a notion that Locke's eighteenth-century radical Whig followers developed into the right to freedom of speech.[28] For Locke, these principles of liberal constitutionalism and the rule of law form the principal line of defense against tyranny. It is only when these institutions fail that the people are thrown back on the ultimate rights of resistance and revolution, with all the violence and bloodshed that they may involve. In short, Locke's account is not meant to endorse a broad right to use force but, so far as possible, to make such force unnecessary.

Blackstone and the English Constitutional Tradition

Now let us turn to Sir William Blackstone's views on the right to arms. In his *Commentaries on the Laws of England,* Blackstone observes that this right of Englishmen is rooted in "the natural right of resistance and self-preservation, when the sanctions of society and laws are found insufficient to restrain the violence of oppression." [29]

This passage is crucial for those who argue that the Second Amendment was intended to protect an individual natural right to self-defense. According to Don Kates, "Blackstone placed the right to arms among 'the absolute rights of individuals at common law.' " "[U]nquestionably," Kates adds, "what Blackstone was referring to was individuals' rights to have and use personal arms for self-protection." [30] Similarly, Joyce Malcolm asserts that "Blackstone emphatically endorsed the view that keeping arms was necessary both for self-defense, 'the natural right of resistance and self preservation,' and 'to restrain the violence of oppression.' " She continues, "Blackstone's comments on this subject are of the utmost importance, since his work immediately became *the* great authority on English common law in both England and America." [31] Indeed, the case can be put even more forcefully. In this passage, Blackstone was describing a right that was protected by an article of the English Bill of Rights of 1689 [32]—a provision that in turn is a plausible antecedent of the Second Amendment. If Blackstone interpreted this English provision in individual rights terms, that would be important evidence that the Second Amendment should be read in the same way. [33]

Although this understanding of Blackstone is superficially attractive, a closer reading shows that it fundamentally misunderstands his position. In fact, Blackstone provides even less support for an individualist interpretation of the right to arms than does Locke.

Blackstone's discussion of the right to arms reads in full as follows:

> The fifth and last auxiliary right of the subject . . . is that of having arms for their defence suitable to their condition and degree, and such as are allowed by law. Which is also declared by the same statute 1 W. & M. st. 2. c. 2 [i.e., the Bill of Rights], and it is indeed, a public allowance under due restrictions, of the natural right of resistance and self-preservation, when the sanctions of society and laws are found insufficient to restrain the violence of oppression. [34]

In exploring this passage, let us begin with Kates's assertion that "Blackstone placed the right to arms among 'the absolute rights of individuals at common law.' "[35] I think it is fair to say that no one who reads Blackstone carefully could come to such a conclusion. It is true that Blackstone discusses the right to arms in a chapter entitled "Of the Absolute Rights of Individuals." As Blackstone makes perfectly clear, however, these consist of the following three articles: (1) the right to personal security, which "consists in a person's legal and uninterrupted enjoyment of his life, his limbs, his body, his health, and his reputation"; (2) the right to personal liberty or freedom of movement; and (3) the right to private property. In other words, Blackstone's "absolute rights" correspond to the classic natural rights of life, liberty, and property. The right to arms, on the other hand, is not an "absolute right" but is one of the "auxiliary subordinate rights of the subject"—a concept to which we shall return shortly.[36]

It is also important to observe that, in Blackstone's usage, "absolute rights" means something quite different than what the term would mean to us today. For Blackstone, absolute rights are those that pertain to the individual as such; they are rights that persons would enjoy even in a state of nature, before the formation of society. Such rights are contrasted with relative rights, which are those that arise from various social relationships. In designating certain rights as "absolute," however, Blackstone does not mean to suggest that they can never properly be restricted. On the contrary, he makes clear that these rights are subject to regulation to protect others and promote the common good.[37] Consistent with this principle, Blackstone notes that the right to arms is limited to "such as are allowed by law."[38]

Finally, we should note that (contrary to Kates's assertion) Blackstone nowhere suggests that the right to arms derives from "the common law."[39] Instead, this is a right that is secured by "the constitution," and in particular by the Bill of Rights.[40]

What is the nature of this right? Contrary to the position taken by Kates, Lund, and Malcolm, there is no reason to believe that Blackstone views it as encompassing an individual right to use arms for self-defense against private violence. Blackstone discusses the personal right to self-defense at three main points in the *Commentaries:* in connection with the right to life, with defense against tortious injury, and with the law of homicide. In none of these passages does he mention a right to possess or use arms for self-protection. The reasons for this omission are not difficult to discern in light of our previous discussion. Although Blackstone holds that individuals are naturally free to "act as [they] think fit, without any restraint or control, unless by the law of nature," he agrees with Locke that this natural liberty is self-defeating, undermining rather than securing individual self-preservation.

> For no man, that considers a moment, would wish to retain the absolute and un-
> controlled power of doing whatever he pleases: the consequence of which is,
> that every other man would also have the same power; and then there would be
> no security to individuals in any of the enjoyments of life.

For this reason, when individuals enter into society, they give up a portion of their natural liberty in exchange for protection under the law, and oblige themselves "to conform to those laws, which the community has thought proper to establish." Individuals do retain a right to defend themselves against imminent violence, for "[s]elf-defence . . . is justly called the primary law of nature," and "is not, neither can it be, in fact, taken away by the law of society." But this right is limited to "sudden and violent cases; when certain and immediate suffering would be the consequence of waiting for the assistance of the law." In all other cases, Blackstone holds that natural liberty is subject to regulation for the preservation of the society and its members.[41] As we have seen, the question of whether individuals should be permitted to own weapons would seem to fall within this general power of the legislature to regulate for the public good, rather than within the narrow exception for imminent self-defense.[42] Nothing in Blackstone's *Commentaries* suggests the contrary.

It appears, then, that Blackstone does not mention an inalienable right to arms for private self-defense because he does not recognize such a right.[43] This is entirely consonant with his general social and jurisprudential views. For Blackstone, human nature is fallen, and human beings are prone to violence and disorder in the absence of effective social constraints. Liberty cannot long exist in the state of nature, which is a "wild and savage" condition, but only within a strong legal and social order. Thus, in contrast to Locke, Blackstone emphasizes not the inalienability of natural rights, but the necessity for those rights to be regulated for the common good. Indeed, Blackstone does not regard even liberty of speech and press as inalienable rights.[44] Under these circumstances, it would be surprising if he considered the possession of arms to be such a right.

If Blackstone's right to arms is not an "absolute right of individuals," nor a right of personal self-defense, then how should it be understood? To answer this question, we must begin with his description of this right as an "auxiliary right." After outlining the three absolute rights, Blackstone remarks that those rights would be a "dead letter" if the constitution had taken no effective steps

> to secure their actual enjoyment. It has, therefore, established certain other aux-
> iliary subordinate rights of the subject, which serve principally as outworks or
> barriers, to protect and maintain inviolate the three great and primary rights, of
> personal security, personal liberty, and private property.

Blackstone proceeds to describe these auxiliary rights as follows:

1. The constitution, powers, and privileges of parliament. . . .
2. The limitation of the king's prerogative, by bounds, so certain and notorious, that it is impossible he should either mistake or legally exceed them without the consent of the people. . . . The former of these, keeps the legislative power in due health and vigour, so as to make it improbable that laws should be enacted destructive of general liberty: the latter is a guard upon the executive power, by restraining it from acting either beyond or in contradiction to the laws. . . .
3. A third subordinate right of every Englishman is that of applying to the courts of justice for redress of injuries. . . .
4. If there should happen any uncommon injury, or infringement of the rights before-mentioned, which the ordinary course of law is too defective to reach, there still remains a fourth subordinate right, appertaining to every individual, namely, the right of petitioning the king, or either house of parliament, for the redress of grievances.[45]

The list then concludes with the "fifth and last auxiliary right," the right of subjects to "hav[e] arms for their defence." When viewed in this context, it is clear that what Blackstone is referring to is not personal self-defense but defense against tyranny. That is what he means when he says that the right becomes important "when the sanctions of society and laws are found insufficient to restrain *the violence of oppression.*"[46]

In short, Blackstone follows Locke in recognizing a "natural right of resistance and self-preservation" against tyrannical rulers.[47] The question then arises as to the nature of this right: is it one that belongs to private individuals or to the people as a whole? Kates, Lund, and Malcolm seem to assume that, since it is described as a "natural right," it must be a right of individuals. Traditionally, however, natural rights could be predicated of collectivities as well as of individuals. For example, Locke declares that, under the fundamental natural "Law of *Self-Preservation,*" "the *Community*" as a whole has a right to defend itself against tyranny.[48] Likewise, while some of Blackstone's auxiliary rights are said to pertain "to every individual," others, such as the "constitution, powers, and privileges of parliament," are public rather than private in nature.[49] When Blackstone refers to the latter as "rights of the subject," then, he must be using "the subject" in a representative or collective sense, and not to refer to individuals as such.

Unfortunately, nothing in Blackstone's discussion of auxiliary rights sheds much light on how the right to resistance is to be understood. Yet he returns to the subject later in Book I, and there he makes his position crystal clear. The question is what may be done "when the contracts of society are in danger of dissolution, and the law proves too weak a defence against the violence of fraud or oppression"—language that echoes his earlier discussion. Here Blackstone rejects two contrary positions. The first is the absolutist doctrine of "unlimited passive obedience," which he derides as slavish and absurd. Yet he also rejects "the other extreme": a view that would "allow to every individual the right of determining [when resistance is appropriate], and of employing private force to resist even private oppression." This doctrine, Blackstone asserts, is

> productive of anarchy, and (in consequence) equally fatal to civil liberty as tyranny itself. For civil liberty, rightly understood, consists in protecting the rights of individuals by the united force of society: society cannot be maintained, and of course can exert no protection, without obedience to some sovereign power: and obedience is an empty name, if every individual has a right to decide how far he himself shall obey.

Instead, Blackstone holds that "resistance is justifiable" only "when the being of the state is endangered, and the public voice proclaims such resistance necessary."[50]

This position dovetails with Blackstone's broader constitutional theory. According to that view, government is founded on an "original contract between king and people," under which the latter promise allegiance and obedience while the former undertakes to protect his subjects. If the king should violate this contract, as James II was found to have done, then it is the people as a whole who are the injured party and who have a right to resist tyranny.[51]

In short, Blackstone's doctrine is not one of private resistance by individuals but of "national resistance by the people." And this in turn provides the key to understanding his view of the right to arms. As we have seen, Blackstone describes this right as simply "a public allowance" of the right to resist oppression.[52] If the right to resistance is one that essentially belongs to the people as a whole, then the same is true of the right to arms. To be sure, Blackstone does not discuss how such arms are to be held: whether by individuals or by the community (for example, in public stores belonging to the militia). But this would appear to be essentially a practical question. As a matter of principle, Blackstone's position is clear: the right to arms recognized by the English Bill of Rights is not intended to allow individuals to possess weapons for their own purposes, but rather to ensure that the people as a whole have the means to resist tyranny. This is a collective right and is subject to collective control. For this reason, there is no conflict between this right and the qualification, recognized by the Bill of Rights as well as by Blackstone, that the right may be regulated by law.[53] Because the right is one that belongs to the people as such, they have the authority to regulate and control that right through their representatives in parliament.

In conclusion, a close reading of Blackstone's *Commentaries* reveals that his view is similar to Locke's.[54] Blackstone does not recognize an inalienable right to have arms for private self-defense, and he understands the right to resistance in collective rather than individual terms. If, as Malcolm argues, Blackstone had a profound influence on the American conception of the right to arms, then here is powerful evidence against—rather than for—the individual rights interpretation of the Second Amendment.

THE MILITIA AND THE RIGHT TO ARMS IN THE EARLY AMERICAN REPUBLIC

After declaring independence from Great Britain, Americans set about the task of drafting constitutions and declarations of rights for their new state governments.[55] These documents provide an invaluable window into American political thought during the period, and shed important light on the meaning of the Second Amendment.

The Right to Arms

How was the right to arms understood in post-Revolutionary America? We can attain great insight on this point by exploring the 1780 Massachusetts Constitution. This document, which was drafted by John Adams, contains the most carefully written of all the state declarations of rights and constitutes one of the best statements "of the fundamental rights of Americans at the end of the Revolutionary period."[56]

In its preamble, the Massachusetts Constitution sets forth the relationship between society and its members. The "people" or "the body-politic" are "formed by a voluntary association of individuals," who come together through "a social compact." What is most remarkable is that, having distinguished between the "people" and "the individuals who compose it," the document then uses these terms in a consistent way throughout. This makes it possible to discern with great clarity how the various rights were understood, and whether they were viewed in individual or collective terms.

The following are some examples of provisions that ascribe rights to "individuals," or to related terms such as "men," "persons," or "subjects":[57]

> Art. I.—ALL MEN are born free and equal, and have certain natural, essential, and unalienable rights; among which may be reckoned the right of enjoying and defending their lives and liberties; that of acquiring, possessing, and protecting property; in fine, that of seeking and obtaining their safety and happiness.

II.— ... (N)O SUBJECT shall be hurt, molested, or restrained, in his person, liberty, or estate, for worshipping God in the manner and season most agreeable to the dictates of his own conscience. . . .

X.—EACH INDIVIDUAL OF THE SOCIETY has a right to be protected by it in the enjoyment of his life, liberty and property, according to standing laws. . . .

XII.— ... (N)O SUBJECT shall be arrested, imprisoned, despoiled, or deprived of his property, immunities, or privileges, put out of the protection of the law, exiled or deprived of his life, liberty, or estate, but by the judgment of his peers, or the law of the land.

XIV.—EVERY SUBJECT has a right to be secure from all unreasonable searches and seizures of his person, his houses, his papers, and all his possessions. . . .

On the other hand, these are some of the passages relating to the rights to "the people":

IV.—*The people* of this commonwealth have the sole and exclusive right of governing themselves as a free, sovereign, and independent State. . . .

V.—All power residing originally in *the people* and being derived from them, the several magistrates and officers of the government vested with authority, whether legislative, executive, or judicial, are their substitutes and agents, and are at all times accountable to them.

VII.—Government is instituted for the common good, for the protection, safety, prosperity, and happiness of *the people* . . . ; therefore *the people* alone have an incontestable, unalienable, and indefeasible right to institute government, and to reform, alter, or totally change the same when their protection, safety, prosperity, and happiness require it.

VIII.—In order to prevent those who are vested with authority from becoming oppressors, *the people* have a right at such periods and in such manner as they shall establish by their frame of government, to cause their public officers to return to private life; and to fill up vacant places by certain and regular elections and appointments.

In this way, the Massachusetts declaration draws a clear and uniform distinction between the rights that belong to individuals and those that belong to the people as a whole. This distinction is followed so carefully that it is observed even when both sorts of rights are implicated. Thus, Article XXIX declares that the independence of the judiciary is essential "for the security of the rights of the people, and of every citizen."

Article XVII of the Massachusetts declaration reads as follows:

The people have a right to keep and to bear arms for the common defence. And as, in time of peace, armies are dangerous to liberty, they ought not to be maintained without the consent of the legislature; and the military shall always be held in an exact subordination to the civil authority and shall be governed by it.

In view of the declaration's careful usage, there can be no question that the "right to keep and bear arms" that it recognizes is one that belongs not to private individuals but to the people in their collective capacity. This is made even more clear by the fact that the right is to bear arms "for the common defence," as well as by the overall concern of the provision: to control the military force of the community and guard against the danger of military tyranny.[58]

I have chosen to focus on the Massachusetts Constitution because of the precision of its language, which strongly illuminates the nature of the rights that it contains. Yet the same distinction between "individuals" (or cognate terms) and "the people" is also generally, although not invariably, observed in the other post-Revolutionary state declarations of rights. When these documents recognize a right to bear arms, they always describe it as a right of "the people," rather than of every "individual" or "man."[59] This is strong evidence that the right was originally understood in collective terms.

The Militia

How did the people exercise their collective right to bear arms? The answer is through the militia. Indeed, most of the state constitutions speak not of a right to bear arms but rather of the importance of a citizen militia.[60] The model for these provisions was established by section 13 of the Virginia Bill of Rights, which asserted:

> That a well-regulated militia, composed of the body of the people, trained to arms, is the proper, natural, and safe defence of a free State; that standing armies, in time of peace, should be avoided, as dangerous to liberty; and that in all cases the military should be under strict subordination to, and governed by, the civil power.

It should be observed that, apart from the first clause, this provision is substantially identical to that contained in the Massachusetts Declaration. In fact, it is not clear that there was any essential difference in meaning between the two versions. Within the militia, the people had a right to bear arms, and they exercised this right through the militia. It seems likely that, for late-eighteenth-century Americans, assertions of the importance of the militia and of the people's right to bear arms were merely two different ways of saying the same thing.

Although never mentioned by Locke, the militia held an important place in eighteenth-century American political thought, with its characteristic synthesis of liberalism and civic republicanism. One way to understand the idea of the militia is through a comparison with the distribution of political authority in the state. According to social contract theory, all political power initially belongs to the community at large. Although it has the right to retain that power, the community generally chooses to delegate it to a particular government. This government need not be democratic in form: nothing in natural rights theory precludes the community from establishing a monarchy, an aristocracy, or some other form of government.[61] As the republican tradition taught, however, if the people were wise, they would not alienate all of their power to the government but would retain as much as possible for themselves. By the time of the Revolution, this had become an article of political faith for Americans.

The idea of a citizen militia can be understood in similar terms. According to Locke, when individuals enter into society, they not only give up the broad right to use force for self-preservation; they also promise to use their "natural force" to assist the community in enforcing the laws and defending against foreign attack. In this way, the community acquires a power to direct the force of all its members. This power is subsequently entrusted to the government. But just as there is a danger that the government will abuse its political authority, so also is there a danger that it will misuse its control over the force of the community by invading the rights of citizens and tyrannizing over them.[62]

For this reason, liberal republicans concluded that it was essential to impose strict constraints on the military power of government. In particular, the community should rely, to the extent possible, not on a regular army but on a militia composed of "the body of the people."[63] Under this regime, the people would retain as much military power as they could in their own hands.[64] This approach, it was believed, would protect liberty in two important ways. First, the existence of a well-armed, trained, and disciplined militia would minimize the need to establish a standing army—an institution that all too easily could come to have a separate interest from that of the people and be made an instrument of tyranny.[65] By contrast, militia members were citizens first and soldiers second; there was little reason to fear that they would turn their arms against themselves, their families, and their neighbors.[66] Second, if the government did seek to tyrannize over the people, its forces would not be able to prevail (so it was hoped) against the united force of the community as embodied in the militia.[67]

This notion of a citizen militia represented an advance in natural rights theory in two respects. First, whereas Locke tended to view the people as an ultimate but dormant power existing outside the government, liberal republicanism integrated the people into the state through the militia, just as they were integrated also through republican political institutions.[68] In this way, liberty was made more secure. Second, if a danger of tyranny should arise, the militia provided an effective means through which the people could exercise their collective rights to resistance and revolution—rights that were affirmed by many of the state constitutions.[69] By contrast, while Locke and Blackstone recognized the people's right to resist tyranny, they were vague about how this could be done.

In these ways, the institution of the militia was intended both to make the people's liberty more secure and to provide a concrete, effective way in which to exercise their natural right to self-preservation in cases of necessity. This was the ideal that was embodied in the state constitutional provisions we have looked at, whether they were phrased in terms of the people's right to bear arms or the importance of the militia. On this reading, these provisions are fully consonant with a collective understanding of the right to arms.

An Examination of Some Evidence for the Individual Rights Interpretation

Before leaving this subject, we should consider two pieces of evidence that are often said to support a right to arms for individual self-defense. The first is Article XIII of the Pennsylvania Declaration of Rights, from 1776, which states that "the people have a right to bear arms for the defence of themselves and the state."[70] Unlike the other provisions we have considered, this one is ambiguous. The question is what the declaration means by "the defence of themselves." On one hand, as Malcolm and others contend, this language could be read to endorse a right to arms for personal self-defense.[71] On the other, "the defence of themselves" could be read to refer to the collective right of the people to defend themselves against internal disorder, external invasion, or governmental oppression.

Although the former possibility cannot be dismissed, a strong case can be made for the latter interpretation. First, as in the other state declarations, the Pennsylvania language on the right to arms appears in a provision that also condemns standing armies and asserts that the military must be strictly subordinate to the civil power.[72] This strongly suggests that the entire provision is concerned with the military power of the state, rather than with the rights of individuals to self-defense.

This interpretation finds further support in the broader context of the provision, the declaration as a whole. After declaring that "every member of the society hath a right to be protected in the enjoyment of life, liberty and property," Article VIII goes on to assert that every individual is therefore "bound to contribute his proportion towards the expence of that protection, and yield his personal service when necessary." The provision recognizes an exception to this principle in cases of religious objection: no "man who is conscientiously scrupulous of bearing arms, [can] be justly compelled thereto, if he will pay

[an] equivalent." In this way, Article VIII equates "bearing arms" with the "personal service" that is required of citizens—that is, with the Lockean duty to employ one's natural force to assist the government in enforcing the laws and protecting the community from attack. This strongly suggests that the declaration uses "bear arms" in a military sense, and that it is in this sense that "the people have a right to bear arms for the defence of themselves and the state." [73] Indeed, the first state constitutions never clearly use the term "bear arms" in any other sense. [74]

There is no persuasive reason, then, to believe that the meaning of Article XIII of the Pennsylvania declaration was substantially different from that of the other declarations we have seen. If, however, that provision is read to encompass a right to arms for individual self-defense, this was a distinctly minority position among the states. [75] And while this language appears in a constitutional amendment recommended by a minority of the ratifying Pennsylvania Convention, it does not appear in the amendments proposed by the majority of any state convention, nor in any version of the Second Amendment as it evolved in the First Congress. [76] Therefore, even if the Pennsylvania provision bore an individual rights meaning, there is little reason to believe that this meaning was incorporated in the Second Amendment.

Finally, recognizing that most state declarations did not expressly recognize an individual right to arms, Malcolm argues that such a right was implicit in other provisions of the state declarations. For example, the first article of the Massachusetts declaration asserted:

> All men are born free and equal, and have certain natural, essential, and unalienable rights; among which may be reckoned the right of enjoying and *defending* their lives and liberties; that of acquiring, possessing, and *protecting* property; in fine, that of seeking and obtaining their safety and happiness.

"It is difficult," Malcolm observes, "to see how the right to defend one's life could be fully exercised if citizens were deprived of the right to be armed." She concludes that "the individual's right to be armed, [even] where not specifically mentioned, is unmistakably assumed." [77]

This argument is unconvincing. To begin with, only a handful of the state declarations refer to a right of "defending their lives and liberties." [78] Most of the declarations contain *neither* this right *nor* the Pennsylvania language that supposedly recognizes an individual right to "bear arms." [79] Moreover, the language will not bear the interpretive weight that Malcolm places on it. When a state declaration speaks of an "unalienable right" to defend life and liberty, that cannot mean that individuals retain as sweeping a right to use force against others as they possess in the state of nature, for such a right would be inconsistent with the very existence of civil society. According to Locke, an individual in the state of nature who judges another to pose an ongoing threat to his life has a right to destroy the other—a right that is unbounded by time or place. This conflict is what Locke calls the state of war. "To avoid this State of War," Locke explains, "(. . . wherein every the least difference is apt to end, where there is no Authority to decide between the Contenders) is one great *reason of Mens putting themselves into Society,* and quitting the State of Nature." Within civil society, the right to use force in self-defense is a narrow one, and does not necessarily include a right to arms.[80] When the opening articles of the Pennsylvania and Massachusetts declarations speak of an inalienable right to defend life, one cannot assume that they mean more than this.[81] Therefore, even if we view these articles solely in doctrinal terms, they do not endorse an individual right to arms.

It would be a mistake, however, to approach these articles solely on a doctrinal level. For their primary purpose is not to secure a specific set of legal rights, but rather to proclaim the natural freedom and equality of individuals and to articulate the fundamental objectives they seek to attain when they establish society and government. Of course, these objectives include defending and protecting their lives, liberties, and properties. But the main way in which individuals do so is not through the use of private force but through the formation of a social order that will protect their rights under the law. It is in this way, above all, that individuals are capable of "seeking and obtaining their safety and happiness."[82] In other words, Article I should be read together with the rest of the Massachusetts Constitution, and in particular with the statement that "[e]ach individual of the society has a right to be protected by it in the enjoyment of his life, liberty and property, according to standing laws."[83]

In short, there is little reason to believe that an individual right to arms was implicit in the language of the few state declarations that mentioned a natural right of "defending life and liberty." Even if there were, however, this would do nothing to advance the case for an individualist reading of the Second Amendment. The "defending life and liberty" language appears in none of the amendments proposed by the state ratifying conventions, nor does it appear in the amendments introduced by Madison in the First Congress. Instead, these proposals speak of "the enjoyment of life and liberty."[84] And as finally adopted, of course, the Bill of Rights contains no provision of the kind. Thus if the individual right to arms is to be found in the "defending life" language, as Malcolm suggests, one can conclude only that this right was not made a part of the federal Constitution.

THE RATIFICATION DEBATE AND THE ADOPTION
OF THE SECOND AMENDMENT

In late-eighteenth-century America, then, the right to bear arms was generally understood to be a collective right that was exercised through a citizen militia. This is the right that was secured by the Second Amendment.

The Debate over the Constitution

When the federal Constitution was proposed in 1787, it was immediately attacked for creating too powerful a national government. Two objections are of particular relevance for our purposes. First, anti-Federalists objected that Congress would have the power to raise a standing army that could be used to destroy public liberty and erect a military despotism.[85] Second, they criticized the provisions of Article I that empowered Congress to provide for organizing and calling forth the militia in order "to execute the Laws of the Union, suppress Insurrections and repel Invasions."[86]

In response, Federalists argued that, far from being a defect in the Constitution, Congress' powers regarding the militia were favorable to liberty, for the best way to avoid the need for a standing army was to have an effective militia.[87] A small army, they argued, might be necessary to defend the country from insurrection or attack.[88] Yet they ridiculed the notion that, within the democratic system envisioned by the Constitution, there was reason to fear the establishment of a military tyranny. As Madison put it in *Federalist #46*:

> That the people and the States should, for a sufficient period of time, elect an uninterrupted succession of men ready to betray both; that the traitors should, throughout this period, uniformily and systematically pursue some fixed plan for the extension of the military establishment; that the governments and people of the States should silently and patiently behold the gathering storm, and continue to supply the materials, until it should be prepared to burst on their own heads, must appear to every one more like the incoherent dreams of a delirious jealousy, or the misjudged exaggerations of a counterfeit zeal, than like the sober apprehensions of genuine patriotism.[89]

Madison added that, even if one were to make such an "[e]xtravagant . . . supposition," the largest standing army that Congress would be able to raise would be no match for "a militia amounting to near half a million of citizens with arms in their hands, officered by men chosen from among themselves, fighting for their common liberties, and united and conducted by governments possessing their affections and confidence."[90] Of course, this statement reflects precisely the same view as the state declarations of rights: it portrays the people as possessing and using arms as members of a citizen militia, for the purpose of collective self-defense.[91]

Another anti-Federalist objection proved more difficult to meet. Article I, section 8, clause 16, empowered Congress to

> provide for organizing, arming, and disciplining, the Militia, and for governing such Part of them as may be employed in the Service of the United States, reserving to the States respectively, the Appointment of the Officers, and the Authority of training the Militia according to the discipline prescribed by Congress.

But suppose, asked George Mason and Patrick Henry in the ratifying Virginia Convention, that "the general government should neglect to arm and discipline the militia?" Could not Congress by that method effectively disarm and destroy the state militias?[92] In response, Madison denied that the Constitution, in "giving the general government the power of arming the militia, takes it away from the state governments. The power is concurrent, and not exclusive." Yet this was hardly the only reasonable interpretation, and it failed to reassure Mason and Henry, who demanded that the Constitution be amended to make clear that the states retained a power to arm the militia.[93]

The Adoption of the Second Amendment

Presumably, it was concerns of this sort that led the Virginia convention to propose the following amendment to the Constitution:

> That the people have a right to keep and bear arms; that a well regulated Militia composed of the body of the people trained to arms is the proper, natural and safe defence of a free State. That standing armies in time of peace are dangerous to liberty, and therefore ought to be avoided, as far as the circumstances and protection of the Community will admit; and that in all cases the military should be under strict subordination to and governed by the Civil power.

This recommendation, which was soon endorsed by the ratifying conventions of New York and North Carolina, became the starting point for the Second Amendment.[94] When Madison introduced his draft of the Bill of Rights in the First Congress in June 1789, he included the following amendment:

> The right of the people to keep and bear arms shall not be infringed; a well armed, and well regulated militia being the best security of a free country: but no person religiously scrupulous of bearing arms, shall be compelled to render military service in person.

As adopted by the House of Representatives, the provision read:

A well regulated militia, composed of the body of the People, being the best security of a free State, the right of the People to keep and bear arms, shall not be
infringed, but no one religiously scrupulous of bearing arms, shall be compelled
to render military service in person.

The Amendment received its final form in the Senate, where it was altered
to read:

A well regulated militia, being necessary to the security of a free State, the right
of the people to keep and bear arms, shall not be infringed.[95]

What light does this legislative history shed on the meaning of the Second
Amendment? To begin with, it is clear that the language proposed by the Virginia, New York, and North Carolina conventions was drawn from the state
declarations of rights. As we have seen, those declarations recognized the
collective right of the people to bear arms through the militia. This is strong
evidence that the Second Amendment was meant to be understood in the
same way.

This interpretation finds further support in the phraseology of the various
drafts of the amendment. First, in exempting conscientious objectors, Madison's draft and the House version both equate "bear[ing] arms" with "render[ing] military service in person." The clear implication is that the right to
"bear arms" relates to service in the militia. Second, both the Virginia proposal
and the House version refer to a militia "composed of the body of the people."
This usage suggests that "the people" who have a "right to keep and bear
arms" are the same as "the body of the people trained to arms" that constitutes
the militia. As in the state declarations of rights, references to the militia and to
the people's right to bear arms appear to be two different ways of saying the
same thing.[96] Nor is this usage an uncommon one: in the Virginia convention,
Madison himself is on record as using "the people" and "the militia" synony-
mously.[97]

In these ways, the development of the constitutional text lends further support to a collective rights interpretation. As for the recorded debates over the
amendment in the First Congress, they are rather brief and unhelpful, focusing
largely on the question of religious exemption from military service.[98] They
do, however, tend to confirm the view that the amendment was concerned with
the institution of the militia and the right to bear arms in that context.[99] On the
other hand, the debates give no indication that the amendment was meant to
protect an individual right to possess arms for one's own purposes, or outside
the context of the militia.[100]

The Meaning and Purposes of the Second Amendment

The Second Amendment, then, recognizes the collective right of the people to keep and bear arms through a civic militia. One virtue of this interpretation is that it is able to read the language of the amendment as a coherent whole. By contrast, supporters of the individual rights interpretation are forced to argue that the amendment "was meant to accomplish two distinct goals": to secure an individual right to arms and to recognize the importance of the militia.[101] On the view advanced here, the amendment does not consist of two disparate parts, but expresses a single unified principle, protecting a right of the people as a whole.

What purposes was this constitutional right meant to serve? First, it was clearly meant to reaffirm the importance of the militia and to ensure that the federal government could not disarm it. In this way, the amendment sought to reduce the need for a standing army.[102]

A more difficult question is whether the amendment was intended to enable the people to resist the national government if it should become tyrannical. As already noted, many of the state constitutions recognized the rights of resistance and revolution, and some of the state ratifying conventions urged the adoption of amendments to reaffirm those rights.[103] In his June 8, 1789, speech, Madison proposed an amendment to declare "[t]hat the people have an indubitable, unalienable, and indefeasible right to reform or change their government, whenever it be found adverse or inadequate to the purposes of its institution."[104] Congress declined, however, to include such a provision in the Bill of Rights. As we have seen, Federalists regarded anti-Federalist fears of tyranny as "extravagant" and "far-fetched."[105] In the wake of Shays's Rebellion and other uprisings, Federalists were more concerned about the danger of unlawful insurrections and insisted that the government must have adequate power to suppress them.[106] Nonetheless, even Federalists recognized in principle that the federal government might become tyrannical, and that in such a case the people would have a natural right of resistance—a right that they could exercise most effectively through the state militias.[107] On the whole, it seems reasonable to conclude that while the Second Amendment itself does not recognize a right of resistance, it was intended to protect an institution, the militia, through which the people could exercise that right if necessary.[108]

In this way, the amendment indirectly secured the collective right to self-preservation discussed by both Locke and Blackstone. On the other hand, there is very little reason to believe that the amendment was intended to protect an individual right to arms for personal self-defense or other purposes. That is not to say, of course, that the possession of arms for these purposes necessarily was unlawful at the time. As this essay has shown, however, the natural rights tradition provided little support for an inalienable individual right to arms, and there is no persuasive evidence that the Second Amendment was intended to secure such a right. Indeed, there was no reason to address this issue in a federal bill of rights: the question of whether and to what extent individuals should be allowed to have weapons for private purposes was properly a matter for the states, through the exercise of their police powers.[109]

It is sometimes argued that even if Second Amendment rights applied only within the militia, the arms themselves were to be provided and owned by individuals.[110] It is true that this was a traditional method of arming the militia, an approach that can be traced from medieval England through the militia laws of the American colonies.[111] By the time of the American Revolution, however, this approach had begun to give way to the more modern view that arming the militia was a public responsibility. In the Articles of Confederation, for example, each state engaged to "always keep up a well regulated and disciplined militia, sufficiently armed and accoutred, and [to] provide and constantly have ready for use, in public stores, . . . a proper quantity of arms, ammunition and camp equipage."[112]

Public provision of arms was not merely an ideal; in post-Revolutionary America it was a necessity. As the historian Michael Bellesiles has shown, the new nation suffered from a desperate shortage of firearms, and even most of the militia lacked such arms.[113] Under these conditions, it was wholly impractical to expect individuals to acquire weapons on their own; if the militia was to be armed, it could only be through governmental action.[114] As Jack Rakove has observed, the Federalists and anti-Federalists were in complete accord on this point; their disagreement focused on whether the states or the federal government should have the greatest authority in this area.[115]

That is not to say, however, that the Second Amendment mandated that arms be provided or owned by the public rather than by individuals. The object of the amendment was to ensure that the national government would not *disarm* the militia—not to specify how the militia's arms should be provided, how they should be held, or who should own them. These matters were left to be settled by militia laws at the state and federal levels.[116] Thus, it is not true that the Second Amendment established an individual right to own arms for militia purposes.

Let us conclude by considering a final objection to the thesis that the Second Amendment right was intended to apply only within the context of the militia. Blackstone associated the right to arms with the collective right to resist tyranny, but he did not expressly connect those rights with a citizen militia.[117] Is it possible that the Second Amendment protects a right to arms not merely within the militia but also for purposes of collective resistance outside that context? There is good reason to be skeptical of such an interpretation. As we have seen, the right to resistance was one that belonged to the people *collectively*. If the people lack effective institutions through which to exercise this right, they can do so only in an informal, unorganized way. If, however, the people have institutions through which to formulate and work their will, including representative government and a citizen militia, then it is natural for the collective right to resistance to be exercised through those channels.[118] Not only is this the most legitimate course, it is also the most effective one, for as both Federalists and anti-Federalists recognized, the unorganized people stand little chance of prevailing against a standing army.[119] At the same time that a right to arms for unorganized resistance has much less value, it also poses greater dangers, since it might well facilitate unlawful insurrections, something that was of great concern during the founding period.[120]

For all of these reasons, it cannot be merely assumed that those who adopted the Bill of Rights desired to recognize a right to arms for unorganized resistance and revolution. To determine whether they did in fact recognize such a right, we must look to the language of the amendment itself. As I have argued, that language is most reasonably construed to secure a right to arms within the context of a "well regulated Militia."

Finally, even if the right to arms for collective resistance was not limited to the militia, that should not place the right beyond the bounds of regulation. As a right that would belong to individuals as members of the people as a whole, the right would be subject to collective control and discipline. Otherwise, the situation that would be created would be the very antithesis of the "well regulated Militia," which it is the stated purpose of the amendment to promote. Moreover, even on this interpretation, the legislature would retain the power to regulate any possession or use of arms that is unrelated to the purpose of collective self-defense.

CONCLUSION

In common with Locke and Blackstone, eighteenth-century Americans believed that the fundamental law of nature was the preservation of mankind. This was a goal that could not be achieved by relying on private force, but only through the united force of the community. Americans further believed that, in a republican government, the people should retain as much control over this force as possible. In this way, they could avoid the dangers posed by a standing army and would also be in a position to resist the government if it should become tyrannical. These functions were to be performed through a well-regulated militia. It was in this context that the people had a right to bear arms, and it was this right that the Second Amendment was meant to protect.

What light does this history shed on how the Second Amendment should be understood today? The idea of a universal civic militia seems very remote from the conditions of modern warfare. And we no longer rely on such a militia to protect us from tyranny. This should not be a subject of regret. Locke, Blackstone, and the American founders regarded armed revolution as a last resort. It meant the breakdown of the constitutional order and a return to the state of war, in which disputes could be resolved only through force. Instead, the founders sought to prevent tyranny primarily through such institutions as representative government, the separation of powers, an independent judiciary, and constitutional protections for individual rights. These institutions have worked so well that the notion of armed revolution has become anachronistic. This is a sign of strength, not weakness, in our constitutional system. In short, the right to arms has evolved from an "auxiliary right" [121] to an archaic one.

That is not necessarily to say that a citizen militia could not be revived.[122] But that can be done only by the people themselves, through their representatives in the state and federal governments. The right secured by the Second Amendment is a collective one, which can be asserted only by the people as a whole. This cannot be done by judicial fiat, any more than the courts are capable of creating other basic social and political institutions. If the Supreme Court were to read an individual right to arms into the Second Amendment, the result would be precisely the opposite of what the founders intended: to entrust the use and regulation of force to the community as a whole.

8: To Hold and Bear Arms: The English Perspective

Lois G. Schwoerer*

For the last quarter of the twentieth century, the Second Amendment to the U.S. Constitution has attracted increasing attention from the general public, legal commentators, and historians of colonial and early national American history. As incidents of gun violence have multiplied, and the public has become polarized into groups that favor gun control versus those who believe in a constitutional right of the individual to own guns, academics have enlarged their efforts to discover exactly what the intentions of our forefathers were in writing the Second Amendment and precisely what that awkwardly worded amendment meant. Interest in the English background to the Second Amendment was marginal for a time, but it has grown as the debate has hardened. In the 1970s and '80s several historians and legal commentators wrote about the English origins of the Second Amendment, but their essays met largely with indifference or criticism.[1]

Then, in 1994, Joyce Lee Malcolm, an American professor specializing in English history who teaches at Bentley College in Massachusetts, recast and enlarged her early work into a book entitled *To Keep and Bear Arms: The Origins of an Anglo-American Right,* which Harvard University Press published.[2] In this book Malcolm presented three major ideas: one, that the medieval English duty of service in the militia and in the *posse comitatus,* imposed theoretically on all males between the ages of sixteen and sixty, was transformed at the time of England's Glorious Revolution in 1688–89 into an individual right to keep and bear arms. She maintained that Article VII of the Declaration of Rights, 1689 (better known as the Bill of Rights, its statutory form), secured that right, writing unguardedly that the convention—that is, the irregularly elected body that drew up the Declaration of Rights—"came down squarely, and exclusively, in favour of an individual right to have arms for self-defence" (pp. 119–120). Two, to explain the undeniable restrictions on the possession of arms in Article VII, Malcolm declared that the restrictions were not really intended and that eighteenth-century legislation, court interpretation, and learned comment clarified the intended meaning of the arms article and that, by the end of the century, it was generally agreed that all Protestants had the right to arms (pp. 123, 128, 129, 134, 138). Three, turning to colonial America, Malcolm asserted that Article VII was an English legacy that influenced the

American drafters of the Second Amendment, who, however, broadened the legacy, sweeping aside "limitations" upon the individual right to possess arms (pp. 151, 153, 161, 162, 163 162). In brief concluding remarks, Professor Malcolm commented on the fate of Article VII in the next centuries, regretting that, although many people wanted to reaffirm it, it was "gently . . . teased from public use" leaving the British people exposed to danger (pp. 165, 176). This provocative and confidently written book provoked great interest and warm approval. At the present time, *To Keep and Bear Arms* plays an important role in discussions of the meaning of the Second Amendment. My essay, however, contests its thesis, attempts to show why it is unacceptable, and offers a reading of the evidence and of the nature of late-seventeenth-century and eighteenth-century English society and thought that is different from that of Professor Malcolm.

To dissent from Malcolm's interpretation, some might say, is foolhardy. After all, her book was enthusiastically received by American historians, legal commentators, and the gun community.[3] Lengthy reviews, warmly praising it, poured from American law journals, including those of the highest reputation. Her argument has been described as "irrefutable," her research in political and legal history as "meticulous," her book as a "foundational text" of the so-called standard modelers.[4] Predictably, the National Rifle Association promoted the book, and reviews in its journal were especially enthusiastic.[5] Less predictably, indeed rather surprisingly, the book found favor with the bench: Supreme Court Justice Anthony Scalia described it as "an excellent study," and Judge Samuel Cummings of the Fifth Circuit Court in Texas, famous for his ruling in the *U.S. vs. Emerson* case, cited Malcolm's book in asserting that the right to bear arms was a legacy of the English Bill of Rights.[6] It has been noted that no scholar has challenged Malcolm in print.[7] That is, strictly speaking, not true, but it is true that, of the formal published reviews, only two—one of them by me—expressed reservations about the thesis and the scholarship,[8] and just two other historians have negatively criticized Malcolm's study in print.[9] In short, Malcolm's thesis has been widely accepted; in some circles it enjoys the status of dogma respecting the English origins of the Second Amendment.

Professor Malcolm asserts that she is a historian, not an advocate, and that she is asking only for a "decent respect" for the past (p. 177). I too lay claim to the high calling of historian and, with Malcolm, believe that knowledge of history is of great value deserving of "decent respect" and more. I suspect that all historians would agree that it is no simple matter to research some historical problem or other, build one's understanding of it on verifiable sources, and present one's account and interpretation with such clarity, grace, and unambiguous evidence as to convince and delight the reader. Historians understand, as students and lay persons sometimes forget, that evidence does not always say the same thing to everyone; different people of good will may interpret it differently. It does not follow, however, that every interpretation is as accurate as every other one. As Michael Dorf remarks in his essay in this collection, "In the end, a satisfying interpretation is not so much one that earns the highest composite score on the relevant factors, nor even one that prevails in a trumping category, but one that best hangs together." [10]

In my view, an issue is more likely to yield its meaning when the words used are dissected in terms of their contemporary signification, when the political, ideological, and socioeconomic context is analyzed, the persons playing a role in it are examined, and the evidence is contemporary and verifiable. [11] These steps are especially important when the evidence is not as full as one would wish, as is the case with the passage of the Declaration of Rights. Virtually unchallenged, Malcolm's thesis has become received wisdom through the circularity of positive comment. To challenge that thesis by offering a different interpretation will, I hope, clarify not only the intellectual and constitutional antecedents but also cast some light on the meaning of the much-disputed Second Amendment to our Constitution.

I

Professor Malcolm's statement and practice suggest that she is an originalist; in other words, she believes in the overriding importance of the original meaning of the English and American Bill of Rights (p. 176 and especially chapter 7). I will follow her in this by presenting my understanding of the drafters' intentions and the resultant meaning of Article VII of the Declaration/Bill of Rights, 1689. [12] It was a tactical victory for the supporters of a claim of rights that a list of thirteen rights was included in the Declaration of Rights along with the offer of the throne to Prince William and Princess Mary of Orange and the other terms of the settlement. [13] To underscore its importance, the Declaration of Rights was carried in a magnificent procession on February 13, 1689 from Westminster Hall to the Banqueting Hall and presented to Prince William and Princess Mary in an elaborate ceremony, events later memorialized in prints. [14] In December 1689, the declaration was transformed into a statute, known to this day as the Bill of Rights, a legal process that endowed all its provisions with statutory authority. The fact that Article VII was a part of the document that presented the terms settling the revolutionary crisis no doubt elevated its political importance, and the fact that the Declaration of Rights was transformed into a statute, of course, gave all the articles statutory authority.

As one might expect, the Declaration of Rights took some days to draft, and over a two week period the entire document, including Article VII, underwent significant amendment. The process began on January 29, 1689, when Anthony Cary, Lord Falkland, a Tory, urged the House of Commons not to think about filling the throne until they had decided "what power . . . to give the Crown . . . and what not." [15] In ways suggestive of the politics that surrounded the passage of the American Bill of Rights, Falkland's initiative concealed a Tory effort to delay a decision on filling the throne by embarrassing and deflecting the attention of Whigs who might be expected to agree to the idea of a statement of rights. [16] Following a lengthy debate in which objections were aired [17] and grievances canvassed, the House concurred with Falkland's proposal and appointed a thirty-nine-member committee, [18] the "Rights Committee," which was dominated by Whig members, to prepare a report. Prominent among the many grievances mentioned in debate were a standing army in peacetime without parliament's consent and the use of the militia (under the command of the king) to disarm and imprison men without cause. Members of the House of Commons, who for years had harangued against these issues, came forward. For example, Sir Richard Temple declared that it was essential to "provide against a standing army without consent of parliament" in peacetime. [19] Serjeant John Maynard denounced the Militia Act and bitterly complained that it was "An abominable thing is disarm the nation, to set up a standing army." [20] Amplifying the point, Hugh Boscawen said, "The Militia, under pretence of persons disturbing the government, disarmed and imprisoned men without cause. I myself was so dealt with." [21]

But no one urged in this or any other debate that the individual had a right to bear arms. Professor Malcolm argues to the contrary, basing her view on elliptically reported comments by The Honorable Heneage Finch, a Tory, in the debate on January 28, 1689. According to notes taken by John Somers (used by Malcolm), Finch said: "The constitution being limited there is a good foundation for defensive arms—It has given us right to demand full and ample security." [22] On those grounds Malcolm asserted that Finch "pressed" the "need for the private possession of weapons to restrain the Crown" (p. 116). In my judgment, her reading of these words is unacceptable. Three separate accounts of this debate have survived: one is by Somers; a second is by Anchitell Grey, who recorded parliamentary debates from 1667 to 1694; and a third is by an anonymous compiler of the debate of January 28. All three record that Finch, a former solicitor-general, was discussing the title to the throne, the subject of the January 28 debate. Focusing on the legal complexities of the vacancy of the throne caused by James II's flight, he was asking members to consider whether the flight was a demise, an abdication, or a desertion. [23] Insisting that he was not excusing James II, Finch declared (in Grey, *Debates*) that he looked with horror on the "invasion of our Religion and Properties," and insisted (according to the anonymous compiler) that he "own[ed] that [King James's] violations were very great and that the taking up arms [against him] was necessary."[24] The compiler's account makes clear that the words "defensive arms" in Somers's "Notes" referred to recent engagements against the army of James II. Finch did not mention, much less press for, an individual right to bear arms. His purpose in the debate, as the three records show, was to urge the case for a regency. It is impermissible, I submit, to interpret Finch's remark as favoring the right of the individual to bear arms. I make the point, for it shows that the right to arms was not regarded as significant enough to be named in the January 29 debate, when grievances and rights were discussed.

On February 2, 1689, the committee presented its report, known as the "Heads of Grievances."[25] The report contained twenty-eight Heads,[26] three of which are pertinent to this discussion. One Head (number 5) declared that "the Acts concerning the Militia are grievous to the Subject." Another (number 6) held that the "raising or keeping a Standing Army within this Kingdom in time of Peace, unless it be with the Consent of Parliament, is against Law." The third (number 7) declared that "it is necessary for the public Safety, that the Subjects, which are Protestants, should provide and keep Arms for their common Defence; and that the arms which have been seized, and taken from them be restored." These military issues—the militia, the standing army, and, mentioned for the first time, provision for the common defense—were clearly important to members of the Rights Committee, for no other topic was addressed in three separate Heads.

Where did the idea of specifying a right of Protestant subjects to possess arms for the common defense come from? The right was not a component of an intellectual tradition, as was the anti-army prejudice and the pro-militia sentiment. The Renaissance heritage, known to all educated men through the works of Erasmus and Sir Thomas More, satirized and condemned war and professional soldiers and favored a system of citizen defense. Machiavelli argued that the military threatens a people's liberty and that in a free state the citizen militia should serve as the armed force; citizens should be armed and trained for service in the militia. James Harrington, the English political theorist, wrote in great detail about military affairs in his *The Commonwealth of Oceana* (1656), which influenced other writers, such as Henry Neville.[27] Harrington worked out a complicated scheme for the militia, based on the wealth of the citizen.[28] An individual right to arms is not considered.

There was no ancient political or legal precedent for the right to arms. The Ancient Constitution[29] did not include it; it was not in Magna Charta, 1215, nor in the Petition of Right, 1628. No early English government would have considered giving the individual such a right. Through the old militia laws— Henry II's Assize of Arms (1181) and Edward I's Statute of Winchester (1285)—early governments had imposed a responsibility on subjects, according to their income, to be prepared to use arms against crime and in defense of community and nation. In 1558 a Tudor law instituted the new office of lord-lieutenant of the county (almost always a peer) and placed the command of the militia in his hands and those of his deputy-lieutenant (usually a member of the gentry). Although ultimate authority over the militia rested with the king and Privy council, actual supervision lay with the peerage and landed gentry.

Game laws[30] also restricted gun possession. The earliest Game Laws, beginning in the fourteenth century, limited hunting to persons of a certain wealth because, it was observed later by King James I, hunting was for gentlemen and "it is not fit that clowns should have these sports." As a twentieth-century historian remarked wittily, the laws "protected pheasants from peasants."[31] When guns came into use, they were added to the list of prohibited weapons. The Game Laws helped to protect the monarch and upper classes against insurrection while at the same time defending their sport and game. The Game Act of 1671 was the most exacting of all. For several reasons, it contained highly restrictive measures, among them limiting the right to have a gun to persons with a freehold of at least £100 a year or a long-term leasehold or copyhold of £150 per year or who were sons and heirs of persons of high degree.[32] This figure may be put in perspective by noting that the annual income of a laborer in the period ranged from £9 to £15 pounds; the average income of a temporal lord was estimated at £3,200.[33]

Other laws also restricted the holding of guns. A nagging fear of all early English governments was riot and social upheaval, and in the sixteenth century Tudor monarchs took steps to control guns. For example, an act of 1541, passed during the reign of Henry VIII, limited the ownership of crossbows and pistols shorter than a specific length to persons with an income of at least £100 and restricted their use by such persons. In 1553 a law of Edward VI required people who "shoot guns" to register with their local justice. In the early seventeenth century, in 1616, King James I issued a proclamation to ban the sale and the wearing and carrying of "Steelets, pocket daggers, picket Dagges and pistols" under pain of imprisonment and censure in the Court of Star Chamber. He described the weapons as "odious and noted Instruments of murther and mischiefe" and declared that he preferred to prevent rather than punish crime.[34] James I and Charles I vigorously enforced the Game Laws.

There were objections and resistance to the Game Laws, but not in terms of a demand for the *right* to possess arms. The right of the individual to bear arms was no part of the Militia Bill debate in 1641.[35] It did not figure in the proposals of the Levellers or Diggers, radicals who might be expected to demand a radical right.[36] Reformers at the time of the Exclusion Crisis (1678–83) did not mention individual arms as a right,[37] nor did radical Whigs.[38] Men who tried to influence members of the 1689 convention by printing their ideas did not refer to it.[39]

Once, during the frenzy of Exclusion, parliamentary critics of the government called for arming Protestants, not as a right but to protect the nation against Catholics. In the spring of 1679 an M.P. wanted a law empowering the people to arm against a king who wished to introduce Popery. Although no one spoke of a *right* of the individual to arm, members of the Commons did want to arm the people for the practical purpose of preserving the nation from Catholicism. Nothing came of this proposal, nor of an address to the king in December 1680 that asked for approval of an association bill, modeled on the Act of Association of 1581, which authorized the upper classes to unite for defense of themselves and the nation were Queen Elizabeth I to be murdered.[40]

The idea, then, of giving individual Protestants the right to provide and keep arms must have been a response to immediate experience. It almost certainly came from members who had received rough treatment at the hands of a zealous militia operating under the command of the king during the two previous reigns. They had already expressed outrage in debate (as we saw), and it is a near certainty that some among them translated their anger into a right of Protestants to provide and keep arms and into the demand that confiscated weapons should be returned. Their actions well illustrate the historicity of interest in specific rights; one historian has put it this way: "A right presupposes a claim; if the claim is not made, the question of a right does not arise."[41] In other words, claims to specific rights emerged out of practical political disputes, not abstract theoretical discussions. At this stage in the drafting process of Article VII, members claimed this right as necessary for the public safety and placed no qualifications on it. This right was drafted, apparently, with hotheaded speed out of deep rage over the treatment that some had endured. It was not a carefully thought out article, as the ready acceptance several days later of the lords' significant amendments indicates.

The authors, however, apparently chose some words with care. "Arms" was selected to describe the weapons that Protestants should "provide and keep for their common defense." In the seventeenth-century the word "arms" meant "firearms . . . such as guns and pistols"; "a defensive or offensive outfit for war."[42] I argue that M.P.s selected the word to signal that they were not providing a right to the individual to have a weapon for the protection of himself, his family, or his house. In a predominantly rural society that had no police force, many persons had some kind of weapon—a club, an ax, a gun, for those purposes. But a right to "arms"—to a "defensive or offensive outfit for war"— that would provide a collective or common defense did require constitutional authority. Further, the words "common defense" evoked the idea of a reformed militia composed of Protestant freeholders and officered by the local aristocracy. A militia had always been regarded as the "common defense" of the nation, an instrument that would provide for public safety but also counterbalance a professional standing army. Moreover, the use of the plural "Subjects, which are Protestants" suggests that the drafters were thinking of a collective, rather than an individual right. A reformed militia was their reference point.

The Prince of Orange's camp influenced the M.P.s Prince William objected to restricting the power of the crown; he wanted a shorter list of rights. So the committee separated the Heads of Grievances into two categories—grievances that required new law to redress and those that affirmed old law.[43] Head V, which demanded "repealing the acts concerning the Militia, and settling it anew," was given first place in the category of issues requiring new law. Head VI, which condemned standing armies in peacetime without the consent of parliament, was placed in the category of reaffirming old law, even though it, too, made new law.[44] Head VII was further revised (as will be discussed) and, although a new law emerged from the revisions, the article was also retained in the category of issues reaffirming old law. Placing Heads VI and VII in the category of reaffirming old law, when in fact they made new law, was not a unique move. As I have shown elsewhere, the House simply declared as old law what they wanted to be old law in a total of eight instances; nine instances, if Head VII is added.

Several further alterations were made to Article VII. First, the form of the verb was changed from *"should* provide and keep arms" to *"may* provide and keep Arms."[45] The change, as Malcolm believes, made "having arms a legal right." I disagree that it "shifted the emphasis away from the public duty to be armed and toward the keeping of arms solely as an individual right" (p. 118). Rather, I hypothesize that the change was made to satisfy the Prince of Orange, who objected to the idea that Protestants *"should* provide and keep Arms." Finally, the word "Subjects" remained in the plural, negating the idea that an individual right was intended.

Article VII now read: "That the Subjects, which are Protestants, may provide and keep Arms, for their common defense."

From February 9 through February 12 the House of Lords made substantive changes to the military articles. In the phrase "provide and keep arms for their common defense," the lords substituted the word "have" for "provide and keep" and deleted the word "common."[46] Malcolm and I agree that the House of Lords and the Prince of Orange regarded the word "provide" as suggesting too much "of preparation for popular rebellion" to be accepted (p. 119). But I dissent from Malcolm's view that, by dropping the word "common," the peers "claimed for the individual a right to be armed" (p. 119). Rather, the word "common" conveyed the idea of a national preparation for the kingdom's defense—as in a reformed militia—a notion that the Prince was unwilling to accept. Furthermore, their lordships added two phrases that negated the idea of granting an individual right to have arms—"suitable to their conditions" and "as allowed by law." These changes to Article VII were accepted without recorded debate by the House of Commons on February 12.[47]

Article VII, as revised, now read: "That the Subjects which are Protestants may have Armes for their defence suitable to their Condition and as allowed by Law." As is plain to see, the language of Article VII had traveled a long way from its first formulation. The words now qualified the right of the subject to have arms in three respects: *religion* (must be Protestant), *socioeconomic status* ("suitable to their condition"), and *law* ("as allowed by law.") One may ask: What kind of right is this that is so severely qualified as to negate the very meaning of a right? Obviously, it is a far cry from our understanding of a right, but would have been familiar to a person in the Middle Ages. Then, and for centuries thereafter, a right meant a power or authority that was exclusive, not held by everyone. Such a right was dependent on property, status, or gift.[48] We cannot know for sure, but probably that understanding was in the minds of the lords who proposed the restrictions and, perhaps, of the House of Commons, which readily accepted them. What are we to make of these limitations?

The first restriction on gun possession was religion—subjects must be Protestants. Now, anyone familiar with the history of sixteenth- and seventeenth-century England would expect that members of the convention would limit such an extraordinary right as that of subjects to have arms for their defense to Protestants. The limitation reflected the fear and loathing of Roman Catholics that had grown and intensified in English society ever since the sixteenth-century Protestant Reformation. By the late seventeenth century, anti-Catholic prejudice was deeply embedded in English culture. In one convention debate, Henry Pollexfen expressed the feeling of the assembly when he declared, "Popery is the fear of the nation."[49] This prejudice had been nourished by a yearly church service of thanksgiving for the timely discovery and foiling of the Gunpowder Plot of 1605 and sharpened by the Popish Plot of 1678–83 said to be aimed at elevating a Catholic to the English throne. To rescue England from a succession of popish kings, a virtual certainty with the birth of King James II's son in June 1688, was one reason for the Revolution of 1688–89. English Protestants were outraged that King Charles II and, even more so, the Catholic King James II, had tried to disarm the militia in Ireland, Scotland, and, to a lesser extent, in England at the same time that they had disarmed Protestant gentlemen. James II had also appointed Catholic officers in his army and had armed his Catholic subjects.[50] As members of the Rights Committee testified in debate, several of them had had their arms confiscated and/or their houses searched. Their outrage was palpable, as we saw. Language that evoked memory of these incidents was insisted upon by the lords, who added the words "at the same time when papists were both armed and

Employed contrary to Law." The majority of English people despised and dis-
trusted Catholics. The point is that restricting the right to have arms to Protestants was a reflection of Early Modern English prejudice against Catholics.
The second and third qualifiers were "suitable to their [Subjects'] condition,
and "as allowed by Law." Malcolm confessed that she found it difficult to explain these amendments, because they made "the assertion of a guaranteed
right for Protestants to have arms seem empty rhetoric" (p. 120). She resolved
her dilemma by recalling that "legislative reforms proposed by the Convention, such as a modification of the Militia Act, had been left to future parlia-
ments. This meant," she reasoned, "[that] the arms article declared a right that
current law negated, with the understanding that future legislation would eliminate the discrepancy" (p. 120). There is no evidence in either the debates of
1689 or in the later legislative record that it was agreed in 1689 that "future legislation would eliminate the discrepancy." In my view the qualifiers conveyed
precisely what members of the convention intended.

The restrictions may be explained by a short excursus into English social
history. The amendments reflected the social and economic prejudices of
upper-class English society, members of which sat in the House of Lords and
the House of Commons. The structure of English society was hierarchical and
stratified, with a tiny minority at the top exercising enormous political, economic, and social authority. It was a society based on inequality, one that recognized social gradations and was sensitive to title, status, role, and wealth.[51] A
telling illustration of this point occurred in one of the convention debates
when a member, in an effort to make a partisan political point, declared that the
convention represented no more than a "4th part of the Nation." He explained
that "there are freeholders under 40 shillings a year & all Copyholders, &
women & Children & Servants" who have no share in parliamentary elections.[52] This remark met with indignant rejoinders, one fellow member
protesting that "we represent the people fully" and speak for those that have a
share in government, "or are fit to have a share in it." This response encapsu-
lates the socially conservative view of the convention.

The social standing of the peers is obvious; perhaps we should remind ourselves that members of the House of Commons enjoyed high economic and social standing, too. The Rights Committee in the Lower House was composed
almost entirely of leaders in parliamentary, political, and legal circles; many
were lawyers; some had connections with members of the lords' Rights Committee either as friends, family, or business associates.[53] The first chairman
of the Commons Rights Committee was Sir George Treby (1634–1700), a
lawyer and past Recorder of London. The second chairman, John Somers
(1651–1716), also a lawyer, was a writer of influential political tracts, junior
counsel (he was thirty-seven years old) for the Seven Bishops at their trial in

June 1688, and, after the Revolution, Lord Chancellor. Such people as these were sensitive to the dangers implicit in allowing *all* Protestants to have arms. There was even a recent incident that might have been in the forefront of their minds: the rampaging of a Protestant mob in London in December 1688, which had caused property and personal damage.[54] Equally to the point is that the possession of arms had always been associated with property and/or income. Subjects' military obligations had been equated with their socioeconomic status in the militia laws going back to the twelfth century, as we have seen. The customs and laws governing both the militia and the feudal array reflected hierarchical social values and fear of arming the lower classes. Weapons in the hands of the "people" were closely regulated by law. The Militia Act of 1662 continued the principle set out in earlier militia laws, that specified the individual's obligation according to his estate. It is no wonder that the House of Commons should have accepted without recorded dissent the two qualifiers introduced by the House of Lords.

Further, the attitude of equating weapons and property was reflected in papers of two members of the convention. Thomas Erle (c. 1650–1720), a member of the House of Commons and an opponent of standing armies, was interested in reforming the militia to prevent an arbitrary monarch from using it for corrupt purposes against his perceived enemies. In a manuscript entitled "Paper of Instructions for the Parliament Meeting after the Revolution" and written probably in early December 1688, Erle spelled out his ideas for protecting the nation.[55] There should be no standing army, and no English monarch should have more guards than did Queen Elizabeth I, King James I, and King Charles I. The militia should be reformed, and only persons of wealth were to serve, for such men had something to lose and could be trusted, Erle believed. In addition to the militia he recommended that men in the counties with an income of £10 and substantial property holders in towns and cities should be provided with a "good musket" to protect the nation against invasion.[56] That idea would have required an amendment to the Game Law of 1671 (discussed below), but Erle argued that other laws protected game and, sounding like a late-twentieth-century defender of guns, declared that a gun was not to blame for the destruction of game; the person who misused it was. It is not certain that Erle presented his ideas in debate, but since he wrote them out it is likely.

Philip Wharton, fourth Baron Wharton (1613–96), a Whiggish member of the House of Lords, also left papers setting out his ideas on remodeling the government, including the militia. Among the points he made was that only freeholders who had an annual income of at least £20 or held a copyhold for life of £30 were to serve in the militia.[57] Equating arms and property is a basic assumption in Wharton's thought, as it was in Erle's. In neither case was an unrestricted individual right to arms under consideration. Thus, in debate and in surviving papers, members of the convention made clear that a qualification for Protestants to have a gun was their social status and economic condition.

The other qualification for possessing arms introduced by the House of Lords was "as allowed by law." What did the peers mean by this phrase? There seem to be two overlapping strands comprising the point the peers were making. Foremost in their minds, I believe, were the old Militia Laws and Game Laws, especially the Game Act of 1671, both of which restricted the possession of weapons to the wealthy. The lords knew well the provisions of the Game Act of 1671, for three members of their Rights Committee had served on the committee to which the Game Bill was referred in 1671. So too did members of the Rights Committee in the House of Commons, for four of them had initiated that Game Bill. Members of both Houses had reason to preserve their hunting privileges and game and to fear the threat to property and person from placing arms in the hands of *all* Protestants. In Article VII they specified that having guns was to be limited according to law, that is, by the laws already on the books that restricted guns to upper-class Englishmen. At the same time, their lordships were underscoring with this restriction the law-making role of parliament. Carl Bogus has insightfully argued that the words were intended to mean that parliament, as the principal law-making body, had the authority to decide which Protestants might have guns.[58] Bogus reasoned that the phrase "as allowed by law" invited the question: "Who makes law?" Members of the convention (which was concerned to do all it could to achieve the sovereignty of parliament) would have certainly answered: "Parliament." Parliament, of course, had been regulating who might have weapons, including guns, for centuries in their Militia Laws and Game Laws. Recently they had done so in the Game Act of 1671. Surely they would do so in future. In other words, the phrase "as allowed by law" invited recognition of parliament's law-making authority in the past, the present, and the future.

Interestingly, the language does not specify "English men," but rather says "Subjects which are Protestants." Thus, logically, properly qualified English women, that is, Protestant women of wealth, who as widows held property of appropriate value, would be allowed to have arms also. In this instance, then, the prejudices of religion, status, and economic standing trumped the prejudice against the female.

In sum, I maintain that Article VII was erected on prejudices: religious, social, and economic. Reflecting social and economic snobbery, Article VII preserved the interests of the upper-class Protestant landowner. It was erected on law—class law—that protected the interests of the well-to-do. The phrase "as allowed by law" may also have signaled the intention that parliament have the authority to make future law regarding who might possess guns. Article VII is properly regarded not as a gun rights law, but as a gun control measure. It gives no right to all Protestants to possess guns; it gives that right to upper-class Protestants. In effect, it armed a small minority—perhaps no more than 3 percent—of the population. This, I submit, was the original meaning of Article VII.

II

What happened to this restrictive right immediately following the Revolution? If we are to believe Joyce Malcolm, members intended to "eliminate the discrepancy" of restrictions in Article VII, and "by the early eighteenth century legislation and court interpretation had made it clear that an individual right to bear arms belonged to all Protestants" (p. 122). No evidence, presented by Professor Malcolm or otherwise uncovered, convincingly supports this argument. Malcolm offered three examples: the first was the March 13, 1689, debate over disarming Catholics. The convention had been transformed into the Convention Parliament at the end of February and the same members were now sitting to take up the pressing issues that confronted the new government.[59] For some members, nothing was more important than protecting the nation against gun-owning Catholics. In debate on doing so, an M.P. remarked that "a way to convict" persons of Catholicism must be contrived else "you cannot disarm them."[60] Malcolm reasoned that "this statement implies that the House clearly meant the new right to have arms to include all Protestants, whatever their condition" (p. 123). In my view, the comment cannot carry that conclusion. The debate was on disarming Catholics; neither Protestants nor an unrestricted right of all of them to have arms was mentioned. If such a right had been intended only a month after crafting Article VII, surely it would have provoked comment. But the bill disarming Catholics passed without comment. The law gave Catholics permission to keep "necessary Weapons" for personal defense, as the Justice of the Peace would allow. The allowance reinforces my point that the convention was guaranteeing a right to certain carefully identified persons to keep "arms" suitable for offensive and defensive warfare; it was not giving a constitutional guarantee to possess a weapon for personal defense.

Malcolm's second example was reform of the militia. Beginning in July 1689 and continuing in the autumn of 1690, M.P.s made repeated attempts to draft a Militia Bill.[61] Their efforts to reform the militia met with failure: unsettled conditions and King William's opposition doomed the project. Malcolm saw a connection between militia reform and the right to possess arms in the failure of militia reform. "Insistence on the principle of a right to be armed," she wrote, "must have seemed adequate protection against forcible disarmament by the militia" (p. 125). She explained that Sir William Williams (1634–1700) willingly delayed reform on those grounds (p. 208, note 25). But Malcolm gave no evidence to show the existence of an "insistence" on the principle of an arms right nor of Williams's interest in that principle. By contrast, J. R. Western, a historian of the militia, explains Williams's willingness to delay militia reform because of his sense of urgency that the nation must move against Catholics, whatever the condition of the militia.[62] In my view, the M.P.s' handling of militia reform does not advance Professor Malcolm's argument.

What the story of attempted militia reform does show is that militia reform—and not allowing all Protestants the right to possess guns—was what seriously engaged the attention of members of the Convention Parliament. If M.P.s had wanted to modify the restrictions in Article VII, they would have taken the time to do so, just as they took the time to introduce bills about the militia. They had other opportunities, of which they did not avail themselves, when over the next eight months or so the Declaration of Rights was transformed into the Bill of Rights. During that process the declaration was amended,[63] but Article VII was not touched. It cannot be said that the committee of eleven members elected on March 5 to manage that transformation was unfamiliar with the details of the declaration. Eight persons who had served on the Rights Committees for the declaration, including Somers and Treby, were elected to the Bill of Rights committee. The proper conclusion is that members ignored Article VII deliberately, because it was no part of their intention to remove the restrictions.

The third "proof" that Malcolm offered was the Game Act of 1693.[64] Stressing that guns were not specifically included in the list of prohibited devices, although admitting that they may have been included under "other instruments," Malcolm declared that "the Whigs" "fought" to assure of the right of gun ownership for all Protestants (p. 126). The "committee," she continued, introduced a rider at the third reading "to enable every Protestant to keep a musket in his House for his defence, not withstanding this or any other Act."[65] It is true that Whigs played a primary role in promoting the rider, but Whig leaders did not take the initiative and the amendment was not a "committee" measure. Rather, the rider was presented by "Mr. Norris," no doubt Thomas Norris (1653–1700) who was on the committee and a Whig, to be sure, but "an inactive Member," no leader.[66] Of the four men who supported Norris, only one was from the committee, Anthony Bowyer (1633–1709), described as voting "steadily as a court Whig," which was not true in this case.[67] These men argued that the rider promoted the security of the government and that all Protestants should be able to defend themselves.[68] The "majority Tory party," Malcolm said, opposed the rider. True again that Sir Christopher Musgrave and Sir Joseph Tredenham, both Tories, led the debate against the rider. But, significantly, Sir John Lowther, a *Court* Whig, joined them, for we can be sure that King William and his friends would not have allowed it to pass. These men insisted that the measure was irregular, one saying that it "savours of the politics to arm the mob, which . . . is not very safe for any government."[69] One may reasonably think that such considerations animated Musgrave and Tredenham (who had served on the Rights Committee) just four years earlier, when Article VII was being drafted.

In any case, the rider was decisively defeated 169 to 65,[70] leaving no doubt that, while minority sentiment for arming all Protestants existed, a decisive majority opposed both it and the notion of modifying the terms of Article VII. As of the early eighteenth century, Article VII and the assumptions underlying it remained intact.

III

Whereas no claim of the right of the subject to have arms was raised before the Revolution of 1688–89, such claims for Protestants were raised during the eighteenth century. They appeared in law cases when a defendant protested being denied a gun, or in tracts at moments of crisis, as, for example, during the run-up to the Militia Bill of 1757, or in parliamentary debate at the time of the Gordon Riots in 1780. As long as there was a threat of foreign invasion from France, Jacobite uprising, or papist coup d'état, some persons would argue for allowing all Protestants to have guns. But as the historian of the Game Laws has remarked, "The spirit of the Game Laws . . . was very much alive in the eighteenth century" and grew stronger over the century.[71] In fact, court decisions and claims did not prevent the Game Acts from being enforced, albeit fitfully, depending upon the attitude of the local gentry,[72] nor eliminate further claims to the right to have arms. These facts alone demonstrate that a constitutional right for all Protestants to have arms was not achieved by the end of the eighteenth century.

Changes that did occur were among the Game Laws, and not in Article VII of the Bill of Rights. Thus, the Game Act of 1706 omitted guns from the list of prohibited weapons, this time deliberately. According to a later account of the debate, a contemporary member of parliament who participated in the discussions objected to including guns because "it might be attended with greate inconvenience."[73] A gun, it was said, is "frequently necessary to be kept and used for other purposes, as the killing of noxious vermin and the like."[74] When used for killing game, then a gun fell under the law. Decisions in two law cases, Rex v. Gardner in 1739 and the other in 1752, reinforced the legality of an individual to have a gun. The court ruled for the defendant charged with gun possession. In both instances, the court accepted the defense argument that a gun was needed for personal defense or "for a farmer to shoot crows."[75] These two law cases apparently were the only pertinent ones, for Malcolm neither discusses nor cites any others.[76] These two rulings favoring gun possession, however, did not put the matter to rest. After each case, outrage that guns were being taken from subjects appeared: the *Craftsman* complained in 1739 that pheasants and partridges were being preserved at "the imminent Hazard of our Liberties."[77] In 1755 John Shebbeare, a Tory polemicist, critical of the government's slowness to proceed with militia reform, wrote a series of letters to and about the English, in which he fumed against the Game Laws for depriving "people of Arms to defend themselves, and thus [making] them slaves by robbing them of the power of resistance."[78] He said it was a "breach" of the Bill of Rights to disarm the populace.[79] He and other Tories (such as William Beckford and John Brown) bitterly attacked the use of standing armies and foreign troops, condemned the denial of arms to the people, and demanded a national militia.[80] They appropriated the anger over that denial and used it as a propaganda ploy, even as the antimilitary ideology had been used during the Restoration. Tories and Patriot Whigs pressed hard for arming the people for service in a militia, which they confidently predicted would remove the need for and rid the country of German mercenaries as well as train the nation in civic virtue. Public opinion, thus aroused, propelled William Pitt to power and led to the passage of the Militia Bill. Ironically, the new militia, although driven by popular and libertarian sentiments, proved unpopular in the event, provoked serious riots, and influenced the nature of political alignments.[81] The point is that printed tracts concerning the Militia Bill of 1757 illustrate the polemical uses of claiming a right to arm.

The Gordon Riots of 1780 were another occasion that provoked outbursts of vehement support for the principle of the right of the individual to possess arms. The context[82] was as follows: The government of Lord North had fallen under increasingly sharp criticism because of military reverses in America and serious problems with France, Spain, and neutral nations. The opposition, under the leadership of such men as Charles James Fox, became radical and factious. In 1778, in an effort to motivate Catholics to enlist in the army, North's government promoted the passage of the Catholic Relief Act, which removed several disabilities from Catholics. Tapping into the deep vein of anti-Catholicism, the Protestant Association, led by its president, the erratic Lord George Gordon, young son of a Scottish noble, organized a mass petition, said to contain 120,000 signatures, for the repeal of the act. When parliament refused an immediate hearing, crowds that had gathered outside Westminister turned angry. Violence soon spread through the city. From Friday June 2 to the following Thursday, June 8, great damage was done to Catholic chapels, houses, and businesses, more than three hundred people were killed in the melee, and more were injured. Some cities in the counties also erupted in riot and mayhem. Order was not restored until the army was finally ordered to act.

An army officer, Jeffrey Lord Amherst, commanded his lieutenant-colonel in London to disarm all residents except those in the militia and others specifically designated to defend the city. Charles Lennox, the third Duke of Richmond, responded indignantly to this move. In speeches in the House of Lords later in the month, he charged that the Bill of Rights guaranteed that "every Protestant subject shall be permitted to arm himself for his personal security, or for the defence of his property." [83] He moved that the order of the army officer be branded as "unwarrantable" because it had violated the "sacred right" of Protestant subjects "to have arms for their defence, suitable to their conditions, and as allowed by law." [84] Although Malcolm makes much of Lennox's remarks (p. 131), it is clear that in his confused speech he ultimately claimed nothing different from the restricted right allowed by Article VII. The Earl of Carlisle, Lord Stormont, and the Lord Chancellor defended the army's actions and Lennox's motion was defeated.

Protests favoring the right of Protestant subjects to be armed were heard outside of parliament. In the summer of 1780, the Yorkshire Association condemned any attempt "to disarm peaceable subjects" who were Protestant.[85] When asked to give his opinion in July 1780, the Recorder of London registered his approval of the associations and of the right of Protestants individually to have arms "and to use them for lawful purposes." It was a right, he said, which "may, and in many cases must, be exercised collectively." [86] Malcolm regards his remarks as "perhaps the clearest summation of the right of Englishmen to have arms" at that time (p. 134). On the other hand, the recorder's use of the words "for lawful purposes" and his reference to "exercising" the right "collectively" may signal that he wanted to guarantee the right of individual Protestants to be armed so that they might serve effectively in the associations. In any case, these remarks did not end the matter. Two years later, an anonymous tract, *Dialogue Between a Scholar and a Peasant* (1782), written by William Jones, again regretted that Englishmen did not have guns and urged them to be prepared—that is, armed—to defend themselves in associations against the government. The tract was published by the radical Society for Constitutional Information and translated into Welsh.[87] These moves provided powerful propaganda. But the moment passed; people turned away from extralegal activities, disavowed radicalism, and lost interest. The government took charge, and the associations in the counties and in London dissolved. Jones was charged with libel and sedition. The fervent expressions of the right of the individual Protestant to be armed came to nothing.

To support her thesis further, Malcolm called upon two great figures in English history, the jurist William Blackstone and the historian Thomas Lord Macaulay. She declared that in his celebrated *Commentaries on the Law of England,* Blackstone endorsed the Whig view that "armed citizens [*sic*] were a necessary check on tyranny" and in doing so transformed the view into "orthodox opinion" (pp. 129–30). It is true that Blackstone identified the right of the subject to possess arms as the fifth "auxiliary right" in protecting freedom, but he was not speaking about an unrestricted right. He wrote:

> The fifth and last auxiliary right of the subject . . . is that of having arms for their defence, suitable to their condition and degree, and such as are allowed by law. Which is also declared by the same statute 1 William and Mary and is indeed a public allowance, under due restraints, of the natural right of resistance and self-preservation, when the sanctions of society and laws are found insufficient to restrain the violence of oppression.[88]

Clearly, Blackstone not only quoted from Article VII but named the Bill of Rights. He summed up by describing the five auxiliary rights as birthrights, "unless where laws of our country have laid them under necessary restraints."[89] In his view the right of the subject to possess arms existed under "due restraints" as spelled out in the Bill of Rights. That right applies, he added, only "when the sanctions of society and laws are found insufficient to restrain the violence of oppression." Blackstone was not advocating an unrestricted right of the individual to possess arms. I agree with Malcolm that Blackstone's remarks are "of the utmost importance" because his *Commentaries* played such a significant role in both England and the colonies (p. 130; also 142–43). That being the case, it is of utmost importance to understand aright what he wrote.

In a different way, Macaulay's views carry an importance equal to those of Blackstone. Quoting a passage from Macaulay's *Critical and Historical Essays, Contributed to the Edinburgh Review*,[90] Malcolm contended that Macaulay advocated the idea that "the Englishman's ultimate security depended not upon Magna Carta or Parliament but upon the power of the sword" (pp. x, 169, 176). It is true that in a review of Henry Hallam's *The Constitutional History of England, from the Accession of Henry VII to the Death of George II,* Macaulay had written: "The great security, the security without which every other would have been insufficient was the power of the sword." But Macaulay was not arguing in this remark for the subject's right to arms. Rather he was discussing the mounting conflict in 1640–41 between Charles I and the parliamentary leaders over the power of the sword, a dispute that moved inexorably toward the passage of the Militia Bill/Ordinance[91] and the outbreak of war. His point was that each side understood the importance of the Militia Bill/Ordinance because the result would place command of the armed forces in the hands of parliament. I know of no place where Macaulay subscribed to an unrestricted right of the subject to possess arms. In fact, he does not even mention the restricted right to arms provided by Article VII in his magisterial *History of England.*

IV

The climax of Joyce Malcolm's argument is that an individual right to bear arms was a heritage of the Bill of Rights that "Englishmen took with them to the American colonies" (p. 134). It was a legacy that "Americans fought to protect in 1775" (p. 134). This heritage, Malcolm contends, had a defining influence on the Second Amendment. The "public" found reassurance when the First Congress "copied English policies"; it was not satisfied "until passage of the Second Amendment" (p. 151). In the Second Amendment Americans went beyond the model provided by Article VII; they removed the restrictions, forbidding "any infringement" upon the right to have arms (p.162). Malcolm maintains that the account in her book "is the key to the meaning and intent of the much-misunderstood Second Amendment" (pp. 150–51).

There is much that is problematic about these assertions. First, Malcolm supplies no notes to them. She does not define "people" nor give proof of the attitude that she assigns them. What evidence is there that the people wanted the Congress to copy English policies or that their "concern" was "not allayed until the passage of the Second Amendment"? What evidence is there that the English Bill of Rights' provision for "individuals to have arms" was before the members of the First Congress? Where is there comment about removing the restrictions in Article VII to ensure no "infringement" on the right to bear arms? While everyone might agree that the English Bill of Rights was of central importance to the colonists,[92] and that members of the First Congress were familiar with all its provisions, the fact is that the record of the debates, as well as the correspondence and other documents relating to the creation of the American Bill of Rights, contain no direct reference to Article VII. When delegates refer to arming the people, they do so in the context of assuring a reliable militia, discussing the question of conscientious objectors, or expressing strong objections to a standing, professional army.[93] One may suggest that the absence of reference to Article VII and its right of the subject to possess arms under restrictions reflects the fact that the article had no relevance to American needs. How could it? The status of the constitutional right of the individual to hold arms in English law in 1789 at the time of the meetings held in Philadelphia to draft the American Bill of Rights remained the terms of Article VII. Those terms had not been changed since the Bill of Rights became law in November 1689. Over the intervening one hundred years no one had stepped forward to introduce an amendment bringing Article VII into conformity with what Professor Malcolm believes to have been the intention of the members of the convention.

True, over the years voices were raised, tracts written, and two law cases decided in favor of the right of the individual to have a gun. These expressions of opinion, however, did not represent majority public opinion nor did they rise to the level of constitutional change. In some instances the charge that the government disarmed subjects and disallowed them the right to hold arms was a propaganda ploy that critics used against the government. It is clear that people may declaim and express their outrage over an issue in parliamentary debate; they may print tracts and pamphlets insisting upon their viewpoint; two law cases may decide an issue in ways that please such people. Yet none of these things creates a constitutional right. The constitutional right of the individual to hold arms at the end of the eighteenth century was what it was at the beginning—a restricted right. If the Americans ignored all these restrictions, as Malcolm claims, then they were not following the English constitutional example.

In point of fact, however, the Americans did follow the English, but not in the way Malcolm thinks. The Americans, like the English, favored the militia, and wrote an awkwardly worded amendment that would assure that the militia would be appropriately armed by the individuals who served in it.

V

This essay began with the hope that, in offering an interpretation different from that of Malcolm in *To Keep and Bear Arms,* it might clarify and illuminate the English intellectual and constitutional antecedents and the meaning of the much-disputed Second Amendment to the U.S. Constitution. In my view, Professor Malcolm's book is a well-written study that advances its argument in compelling terms, sometimes in unguarded language. But despite the trappings of historical scholarship, the analysis of text and context is sometimes open to question; the research is not meticulous; and the argument is not irrefutable. In offering an opposing perspective, I contend that Englishmen did not secure to "ordinary citizens" the right to possess weapons. Article VII of the Bill of Rights did secure the right to arms to English subjects, according to their religion, as was "suitable" to their economic standing, and "according to the law" that governed such matters; in other words, to upper-class Protestants. The Article is an excellent example of class law and of law erected on religious, social, and economic prejudices. It was a reaction to the policies of King Charles II and his Catholic brother, King James II, and reflected the hatred of standing armies in time of peace and the conviction that the militia, as an instrument that was effectively controlled by parliament and the upper classes, could provide a safeguard against standing armies and an absolute King. Drafted by upper-class Protestants who had their own interests at heart, Article VII was a gun control measure.

Throughout the eighteenth century, protests against disarming subjects and fervent assertions that the right of gun possession applied to every Protestant appeared at moments of crisis and sometimes were used as a propaganda weapon against the government. At the end of the eighteenth century, after winning the war against Great Britain, the American colonists drew up a written constitution, and soon thereafter added to it a series of amendments. The delegates to the First Congress were aware of the English precedents, including Article VII; some delegates insisted that they laid claim to all the rights of Englishmen. But there is no evidence that they regarded Article VII as the source of the Second Amendment to their own Bill of Rights. Why should they have, when that Article restricted a right to guns in ways entirely unacceptable to them?

In short, Professor Malcolm's book does not, as she claims, "set the American controversy over the meaning of the Second Amendment . . . upon a foundation of fact." [94] The fact is, there was no unrestricted English right of the individual to possess guns for the colonists to inherit.

9. Disarmed by Time: The Second Amendment and the Failure of Originalism

DANIEL A. FARBER*

When the Almighty Himself condescends to address mankind in their own language, his meaning, luminous as it must be, is rendered dim and doubtful by the cloudy medium through which it is communicated.

Federalist 37, James Madison

According to the received wisdom, the Second Amendment is little more than a footnote to the militia clauses of the Constitution, themselves virtually irrelevant to today's military.[1] This conventional view has been challenged by revisionist scholars.[2] Now claiming for their own view the title of "standard model," revisionists contend that the framers had a far more sweeping vision of the "right to keep and bear arms." In their view, the Constitution protects the individual's right to own guns for self-defense, hunting, and resistance to tyranny.

Unlike Madison, these scholars find no room for uncertainty about the historical meaning of constitutional language. "The Second Amendment," we are told by one scholar, "is thus not mysterious. Nor is it equivocal. Least of all is it opaque."[3] The meaning of the "right to bear arms," says another, "seems no longer open to dispute," and "an intellectually viable response . . . has yet to be made."[4]

The revisionists' confidence about the original understanding of the Constitution is the foundation for their reinterpretation of the Second Amendment.[5] The appropriate role of original intent in constitutional law has been debated for the past two decades.[6] That debate should, if nothing else, caution against this sense of certainty about the import of historical materials for present-day constitutional issues such as gun control.

Reading the historical record on the right to bear arms turns out to be a difficult exercise, full of perplexities.[7] Even if we had a definitive answer that turned out to favor the revisionists, the claim that original intent should always trump contemporary legislative decisions is itself problematic. These defects in originalism are familiar to constitutional scholars. What may be less familiar is the almost uncanny way in which these flaws are reproduced in the literature on the Second Amendment.

History cannot provide the kind of unshakeable foundation for gun rights that some scholars have sought. Indeed, there is something profoundly amiss about the notion that the Constitution's meaning today should be settled first and foremost by a trip to the archives. The effort to apply this notion to an issue as contemporary and hotly contested as gun control only seems to underscore the fundamental peculiarity of the originalist approach to constitutional law.[8]

Given the deep flaws in originalism, its continuing appeal may seem mysterious. For its more sophisticated adherents, it may appeal in part as a value-neutral method of decision and in part as a solution to the counter-majoritarian difficulty—perhaps a solution they would admit to be flawed, yet better than the alternatives. For less sophisticated adherents, however, originalism may have another, more visceral appeal. It harkens back to an earlier, purer age, wherein today's petty political concerns and squalid politicians can be replaced with great statesmen devoted to high principle. This implicit appeal to a nobler, more heroic past may have particular resonance in the context of the Second Amendment, where it brings to mind visions of minutemen and frontier lawmen, valiantly defending justice and freedom with their guns. These mythic versions of the past, however, can only obscure the all-too-real issues facing our society today. Being inspired by myth is healthy; being ruled by it is unsafe.

THE FEASIBILITY OF ORIGINALIST INTERPRETATION

Before turning to the question of whether the historical evidence *should* control the meaning of the Second Amendment, we may begin with the question of whether it *can* be controlling. In short, can judges and other decision makers determine the "original understanding" of the Second Amendment in a sufficiently unambiguous, accurate manner to justify putting such heavy reliance on the historical record?

The first question is whether judges can determine the framing generation's understanding of the Second Amendment with any confidence. Various methodological problems may make it difficult to do so, and, of course, if judges cannot determine original intent, they cannot make it the basis for interpretation.

Before considering the special problems of interpreting historical documents from past centuries, it is worth bearing in mind that interpretation is a problematical task even without these additional difficulties. The fundamental question is whether someone who keeps a gun for use in hunting or against burglars is "keeping and bearing arms" within the meaning of the Second Amendment.[9] The Supreme Court has not found it easy to answer similar questions even without the extra burden of historical interpretation.

In a series of recent cases, for example, the Supreme Court has struggled to interpret seemingly commonplace phrases relating to the use and possession of guns. These cases involved contemporary statutes with none of the obscurities that impede our understanding of texts from the more distant past. Yet the Supreme Court found itself deeply divided on basic definitional questions. Is a person with a gun in a locked car trunk guilty of "carrying a firearm"? Yes, according to five Justices; absolutely not, said the four dissenters.[10] Does a person under similar circumstances "use" the gun (another phrase in the same statute)? No, said a unanimous Court.[11] But does a person who trades a gun for drugs "use" the gun in a drug deal? Six Justices said yes; Justice Scalia and two others thought this was clearly wrong.[12] Such interpretative problems accumulate compound interest as linguistic understandings and legal contexts shift over time. If we are not sure what Congress meant only a few years ago by references to carrying or using a firearm, we are likely to face even greater difficulties in determining what Congress meant two centuries ago by the phrase "keep and bear Arms."

Indeed, the historical inquiry required by originalism is not an easy one, as Justice Scalia has explained:

> [I]t is often exceedingly difficult to plumb the original understanding of an ancient text. Properly done, the task requires the consideration of an enormous mass of material. . . . Even beyond that, it requires an evaluation of the reliability of that material. . . . And further still, it requires immersing oneself in the political and intellectual atmosphere of the time. . . . It is, in short, a task sometimes better suited to the historian than the lawyer.[13]

Justice Scalia cannot be accused of overstating the burden that originalism places on judges. The difficulty of the necessary research is not to be minimized. To begin with, the historical record, while voluminous in some respects, is incomplete just where it would be most helpful. As background to the Second Amendment, we would like to know the original understanding of the militia clauses of the Constitution. It would be particularly useful to understand the views of the specific individuals who drafted or ratified the document. The documentary record is unsatisfactory on either score. As to the Constitutional Convention, our best source is Madison's notes. But the notes are far from being verbatim, including less than ten percent of the total proceedings.[14] The records of the ratification debates are even worse, regarded by historians as paying scant attention to accuracy at best.[15] The debates of the First Congress covering the Bill of Rights—including the Second Amendment—were not recorded at all in the Senate, and were recorded in the House by one Thomas Lloyd. Lloyd's accuracy had never been good, and by 1789 his "technical skills had become dulled by excessive drinking."[16]

Moving beyond the official debates, we also have access to a flood of published materials debating the Constitution, such as *The Federalist Papers,*[17] but it is always unclear how these materials were viewed by their readers; indeed, it is not necessarily clear who those readers might have been.[18] We can also turn to the general intellectual context, but that, too, can be difficult to reconstruct and apply to specific legal issues.[19] In short, the further we get from the decision-making process itself, the more material we have available but the harder it is to digest this material and evaluate its significance, particularly for amateur historians such as judges.

Evaluating these materials, along with the earlier American and English materials that provide their context, is no easy task. Judges, after all, have not been chosen on the basis of their skills as historians—nor, on the whole, are law professors renowned for the depth of their historical knowledge of early American history.[20] By most accounts, for instance, the Supreme Court's recent rulings on state sovereign immunity reflect a high degree of historical ineptitude.[21] Historical interpretation is also made more difficult by the nature of democratic decision making: for law to be made, a majority or super-majority must favor it, but they need not agree among themselves about exactly what it means, so we have no reason to assume that any consensus about the meaning of the provision actually existed.

The difficulty of extracting clear messages from these messy historical materials is amply illustrated within Second Amendment scholarship. When examining the contending positions of these scholars, it is hard not to sympathize with a leading judge's lament about the difficulty of working with legislative history:

> A Sherlock Holmes could work through the clues, and those most reliable, and draw unerring inferences. Alas, none of us is a worthy successor to Holmes . . . We hear in the debates what we prefer to hear—and our preferences differ widely. Even when all of us hear the same thing, a search for those clues consumes resources but does not yield rewards comparable to the effort invested.[22]

This is not to say that historical interpretation is wholly indeterminate. Rather, it is to question whether historical research is a viable way for judges and lawyers to find definitive answers to concrete legal questions.

To document fully this assertion with a detailed analysis of the historical debate over the Second Amendment would be to write an article—more likely a book—about Second Amendment history, not an essay about originalism. But we can begin to see the problems that a judge would confront by considering some of the opposing assertions that she would have to resolve. Consider as examples a half dozen of the dueling historical views that the judge would confront:

1. Claim: Madison gave his "imprimatur" to a description of the Second Amendment by a fellow Federalist, who described it as guaranteeing against the confiscation of private arms.[23]

   Counterclaim: "Madison's letter is polite and general, not a discussion of any substantive point Coxe made." Indeed, Coxe's treatment of the establishment clause was quite contrary to Madison's views, but Madison did not mention the disagreement.[24]

2. Claim: The Framers did not contemplate extensive gun regulation: "Well regulated" meant well drilled or practiced.[25]

   Counterclaim: Every state had substantial gun regulation when the Second Amendment was adopted.[26]

3. Claim: "If any group of persons deserves the label 'pro-gun,' it is . . . the Founders themselves."[27]

   Counterclaim: Gun use was not widespread. Only 14 percent of population owned guns (many of which were broken).[28]

4. Claim: "[T]he Framers' militia was not an elite fighting force but the entire citizenry of the time: all able-bodied adult white males."[29]

   Counterclaim: Leaders such as Hamilton and Washington realized that the general militia was impotent and contemplated "a select corp of moderate size."[30] About 40 percent of citizens were disbarred from militia service because of failure to demonstrate their loyalty.[31]

5. Claim: Based on their own Revolutionary experience, "the last thing the Framers would have done is to deny the People the means of armed insurrection."[32]

   Counterclaim: Key framers like Madison, Hamilton, and Washington were horrified by insurrections and intended the Constitution to provide the means for suppressing them.[33]

6. Claim: To "keep" arms in eighteenth-century usage meant to have them in one's personal possession.[34]

   Counterclaim: To "keep" arms in eighteenth-century usage meant to hold them in a communal military arsenal.[35]

Surely, there is much to be written—even more surely, more yet *will* be written—on all of these and many other similar issues. The question is not whether, in the end, some answers to these historical questions will prove to be more strongly supported by the record than others. Rather, the question is whether we think judges are likely to do a very good job in resolving these issues—a good enough job to justify using historical research as the means of

deciding cases regarding the Second Amendment or other constitutional issues.[36] Given their limited time and training—not to mention their very mixed
record in attempting to identify original intent in other areas—it is hard to be
optimistic about the prospects for success by these amateur historians in black
robes.

Was Originalism the Original Understanding?

The question of originalism can itself be approached from an originalist perspective, by asking whether the framers expected their intentions to control
subsequent interpretation of the Constitution. This issue seems particularly
relevant for the "original understanding" mode of originalism, which focuses
on the way the text would have been understood by contemporary readers
rather than on the intentions of the author.[37]

If such readers were trying to be sure of the meaning of some part of the constitutional text, they would naturally bring into play whatever conventions existed at the time for interpreting such texts. Some, of course, would be general
linguistic conventions, common to the whole community, but others might be
more specifically legal. Thus, an eighteenth-century reader with legal training
would presumably have expected the document to be interpreted in line with
existing legal conventions, and those conventions would themselves enter into
his own interpretation. For instance, if he expected the Constitution to be interpreted based on the views of its framers, such as Madison and Hamilton, a
contemporary reader would have felt entitled to rely on their public statements, knowing that those statements would also carry weight with later interpreters. On the other hand, if he expected interpretation to be more pragmatic,
his own understanding of the text's legal meaning would place more weight on
practical considerations to resolve ambiguities.

Like most historical questions, this one is not free from doubt. But the best
scholarship on the subject suggests that the framing generation would not have
expected interpretation to turn on the subjective intent of the "authors"—in
this case, the drafters and ratifiers. Indeed, they probably would not have
thought extrinsic evidence such as the debates of the time could be considered
to resolve ambiguities.[38] (The evidence is somewhat less clear on this point
concerning the intent of the ratifiers, as opposed to the drafters in Philadelphia,[39] but, as we have seen, the historical record regarding the ratifiers' views
is much less satisfactory, making reliance on those views difficult as a practical
matter.) Indeed, even at the time, ratifiers in one state would have had little reason to know what had been said about the Constitution in the debates elsewhere.

If they would not have looked to the debates as dispositive evidence, how would the ratifiers or the "reasonable contemporary reader" have gone about interpreting the text? With respect to the Second Amendment, one much-mooted question is whether the introductory purpose clause relating to the militia would have placed some limit on the operational "right to bear arms" clause.[40] Eugene Volokh argues, for instance, that "the justification clause can't take away what the operative clause provides."[41] On the other hand, the justification clause might arguably suggest a narrow reading of the operative clause. Thus, by analogy, the argument for limiting the First Amendment to explicitly political speech would surely be strengthened if that amendment had been written like the Second, perhaps along the following lines: "A well-informed electorate being essential to a free state, the freedom of speech and of the press shall not be abridged."

For the originalist, the question should not be which of these lines of argument seems plausible today, but rather which interpretative strategy would have seemed stronger in the 1790s. Americans had had little experience in interpreting constitutional provisions at that point, but they were heirs to centuries of experience in the similar enterprise of interpreting statutes. A reasonable and well-informed lawyer might well have expected the same methods to apply to constitutional provisions, and this expectation would shape his own interpretation of constitutional language.

Such a late-eighteenth-century legal reader might well have thought that the purpose of a provision could be used to cut back from its otherwise plain language. After a careful review of the early American cases, William Eskridge found that courts felt free to go beyond statutory language and resort to the "equity of the statute."[42] For instance, in one case, the court said it did not feel "bound by the strictly grammatical construction of the words of the act" but would instead adopt a construction "free from those inconveniences which must flow from any other interpretation."[43] Similarly, Blackstone endorsed the principle that the law ceases where its purpose ends, and maintained that courts must sometimes adapt statutes to circumstances unforseen by the legislators.[44] After another careful look at early Anglo-American practice, John Manning concurred that resort to the "equity of the statute" was an accepted canon of statutory construction before the Constitution was adopted, including "the judge's power not only to extend, but also to restrict, statutory words in the name of equity."[45] The possibility of equitable construction would color a sophisticated reader's approach to the constitutional text.

In short, to determine the original understanding, we need to take into account the interpretative methods that a contemporary reader might have employed. We need to remember that an eighteenth-century reader—whether a member of Congress, a ratifier, or even a hypothetical reasonable person—would not necessarily have thought it appropriate to look to the Second

Amendment's legislative history. Such a reader might also have expected the right to bear arms to be construed restrictively in light of the express purpose of the amendment to strengthen the militia.

At least, we have no reason to assume away these possible readings; and even if we would not be inclined to adopt similar methods of interpretation ourselves today, the relevant question for an originalist ought to be what method of interpretation shaped the understanding of the text by readers of the time. The eighteenth century was entitled to understand the import of texts in its own way rather than in ours, and if we want to know how those texts were used at the time, it is those methods of interpretation we must consider. Of course, this only adds another layer of difficulty to the originalist's task.

The Ambiguity of "Intent"

Another difficulty of implementing originalism is deciding what level of intent we are interested in at the most concrete level. We might consider the relevant intent or understanding to consist of a kind of checklist of allowable and prohibited acts, so that the ordinary reader of the Second Amendment might have understood that it did or did not protect, for example, the use of muskets for hunting. But this way of thinking about intent is notoriously unsatisfactory.[46] Focusing solely on the concrete applications anticipated by the framers makes it difficult or impossible to justify decisions, such as the school desegregation cases, that by common agreement were correct in their outcomes.[47] As Mike McConnell points out, it is also important not to "confuse the founders' expectations about how the nation would be governed under the Constitution with the founders' understanding of the meaning of the Constitution."[48] Yet more abstract interpretations also raise problems. Moving from specific understandings about particular fact patterns to more general principles is no easy matter.[49] Moreover, once we move away from explicit consensus about concrete applications to more general concepts, interpretation can become quite an open-ended process. For this reason, Judge Robert Bork argued for keeping interpretation at a relatively low level of generality.[50] Thus, when we say we are in search of the "original understanding," it is not entirely clear what it is that we hope to find.

We have considered the problems of determining whether a particular "intent" or "understanding" is well supported by the historical record compared to the alternatives. But even once we surmount those problems, we may discover that this was not after all the *kind* of intent (or understanding) that we were looking for. As Jack Rakove points out, much of the debate over the interpretation of the Second Amendment involves the extent to which we should restrict ourselves to the specific historical context of enactment, as opposed to considering the broad theories of government that were common at the time.[51] The supporters of a narrow interpretation would prefer to define the original understanding at a low level of generality, while those seeking a broad interpretation would prefer to define the original understanding far more abstractly. There is no agreement on any general principle for choosing the right level of generality.

Supporters of a narrow construction might also charge their opponents with confusing expectations with meaning. Even granting the factual claims made in favor of a broad right to bear arms, they might argue, those factual claims are not probative of the original understanding. Suppose, for example, that the framers did believe that the militia would be constituted of the entire population and would keep their arms at home ready for use. Suppose in addition that they believed arming the militia would create a possible check against usurpation by the federal government and would aid individuals in exercising their rights to personal self-defense. Still, how do we tell whether these various beliefs were anything more than predictions about how things would work out, as opposed to an understanding of the *meaning* of the amendment? If we had asked the framers this question, they might have thought we were engaging in the kind of hair-splitting they themselves might have associated with medieval philosophy—yet implementing originalism requires us to make just these sorts of fine distinctions.

In the absence of any consensus about how to choose the proper level of generality or distinguish meanings from expectations, originalists who agree about the historical facts can nevertheless reach quite different legal conclusions. This makes originalism all the less likely to constrain judicial interpretation of the Constitution, which is one of its main goals.

The Problem of Stare Decisis

Most originalists agree that the original understanding is not everything: originalism must leave some room for upholding precedent in order to maintain legal stability. As Henry Monaghan once explained, the "expectations created by [precedent] render unacceptable a full return to original intent theory in any pure, unalloyed form"; while "original intent may constitute the starting point" of interpretation, some theory of precedent is "needed to confine its reach."[52]

More recently, Justice Scalia has also stressed precedent as a limit on originalism. Despite its centrality in his thinking about judicial review, originalism plays little role in some of Justice Scalia's most notable opinions. For instance, he does not apply it to the First Amendment, an area in which he has been a staunch supporter of free speech. He defends his First Amendment decisions as applications of "long-standing and well-accepted principles (not out of accord with the general practices of our people, whether or not they were constitutionally required as an original matter) that are effectively irreversible." He defends this use of precedent because, given the existence of an ongoing system of law, originalism cannot hope to remake the world from scratch, and must take as givens such settled points as the legitimacy of judicial review and the unconstitutionality of the Alien and Sedition Acts of 1798. Thus, Justice Scalia says, "originalism will make a difference," "not in the rolling back of accepted old principles of constitutional law but in the rejection of usurpatious new ones." [53]

Justice Scalia has also recognized a closely related restraint against reopening settled questions. His dissent in the patronage contracting cases is a good illustration of his use of tradition. In previous cases, the Court had held that hiring or firing employees based on their party affiliation violated their First Amendment rights. In two 1996 cases, the Court applied this rule to government contractors. [54] Justice Scalia's dissent was joined only by Justice Thomas. Scalia protested that "like rewarding one's allies, the correlative act of refusing to reward one's opponents . . . is an American tradition as old as the Republic." In his view, this history was dispositive:

> If that long and unbroken tradition of our people does not decide these cases, then what does? The constitutional text is assuredly as susceptible of one meaning as of the other; in that circumstance, what constitutes a "law abridging the freedom of speech" is either a matter of history or else it is a matter of opinion. Why are not libel laws such an "abridgement"? The only satisfactory answer is that they never were. What secret knowledge, one must wonder, is breathed into lawyers when they become Justices of this Court, that enables them to discern that a practice which the text of the Constitution does not clearly proscribe, and which our people have *regarded* as constitutional for 200 years, is in fact unconstitutional? [55]

More generally, Justice Scalia insisted (quoting from his own dissent in an earlier case), when a "practice not expressly prohibited by the text of the Bill of Rights bears the endorsement of open, widespread, and unchallenged use that dates back to the beginning of the Republic, we have no proper basis for striking it down." Rather than subjecting such practices to current constitutional doctrines, "such traditions are themselves the stuff out of which the Court's principles are to be formed"—the "very points of reference by which the legitimacy or illegitimacy of *other* practices is to be figured out." [56]

As with almost everything about the Second Amendment, there is controversy about the precise meaning of the current precedents. Akhil Amar, who has taken an expansive view of the right to bear arms, concedes that the lower courts have firmly embraced the opposing view "that the Amendment was about a militia, not individually armed citizens," and as a "corollary that there is no individual right to bear arms."[57] The Supreme Court jurisprudence is less recent and sparser but is at least not inconsistent with the more recent consensus in the lower federal courts. The Supreme Court case most directly on point rejects a Second Amendment defense to a charge of possessing a sawed-off shotgun on the ground that "possession or use" of the weapon lacked any "reasonable relationship to the preservation or efficiency of a well regulated militia." That opinion is neither recent nor entirely unamibguous. But the more recent decisions of the federal circuit courts are unified in upholding gun control, and the Court has not chosen to revisit the issue in any of the many recent cases it has decided pertaining to firearms. In short, no federal gun control law has ever been declared a violation of the Second Amendment by a federal appellate court.

Does this line of authority, combined with the history of gun regulation in America, amount to the kind of precedent or "tradition of our people" that Justice Scalia would respect? The only honest answer is that no confident answer is possible. Originalism simply offers no clear-cut answer to the problem of when the need for legal stability precludes recourse to the original intent. Justice Scalia himself has provided no clear definition of binding traditions and no rule for applying stare decisis. What is required is seemingly an act of judgment—just the kind of value judgment that originalism was supposed to avoid.[58] Perhaps Justice Scalia would find the conventional understanding too entrenched to challenge; he reached a similar conclusion in the Eleventh Amendment area, where the conventional understanding seemed no more solidly established.[59] Until he actually confronts the issue, however, one cannot be sure what he or any other originalist would actually decide.

NORMATIVE DIMENSIONS OF ORIGINALISM

Originalism requires judges to make difficult historical judgments with little training in doing so; it gives no guidance about how concretely or abstractly to define the original understanding or about how to distinguish the framers' understanding of the text from their expectations about its implementation; and it leaves open the difficult problem of when to relinquish original understandings in favor of precedent or tradition. Furthermore, as practiced today, it may not even correspond with the methods used by the framers themselves to understand the text, so the so-called original understanding may not reflect the understanding of the framers of how the provision would be applied under new circumstances. In short, with the best will in the world, judges who practice originalism will find themselves in vast disagreement over the meaning of the Second Amendment. Thus, if it is intended to constrain judges, original-ism is a failure.

Even apart from these difficulties of implementation, the question remains whether we would want to implement originalism if we could. The Second Amendment is a good illustration of why we should not want to be bound by the original understanding. Originalists claim that only originalism can recon-cile judicial review with majority rule and make the Supreme Court something other than a super-legislature. In reality, however, the Justices do not need to give up their bar memberships and join the American Historical Society in order to do their jobs properly. The conventional methods of constitutional law are completely legitimate and adequate to the task at hand. Originalism's greatest failing—in contrast to the conventional process of common law deci-sion making—is its inability to confront historical change. We should reject the originalist's invitation to ignore all of the history that has transpired since 1790 when we interpret the Constitution.

Majoritarianism Concerns

Originalism has generally been tied to majoritarianism.[60] As Edwin Meese once explained it, the logic is simple: "[t]he Constitution is the fundamental will of the people; that is the reason the Constitution is the fundamental law"—hence, "[t]o allow the courts to govern simply by what it views at the time as fair and decent, is a scheme of government no longer popular; the idea of democracy has suffered."[61] Or, as John Ely put it, under the originalist view "the judges do not check the people, the Constitution does, which means the people are ultimately checking themselves."[62]

It seems doubtful that the eighteenth-century ratification process was dem-ocratic enough to support this claim. One of the standard criticisms is that it represented only propertied white males.[63] Moreover, there may be special reasons to be concerned about this lack of representativeness in connection with the Second Amendment itself. The Second Amendment may have been not merely "of the white people" and "by the white people" but also, at least to an extent, "for the white people."

Carl Bogus has suggested that a major motivation for passage of the Second Amendment may have been the militia's role in suppressing resistance by slaves.[64] Most of his evidence is admittedly circumstantial,[65] based on the known weakness of the militia as a military force[66] compared with its useful-ness in slave patrols and putting down slave revolts.[67] Besides the circumstan-tial evidence, however, Bogus does cite at least one disturbing piece of more direct evidence, in the form of Patrick Henry's concern that Congress might prevent the use of the state militia "[i]f there should happen an insurrection of slaves." [68] If Bogus's evidence is not enough to brand the Second Amendment as pro-slavery, it is at least enough to remind us that not all of the framers' motives were equally worthy of our respect.

Quite apart from these specific questions about the Second Amendment's pedigree, originalism seems to misconceive the connections between majoritarianism, constitutionalism, and judicial review. Taking majority rule as the sole foundational constitutional norm, originalism struggles to justify judicial review as enforcing the decisions of an earlier and more potent majority. This concern about majoritarianism is quite understandable. *Of course* majority rule is important, and *of course* judges should exercise restraint in reviewing the work of elected officials. But we have sometimes seemed so preoccupied with the tension between judicial review and majority rule that it has threatened to become a fetish. [69] When judicial review seemed to be a uniquely American institution, shared by no other democracy, perhaps it was natural to regard it as an anomaly in urgent need of justification. Today, this impulse seems anachronistic. Democratic governments around the world have now adopted judicially enforceable written constitutions, featuring various protections for individual rights against majority action. [70] What is in need of justification and legitimization now is less judicial review than its absence. [71] We need not mangle our methods of constitutional interpretation out of anxiety about the legitimacy of judicial review.

Reliance on the norm of majority rule is a particularly bad argument for Second Amendment originalism. This argument may have some appeal when the courts use nonoriginalist reasoning to strike down laws with broad popular support. In that setting, a turn toward originalism actually would strengthen majority rule, albeit at the possible expense of other constitutional values. But here, the shoe is on the other foot. Second Amendment originalism aims not to strengthen majority rule but to weaken it by limiting the majority's right to legislate in an important area of public policy.

Some arguments for a broad reading of the Second Amendment pose a different kind of threat to majority rule. The "insurrectionist" argument for the right to bear arms celebrates armed revolt against the government—reading the amendment to guarantee "the People's access to bullets as well as ballots." [72] In a democracy, however, this almost inevitably means the right of a minority to rebel when it sees a threat to its fundamental rights, for the majority can protect itself quite adequately with ballots. If we accept the legitimacy of this minority threat to revolt, we place a restraint on majority rule. Even apart from the remote chance that the threat will be implemented, its mere existence places a restraint on majority rule. It was for this reason that, the last time the insurrectionist card was played, President Lincoln argued that the real question was whether "any government so constituted"—any government "of the people, by the people, and for the people"—could long endure, or whether such a government must inevitably be subject to coercive threats by disgruntled minorities. If judicial review poses a countermajoritarian "difficulty," the insurrectionist reading of the Second Amendment threatens a countermajoritarian debacle.

The effort to equate the original understanding with the will of the people, and to equate both with constitutionalism, is dubious in any event. In the context of the Second Amendment, however, it is particularly tenuous.

The Nature of the Judicial Role

Other arguments for originalism rest on the nature of the judicial role. Justice Scalia argues that originalism, despite its problems, is the only way to restrain judicial discretion. Speaking of the traditional common law approach to judging, he says that it "would be an unqualified good, were it not for a trend in government that has developed in recent centuries, called democracy." Scalia's main priority is properly confining the role of judges—as he says in his response to Professor Gordon Wood: "I am sure that we can induce judges, as we have induced presidents and generals, to stay within their proper governmental sphere." Note in this regard that one of his main arguments for originalism is that it counters the tendency of judges to be swayed by their personal predilections, which he calls the "principal weakness of the system." [73]

Justice Scalia is too quick to dismiss the common law method, which is a central feature of American constitutional law. [74] Even some writers with a strong originalist bent, like Michael McConnell, seem to acknowledge a role for common law evolution. [75] At least since Karl Llewellyn—if not since Justice Holmes—American legal pragmatists have defended just this type of common law reasoning. The fullest recent attempt to justify this process comes from Cass Sunstein. He argues that we often make the best collective decisions (particularly collectively) on the basis of what he calls incompletely theorized agreements. These agreements represent a consensus on the proper outcome in a given case, with only a partial attempt to work out a theoretical justification. [76] These incompletely theorized agreements are particularly prominent in law—enough so that, for many lawyers, the only odd thing about the idea of an incompletely theorized agreement is that it seems to imagine the possibility of the other kind! (What lawyer has ever negotiated a completely theorized agreement or even had reason to read one? Indeed, one of the least plausible aspects of the recent efforts to expand the Second Amendment is the attempt to portray the amendment as embodying a complete theory of government.) As Sunstein explains, agreement about legal issues often "involves a specific outcome and a set of reasons that do not venture far from the case at hand. High-level theories are rarely reflected explicitly in law." [77]

An economist was once defined as someone who tries to prove that what is actually happening is theoretically possible. The efforts of legal philosophers to validate the common law method have something of this flavor. The fact is that English courts have been using this method since the Middle Ages, and our Supreme Court has been deciding cases without the benefit of a grand theory since it issued its first opinion. It seems a little late in the day to argue that the method does not work. Orville and Wilbur may not have known much aeronautical theory, but the plane did get off the ground.

The real concern of the originalists is not that the process is nonfunctional, but that it gives judges too much leeway. [78] Judges do have leeway, which they sometimes exercise in ways that not all of us like. But this is a condition without a cure, other than simply killing the patient. In particular, originalism will not cure the problem of judicial discretion. In practice, recourse to original intent simply fails to place sharp constraints on judges. Justice Scalia himself has not succeeded in purging his own decisions of personal value judgments, which flourish despite his attachment to originalism. [79] Nor have the efforts of other members of the Court been successful in this regard—for instance, in the Eleventh Amendment area, the Court has come to historical conclusions that are almost unanimously rejected by scholars. [80]

The Second Amendment once again provides an apt illustration of the defects of originalism. If the original understanding is to constrain judicial discretion, it must be possible to ascertain that understanding in a reasonably indisputable way. But, as discussed, it is not even possible to give a clear-cut definition of what constitutes the original "understanding," as opposed to the original "expectation" or the original "applications" associated with a constitutional provision. And having cleared that hurdle, formidable difficulties confront the originalist judge, including a historical record that combines enormous volume with frustrating holes in key places; a complex intellectual and social context; and a host of interpretative disputes. If we do not trust judges to correctly interpret and apply their own precedents—a skill they were supposedly taught in law school and have practiced throughout their professional lives—it is debatable whether we should trust them to interpret and apply a mass of eighteenth-century archival documents.

Fidelity and Change

Originalism is an effort to fix the meaning of the Constitution once and for all at its birth. But there is an opposing view, one most eloquently expressed by Justice Holmes:

> [W]hen we are dealing with words that also are a constituent act, like the Constitution of the United States, we must realize that they have called into life a being the development of which could not have been foreseen completely by the most gifted of its begetters. It was enough for them to realize or to hope that they had created an organism; it has taken a century and has cost their successors much sweat and blood to prove that they created a nation. The case before us must be considered in the light of our whole experience and not merely in that of what was said a hundred years ago.[81]

The Second Amendment is among the provisions of the Constitution that seem most to call out for Holmes's approach. For the historical changes relating to the "right to bear arms" have been far-reaching indeed.

Some of those changes relate directly to the two subjects of the Second Amendment: firearms and the militia. There is first of all the disappearance of the kind of militia contemplated by the framers. As Akhil Amar explains, perhaps with some regret:

> [T]he legal and social structure on which the amendment is built no longer exists. The Founders' juries—grand, petit, and civil—are still around today, but the Founders' militia is not. America is not Switzerland. Voters no longer must show up for militia practice in the town square.[82]

Another relevant change is the development of professional police departments, which limit the need for individuals and groups to engage in self-help.[83] Because these changes, unanticipated by the framers, undermined the asserted original purpose of the Second Amendment, its application today becomes problematic.[84]

Apart from these changes relating directly to the amendment's subject matter, broad changes in the constitutional landscape are also relevant. One watershed is the Civil War, which undermines the insurrectionist argument that armed revolt is a constitutionally sanctioned check on federal power.[85] Perhaps one should just say that the constitutionality of insurrection was decisively rejected. One might even cite in this regard the decisive ruling on this point at the Appomattox courthouse in the case of *Grant v. Lee*—a "ruling" of more decisive constitutional importance than many a Supreme Court decision, or even some constitutional amendments.

Perhaps there may be those who reject the validity of the decision at Appomattox even today. What cannot be disputed as a lesson of the Civil War, however, is that insurrection is not an acceptable practical check on the federal government. Quite apart from the question of whether insurgents could defeat a modern army, the lesson of the Civil War suggests that the costs of exercising this option would simply be unbearable: if a similar percentage of the current population died during such an insurgency today, we would be talking about five million deaths.[86] Brave talk about insurrection is one thing; "paying the butcher's bill" is quite another. Perhaps the framers can be forgiven for failing to appreciate this reality; it is much harder to excuse similar romanticism today.

The Civil War also transformed our concept of the relationship between the state and federal governments. The Second Amendment, at least if revisionist scholars are to be believed, was based on the threat a powerful national government posed to liberty. But one effect of the Civil War was to cement the federal government's role as a guarantor of liberty. Since the time of the Fourteenth Amendment, rather than state and local communities being seen as bulwarks of freedom against the federal leviathan, the federal government has been pressed into service to defend liberty. The Fourteenth Amendment arose in part out of a sense of the obligation of the federal government to protect the rights of its citizens, by force if necessary, whether the threat came from a foreign nation or a state or local government.[87]

Thus, rather than entrusting liberty to the "locals," the Fourteenth Amendment calls into play federal judicial and legislative power to ensure that the states respect individual rights. This realignment of the federal government as friend rather than threat to liberty underlies much of our modern Supreme Court jurisprudence and a plethora of twentieth-century civil rights legislation. This fundamental reassessment of the relationship between federal power and liberty would make the independent state and local militia as much a threat to liberty as a protector of it.

If the insurrectionist argument is at odds with the lessons of the Civil War, the self-defense argument for constitutional protection clashes with the modern regulatory state. It is a commonplace that the New Deal was a "watershed" in the development of the regulatory state,[88] enough so to lead one prominent theorist to build a whole theory of constitutional interpretation around this shift.[89] But the New Deal was only the beginning. In the 1960s and '70s came a new wave of legislation covering matters such as consumer protection, discrimination law, and the environment.[90] As a result, we live in a world where citizens routinely rely on the federal government, rather than self-help, to protect them against a host of threats.

Today, we expect federal protection against everything from potentially dangerous traces of pesticides in our foods to unwanted sexual overtures in the workplace. In this context, the notion that the government cannot protect us from the dangers of firearms seems like an odd relic of an earlier laissez-faire period. Indeed, it seems peculiar at best to say that the government can constitutionally protect us from one kind of hostile environment—coworkers displaying lewd pictures—but not from a more dramatic kind of hostile environment, such as neighbors carrying Uzis.

The point here is not that the Second Amendment is an anachronistic text that ought to be ignored, or that its interpretation should necessarily be narrowed in light of these later developments. It is not even that these later developments are fundamentally correct. What is wrong with originalism is that it seeks to block judges from even considering these later developments, which on their face seem so clearly relevant to the legitimacy of federal gun control efforts. Try as they may, however, it seems unlikely that judges can avoid being influenced by these realities.

CONCLUSION

What do we learn about originalism from the Second Amendment debate? What do we learn about the Second Amendment from the originalism debate?

One set of lessons relates to constitutional interpretation. The Second Amendment shows how the standard academic criticisms of originalism are not just academic quibbles; they identify real and troubling flaws. The debate about the Second Amendment vividly illustrates critical problems with originalism:

- The historical record concerning the right to bear arms is difficult for non-historians such as judges to evaluate, requiring a high level of historical expertise to evaluate the credibility and import of the evidence.[91]
- Originalism might not accurately reflect the way in which contemporary readers understood the document; in particular, it may underestimate their willingness to contemplate limiting the "right to bear arms" clause in light of the purpose clause.[92]
- The original understanding of the Second Amendment can be defined at different levels of generality, and the interpretation will depend on the choice of level as well as on how we distinguish the original "understanding" from mere original "expectations."[93]
- Originalism, to be a realistic option, must acknowledge stare decisis, yet it does not provide us with clear guidance about whether the current Second Amendment case law should stand.[94]
- Although originalism claims simply to be enforcing the will of "We the Peo-

ple," the Second Amendment may show how originalism undermines majority rule.[95]
- Because of the difficulties judges would face in basing their decisions on purely historical grounds, originalism would not eliminate the role of personal values in judging.[96]
- Originalism forces us to ignore the ways our world has changed since the eighteenth century: the Civil War and its aftermath have cut the ground away from the notion of insurrection as a protection of liberty against federal power; and the New Deal and *its* aftermath have created a world in which we customarily turn to the regulatory state, rather than self-help, to protect ourselves from threats.[97]

It would, in short, be a serious mistake for judges to use originalism as their recipe for interpreting the Second Amendment or other ambiguous constitutional language. The fact that the arguments against this approach are familiar does not make them any less damaging.

At a more fundamental level, however, the lesson is not simply that originalists are wrong about how judges should read the Constitution. More important, they are wrong about the nature of the Constitution itself. In general, disputed constitutional provisions cannot simply be applied on the basis of whatever examples were discussed at the time, and so it is natural for originalists to attempt instead to reconstruct the theories underlying those provisions. This effort to theorize constitutional provisions is quite evident with the Second Amendment originalists we have discussed,[98] but it is equally clear in the efforts of other originalists to find in the original understanding some unified theory of executive power or of federalism. But to look for an underlying theory is to misconceive the nature of the constitutional enterprise. Unlike physics, law does not lend itself to a "standard model" or a grand unified theory.

While the framers were indeed "concerned with such fundamental questions as the nature of representation and executive power,"[99] they were also engaged in "a cumulative process of bargaining and compromise in which a rigid adherence to principle yielded to the pragmatic tests of reaching agreement and building coalitions."[100] In short, they were doing their best to create a viable set of democratic institutions, a task that required the utmost attention to both principle and pragmatism. Their task was not to agree on a theory but to create the basis for a working democracy. We hardly do justice to the spirit of their undertaking if we treat the resulting document as *their* Constitution alone rather than being ours as well. The last thing they would want would be for us to be ruled by false certainties about their intentions, an invitation we have received all too often with respect to the Second Amendment.

10. What Does the Second Amendment Mean Today?

Michael C. Dorf*

A growing body of legal scholarship argues that the Second Amendment protects a right of individuals to possess firearms, regardless of whether those individuals are organized in state militias.[1] Proponents of this individual rights view[2] do not merely disagree with those who champion the competing view that the Second Amendment poses few if any obstacles to most forms of gun control legislation by the state or federal governments. Judged by the titles of their writings, many of the individual rights scholars appear to believe that the Second Amendment has been subject to uniquely shabby treatment by the courts and, until recently, academic commentators.

For example, Sanford Levinson titles an important essay "The Embarrassing Second Amendment,"[3] thereby suggesting that any interpretation less robust than the one favored by the National Rifle Association (NRA) must be the product of result-oriented scholarship. The Second Amendment, Levinson implies, protects an individual right to own guns, and that is embarrassing to liberals who favor gun control.

In the same vein, Eugene Volokh titles a recent essay "The Amazing Vanishing Second Amendment."[4] Volokh argues that the interpretive moves that have been used to restrict the Second Amendment's scope are unprincipled because they would be unacceptable in other contexts.[5] Similar claims permeate the individual rights literature.[6]

Nonetheless, the Second Amendment has not been unfairly orphaned. The courts and commentators that reject the individual rights scholars' claims are justified in doing so by the application of the same criteria of interpretation commonly applied to other constitutional provisions. A nonexclusive list of the relevant factors includes: precedent, text, original understanding, structural inference, postadoption history, and normative considerations.

Champions of the individual rights interpretation of the Second Amendment may believe that these criteria are wrongheaded or illegitimate in all contexts. For example, many individual rights scholars appear to believe that original meaning is the sole criterion of constitutional interpretation.[7] But if that is their premise, they cannot contend that nonoriginalist interpretation of the Second Amendment is anything like a *unique* mistake. Many of the foundational doctrines of our current constitutional regime do not comport with the original understanding of the Constitution or its amendments. The requirement of equal population apportionment for state legislative districts, the invalidity of de jure racial segregation, and the breadth of federal power under the Commerce Clause (even after some recent Supreme Court decisions cutting it back) are all at odds with the dominant understandings of those who adopted the relevant constitutional provisions. Original understanding is not the sole, nor even the principal, measure of a constitutional interpretation's correctness.[8] If the individual rights interpretation of the Second Amendment rests on contrary premises, its proponents must persuade us to abandon much more than gun control.

It has become customary to contrast the individual rights view of the Second Amendment with what is often called the collective rights interpretation.[9] Under the latter, the Second Amendment protects some right of state militias against undue federal interference but no right of individuals against either federal or state regulation.[10] Although I am sympathetic to the collective rights view, I acknowledge that the Second Amendment is and has always been somewhat puzzling. Motivated in large measure by the founders' distrust of standing armies, even on the broadest reading the Second Amendment does nothing to prevent the federal government from maintaining a standing army.

So, too, the right of insurrection that is sometimes offered as a normative justification for a right to possess firearms has been emphatically rejected by our constitutional history. When *individuals* attempted to exercise a right to rebel during the Whiskey Rebellion of 1794, President Washington called forth the militia (the institution at the heart of the Second Amendment) to suppress the rebels. The only serious attempt by the *states* to exercise a right of rebellion led to the Civil War.

Accordingly, the Second Amendment is probably best read as preventing the federal government from abolishing state militias. Before coming to that conclusion, however, we must examine the canonical forms of constitutional argument.

PRECEDENT

The Second Amendment provides: "A well regulated Militia, being necessary to the security of a free State, the right of the people to keep and bear Arms, shall not be infringed." Although judges and scholars customarily list authoritative text as the first consideration in ascertaining meaning, I shall briefly defer consideration of the Second Amendment's text as such. I do so, not simply because the Second Amendment lacks a "plain meaning," but because, contrary to conventional wisdom, constitutional doctrine typically trumps constitutional text—at least absent arguments of sufficient strength to justify overruling established precedent. For example, there is a familiar and powerful textual argument that the Fourteenth Amendment's prohibition on state deprivations of liberty without due process implicitly authorizes such deprivations where adequate procedures are followed. Yet even the staunchest critics of particular doctrines adopted in the name of "substantive due process" would not so limit the clause; at a minimum, they accept that the Fourteenth Amendment has the substantive effect of making most of the Bill of Rights applicable to the states, and not just to the federal government. An argument that, say, the First Amendment poses no obstacle to a state imposing viewpoint-based regulations on speech would face an insurmountable doctrinal hurdle. Similarly, references in the case law to "the dormant Commerce Clause"[11] suggest that there is an express provision of the Constitution restricting the states' ability to enact discriminatory or unduly burdensome regulations of interstate commerce, when the text of Article I, section 8, clause 3, appears to be nothing more than a grant of power to Congress. Numerous other examples could be adduced in which sound textual arguments would stand no realistic chance of prevailing because of contrary doctrine. Therefore, it is appropriate in interpreting the Second Amendment or any constitutional provision to begin with precedent rather than text. Let us turn, then, to the cases.

The Supreme Court has never upheld an individual's Second Amendment objection to prosecution under a law regulating firearms. Two nineteenth-century decisions, *United States v. Cruikshank*[12] and *Presser v. Illinois*,[13] held that the Second Amendment does not apply to the states. Although these decisions postdated the enactment of the Fourteenth Amendment, they predated the modern cases holding that the Fourteenth Amendment incorporates most of the provisions of the Bill of Rights. To the extent that *Cruikshank* and *Presser* simply rely on the old view that the Bill of Rights does not apply to the states,[14] they might appropriately be reexamined. This does not, of course, mean that the Second Amendment necessarily applies to the states. Upon reexamination, we might conclude, for example, that the Second Amendment prohibits the federal government from asserting some measure of control over state units of the National Guard; such a limit on the federal government for the *benefit* of the states could not readily be applied *against* the states. On the other hand, if the Second Amendment protects a right of individual firearm ownership against federal interference, there would be no analytical difficulty in applying a parallel limit against the states.

The leading case involving the Second Amendment as a limit on federal action is *United States v. Miller*.[15] There the Court rejected the claim that the

Second Amendment protected a private right to possess a sawed-off shotgun because there was no evidence that such possession bore "some reasonable relationship to the preservation or efficiency of a well regulated militia."[16]

Individual rights scholars correctly point out that *Miller* might plausibly be read to suggest a negative pregnant: "if the sawed-off shotgun had been a militia weapon, then," on this reading, the defendants "would have had a constitutional right to possess it."[17] By further implication, in general, individuals would have a Second Amendment right to private possession of whatever weapons might be useful in military service. *Miller* approvingly describes state statutes in force at the time of the adoption of the federal Constitution organizing militias out of the (adult white male) citizens, who (according to the statutes) were to bring their own weapons when called to muster.[18] When not called to muster, the argument goes, the people are entitled to, in the terms of the Second Amendment, "keep" their weapons.

Miller itself does not exclude this possibility; but neither does *Miller* compel it. Indeed, we extrapolate from the logic of *Miller* at our peril, because, under modern conditions, it would seem to grant the most constitutional protection to just those weapons that are least suitable to private possession—distinctly military "arms" such as tanks, attack helicopters, rocket launchers, or even nuclear weapons.[19]

More important, the Supreme Court has not read *Miller* to imply anything resembling an individual right to firearms possession. For example, in a 1980 case, *Lewis v. United States*,[20] the Court upheld a federal statute prohibiting a convicted felon from possessing firearms. If the Court had been interested in safeguarding an individual right of firearms possession for law-abiding citizens, it could have relied on the fact that prohibitions on firearms possession by felons date back to colonial times.[21] Yet the *Lewis* Court went considerably further in undermining constitutional protection for an individual right. It cited *Miller* for the proposition that the statute at issue did not "trench upon any constitutionally protected liberties."[22]

Or consider *Adams v. Williams,* which rejected a Fourth Amendment challenge to a "stop-and-frisk" based on an informant's tip that the defendant was in illegal possession of narcotics and a handgun.[23] Dissenting, Justice Douglas, joined by Justice Marshall, argued that the danger to the police in street encounters with suspects stemmed not from the niceties of the Fourth Amendment but from the state's failure to enact strict gun control laws. Citing *Miller,* Justice Douglas opined that "[t]here is no reason why all pistols should not be barred to everyone except the police."[24] No member of the Court took issue with this statement.

These decisions suggest that, without directly facing the question, the Supreme Court has come to understand *Miller* as standing roughly for the collective rights view of the Second Amendment.[25] With one recent exception, the lower federal courts have also understood *Miller* this way.[26] As a matter of doctrine, the most that can be said for reading the Second Amendment as conferring an individual right to own and carry firearms is that constitutional precedent does not pose an insuperable obstacle to that reading, although its adoption would mark a substantial change in the prevailing view, and presumably would have to satisfy the criteria ordinarily thought to justify a departure from precedent.

Before moving to textual arguments, I should consider an objection to the conclusion that existing precedents stand against the individual rights view: *Miller* did not actually hold that the Second Amendment protects no individual right to firearms possession, so cases or individual opinions treating *Miller* as if it did are not entitled to the weight of precedent. This is not a trivial objection; however, and this is the point I wish to emphasize, the objection applies to much more than Second Amendment jurisprudence. For example, much of the rationale for the Supreme Court's decision in *Brown v. Board of Education*[27] rested on an examination of the harms caused by racial segregation in *education*[28]; yet the Court, without explanation, rapidly applied *Brown* to invalidate racial segregation in a wide variety of other contexts.[29]

Nor has this process of precedent setting without judicial opinion been confined to the *expansion* of individual rights. As in the interpretation of the Second Amendment so, too, have First Amendment rights been *restricted* to less than they might have been by somewhat unreflective citation. For example, current First Amendment law affords less protection to labor picketing than to otherwise comparable speech outside the labor context.[30] The difference in treatment is essentially a historical legacy: labor decisions predating modern free speech doctrine continue to be cited as good law, and, for that reason, remain good law.[31] Furthermore, as Justice Kennedy has noted, even the now canonical view that content-based regulation of speech can be justified if strictly necessary to further a compelling state interest came into being by a series of sloppy citations.[32] Yet despite his well-documented protest, Justice Kennedy convinced none of his colleagues to reexamine the test.

These examples illustrate a quite basic point that the objection under consideration ignores: the force of doctrine qua doctrine does not rest on how it came into being any more than it rests upon the soundness of the arguments that can be advanced for it. The main point of following precedent is to follow it when there is a plausible argument that it is wrong. There are, of course, occasions when constitutional precedents are abandoned because they are very clearly wrong or because they have become unworkable, and some (including me) have argued that the Supreme Court should be willing to reexamine its precedents more frequently than it does.[33] But as a matter of precedent understood in the conventional way, the case for the individual rights view of the Second Amendment remains a very weak one. To put the matter in lawyerly terms, champions of the individual rights view of the Second Amendment must satisfy a heavy burden of persuasion. They must make an overwhelming rather than a just barely convincing case for their view. Turning to the remaining criteria of constitutional interpretation, we will see that this is a tall order.

TEXT

Recall the text of the Second Amendment: "A well regulated Militia, being necessary to the security of a free State, the right of the people to keep and bear Arms, shall not be infringed." The preamble is arresting. Only one other operative provision of the Constitution contains anything resembling it. Article I, section 8, clause 8, gives Congress the power "[t]o promote the Progress of Science and useful Arts, by securing for limited Times to Authors and Inventors the exclusive Right to their respective Writings and Discoveries." What are we to make of such preambles? One answer would be to treat them as purely hortatory. But even if one believes (as I do not) that, in general, the interpretation of authoritative text should proceed without any consideration of the background purposes of its adopters, surely that principle of construction does not apply when the lawmakers have stated their purpose in equally authoritative text. The Second Amendment's preamble is no scrap of legislative history taken from a largely overlooked committee report or poorly attended floor debate. It is part of the Constitution and should therefore inform our understanding of the rest of the sentence of which it is a part.

The Preamble to the Constitution as a whole provides a useful parallel. Although it creates no judicially enforceable rights or duties directly, the Preamble has been used, quite appropriately, to shed light on the meaning of other judicially enforceable provisions.[34] I am suggesting that a similar use should be made of the Second Amendment's preamble—and, although this is beyond the scope of my argument here, the preamble to the Copyright and Patent Clauses as well. To the extent that we are unsure what a right to keep and bear arms entails, the Second Amendment's preamble provides guidance.

The relevance of the Second Amendment's preamble to its meaning would seem so obvious as not to need justifying were it not for academic efforts to minimize its weight.[35] For example, Volokh points out that provisions of state constitutions of the founding era commonly contained preambles of the sort we see in the federal Constitution's Second Amendment. Those provisions involved not only the right to bear arms but a diverse collection of other rights, including freedom of speech and the press, the right to trial by a local jury, and many more.[36] Volokh draws two inferences from the existence of these provisions: first, the framers' decision to include a preamble in the Second Amendment was mere stylistic happenstance, to which virtually no significance can be attributed.[37] Second, reading the contemporaneous state constitutional provisions alongside the Second Amendment drives home the lesson that, even when a constitutional provision's operative clause is over- or under-inclusive with respect to its justification clause, it is still the operative clause, and not the justification clause, that controls.[38] Although we might not think "that entirely unfettered freedom of speech in the legislature"[39] is, in the words of the justification clauses of the Speech and Debate Articles of the Massachusetts, New Hampshire, and Vermont constitutions, "essential to the rights of the people,"[40] we would nonetheless be obliged to give full effect to the operative language of those provisions. Volokh argues for similar treatment for the Second Amendment: even if we no longer believe that "A well regulated Militia" is "necessary to the security of a free State," we nonetheless must respect "the right of the people to keep and bear Arms."

Although I agree with the overall thrust of Volokh's argument, it does not, in my view, carry us very far in the direction of the individual rights interpretation of the Second Amendment. I should begin by noting my substantial disagreement with Volokh's first inference. As a matter of *textual* interpretation of the Second Amendment, it is largely irrelevant that clause preambles are commonplace in *other* documents. In the United States Constitution, the inclusion of a preamble marks the Second Amendment as extraordinary. The frequent use of clause preambles in contemporaneous documents does, I concede, shed some light on the subjective intent of those who drafted the Second Amendment as well as, perhaps, the most common understanding of the political community at the time. However—and here Volokh's second argument undermines his first—it is the text itself, not the subjective intent of the drafters nor even the background understanding of the time, that was enacted. In the case of the Second Amendment as it appears in the federal Constitution, that text is striking for containing its own preamble.

I do not read Volokh as ultimately disagreeing. He says: "To the extent the operative clause is ambiguous, the justification clause may inform our interpretation of it, but the justification clause can't take away what the operative clause provides."[41] I agree, as, apparently, does David Williams—one of the principal champions of the collective rights interpretation of the Second Amendment.[42] The real disagreement between Volokh, on the one hand, and Williams and myself, on the other, has nothing to do with the general function of clause preambles; instead, we disagree over whether the operative clause standing alone is ambiguous. In my view, protecting a "right of the people to keep and bear Arms" is a sufficiently odd way of protecting an individual right to possess firearms for rebellion, self-defense, or hunting as to provoke further inquiry.

As I note below, at the time of the founding, the phrase "bear arms" was most commonly used in a military setting, and even today it carries a military connotation. This is not to say that people do not use the phrase to refer to individual firearm possession—they do. However, many of the people who use the term that way do so for a distinctly political purpose: they aim to associate the language of the Second Amendment with private firearms possession for rebellion, self-defense, or hunting. For example, the home page of the NRA touts all that the organization does for "your Second Amendment right to keep and bear arms."[43] The political import of this use of the Second Amendment's language is difficult to miss. By repeatedly associating the Second Amendment's language with its own political aims, the organization increases the likelihood that, over time, the language will simply come to be synonymous with those aims.

A strict originalist would object that, to the extent that the NRA uses the words of the Second Amendment to mean something different from their common understanding in 1791, the new usage should have no bearing on authoritative constitutional interpretation. However, I am not a strict originalist and would therefore eschew this objection. Abolitionists were fully entitled to invoke the Declaration of Independence's statement that "[a]ll men are created equal" in pursuit of ends that its drafters would have rejected.[44] Even without accompanying changes in constitutional text, constitutional change can legitimately come about because of a political struggle that aims to capture hearts and minds through language.[45]

Therefore, I do not question the legitimacy of the NRA's efforts to tie the language of the Second Amendment to its political agenda. Should those efforts succeed, and should the language of the Second Amendment widely come to be understood as synonymous with a right to private possession of firearms for rebellion, self-defense, or hunting, the plain-meaning argument for that interpretation would be accordingly strengthened. However, and this is the critical point, the NRA has not (yet) won its battle. The meaning of "the right to keep and bear arms" remains hotly contested in a way that other formerly contested questions of constitutional meaning—such as whether the most blatant forms of sex discrimination deny the equal protection of the laws—do not. For the time being at least, for a large number of reasonable interpreters, perhaps a majority, the phrase "keep and bear arms" is a sufficiently awkward way to protect a right of armed rebellion, self-defense, or hunting to warrant a search for some alternative interpretation.

Yet considered in the light of twenty-first-century conditions and sensibilities, the Second Amendment is baffling. What exactly is the militia, and how does protecting a right to keep and bear arms contribute to a "well-regulated" one? We are accustomed to thinking that rights act to impede rather than to further government regulation. Perhaps the answer is that "the people" who have a right to keep and bear arms are the people in a collective capacity,[46] so that the right at stake is, at least in substantial measure, what Benjamin Constant famously called a "liberty of the ancients"—a collective right of self-governance—rather than a "liberty of the moderns"—a right against the government.[47] But if this is so, the individual rights scholars like to ask, how do we account for the fact that other provisions of the Bill of Rights, which we understand as rights against the government, use the very same term, "the people"?[48]

The short answer is that the Constitution was the product of human hands and, therefore, there would be nothing particularly odd if it used the same word to mean different things in different contexts: to assume otherwise is to commit "the fallacy of *hyper-integration*—of treating the Constitution as a kind of seamless web."[49] Nonetheless, individual rights scholars pursue just this course.

Many individual rights scholars say that the militia and the people are one and the same. They frequently quote founding-era statements equating the militia with the people, such as the following remark by George Mason: "Who are the militia?[50] They consist now of the whole people." Yet the individual rights scholars rarely cite the remainder of Mason's observation, which reveals that he understood near-universal militia service to be subject to legislative abolition, absent contrary language in the Constitution. He stated: "I cannot say who will be the militia of the future day."[51] Nor do the individual rights scholars note that the debate from which this quotation is taken focused on the balance of power between the state and federal governments.[52]

Moreover, the individual rights scholars' equation of the militia and the people leads to considerable modern interpretive difficulty. If the "people" of the Second Amendment are the same "people" we encounter elsewhere in the Constitution, then the "militia" of the Second Amendment must also be the "militia" of Articles I and II, and individual rights scholars indeed assume as much.[53] Yet *Perpich v. Dod,*[54] a unanimous 1990 ruling of the Supreme Court, treats the militia of Articles I and II as identical to Congress's statutory definition of the militia.[55] That statutory definition expressly excludes women who are not members of the National Guard and men who are not able-bodied and (unless they are former members of the regular armed forces who enlisted in the National Guard before they turned sixty-four) under forty-four years of age.[56]

Thus, the individual rights scholars' theory would deny a right to own or possess firearms to the disabled, to most women, to most middle-aged men, and to all older Americans. Worse still, because the militia of Articles I and II equals the militia of the Second Amendment equals the people of the Second Amendment equals the people of the other provisions of the Constitution, *all constitutional liberties* would appear to be ruled out for these groups, which comprise a majority of the adult population.

How can the individual rights scholars avoid these absurd implications? They might argue that *Perpich* is simply wrong, although they would face a stiff burden of persuasion in contesting a unanimous decision (authored by Justice Stevens, a Bronze Star Navy veteran) and a congressional interpretation that has not changed significantly in nearly a century.[57] Alternatively, the individual rights scholars could say that the militia and the people were thought to be synonymous in 1791 but that the meanings of the terms have since diverged. Yet such an approach would explain *Perpich* by conceding that the meaning of words in the Second Amendment can change over time, a concession that would seem fatal for the more strongly originalist variants of the individual rights theory. We will see next how, even without this difficulty, the original understanding provides at best tenuous support for the individual rights view.

ORIGINAL UNDERSTANDING AND STRUCTURAL INFERENCE

Professional historians seem to enjoy chiding judges and legal academics for the way the latter employ historical material. The charge typically takes one or more of three forms. First, historians object to what they see as incompetence.[58] Second, they decry the pervasiveness of "law office history," in which advocates "pick and choose facts and incidents ripped out of context that serve their purposes."[59] Painful though they may be, these two criticisms are well taken: who could defend incompetent or biased work?

The third common criticism is more problematic, however. Some historians—especially those who are not also lawyers—labor under the misimpression that constitutional interpretation aspires to recapture original meaning and nothing else, so that nonoriginalist decisions are, ipso facto, the product of incompetent historical understanding or illegitimate usurpation. For example, upon concluding that the founders intended the Second Amendment to protect a private right of armed self-defense and revolution, Joyce Malcolm asserts—without any discussion of nonhistorical forms of constitutional argument—that to take a different view of the Second Amendment in modern times is to engage in "misinterpretation."[60] If we disagree with the founders' views, as she understands them, the only legitimate path is constitutional amendment.[61] Daniel Lazare makes the identical move, although he is considerably less sanguine than Malcolm, both because he takes a dimmer view of the wisdom of an armed populace and because he acknowledges the near impossibility of securing a constitutional amendment.[62] Malcolm, Lazare, and many others writing in the field thus appear to be laboring under what James Fleming has aptly called the "originalist premise."[63]

As I have argued at length elsewhere, the original understanding of very old provisions of the Constitution is relevant to modern interpretation, but not in the reductionist way that strict originalists and some historians commonly assume. The relevance of original understanding takes three principal forms. First, if phrases like "keep and bear arms" or

> "well regulated Militia" ha[ve] no commonly accepted modern usage, a [modern] interpreter would first wish to discern [their] meaning in the eighteenth century and then to translate that meaning into modern English. [T]o the extent that *text* matters to the modern interpreter, it sometimes will be nearly impossible to make any sense out of the text without understanding an earlier historical context.[64]

Second, "we care about what the framers thought because, whether we like it or not, our own understanding has been shaped against the backdrop of theirs."[65] And third, "we believe that the Founders of the Republic had insight into the problems of government which their handiwork addressed."[66] I have referred to the second and third reasons for caring about the original understanding as *ancestral* and *heroic* originalism, respectively.[67] We clearly have sound reasons for studying the original understanding, although "[n]othing in this enterprise commits the modern reader to seeking or to following the intentions of the eighteenth-century adopters of the language."[68] In this spirit, let us look to the original understanding of the Second Amendment.

A historian interested in unearthing the founders' full views on the right to keep and bear arms would no doubt begin with the seventeenth-century English experience, culminating in the English Bill of Rights of 1689.[69] From this experience, Americans drew the Whig lesson that standing armies—a somewhat ambiguous idea even in the eighteenth century—posed a serious threat of tyranny.[70] They "also had firsthand experience with European military practices that reinforced political theory and identified the standing army in American minds as a foreign, anti-libertarian institution."[71] Remote and local experience came together in the Revolutionary War. Among the colonists' principal complaints against George III was his use of the military against the civilian population. In the words of the Declaration of Independence, "He has kept among us, in times of peace, Standing Armies without the Consent of our legislatures. He has affected to render the Military independent of and superior to the Civil power."[72]

Many colonists believed that severing the tie to England was not by itself sufficient to avert such harms. Even as the Revolutionary War was being fought, they included in the Articles of Confederation provisions designed to ensure that domestic government would not become tyrannical in the way that George III's rule had. Article VI prohibited states from maintaining a peacetime navy or a peacetime standing army without congressional authorization and obligated the states to equip and train a militia. Article IX authorized Congress to maintain a national navy and to requisition state forces for a national army, but required a super-majority for waging war. The Articles thus employed civilian control of the military and the continued existence of state militias as the means to avert tyranny.

The original Constitution further concentrated military power in the federal government. Federalists who had seen the Continental army outperform the militia during the Revolution—including, especially, George Washington—favored a strong national military force,[73] while most anti-Federalists grudgingly accepted the need for some national military institutions.[74] In the Constitution that emerged, civilian control of the military was assured through both the executive and legislative branches. The president was designated commander in chief of federal forces and of the state militias when called into service, while Congress was granted authority over funding, maintenance, training, and use of federal land and naval forces, as well as state militias. No provision of the original Constitution exactly paralleled the Articles' requirement that states maintain their militias, although one can probably be inferred from the assumption that militias would exist to be called upon by the federal government and from the reservation to the states of the power of "[a]ppointment of the Officers, and the Authority of training the Militia according to the discipline prescribed by Congress."[75]

The story of the ratification debate is a familiar one. Anti-Federalists objected to the strength of the federal government. To the extent that opponents of ratification worried about arms, their principal concern was that the federal government would establish a standing army.[76] Ratification was obtained through a bargain. "[I]n order to gain acceptance of their handiwork, the Federalists had to commit themselves, unofficially, to the formulation of a bill of rights when the first Congress met in 1789."[77] The ultimately enacted Bill of Rights contained what is now the Second Amendment.

And therein lies the puzzle, for the Second Amendment does nothing to prevent the maintenance of a federal standing army, nor does it remotely insulate state militias from federal control.[78] Congress retains the authority to prescribe training for state militias and to call them into federal service, while the president commands them when thus called. Why, then, did anti-Federalists and others who disdained standing armies settle for the Second Amendment?

One possibility is that the founders were principally interested in protecting an individual right to rebellion and self-defense, but there are at least two other, in my view more plausible, explanations of the apparent mismatch between the Second Amendment and the goals of those who feared federal power. First, some, perhaps most, of the framers and ratifiers of the Second Amendment may have believed that it would serve to negate the inference from the 1787 text that standing federal forces were anything more than a necessary evil. As Madison argued, removing federal control of the militia would have left the federal government more, rather than less, dependent on a standing army.[79] In an era before judicial review was firmly established as the principal means of enforcing constitutional safeguards, the Second Amendment would have been understood as a reminder to Congress to prefer defense by militia to defense by standing army.[80]

A second possibility is that the Second Amendment was intended to protect the *states'* right of organized resistance against federal tyranny. Once again, Madison is instructive. In *Federalist* 46, he explains why, given the representation of the states in the federal government, resort to such resistance would not be necessary. But, he goes on, "[e]xtravagant as the supposition is" that the federal government would accumulate a standing military force for the purpose of destroying the states,

> let it, however, be made. Let a regular army, fully equal to the resources of the country, be formed; and let it be entirely at the devotion of the Federal Government; still it would not be going too far to say, that the State Governments, with the people on their side, would be able to repel the danger. The highest number to which, according to the best computation, a standing army can be carried in any country, does not exceed one hundredth part of the whole number of souls; or one twenty-fifth part of the number able to bear arms. This proportion would not yield, in the United States, an army of more than twenty-five or thirty thousand men. To these would be opposed a militia amounting to near half a million of citizens with arms in their hands, officered by men chosen from among themselves, fighting for their common liberties, and united and conducted by Governments possessing their affections and confidence. It may well be doubted, whether a militia thus circumstanced could ever be conquered by such a proportion of regular troops.[81]

Some scholars point to *Federalist* 46—especially Madison's statement, immediately following the text quoted above, that "over the people of almost every other nation," Americans possess "the advantage of being armed"[82]—in support of the individual rights interpretation of the Second Amendment.[83] Yet the armed resistance Madison contemplates in *Federalist* 46 quite clearly occurs under the official aegis of the states—not by self-styled patriots. The founding generation's conception of armed resistance, indeed the whole concern over standing armies, is probably best understood in federalism terms, as part of a struggle between the states and the federal government rather than between individuals and (either state or federal) government.

What of Madison's assumption that the people would have arms? It is possible that the assumption was simply inaccurate? Based on his examination of probate records and gun censuses, Michael Bellesiles contends that relatively few people in colonial America owned working guns.[84] Moreover, as Garry Wills explains, Bellesiles's conclusion is consistent with other evidence tending to show that the notion of founding-era militias comprising nearly all able-bodied adult white males was never more than a myth.[85] The romantic attachment to the militia arose, Wills contends, because of their role in keeping order on the home front—protecting against, among other things, Indian attacks and slave revolts[86]—while the Continental army won the war against the British. However, questions have been raised about Bellesiles's methods and results,[87] and historians will undoubtedly continue to debate the extent of gun ownership in early America for some time.

Does it matter whether the founders' assumptions about an armed populace were in error? That depends on the reasons we have for caring about the founders' views. Recall my categories of ancestral and heroic originalism. Within the *ancestral* category, if we discover that their understanding of the facts was false, "we may discount their views."[88] The same logic applies within the *heroic* category, when the framers' values are simply too distasteful to count as support for a given proposition.[89]

It is in this spirit, I believe, that Carl Bogus offers his discovery that many of the supporters of the Second Amendment feared that the federal government would disarm the militia, and thus disempower the principal mechanism for suppressing slave revolts. Hence he concludes his study: "The Second Amendment takes on an entirely different complexion when instead of being symbolized by a musket in the hands of the minuteman, it is associated with a musket in the hands of the slave holder."[90] As I have argued elsewhere, ancestral and heroic originalism better capture the relevance of original understanding to constitutional interpretation than does the social contract theory of strict originalism. Accordingly, the historical work of scholars like Bellesiles and Bogus—if correct in their conclusions—substantially undermines the individual rights position.

Of course, advocates of the individual rights position may fare better with respect to the first reason I identified above for caring about original meaning—to understand, in historical context, what the people who adopted the Second Amendment had in mind. If, in 1791, the language of the Second Amendment was widely understood to protect an individual right to firearms possession, then that fact must count somewhat in favor of such a contemporary reading—regardless of how widespread gun ownership actually was at the time. For this inquiry, the crucial issue is the meaning of words, not the facts on the ground. Thus we come to the question: How were the words of the Second Amendment understood at the time of its adoption?

Begin with the question of who are the militia of the Second Amendment's preamble. Akhil Amar gives a concise statement of the individual rights perspective: "Nowadays," he writes,

> it is quite common to speak loosely of the National Guard as "the state militia," but two hundred years ago, any band of paid, semiprofessional, part-time volunteers, like today's Guard, would have been called "a *select* corps" or "*select* militia"—and viewed in many quarters as little better than a standing army.[91]

Here Amar appears to assume a false universality of militia service. Nonetheless, it could be argued that this false assumption reflected founding-era ideology, and that ideology underlies the Second Amendment. On this reading, the "militia" of the Second Amendment's preamble is synonymous with the "people" of its operative clause, which in turn refers to the people in their individual capacities.

Putting aside the anomaly this reading creates given the long-standing congressional and judicial understanding of "militia," this is a plausible account of how many eighteenth-century readers would have approached the language, although certainly there would have been many readers—including such significant figures as George Washington—who would not have shared the ideological gloss, and thus would have distinguished the militia from the people. Still, even if we score the debate over the original understanding of "militia" as a bare victory for the individual rights scholars, we are left with the question of what "bear arms" meant.

As overwhelmingly understood, the term had a military connotation.[92] Although there is no true substitute for the professional historian's thorough immersion in the original sources of the day, computer databases can assist the amateur historian in getting a feel for how terms were used. Searching for the phrase "bear arms" in the Library of Congress's database of congressional and other documents from the founding era produces a great many references, nearly all of them in a military context.[93] To be sure, one can find the occasional disparate usage, especially among Pennsylvanians. For example, the 1776 Pennsylvania Constitution provided, in part: "The people have a right to bear arms for the defense of themselves and the State."[94] Some Pennsylvania anti-Federalists went even further, proposing an amendment that would have stated, in part, "That the people have a right to bear arms for the defence of themselves and their own State, or the United States, or for the purpose of killing game."[95] But while these uses show that the phrase "bear arms" could be, and sometimes was, adapted to include activities outside of the organized military,[96] they hardly cast doubt on the dominant usage.

Despite these reasons to be cautious, there are, in my view, three nonfrivolous (but ultimately unpersuasive) reasons why one might conclude that when it was adopted the Second Amendment conferred an individual right to own firearms. First, as Volokh notes, a right to bear arms appeared in state constitutions of the founding era, where it would have had nothing to do with federalism.[97] He therefore infers that at the founding a right to bear arms—whether it appeared in a state or the federal constitution—was understood as a right of the individual *against* the government.

There is some plausibility to this argument, I admit, but it may anachronistically interpret rights. Although Republican Revivalists have no doubt sometimes overstated their case, they are surely correct that the modern liberal conception of rights as trumps or shields against the state was not universally accepted at the founding.[98] In a period of intellectual upheaval over the meaning of most public institutions, there would have been nothing especially anomalous about a state constitution using the language of rights to protect a liberty of the ancients.[99] Moreover, even if Volokh's reading of the state constitutions of the day is correct, the phrase "bear arms" might well have meant something quite different in the federal Constitution, where, as all acknowledge, it was inspired by fears about the relative strength of the state and federal governments. Most important, as Saul Cornell cautions, it is easy to (mis)read the founding generation through the prism of the modern understandings of rights. The Pennsylvania Constitution coexisted with a loyalty-oath requirement that made quite clear that the right to arms, even for self-defense, was reserved for those deemed trustworthy by the state.[100] Similar restrictions in other colonies and states[101] indicate that even some of the seemingly more expansive protections for arms-bearing in founding-era state constitutions were probably understood to confer something less than an individual right against the state.

The second plausible historical basis for the individual rights interpretation of the Second Amendment is that many people in the late eighteenth century believed they had such a right. It is undoubtedly an oversimplification to believe that there was a single, well-understood "philosophy" that entitled all adult white male citizens to possess arms.[102] Still, one can find evidence that such a view was widely held. Blackstone wrote of the people's limited right "of having arms for their defense"[103] and his views were quite influential in the colonies. But such a right may well have been understood as a natural right,[104] quite distinct from the positive rights set out in the Constitution. Although there were certainly some people among the founding generation who believed that the Constitution protected all natural rights, the distinction between natural and positive law was generally understood, if controversial, at the founding.[105] Thus, even if some of the founders equated their natural law views about arms ownership with the Second Amendment's meaning,[106] it does not follow that they enacted their assumption into law—either as a matter of eighteenth- or twenty-first-century logic.

This leads me to the third and final plausible (but, again, ultimately unpersuasive) historical basis for the individual rights interpretation—the text itself. The Second Amendment protects a right not only to "bear" but also to "keep" arms. It is possible that some people understood "keep" to broaden the military connotation that "bear" would otherwise assume. A militiaman would "bear" arms only while on active duty, but when not called to muster he would "keep," that is, maintain private possession of, his weapon—therefore having it readily available to deter tyranny, for self-defense, and even for killing game.

The principal difficulty with this last argument is that "keep and bear" appears to have been understood as a unitary phrase, like "cruel and unusual" or "necessary and proper." I have not come across any documents of the period that parse the phrasing as finely as I have suggested. However, I must acknowledge that if the distinction between unspoken assumptions and enacted text can be invoked against a proposed interpretation, it can also be invoked in favor of that interpretation, and so it is possible that the plain meaning of "keep" would have been sufficient to connote an individual right. But then, ironically, our detour through eighteenth-century history will have left us more or less where we began: puzzling over the naked text.

While we are revisiting the text, we may wish to pay attention, finally, to "arms." Even if we assume that the individual rights interpretation of the Second Amendment best reflects the original understanding, we still must face the question of what "arms" it protects today. As Wills notes, at the founding very few Americans possessed pistols or rifles, which were not, in any event, considered effective military weapons.[107] Therefore, when the ratifiers of the Second Amendment saw the word "arms," they would have likely thought of muskets.

An originalist of the narrowest sort might therefore conclude that even today "arms" means muskets no more advanced than those commonly available in 1791. Even if we properly reject that narrow approach, we are left with the quite subjective task of applying the founders' understanding of arms to a world they could not have anticipated.[108] There is no obviously correct "translation."[109] Chemical and biological weapons seem clearly out, but why? Is it because of the enormous harm they can cause? That reasoning could also support a ban on nearly all modern firearms—which are, of course, much more accurate and powerful than the Revolutionary-era musket.

These sorts of difficulties are not unique to the Second Amendment. Technologically advanced forms of surveillance call for similar judgments under the Fourth Amendment, for example. And when the Supreme Court decided that radio and television can be subject to more extensive regulation than newspapers,[110] it was, in some sense, applying the founders' understanding of the First Amendment's protection for "freedom . . . of the press" to (its arguably misguided understanding of) the electromagnetic spectrum. But the judgments that these sorts of cases require are not, primarily, historical ones; they are normative.

POSTADOPTION HISTORY

The difficulties we encounter in applying the Second Amendment to modern circumstances should focus our attention on how the world has changed since the founding. There are numerous salient differences between the modern world and the one the framers inhabited. The American frontier is closed; many of us live in large, densely populated cities or suburbs; our population is much more heterogeneous than it was; in both absolute and per capita terms we have substantially more firearms than at the founding, and those we have are much more potent; the United States has become the leading military power in the world; and judicial review has emerged as a leading mechanism for preserving basic liberty and thus preventing tyranny. These and other developments indicate that even if we had located a completely clear consensus concerning the meaning of the Second Amendment at the founding, and even were we committed to a static view of constitutional meaning, we would face a difficult interpretive task in applying the founding-era understanding to modern circumstances. For those, like myself, not committed to a static view, the difficulties multiply.

A full treatment of the subject would inquire how the prevailing understandings of the Second Amendment have changed over time, beginning at the founding and taking us right to the present moment, through a process that Barry Friedman and Scott Smith have aptly termed "sedimentary."[111] My condensed account may appear to leave out many developments, especially those of the very recent past, but we do well to recall that "because all of our accumulated history is immanent in us, our constitutional commitments may be found in more recent, rather than more ancient, history."[112] The impact of recent history will be felt still more directly when we turn to normative considerations.

Perhaps at the founding it was plausible to interpret the Second Amendment as reserving to the states a right of rebellion should the federal government become tyrannical. In my view, even then it was not plausible (in the sense of workable) to assign this right of rebellion to individuals, as was demonstrated by the role of the militia in putting down Shays's Rebellion[113] on the eve of the Constitutional Convention and (after considerable delay) the Whiskey Rebellion[114] just three years after the adoption of the Second Amendment. On both occasions, self-styled patriots objected to what they saw as acts of tyranny—in the former instance, by the government of Massachusetts; in the latter, by the federal government. Yet when the rebels took up arms, they were put down by the militia because, in the unsurprising judgment of the properly constituted governments, no tyrannical conditions justified the revolt. These events demonstrated in the founding era what acts by the likes of Timothy McVeigh have demonstrated in our own time: that placing a right to rebel against tyranny in the hands of individuals risks violence by every would-be Spartacus.

Does a right of rebellion lodged in the hands of the states stand on a firmer footing than an individual right to rebel? Unlike self-promoting demagogues and other rash individuals or private groups, we might imagine that the states in their official capacities would be motivated to act only in a true crisis of the sort Madison describes in *Federalist* 46. However, even in the eighteenth century, this was a dubious strategy, as was illustrated by the failed attempt by Madison and Jefferson to rouse the state legislatures in defiance of the Sedition Act through the Virginia and Kentucky Resolutions. As a result of that failure, those who feared excess federal power chose a new strategy that has been effective ever since—they shifted the locus of opposition to federal policy from the states to a newly organized opposition political party.[115]

Notwithstanding this shift, prior to the Civil War perhaps it still might have been thought that state-organized armed resistance remained available as the ultimate check on federal power. That bloody conflagration taught otherwise. In some sense, of course, as Amar argues, the taking up of arms by the Confederacy was an "abuse" of the right of resistance because "none of the constitutional prerequisites for this ultimate form of self-help had been met."[116]

But this observation merely highlights the impracticality of a state right of rebellion. We reject an *individual* right of insurrection limited to those occasions that truly justify insurrection because we rightly fear that too many individuals will try to use the right when it is not justified. Timothy McVeigh's invocation of Jefferson upon his arrest is a chilling case in point. He wore emblazoned on his shirt Jefferson's statement that "[t]he tree of liberty must be refreshed from time to time with the blood of patriots and tyrants."[117]

So, too, may we rightly reject a *state* right of insurrection limited to those occasions that truly justify insurrection because we rightly fear that states will try to use the right when it is not justified. McVeigh completes the circle in grisly fashion. The shirt that bore Jefferson's words on the back, paid homage on the front to John Wilkes Booth, carrying his image, as well as Lincoln's, along with Booth's words uttered at the moment of assassination: "Sic Semper Tyrannis."[118]

Nonetheless, even if, convinced by the lessons of our history, one concludes that there is no constitutionally protected right of rebellion, it would still be possible to defend an armed populace on the ground that it poses the *threat* of rebellion or resistance and that is what keeps the government in line. Just as nuclear arms are more useful as a deterrent than in war, so, it could be argued, an individual (or, for that matter, a state) right to bear arms acts as a sword of Damocles.

Yet if we accept this logic—which is dubious even in the case of nuclear weapons[119]—we undermine one of the main protections against tyranny in the modern age: the right of free speech. Modern free speech law—which is much more permissive than the original understanding of free speech—draws a critical distinction between speech and action.[120] However difficult the task of distinguishing "advocacy of abstract doctrine and advocacy directed at promoting unlawful action,"[121] and even if expressive conduct is "100% action and 100% expression,"[122] there is no plausible argument that stockpiling weapons is protected expression. Yet if the right to own but not use weapons is protected as a means of deterring tyranny, must the government wait to act until the weapons are actually used? It is difficult to see how the government could intervene to prevent serious harm at an earlier point *except* by distinguishing among the political aims of weapons owners. It would be a bizarre doctrine indeed that permitted one either to teach the (abstract) necessity of overthrowing the government *or* to stockpile weapons, but not to engage in both otherwise protected activities. The point is not simply that, as the putative right of insurrection has come to be seen as less useful, the right of free speech has taken over some of the work of preserving liberty.[123] The point is that a right of private possession of firearms may actually impede the right of free speech in doing that work.

The emergence of organized police forces is another important development that bears on the application of the Second Amendment to modern circumstances. "In the eighteenth century the primary responsibility of the militia was not public defense but internal security."[124] Professional police forces as we know them today were first created in the nineteenth century.[125] Prior to the emergence of the police, ordinary citizens would bring what arms they had in response to a "hue and cry" or when serving on a *posse comitatus*.[126]

It is not immediately clear whether the nonexistence of professional police at the founding strengthens or weakens the individual rights thesis. On a narrowly originalist reading, this fact serves to highlight that arms possession by members of the militia was not a strictly military function in the sense of responding to external threats; it included protecting one's self and one's neighbors from all manner of threats. If ordinary (white male) civilians performed functions at the founding like those subsequently assumed by the police, then, on narrowly originalist premises, it follows that they may perform such functions today, and this would include possessing firearms.

On the other hand, the nonexistence of professional police at the founding may have an impact on what purpose the right to keep and bear arms served then, and thus, on a less narrowly originalist approach to interpretation, should tell us something about how to fulfill that purpose today. To the extent that the Second Amendment "right" to bear arms was in substantial measure a duty of the responsible citizenry to participate in the collective self-defense of the community,[127] i.e., to the extent that it was understood as a liberty of the ancients, the government may be understood to respect that right today by maintaining professional police.

If we take this latter approach, further questions arise. If the state fails to provide adequate police protection against private violence, do individuals then have a right to resort to armed self-help? Or, more radically, does the Second Amendment imply a right to adequate policing, enforceable by the judiciary if not by self-help? There are nonfrivolous moral arguments for such entitlements, whether or not they are rooted in the Second Amendment.

One difficulty with describing the Second Amendment as an antiquated police provision is the fact that the nation hardly outgrew the idea of privately owned arms for self-defense the moment professional police came on the scene. Throughout the nineteenth century, much of America remained a frontier society, and armed self-help was widespread even in urban centers: in the middle of the nineteenth century, a prominent New York City businessman reported that, due to fears of mob violence, "most of his friends never left home without a pistol."[128]

Indeed, the use of privately owned firearms for self-defense seemed to increase, rather than decrease, even as police forces came on the scene, and for many the language of arms-bearing came to be associated with self-defense. This is hardly to say that the Second Amendment was completely transformed into a private right during the nineteenth century. The connection between arms-bearing and the safeguarding of democracy persisted.[129] But even if one can quibble over the details of the tale he tells, Amar is generally correct in claiming that, between the founding and Reconstruction, the right to bear arms came to be understood less in terms of states' collective interests against the government and more in terms of individuals' rights against state interference with their efforts to protect themselves against private violence.[130]

How much modern interpretive weight should be given to the fact that the ideology of gun ownership for self-defense seems to have grown, rather than diminished, during the nineteenth century? The most straightforward answer is: not much. We began the present inquiry by noting that at the founding the militia served a function now generally served by the professional police. At some point between the founding and the present, many people thought that private arms for self-help against private violence had taken over (at least part of) the function of the militia. Eventually, with the closing of the frontier and the increasing professionalization of police forces, fewer people came to hold that view. If we want to know how the founders' conception of the militia and arms-bearing applies in the modern world, it is not at all clear that we should focus much attention on the world as it was during the intermediate period of the nineteenth century. The most salient question would seem to be: Given conditions as they are *now,* how do we best understand the founders' text?

However, before concluding that nineteenth-century attitudes toward arms-bearing have little direct relevance to the twenty-first-century meaning of the Second Amendment, we must confront an argument that would give critical importance to the nineteenth-century—or, to be more precise, the 1868—understanding of the right to bear arms. Amar contends that when the Fourteenth Amendment was ratified in 1868, a right to bear arms was understood by Reconstruction Republicans and others as a right of armed self-defense against private violence. The struggle against slavery had, to use the vocabulary of the nineteenth century, moved arms-bearing from the class of *political* rights like voting, which belonged only to full members of the political community, into the class of personal or civil rights like personal security, possessed by all citizens—including white women and, following the Thirteenth and Fourteenth Amendments, blacks.[131] In Amar's view, if a provision of the Bill of Rights "is a personal privilege—that is, a private right—of individual citizens, rather than a right of states or the public at large," the Privileges or Immunities Clause of the Fourteenth Amendment prohibits states from infringing it.[132] Thus, he concludes, the Fourteenth Amendment protects at least a limited private right of arms for self-defense.[133]

One consequence that seems to follow from this theory is that *"federal* gun control legislation would be essentially invulnerable under the Second Amendment provided the state militia were not undermined, while *state and local* gun control legislation would have to satisfy some heightened form of scrutiny."[134] Yet that is a strikingly odd result, given that the only express reference to arms-bearing appears in the provision that limits the federal government.

The oddity could be avoided if one imagined that the enactment of the Fourteenth Amendment simultaneously changed the meaning of the Second, by a "feedback effect"[135] that Laurence Tribe labels "time travel."[136] Although one might be appropriately skeptical of any interpretive method called time travel, the phenomenon is in fact quite familiar. Aside from constitutional amendments that expressly repeal or modify earlier-enacted provisions, the most famous example of constitutional time travel is, of course, *Bolling v. Sharpe*,[137] in which the Supreme Court held that the Fifth Amendment Due Process Clause—ratified by slaveholders in 1791—prohibited de jure racial segregation in District of Columbia public schools.

Yet the theory of *Bolling* most certainly was not that the framers and ratifiers of the Fourteenth Amendment intended to prohibit de jure segregation. To the contrary, *Brown v. Board of Education*,[138] to which *Bolling* was a companion, found the evidence of the original meaning of the Fourteenth Amendment "inconclusive."[139] *Bolling* itself was even more self-consciously presentist, justifying its conclusion on the ground that any other result would be "unthinkable."[140] Clever lawyers can concoct all sorts of arguments for why *Bolling* is no more problematic than *Brown*,[141] but for an originalist that still leaves the puzzle of *Brown* itself. And despite some determined revisionism, the overwhelming weight of historical evidence indicates that *Brown* is contrary to the original understanding of the Fourteenth Amendment.[142]

Thus, upon inspection, *Bolling* undermines, rather than supports, a reconstructed individual right to own firearms based on the Amar/Tribe approach, because *Bolling* decidedly rejects the idea that the enactment of the Fourteenth Amendment updated the meaning of the Fifth (or the Second) Amendment from 1791 to 1868 and froze it there. Instead, *Bolling* reflects the commonsense idea that experience over time can prompt a reexamination of the meaning of prior commitments, at least where those commitments are embodied in capacious text. In short, on any plausible reading, *Bolling* and *Brown* stand for the proposition that the meaning of a constitutional provision need not be fixed by the concrete intentions, expectations, or understandings of its adopters.[143]

Nor do Amar and Tribe subscribe to narrow originalism. Tribe may have backed away somewhat from the view of the Second Amendment that he and I set forth a decade ago—that it is "most plausibly . . . read to preserve a power of the state militias against abolition by the federal government,"[144]—but I do not read any of his recent work as disavowing the more general point that "we must look beyond the specific views of the framers to apply the Constitution to contemporary problems."[145]

As for Amar, he proclaims himself an eclectic who accepts the legitimacy of textual, historical, structural, prudential, doctrinal, and ethical forms of argument in constitutional interpretation.[146] Moreover, read as a whole, *The Bill of Rights*—the book in which Amar sets forth his narrative of the Reconstruction-era transformation of the Second Amendment and the Bill of Rights more generally—does not claim that the transformation was completed upon the enactment of the Fourteenth Amendment. For example, his discussion of the First Amendment explains how modern Supreme Court doctrine could be supported by drawing upon historical analogies to Reconstruction,[147] but he certainly does not argue that the framers and ratifiers of the Fourteenth Amendment understood it to enact modern First Amendment doctrine as such. Moreover, when Amar turns to drawing broad lessons, his goal seems to be primarily to set the record straight—to replace the mistaken notion that we inherited our freedoms directly from the founding with a more accurate picture that celebrates the role of Reconstruction Republicans.[148]

Setting the record straight about the historical origins of our freedoms need not entail interpreting the Constitution in a narrowly originalist fashion. Amar and Tribe could be right that by 1868 the background understanding of arms-bearing had evolved to the point where a private right of gun ownership was generally thought to be among the privileges and immunities of national citizenship. But just as the original "Second Amendment did not enact the background understanding"[149] circa 1791, neither did the Fourteenth Amendment—the text of which does not expressly mention arms at all—enact the background understanding circa 1868.

NORMATIVE CONSIDERATIONS

Our considerations of precedent, text, structure, and history have not been value free. In trying to give coherence to case law or to draw lessons from historical experience, we have necessarily been engaged in a somewhat normative enterprise. I now consider normative arguments more directly. In doing so, I acknowledge that there exists substantial disagreement about the questions under consideration. But the fact that some people will disagree with an argument is no reason not to make it.

Let us begin with the insurrectionist argument for an individual right to own firearms. An armed populace, the argument goes, will be able to resist a tyrannical government. Indeed, the mere fact that the people have arms will deter would-be tyrants from seizing the reins of government for oppressive purposes.

There is a nonconsequentialist and a consequentialist form of this argument. The nonconsequentialist form links the people's right to arms with self-government. In the natural law language of the Declaration of Independence, governments derive "their just powers from the consent of the governed, [and] whenever any Form of Government becomes destructive of [humans' unalienable rights], it is the Right of the People to alter or to abolish it."[150] Yet if the right of rebellion is understood in nonconsequentialist terms, it would seem to inhere not in individuals but in political communities. Individuals may have a right to *participate* in self-government, but only the people in a collective capacity have a right of self-government as such. Thus, the nonconsequentialist claim that self-government entails a right to alter (or restore) the form of government by force cannot by itself justify an individual right to arms.

Notice I do not say that one could not posit a nonconsequentialist individual right to use force against tyrannical exercises of government authority. One might think that individuals have a right to own firearms so that any time the government attempted to violate their rights, they could resist or threaten resistance with force. But while such a radically libertarian, indeed positively anarchistic, view would be internally consistent, it is not the standard insurrectionist account. In the standard account, the armed population stands ready to defend the political community as a whole against tyrants, not to defend every member of the community against every possible violation of rights.

Nonetheless, one might still invoke notions of self-government to justify an individual right to own arms. It could be argued that an individual right to own arms provides the people in their collective capacity with the means to resist or deter tyranny. This is a consequentialist or empirical rather than a nonconsequentialist claim. It asserts that an individual right to own arms will aid in the preservation of democracy.

Is the empirical claim true? Widespread individual ownership of and skill in using firearms arguably increase a nation's ability to resist foreign armies and thus deter foreign attack. It is possible to draw such a lesson from the experience of Soviet forces in Afghanistan, although for much of the occupation the mujahideen received sophisticated military equipment from the West and the Islamic world.[151] But even granting that it is more difficult for an invading force to subdue an armed population than an unarmed one, it is simply fantastic to suppose that a power bent on occupying the United States would be undeterred by our conventional and nuclear military forces, yet given pause by the prospect of resistance from individuals. The twenty-first-century American insurrectionist claim for arms therefore must rest on an argument about their utility in resisting tyranny by our own government.

Does an individual right to own arms in fact aid in the preservation of democracy against threats by a nation's own leaders? Certainly we can imagine circumstances in which the answer would be yes. Imagine a fledgling democracy in which there is reason to fear the despotic tendencies of the highest elected official. The knowledge that people demonstrating against one of the would-be despot's policies are armed might well cause him to hesitate before ordering his troops to march against the demonstrators. Then again, one might conclude that, even if such scenarios are possible, a heavily armed populace itself poses risks to democracy. It is a striking fact that none of the constitutions written since the fall of communism—under circumstances in which fears of reversion to dictatorship were hardly fantastic—contains a provision explicitly protecting a right of arms. Construing the United States Constitution to confer a robust individual right of gun ownership would, to my knowledge, render it unique. Even in Switzerland, where there is a tradition of universal military service and private gun ownership, the constitution contains no such right.[152]

Moreover, even if one believes that a private right of gun ownership is valuable in a new democracy, in a mature democracy like the United States, other rights—especially the right of free speech—perform the day-to-day task of ensuring that the government serves the people. Above I suggested that robust judicial protection for an individual right of gun ownership could undermine protection for freedom of speech because it would problematize the line between abstract advocacy and dangerous conduct. It might also be thought that, to the extent that widely available guns contribute to crime, they trigger aggressive policing tactics that undermine Fourth Amendment liberties, as well as policies of mass incarceration that sit uncomfortably with the ideals of a free society.

In short, if the Second Amendment ever did protect an individual right to gun ownership for insurrectionist reasons, the desuetude into which that right has apparently fallen may reflect more than just archaic language. I am suggesting that whatever democracy-reinforcing effects a private right to own firearms may be thought to have tend to decay over time. As the democracy matures, the risk that a tyrant will seize the reins of government diminishes, and the threats to liberty come from more mundane abuses. In such times, robust protection for a private right to own firearms actually may impede robust protection for the civil and political rights needed to guard against such mundane but hardly trivial abuses.

There is no guarantee that even a mature democracy such as our own will not give way to tyranny. The hypothesis that any given society will be better able to preserve its democracy without an individual right to firearms than it can with one cannot be proven in any strict sense. Nonetheless, the factors identified above suggest that this is the safer bet. Although there are recent examples of democracy giving way to military rule in our own hemisphere, typically it was the existence of armed revolutionaries or the perceived threat of disorder that was used as a justification for the coup. It is therefore quite possible that a formal right of firearms ownership would have only increased the frequency of these occurrences. In any event, the fragility of Latin American democracy in the twentieth century seems much more a product of weak traditions of civilian control over the military than a product of the status of firearms rights.

In evaluating the likely costs and benefits that an individual right to firearms ownership would confer on democracy, we make a complicated prediction in the face of considerable uncertainty. I have offered some reasons to think that a robust individual right to own firearms is unnecessary to, and may actually impede the chances for, the survival of our democracy.

Nevertheless, insurrection is not the only possible normative basis for an individual right to own firearms. Self-defense provides a somewhat stronger justification. Even if the government provides police protection, some acts of private violence will occur. Should innocent, otherwise law-abiding citizens have the right to own firearms to protect themselves in the event that they are the targets of such private violence?

The most common argument for most forms of gun control—from laws prohibiting the carrying of concealed weapons, to those requiring trigger locks, even to near-complete bans on possession—is that firearms possession does not make for greater safety but actually increases the risk of injury or death. A (hand)gun obtained for defense against felons has a greater chance, gun control advocates say, of being used opportunistically against a family member or discharging accidentally.[153] Others contest these claims. They argue that accidental firearms deaths are rare,[154] and that widespread firearm ownership reduces (or at least does not increase) violent crime because criminals are deterred by the risk to themselves if they attack armed law-abiding citizens.[155] Still others point to the unreliability of the data used to support the safety-enhancing effects of gun ownership.[156]

The complicated empirical and policy judgments required to sort out these conflicting claims seem best suited to legislative judgment. There is no reason to think that the legislative process currently excludes the perspectives of those who oppose various forms of firearm regulation. Indeed, whatever its precise strength, the fact that the "gun lobby" is widely recognized as wielding substantial legislative influence indicates that, unlike racial minorities, for example, gun control opponents cannot be characterized as the victims of a process failure.[157]

However, those who support gun rights contend that because gun control laws limit a constitutional right, the burden of persuasion rests with the government.[158] If we accept their premise, the point is largely correct. Although we can imagine a regime in which a right to firearms coexists with extensive regulation—indeed, that appears to be a fairly apt description of the colonial and founding eras[159]—under modern doctrine, the recognition of a constitutional right typically means that the government bears the burden of persuading a court that the regulation is necessary.

Yet the premise of the gun advocates' argument begs the central question of whether there is a constitutional right to gun ownership. If constitutional text, structure, history, and precedent led us to conclude that there is a Second

Amendment right to own firearms for self-defense, then the persuasion burden would fall on those who sought to limit that right. But our inquiry to this point does not establish such a right, and we have turned to normative arguments to see whether they provide a clear basis for inferring one. Therefore, the persuasion burden does not fall on those who would limit rights of gun ownership, and, absent a contrary showing, lawmakers are entitled to infer that there is some causal relation between the widespread availability of firearms in the United States and the significantly higher rates of gun violence here than in otherwise similar countries that regulate firearms more strictly.[160]

Still, the question of whether there should be a right to own or possess firearms is not simply a matter of calculating the likely consequences of such a right. If we say that legislatures are justified in enacting gun control measures on the ground that, on the whole, these laws increase personal security, the deontologist will object to the sacrifice of some individuals' right of personal security. If owning a firearm makes one law-abiding citizen safer, the argument goes, that individual claims the government cannot prohibit such ownership for the benefit of others. This claim calls to mind Ronald Dworkin's familiar thesis that rights may not be overridden based on a calculation of costs and benefits,[161] but as we shall see, the claim fails to establish a Second Amendment right of armed self-defense.

Consider three schematic cases. A believes that her ownership of a firearm makes her substantially safer while increasing the risk of injury or death of innocent third parties at most marginally. Perhaps A believes that it even makes innocent third parties, in the aggregate, safer. In fact, however, A is mistaken. A's ownership of a firearm increases the risk of death or injury to herself as well as to innocent third parties. B's ownership of a firearm increases the risk of death or injury to innocent third parties to a greater degree than it increases her own safety, but it does increase her own safety somewhat. C's ownership of a firearm actually does make her substantially safer while increasing the risk of injury or death of innocent third parties at most marginally. Perhaps it even makes innocent third parties, in the aggregate, safer.

A presents the weakest claim for a right to firearms ownership. Some constitutional rights are best understood as protecting decisional autonomy, and are in this sense rights to be wrong. For example, even if we knew to a certainty that, contrary to the expectations of a pair of lovers, their marriage would prove to be a source of nothing but misery to them, we would not grant the government the power to prevent them from marrying one another. Part of what makes the decision whether to marry or to have children valuable is that it is one's own decision. One could conceive of a right to safety in these terms—as a right to *decide* whether and how to protect oneself against private violence— but the right then loses most of its moral force. A is entitled to hold all manner of beliefs, but when acting on those beliefs risks serious physical harm to herself and others; something more than the fact that A holds a belief is needed to prevent the government from intervening.

B has a stronger claim than A. Nevertheless, B's proposed conduct harms third parties, thereby making it a poor candidate for a right. Moreover, why should the government prefer B's claim to personal safety over those of third parties when the latter are, by hypothesis, stronger?

B might say that her claim is a composite of safety and liberty: in the interest of third parties, the government proposes not only to decrease her safety but also to limit her freedom to own a firearm. Phrased in this way, it looks as if the government is singling out B for a burden, the benefit of which it confers on others. Yet it should be recalled that the law imposes the reciprocal burden on all. The third parties whose safety the gun control law enhances will also have their own freedom to own firearms restricted. Thus, unless the aspect of B's freedom that is limited is itself highly prized—and this is the very issue in dispute—the safety interests of the third parties will justifiably outweigh the combination of B's safety claim plus her liberty claim.

C presents a strong claim because the reduction in C's safety (and freedom) carries no substantial compensating benefit for herself or others. The main problem with C's claim is the difficulty, *ex ante*, of distinguishing C from A (or B). Nearly everyone who claims a right to own firearms will believe that she is a C, or, at worst, a B. (By comparison, in one well-known study, 90 percent of people surveyed rated themselves as above-average drivers.[162]) At the very least, this suggests that the government may legitimately require trigger locks, safety education, and similar measures as a condition of firearm ownership licensing, thereby weeding out A's and converting some of them into C's. But even these measures will not be deemed sufficient if the government has a reasonable basis to conclude that firearms possession by properly certified individuals on the whole increases the risk of death or injury—because accidents still happen, because the firearm remains available to otherwise cautious people should they become enraged, and because criminals who have a substantial reason to believe their victims are armed may more readily resort to violence themselves.

Ex post, matters may look somewhat different. Imagine that the government bans firearm possession, but C (who really is a C) decides to carry a weapon nonetheless. If C uses the firearm in justifiable self-defense, should C have a necessity defense to a charge of illegal possession? C might say that any basis for thinking she was really an A is removed by the facts of her case. However, to give C such a defense would rob the general prohibition of most of its deterrent effect. Many A's, thinking themselves C's, will reason that they can safely violate the possession prohibition because their violation would likely come to light only in the event that they use the firearm, and because they (erroneously) believe they would only use the firearm justifiably, they reason that they could not be prosecuted. Thus, if we conclude that the difficulty of distinguishing A's from C's *ex ante* justifies prohibiting firearm possession even by C's, we would likely also conclude that in order to be able to enforce the prohibition, we must disallow a necessity defense by C.

This result may seem somewhat harsh, and I admit that I am not entirely comfortable with it. We justified a reduction in B's safety on the ground that B was endangering third parties. C, by contrast, does not endanger third parties. How can the harmful effects of A's conduct justify a limit on C's ability to protect herself from attack? There is no good answer to this question other than to say that sometimes the good of the community justifies imposing general burdens that are irreducibly imprecise.

Even if we find this response unconvincing, it is worth pausing to notice that the normative arguments we have considered for some limited right of armed self-defense do not track the Second Amendment at all closely. There is the initial problem of grafting a self-defense justification onto a text that speaks in what appear now, and were understood at the founding, to be military terms. In addition, a right to own or possess firearms is at most an indirect means of protecting the right of personal security. If the latter can be protected as or nearly as effectively by other means—such as police protection or nonlethal weapons—the argument for a right to firearms is accordingly weaker.

Finally, there is the problem that the self-defense argument hardly justifies a right to own or possess firearms for all of "the people." At most, the arguments considered justify exemptions from general prohibitions for particular individuals in particular circumstances. The question of who, if anyone, should be entitled to a right to own, possess, or use firearms, and under what circumstances, raises difficult issues of substantive criminal law. To the extent that these are also issues of constitutional law, they are probably better analyzed under the Due Process Clauses of the Fifth and Fourteenth Amendments than by attempting to shoehorn them into the Second Amendment.

Is the Second Amendment an Anachronism?

A recent article by Stephen Halbrook and David Kopel accuses critics of the individual right interpretation of adopting a " 'nihilist theory' of the Second Amendment."[163] The amendment must do *something*, they say; otherwise there was no need to bother adding it. To the extent that Halbrook and Kopel issue a historical challenge, we have a plausible answer: the framers and ratifiers of the Second Amendment were principally worried about a standing federal army. By protecting state militias against abolition they hoped to reduce federal reliance on a standing army and, in the event of federal tyranny by a standing army, to provide the states with the means to resist.[164]

This response may seem less than fully satisfactory because we do not share the founders' distrust of standing armies or their faith in militias. Our national defense now rests almost entirely with federal forces and, following the Civil War, the notion of an armed clash between the federal government and some number of states has been understood not as our last defense against tyranny but as the paradigmatic national catastrophe. Thus, the *something* that the Second Amendment accomplished at the founding looks now like a nothing. To avoid rendering the Second Amendment a modern nullity, the Halbrook/ Kopel argument implies, we should adopt the individual rights interpretation—even if that is ahistorical.

However, it is decidedly not true that preserving state militias against federal abolition serves *no* modern purpose. To be sure, giving full effect to the spirit of the Second Amendment would potentially require overruling the Supreme Court's decision in the *Selective Draft Law Cases*,[165] which upheld Congress's authority to incorporate National Guard and National Guard Reserve troops into the regular army. But those cases are fully consistent with the letter of the Second Amendment as I have explained it: relying on the militia clauses but not the Second Amendment, the Court said that even though Congress might choose to incorporate militia members into the national army, its power to train and discipline the militia would, in general, obviate "the necessity for exercising the army power."[166] The Second Amendment still reinforces this idea, just as the Tenth Amendment reinforces the notion of enumerated powers in Article I.

This last suggestion also provides a response to the charge that interpreting the Second Amendment merely to preserve state militias renders it redundant with the militia provisions of Articles I and II. The response is: so what? There is in fact no interpretive canon requiring that every constitutional provision have some effect not attributable to some other provision. For example, under the Supreme Court's modern interpretation of the Commerce Clause, Congress may regulate intra-state economic activity that has a substantial effect on interstate commerce.[167] Under that test, many of the powers articulated elsewhere in Article I are unnecessary. Among the provisions rendered surplusage by the modern interpretation of the Commerce Clause are the power: "To establish . . . uniform Laws on the subject of Bankruptcies"[168]; "[t]o Coin Money"[169]; "[t]o provide for the Punishment of counterfeiting"[170]; and to issue copyrights and patents.[171] It was just this redundancy that led Justice Thomas, concurring in *United States v. Lopez*,[172] to complain that the Court's interpretation of the Commerce Clause warranted reexamination.[173] None of his colleagues took the offer seriously. Thus, on the question that was most central to the debate over ratification of the Constitution—the scope of Congress' enumerated powers—we find that whole clauses have been rendered superfluous by the modern understanding.

There are additional examples of constitutional provisions that have been rendered superfluous by expansive interpretation of other provisions or changed circumstances. Congress' power to "grant Letters of Marque and Reprisal"[174] was rendered useless by the 1856 Declaration of Paris (even if in principle the United States could renounce the declaration).[175] The limitation of the Seventh Amendment's guarantee of a civil jury trial right to cases in which the amount in controversy exceeds "twenty dollars" has been entirely eaten away by inflation. And given the Supreme Court's ruling that the Free Exercise Clause prohibits discriminatory but not nondiscriminatory burdens on religion,[176] it is not clear that the Free Exercise Clause adds anything to the Establishment Clause and the Equal Protection Clause (or in the case of the federal government, the equal protection component of the Fifth Amendment Due Process Clause).[177]

Even if we disagree with the particulars of any of these developments—perhaps we think the Seventh Amendment has earned a cost of living adjustment—the more general phenomenon makes perfect sense. The Constitution is not the work of an omniscient deity who foresaw all future developments and chose only those words that were indispensable for all circumstances.[178] Furthermore, because it is phrased in general language and so very difficult to amend, its interpretation calls for some degree of flexibility.[179] It should hardly surprise us that, over the course of more than two centuries, some provisions of the Constitution faded in importance or were rendered redundant by the sensible expansive interpretation of others. Certainly the Second Amendment's fate has hardly been unique in this respect.

In my view, there remains one minor difficulty with interpreting the Second Amendment solely to preserve state militias: even if we reject the view that the "militia" is now synonymous with "the people," and even if "the people" as understood in the late eighteenth century were understood as not exactly collective or individual in the way we use those terms today, the individual rights scholars who argue that the term "the people" *now* generally means individuals make a legitimate point. Perhaps we should try to understand the Second Amendment as preserving *some* individual right. However, engaging in this exercise in creative anachronism hardly compels *the* individual right to own and possess firearms.

One possibility we considered previously would be to recognize a limited right of armed self-defense. I noted above the awkward fit between the scope of the right that might be justified and the Second Amendment's reference to all of "the people." We might remedy that problem by emphasizing the militia's original role as a primitive police force: perhaps the right that inheres in all of the people is a right to adequate police protection. The issue is hardly hypothetical. Minority communities have long complained that the police provide them with inadequate protection. Of course, a right of self-help against private violence would not address the related problem of abusive treatment of racial minorities by the police themselves. Borrowing a page from the broad notion of "self-defense" favored by the Black Panther Party, one might think that the solution to this problem is also private arms, but this view sounds dangerously similar to a private right of insurrection; reforms of police practices would seem a much more appropriate course.[180]

A second possibility would be to recognize a right of law-abiding citizens, upon successful completion of a safety course, to own or possess a small number of long-barreled guns.[181] As Wills notes, pistols were virtually unknown at the founding, except for dueling among aristocrats.[182] Merging narrowly understood history with the narrow letter of *Miller,* we might say that the Second Amendment protects a right to guns similar to those that were deemed useful to the militia at the founding.

A long-guns-only interpretation would have two pragmatic virtues as well. First, it would not threaten hunters, an important political constituency. Second, a distinction between long guns and handguns may make policy sense. Although handguns comprise roughly one-third of all firearms in the United States, they account for more than three-fourths of firearm homicides, and more than half of all homicides.[183] An effective ban on handguns would undoubtedly shift some gun violence from handguns to other weapons, but some substantial reduction in total violence would probably result.

Both of the foregoing proposals—a limited right of self-defense and a limited right to own or possess long guns—lack any direct connection to the military focus of the Second Amendment. My final proposal would address that deficiency. Even if we do not share the founders' skepticism of standing armies, we may well sympathize with the ideal of the citizen-soldier in the following sense: we are rightly concerned by large gaps between martial and civilian values. Nuremberg and My Lai teach that, notwithstanding the importance of military discipline, the duty to follow orders does not excuse members of the armed services of their duty to follow minimal rules of human decency. The Iran-Contra affair provides a warning about how ready military officials may be to execute policy contrary to law if they are convinced that the civil authorities will turn a blind eye. The ideal of a citizen-soldier in the sense of a service member who is both of the people and subject to civilian control is thus very much a modern ideal.

How does the Second Amendment speak to this ideal in modern times? By providing a right of the people to keep and bear arms—that is, a right to serve in the military. Of course the government need not accept anyone who wishes to serve in the military. Exclusions based on physical fitness, military need, criminal record, and so forth, would be perfectly appropriate. But wholesale exclusions based on stereotypical assumptions would not be consistent with the ideal of armed forces drawn from "the people." On this reading, the most substantial effect of the Second Amendment today would be to invalidate official military discrimination on the basis of sex and sexual orientation.[184]

This proposal is not nearly as odd as it first appears. Its great virtue is its synthesis of the founding and Reconstruction *as those periods are now understood.* Recall Amar's contention that the Second Amendment means today what it meant circa 1868. This approach depends not only on saddling us with Reconstruction-era views about arms-bearing, but also relies on the old distinction between civil and political rights, which Amar aptly characterizes as dividing people into "First Class Citizens" and "members of the larger society."[185] However, even if those who framed and ratified the Reconstruction amendments still thought in these terms, in our times the central meaning of those amendments is that there can be no division of citizens into classes. The idea that "[t]here is no caste here"[186] has become a fixed star in our constitutional constellation.

Understanding the core meaning of the Reconstruction amendments in these terms also explains how the Second Amendment could be read to speak to the composition of federal forces and not just state militias. It is not just that the operative clause makes no reference to state as opposed to federal forces. The anti-caste principle has become so central to our *modern* understanding of the entire Constitution that it infuses the whole.[187]

To be sure, none of these alternative readings is clearly superior to viewing the Second Amendment as simply a limit on Congress' ability to abolish state militias. The alternatives are offered for those who believe—erroneously, in my view—that every constitutional provision must play a substantial role in shaping the proper scope of government authority. As the last of my proposals shows, however, we should not assume that giving the Second Amendment bite necessarily means giving civilians guns.

CONCLUSION

I have proceeded here on the assumption that something important is at stake in the academic debate over how to interpret the Second Amendment. Yet most "contemporary gun control proposals, which by and large do not seek to ban all firearms, but seek only to prohibit a narrow type of weaponry (such as assault rifles) or to regulate gun ownership by means of waiting periods, registration, mandatory safety devices, or the like . . . are plainly constitutional,"[188] even under the individual rights view of the Second Amendment. An originalist could find the justification for the contemporary proposals in analogous provisions in force during colonial times and at the time of the founding.[189] A doctrinalist would note that recognition of a constitutional right—whether to free speech or to the possession of firearms—can be limited if the limitation is necessary to further a compelling government interest such as public safety.[190]

Nevertheless, the debate over the scope of the Second Amendment is not merely an academic one. Even if modest gun control proposals are consistent with the individual rights view of the Second Amendment, at some point, federal, state, or local lawmakers may conclude that a complete or near-complete ban on private possession of handguns is needed to reduce the level of violent crime in the United States to that of other industrialized nations. Such an immodest measure would be well-nigh impossible to justify if one accepted the conventional individual rights view.

To be sure, a technical legal solution would remain available: we could say that there is an individual right to possess firearms, but it must yield to the compelling interest in preventing violent crime. Yet if a compelling interest overrides a right in nearly every circumstance in which the right may be exercised, one might as well say that there is no right. One of the main arguments against finding in the Second Amendment an individual right to firearm possession is that such a right would endanger public safety. If a court were to find that, notwithstanding the threat to public safety, the Second Amendment protects an individual right to firearm possession, it is highly unlikely that the same court would go on to find a compelling interest that would justify strong gun control measures. Thus, it makes a great deal of practical difference whether or not the advocates of the individual rights view prevail in the courts.

Should they so prevail? Judged by the conventional criteria of constitutional adjudication, the case for a robust individual right to own firearms enforceable against either the federal or state governments has not been made. To be sure, this is not to say that the conventional criteria are correct. Critics of existing constitutional jurisprudence abound. The most common criticism points to the "countermajoritarian difficulty,"[191] objecting to the Court's power to nullify democratically chosen policies. Of course, that is not the complaint of the advocates of the individual rights interpretation of the Second Amendment. In their view, the courts have been insufficiently countermajoritarian.

What infuriates the individual rights scholars who oppose gun control—and embarrasses those who favor it—is their perception of a political double standard. Even if we grant that the Second Amendment's text does not unambiguously guarantee an individual right of firearm ownership and possession, they say, surely there is greater textual support for such a right than for other rights the Court has recognized, such as the right to contraception,[192] the right to abortion,[193] or the right of minor first cousins to live together with their grandmother.[194]

Note the understanding of constitutional interpretation implied by this criticism: surrounding the core of each textual provision are concentric circles of related values; if a right is recognized at some distance from the core then, a fortiori, all rights at lesser distances must be recognized as well. Thus, if contraception lies at distance X from the Fourth Amendment (and other provisions), recognition of a constitutional right to contraception implies recognition of a right of armed self-defense, provided that such a right lies less distance than X from the Second Amendment.

Although this view of constitutional interpretation finds some superficial support in the Court's discussion of "penumbras" and "emanations" in *Griswold v. Connecticut*,[195] it is deeply flawed. The right to scream profane threats at passersby is arguably closer to the text of the First Amendment than is the right to publish on the Internet a statement of political support for a presidential candidate; the former is literally "speech," while the latter employs neither vocal cords nor a printing press. Yet no one would seriously argue that protection of the latter implies protection of the former. To the extent that talk of penumbras and emanations leads us to think that constitutional interpretation in hard cases is a matter of measuring the distance from the text, it is simply another unsuccessful effort to banish value judgments from constitutional interpretation.[196]

The existence of a large body of Supreme Court decisions recognizing constitutional rights that are not expressly articulated in the text means that we cannot rule out the individual rights view of the Second Amendment on textual grounds alone. The champions of the individual rights view are entitled to have their arguments heard. However, that does not mean that they are entitled to have their arguments accepted, unless, as judged by the admittedly somewhat value-laden criteria of constitutional interpretation, the arguments are convincing. As I have endeavored to show here, on the whole these criteria point away from the individual rights interpretation.

Notes

1. THE HISTORY AND POLITICS OF SECOND AMENDMENT SCHOLARSHIP: A PRIMER

* Carl T. Bogus, symposium editor, teaches jurisprudence, torts, products liability, and evidence at Roger Williams University School of Law. He is the author of *The Hidden History of the Second Amendment* (U.C. DAVIS LAW REVIEW), in which he argued that the Second Amendment was written to assure the South that Congress would not undermine the slave system by disarming the state militia, on which the South relied for slave control. His many writings about guns include: *Gun Litigation and Societal Values* (CONNECTICUT LAW REVIEW); *Race, Riots and Guns* (SOUTHERN CALIFORNIA LAW REVIEW); and *The Strong Case for Gun Control* (AMERICAN PROSPECT). In 1991, he recieved the Ross Essay Award from the American Bar Association for *The Invasion of Panama and the Rule of Law* (INTERNATIONAL LAWYER). Professor Bogus testified about the Second Amendment before the U.S. Senate Judicial Committee's Subcommittee on the Constitution in 1998. His book, WHY LAWSUITS ARE GOOD FOR AMERICA: DISCIPLINED DEMOCRACY, BIG BUSINESS AND THE COMMON LAW, was published by New York University Press in 2001.

1. Some include within this list a fourth case, *Miller v. Texas* 153, U.S. 535 (1894). However, here the Court merely found that there was no federal question and dismissed the case on jurisdictional grounds.

2. U.S. v. Cruikshank, 92 U.S. 542 (1876).

3. Presser v. Illinois, 116 U.S. 252 (1886).

4. U.S. v. Miller, 307 U.S. 174 (1939).

5. The Court wrote:

   > The Constitution as originally adopted granted to Congress power—"To provide for calling forth the Militia to execute the Laws of the Union, suppress Insurrections and repel Invasions; To provide for organizing, arming and disciplining, the Militia, and for governing such Part of them as may be employed in the Service of the United States, reserving to the States respectively, the Appointment of Officers, and the Authority of training the Militia according to the discipline prescribed by Congress." U.S.C.A.Const. art. 1, § 8. With obvious purpose to assure the continuation and render possible the effectiveness of such forces the declaration and guarantee of the Second Amendment were made. It must be interpreted and applied with that end in view.

   U.S. v. Miller, *supra* note 4, at 178.

6. *E.g.,* U.S. v. Tot, 131 F.2d 261, 266 (3rd Cir. 1942), *rev'd on other grounds* 319 U.S. 463 (1943); U.S. v. Johnson, 497 F.2d 548, 550 (4th Cir. 1974); Stevens v. U.S., 440 F.2d 144, 149 (6th Cir. 1971); Quilici v. Village of Morton Grove, 695 F.2d 261, 270 (7th Cir. 1982); U.S. v. Nelson, 859 F.2d 1318, 1320 (8th Cir. 1988); Fresno Rifle and Pistol Club, Inc. v. Van de Kamp, 746 F.Supp. 1415, 1418 (E.D. Cal. 1990); Vietnamese Fishermen's Assn. v. Knights of the Ku Klux Klan, 543 F.Supp. 198, 210 (S.D. Texas 1982).

7. Eleven articles discussing the Second Amendment were published during this seventy-three year period. All endorsed the collective rights model. Robert J. Spitzer, *Lost and Found: Researching the Second Amendment,* Chapter 2, at Table 1 [hereinafter Spitzer, *Lost and Found*].

8. Stuart R. Hays, *The Right to Bear Arms: A Study in Judicial Misinterpretation,* 2 WM. & MARY L. REV. 381 (1960).

9. Spitzer, *Lost and Found, supra* note 7 at 25.

10. *Id.* at 381 n.2.

11. *Id.* at 397.

12. *See* 51 A.B.A. J. 554 (1965).

13. *See* Josh Sugarmann, *National Rifle Association: Money, Firepower, Fear* 36 (1992).

14. *Id.* at 35.

15. *Id.* at 37.

16. *Id.* at 37 (quoting Dodd).

17. *Id.* at 36–37 (quoting Rummel).

18. Robert A. Sprecher, *The Lost Amendment*, 51 A.B.A. J. 554, and 665 (1965).

19. *Id.* at 669.

20. Frederick J. Kling, *Restrictions on the Right to Bear Arms: State and Federal Firearms Legislation*, 98 U. PA. L. REV. 905, 908–11 and 919 (1950).

21. *Id.* at 906.

22. Spitzer, *Lost and Found, supra* note 7 at 25.

23. *Id.*

24. David I. Caplan (three articles): *Restoring the Balance: The Second Amendment Revisited*, 5 FORDHAM URBAN L.J. 31 (1976); *Handgun Control: Constitutional or Unconstitutional? A Reply to Mayor Jackson*, 10 N.C. CENTRAL L.J. 53 (1978); *The Right of the Individual to Bear Arms: A Recent Judicial Trend*, DET. C.L. REV. 789, 789 n.[†] (1982) (identifying Caplan as voluntary counsel to the Federation of New York State Rifle & Pistol Clubs).

Robert Dowlut (three articles): with Janet A. Knoop, *State Contributions and the Right to Keep and Bear Arms*, 7 OKLA. CITY L. REV. 177 (1982); *The Right to Arms: Does the Constitution or the Predilection of Judges Reign?*, 36 OKLA. L. REV. 65, 65 n.[*] (1983); *Federal and State Constitutional Guarantees to Arms*, 15 U. DAYTON L. REV. 59, 59 n.[*] (1989).

Although the 1982 and 1983 articles identify Dowlut only as a member of the D.C. bar, in 1982 he identified himself elsewhere as a lawyer in the Office of General Counsel of the NRA. *See* Report of the Subcommittee on the Constitution of the Committee on the Judiciary, U.S. Senate, 97th Cong., 2d sess., *The Right to Keep and Bear Arms*, 83–109 (1982) ("Other Views"). The 1989 article identifies Dowlut as Deputy General Counsel for the NRA.

Richard E. Gardiner (one article): *To Preserve Liberty–A Look at the Right to Keep and Bear Arms*, 10 N. KY. L. REV. 61, 61 n.[*] (1982) (identifying Gardiner as NRA Assistant General Counsel).

Alan M. Gottlieb (one article): *Gun Ownership: A Constitutional Right*, 10 N. KY. L. REV. 113, 113 n.[*] (1982) (identifying Gottlieb as president of the Second Amendment Foundation and chairman of the Citizens Committee for the Right to Keep and Bear Arms).

Stephen P. Halbrook (six articles): *Encroachments of the Crown of Liberty of the Subject: Pre-Revolutionary Origins of the Second Amendment*, 15 U. DAYTON L. REV. 91 (1989); *What the Framers Intended: A Linguistic Analysis of the Right to "Bear Arms,"* 49 LAW & CONTEMP. PROBS. 401 (1986); *The Right to Bear Arms in the First State Bills of Rights: Pennsylvania, North Carolina, Vermont, and Massachusetts*, 10 VT. L. REV. 255 (1985); *Tort Liability for the Manufacture, Sale, and Ownership of Handguns?*, 6 HAMLINE L. REV. 351 (1983); *To Keep and Bear Their Private Arms: The Adoption of the Second Amendment, 1787–1791*, 31 N. KY. L. REV. 13 (1982); *The Jurisprudence of the Second and Fourteenth Amendments*, 4 GEO. MASON U.L. REV. 1 (1981). Halbrook also produced two other law review articles that, although not included in Spitzer's list because they do not deal centrally with the Second Amendment, are related to the right to bear arms: *The Right to Bear Arms in Texas*, 41 BAYLOR L. REV. 629 (1989); *Firearms, the Fourth Amendment, and Air Carrier Security*, 53 J. AIR L. & COM. 585 (1987).

Although in these articles Halbrook identifies himself only as an attorney in Fairfax, Virginia, in 1986 he told a federal district court that he was a lawyer in the Office of General Counsel of the NRA. *See Oefinger v. D.L.O. Manufacturing and Importing*, 1986 U.S. Dist. LEXIS 18370 (D.D.C. 1986).

Don B. Kates, Jr. (two articles): *The Second Amendment: A Dialog*, 49 L. & CONTEMP. PROBS 143 (1986); *Handgun Prohibition and the Original Meaning of the Second Amendment*, 82 MICH. L. REV. 204 (1983).

Kates has represented the Second Amendment Foundation. *See Quilici v. Second Amendment Foundation*, 769 F.2d 414, 415 (7th Cir. 1985).

25. STEPHEN P. HALBROOK, FREEDMAN, THE FOURTEENTH AMENDMENT, AND THE RIGHT TO BEAR ARMS, 1866–76 (1998); TARGET SWITZERLAND: SWISS ARMED NEUTRALITY IN WORLD WAR II (1998); FIREARMS LAW DESKBOOK (1995); A RIGHT TO BEAR ARMS: STATE AND FEDERAL BILLS OF RIGHTS AND CONSTITU-

TIONAL GUARANTEES (1989); THAT EVERY MAN BE ARMED: THE EVOLUTION OF A CONSTITUTIONAL RIGHT (1984).

DON B. KATES, JR. & GARY LLECK, THE GREAT AMERICAN GUN DEBATE: ESSAYS ON FIREARMS AND VIO-LENCE (1997); FIREARMS AND VIOLENCE, ISSUES OF PUBLIC POLICY (DON B. KATES ED., 1984); RESTRICT-ING HANDGUNS: THE LIBERAL SKEPTICS SPEAK OUT (DON B. KATES ED., 1979).

26. Halbrook: In addition to the articles cited in *supra* note 24, Halbrook's law review writings include: *Congress Interprets the Second Amendment: Declarations by a Co-Equal Branch on the Individual Right to Keep and Bear Arms,* 23 TENN. L. REV. 597 (1995); *Personal Security, Personal Liberty, and "the Constitutional Right to Bear Arms": Visions of the Framers of the Fourteenth Amendment,* 5 SETON HALL CONST. L.J. 341 (1995); *Second-Class Citizenship and the Second Amendment in the District of Columbia,* 5 GEO. MASON U.C.R. L.J. 601 (1995); with Richard E. Gardiner, *NRA and Law Enforcement Opposition to the Brady Act,* 10 ST. JOHN'S J. LEGAL COM. 13 (1994); *Ration-ing Firearm Purchases and the Right to Keep and Bear Arms: Reflections on the Bills of Right of Virginia, West Virginia, and the United States,* 96 W. VA. L. REV. 1 (1993); *The Right of the People or the Power of the State: Bearing Arms, Arming Militias, and the Second Amendment,* 26 VAL. U.L. REV. 131 (1991).

Kates: In addition to the writings listed in *supra* note 24, Kates's law review articles include: with Daniel D. Polsby, *Causes and Correlates of Lethal Violence in America: American Exceptionalism,* 69 U. COLO. L. REV. 969 (1998); with Randy E. Barnett, *Under Fire: The New Consensus on the Second Amendment,* 45 EMORY L.J. 1139 (1996); with Daniel D. Polsby, *Book Review: Of Genocide and Disar-mament,* 86 J. CRIM. L. & CRIMINOLOGY 247 (1995); *Bigotry, Symbolism and Ideology in the Battle over Gun Control,* 31 PUB. INTEREST L.J. 1992; *Gun Control: Separating Reality from Symbolism,* 20 J. CON-TEMP. L. 353 (1994); *The Second Amendment and the Ideology of Self-Protection,* 9 CONST. COMM. 87 (1992); *The Value of Civilian Handgun Possession as a Deterrent to Crime or a Defense Against Crime,* AM. J. CRIM. L. 113 (1991).

27. *See, e.g.,* Halbrook: *The Gun Question: Our Right to Bear Arms,* HOUSTON CHRON., July 30, 1995, Outlook Section at 1; *The Second Amendment Stands,* USA TODAY, Jan. 16, 1991, at 8A. Kates: *Fore-father's Firm on Bearing Arms,* CHICAGO TRIB., Dec. 14, 1983, §1 at 21; *Shot Down: Cops, Criminals, and Criminologists are Equally Skeptical about Firearm Prohibition,* NAT'L REV., March 6, 1995, at 49.

28. *See, e.g., Gun Rights by Don Kates, Jr.: New Scholarship on the Right to Arms,* HANDGUNS, June 2000, at 32.

29. *www.nrahq.org/store* (visited May 17, 2000).

30. Halbrook: *members.aol.com/protell* (visited May 16, 2000); Kates: *www.donkates.com* (visited May 17, 2000). Consistent with their similarities, and with the personal aspect they seek to convey to their public, Halbrook and Kates each make a point of telling visitors that his Web site is maintained by his wife.

31. STEPHEN P. HALBROOK, THAT EVERY MAN BE ARMED: THE EVOLUTION OF A CONSTITUTIONAL RIGHT 195 (1984).

32. *Id.* at 77.

33. JOYCE LEE MALCOLM, TO KEEP AND BEAR ARMS: THE ORIGINS OF AN ANGLO-AMERICAN RIGHT (1994) [hereinafter Malcolm, *To Keep and Bear Arms*].

34. Randy E. Barnett and Don B. Kates, *Under Fire: The New Consensus on the Second Amendment,* 45 EMORY L.J. 1139, 1187 (1996). *See also* Robert J. Cottrol and Raymond T. Diamond, *The Fifth Auxil-iary Right,* 104 YALE L.J. 995 (1995); Nelson Lund, *The Past and Future of the Individual's Right to Arms,* 31 GA. L. REV. 1, 6 (1996); Glenn Harlan Reynolds, *A Line of Defense,* A.B.A. J., Aug. 1994, at 94 (reviewing Malcolm's book).

35. *Book Review,* AM. RIFLEMAN, April 1994, at 27. *See also* Wayne LaPierre, *Guns, Crime, and Freedom* 14–15 (1994). LaPierre is the chief executive officer of the NRA.

36. ANTONIN SCALIA, A MATTER OF INTERPRETATION: FEDERAL COURTS AND THE LAW 136–37 n.13 (1997).

37. *Declaration of Rights* art. 7. The declaration may be found in Lois G. Schwoerer, *The Declaration of Rights,* 1689 (1981) (Appendix 1).

38. The two most notable earlier criticisms may be found in: Carl T. Bogus, *The Hidden History of the Second Amendment,* 31 U.C. DAVIS L. REV. 309, 375–86 (1998); and Garry Wills, *To Keep and Bear Arms,* N.Y. REV. OF BOOKS, Sept. 21, 1995, at 62.

39. Sanford Levinson, *The Embarrassing Second Amendment*, 99 YALE L.J. 637 (1989).

40. *Id.* at 642.

41. *Id.* at 650–51.

42. "I cannot help but suspect that the best explanation for the absence of the Second Amendment from the legal consciousness of the elite bar, including that component found in the legal academy, is derived from a mixture of sheer opposition to the idea of private ownership of guns and the perhaps subconscious fear that altogether plausible, perhaps even 'winning,' interpretations of the Second Amendment would present real hurdles to those of us supporting prohibitory regulation," Levinson wrote. *Id.* at 642. "Perhaps 'we' might be led to stop referring casually to 'gun nuts,' " he wrote at another point. *Id.* at 659.

43. Sanford Levinson, *Democratic Politics and Gun Control*, 1 RECONSTRUCTION 137, 140 (1992).

44. *Id.* at 138.

45. *Id.* at 141.

46. *See, e.g.,* Cynthia Tucker, *NRA Spins its Lies Like a Gunslinger*, ATLANTA J. & CONSTITUTION, March 19, 2000, at 5G; Welton Jones, *Death in the Afternoon—Blame the Tools, not the Creators*, SAN DIEGO UNION-TRIBUNE, May 9, 1999, at E-1; William Booth, *Dole Doesn't Make Teens' Top 10: Parents, Wary of Political Crisis Worry about Pop Culture*, WASH POST., June 5, 1995, at A1; William Raspberry, *Problem Is Much Deeper: Gun Control Won't Stop the Killing in our Cities*, ATLANTA J. & CONSTITUTION, Aug. 24, 1994, at A12; James Brooke, *Brazil Is Now Leading Foreign Supplier of Handguns to U.S.*, N.Y. TIMES, Aug. 21, 1994, §1 at 6 (all mentioning the slogan, "When guns are outlawed, only outlaws will have guns").

47. *See, e.g.,* George P. Will, *The Embarrassing Second Amendment*, ST. PETERSBURG TIMES, March 21, 1991, at 23A; Michael Kinsley, *Second Thoughts: TRB-Gun Control Unconstitutional*, NEW REPUBLIC, Feb. 26, 1990, at 4; Michael Isikoff, *NRA Pushes Machine Gun Ownership*, WASH. POST, Dec. 28, 1990, at A17.

48. A Westlaw search conducted in the TP-All file on May 18, 2000, indicated that *The Embarrassing Second Amendment* has been cited in 195 law review articles.

49. *See* Bogus, *The Hidden History of the Second Amendment, supra* note 38, 318 n.37 (1998).

50. *See* Spitzer, *Lost and Found, supra* note 7 at 34; and *The AALS Directory of Law Teachers 1999–2000*, 764 (reporting that Olson joined the NRA Board in 1991).

51. Advertisement titled "An Open Letter on the Second Amendment," copyrighted 1995 by Academics for the Second Amendment (on file with author).

52. *See* Wendy Kaminer, *Second Thoughts on the Second Amendment*, ATLANTIC MONTHLY, March 1996, at 32.

53. Spitzer, *Lost and Found, supra* note 7 at 34.

54. *Id.*

55. Akhil Reed Amar, *The Bill of Rights and the Fourteenth Amendment*, 101 YALE L. J. 1193, 1205–11, 1261–62 (1992) [hereinafter Amar, *Fourteenth Amendment*]; Akhil Reed Amar, *The Bill of Rights as a Constitution*, 100 YALE L. J. 1131, 1162–75 (1991) [hereinafter Amar, *Constitution*]. *See also* AKHIL REED AMAR, THE BILL OF RIGHTS: CREATION AND RECONSTRUCTION 46–59 (1998).

56. Amar, *Fourteenth Amendment, supra* note 55 at 1164.

57. *Id.* at 1165.

58. *Id.* at 1165–66.

59. *Id.* at 1166 n.163.

60. The Constitution provides:

> The Congress shall have Power . . . To provide for organizing, arming, and disciplining, the Militia, and for governing such Part of them as may be employed in the Service of the United States, reserving to the States respectively, the Appointment of the Officers, and the Authority of training the Militia according to the discipline prescribed by Congress.

U.S. CONST. art. I, § 8.

61. Writing in the *Federalist Papers*, Hamilton made it clear that the Constitution gives Congress the authority to organize the militia as it sees fit, adding: "What plan for the regulation of the militia may be pursued by the national government is impossible to be foreseen." THE FEDERALIST No. 29 (Alexander Hamilton). Stressing that he was offering his personal opinion only, Hamilton stated he would

advise Congress to opt for a "select corps of moderate size." *Id.* Though some of Madison's writings may be read as an endorsement of a universal militia, he made it clear that the militia were to be organized by Congress. THE FEDERALIST Nos. 53 and 65 (both James Madison). Moreover, Madison, who was the principal author of both the militia clause in Article I, section 8, and the Second Amendment, stated that the Bill of Rights did not change any of the principal structure or principles of the Constitution. Remarks of James Madison, House of Representatives, June 8, 1789, in CREATING THE BILL OF RIGHTS: THE DOCUMENTARY RECORD FROM THE FIRST FEDERAL CONGRESS 63 Helen E. Veit, et al., eds., (1991).

62. *See* Michael C. Dorf, *What Does the Second Amendment Mean Today?,* Chapter 10, at 255.

63. William Van Alstyne, *The Second Amendment and the Personal Right to Arms,* 43 DUKE L.J. 1236 (1994).

64. The strongest passage reads as follows:

> There is, to be sure, in the Second Amendment, an express reference to the security of a *"free* State." It is not a reference to *the* Security of THE STATE. There are doubtless certain national constitutions that put a privileged emphasis on the security of "the state," but such as they are, they are all *unlike* our Constitution. . . . Accordingly, such constitutions make no reference to any right of the people to keep and bear arms, apart from state service. And why do they not do so? Because, in contrast with the premises of constitutional government in this country, they reflect the belief that recognition of any such right "in the people" might well pose a threat to the security of "the state." In view of these different constitutions, it is commonplace to find that no one within the state other than its own authorized personnel has any right to keep and bear arms—a view emphatically rejected, rather than embraced, however by the Second Amendment. . . .

Id. at 1244 (citations omitted).

65. LEONARD W. LEVY, ORIGINS OF THE BILL OF RIGHTS 133–49 (1999).

66. *Id.* at 134.

67. *Id.* at 135.

68. *Id.* at 133.

69. *Id.* at 148.

70. *Id.* at 149 (quoting the Supreme Court in *Dennis v. U.S.* regarding the proposition that allowing preparation for revolution leads to anarchy).

71. *Id.*

72. *Id.*

73. LAURENCE H. TRIBE, 1 AMERICAN CONSTITUTIONAL LAW (3d ed., 2000).

74. Tony Mauro, *Scholar's Views on Arms Rights Anger Liberals,* USA TODAY, Aug. 27, 1999, at 4A.

75. *See, e.g.,* William Glaberson, *Right to Bear Arms: A Second Look,* N.Y. TIMES, May 30, 1999, §4 at 3; Mauro, *supra* note 74.

76. Charlton Heston, *President's Column,* AMERICAN HUNTER, Nov. 1, 1999, at 12 (available on LEXIS ALLNEWS database).

77. Tribe, *supra* note 73 at 903.

78. *See id.* at 898 (especially note 213), and 901–02 (especially the last paragraph of note 221).

79. *Id.* at 902 n.221.

80. "[T]he federal government may not disarm individual citizens without some unusually strong justification consistent with the authority of the states to organize their own militias," Tribe wrote. *Id.* at 902 n. 221.

81. *Id.* at 899.

82. *Id.* at 902.

83. *Id.* at 896 (emphasis added).

84. Akhil Reed Amar, *Second Thoughts: What the Right to Bear Arms Really Means,* NEW REPUBLIC, July 12, 1999, at 24 [hereinafter Amar, *Second Thoughts*].

85. Laurence H. Tribe and Akhil Reed Amar, *Well Regulated Militias, and More,* N.Y. TIMES, Oct. 28, 1999, at A31.

86. *Id.*

87. Amar, *Second Thoughts, supra* note 84, at 27.

88. The ad was published in the *New York Times* on March 27, 2000, on the op-ed page (A-27). The letter is available on the Web site of the sponsoring organization, the Legal Community Against Vio-

lence, *www.lcav.org* (visited June 2, 2000). I was also, along with Tribe and Amar, both a signatory of the letter and an active participant in helping to organize the project.

89. Tribe and Amar, *supra* note 85.

90. *Id.* at 26.

91. Amar expressly contradicts the Constitution on this key point. "A modern translation of the amendment might be: 'An armed and militarily trained citizenry being conducive to freedom, the right of the electorate to organize itself militarily shall not be infringed,'" he writes. *Id.* at 24–25. That is, while the Constitution says the militia is organized by Congress, Amar says that, in some unexplained fashion, the electorate organizes itself into the militia. What does Amar mean by using the word "electorate" rather than "people" or "citizenry?" Is he implying the people organize themselves into the militia at the ballot box, perhaps by voting for members of Congress? Amar does not say.

92. *See* Frank R. Shapiro, *The Most-Cited Legal Scholars,* 29 J. LEG. STUDIES 409, 424–26 (2000); and James Lindgren and Daniel Seltzer, *The Most Prolific Law Professors and Faculties,* 71 CHICAGO-KENT L. REV. 781, 796 (1996).

93. *See* Scott Heller, *The Right to Bear Arms: Some Prominent Legal Scholars are Taking a New Look at the Second Amendment,* CHRONICLE OF HIGHER EDUC., July 21, 1995, at A8.

94. Brief for Amicus Curiae Academics for the Second Amendment, U.S. v. Lopez, U.S. (No. 93–1260)(available on LEXIS in GENFED/BRIEFS file) [hereinafter "A2A Brief"]. Similar lists are set forth in David B. Kopel and Christopher C. Little, *Communitarians, Neorepublicans, and Guns: Assessing the Case for Firearms Prohibition,* 56 MD. L. REV. 438, 523 n.445 (1997), and Randy E. Barnett and Don B. Kates, *Under Fire: The New Consensus on the Second Amendment,* 45 EMORY L.J. 1139, 1143–44 nn.12–13 (1996). However, as Spitzer's research shows, though a majority of law review articles since 1980 have supported the individual rights model, the numbers were never as lopsided as suggested.

95. A2A Brief, *supra* note 94.

96. Glenn Harlan Reynolds, *A Critical Guide to the Second Amendment,* 62 TENN. L. REV. 461, 463 (1995).

97. Printz v. United States, 117 S. Ct. 2365, 2385–86 n.2 (1997) (Thomas, J. concurring). On the other hand, Justice Souter, joined by Justices Stevens, Ginsburg, and Breyer, has hinted that the Second Amendment might grant a collective right. *See* United States v. Morrison, 120 S.Ct. 1740, 1765 n.11 (May 15, 2000) (Souter, J. dissenting).

98. Antonin Scalia, *A Matter of Interpretation: Federal Courts and the Law* 136–37 n.13 (1997).

99. *See* GARRY WILLS, A NECESSARY EVIL: A HISTORY OF AMERICAN DISTRUST OF GOVERNMENT 25–41, 112–33, 159, 191–260 (1999); and Wills, *supra* note 38, at 62.

100. MICHAEL A. BELLESILES, ARMING AMERICA: THE ORIGINS OF A NATIONAL GUN CULTURE (2000); Michael A. Bellesiles, *Gun Laws in Early America: The Regulation of Firearms Ownership 1607–1794,* 16 LAW & HIST. REV. 567 (1998); Michael A. Bellesiles, *The Origins of Gun Culture in the United States, 1760–1865,* 83 J. AM. HIST. 425 (1996).

101. Saul Cornell, *Commonplace or Anachronism: The Standard Model, The Second Amendment, and the Problem of History in Contemporary Constitutional Theory,* 16 CONST. COMMENTARY 221 (1999). Three worthwhile comments on Cornell's article follow in the same journal issue.

102. Don Higginbotham, *The Federalized Militia Debate: A Neglected Aspect of Second Amendment Scholarship,* 55 WM. & MARY Q. 39 (1998).

103. Bogus, *The Hidden History of the Second Amendment, supra* note 38.

2. LOST AND FOUND: RESEARCHING THE SECOND AMENDMENT

* Robert J. Spitzer is Distinguished Service Professor of Political Science at the State University of New York, College at Cortland. He is the author of seven books including PRESIDENT AND CONGRESS (McGraw-Hill); THE POLITICS OF GUN CONTROL (Chatham House); THE RIGHT TO BEAR ARMS (ABC-CLIO); and THE ESSENTIALS OF AMERICAN POLITICS (W. W. Norton). In addition, Professor Spitzer is the editor of four other books, including POLITICS AND CONSTITUTIONALISM (Praeger), and CONSTITUTIONALISM, INSTITUTIONS, AND IMPLICATIONS OF POWER (University Press of Kansas), and is the book series general editor for the Series on American Constitutionalism published by SUNY

Press. Professor Spitzer is also the author of more than one hundred articles and book chapters on a variety of American political subjects. He currently is vice president and president-elect of the Presidency Research Group of the American Political Science Association. He has testified before Congress on several occasions, including before the U.S. Senate Judiciary Committee's Subcommittee on the Constitution, Federalism, and Property Rights, at its hearing about the Second Amendment in 1998.

1. Warren Burger, *The Right to Bear Arms*, PARADE, January 14, 1990, 5.
2. *Creating the Bill of Rights* 182–84, 198–99, Helen E. Veit, Kenneth R. Bowling, and Charlene Bangs Bickford, eds., 1991; ALEXANDER HAMILTON, JAMES MADISON, AND JOHN JAY, THE FEDERALIST PAPERS 24, 25, 28, 29, and 46 (1961); GARRY WILLS, A NECESSARY EVIL 119–21 (1999).
3. *See* U.S. v. Cruikshank, 92 U.S. 542 (1876); Presser v. Illinois, 116 U.S. 252 (1886); Miller v. Texas, 153 U.S. 535 (1894); and U.S. v. Miller, 307 U.S. 174 (1939). The court acknowledged this line of cases in Lewis v. U.S., 445 U.S. 90 (1980). A list of the pertinent federal court rulings appears in note 65. *See* SPITZER, THE POLITICS OF GUN CONTROL, chap. 2, for a fuller discussion of these cases.
4. ALLAN R. MILLETT AND PETER MASLOWSKI, FOR THE COMMON DEFENSE: A MILITARY HISTORY OF THE UNITED STATES (1984). The authors quote Rep. Jabez Upham, who observed in 1808 during debate in the House of Representatives that reliance on citizen militias "will do very well on paper; it sounds well in the war speeches on this floor. To talk about every soldier being a citizen, and every citizen being a soldier, and to declaim that the militia of our country is the bulwark of our liberty is very captivating. All this will figure to advantage in history. But it will not do at all in practice" (129).
5. Keith A. Ehrman and Dennis Henigan, *The Second Amendment in the Twentieth Century: Have You Seen Your Militia Lately?* UNIVERSITY OF DAYTON LAW REVIEW 15 (Fall 1989): 36. *See also* JAMES M. MCPHERSON, BATTLE CRY OF FREEDOM 317 (1988); WILLIAM RIKER, SOLDIERS OF THE STATES: THE ROLE OF THE NATIONAL GUARD IN AMERICAN DEMOCRACY (1957), chap. 3.
6. 32 Stat. 775–80 (1903); 39 Stat. 166 (1916). *See also* MILLETT AND MASLOWSKI, FOR THE COMMON DEFENSE 247–49; RIKER, SOLDIERS OF THE STATES; and JERRY COOPER, THE RISE OF THE NATIONAL GUARD (1997).
7. I decline to use the term "standard modelers" or "standard model" to refer to those who advocate alternate views of the Second Amendment, as this term implies something standard, orthodox, or historically mainstream about this point of view, which, in my view, is not the case.
8. Collin Levey, *Liberals Have Second Thoughts on the Second Amendment,* WALL STREET JOURNAL, November 22, 1999.
9. Recent cites of this early version of Madison include in SPITZER, THE POLITICS OF GUN CONTROL 34 (1995 edition), which in turn appeared in CREATING THE BILL OF RIGHTS 10 (1991 edition).
10. *See* SPITZER, THE POLITICS OF GUN CONTROL 25–27.
11. THOMAS JEFFERSON, THE WRITINGS OF THOMAS JEFFERSON 415, Andrew A. Lipscomb, ed. (1904).
12. William Glaberson, *Right to Bear Arms: A Second Look,* NEW YORK TIMES, May 30, 1999.
13. William Safire, *An Appeal for Repeal,* NEW YORK TIMES, June 10, 1999; Walter Shapiro, *It's High Time to Gun Down the 2nd Amendment,* USA TODAY, September 17, 1999; Daniel Lazare, *Your Constitution Is Killing You,* HARPER'S MAGAZINE, October 1999, 57–65.
14. Levey, *Liberals Have Second Thoughts on the Second Amendment,* WALL STREET JOURNAL.
15. For example, legal writer and individualist architect Don B. Kates edited a book titled RESTRICTING HANDGUNS: THE LIBERAL SKEPTICS SPEAK OUT (1979), which was consciously compiled to marshal "liberal skepticism about 'gun control.' " (1–2) Similarly, criminologist Gary Kleck, who argues in his writings against stronger gun controls, argues strenuously, even vehemently, that he is a good liberal. At the start of two books, he provides an "Author's Voluntary Disclosure Notice" that trumpets his devotion to liberal causes and organizations. In his book TARGETING GUNS (1997), vi, he writes of himself: "The author is a member of the American Civil Liberties Union, Amnesty International USA, Independent Action, Democrats 2000, and Common Cause, among other politically liberal organizations. He is a lifelong registered Democrat, as well as a contributor to liberal Democratic candidates. He is not now, nor has he ever been, a member of, or contributor to, the National Rifle Association, Handgun Control, Inc. nor any other advocacy organization, nor has he received funding for research from any such organization." One presumes this is offered somehow to enhance his credibility, although it is difficult to see how such an exuberant embrace of partisan political organizations, and rejection of others, can be considered a sign of objectivity. Unintentional hilarity aside,

Kleck's personal proclamation does provide a diversion from an assessment of Kleck's work based on its objective merit.

16. Andrew Jay McClurg refers to this as the fallacy of diversion, defined as "distorting the reasoning process in ways intended to make the audience lose track of or ignore the real point." *The Rhetoric of Gun Control,* 42 THE AMERICAN UNIVERSITY LAW REVIEW 81 (1992).

17. Most notably, see R. E. Barnett and D. B. Kates, *Under Fire: The New Consensus on the Second Amendment,* 45 EMORY LAW JOURNAL 1139–59 (1996). As the subtitle states, the authors seek to assert that the individualist view has become the new academic consensus.

18. Lazare, *Your Constitution Is Killing You,* 58. Emphasis in original.

19. Quoted in *Id.* at 59.

20. Shapiro, *It's High Time.*

21. Much of this line of analysis relies on supporting quotes accidentally or willfully pulled out of context that, when examined in context, support the court view. To pick an example, Stephen P. Halbrook quotes Patrick Henry's words during the Virginia ratifying convention as saying, "The great object is, that every man be armed. . . . Every one who is able may have a gun." *To Keep and Bear Their Private Arms: The Adoption of the Second Amendment, 1787–1791,* 10 NORTHERN KENTUCKY LAW REVIEW 25 (1982). This quote would seem to support the view that at least some early leaders advocated general popular armament aside from militia purposes. Yet here is the full quote from the original debates: "May we not discipline and arm them [the states], as well as Congress, if the power be concurrent? so that our militia shall have two sets of arms, double sets of regimentals, &c.; and thus, at a very great cost, we shall be doubly armed. *The great object is, that every man be armed.* But can the people afford to pay for double sets of arms, &c.? *Every one who is able may have a gun.* But we have learned, by experience, that, necessary as it is to have arms, and though our Assembly has, by a succession of laws for many years, endeavored to have the militia completely armed, it is still far from being the case." JONATHAN ELLIOT, 3 DEBATES IN THE SEVERAL STATE CONVENTIONS ON THE ADOPTION OF THE FEDERAL CONSTITUTION 386 (1836); emphasis added. It is perfectly obvious that Henry's comments are in the context of a discussion of the militia, and the power balance between the states and Congress. For further discussion of this defective research, see Jack N. Rakove's article in this book. Garry Wills's conclusion about this literature is less charitable. Speaking about the individualist writers, he says that "it is the quality of their arguments that makes them hard to take seriously." *To Keep and Bear Arms,* THE NEW YORK REVIEW OF BOOKS, September 21, 1995, 62.

22. *See* Presser v. Illinois, 116 U.S. 252 (1886) at 265-66.

23. Michael A. Bellesiles, *The Origins of Gun Culture in the United States, 1760–1865,* 83 JOURNAL OF AMERICAN HISTORY 426, 428 (1996).

24. SPITZER, THE POLITICS OF GUN CONTROL, 28.

25. *See* 10 U.S.C. 311 (1983).

26. JOHN SHY, A PEOPLE NUMEROUS AND ARMED 31 (1990).

27. Shy cites as a telling example of the problem of internal security the fact that militias in the South increasingly were used as "an agency to control slaves, and less [as] an effective means of defense." A PEOPLE NUMEROUS AND ARMED 37. Carl T. Bogus argues persuasively that the Second Amendment was supported by the southern states precisely because they were seeking a guarantee to continue to use militias for this purpose. *The Hidden History of the Second Amendment,* 31 U.C. DAVIS LAW REVIEW 375–86 (1998).

28. SHY, A PEOPLE NUMEROUS AND ARMED 37–38.

29. Saul Cornell, *Commonplace or Anachronism: The Standard Model, the Second Amendment, and the Problem of History in Contemporary Constitutional Theory,* 16 CONSTITUTIONAL COMMENTARY 235 (1999).

30. SHY, A PEOPLE NUMEROUS AND ARMED 36–38.

31. Obviously, the Second Amendment is talking about only those people who could serve in a militia, as the Supreme Court made clear in Presser. This argument is raised in Robert Dowlut, *The Right to Arms: Does the Constitution or the Predilection of Judges Reign?* 36 OKLAHOMA LAW REVIEW 93–94 (1983). In *Fresno Rifle & Pistol Club v. Van De Kamp,* the court of appeals rejected the idea that the phrase "the people" had the same, uniform meaning throughout the Bill of Rights (965 F.2d 723; 9th Cir. 1992); No. 91-15466, at 5938-39.

Some law journal articles have asserted that a 1990 Supreme Court case, *U.S. v. Verdugo-Urquidez*

(494 U.S. 259), ruled that the phrase "the people" in the Second Amendment meant all citizens. *See, e.g.,* W. Van Alstyne, *The Second Amendment and the Personal Right to Arms,* 43 DUKE LAW JOURNAL 1243, n.19 (1994); G. L. Shelton, *In Search of the Lost Amendment: Challenging Federal Firearms Regulation Through the "State's Right" Interpretation of the Second Amendment,* 23 FLORIDA STATE UNIVERSITY LAW REVIEW 105–39 (1995); R. J. Larizza, *Paranoia, Patriotism, and the Citizen Militia Movement: Constitutional Right or Criminal Conduct?* 47 MERCER LAW REVIEW 605 (1996). Such interpretations are false, as the Verdugo-Urquidez case has nothing to do with interpreting the Second Amendment. In fact, the case deals with the Fourth Amendment issue of whether an illegal alien from Mexico was entitled to constitutional protection regarding searches. In the majority decision, Chief Justice Rehnquist discussed the meaning of the phrase "the people," given that the phrase appears not only in several parts of the Bill of Rights but also in the Constitution's preamble, in order to determine its applicability to a noncitizen. Rehnquist speculated that the phrase "seems to have been a term of art" (at 265) that probably pertains to people who have developed a connection with the national community. Rehnquist's speculations about whether the meaning of "the people" could be extended to a noncitizen, and his two passing mentions of the Second Amendment in that discussion, shed no light, much less legal meaning, on this amendment.

32. JOEL SAMAHA, CRIMINAL LAW 230–76 (1993); AMERICAN LAW INSTITUTE, 1 MODEL PENAL CODE AND COMMENTARIES 380–81 (1985); BLACK'S LAW DICTIONARY 707 (1983).

33. 1 U.S. Stat. 264.

34. 10 U.S.C. 331-334.

35. ROSCOE POUND, THE DEVELOPMENT OF CONSTITUTIONAL GUARANTEES OF LIBERTY 90–91 (1957).

36. Donald L. Beschle, *Reconsidering the Second Amendment: Constitutional Protection for a Right of Security,* HAMLINE LAW REVIEW 95 (1986).

37. Cornell, *Commonplace or Anachronism,* 238.

38. As Justice Robert Jackson noted in *Terminello v. Chicago* (337 U.S. 1, 1949; at 37): "The choice is not between order and liberty. It is between liberty with order and anarchy without either. There is danger that if the Court does not temper its doctrinaire logic with a little practical wisdom, it will convert the constitutional Bill of Rights into a suicide pact." Even though the truth of this conclusion is clear enough, Akhil Amar and Alan Hirsch do not accept it, arguing that "the Framers did envision the militia playing precisely this double role" of both suppressing revolt and fomenting it. They offer this argument without providing any sources or documentation to support the claim that the framers endorsed this insurrectionist purpose of the militias. Then, even more puzzling, they retreat from their argument that some portion of the Constitution or Bill of Rights supports armed revolt against the government by saying that the case for violent revolution made by the Declaration of Independence was changed by the Constitution, which "endorsed a new kind of revolution, a peaceful means of altering or abolishing the government" by "ballots rather than bullets." They conclude with, "It may be a mistake to think of the right to armed revolt as a 'constitutional' right." At last, they get it right. AKHIL REED AMAR AND ALAN HIRSCH, FOR THE PEOPLE 174–76 (1998). Amar and Hirsch seek to rebut the arguments of Dennis Henigan, *Arms, Anarchy, and the Second Amendment,* 26 VALPARAISO UNIVERSITY LAW REVIEW 107–29 (Fall 1991).

39. *See, e.g.,* Glenn Harlan Reynolds, *The Right to Keep and Bear Arms Under the Tennessee Constitution,* 61 TENNESSEE LAW REVIEW 669 (1994); David E. Vandercoy, *The History of the Second Amendment,* 28 VALPARAISO UNIVERSITY LAW REVIEW 1009 (1994); Williams, *The Militia Movement and Second Amendment Revolution,* 886, n.13.

40. Sanford Levinson, *The Embarrassing Second Amendment,* 99 THE YALE LAW JOURNAL 642, 650–51 (1989).

41. *See, e.g.,* Larizza, *Paranoia, Patriotism, and the Citizen Militia Movement,* 581–636; N. Lund, *The Second Amendment, Political Liberty, and the Right to Self-Preservation,* 39 ALABAMA LAW REVIEW 103–30 (1987); Reynolds, *The Right to Keep and Bear Arms Under the Tennessee Constitution,* 647–73; Van Alstyne, *The Second Amendment and the Personal Right to Arms,* 1236–55. A particularly egregious example of this is David C. Williams, who says flatly that the Second Amendment "guarantees to citizens the right to own arms, so as to be ready to make a revolution." *The Militia Movement and Second Amendment Revolution,* 886, n.13.

42. For an extended, classic discussion of the meaning and origins of the modern concept of revolution, see HANNAH ARENDT, ON REVOLUTION, chap. 1, 1963.

43. Bogus, *The Hidden History of the Second Amendment*, 386.
44. A few classics in the field include ARENDT, ON REVOLUTION; JOHN DUNN, MODERN REVOLUTIONS (1972); BARRINGTON MOORE, SOCIAL ORIGINS OF DEMOCRACY AND DICTATORSHIP (1966); ERIC R. WOLF, PEASANT WARS OF THE TWENTIETH CENTURY (1969). One commentator who offers meaningful and valuable analysis of the military consequences of revolutions and peasant uprisings is Colonel Charles J. Dunlap, *Revolt of the Masses: Armed Civilians and the Insurrectionary Theory of the Second Amendment*, 62 TENNESSEE LAW REVIEW 643–77 (1995).
45. Barnett and Kates, *Under Fire*, 1141; R. G. Cottrol and R. T. Diamond, *The Second Amendment: Toward an Afro-Americanist Reconsideration*, 80 THE GEORGETOWN LAW JOURNAL 311 (1991); N. J. Johnson, *Beyond the Second Amendment: An Individual Right to Arms Viewed Through the Ninth Amendment*, 24 RUTGERS LAW JOURNAL 72 (1992); Levinson, *The Embarrassing Second Amendment*, 658; Lund, *The Second Amendment*, 226; Reynolds, *The Right to Keep and Bear Arms*, 647; Shelton, *In Search of the Lost Amendment*, 108–10.
46. Barnett and Kates, *Under Fire*, 1141; S. Bursor, *Toward a Functional Framework for Interpreting the Second Amendment*, 74 TEXAS LAW REVIEW 1126 (1996); D. B. Kates, *The Second Amendment and the Ideology of Self-Protection*, 9 CONSTITUTIONAL COMMENTARY 361 (1992).
47. Cottrol and Diamond, *The Second Amendment*, 310; S. A. Halbrook, *Jurisprudence of the Second and Fourteenth Amendments*, 4 GEORGE MASON UNIVERSITY LAW REVIEW 1 (1981); D. T. Hardy, *Armed Citizens, Citizen Armies: Toward a Jurisprudence of the Second Amendment*, 9 HARVARD JOURNAL OF LAW AND PUBLIC POLICY 559 (1986); Levinson, *The Embarrassing Second Amendment*, 641; Lund, *The Second Amendment*, 226; Van Alstyne, *The Second Amendment and the Personal Right to Arms*, 1239–40.
48. A. R. Amar, *The Bill of Rights and the Fourteenth Amendment*, 101 YALE LAW JOURNAL 1264 (1992); Hardy, *Armed Citizens, Citizen Armies*, 559–60; D. B. Kates, *Handgun Prohibition and the Original Meaning of the Second Amendment*, 82 MICHIGAN LAW REVIEW 214, 218 (1983); Levinson, *The Embarrassing Second Amendment*, 654; Lund, *The Second Amendment*, 225; T. M. Moncure, *The Second Amendment Ain't About Hunting*, 34 HOWARD LAW JOURNAL 592 (1991); G. H. Reynolds, *A Critical Guide to the Second Amendment*, 62 TENNESSEE LAW REVIEW 498 (1995); J. R. Wagner, *Gun Control Legislation and the Intent of the Second Amendment: To What Extent Is There an Individual Right to Keep and Bear Arms?* 37 VILLANOVA LAW REVIEW 1410 (1992).
49. I conducted my search at the Cornell University Law Library. The earliest printed edition of the *Index to Legal Periodicals* in the library was titled *An Index to Legal Periodical Literature*, by Leonard A. Jones (1888). It indexed articles from 158 law journals and reviews written prior to 1887. I excluded from my search books, as well as articles, on the Second Amendment appearing in the publications of other disciplines, such as history, since my deliberate purpose is to chronicle publications on this subject within the law journal community, where virtually all of this writing has taken place. In my search, I used the *Index* cites to identify articles that likely considered Second Amendment issues, and to weed out those that did not. Based on a list of likely candidates drawn from the *Index*, I then went to the bound volumes of law journals to personally examine each article, to see if it did in fact analyze the Second Amendment, and to then discern the article's spin, which then constituted the bibliographic data found in this article's Appendix.
50. *The Constitutional Right to Keep and Bear Arms and Statutes Against Carrying Weapons*, 46 AMERICAN LAW REVIEW 778 (1912).
51. *Right to Bear Arms*, 16 LAW NOTES 207–8 (1913).
52. Lucilius A. Emery, *The Constitutional Right to Keep and Bear Arms*, 28 HARVARD LAW REVIEW 476 (1915).
53. *Id.* at 477.
54. S. R. Hays, *The Right to Bear Arms, A Study in Judicial Misinterpretation*, 2 WILLIAM AND MARY LAW REVIEW 403 (1960).
55. Compare with Lois G. Schwoerer's article in this book.
56. Hays, *The Right to Bear Arms*, 397.
57. *Id.* at 401.
58. *Id.* at 399.
59. *Id.* at 400, n.82 and 84; 402, n.88.
60. According to the Alumni Office at the College of William and Mary School of Law, Hays received his

undergraduate B.A. degree from William and Mary in 1957, and a B.C.L. degree from the law school in 1960. Hays also served as an editor of the *William and Mary Law Review,* had been a hunter and gun collector since before his law school days, and also had become a life member of the National Rifle Association before law school (correspondence with the author, December 15, 1999).

61. D. B. Kates has been quick to mischaracterize the literature, saying that before the 1980s there was "scant historical support" for the court/collectivist view (an assertion contradicted by the bibliographic data presented here), and as seen also in his false assertion that "thirty-six law review articles" addressed the Second Amendment from 1980 to the early 1990s, and that "only four" take the court/collectivist view. According to Table 1, thirty-eight articles dealt with the subject from 1980–89, with another twenty-four published from 1990–93 (the year before the publication of Kates's article; see Appendix to this article), totaling sixty-two articles. Of the sixty-two, twenty-six take the court/collectivist view, not four. *Gun Control: Separating Reality from Symbolism,* 20 JOURNAL OF CONTEMPORARY LAW 359 (1994).

62. JACK PELTASON, CORWIN AND PELTASON'S UNDERSTANDING THE CONSTITUTION 168 (1988).

63. IRVING BRANT, THE BILL OF RIGHTS 486 (1965).

64. Edward Dumbauld says, "The Second and Third Amendments stand simply as the empty symbol of what remains a living American ideal: the supremacy of the civil power over the military." He also notes that "these amendments are defunct in practice." THE BILL OF RIGHTS 62–63 (1957). *See also* JOHN SEXTON AND NAT BRANDT, HOW FREE ARE WE? 209–10 (1986). In the words of Robert A. Rutland, the Second Amendment (along with the Third, having to do with the quartering of troops in peoples' homes) has become "obsolete." THE BIRTH OF THE BILL OF RIGHTS 229 (1955). Standard legal reference works used by lawyers and judges parallel this perspective. *See* AMERICAN LAW REPORTS, FEDERAL 700–29 (1983). In 1975, the American Bar Association endorsed the understanding that the Second Amendment is connected with militia service, as has the American Civil Liberties Union. See A. J. Dennis, *Clearing the Smoke,* 29 AKRON LAW REVIEW 65, n.29 (1995).

65. Hickman v. Block, 81 F.3d 98; 9th Cir., 1996, at 101. *See also* U.S. v. Nelson, 859 F.2d 1318, (8th Cir. 1988), at 1320. Other federal court rulings making the same point include: Cases v. U.S., 131 F.2d 916, 922–23 (1st Cir. 1942), cert. denied sub nom Velazquez v. U.S., 319 U.S. 770 (1943); U.S. v. Tot, 131 F.2d 261, 266 (3d Cir. 1942), reversed on other grounds, 319 U.S. 463 (1943); U.S. v. Johnson, 441 F.2d 1134, 1136 (5th Cir. 1971); U.S. v. McCutcheon, 446 F.2d 133, 135–36 (7th Cir. 1971); Stevens v. U.S., 440 F.2d 144, 149 (6th Cir. 1971); Cody v. U.S., 460 F.2d 34, 36–37 (8th Cir. 1972), cert. denied, 409 U.S. 1010 (1972); Eckert v. City of Philadelphia 3d Cir. 1973; U.S. v. Day, 476 F.2d 562, 568 (6th Cir. 1973); U.S. v. Johnson, 497 F.2d 548, 550 (4th Cir. 1974); U.S. v. Warin, 530 F.2d 103, 106 (6th Cir. 1976), cert. denied, 426 U.S. 948 (1976); U.S. v. Graves, 554 F.2d 65, 66–67 (3d Cir. 1977); U.S. v. Oakes, 564 F.2d 384, 387 (10th Cir. 1977), cert. denied, 435 U.S. 926 (1978); Quilici v. Village of Morton Grove, 695 F.2d 261, 270 (7th Cir. 1982), cert. denied, 464 U.S. 863 (1983); Thomas v. Members of City Council of Portland, 730 F.2d 41 (1st Cir. 1984); Farmer v. Higgins, 907 F.2d 1041 (11th Cir. 1990), cert. denied, 111 S.Ct. 753 (1991); Fresno Rifle & Pistol Club v. Van de Camp, 965 F.2d 723 (9th Cir. 1992); Hickman v. Block, 81 F.3d 168 (9th Cir. 1996); U.S. v. Wright, 117 F.3d 1265, 1273 (11th Cir. 1997); Peoples Rights Organization, Inc. v. City of Columbus, 152 F.3d 522, 539 (6th Cir. 1998); U.S. v. Napier, 233 F.3d 394 (6th Cir. 2000); U.S. v. Metcalf, 221 F.3d 1336 (6th Cir. 2000), cert. denied; U.S. v. Finitz, 2000 WL 1171139 (9th Cir. Aug. 17, 2000); U.S. v. Hancock, 231 F.3d 557 (9th Cir. 2000). *See also* Burton v. Sills, 394 U.S. 812, 1969, where a Second Amendment appeal was "dismissed for want of a substantial federal question."

66. 138 L Ed 2d 914 (1997), at 946–47.

67. Antonin Scalia, *Common-Law Courts in a Civil-Law System,* in A MATTER OF INTERPRETATION: FEDERAL COURTS AND THE LAW 3, 43 Amy Gutmann ed. (1997).

68. The case raises a host of questions, not the least of which is that it relies almost exclusively on the individualist law journal literature, and ignores the three nineteenth-century Supreme Court cases on the Second Amendment, saying simply that they are not "modern." 1999 WL 181663 (N.D. Tex.) at 11. Since this case is on appeal as of this writing, it is not analyzed here.

69. Thomas M. Moncure says that the three nineteenth-century cases "are as unillustrative as they are unpleasant." Whether true or not, I know of no legal doctrine that invalidates cases because of these traits. *The Second Amendment Ain't About Hunting,* 34 HOWARD LAW JOURNAL 592 (1991).

70. The late Supreme Court Justices John Marshall Harlan, William O. Douglas, and Hugo Black ar-

gued for total incorporation of the Bill of Rights, but no one else on the court has since embraced such an argument. The first incorporation case applied the Fifth Amendment protection to the states pertaining to just compensation in cases of eminent domain in *Chicago, Burlington, and Quincy Railroad v. Chicago,* 166 US 226 (1897). Other significant incorporation cases included First Amendment free speech in *Gitlow v. New York,* 268 US 652 (1925); First Amendment press freedom in *Near v. Minnesota,* 283 US 697 (1931); First Amendment religious freedom in *Hamilton v. Regents of the University of California,* 293 US 245 (1934); First Amendment freedom of assembly and petitioning the government for redress of grievances, *De Jonge v. Oregon,* 299 US 353 (1937); Fourth Amendment search and seizure in *Mapp v. Ohio,* 367 US 643 (1961); Sixth Amendment right to counsel in *Gideon v. Wainwright,* 372 US 335 (1963); and Fifth Amendment protection against double jeopardy in *Benton v. Maryland,* 395 US 784 (1969). For an excellent summary of incorporation, see HENRY J. ABRAHAM, FREEDOM AND THE COURT (1972), chap. 3. *See also* BRANT, THE BILL OF RIGHTS, chaps. 27–40.

71. *See* RICHARD C. CORTNER, THE SUPREME COURT AND THE SECOND BILL OF RIGHTS 279 (1981).

72. The Courts of Appeal have repeatedly recognized the validity of the earlier Supreme Court cases dealing with the Second Amendment. Some individualist writers misconstrue incorporation entirely. Halbrook, for example, claims that the *Presser* case "plainly suggests that the second amendment applies to the States through the fourteenth amendment" when in fact the court said precisely the opposite. *To Keep and Bear Their Private Arms,* 85.

73. STEPHEN P. HALBROOK, THAT EVERY MAN BE ARMED 112 (1984).

74. ALFRED AVINS, THE RECONSTRUCTION AMENDMENTS' DEBATES 219 (1967).

75. M. J. Quinlan makes the same error in *Is There a Neutral Justification for Refusing to Implement the Second Amendment or Is the Supreme Court Just 'Gun Shy'?* 22 CAPITAL UNIVERSITY LAW REVIEW 661 (1993).

76. AKHIL REED AMAR, THE BILL OF RIGHTS 259 (1998). Amar concludes that the Second Amendment "was reglossed by a later constitutional text [i.e., the Fourteenth Amendment]." (297) Amar cites the same kind of sources as Halbrook to support his "floor wax" theory of this supposed relationship between the two amendments. In his analysis, Amar confuses politics and law, citing congressional debate over southern turmoil to support his argument, yet he never cites, or even mentions, the *Cruikshank* or *Presser* cases (or for that matter *Miller v. U.S.*), which falsify his argument.

77. Quinlan, *Is There a Neutral Justification,* 662.

78. *Id.*

79. STEPHEN P. HALBROOK, FREEDMEN, THE FOURTEENTH AMENDMENT, AND THE RIGHT TO BEAR ARMS, 1866–1876 viii (1998).

80. *Id.* at 43. *See also* 71.

81. Akhil Reed Amar also wants to argue for a kind of total incorporation by saying that "the Second Amendment right to bear arms—and presumably all other rights and freedoms in the Bill of Rights—were encompassed by both the Freedman's Bureau Act and its companion Civil Rights Act. (Of course, adoption of both Acts presupposed congressional power to impose the general requirements of the Bill of Rights on states. [Rep.] Bingham . . . denied that Congress had such power, and therefore argued that a constitutional amendment was required to validate the Civil Rights Act.)" Amar does note the key difference between the two bills and the Fourteenth Amendment. *The Bill of Rights and the Fourteenth Amendment,* 101 YALE LAW JOURNAL 1245, n.228 (1992).

82. U.S. v. Cruikshank, 92 US 542 (1876), at 553. Halbrook erroneously asserts that, in the *Cruikshank* case, "the Supreme Court did not consider whether the Fourteenth Amendment incorporated the rights to assemble and keep and bear arms against the states." FREEDMEN, THE FOURTEENTH AMENDMENT, 172.

83. ABRAHAM, FREEDOM AND THE COURT, 43.

84. ANDREA L. BONNICKSEN, CIVIL RIGHTS AND LIBERTIES 2 (1982).

85. WILLS, A NECESSARY EVIL, 257–58.

86. Barnett and Kates, *Under Fire. See also* Bursor, *Toward a Functional Framework for Interpreting the Second Amendment,* 1125–51.

87. Rosa Ehrenreich, *Look Who's Editing,* LINGUA FRANCA 58–63 (1996); Bernard J. Hibbitts, *Last Writes? Reassessing the Law Review in the Age of Cyberspace,* 71 NEW YORK UNIVERSITY LAW REVIEW 615–88 (1996); Christopher Shea, *Students v. Professors,* THE CHRONICLE OF HIGHER EDUCATION, June

2, 1995, A33-34. Faculty oversight has actually declined since 1970, although there has been a recent revival of the call for greater faculty control. Roger C. Cramton, *"The Most Remarkable Institution"*: *The American Law Review*, 35 JOURNAL OF LEGAL EDUCATION 6 (1986).

88. Ehrenreich, *Look Who's Editing*, 60. Having taught students, and graded student papers, for more than twenty years, I am struck by the fact that students would typically identify two traits of writing, commonly found in law journals, as signs of excellence: length (the longer a work is, the better it must be) and the number of footnotes (more equalling better).

89. The law school community has engaged in much soul-searching and self-criticism on this matter, going back many decades. *See Special Issue*, 30 AKRON LAW REVIEW (1996); *Special Issue*, 47 STANFORD LAW REVIEW (1995); *Symposium on Law Review Editing: The Struggle Between Author and Editor Over Control of the Text*, 61 CHICAGO-KENT LAW REVIEW (1994). Oliver Wendell Holmes, Jr., brushed law reviews aside as the "work of boys." Quoted in Hibbitts, *Last Writes?*, 631.

90. Hibbitts, *Last Writes?*, 647-48. Despite continued, even growing criticism of student control of law reviews, students continue to control an ever-growing number of such publications.

91. Cramton, *"The Most Remarkable Institution,"* 8.

92. It may also be that intellectual traits stemming from legal training contribute to the trends described here, such as the adversarial principle and the reasonable doubt standard, but these questions are beyond the scope of this article.

93. Wills, *To Keep and Bear Arms*, 71.

94. For more on the argument that the legal profession's norms encourage modes of thought that are uniquely different from other professions, and that encourage some of the problems described here, see MARK C. MILLER, THE HIGH PRIESTS OF AMERICAN POLITICS (1995).

95. Theodore J. Lowi, *The State in Political Science: How We Become What We Study*, 86 AMERICAN POLITICAL SCIENCE REVIEW 1 (1992).

96. *See* SPITZER, THE POLITICS OF GUN CONTROL, chaps. 4 and 5.

97. Of the forty-eight academics whose names appeared in the A2A ad, thirty-three listed law school affiliations. Reprinted in the NATIONAL REVIEW, March 15, 1993, 23.

98. Scott Heller, *The Right to Bear Arms*, THE CHRONICLE OF HIGHER EDUCATION, July 21, 1995, A8, 12; Jan Hoffman, *Fund Linked to N.R.A. Gave $20,000 for Goetz's Defense*, NEW YORK TIMES, April 16, 1996.

99. A. D. Herz, *Gun Crazy: Constitutional False Consciousness and Dereliction of Dialogic Responsibility*, 75 BOSTON UNIVERSITY LAW REVIEW 138, n.358 (1995).

100. The Lawyer's Second Amendment Society publishes *The Liberty Pole* six times a year, a newsletter that advances its constitutional arguments.

101. In particular, individualist authors including Caplan, Dowlut, Gardiner, Halbrook, Kates, Moncure, and Tahmassebi are employed by, or have worked for, the NRA or other gun groups. These seven individuals alone account for twenty-seven of the articles listed in this article's Appendix (this count does not include other articles pertaining to gun control not authored or coauthored by these individuals that do not appear on this list by virtue of the fact that they do not dwell on the Second Amendment). Caplan has served on the governing board of the National Rifle Association, and as counsel to two New York State gun groups. See *Constitutional Rights in Jeopardy: The Push for "Gun Control,"* a publication of the NRA, 1998. Dowlut, Gardiner, Moncure, and Tahmassebi have all worked for the Office of the General Counsel of the NRA; see Subcommittee on the Constitution, Judiciary Committee, U.S. Senate, *The Right to Keep and Bear Arms*, 97th Cong., 2d sess. (1982), iii; T. M. Moncure, *Who Is the Militia*, 19 LINCOLN LAW REVIEW 1 (1990); S. B. Tahmassebi, *Gun Control and Racism*, 2 GEORGE MASON UNIVERSITY CIVIL RIGHTS LAW JOURNAL 67 (1990). Halbrook is a leading lawyer for the NRA cause, having argued such cases as *Printz v. U.S.* For example, during hearings held before the Subcommittee on the Constitution, Judiciary Committee, U.S. Senate, held in Washington, D.C., on September 23, 1998, Halbrook advised NRA president Charlton Heston during Heston's testimony before the committee. Oddly, Halbrook does not mention his long association with the NRA when identifying himself. In his book *Freedmen, the Fourteenth Amendment, and the Right to Bear Arms, 1866-1876* (1998), he identifies himself as having argued Printz before the Supreme Court, but beyond that says only that he "practices law in Fairfax, Virginia." Fairfax is the home of the NRA. Kates is a longtime gun activist who is a regular contributor to anti–gun control publications and adviser to anti-control activists. *See, e.g., Readers Write*, AMERICAN RIFLEMAN, February 1994, 10. He authors a regular column called "Gun Rights" that appears in the magazine *Hand-*

guns. Dennis A. Henigan is chief counsel for Handgun Control, Inc., and is the author of two collec-
tivist articles listed in the Appendix. No other court/collectivist author listed has authored more than
two articles. I do not attach particular significance to these interest-group associations, however, because the key issue is the willingness of law journals to accept and print these articles rather than the
occupational backgrounds or ideological predilections of the authors.
102. Bogus, *The Hidden History of the Second Amendment,* 316.
103. 138 L Ed 2d 914 (1997), at 946–47.
104. CLEMENT E. VOSE, CAUCASIANS ONLY: THE SUPREME COURT, THE NAACP, AND THE RESTRICTIVE COVENANT
    CASES 68 (1959). *See also* 69–71, 161, 175–76.

3 THE SECOND AMENDMENT IN ACTION

 * Michael A. Bellesiles teaches legal history at Emory University and has also taught at Oxford and
   Stanford universities. He is the author of REVOLUTIONARY OUTLAWS: ETHAN ALLEN AND THE STRUG-
   GLE FOR INDEPENDENCE ON THE EARLY AMERICAN FRONTIER (University Press of Virginia) and
   ARMING AMERICA: THE ORIGINS OF A NATIONAL GUN CULTURE (Alfred A. Knopf), for which he received the Bancroft Prize; the editor of three books, including LETHAL IMAGINATION: VIOLENCE AND
   BRUTALITY IN AMERICAN HISTORY (New York University Press); and the author of more than thirty
   professional articles and book chapters. Professor Bellesiles is the only person to ever win both of the
   top article-of-the-year prizes from the Organization of American Historians: the Louis Pelzer Award
   in 1986 and the Binkley-Stephenson Award in 1996.
 1. 44 GUNS & AMMO 37–38 (November 1999).
 2. 10 LINGUA FRANCA 32 (February 2000).
 3. *Id.* at 32.
 4. Randy E. Barnett and Don B. Kates, *Under Fire: The New Consensus on the Second Amendment,* 45
    EMORY LAW JOURNAL 1141 (1996).
 5. Quoted in Daniel Lazare, *Your Constitution Is Killing You,* HARPER'S MAGAZINE, 59 (October 1999).
 6. *See, e.g.,* the forums in 62 TENNESSEE LAW REVIEW (1995) and 16 CONSTITUTIONAL COMMENTARY (1999).
 7. HELEN AUGUR, THE SECRET WAR OF INDEPENDENCE 13–20, 51–91 (1955); SAMUEL FLAGG BEMIS, THE
    DIPLOMACY OF THE AMERICAN REVOLUTION 24–37, 48–54 (1935); Elizabeth Miles Nuxoll, "Congress
    and the Munitions Merchants: The Secret Committee of Trade during the American Revolution,
    1775–1777," 112–72, 343–421 (Ph.D. diss., 1979); 1, 2 HISTOIRE DE LA PARTICIPATION DE LA FRANCE A
    L'ETABLISSEMENT DES ETATS-UNIS D'AMERIQUE (Henri Doniol ed., 1886–1892).
 8. LAWRENCE DELBERT CRESS, CITIZENS IN ARMS: THE ARMY AND THE MILITIA IN AMERICAN SOCIETY TO THE
    WAR OF 1812 75–93 (1982); MICHAEL A. BELLESILES, ARMING AMERICA: THE ORIGINS OF A NATIONAL GUN
    CULTURE chs. 6 and 7 (2000).
 9. THE DIARY OF WILLIAM MACLAY AND OTHER NOTES ON SENATE DEBATES 246 (Kenneth R. Bowling and
    Helen E. Veit eds., 1988).
10. ROBERT J. TAYLOR, WESTERN MASSACHUSETTS IN THE REVOLUTION ch. 6 (1954); DAVID P. SZATMARY,
    SHAYS' REBELLION: THE MAKING OF AN AGRARIAN INSURRECTION ch. 2 (1980).
11. ACTS AND LAWS OF MASSACHUSETTS, 1786 494–95, 497, 502–03, 510 (1786); Massachusetts Senate to
    Governor Bowdoin, Feb. 4, 1787, Massachusetts Archives, State House (Boston); *Address to the Peo-
    ple* from the General Court, HAMPSHIRE GAZETTE, Dec. 3, 1786; William Shepard to Bowdoin, Jan. 26,
    1787, and Benjamin Lincoln to Bowdoin, Jan. 28, 1787 in Joseph P. Warren, *Documents relating to
    Shays' Rebellion,* 2 AMERICAN HISTORICAL REVIEW 694–96 (1897); SZATMARY, SHAYS' REBELLION
    70–105.
12. George Washington to James Madison, Nov. 5, 1786, 29 THE WRITINGS OF GEORGE WASHINGTON FROM
    THE ORIGINAL MANUSCRIPT SOURCES, 1745–1799 50–52 (John C. Fitzpatrick ed., 1931–1944). On the
    impact of Shays's Rebellion on the militia's reputation, see CRESS, CITIZENS IN ARMS 95–98.
13. George Washington to Benjamin Lincoln, Feb. 24, 1787, 29 WRITINGS OF WASHINGTON 168.
14. 1 WESTERN MASSACHUSETTS: A HISTORY, 1636–1925 183 (John Lockwood et al., 1926).
15. 1 THE RECORDS OF THE FEDERAL CONVENTION OF 1787 19–20, 25, 293 (Max Farrand ed., 1937); *id.* at 2:
    47. See also THE FEDERALIST NO. 29.
16. 2 THE RECORDS OF THE FEDERAL CONVENTION 220–22, 330–31. The debate over the federal regulation

of the militia may be followed through the records. *See especially id.* at 2: 47–49, 133–37, 144–48, 159, 168, 174, 182, 316–18, 323–33, 352–56, 368, 380–90, 459, 466–67, 602, 656, 662.

17. James Madison to Thomas Jefferson, Oct. 24, 1787, 10 THE PAPERS OF JAMES MADISON 212–14 (William T. Hutchinson, et al. eds., 1962–1991); JACK N. RAKOVE, DECLARING RIGHTS: A BRIEF HISTORY WITH DOCUMENTS 147–66 (1998). *See generally* H. Jefferson Powell, *Rules for Originalists*, 73 VIRGINIA LAW REVIEW 673–84 (1987); JACK N. RAKOVE, INTERPRETING THE CONSTITUTION: THE DEBATE OVER ORIGINAL INTENT (1990); RAKOVE, ORIGINAL MEANINGS: POLITICS AND IDEAS IN THE MAKING OF THE CONSTITUTION (1997).

18. 2 RECORDS OF THE FEDERAL CONVENTION 207.

19. *Id.* at 386–87.

20. Don Higginbotham, *The Federalized Militia Debate: A Neglected Aspect of Second Amendment Scholarship*, 55 WILLIAM AND MARY QUARTERLY 44 (1998); 2 RECORDS OF THE FEDERAL CONVENTION 182, 323, 330–33, 352–56, 380–90.

21. Don Higginbotham, *The Second Amendment in Historical Context*, 16 CONSTITUTIONAL COMMENTARY 263–68 (1999).

22. Michael Bellesiles, *Gun Laws in Early America: The Regulation of Firearms Ownership, 1607–1794*, 16 LAW AND HISTORY REVIEW 567–89 (1998).

23. The precise concept of eminent domain was not known under English common law; until the 1770s the taking of property by the sovereign required a special act of parliament. WILLIAM BLACKSTONE, 1 COMMENTARIES ON THE LAWS OF ENGLAND 138–39, 222, 290–96 (1979); *id.* at 4: 154–59; FORREST MCDONALD, NOVUS ORDO SECLORUM: THE INTELLECTUAL ORIGINS OF THE CONSTITUTION 9–24 (1985).

24. *See, e.g.*, 1 THE PUBLIC RECORDS OF THE COLONY OF CONNECTICUT 351 (J. Hammond Trumbull et al. eds., 1850–90); *id.* at 2: 217, 8: 380; 9: 341–44, 473, 580; 29 ARCHIVES OF MARYLAND 10–11, 47, 98, 153–55, 237–39, 376–78 (William H. Browne, et al. eds., 1883–1972); *id.* at 30: 20–21, 38–39, 461–63; 42: 87–90; 2 THE STATUTES AT LARGE OF SOUTH CAROLINA 15 (Thomas Cooper and David J. McCord eds., 1836–41); 10 THE STATE RECORDS OF NORTH CAROLINA 158 (Walter Clark ed., 1886–1909); ROBERT M. CALHOON, THE LOYALISTS IN REVOLUTIONARY AMERICA, 1760–1781 281–311, 397–414, 439–78 (1965); ALEXANDER C. FLICK, LOYALISM IN NEW YORK DURING THE AMERICAN REVOLUTION 58–94 (1901); ROBERT S. LAMBERT, SOUTH CAROLINA LOYALISTS IN THE AMERICAN REVOLUTION 33–58 (1987).

25. SELECT DOCUMENTS ILLUSTRATIVE OF THE HISTORY OF THE UNITED STATES, 1776–1861 9 (William McDonald, ed., 1903).

26. Higginbotham, *The Federalized Militia Debate*, 41; SOURCES AND DOCUMENTS ILLUSTRATING THE AMERICAN REVOLUTION 151 (Samuel E. Morison, ed., 1929).

27. ANON., MILITIA LAWS OF THE UNITED STATES AND MASSACHUSETTS (1836), 1–2.

28. Quoted, John K. Rowland, "Origins of the Second Amendment" 410 (Ph.D. diss., 1978).

29. RAKOVE, DECLARING RIGHTS 86–87; 9 THE STATUTES AT LARGE OF PENNSYLVANIA 110–14, 346–48 (James T. Mitchell and Henry Flanders eds., 1903); Saul Cornell, *Commonplace or Anachronism: The Standard Model, the Second Amendment, and the Problem of History in Contemporary Constitutional Theory*, 16 CONSTITUTIONAL COMMENTARY 221–46 (1999).

30. Higginbotham, *The Federalized Militia Debate*, 40.

31. Patrick Henry, June 5, 1788, 9 THE DOCUMENTARY HISTORY OF THE RATIFICATION OF THE CONSTITUTION 954–59 (Merrill Jensen et al. eds., 1976–1995); CRESS, CITIZENS IN ARMS, 98–102; Lyle D. Brundage, "The Organization, Administrations, and Training of the United States Ordinary and Volunteer Militia, 1792–1861" 41 (Ph.D. diss., 1958). For additional anti-Federalist views on the militia, see 1 DOCUMENTARY HISTORY OF THE RATIFICATION 482, 539–40; *id.* at 2: 37–38, 60, 184–85, 290–92, 318–19, 3: 20–22, 30–31, 408–412, 4: 58.

32. 3 RECORDS OF THE FEDERAL CONVENTION 272. For Martin's response, see *id.* at 286–95; Landowner #10, 16 DOCUMENTARY HISTORY OF THE RATIFICATION 267.

33. Higginbotham, *The Federalized Militia Debate*, 49; 9 DOCUMENTARY HISTORY OF THE RATIFICATION, 1014, 1074, 1102; *id.* at 10: 1288–96, 1311–12, 1324–25, 1486, 1531; a point also made in FEDERALIST 29 and FEDERALIST 46.

34. Higginbotham, *The Federalized Militia Debate*, 50; CRESS, CITIZENS IN ARMS 102–109.

35. 2 DOCUMENTARY HISTORY OF THE RATIFICATION 318–19.

36. *Id.* at 2: 420; ALEXANDER HAMILTON, JAMES MADISON, AND JOHN JAY, THE FEDERALIST, OR THE NEW CON-

STITUTION 161 (1979). See also *id.* at 151–56 (24), 180–86 (29), 313–20 (46); 1 DOCUMENTARY HISTORY OF THE RATIFICATION 435–36; *id.* at 3: 321–22, 401–402, 457, 508, 532, 4: 125, 265–67, 419.

37. Higginbotham, *The Federalized Militia Debate,* 48; CREATING THE BILL OF RIGHTS: THE DOCUMENTARY RECORD FROM THE FIRST FEDERAL CONGRESS 12, 30, 38–39n, 182–85, 267 (Helen E. Veit et al. eds., 1991).

38. 14 DOCUMENTARY HISTORY OF THE FIRST FEDERAL CONGRESS 173 (William C. diGiacomantonio et al. eds., 1996); Higginbotham, *The Federalized Militia Debate,* 48; Stuart Leibiger, *James Madison and Amendments to the Constitution, 1787–1789: 'Parchment Barriers,'* 59 JOURNAL OF SOUTHERN HISTORY 441–68 (1993).

39. Carl T. Bogus, *The Hidden History of the Second Amendment,* 31 U.C. DAVIS LAW REVIEW 352 (1997).

40. DECLARING RIGHTS 176–77.

41. CREATING THE BILL OF RIGHTS 182–84, 198–99; *see also id.* at 4, 30, 37–41, 48, 247–48, 293. Roger Sherman's version of the Bill of Rights, which played a key role in the congressional debates, addresses only the militia, with no reference to a right to bear arms. *Id.* at 266–68.

42. 1 Stat. 264 (May 2, 1792); MILITIA LAWS 16; Bellesiles, *Gun Laws in Early America.*

43. JOEL BARLOW, ADVICE TO THE PRIVELEGED ORDERS OF EUROPE 45–46 (London, 1792; 1956); JOHN TAYLOR, AN INQUIRY INTO THE PRINCIPLES AND POLICY OF THE GOVERNMENT OF THE UNITED STATES (1814), quoted in CRESS, CITIZENS IN ARMS 158; WALTER MILLIS, ARMS AND MEN: A STUDY IN AMERICAN MILITARY HISTORY 38–39 (1956); Michael Bellesiles, *Suicide Pact: New Readings of the Second Amendment,* 16 CONSTITUTIONAL COMMENTARY 247–62 (1999).

44. *1 Stat. 381 (June 5, 1794); 3 DEBATES AND PROCEEDINGS IN THE CONGRESS, 343–48, 762–90 (1834–1856); RICHARD H. KOHN, EAGLE AND SWORD: THE BEGINNINGS OF THE MILITARY ESTABLISHMENT IN AMERICA, 120–23, 145–48 (1975); CRESS, CITIZENS IN ARMS, 130–34.

45. THOMAS P. SLAUGHTER, THE WHISKEY REBELLION: FRONTIER EPILOGUE TO THE AMERICAN REVOLUTION 192–206 (1986).

46. *Id.* at 205–206.

47. Frank A. Cassell, "Samuel Smith: Merchant Politician, 1792–1812," 44–45 (Ph.D. diss., 1968); THE COLUMBIAN CHRONICLE, Jan. 23, 1795; Martin K Gordon, "The Militia of the District of Columbia, 1790–1815," 32 (Ph.D. diss., 1975); Richard H. Kohn, *The Washington Administration's Decision to Crush the Whiskey Rebellion,* 59 JOURNAL OF AMERICAN HISTORY 567–84 (1972); RUSSELL F. WEIGLEY, HISTORY OF THE UNITED STATES ARMY 100–103 (1967); SLAUGHTER, THE WHISKEY REBELLION 206–221; Saul Cornell, *Aristocracy Assailed: The Ideology of Backcountry Anti-Federalism,* 66 JOURNAL OF AMERICAN HISTORY 1148–72 (1990).

48. Meriwether Lewis to Lucy Marks, Oct. 4, 1794, Meriwether Lewis Papers, Missouri State Historical Society.

49. UNITED STATES CONGRESS, AMERICAN STATE PAPERS: DOCUMENTS, LEGISLATIVE AND EXECUTIVE, OF THE CONGRESS OF THE UNITED STATES, class V: 1 MILITARY AFFAIRS, 69–70 (1832–61).

50. CRESS, CITIZENS IN ARMS 128; Cornell, *Commonplace or Anachronism,* 231–37, 242–46.

51. WILLIAM FINDLEY, HISTORY OF THE INSURRECTION IN THE FOUR WESTERN COUNTIES OF PENNSYLVANIA 165–68 (1796); Washington's Sixth Annual Message to Congress, Nov. 19, 1794, 34 WRITINGS OF WASHINGTON, 3–6, 34–35; General Smith to the Maryland Troops, Nov. 15, 1794, 4 PENNSYLVANIA ARCHIVES 253–54 (Samuel Hazard et al. eds., 1852–1935); 4 DEBATES AND PROCEEDINGS IN THE CONGRESS 1067–71, 1214–20.

52. West Point Waste Books, 1784–92, USMA Library West Point; WILLIAM GUTHMAN, MARCH TO MASSACRE: A HISTORY OF THE FIRST SEVEN YEARS OF THE UNITED STATES ARMY, 1784–1791 93 (McGraw-Hill, 1975).

53. 14 DOCUMENTARY HISTORY OF THE FIRST FEDERAL CONGRESS 56, 84, 93–94; *see also id.* at 48–76, 102–132, 161–67.

54. FRIEDRICH W. L. G. A. BARON VON STEUBEN, A LETTER ON THE SUBJECT OF AN ESTABLISHED MILITIA 7–8 (1784); George Washington to Alexander Hamilton, May 2, 1783, 26 WRITINGS OF WASHINGTON 388–89; HENRY KNOX, A PLAN FOR THE GENERAL ARRANGEMENT OF THE MILITIA OF THE UNITED STATES (1786); CRESS, CITIZENS IN ARMS 84–85, 90–92.

55. 1 AMERICAN STATE PAPERS: MILITARY AFFAIRS 6–13; Knox to the Speaker of the House, Jan. 18, 1790, 2 DEBATES AND PROCEEDINGS IN THE CONGRESS 2087–2107.

56. 2 DOCUMENTARY HISTORY OF THE RATIFICATION 509.

57. See George Mason's speech to the Virginia Convention, *id.* at 10: 312; "Federal Farmer" [perhaps Melancton Smith], "An Old Whig" [perhaps Smilie], 2 THE COMPLETE ANTI-FEDERALIST 224–27, 341–42 (Herbert J. Storing ed., 1981); *id.* at 3: 49; EDMUND S. MORGAN, INVENTING THE PEOPLE: THE RISE OF POPULAR SOVEREIGNTY IN ENGLAND AND AMERICA 173 (1988); DIARY OF WILLIAM MACLAY 245; WEIGLEY, HISTORY OF THE UNITED STATES ARMY 89–94; 2 DEBATES AND PROCEEDINGS IN THE CONGRESS 1804–26; THEODORE J. CRACKEL, MR. JEFFERSON'S ARMY: POLITICAL AND SOCIAL REFORM OF THE MILITARY ESTABLISHMENT, 1801–1908 162–64 (1987); CRESS, CITIZENS IN ARMS 119–21.

58. Harrison Gray Otis in the House of Representatives, 10 DEBATES AND PROCEEDINGS IN THE CONGRESS 304–306; 1 AMERICAN STATE PAPERS: MILITARY AFFAIRS 133–35, 142–44; CRESS, CITIZENS IN ARMS 136–49; CRACKEL, MR. JEFFERSON'S ARMY 17–35.

59. JAMES ROGER SHARP, AMERICAN POLITICS IN THE EARLY REPUBLIC: THE NEW NATION IN CRISIS 203 (1993); Adrienne Koch and Henry Ammon, *The Virginia and Kentucky Resolutions,* 5 WILLIAM AND MARY QUARTERLY 163–65 (1948); RICHARD R. BEEMAN, THE OLD DOMINION AND THE NEW NATION, 1788–1801 202 (1972).

60. SHARP, AMERICAN POLITICS IN THE EARLY REPUBLIC 222; LISLE A. ROSE, PROLOGUE TO DEMOCRACY: THE FEDERALISTS IN THE SOUTH, 1789–1800 219–23 (1968).

61. SHARP, AMERICAN POLITICS IN THE EARLY REPUBLIC 252; quoting the GENERAL ADVERTISER, Dec. 11, 1800.

62. Gordon, *The Militia of the District of Columbia,* 38, 40.

63. *Id.* at 36–37.

64. *Id.* at 58–59; THE TIMES AND ALEXANDRIA ADVERTISER, May 18, 1798, 21, 31; Roger West to James Wood, June 6, 1798, Statement of Public Arms, June 22, 1799, 8 CALENDAR OF VIRGINIA STATE PAPERS AND OTHER MANUSCRIPTS 487–88, (William P. Palmer et al. eds., 1875–1893); *id.* at 9: 31–32.

65. James McHenry to Harrison Gray Otis, Jan. 31, 1800, 1 AMERICAN STATE PAPERS: MILITARY AFFAIRS 142.

66. THE TWO TRIALS OF JOHN FRIES ON AN INDICTMENT OF TREASON 21, 75 (Thomas Carpenter comp., 1800); STATE TRIALS OF THE UNITED STATES 545 (Francis Wharton, ed., 1849); SHARP, AMERICAN POLITICS IN THE EARLY REPUBLIC 209–210; Peter Levine, *The Fries Rebellion: Social Violence and the Politics of the New Nation,* 40 PENNSYLVANIA HISTORY 241–58 (1973).

67. Alexander Hamilton to James McHenry, March 18, 1799, 22 THE PAPERS OF ALEXANDER HAMILTON 552–53 (Harold C. Syrett and Jacob E. Cooke eds., 1961–1979); Levine, *Fries Rebellion,* 249–50.

68. SHARP, AMERICAN POLITICS IN THE EARLY REPUBLIC 268; quoting John Beckley to A. Gallatin, Feb. 15, 1801, Gallatin Papers, New York Historical Society.

69. SHARP, AMERICAN POLITICS IN THE EARLY REPUBLIC 269.

70. *Id.* at 270; T. M. Randolph to James Monroe, Feb. 14, 1801, Monroe Papers, Library of Congress.

71. SHARP, AMERICAN POLITICS IN THE EARLY REPUBLIC 269; Thomas McKean to Thomas Jefferson, Mar. 19, 1801, McKean papers, Historical Society of Pennsylvania.

72. Gordon, *The Militia of the District of Columbia,* 84.

73. Act of 1778, 19 THE COLONIAL RECORDS OF THE STATE OF GEORGIA: STATUTES COLONIAL AND REVOLUTIONARY, 1774 to 1805 104 (Alfred D. Candler ed., 1911).

74. 1 A COMPILATION OF THE MESSAGES AND PAPERS OF THE PRESIDENTS 57 (James Richardson, comp., 1897–1917).

75. Alexander Hamilton, *Final Version of the Report of Manufactures,* Dec. 5, 1791, 10 THE PAPERS OF ALEXANDER HAMILTON 317.

76. *See, e.g.,* 3 THE STATUTES AT LARGE OF VIRGINIA, 1792–1806 18 (Samuel Shepard comp., 1835).

77. MILITIA LAWS 8–10, 13; 1 U.S. STATUTES 271–74 (reenacted Feb. 2, 1813, *id.* at 2: 797); 3 DEBATES AND PROCEEDINGS IN THE CONGRESS 1392–95; KOHN, EAGLE AND SWORD 128–35. *See also* acts on the calling out of the militia, 1 U.S. STATUTES, 264 (May 2, 1792), 424 (Feb. 28, 1795; repealed 1861), *id.* at 2: 241 (March 3, 1803), 383–84 (April 18, 1806), 478–79 (March 30, 1808), 705–07 (April 10, 1812; reenacted 1814).

78. JAMES E. HICKS, 1 NOTES ON UNITED STATES ORDNANCE 14 (1940); REPORT OF THE COMMITTEE OF COMMERCE AND MANUFACTURES, TO WHOM WERE REFERRED THE PETITIONS OF THE MANUFACTURERS OF GUNPOWDER (1802), n.p.

79. Knox to the Senate, Dec. 16, 1793, George Washington to Congress, Jan. 21, 1790, 1 AMERICAN STATE PAPERS: MILITARY AFFAIRS 7–8, 44; Brundage, *Organization, Administrations, and Training,* 53.

80. Pickney to the House, Nov. 30, 1792, Moultrie to the House, Dec. 14, 1792, in JOURNALS OF THE HOUSE OF REPRESENTATIVES, 1792–1794 38–39, 182 (Michael E. Stevens ed., 1988).

81. *Id.* at 233, 285, 421–22, 440, 499–500.

82. Gordon, *Militia of the District of Columbia,* 21–22; JOHN K. MAHON, THE AMERICAN MILITIA: DECADE OF DECISION, 1789–1800, 14 (1960).

83. 1 AMERICAN STATE PAPERS: MILITARY AFFAIRS 69–70.

84. *Id.* at 44; RAPHAEL P. THIAN, LEGISLATIVE HISTORY OF THE GENERAL STAFF OF THE ARMY OF THE UNITED STATES, 1775–1901 (1901), 569–72; MERRITT ROE SMITH, HARPERS FERRY ARMORY AND THE NEW TECHNOLOGY: THE CHALLENGE OF CHANGE (1977).

85. HICKS, 1 NOTES ON UNITED STATES ORDNANCE 14–18; SIMEON N. D. NORTH AND RALPH H. NORTH, SIMEON NORTH, FIRST OFFICIAL PISTOL MAKER OF THE UNITED STATES 18–19 (1913); GEORGE D. MOLLER, MASSACHUSETTS MILITARY SHOULDER ARMS, 1784–1877 26–27 (1988); JAMES A. HUSTON, LOGISTICS OF LIBERTY: AMERICAN SERVICES OF SUPPLY IN THE REVOLUTIONARY WAR AND AFTER 312–14 (1991).

86. Secretary of War to the Senate, Dec. 12, 1798, 1 AMERICAN STATE PAPERS: MILITARY AFFAIRS 110; FELICIA J. DEYRUP, ARMS MAKERS OF THE CONNECTICUT VALLEY 37 (1948). DEYRUP, ARMS MAKERS OF THE CONNECTICUT VALLEY 37. *See also* Eli Whitney Papers, Yale University Library; JEANNETTE MIRSKY AND ALLEN NEVINS, THE WORLD OF ELI WHITNEY 206–65 (1952); 1 A COLLECTION OF ANNUAL REPORTS AND OTHER IMPORTANT PAPERS RELATING TO THE ORDNANCE DEPARTMENT, 1812–1889 (Stephen Vincent Benét comp., 1890).

87. 1 A COLLECTION OF ANNUAL REPORTS 37, 233; SMITH, HARPERS FERRY 69.

88. 1 AMERICAN STATE PAPERS: MILITARY AFFAIRS 162, 198–99, 215–17.

89. *Id.* at 190.

90. 27 DEBATES AND PROCEEDINGS IN THE CONGRESS 1002–1005, 1019–45, 2175–97.

91. 2 U.S. STATUTES 490; MILITIA LAWS 16–17.

92. Michael Bellesiles, *The Origins of American Gun Culture, 1760–1865,* 83 JOURNAL OF AMERICAN HISTORY 425–55 (1996).

93. 1 A COMPILATION OF THE MESSAGES AND PAPERS OF THE PRESIDENTS.

94. HICKS, 2 NOTES ON UNITED STATES ORDNANCE 24.

95. 1 AMERICAN STATE PAPERS: MILITARY AFFAIRS 328, 335–37; HICKS, 1 NOTES ON UNITED STATES ORDNANCE 32–35; *id.* at 2: 20–25, 29, 35–36, 115–28; 1 A COLLECTION OF ANNUAL REPORTS . . . ORDNANCE DEPARTMENT, 113, 177; DEYRUP, ARMS MAKERS OF THE CONNECTICUT VALLEY 41–42.

96. 2 AMERICAN STATE PAPERS: DOCUMENTS, LEGISLATIVE AND EXECUTIVE, OF THE CONGRESS OF THE UNITED STATES, class III: FINANCE, 687, 696 (1832–59).

97. Benjamin Tallmadge to Ebenezer Huntington, Dec. 18, 1809, Huntington to Tallmadge, Jan. 5, 1810, 1 AMERICAN STATE PAPERS: MILITARY AFFAIRS 264–65.

98. MAXIMILLIAN GODEFROY, MILITARY REFLECTIONS, ON FOUR MODES OF DEFENCE, FOR THE UNITED STATES 22 (1807); JOSEPH PRIESTLEY, LECTURES ON HISTORY, AND GENERAL POLICY (1803); JOHN TAYLOR, AN INQUIRY INTO THE PRINCIPLES AND POLICY OF THE GOVERNMENT OF THE UNITED STATES (1814); ANNALS OF CONGRESS, 12th Cong., 2d sess. (House), 630 (1814).

99. DAVID HUMPHREYS, CONSIDERATIONS ON THE MEANS OF IMPROVING THE MILITIA FOR THE PUBLIC DEFENCE 16 (1803).

100. 1 AMERICAN STATE PAPERS 266–27. *See also* ANNALS OF CONGRESS, 12th Cong., 2d sess. (House), 923–28.

101. 2 AMERICAN STATE PAPERS: MILITARY AFFAIRS 429.

102. Bogus, *The Hidden History of the Second Amendment.*

103. *See, e.g.,* 3 STATUTES AT LARGE OF VIRGINIA 11–18; H. M. HENRY, THE POLICE CONTROL OF THE SLAVE IN SOUTH CAROLINA (1914); JOHN HOPE FRANKLIN, THE MILITANT SOUTH, 1800–1861 72–98 (1956).

104. Sally E. Hadden, "Law Enforcement in a New Nation: Slave Patrols and Public Authority in the Old South, 1700–1865" (Ph.D. diss., 1993).

105. DOUGLAS R. EGERTON, GABRIEL'S REBELLION: THE VIRGINIA SLAVE CONSPIRACIES OF 1800 and 1802 50–68 (1993).

106. *Id.* at 72, 75-79.

107. *Id.* at 76; William Wilkinson to James Monroe Oct. 1, 1800, Executive Papers, Negro Insurrection, Virginia State Library; NORFOLK HERALD, Oct. 2, 1800; VIRGINIA ARGUS (Richmond), Oct. 10, 1800.

108. EGERTON, GABRIEL'S REBELLION 77; James Callender to Thomas Jefferson, Sept. 13 or 18, 1800, Jefferson Papers, Library of Congress; John Randolph to Joseph Nicholson, Sept. 26, 1800, Nicholson Papers, Library of Congress.

109. Thomas Newton to James Monroe, Dec. 29, 1800, John Bracken to Monroe, Sept. 20, 1800, Executive Papers, Negro Insurrection, Virginia State Library; EGERTON, GABRIEL'S REBELLION 75, 77.

110. EGERTON, GABRIEL'S REBELLION 133–34; James Monroe to Richard Adams, July 26, 1802, Letterbook, Executive Papers, Virginia State Library.

111. EGERTON, GABRIEL'S REBELLION 173; Howard to William Preston, Oct. 25, 1800, Preston Family Papers, Library of Congress.

112. *See, e.g.,* 16 STATUTES AT LARGE 109–10; *id.* at 9: 268, 12: 182; JUNE PURCELL GUILD, BLACK LAWS OF VIRGINIA 96–97, 106–107 (1969); THEODORE B. WILSON, THE BLACK CODES OF THE SOUTH 24–30 (1965); HENRY, POLICE CONTROL OF THE SLAVE 99–106.

113. State v. Newson 27 NC 250 (1844).

114. JOHN R. ELTING, AMATEURS, TO ARMS!: A MILITARY HISTORY OF THE WAR OF 1812 2 (1995); R. ERNEST DUPUY AND TREVOR N. DUPUY, THE ENCYCLOPEDIA OF MILITARY HISTORY FROM 3500 B.C. TO THE PRESENT 756, 765 (2d ed., 1986); CRACKEL, MR. JEFFERSON'S ARMY 98–125; C. EDWARD SKEEN, CITIZEN SOLDIERS IN THE WAR OF 1812 1–3, 39–61 (1999).

115. 1 AMERICAN STATE PAPERS: MILITARY AFFAIRS 491–92.

116. 1 THE HISTORICAL REGISTER OF THE UNITED STATES 59 (T. H. Palmer, ed., 1814–16); 1 AMERICAN STATE PAPERS: MILITARY AFFAIRS 323; 6 OFFICIAL LETTER BOOKS OF W. C. C. CLAIBORNE, 1801–1816 179–80, 218–19 (1917).

117. *Pennsylvania Militia,* 3 NILES' WEEKLY REGISTER 240 (Dec. 12, 1812); 1 AMERICAN STATE PAPERS: MILITARY AFFAIRS 338; Lenoir quoted, SKEEN, CITIZEN SOLDIERS 52; ANNALS OF CONGRESS, 12th Cong., 1st sess. (Senate), 283. *See also* 2 NILES' WEEKLY REGISTER 274 (June 27, 1812); *id.* at 3 (Sept. 26, 1812): 50, (Oct. 24, 1812): 115–16, (Dec. 12, 1812): 209–211; SKEEN, CITIZEN SOLDIERS 72–77.

118. CRESS, CITIZENS IN ARMS 152.

119. 1 AMERICAN STATE PAPERS: MILITARY AFFAIRS 337; Gordon, *The Militia of the District of Columbia,* 301–303; ALEXANDRIA GAZETTE, June 17, 19, 1812; NATIONAL INTELLIGENCER, May 14, 19, June 2, 13, 20, 1812; OFFICIAL LETTERS OF THE MILITARY AND NAVAL OFFICERS OF THE UNITED STATES (John Brannan, ed., 1823, 1971), 103, 109; 6 OFFICIAL LETTER BOOKS OF CLAIBORNE 231–32.

120. EDWARD D. INGRAHAM, A SKETCH OF THE EVENTS WHICH PRECEDED THE CAPTURE OF WASHINGTON 44–45 (1849); ELTING, AMATEURS, TO ARMS! 198–243.

121. 1 AMERICAN STATE PAPERS: MILITARY AFFAIRS 554, 563–64.

122. Though he called it the Fifth Amendment. 5 Wheat. 1 (1820) at 52.

123. *Id.* at 54, 76.

124. 12 Wheat. 19 (1827).

125. 1 Stat. 264 (May 2, 1792); 1 Stat. 381 (June 5, 1794); 2 DIGEST OF STATUTE LAWS OF KENTUCKY 1289–90 (C. S. Morehead and Mason Brown eds., 1835); Bliss v. Commonwealth 2 Litt. (Ky) 90, 13 Am. Dec. 251 (1822); Aymette v. State 21 Tenn. 154, 158 (1840). *See also* The State v. Reid, I Ala. 612 (1840), in which the court declared that neither the federal nor state constitutions "expressly nor by implication, denied to the Legislature, the right to enact laws in regard to the manner in which arms shall be borne." *Id.* at 616.

126. 4 Stat. 730 (June 30, 1834).

127. WILLIAM T. MINOR, MESSAGE OF HIS EXCELLENCY WILLIAM T. MINOR, GOVERNOR OF CONNECTICUT 19 (1856); JOSEPH D. WILLIAMS, ANNUAL REPORT OF THE ADJUTANT GENERAL OF THE STATE OF CONNECTICUT FOR THE YEAR 1857 26–27 (1858); Gates, *Disorder and Social Organization,* 251–55; WILLIAM A. BUCKINGHAM, MESSAGE OF HIS EXCELLENCY WILLIAM A. BUCKINGHAM, GOVERNOR OF CONNECTICUT 13 (1859); JEROME B. LUCKE, HISTORY OF THE NEW HAVEN GRAYS 135 (1876).

128. Cornell, *Commonplace or Anachronism,* 221–46; Bellesiles, *Suicide Pact,* 247–62.

129. BENJAMIN L. OLIVER, THE RIGHTS OF AN AMERICAN CITIZEN; WITH A COMMENTARY ON STATE RIGHTS 177–78 (1832, 1970).

130. 1 LAWS OF THE STATE OF TENNESSEE . . . 1715–1820 710 (Edward Scott comp., 1821).

131. LOUISIANA DIGEST, 1804–1841 13 (Meinrad Greiner, comp., 1841); ACTS OF LOUISIANA, 1813 172–74 (1813).

132. *See, e.g.,* the constitutions of Pennsylvania (1790), Kentucky (1792 and 1799), Connecticut (1818), Mississippi (1817), and Maine (1819).

133. ILLINOIS REVISED LAWS, 1832–1833, 202 (1833); OHIO ACTS, FIFTY-THIRD GENERAL ASSEMBLY, 2d sess., JANUARY, 1859 56–57 (1859). *See also* LAWS OF INDIANA (1831), 192; State v. Mitchell 3 Blackf. Rep. 229.

134.   DIGEST OF STATUTE LAWS OF GEORGIA, 1851 848 (1851).
135.   1 Kelly 243.
136.   RAKOVE, ORIGINAL MEANINGS.

4   THE SECOND AMENDMENT:
THE HIGHEST STAGE OF ORIGINALISM

*   Jack N. Rakove is the Coe Professor of History and Professor of Political Science at Stanford University, where he teaches courses in early American history and the origins and interpretation of the Constitution. He is the author of four books: THE BEGINNINGS OF NATIONAL POLITICS: AN INTERPRETIVE HISTORY OF THE CONTINENTAL CONGRESS (Alfred A. Knopf); JAMES MADISON AND THE CREATION OF THE AMERICAN REPUBLIC (Little Brown); DECLARING RIGHTS: A BRIEF HISTORY WITH DOCUMENTS (Bedford Books); and ORIGINAL MEANINGS: POLITICS AND IDEAS IN THE MAKING OF THE CONSTITUTION (Alfred A. Knopf), which won the 1997 Pulitzer Prize in History, the 1997 Fraunces Tavern Museum Book Award, and the 1998 Society of the Cincinnati Book Prize. He is also the editor of INTERPRETING THE CONSTITUTION: THE DEBATE OVER ORIGINAL INTENT (Northeastern University Press), and JAMES MADISON: WRITINGS (Library of America). He has contributed articles and chapters to numerous scholarly collections and law reviews, including the *Stanford Law Review, University of Chicago Law Review, Yale Law Journal,* and *Yale Journal of Law and Humanities.*

1.   For further elaboration of these points, see the opening pages of the original version of this essay, published in 76 CHICAGO KENT LAW REVIEW (2000). Readers are alerted that the original version is also more extensively annotated with references to both primary sources and secondary writings.

2.   Skeptical as I am of the view that this interpretation merits description as the "standard model," I will henceforth refer to it as the individual rights interpretation.

3.   For a good example of this phenomenon, see Randy Barnett and Don B. Kates, *Under Fire: The New Consensus on the Second Amendment,* 45 EMORY L. J. 1131 and passim (1996), largely devoted to rebutting Andrew Herz, *Gun Crazy: Constitutional False Consciousness and Dereliction of Dialogic Responsibility* 75 BOSTON UNIV. L. R. 57–153 (1995). One would not want to suggest, however, that Herz's essay is itself a model of scholarly decorum.

4.   STEPHEN HALBROOK, THAT EVERY MAN BE ARMED: THE EVOLUTION OF A CONSTITUTIONAL RIGHT x–xii (1984).

5.   In this article, I do not address the distinct claims about the relation between the Fourteenth Amendment and the right to bear arms that might be made under the aegis either of the original meaning of the former, especially as it related to the plight of the African-American freemen of the Reconstruction South, or the various theories of incorporation that lie at the heart of so much modern constitutional jurisprudence.

6.   This is not to deny that serious arguments can be made in favor of the deterrent value of firearms. But to reason about firearms about the basis of whether their availability does more to promote violent crime and accidental mayhem, on the one hand, or to deter crime, on the other, is to reason on decidedly nonoriginalist grounds.

7.   Anyone consulting the index to the respective volumes of the DOCUMENTARY HISTORY OF THE RATIFICATION OF THE CONSTITUTION will discover only scattered entries under the heading "Arms, Right to Bear," in contrast to numerous entries under headings like "Army, Standing" and "Militia."

8.   On this point, see especially MARY ANN GLENDON: RIGHTS TALK: THE IMPOVERISHMENT OF POLITICAL DISCOURSE (1991).

9.   For further discussion, see DONALD S. LUTZ, POPULAR CONSENT AND POPULAR CONTROL: WHIG POLITICAL THEORY IN THE EARLY STATE CONSTITUTIONS 59–71 (1980); GORDON S. WOOD, THE CREATION OF THE AMERICAN REPUBLIC 271–73 (1969); AMAR, BILL OF RIGHTS, 131–132; and JACK N. RAKOVE, DECLARING RIGHTS: A BRIEF HISTORY WITH DOCUMENTS (1997), in which I attempt to trace the ambiguities in American thinking about the exact juridical authority and reach of declarations of rights.

10.   It would be interesting to test this proposition against the historical record of how revolutions actually succeed, and in the process differentiating revolutions wherein the authority of an entrenched regime actually collapsed from civil wars in which two well-armed camps contended for victory against each other.

11.   In stating this point, I refer especially to WILLIAM J. NOVAK, THE PEOPLE'S WELFARE: LAW AND REG-

ULATION IN NINETEENTH-CENTURY AMERICA (1980), a work that is admittedly concerned with the post-Revolutionary era. Yet Novak's account is also fully consistent with the description of eighteenth-century political economy provided in such classic works as OSCAR HANDLIN AND MARY FLUG HANDLIN, COMMONWEALTH: A STUDY OF THE ROLE OF GOVERNMENT IN THE AMERICAN ECONOMY, 1774–1861 (1947). There is no reason to think that the Revolutionary era—whatever other changes it introduced in constitutional theory—engendered a shift in underlying understandings of the inherent police power of the states.

12. This is in fact a mantra encountered in most writings favoring the individual rights interpretation. See JOYCE LEE MALCOLM, TO KEEP AND BEAR ARMS: THE ORIGINS OF AN ANGLO-AMERICAN RIGHT 162 (1994); Sanford Levinson, *The Embarrassing Second Amendment,* 99 YALE LAW JOURNAL 645 (1989); HALBROOK, THAT EVERY MAN BE ARMED 83.

13. THE FEDERALIST NO. 37, in 15 DOCUMENTARY HISTORY OF THE RATIFICATION OF THE CONSTITUTION 346 (J. Kaminski and G. Saladino eds., 1993).

14. For further discussion, see JACK N. RAKOVE, ORIGINAL MEANINGS: POLITICS AND IDEAS IN THE MAKING OF THE CONSTITUTION 11–22, 27 (1996).

15. For further discussion of this distinction between framer-intent and ratifier-understanding, see RAKOVE, ORIGINAL MEANINGS 7–11, and Charles A. Lofgren, *The Original Understanding of Original Intent?* in INTERPRETING THE CONSTITUTION: THE DEBATE OVER ORIGINAL INTENT 117–50 (J. Rakove, ed., 1990).

16. Madison's preparations for 1787 and 1789 are described in RAKOVE, ORIGINAL MEANINGS, 42–56, 330–36. His seemingly disparaging comment about the project of amendments was made in a letter to Richard Peters, August 19, 1789, 12 PAPERS OF JAMES MADISON 346–47 (R. Rutland ed., 1979). His speech of June 8 introducing the amendments can be found *id.* 196–209. Madison culled the proposals from a pamphlet published in the fall of 1788: THE RATIFICATIONS OF THE NEW FEDERAL CONSTITUTION, TOGETHER WITH THE AMENDMENTS, PROPOSED BY THE SEVERAL STATES (1788).

17. ROBERT A. GOLDWIN, FROM PARCHMENT TO POWER: HOW JAMES MADISON USED THE BILL OF RIGHTS TO SAVE THE CONSTITUTION 167–73 (1997).

18. For general discussion, see RAKOVE, ORIGINAL MEANINGS, 330–336, and Paul Finkelman, *James Madison and the Bill of Rights: A Reluctant Paternity,* SUPREME COURT REVIEW (1990), 301–47.

19. One can only wonder whom David Williams means to identify when he speaks of "the Anti-Federalist framers of the Second Amendment." David C. Williams, *Civic Republicanism and the Citizen Militia: The Terrifying Second Amendment,* 101 YALE L. J. 584 (1991). For another analysis that seems to rest on the same presumption, see AKHIL REED AMAR, THE BILL OF RIGHTS: CREATION AND RECONSTRUCTION 51–52 (1998).

20. James Madison, Speech of August 13, 1789, 12 PAPERS OF MADISON 333.

21. Here I obviously rely on GORDON S. WOOD, THE CREATION OF THE AMERICAN REPUBLIC, 1776–1787 (1969).

22. RICHARD PRIMUS, THE AMERICAN LANGUAGE OF RIGHTS (1999).

23. This third mode of analysis arguably blurs the difference between mere textualism and originalism, for it requires a turn to legislative history (or its equivalent) in order to ascertain how the intentions of the document's framers were reflected in their final editorial decisions about the text. Given the absence of recorded congressional debate about the key changes in the text of the Second Amendment, however, it seems useful to treat these editorial revisions as a mode of primarily textual analysis, the more so when we have to infer intention from changes between drafts.

24. The idea that "people" always means "individuals" is open to challenge, however. One does not have to read very far in the Constitution to learn that the House of Representatives will be "chosen . . . by the People of the several States," but that this people actually consists of a rather smaller set of "Electors." U.S. CONST., art. I, sect. 2.

25. THE COMPLETE BILL OF RIGHTS: THE DRAFTS, DEBATES, SOURCES, AND ORIGINS 169 (N. Cogan ed., 1997). Malcolm erroneously claims that "Madison's original version of the amendment, as well as those suggested by the states, described the militia as either 'composed of' or 'including' the body of the people." TO KEEP AND BEAR ARMS at 162–63. Madison's version did neither. Malcolm also notes that "not one of the ninety-seven distinct amendments proposed by the state ratifying conventions asked for a *return* of any control that had been allocated to the federal government over the militia." *Id.* at 163. But the eleventh amendment proposed by the Virginia convention declares: "That each

State respectively shall have the power to provide for organizing, arming, and disciplining its own militia, whensoever Congress shall omit or neglect to provide for the same. That the militia shall not be subject to martial law, except when in actual service in time of war, invasion or rebellion, and when not in the actual service of the United States, shall be subject only to such fines, penalties and punishments, as shall be directed or inflicted by the laws of its own State." 10 DOCUMENTARY HISTORY OF THE RATIFICATION OF THE CONSTITUTION 1554 (J. Kaminski and G. Saladino eds., 1993).

26. ". . . that standing armies, in time of peace, are dangerous to liberty, and therefore ought to be avoided, as far as the circumstances and protection of the community will admit." *Id.* at 182–83. This wording, of course, illustrates the idea that a bill of rights could consist not of legally enforceable claims but rather of general principles for the guidance of officials and citizens.

27. The clause granting exemptions from militia service to religious objectors was derived from the nineteenth amendment recommended by the Virginia convention.
    Whether Madison was thinking of two rights (arms-bearing distinguished from the security provided by the militia) is, however, far from certain. The use of "being" can still be read to imply that the militia clause modifies the arms-bearing one (semi-colon be damned, so to speak); while if the militia clause serves as a preamble to the "religiously scrupulous" one, the use of the conjunction "but" would appear superfluous.

28. Malcolm errs in noting that Madison's amendments were referred to a three-member committee (Madison, Roger Sherman, and John Vining). TO KEEP AND BEAR ARMS 160. After being introduced on June 8, the amendments were referred to a committee of the whole House, and then, after the House failed to address the issue, to a committee of one member from each state, appointed on July 21, which in turn reported on July 28. 3 DOCUMENTARY HISTORY OF THE FIRST FEDERAL CONGRESS OF THE UNITED STATES OF AMERICA 84, 117, 124 (Linda Grant DePauw ed., 1977).

29. COMPLETE BILL OF RIGHTS at 170.

30. COMPLETE BILL OF RIGHTS 174–76.

31. Notes for speech in Congress [ca. June 8, 1789], 12 PAPERS OF MADISON 193–94. The use of "private rights" is further separated from the reference to 1689 by a new heading: "Bills of Rights—useful—not essential." Perhaps not surprisingly, Halbrook omits this intervening statement when he quotes Madison's outline, without inserting the required ellipses. HALBROOK, THAT EVERY MAN BE ARMED, 76.

32. AMAR, BILL OF RIGHTS 51–52. The argument for "stylistic shortening" seems to have two parts: one holding that the formula defining the militia as the people was unnecessary because redundant of common usage; the other suggesting that the insertion of this phrase would have rendered the amendment a more awkward text, presumably by repetition of the phrase, "the people." For similar attempts to argue away the significance of this revision, see MALCOLM, TO KEEP AND BEAR ARMS, 161; and David C. Williams, *The Militia Movement and Second Amendment Revolution: Conjuring with the People,* 81 CORNELL L. R. 907 (1996).

33. AMAR, BILL OF RIGHTS 56. Amar further tells us that "jealousy and vigilance are at the heart of the amendment's gloss on clause 16 [the Militia Clause of art. I, sect. 8]," and that he has "emphasized republican ideology about militias and armies because that ideology was expressly written into the amendment's preamble." *Id.* at 56. Had that ideology really been "expressly written" into the preamble, we would expect to find the usual admonition against standing armies present; its absence, like the omission of the word "expressly" from the Tenth Amendment, reminds us that the spokesmen for the traditional "anti-Federalist and republican ideology" were not in a position to dictate the content of the Bill of Rights.

34. The debate at Philadelphia is completely ignored, for example, in HALBROOK, THAT EVERY MAN BE ARMED, which adroitly skips from provisions in the state constitutions to the ratification debate without bothering to stop at Philadelphia. The convention is similarly ignored in the leading article by Don B. Kates, Jr., *Handgun Prohibition and the Original Meaning of the Second Amendment,* 82 MICHIGAN LAW REVIEW 204 (1983). There is a brief but rather garbled discussion in MALCOLM, TO KEEP AND BEAR ARMS 152–55.

35. 1 DOCUMENTARY HISTORY OF FIRST CONGRESS 158.

36. HALBROOK, THAT EVERY MAN BE ARMED, 8.

37. 2 RECORDS OF THE FEDERAL CONVENTION OF 1787 187 (M. Farrand ed., 1966).

38. *Id.* at 330–31. Madison's notes make Mason's reference to the select militia slightly ambiguous; the relevant passage reads: "Mr. Mason—had suggested the idea of a select militia." This seems to be a

response to Dickinson, but it is possible that Mason meant that he, too, had that idea originally in mind.

39. *Id.* at 332–33.
40. *Id.* at 384–85.
41. The three motions came respectively from Roger Sherman; Jonathan Dayton; and, again, from Ellsworth and Sherman; they can be found *id.* at 385–86.
42. *Id.* at 385.
43. *Id.* at 386–87.
44. The locus classicus of this interpretation is BERNARD BAILYN, THE IDEOLOGICAL ORIGINS OF THE AMERICAN REVOLUTION (enlarged edition, 1992 [1967]). The relation between this ideology and American attitudes toward an armed citizenry was explored in two leading articles: Robert E. Shalhope, *The Ideological Origins of the Second Amendment,* 69 JOURNAL OF AMERICAN HISTORY 599 (1982), and Lawrence D. Cress, *An Armed Community: The Origins and Meaning of the Right to Bear Arms,* 71 JOURNAL OF AMERICAN HISTORY 22 (1984).
45. THE FEDERALIST NO. 29, 15 DOCUMENTARY HISTORY OF RATIFICATION 318–22. As the editors note (*id.* at 318) this essay was originally number 35 in the newspaper publication, but became number 29 in the first bound edition, the M'Lean edition published in the spring of 1788.
46. It is worth noting that, in Hamilton's view, this select militia would still comprise "citizens" linked in fellow feeling not to the dragoons of the national army but to their "fellow citizens" in the states. *Id.* at 320.
47. RAKOVE, ORIGINAL MEANINGS 110–112, 116–118.
48. 2 DOCUMENTARY HISTORY OF RATIFICATION 597–98, 623–24.
49. See the discussion in Saul Cornell, *Commonplace or Anachronism: The Standard Model, the Second Amendment, and the Problem of History in Contemporary Constitutional Theory,* 16 CONSTITUTIONAL COMMENTARY 228–37 (1999).
50. The state's western boundary marked the easternmost boundary of the national domain created by the process of state cessions completed in 1784.
51. *The Address and Reasons of Dissent of the Minority of the Convention of the State of Pennsylvania to their Constituents,* first published in the PA. PACKET, Dec. 18, 1787, reprinted in 2 DOCUMENTARY HISTORY OF RATIFICATION 617–40.
52. *Id.* at 630–31.
53. *Id.* at 637–39.
54. Noah Webster, writing as "America," N. Y. DAILY ADVERTISER, Dec. 31, 1787, 15 DOCUMENTARY HISTORY OF RATIFICATION 199.
55. 10 DOCUMENTARY HISTORY OF RATIFICATION 1312.
56. *Id.* For truncated citations, see Don B. Kates, *Handgun Prohibition,* 82 U. MICH. L. R. 216 n. 51 (1983); HALBROOK, THAT EVERY MAN BE ARMED 74; Levinson, *Embarrassing Second Amendment,* 647.
57. One noteworthy exception is Carl T. Bogus, *The Hidden History of the Second Amendment,* 31 U. C. DAVIS LAW REVIEW 309 (1997), which uses this debate, however, primarily to stress the relation in Virginia between fears of slave insurrection and the militia question more generally.
58. 10 DOCUMENTARY HISTORY OF RATIFICATION 1270–71. For the identification of Keith, see *id.* at 1298 n. 11.
59. *Id.* at 1272. Mason's general argument echoes one made by Luther Martin, the Maryland delegate who left the Federal Constitutional Convention prior to adjournment and who then subsequently opposed ratification. Martin complained that the Constitution would "enable the government totally to discard, render useless, and even disarm the militia, when it would remove them out of the way of opposing its ambitious views." The national government, he continued, has "the powers, by *which only* the militia can be organized and armed, and by the neglect of which they may be rendered utterly useless and insignificant, when it suits the ambitious purposes of government." Martin, *To the Citizens of Maryland,* MD. JOURNAL, March 18, 1788, in 16 DOCUMENTARY HISTORY OF RATIFICATION 419 (1986).
60. *Id.* at 1273.
61. *Id.* at 1276.
62. *Id.* at 1280.
63. *Id.* at 1289.
64. *Id.* at 1304–1305 (Henry), 1305–1306 (Grayson). The latter went on to repeat the idea that Congress

might be free to "entirely neglect" arming the militia in particular states. This in turn led him to distinguish the deprived situation of the militia in Scotland and Ireland from that in England, which had "an excellent militia law . . . such as I wish to be established by the General Government." And what did this mean in practice? "They have 30,000 select militia in England," Grayson noted approvingly. *Id.* at 1306. Of course, according to individual rights advocates, the idea of a select militia is exactly what Americans were supposed to revile. Unfortunately, Grayson did not have the advantage of reading the contemporary "scholarly consensus" on this point.

65. *Id.* at 1306–1307.
66. *Id.* at 1312.
67. THE FEDERALIST NO. 46, 15 DOCUMENTARY HISTORY OF RATIFICATION 492–93.
68. As I have argued elsewhere, the fear of consolidation was the great controlling theme in anti-Federalist polemics. RAKOVE, ORIGINAL MEANINGS, 148–49, 181–88.
69. It took a lot to get Madison to crank out a truly pungent phrase, but here he observed that these descriptions of a tyranny imposed by military despotism were "more like the incoherent dreams of a delirious jealousy, or the misjudged exaggerations of a counterfeit zeal, than like the sober apprehensions of genuine patriotism." Fed. 46, 15 DOCUMENTARY HISTORY OF RATIFICATION 492.
70. *Id.* at 492–93. For representative examples of partial quotations, see Kates, *Handgun Prohibition* 228 (1983); HALBROOK, THAT EVERY MAN BE ARMED, 67–68.
71. 17 DOCUMENTARY HISTORY OF RATIFICATION 362.
72. HALBROOK, THAT EVERY MAN BE ARMED, 70–72. Halbrook notes that "most of Lee's proposals [that is, the Federal Farmer's] were subsequently adopted in the Bill of Rights, and some with almost identical wording," but in fact the LETTERS FROM THE FEDERAL FARMER contain no such draft of a bill of rights. On the other hand, as a member of the Continental Congress reviewing the Constitution in late September 1787, Lee had in fact attempted to append a declaration of rights, but his articles contained no mention of the right to bear arms. The only relevant proposal in Lee's draft amendments was a statement "That standing Armies in times of peace are dangerous to liberty, and ought not to be permitted unless assented to by two thirds of the Members composing each house of the legislature under the new constitution." 13 DOCUMENTARY HISTORY OF RATIFICATION 239; on Lee's efforts to secure amendments, see RAKOVE, ORIGINAL MEANINGS, 108–110.
73. 17 DOCUMENTARY HISTORY OF RATIFICATION 362–63.
74. MALCOLM, TO KEEP AND BEAR ARMS 150–151.
75. THE FEDERALIST NO. 47, in 15 DOCUMENTARY HISTORY OF RATIFICATION 499–507.
76. "That the Subjects which are Protestants may have Armes for their defence Suitable to their Condition and as allowed by Law."
77. See the useful summary of this point in FORREST MCDONALD, NOVUS ORDO SECLORUM: THE INTELLECTUAL ORIGINS OF THE CONSTITUTION 10–36 (1985).
78. MALCOLM, TO KEEP AND BEAR ARMS, 138–41.
79. 5 FOUNDERS CONSTITUTION 7, 3.
80. *Id.* at 148–49.
81. *Id.* at 162.
82. As Michael Bellesiles notes, perhaps the most important development in the battlefield use of firearms in the eighteenth century came when the Duke of Cumberland realized the advantage of affixing a socket bayonet to the end of a musket, enabling soldiers to fire (or receive) a single volley, and then charge the enemy to inflict more devastating casualties with the blade than they could ever attain with the ball. MICHAEL BELLESILES, ARMING AMERICA: THE ORIGINS OF A NATIONAL GUN CULTURE 144–46 (2000).
83. On this general point, compare BAILYN, IDEOLOGICAL ORIGINS (enlarged edition) with the classic essay by Cecilia Kenyon, *Men of Little Faith: The Anti-Federalists on the Nature of Representative Government,* 12 WILLIAM AND MARY QUARTERLY 3 (1955); and see RAKOVE, ORIGINAL MEANINGS 149–60. There is an extensive scholarly literature that seeks to differentiate Federalists and anti-Federalists in terms of qualities of mind, attitudes toward change, and the capacity (we might now say) to think "outside the box" of received authority.
84. Lawrence D. Cress, *An Armed Community: The Origins and Meaning of the Right to Bear Arms,* 71 JOUR. OF AMERICAN HISTORY 22–42 (1984); Don Higginbotham, *The Federalized Militia Debate: A Neglected Aspect of Second Amendment Scholarship,* 55 WILLIAM AND MARY QUARTERLY 39–58 (1998).

85. See the brilliant essay by John Shy, *The American Revolution: The Military Conflict Considered as a Revolutionary War,* originally published in ESSAYS ON THE AMERICAN REVOLUTION (J. Hutson and S. Kurtz eds., 1973).

86. One might express some skepticism about the accuracy of Jefferson's statement of 1778, when (in a letter to an Italian correspondent about music) he explained why he thought American casualties might be half those of the British army thus: "This difference is ascribed to our superiority in taking aim when we fire; every soldier in our army having been intimate with his gun from his infancy." Letter of Jefferson to Giovanni Fabbroni, June 8, 1778, in THOMAS JEFFERSON: WRITINGS 760 (M. Peterson ed., 1984).

87. BELLESILES, ARMING AMERICA, passim. For a preliminary report of findings, see Bellesiles, *The Origins of Gun Culture in the United States, 1760–1865,* 83 JOUR. OF AMERICAN HISTORY 425 (1996).

88. GLENDON, RIGHTS TALK 47.

89. James Madison to Thomas Jefferson, Oct. 17, 1788, JAMES MADISON: WRITINGS 420 (J. Rakove ed., 1999).

90. Speech of June 8, 1789, *id.* at 441, 444. In rejecting these statements, Congress may have been acting on the same assumptions that Edmund Randolph had voiced at the Federal Constitutional Convention two years earlier, when, as a member of the Committee of Detail, he noted that the national constitution need not come adorned with the rhetorical flourishes that accompanied the state constitutions. Such a "display of theory, howsoever proper in the first formation of state governments, *is* unfit here; since we are not working on the natural rights of men not yet gathered into society, but upon those rights, modified by society, and *interwoven with* what we call the rights of states." SUPPLEMENT TO MAX FARRAND'S THE RECORDS OF THE FEDERAL CONVENTION OF 1787, 183 (J. Hutson ed., 1987)

91. Eugene Volokh, *The Commonplace Second Amendment,* 73 N.Y.U.L.R. 793 (1998). Volokh conveniently provides an appendix of similarly styled articles; *id.* at 814–821.

92. The leading scholar working on this issue is David Williams, who has argued in various places that while the Second Amendment was framed to express or confirm a popular right of revolution, that right is now obsolete because no unitary people of the kind imagined by the theorists of the eighteenth century could ever again form. At the same time, Williams denies that the amendment recognizes a constitutionally protected private right of self-defense. For Williams's various expositions of his ideas, see: *Civic Republicanism and the Citizen Militia: The Terrifying Second Amendment,* 101 YALE L. J. 551 (1991); *The Militia Movement and Second Amendment Revolution: Conjuring with the People,* 81 CORNELL L. R. 879 (1996); and *The "Conservative" Right to Constitutional Revolution,* 32 HARVARD CIVIL RIGHTS-CIVIL LIBERTIES L. R. 413 (1997).

93. Letter to Thomas Jefferson of Oct. 17, 1788, MADISON: WRITINGS 420.

94. MALCOLM, TO KEEP AND BEAR ARMS, 163.

5. "A WELL REGULATED MILITIA": THE SECOND AMENDMENT IN HISTORICAL PERSPECTIVE

* Paul Finkelman is the Chapman Distinguished Professor at the University of Tulsa College of Law. Before joining the Tulsa faculty, Professor Finkelman was the John F. Seiberling Professor of Constitutional Law at the University of Akron. He has also held visiting chairs at the University of Miami, Cleveland State University College of Law, and Hamline law schools. He is the author of more than eighty scholarly articles, an editor of five books, and author or co-author of seven books, including AN IMPERFECT UNION: SLAVERY, FEDERALISM, AND COMITY (University of North Carolina Press); SLAVERY AND THE FOUNDERS: RACE AND LIBERTY IN THE AGE OF JEFFERSON (M.E. Sharpe); and SLAVERY IN THE COURTROOM (Library of Congress), which won the Joseph L. Andrews Award from the American Association of Law Libraries.

1. 1 THE PAPERS OF GEORGE MASON (Robert Rutland, ed., 1970).

2. James Madison to Edmund Randolph, June 15, 1789, in 12 THE PAPERS OF JAMES MADISON (Charles F. Hobson and Robert Rutland, eds., 1979). [Hereinafter cited as MADISON PAPERS.]

3. 1 THE RECORDS OF THE FEDERAL CONVENTION OF 1787 18–19 (Max Farrand, 1966). [Hereinafter cited as FARRAND, RECORDS.]

4. For a critique of the collection that discusses its limitations, see Paul Finkelman, *Antifederalists: The Loyal Opposition and the American Constitution,* 70 CORNELL LAW REVIEW (1984).

5. SAUL CORNELL, THE OTHER FOUNDERS: ANTI-FEDERALISM AND THE DISSENTING TRADITION IN AMERICA, 1788–1828 (1999), at 34.

6. *Address and Reasons of Dissent of the Minority of the Convention of the State of Pennsylvania to their Constituents,* 2 THE DOCUMENTARY HISTORY OF THE RATIFICATION OF THE CONSTITUTION 623 (Merrill Jensen, ed., 1976). [Hereinafter cited as HISTORY OF RATIFICATION.]

7. *Address of the Minority of the Maryland Ratifying Convention,* in 5 THE COMPLETE ANTI-FEDERALIST 92–100 (Herbert J. Storing, ed., 1981). Storing quoted in headnote at 92. [Hereinafter COMPLETE ANTI-FEDERALIST.]

8. ROBERT RUTLAND, THE ORDEAL OF THE CONSTITUTION: THE ANTIFEDERALISTS AND THE RATIFICATION STRUGGLE (1966), at 255–66. Jay quoted at 259. Even delegates from upstate were "reluctant" to vote against the wishes of New York City. LINDA GRANT DE PAUW, THE ELEVENTH PILLAR: NEW YORK STATE AND THE FEDERAL CONSTITUTION (1966), at 229. New York's proposed amendments are printed in CREATING THE BILL OF RIGHTS: THE DOCUMENTARY RECORD FROM THE FIRST FEDERAL CONGRESS (Helen E. Veit, Kenneth R. Bowling, and Charlene Bangs Bickford, eds., 1991), at 21–28. [Hereinafter cited as CREATING THE BILL OF RIGHTS.]

9. These are all found in CREATING THE BILL OF RIGHTS, at 14–28.

10. *Address and Reasons of Dissent of the Minority of the Convention of the State of Pennsylvania to their Constituents,* in 2 HISTORY OF RATIFICATION 623; BERNARD SCHWARTZ, THE ROOTS OF THE BILL OF RIGHTS (1971) 662–673; *Address of the Minority of the Maryland Ratifying Convention,* 5 COMPLETE ANTI-FEDERALIST 92–100.

11. Kenneth Bowling, *"A Tub to the Whale": The Founding Fathers and the Adoption of the Bill of Rights,* 8 JOURNAL OF THE EARLY REPUBLIC 223, at 228 (1988). See also Richard E. Ellis, *The Persistence of Antifederalism after 1789,* in BEYOND CONFEDERATION: ORIGINS OF THE CONSTITUTION AND AMERICAN NATIONAL IDENTITY (Richard Beeman, Stephen Botein, and Edward C. Carter, II, eds., 1987), at 297. "The amendments proposed by the states fall into two categories. The first limited the authority of the central government over individuals. . . . The amendments of the second group were both substantive and structural."

12. Richard Henry Lee and William Grayson to the Speaker of the House of Representatives in Virginia, Sept. 28, 1789, in 2 THE LETTERS OF RICHARD HENRY LEE (James Curtis Ballagh, ed., reprint ed., 1970), at 507–08 [Hereinafter cited as LETTERS OF LEE]; James Madison to Thomas Jefferson, Dec. 9, 1787, in 10 MADISON PAPERS 312.

13. CREATING THE BILL OF RIGHTS, at 17–19.

14. *Id.* at 19.

15. *Id.* at 19–21.

16. *Id.* at 21–28, 14–15, 16–17.

17. James Madison to Tench Coxe, July 30, 1788, in 11 MADISON PAPERS 210; *see also* RUTLAND, THE ORDEAL OF THE CONSTITUTION, 301.

18. U.S. CONSTITUTION, art. I, sec. 8, cls. 11–16; art. I, sec. 10, cl. 3; art. II, sec. 1, cl. 1.

19. U.S. CONSTITUTION, art. I, sec. 8, pars. 1 and 16.

20. 2 FARRAND, RECORDS 385 (debate of August 23).

21. Franklin in the LONDON CHRONICLE, November 8, 1770, quoted in JOHN PHILIP REID, IN DEFIANCE OF THE LAW: THE STANDING-ARMY CONTROVERSY, THE TWO CONSTITUTIONS, AND THE COMING OF THE AMERICAN REVOLUTION (1981), at 15.

22. The phrase "quartering troops" actually evokes two different issues. One was the presence of a large standing army in colonial cities. For example, relative to its size the British placed huge numbers of troops in Boston. Neither the Constitution nor the Bill of Rights prevents Congress from quartering large numbers of troops among us. The second aspect of "quartering troops" stemmed from the British policy of forcing colonists to provide lodging for soldiers. No one at the convention contemplated the national government ever doing this, except in an emergency. Anti-Federalists, however, remembering British practice and fearful of the new national government, complained that this might occur. Thus the First Congress in what became the Third Amendment banned the practice, except in time of war.

23. *Address and Reasons of Dissent of the Minority of the Convention of the State of Pennsylvania to their*

Constituents, in 2 HISTORY OF RATIFICATION, at 623. Near the end of the Pennsylvania ratifying convention delegate Robert Whitehill offered most of these provisions as a series of amendments to the Constitution, but the convention rejected them.

24. Number one of the *Reasons of Dissent* declared: "That the right of conscience shall be held inviolable. . . ." at DOCUMENTARY HISTORY, at 623.

25. Number six of the *Reasons of Dissent* declared: "That the people have a right to the freedom of speech, of writing and publishing their sentiments, therefore, the freedom of the press shall not be restrained by any law of the United States." *Id.* Curiously, this is one of the very few anti-Federalist documents to use the term "freedom of speech." The fact that Madison included "speech" in the First Amendment may indicate his use of the *Reasons of Dissent.*

26. Number five of the *Reasons of Dissent* declared: "That warrants unsupported by evidence, whereby any officer or messenger may be commanded or required to search suspected places or to seize any person or persons, his or their property, not particularly described, are grievous and oppressive, and shall not be granted either by the magistrates of the federal government or others." *Id.*

27. Number three of the *Reasons of Dissent* declared: "That . . . no man be deprived of his liberty, except by the law of the land or the judgment of his peers." *Id.*

28. Number three of the *Reasons of Dissent* further declared: "That in all capital and criminal prosecutions, a man has a right to demand the cause and nature of his accusation . . . to be heard by himself and his counsel; to be confronted with the accusers and witnesses; to call for evidence in his favor, and a speedy trial by an impartial jury of his vicinage. . . ." *Id.*

29. Number two of the *Reasons of Dissent* declared: "That in controversies respecting property, and in suits between man and man, trial by jury shall remain as heretofore, as well in the federal courts, as in those of the several states." *Id.*

30. Number four of the *Reasons of Dissent* declared: "That excessive bail ought not to be required, nor cruel and unusual punishments inflicted." *Id.* Except for changing "ought" to "shall," this is the exact wording of what became the Eighth Amendment.

31. The second paragraph of Number Eleven asserted:

> That the sovereignty, freedom, and independency of the several states shall be retained, and every power, jurisdiction, and right which is not by this constitution expressly delegated to the United States in Congress assembled.

32. DOCUMENTARY HISTORY, at 623–624.

33. *Id.*

34. *Id.*

35. *Id.*

36. *Id.* at 1217.

37. In his message to the people of South Carolina during the Nullification crisis, President Jackson noted that

> The war into which we were forced to support the dignity of the nation and the rights of our citizens might have ended in defeat and disgrace, instead of victory and honor, if the States who supposed it a ruinous and unconstitutional measure had thought they possessed the right of nullifying the act by which it was declared and denying supplies for its prosecution.

Proclamation by Andrew Jackson, President of the United States, December 10, 1832, in 3 A COMPILATION OF THE MESSAGES AND PAPERS OF THE PRESIDENTS 1203, at 1205, 1217 (James D. Richardson, ed., 1897). Had the militias been immune from federal control, the states would have been able to prevent the prosecution of the war *without* actually having to nullify the declaration of war.

38. Paul Finkelman, *Legal Ethics and Fugitive Slaves: The Anthony Burns Case, Judge Loring, and Abolitionist Attorneys* 17 CARDOZO LAW REVIEW (1996).

39. Don Higginbotham, *The Federalized Militia Debate: A Neglected Aspect of Second Amendment Scholarship,* 55 WILLIAM AND MARY QUARTERLY 43–44 (1998).

40. Michael A. Bellesiles, *Gun Laws in Early America: The Regulation of Firearms Ownership, 1607–1794,* 16 LAW AND HISTORY REVIEW 567 at 587 (1998).

41. In the nineteenth century Americans organized military expeditions against Cuba and Nicaragua. These preparations began with the accumulation of weapons for the invasion. Such an invasion, then or now, might easily drag the nation into a foreign war. Yet, presumably under the Pennsylvania

minority's proposal, the government could not stop the accumulation or export of weapons. *See, e.g.,* ALBERT Z. CARR, THE WORLD OF WILLIAM WALKER: A BIOGRAPHY (1963).

42. 1 FARRAND, RECORDS 18–19; on Shays's Rebellion see Higginbotham, *Federalized Militia Debate,* at 43–44.

43. It is worth noting that colonies regulated the sale of guns to Indians; it would seem odd that the framers of the Second Amendment might jeopardize such regulation with a sweeping personal right to own weapons. *See* Michael A. Bellesiles, *Gun Laws in Early America,* at 584.

44. Paul Finkelman, *James Madison and the Adoption of the Bill of Rights: A Reluctant Paternity,* 1990 SUPREME COURT REVIEW 301–47 (1991). [Hereinafter Finkelman, A RELUCTANT PATERNITY]; 1 ANNALS OF CONGRESS 453, (1st Cong., 1st sess.); James Madison to Edmund Randolph, June 15, 1789, 12 MADISON PAPERS 219.

45. The "tub to the whale" was a maritime expression. If a whale appeared to be attacking a ship sailors would throw an empty tub into the ocean, hoping to distract the whale, so that it would leave the ship alone. See Kenneth Bowling, *"A Tub to the Whale",* 223.

46. The sixth was New York, which had elected an overwhelmingly anti-Federalist ratifying convention, but which became strongly Federalist after the adoption of the Constitution. The order of ratification is found in CHARLES C. TANSILL, DOCUMENTS ILLUSTRATIVE OF THE FORMATION OF THE UNION OF AMERICAN STATES 1065 (1927).

47. Richard Henry Lee and William Grayson to the Speaker of the House of Representatives in Virginia, Sept. 28, 1789, 2 LETTERS OF LEE 507–08; Brent Tarter, *Virginians and the Bill of Rights,* in THE BILL OF RIGHTS: A LIVELY HERITAGE 13–14 (Jon Kukla, ed., 1987).

48. *See generally* Paul Finkelman, *Turning Losers into Winners: What Can We Learn, If Anything, From the Antifederalists?* 79 TEXAS LAW REVIEW 849–94 (2001).

49. CREATING THE BILL OF RIGHTS, at 19, 17.

50. Speech of James Madison, June 8, 1789, in CREATING THE BILL OF RIGHTS, at 79.

51. *See* Paul Finkelman, *The Ten Amendments as a Declaration of Rights,* 16 SOUTHERN ILLINOIS UNIVERSITY LAW JOURNAL 351–96 (1992). Here I reject the clever but unpersuasive arguments in Akhil Reed Amar, *The Bill of Rights as a Constitution,* 100 YALE LAW JOURNAL 1131 (1991).

52. James Madison to Thomas Jefferson, Dec. 9, 1787, in 10 MADISON PAPERS, at 312.

53. Finkelman, *Antifederalists: The Loyal Opposition and the American Constitution.*

54. U.S. CONSTITUTION, art. I, sec. 8, cl. 6, 9, 15; sec. 9, cl. 1; sec. 8, cl. 3; art. IV, sec. 4.

55. Speech of Alexander Hamilton in the New York Assembly, January 19, 1787, in 4 THE PAPERS OF ALEXANDER HAMILTON 706 (1962).

56. Henry Knox to John Sullivan, May 21, 1787, in 3 FARRAND, RECORDS 13.

57. 2 FARRAND, RECORDS 332; 1 *Id.* at 426; *Id.* at 532.

58. THE FEDERALIST NO. 9, in THE FEDERALIST PAPERS (Garry Wills, ed., 1982), at 37–38. [Hereinafter cited by the number of the essay and a page number to this volume, except as otherwise noted.]

59. George Washington to Thomas Jefferson, May 30, 1788, in 3 FARRAND, RECORDS 31.

60. James Madison to Thomas Jefferson, September 6, 1787, 10 MADISON PAPERS 163–64; Madison to Jefferson, October 24, 1787, *Id.* at 212.

61. CREATING THE BILL OF RIGHTS, at 17, 22. Certainly the Southern framers anticipated the possibility of disarming slave rebels, free blacks, and people who might aid them.

62. Finkelman, *A Reluctant Paternity.* James Madison to Edmund Randolph, June 15, 1789; Madison to Edmund Pendleton, June 21, 1789; and Madison to Samuel Johnston, June 21, 1789, 12 MADISON PAPERS 219, 253, 250; *see also,* Madison to Tench Coxe, June 24, 1789, and Madison to George Nichols, July 5, 1789, *Id.* at 257, 282.

63. DECLARATION OF INDEPENDENCE, Preamble, paragraph 2.

64. James McClurg to James Madison, Richmond, August 5, 1787, in SUPPLEMENT TO MAX FARRAND'S THE RECORDS OF THE FEDERAL CONVENTION OF 1787 (James H. Hutson, ed., 1987) 205, quoted at 206.

65. [Oliver Ellsworth], *A Landholder IX* CONNECTICUT COURANT December 31, 1787, reprinted in 3 DOCUMENTARY HISTORY 515.

66. *Proclamation by Andrew Jackson, President of the United States,* December 10, 1832, in 3 MESSAGES AND PAPERS OF THE PRESIDENTS 1203, at 1216.

67. *Id.* at 389–90.

68. George Washington, *Sentiments on a Peace Establishment*, in 26 THE WRITINGS OF GEORGE WASHINGTON FROM THE ORIGINAL MANUSCRIPT SOURCES 374–98 (John C. Fitzpatrick, ed., 1931–44); Michael A. Bellesiles, *The Origins of Gun Culture in the United States, 1760–1865*, 425 JOURNAL OF AMERICAN HISTORY 429 (1996); Higginbotham, *The Federalized Militia Debate*, at 42.

69. U.S. CONSTITUTION, art. I, sec. 8, cl. 15.

70. Philadelphians IX, from PHILADELPHIA FREEMAN'S JOURNAL February 6, 1788, in 16 DOCUMENTARY HISTORY OF RATIFICATION 57. *Essay by a Farmer and Planter*, in 5 COMPLETE ANTI-FEDERALIST 76. Arguments like this underscore James Madison's belief that the anti-Federalists were mostly unwilling to pay national taxes. Madison to Tench Coxe, July 30, 1788, 11 MADISON PAPERS 210. *See also* RUTLAND, THE ORDEAL OF THE CONSTITUTION, at 301.

71. A Columbian Patriot [Mercy Otis Warren], *Observations on the Constitution*, in 4 COMPLETE ANTI-FEDERALIST 277.

72. John DeWitt, *Letter V: To the Free Citizens of the Commonwealth of Massachusetts*, 4 COMPLETE ANTI-FEDERALIST 37; *Brutus VIII*, NEW YORK JOURNAL, January 10, 1788, in 15 DOCUMENTARY HISTORY OF THE RATIFICATION 336.

73. *Brutus VIII*, in 15 DOCUMENTARY HISTORY OF THE RATIFICATION 335.

74. *Debate in the House of Representatives*, 1 ANNALS OF CONGRESS 749–52 (debate of August 17, 1789, PHILIP KURLAND AND RALPH LERNER, 5 THE FOUNDERS' CONSTITUTION (1987) 210.

75. Speech of Burke, 1 ANNALS OF CONGRESS 774 (1st Cong., 1st sess., debate of August 15, 1789). On this issue see, generally, Kenneth Bowling, *"A Tub to the Whale."* George Mason thought Madison's proposals were "Milk & Water propositions," while Senator Richard Henry Lee dismissed them as "not similar" to the amendments proposed by the Virginia ratifying conventions. Both quoted in Bowling, *"A Tub to the Whale,"* at 233.

76. Higginbotham, *The Federalized Militia Debate*, at 40.

77. Aymette v. State, 21 Tenn. 154 (1840), at 158, 161. Michael A. Bellesiles, *Gun Laws in Early America: The Regulation of Firearms Ownership, 1607–1794*, 16 LAW AND HISTORY REVIEW 567 at 587 (1998).

78. The earliest of "bare" arms supports the notion that the phrase has a military meaning. Thus, in *Beowulf*, line 437–39, we find:

> that I bear sword and ample shield
> yellow disc, to battle, but I with (my) grasp shall
> grapple with enemy, and for life contend
> foe against foe . . .

THOMAS J. MCLEOD, BEOWULF: AN INTERLINEAR TRANSLATION (1970). References to "taking arms" or bearing arms contemporaneous with the adoption of the Bill of Rights are also in the context of military service. *See, e.g.*, WILLIAM ROBERTSON, 1 THE HISTORY OF THE REIGN OF CHARLES THE FIFTH (1770) 316; THE VOIAGE AND TRAVAILE OF SIR JOHN MAUNDERVILE, KT. (J. O. Halliwell, ed., 1883, reprint of edition of 1725), at 65.

79. *Amendments Proposed by the New Hampshire Convention*, CREATING THE BILL OF RIGHTS, at 17.

80. *Id.*

81. Lawrence Delbert Cress, *A Well-Regulated Militia: The Origins and Meaning of the Second Amendment*, in THE BILL OF RIGHTS: A LIVELY HERITAGE (Jon Kukla, ed., 1987), at 62.

82. Higginbotham, *The Federalized Militia Debate*, at 43, 44.

83. Sanford Levinson, *The Embarrassing Second Amendment*, 99 YALE LAW JOURNAL 637, at 645 (1989).

84. *Id.* at 645.

85. *Id.*

86. PENNSYLVANIA CONSTITUTION OF 1776, Declaration of Rights, art. XIII.

87. In the context of the clause it might, however, be seen as a collective right to defend the community, against rioters or organized criminals, and thus imply the militia could be called out for more than defense of the state.

88. Or to frighten a former spouse. *See* U.S. v. Emerson, 46 F.Supp.2d 598 (1999).

89. The government could prohibit hunting on federal lands, but not presumably carrying weapons on federal lands.

90. George Washington, *Sentiments on a Peace Establishment*, in 26 THE WRITINGS OF GEORGE WASHINGTON FROM THE ORIGINAL MANUSCRIPT SOURCES 389 (1931–44).

91. James Madison to Edmund Randolph, June 15, 1789, 12 MADISON PAPERS 219.

92. Bellesiles, *The Origins of Gun Culture in the United States,* at 428–30; "An act for the recovery of arms and accouterments belonging to the state," Act of October 21, 1782, VA. ACTS OF 1782, chap. XII.

93. [Noah Webster], *A Citizen of America,* AN EXAMINATION INTO THE LEADING PRINCIPLES OF THE FEDERAL CONSTITUTION PROPOSED BY THE LATE CONVENTION HELD AT PHILADELPHIA (Philadelphia, 1787), reprinted in PAMPHLETS ON THE CONSTITUTION OF THE UNITED STATES (Paul Leicester Ford, ed., 1888), at 52.

94. [Oliver Ellsworth], *A Landholder, VI,* December 10, 1787, in 3 DOCUMENTARY HISTORY OF RATIFICATION 490.

6. MUTING THE SECOND AMENDMENT:
THE DISAPPEARANCE OF THE CONSTITUTIONAL MILITIA

*   H. Richard Uviller is the Arthur Levitt Professor at Columbia Law School, where he teaches courses on criminal procedure and evidence. He is the author of numerous scholarly articles and of four books: THE TILTED PLAYING FIELD: IS CRIMINAL JUSTICE UNFAIR? (Yale University Press); VIRTUAL JUSTICE: THE FLAWED PROSECUTION OF CRIME IN AMERICA (Yale University Press); THE PROCESSES OF CRIMINAL JUSTICE (West Publishing Company); and TEMPERED ZEAL: A CRIMINAL LAW PROFESSOR'S YEAR ON THE STREETS WITH THE NEW YORK CITY POLICE (Contemporary Books). His articles about the criminal process, evidence, and prosecutorial responsibility have appeared in the *Columbia, Duke, Michigan, University of Pennsylvania,* and *Vanderbilt* law reviews, among many others. Professor Uviller is a member of the American Law Institute and the Lawyer's Committee on Violence, and previously served on the Advisory Committee on Criminal Law and Procedure for the Office of Court Administration.

**   William G. Merkel received his B.A. in history with departmental honors from Johns Hopkins in 1988. In 1996 he graduated from Columbia Law School, where he was a Harlan Fiske Stone Scholar, a Westmoreland Davis Fellow, and president of the Criminal Law Society, as well as the recipient of a Foreign Language and Area Studies Fellowship from the Department of Education. After practicing with a major Washington, D.C. law firm, Mr. Merkel returned to graduate studies in 1998. He is currently nearing completion of an Oxford University doctoral dissertation in modern history, entitled *Liberty, Racism, and Anti-Slavery: A Re-Evaluation of Thomas Jefferson, His Critics, and His Legacy.*

1.   One commentator, Eugene Volokh, argues that the structure of the Second Amendment is really not unusual after all. While no other provision in the Federal Bill of Rights features a "justification clause" [we prefer to label the amendment's initial phrase a "purpose clause"], Volokh points out that such constructions were not uncommon in state bills of rights of the founding period. *See The Commonplace Second Amendment,* 73 N.Y.U. L. REV. 793 (1998).

2.   *See, e.g.,* Keith A. Ehrman and Denis A. Henigan, *The Second Amendment in the Twentieth Century: Have You Seen Your Militia Lately,* 15 U. DAYTON L. REV. 5 (1989), and Andrew D. Herz, *Gun Crazy: Constitutional False Consciousness and Dereliction of Dialogic Responsibility,* 75 B.U. L. REV. 57 (1995).

3.   One of the most forceful expositors of this viewpoint is Eugene Volokh. *See The Commonplace Second Amendment, supra* note 1.

4.   *See, e.g.* Glenn Harlan Reynolds, *A Critical Guide to the Second Amendment,* 62 TENN. L. REV. 461, 466–67 (1995); Randy Barnett and Don B. Kates, *Under Fire: The New Consensus on the Second Amendment,* 45 EMORY L. J. 1139 (1996); Stephen P. Halbrook, *Congress Interprets the Second Amendment: Declarations by a Co-Equal Branch on the Individual Right to Keep and Bear Arms,* 62 TENN. L. REV. 597, 598 (1995); and Joyce Lee Malcolm, *The Right of the People to Keep and Bear Arms: The Common Law Tradition,* 10 HASTINGS CONST. L.Q. 285, 314 (1983). By stating that individual rights interpreters of the Second Amendment view gun possession as "an entitlement immune from government curtailment," we do not mean to imply that all adherents of the individual rights view necessarily rule out reasonable government regulation of what they see as a protected activity. Preeminently, three of the most respected members of the orthodox legal academy to embrace an individual rights reading of the Second Amendment emphasize that this right—like the other individual rights protected in the first eight amendments—should be subject to reasonable regulation. *See, e.g.,*

Laurence H. Tribe & Akhil Reed Amar, *Well-Regulated Militias, and More,* N.Y. TIMES, March 27, 2000, at A27; William Van Alstyne, *The Second Amendment and the Personal Right to Arms,* 43 DUKE L.J. 1236, 1253–54 (1994).

5. *See* H. Richard Uviller and William G. Merkel, *The Second Amendment in Context: The Case of the Vanishing Predicate,* 76 CHI-KENT L. REV. 403, 432–70 (on fears of standing armies, the militia, and the right to arms in republican ideology), 480–94 (on the role of anti-army ideology in the anti-Federalist campaign for a bill of rights), and 495–511 (on the drafting history of the Second Amendment). [Hereinafter *The Second Amendment in Context.*]

6. The progenitive English Bill of Rights of the seventeenth century conditioned the right to "have Arms" on station and Protestantism—class and religion-based restrictions that the Americans elected not to incorporate into the Bill of Rights of 1789. *Compare* An Act Declaring the Rights and Liberties of the Subject and Settling the Succession of the Crown (Bill of Rights), 1689, 1 W. & M., Sess. 2, ch. 2, 7 (Eng.) ("That the Subjects which are Protestants may have Arms for their Defence suitable to their Conditions and as allowed by Law."), *with* U.S. CONST. amend. II. *See also* detailed discussion *infra* notes 178–201 and accompanying text.

7. The ancient right figured highly in Blackstone's reckoning, not as one of the three primary (natural) rights (personal security, personal liberty, private property), but as one of the five auxiliary (political) rights without which the primary rights would be "dead letter[s]." *See* 1 WILLIAM BLACKSTONE, COMMENTARIES *140–45. Blackstone described these five auxiliary rights as (1) the constitution, powers and privileges of Parliament; (2) the limitation of the king's prerogative; (3) the right to apply to the courts of justice for redress of injuries; (4) the right of petitioning the king or either house of Parliament for redress of grievances; and (5) the right of subjects to have arms for their defense. *See id.* at *141–45; *see also* 1 EDWARD COKE, THE FIRST PART OF THE INSTITUTES OF THE LAWS OF ENGLAND; OR A COMMENTARY UPON LITTLETON § 71.a. (19th ed. 1853). At first blush, Blackstone may appear to endorse an unbridled right to arms for defense of self as well as realm and weal, but it is well to note that in the context of his times, Blackstone took for granted a high degree of regulation, circumscription, and exclusion to the right to arms he described.

8. There were, of course, exceptions to this general consensus, chiefly among the arch-Federalists. Many veterans of the Revolutionary officer cadre did not consider the militia necessary (or even useful to) the preservation of national security. *See* RUSSELL F. WEIGLEY, HISTORY OF THE UNITED STATES ARMY (Ind. Univ. Press 1984)(1967) 80–81, 88; *see also* discussion in Uviller & Merkel, *The Second Amendment in Context,* at 467–69. Alexander Hamilton went further—he did not believe the militia useful to the preservation of political liberty. Hamilton's view of the militia's inutility to the conservation of liberty has much to do with his conception of the type of liberty sound government was designed to secure. To Hamilton, liberty meant no more than the ability of the financial and commercial classes to rely on a strong executive's ability to check the mobocracy, and to this end the militia was hardly a useful tool at all, but rather a foil. *See* Williams, *supra* note 74, at 575–76. *But see* LANCE BANNING, THE JEFFERSONIAN PERSUASION: EVOLUTION OF A PARTY IDEOLOGY *passim* (1978) (discussing the republican conception of Hamilton's politics).

9. *See generally* Uviller & Merkel, *The Second Amendment in Context,* at 484–86. Regarding the "marginal" voices outside of New Hampshire, see Saul Cornell, *Commonplace or Anachronism,* 16 CONST. COMMENTARY 221, 232–234 (1999) (discussing the significance [or otherwise] of the call to protect a private right to arms included in the "Dissent of the Minority" of the Pennsylvania Ratification Convention of 1787), but see Garry Wills, *Why We Have No Right to Keep and Bear Arms,* N.Y. REV. OF BOOKS, Sep. 21, 1995, 62, 65–66 (arguing that this "Dissent" represented no more than the ramblings of a single eccentric). *See also* Robert E. Shalhope, *To Keep and Bear Arms in the Early Republic,* 16 CONST. COMMENTARY 269, 277–78, describing several Massachusetts petitions of 1780 demanding a state level constitutional right to arms for private purposes (the petitions failed to bring about alteration of the Massachusetts Declaration of Rights).

10. For a fuller discussion, see Uviller & Merkel, *The Second Amendment in Context, passim.*

11. For a detailed analysis of this passage, along with other utterances from the ratification period in favor of and against constitutional protection for a communal or private right to arms, *see id.,* 480–495.

12. Robert E. Shalhope, *The Ideological Origins of the Second Amendment,* 69 J. AM. HIST. 599, 611 (1982). It should be noted that when Shalhope wrote this article, he rejected the claim we make here that the right to keep and bear arms has no meaning outside the militia context. *See id.* at 614. More

recently, however, Shalhope has modified his position, and criticized standard modelers for uncoupling the right to arms from its historic context; see Shalhope, *To Keep and Bear Arms in the Early Republic*, 16 CONST. COMMENTARY, 269, 270 (1999).

13. *See* Garry Wills, *supra*, note 9, 62, 64.

14. *See, e.g.*, JOSEPH STORY COMMENTARIES ON THE CONSTITUTION OF THE UNITED STATES, §§ 1896–97, 607–608 (2d ed. 1851 [1833]).

15. *See* discussion in Uviller & Merkel, *The Second Amendment in Context*, at 556–558.

16. For a discussion of Madison's conversion to the cause of a bill of rights and his role in drafting the Second Amendment, see Uviller & Merkel, *The Second Amendment in Context*, 493–96. On the perceived danger of standing armies, *see id.* at 456–459, 480–494, and David C. Williams, *Civic Republicanism and the Citizen Militia: The Terrifying Second Amendment*, 101 YALE L. J. 551, ** (1991).

17. For an excellent summary of some of the most influential approaches to originalism, see Jack Rakove's insightful *Introduction* to INTERPRETING THE CONSTITUTION: THE DEBATE OVER ORIGINAL INTENT 3, 3–10 (Jack N. Rakove ed., 1990). For a classic exposition of the viewpoint that we are expressly bound by the original meaning of constitutional and statutory text, *see* ANTONIN SCALIA, A MATTER OF INTERPRETATION: FEDERAL COURTS AND THE LAW (1990). *See also* the intelligent commentaries of Gordon S. Wood, Laurence Tribe, Mary Ann Glendon, and Ronald Dworkin contained in Justice Scalia's just referenced work.

18. Since the First Congress took the pains to express its intent in the language of the Second Amendment itself—something it did for none of the other amendments in the Bill of Rights—this intention became incorporated into the Constitution by the amendment's ratification. Therefore, the legislative intent behind the right to keep and bear arms demands particular fidelity; indeed, one could argue it becomes determinative of the scope of the right protected. For a contrary argument, see Volokh, *supra* note 1 at 801–804.

19. But see Volokh, *supra* note 1 at 80 for the argument that "the justification clause [i.e., the purpose clause] may aid in construction of the operative clause but may not trump the meaning of the operative clause." David C. Williams takes issue with Professor's Volokh's contention in *The Unitary Second Amendment*, 73 N.Y.U. L.REV. 822 (1998). Volokh sur-replies to Williams in *The Amazing Vanishing Second Amendment*, 73 N.Y.U. L.REV. 831 (1998).

20. 496 U.S. 334, 340 (1990).

21. *Id.* (footnotes omitted).

22. *See* U.S. CONST. art. I, §§ 8, 12; *id.* art. II, § 2; discussion in Uviller & Merkel, *The Second Amendment in Context*, 477–480.

23. *See* discussion in Uviller & Merkel, *The Second Amendment in Context*, 500–09.

24. *Perpich*, 496 U.S. at 342.

25. The Act of Sept. 29, 1789, ch. 25, § 1, 1 Stat. 95, 95–96, legalizing the army inherited from the Confederation government, confirmed an earlier act authorizing a force of 840, but only 672 were actually in service at this time. *See* WEIGLEY, *supra* note 8, at 89.

26. *See* 1 SAMUEL ELIOT MORISON ET AL., THE GROWTH OF THE AMERICAN REPUBLIC 235–36 (7th ed. 1980).

27. *Cf.* MARCUS CUNLIFFE, SOLDIERS AND CIVILIANS: THE MARTIAL SPIRIT IN AMERICA, 1775–1865, at 43–48, 182–84 (1968); WEIGLEY, *supra* note 8, at 88–91.

28. *See* WEIGLEY, *supra* note 8, at 79–80, 85–86; *see also* Uviller & Merkel, *The Second Amendment in Context*, at 470–73.

29. *See* WEIGLEY, *supra* note 8, at 81–82; *see also* Uviller & Merkel, *The Second Amendment in Context*, Part at 470–73.

30. *See* CUNLIFFE, *supra* note 27, at 182–83.

31. *See* 1 ANNALS OF CONG. 442, 446–48 (Joseph Gales & William Seaton eds., 1789), *see gen.* Uviller & Merkel, *The Second Amendment in Context*, 497.

32. *See* CUNLIFFE, *supra* note 27, at 182–83.

33. *See* WEIGLEY, *supra* note 8, at 89.

34. *See* CUNLIFFE, *supra* note 27, at 180–83; *id.* at 45–48 (analyzing THE FEDERALIST NOS. 24–26 [Alexander Hamilton]).

35. Henry Knox, *A Plan for the General Arrangement of the Militia of the United States* (1790), *in* 1 AMERICAN STATE PAPERS: MILITARY AFFAIRS 6–13 (Walter Lowrie & Matthew Clarke eds., 1832) [hereinafter Knox Plan]. The Knox Plan can also be found in 1 ANNALS OF CONG. app. at 2141–61 (Joseph Gales &

William Seaton eds., 1790). The Knox Plan largely traced Knox's 1786 proposal to the Confederation Congress. *See* WIEGLEY, *supra* note 8, at 89; CUNLIFFE, *supra* note 27, at 182–84; Uviller & Merkel, *The Second Amendment in Context*, 473. Knox read his plan aloud to Congress and lobbied hard for its adoption. During Washington's first administration, cabinet officers followed the British practice of appearing in person before the legislature to advocate legislation and answer questions. This practice was abandoned after the president himself decided it would be improper to appear in person before Congress to debate the merits of pending legislation.

36. Knox Plan, *supra* note 35, at 8–10.

37. *Id.* at 6.

38. *Id.*

39. A telling criticism of plans to base the nation's defense policy on a revitalized militia focused on the economic and social dislocation associated with militia members' extended absences from home and family. Consider Alexander Hamilton's reservations expressed in FEDERALIST 29:

> To oblige the great body of the yeomanry and of the other classes of citizens to be under arms for the purpose of going through military exercises and evolutions, as often as might be necessary to acquire the degree of perfection which would entitle them to the character of a well-regulated militia, would be a real grievance to the people and a serious public inconvenience and loss. It would form an annual deduction from the productive labor of the country to an amount which calculating upon the present numbers of the people, would not fall far short of a million pounds. To attempt a thing which would abridge the mass of labor and industry to so considerable an extent would be unwise: and the experiment, if made, could not succeed, because it would not long be endured.

THE FEDERALIST NO. 29, at 209–10 (Alexander Hamilton) (Isaac Kramnick ed., 1987).

40. *See* CUNLIFFE, *supra* note 27, at 183.

41. Uniform Militia Act of 1792, ch. 33, § 1, 1 Stat. 271, 271, *repealed by* Dick Act, ch. 196, 32 Stat. 775 (1903).

42. *Id.*

43. It is interesting to note that Professor Michael Bellesiles misquotes this statute in his controversial ARMING AMERICA. Arguing that lawmakers and administrators envisioned government arming of the militia from the very beginning, Bellesiles writes that the Militia Act required that "citizens so enrolled, shall be . . . constantly provided with a good musket or firelock." MICHAEL A. BELLESILES, ARMING AMERICA: THE ORIGINS OF A NATIONAL GUN CULTURE, 230 (2000). Thus, Bellesiles would seemingly shift the onus of arming from militiamen to government. The act, however, clearly mandated that citizens arm themselves (but made no mention that they should do so "constantly"), *see* I Stat. 271, quoted in main text *supra*. In a sense, Bellesiles is not that far off the mark, for, as he ably demonstrates by references throughout his book to numerous other sources such as letters from militia commanders to their superiors and censuses of gun ownership and militia enrollment, the private arming paradigm nearly always failed. In practice, government assumed the responsibility of arming the militia in perceived times of danger, or at the very least took upon itself the task of supplementing privately held arms by public requisition and procurement.

44. *Id.*

45. *See id.*

46. *See* J.G.A. POCOCK, THE MACHIAVELIAN MOMENT: FLORENTINE POLITICAL THOUGHT AND THE ATLANTIC REPUBLICAN TRADITION 414, 416–17 (1975) (discussing the sacrosanct status of the historic English county militia under the "ancient" constitution venerated by the Real Whigs); WEIGLEY, *supra* note 6, at 101 (describing the federalized militia President Washington led out against the Whiskey Rebellion as the "Army of the Constitution").

47. Uniform Militia Act of 1792, ch. 33, § 1, 1 Stat. 271, 271, *repealed by* Dick Act, ch. 196, 32 Stat. 775 (1903). While the rifles described in the Act of 1792 were useful for private purposes as well as military ones, the muskets—less expensive to acquire and far more common than rifles among both regulars and militiamen—had little utility outside a military context because of their notorious inaccuracy. A company arrayed along a firing line two or three tiers deep became effective in the military parlance of the day because of "volume of fire." *See* WEIGLEY, *supra* note 8, at 21. In a crack eighteenth-century regiment, soldiers were expected to load and fire three times per minute, but were not instructed to aim at a particular target. As an enemy formation closed within range, it could thus expect to meet a hail of musket balls, with one rank of a three-tiered formation firing every ten seconds.

See generally GEOFFREY PARKER, THE MILITARY REVOLUTION: MILITARY INNOVATION AND THE RISE OF THE WEST, 1550–1800, 147–48 (1988). But even a good shot could not consistently hit a barn door with a musket fired at sixty paces. Michael A. Bellesiles, *The Origins of Gun Culture in the United States, 1760–1865*, 83 J. AM. HIST. 425, 436 (1996).

48. The states were required to furnish the secretary of war with an annual report on their militia. According to Marcus Cunliffe, "[e]ven from the outset the reports were scrappy, in some cases nonexistent." CUNLIFFE, *supra* note 27, at 185. Jefferson, in his final State of the Union address, delivered on November 8, 1808, remarked to Congress, "[i]t is . . . incumbent on us, at every meeting, to revise the condition of the militia. . . . Some of the States have paid a laudable attention to this object; but every degree of neglect is to be found among others." 9 THE WRITINGS OF THOMAS JEFFERSON 213, 223 (Paul Leicester Ford ed., 1898). Delaware and Mississippi (following its admission in 1817) routinely failed to file reports; by the 1830s, only Massachusetts and Connecticut were reporting some semblance of an organized general militia. *See* CUNLIFFE, *supra* note 27, at 211. Delaware did away with fines for nonattendance at militia musters in 1814; most states that revised their constitutions during the Jacksonian period incorporated abolition of imprisonment for nonpayment of fines for nonattendance as part of their new fundamental law. *See id.* Compulsory militia service was abolished by law in Massachusetts in 1840; in Maine, Vermont, and Ohio in 1844; in Connecticut and New York in 1846; in Missouri in 1847; and in New Hampshire in 1851. *See id.*

49. *See* Dick Act, ch. 196, 32 Stat. 775 (1903).

50. The Uniform Militia Act of 1792 was supplemented by the Calling Forth Act of 1795, which provided in part:

> That whenever the United States shall be invaded, or be in imminent danger of invasion from any foreign nation or Indian tribe, it shall be lawful for the President of the United States to call forth such number of the militia of the state, or states, most convenient to the place of danger, or scene of action, as he may judge necessary to repel such invasion, and to issue his orders for that purpose, to such officer or officers of the militia, as he shall think proper.

Act of Feb. 28, 1795, ch. 36, § 1, 1 Stat. 424, 424.

51. The uncharacteristically large regular army of the War of 1812, which swelled to about 35,000 by 1814 and would have numbered over 60,000 if recruited to authorized strength, was quickly demobilized following the Treaty of Ghent. *See* WEIGLEY, *supra* note 8, at 120-21. Congress scaled back the regular force to 6,000 men by 1821. *Id.* at 139-40. Monroe's young, then ardently nationalistic, secretary of war, John C. Calhoun, proposed a variety of precocious reforms to render the streamlined force effective, including a peacetime general staff and a system of expansibility to absorb trained reserves into regular units in the event of emergency. *See id.* at 141-43. Congress ignored the secretary's proposals. *See id.* at 142. The reforms Calhoun envisioned were not implemented until the eve of World War I. *See id.* at 142-43.

52. Poinsett's plan would have divided the country into eight militia districts, each with a force of 12,500 in active service and another 12,500 in ready reserve, giving the nation an enormous organized militia of 200,000. *See* CUNLIFFE, *supra* note 27, at 197. Congress rejected it out of hand. *See id.* at 197-99. The unpopularity of Poinsett's proposal contributed substantially to Van Buren's defeat by William Henry Harrison in the presidential election of 1840. *See id.* at 198-99. Antimilitary rhetoric, broadsheets, and pamphlets—still classically republican in tone—took a prominent place in the first stump and whistle-stop campaign. *See id.*

53. *See id.* at 184.

54. *See* Dick Act, ch. 196, 32 Stat. 775 (1903); *see also* detailed discussion *infra* notes 556-57 and accompanying text.

55. Opponents of America's expansion overseas and emergence as a colonial/military power during the Spanish-American War generally preferred to rely on America's geographic isolation, coastal artillery, the navy, or simply naïve pacifism for security. While arguments that citizen-soldiers were better suited to defend a democracy than career professionals were commonplace at the turn of the twentieth century, no one then seriously argued that soldiers as lightly trained and disciplined as the founding-era general militia had been could serve any serious military purpose.

56. *Cf.* CHRISTOPHER HILL, GOD'S ENGLISHMAN: OLIVER CROMWELL AND THE ENGLISH REVOLUTION, 85–86 (Norman F. Cantor ed., 1970). As Hill explains:

Parliament . . . resolved on 18 February [1647] to disband the Army without making any provision for payment of arrears or pensions for widows and orphans of those killed in Parliament's service, or even for indemnity for illegal actions committed under orders during the fighting. The troops might be permitted to re-enlist for service in Ireland . . . [but would receive no other compensation]. The rank and file of the Army were at once up in arms. During March . . . regiments . . . appointed Agitators or delegates to represent them.

Id. The consequent politicization of the English army (along with the intransigence of king and Presbyterians in parliament and revolts in the provinces) led within a year to the second civil war. *See id.* at 88–97.

57. *See* WEIGLEY, *supra* note 8, at 77–78.

58. *See id.* at 77; DANIEL J. BOORSTIN, THE AMERICANS: THE COLONIAL EXPERIENCE, 371 (1958).

59. *See* WEIGLEY, *supra* note 8, at 78.

60. *See id.* at 84.

61. *See id.;* GORDON S. WOOD, THE CREATION OF THE AMERICAN REPUBLIC, 1776–1787, 465, 498 (1969).

62. *Cf.* POCOCK, *supra* note 46, at 528.

63. *See id.* at 414, 416–17, Uviller & Merkel, *The Second Amendment in Context,* at 517; LOIS G. SCHWOERER, NO STANTING ARMIES! THE ANTIARMY IDEOLOGY IN SEVENTEENTH CENTURY ENGLAND, 13 (1974).

64. *See* WEIGLEY, *supra* note 8, at 100–02.

65. *See* WILLIAM H. REHNQUIST, GRAND INQUESTS: THE HISTORIC IMPEACHMENTS OF JUSTICE SAMUEL CHASE AND PRESIDENT ANDREW JOHNSON 48–49 (1992).

66. For a detailed (if somewhat hostile) account of Hamilton's scandals, resignation, and continued influence, *see generally* DUMAS MALONE, JEFFERSON AND HIS TIME: JEFFERSON AND THE ORDEAL OF LIBERTY, 325–34 (1962).

67. *See* WEIGLEY, *supra* note 8, at 101–03.

68. *See* DUMAS MALONE, JEFFERSON AND HIS TIME: JEFFERSON THE PRESIDENT, FIRST TERM, 1801–1805, at 6–7, 10–11 (1970). There is documentary evidence that 20,000 Pennsylvania militia were held ready to intervene in the winter of 1801, but only in the event that the electoral college chose someone other than Jefferson or Burr as president, thereby effectively staging a coup. *See* Letter from Thomas McKean to Thomas Jefferson (Mar. 21, 1801), *discussed in* MALONE, *supra,* at 10–11.

69. Hamilton, it turns out, was prophetic. A year after fatally wounding Hamilton in a duel in Weehawken, New Jersey, former vice president Burr did conspire to commit treason against the Republic by handing over the old Southwest to Spain and setting himself up as a sort of military vice-royal in New Orleans. He was acquitted of treason in a highly politicized trial presided over by Chief Justice Marshall in Richmond, in part because the scheme he orchestrated with General Wilkinson was poorly planned and ill conceived and thus not clearly documented, but there can be little doubt as to Burr's treacherous intent. For a comprehensive (if pro-Jeffersonian) account of the Burr treason affair, see DUMAS MALONE, JEFFERSON AND HIS TIME: JEFFERSON THE PRESIDENT, SECOND TERM, 1805–1809, at 215–346 (1974).

70. *See* RICHARD HOFSTADTER, THE IDEA OF A PARTY SYSTEM: THE RISE OF LEGITIMATE OPPOSITION IN THE UNITED STATES, 1780–1840, at 128 (1969).

71. *See* CUNLIFFE, *supra* note 27, at 202–12.

72. *See* Bellesiles, *Origins of Gun Culture, supra* note 47, at 425.

73. *See* CUNLIFFE, *supra* note 27, at 206–07.

74. *See id.* at 205. The fine is roughly equivalent to $1,000 by today's standards.

75. *See id.* at 205–06.

76. *See id.* at 205.

77. *See id.* at 207.

78. *See id.* at 202–03.

79. *See* WEIGLEY, *supra* note 8, at 125.

80. Article II, section 2, clause 1, of the Constitution provides that "The President shall be Commander in Chief of the Army and Navy of the United States, and of the militia of the several States, when called into the actual Service of the United States." But the president's powers as commander in chief of the militia remain circumscribed by the scope of Congress' power to call the militia into federal service in the first place. Article I, section 8, clause 15, provides "The Congress shall have Power . . . [t]o provide for calling forth the Militia to execute the Laws of the Union, suppress Insurrections and

repel Invasions." The clearest exposition of the territorial limitations of this power is Attorney General Wickersham's in his 1912 opinion discussed *infra*. There, the attorney general wrote,

> The plain and certain meaning and effect of this constitutional provision is to confer upon Congress the power to call out the militia "to execute the laws of the Union" within our own borders where, and where only, they exist, have any force, or can be executed by any one. This confers no power to send the militia into a foreign country to execute our laws which have no existence or force there and can not be there executed.

29 Op. Att'y Gen. 322, 327 (1912).

81. The Calling Forth Act of 1795 (really a series of amendments to the Uniform Militia Act of 1792) authorized the president to call up the militia when the country faced "imminent danger of invasion." Act of Feb. 28, 1795, ch. 36, § 1, 1 Stat. 424, 424. According to Professor Weigley, Governor Roger Griswold of Connecticut

> asserted that militia could not lawfully be offered since the state officials knew of no declaration by the President that an invasion had taken place. Secretary (of War) Eustis replied that the President declared that an imminent danger of invasion existed. Governor Griswold in turn argued that war was not invasion and the presence of a hostile fleet off the coast represented only a "slight danger of invasion, which the Constitution could not contemplate."

WEIGLEY, *supra* note 8, at 125.

82. *See id.*

83. 25 U.S. (12 Wheat.) 19 (1827). Jacob E. Mott, a private in the New York militia, refused to obey President Madison's August 1814 order to make muster under federal command in New York City to fight against British forces. *See id.* at 21–22. At a subsequent court martial, Mott was fined $96, which he refused to pay. *See id.* at 36. Mott was then sentenced to one year's imprisonment, while Martin, a U.S. Marshal, executed a forfeiture of Mott's personal property to satisfy the fine. *See id.* at 23. A New York court allowed Mott to replevin his goods from Martin, who, after an unavailing appeal to the New York Senate, which then sat as that state's highest court of appeals, sought relief from the U.S. Supreme Court. *See id.* at 28. In reversing the replevin judgment, Justice Story passed on the Calling Forth Act of 1795 and on the question of ultimate command authority over the militia. He rejected out of hand Mott's constitutional argument that the president's judgment as to whether the danger of invasion warranted calling forth the militia was subject to the review of state officers and militiamen. *See id.* at 32–33. Executive authority, Justice Story held, could not practically be fettered by an implied license for de novo review at each subordinate level. Presidential authority under the Calling Forth Act was supreme, and must not be checked by the second-guessing of any soldier or officer, including the governor of a state. *See id.* at 33. Thus, twelve years after the end of the War of 1812, it was firmly settled that the New England governors had acted unconstitutionally in refusing to follow Madison's orders to deploy their states' militia across state lines, and that supreme command of any militia called into federal service rested squarely with the president. *See id.* at 31–32. Story did not reach the question of whether the governors might constitutionally withhold consent for presidentially ordered militia service in foreign territory, which itself appeared facially unconstitutional.

84. Perpich v. Department of Defense, 496 U.S. 334, 354 (1990).

85. *See* WEIGLEY, *supra* note 8, at 183, 297, 324–25, 337–38, 340, 348–49, 401–02.

86. *See id.* at 120.

87. *See id.* at 122.

88. 1 SAMUEL ELIOT MORISON ET AL., THE GROWTH OF THE AMERICAN REPUBLIC 377 (6th ed. 1969).

89. *See* THE FEDERALIST NO. 46, *supra* note 34, at 301.

90. *See* WEIGLEY, *supra* note 8 at 131.

91. HENRY ADAMS, THE WAR OF 1812 (H. A. Deweerd ed. 1999 [1944] [excerpted from ADAMS, HISTORY OF THE UNITED STATES 1801–1817, 8 Vols., (1889–91)]), 179.

92. WEIGLEY, *supra* note 8, at 131.

93. *See id.* at 597–98.

94. *See* Bellesiles, *Origins of Gun Culture, supra* note 47, at 430 (on the declining percentage of militia members possessing firearms [1803: 235,000 of 524,000; 1810: 308,000 of 678,000; 1820: 400,000 of 837,000; 1830: 359,000 of 1,129,000]). Also consider the 1855 comments of New York's adjutant

general J. Watts de Peyester regarding his own troops: "We always associate the term militia with the rag-tag and bob-tail assemblages armed with broomsticks, cornstalks and umbrellas." *Id.* at 433; *see also* CUNLIFFE, *supra* note 27, at 205.

95. Speech to the Springfield Scott Club (Aug. 14, 1852), *in* 2 THE COLLECTED WORKS OF ABRAHAM LINCOLN 135, 149–50 (Roy P. Basler ed., 1953).

96. On the eve of the Civil War, many states' adjutants general listed *only* volunteer units in their organizational charts. *See* CUNLIFFE, *supra* note 27, at 220–22.

97. Urban Volunteer Companies were by no means an exclusively northern phenomenon. For a fascinating sociocultural description of Richmond's volunteer regiments during the late antebellum years (including detailed treatments of the "Light Blues" and "Grays," the city's best-known companies), see GREGG D. KIMBALL, AMERICAN CITY, SOUTHERN PLACE: A CULTURAL HISTORY OF ANTEBELLUM RICHMOND, *passim* (2000).

98. *See* CUNLIFFE, *supra* note 27 at 88–95, 227, 230.

99. *See id.* at 203 on Jefferson Davis's Mississippi Rifles; *id.* at 252–54 on the role of established, elite Volunteer units during the initial defense of Washington in 1861; *id.* at 5–7 on the Zouaves and other gaily uniformed Volunteers at First Bull Run.

100. Some companies even maintained their own armories under state license, or rented neglected arsenals from their local government. *See id.* at 219–20; *cf. id.* at 227. *But see also* Michael Bellesiles's treatment of the antebellum volunteers in *Arming America.* In keeping with his overall argument that the federal government played a determining role in creating an American gun culture and an armed populace, Bellesiles stresses that even the most exclusive volunteer militia units with the most expensive uniforms and accoutrements not infrequently received or cajoled federally financed arms from state arsenals. *See id.* at 387–406 *passim.*

101. On the states' role in providing arms for militia members prior to 1792, see Bellesiles, *Origins of Gun Culture, supra* note 47, at 581, 585 (regarding Virginia and Connecticut, respectively). On federal dissatisfaction with state efforts to arm the militia to come into compliance with the 1792 Act, see *id.* at 429–35; CUNLIFFE, *supra* note **, at 192–203, 209–12.

102. Act of July 6, 1798, ch. 65, § 1, 1 Stat. 576, 576.

103. Act of Apr. 23, 1808, ch. 55, § 1, 2 Stat. 490, 490, *analyzed in* CUNLIFFE, *supra* note 27, at 193. The law remained on the books until 1887, when Congress increased the annual militia appropriation to $400,000. *See* discussion *infra,* text accompanying n. 134.

104. *See* Uniform Militia Act of 1792, ch. 33, § 1, 1 Stat. 271, 271, *repealed by* Dick Act, ch. 196, 32 Stat. 775 (1903). For an analysis of the Uniform Militia Act of 1792, *see supra,* discussion accompanying notes 40–47; CUNLIFFE, *supra* note 27, at 184; WEIGLEY, *supra* note 8, at 93–94.

105. *See* CUNLIFFE, *supra* note 27, at 193, 209–11.

106. *See* WEIGLEY, *supra* note 8, at 195 (discussing Southern rearmament after Kansas); CUNLIFFE, *supra* note 27, at 209–12 (discussing prior nationwide indifference).

107. *See* WEIGLEY, *supra* note 8, at 201–04.

108. *See* WEIGLEY, *supra* note 8, at 204; Frederick Bernays Wiener, *The Militia Clause of the Constitution,* 54 HARV. L. REV. 181, 191 (1940).

109. *See* WEIGLEY, *supra* note 8, at 246.

110. *Id.* at 203–04.

111. An excellent account of the constitutional foundations of compelled military service during the Civil War can be found in David Yassky, *The Second Amendment in Context,* ** MICH. L. REV. (2001). Our account of the constitutional dimensions of Civil War conscription also draws heavily on HAROLD M. HYMAN AND WILLIAM WIECEK, EQUAL JUSTICE UNDER LAW: CONSTITUTIONAL DEVELOPMENT 1835–1875, 232–278 (1984), and HAROLD M. HYMAN, A MORE PERFECT UNION: THE IMPACT OF CIVIL WAR AND RECONSTRUCTION ON THE CONSTITUTION, 141–224 (1973).

112. On December 31, 1860, eleven days after South Carolina's secession and just before its winter recess, the 36th Congress had authorized increasing the size of the 15,000-strong peacetime army by eleven regiments, or 11,000 men, see WEIGLEY, *supra* note 8 at 199–200.

113. *See id.* at 209.

114. *See id.* at 205.

115. *See id.* at 207–08.

116. The Class II List included males aged twenty to thirty-five and unmarried men thirty-five and over,

while the Class I List comprised married men over thirty-five. The Class II list was to be exhausted before any names were selected from Class I. Only sons of widows, widowers, and infirm parents were exempted entirely. *See id.* at 208–210.

117. *See* ERIC FONER, RECONSTRUCTION: AMERICA'S UNFINISHED REVOLUTION, 33 (1989).

118. *See* WEIGLEY, *supra* note 8 at 211–13, 215.

119. *See* MARTHA DERTHICK, THE NATIONAL GUARD IN POLITICS, 13 (1965); SCOTT SKOWRONEK, BUILDING A NEW AMERICAN STATE: THE EXPANSION OF NATIONAL ADMINISTRATIVE CAPACITIES, 104–05 (1982).

120. *See* SKOWRONEK, *supra* note 119, at 92–95.

121. *See id.* at 93.

122. *See id.* at 104–05.

123. *See* Presser v. Illinois, 116 U.S. 252, 267 (1886). *Presser* is discussed in detail in Uviller & Merkel, *The Second Amendment in Context* notes 38–53 and accompanying text.

124. *See generally* Bellesiles, *Origins of Gun Culture, supra* note 47, at 453 (citing Russell Stanley Gilmore, "Crackshots and Patriots: The National Rifle Association and America's Military-Sporting Tradition, 1871–1929" [1974; unpublished Ph.D. dissertation, University of Wisconsin, on file with the University of Wisconsin Library]); AMERICANS AND THEIR GUNS: THE NATIONAL RIFLE ASSOCIATION STORY THROUGH NEARLY A CENTURY OF SERVICE TO THE NATION (James B. Trefethen compiler & James E. Serven ed., 1967).

125. *See* SKOWRONEK, *supra* note 119, at 85.

126. *See* Bellesiles, *Origins of Gun Culture, supra* note 47, at 435.

127. *See* DERTHICK, *supra* note 119, at 22.

128. *See generally* WEIGLEY, *supra* note 108, at 298–305. It should perhaps be added that, thanks to America's vast naval and industrial superiority, the outcome of this war was never in doubt.

129. *See* Dick Act, ch. 196, § 1, 32 Stat. 775, 775 (1903). For analyses of the Dick Act, see Perpich v. Department of Defense, 496 U.S. 334, 342 (1990); DERTHICK, *supra* note 119, at 26–27; WEIGLEY, *supra* note 8, at 320–22; Wiener, *supra* note 108 at 193–96. The Act provided in relevant part:

> That *the militia* shall consist of every able-bodied male citizen of the respective States, Territories, and the District of Columbia, and every able-bodied male of foreign birth who has declared his intention to become a citizen, who is more than eighteen and less than forty-five years of age, and shall be divided into two classes—the organized militia, to be known as the National Guard of the State, Territory, or District of Columbia, or by such other designations as may be given them by the laws of the respective States or Territories, and the remainder to be known as the Reserve Militia.

Dick Act, ch. 196, § 1, 32 Stat. 775, 775 (1903) (emphasis added).

130. *See* Dick Act, ch. 196, § 3, 32 Stat. 775, 775–76 (1903).

131. *See* Militia Reform Act of 1908, ch. 204, § 1, 35 Stat. 399, 399.

132. *See* 29 Op. Att'y Gen. 322 (1912).

133. *See* WEIGLEY, *supra* note 8, at 324–25.

134. *See generally id.* at 344–47.

135. *See* National Defense Act of 1916, ch. 134, § 1, 39 Stat. 166, 166.

136. *See* WEIGLEY, *supra* note 8, at 348.

137. *See id.*

138. *See id.* at 344–50.

139. *See id.* at 375–76.

140. *See id.* at 356–58.

141. *See id.* at 386–87.

142. *See* SKOWRONEK, *supra* note 119, at 244; WEIGLEY, *supra* note 8, at 397–400.

143. *See* WEIGLEY, *supra* note 8, at 395–400.

144. *See* DERTHICK, *supra* note 119, at 44–47, 49; *id.* at 93–107 (regarding the NGA's lobbying machine of the forties and fifties). On the lobbying effectiveness of Palmer, Reckord, and the NGA during the interwar years, see *id.* at 94.

145. Eventually, in 1952, Congress abandoned the requirement of an emergency and gave the president essentially discretionary authority to call up National Guard units with gubernatorial consent. *See* Perpich v. Department of Defense, 496 U.S. 334, 346 (1990).

146. *See* WEIGLEY, *supra* note 8, at 401.

147. *See id.*

148. The dual enlistment system continues in force to this day. In the words of Justice Stevens,

> Since 1933 all persons who have enlisted in a State National Guard unit have simultaneously enlisted in the National Guard of the United States. . . . [U]nder the "dual enlistment" provisions of the statute that have been in effect since 1933, a member of the Guard who is ordered to active duty in the federal service is thereby relieved of his or her status in the State Guard for the entire period of federal service.

> *Perpich,* 496 U.S. at 345–46.

149. *See* Act of June 15, 1933, ch. 87, 48 Stat. 153.

150. Wiener, *supra* note 108, at 209. Wiener adds, "The 1933 Act proved conclusively that a well-regulated militia is impossible of attainment under the militia clause, and can be organized only by resort to the plenary and untrammeled powers under the army clause." *Id.*

151. *See* WEIGLEY, *supra* note 8, at 420.

152. *See id.* at 436.

153. *See id.* at 486.

154. *See id.*

155. Prominent cases of governors ordering state militia to defy federal court orders relating to desegregation include actions by John Patterson of Alabama in 1956 (Autherine Lucy case), Orval Faubus of Arkansas in 1957 (high school integration), and Ross Barnett of Mississippi in 1962 (state university integration). In each instance, the state militia was subsequently federalized by order of the president (i.e., called up into National Guard duty), and ordered to enforce federal law. The most famous case is that of Alabama governor George Wallace in 1963. Wallace responded to a federal injunction preventing state troopers from obstructing integration by replacing the troopers with militia. President Kennedy federalized the guardsmen, who reluctantly ordered the governor to stand aside from a schoolhouse door he had ostentatiously obstructed. *See* DAN T. CARTER, THE POLITICS OF RAGE 113, 154 (1995); CHARLES & BARBARA WHALEN, THE LONGEST DEBATE: A LEGISLATIVE HISTORY OF THE 1964 civil rights act, 33–34 (1985). Interestingly, after his election in 1962 Wallace toyed with the idea of forming an irregular state militia apart from the National Guard, which would not have been subject to presidential command and thus could have conscientiously followed the governor's orders to enforce segregation. *See* CARTER, *supra,* at 113.

156. *See* WEIGLEY, *supra* note 8, at 497.

157. *See generally* ROBERT MIDDLEKAUFF, THE GLORIOUS CAUSE: THE AMERICAN REVOLUTION, 1763–1789, 575–81 (1982) (regarding the Revolutionary War); 1 MORISON ET AL., *supra* note 88, at 384–85 (regarding the War of 1812).

158. *See generally* WEIGLEY, *supra* note 8, at 184–85.

159. On the similarity of Northern and Southern militia and military cultures in the antebellum years and the insubstantiality of the Southern chivalric myth, *see* CUNLIFFE, *supra* note 27, at 337–384.

160. *See generally* WEIGLEY, *supra* note 8, at 305, 307, 309.

161. *See generally id.* at 497.

162. *See generally id.* at 486–87, 497.

163. *See id.* at 498.

164. *See id.* at 500.

165. *See id.* at 525–26, 535–36.

166. *See id.* at 533–34.

167. *See id.*

168. *See id.* at 508.

169. *See id.*

170. *See id.*

171. *See generally id.* at 509–10, 534–35.

172. *See id.* at 558.

173. *See generally id.* at 578–92.

174. In Eisenhower's words:

> This conjunction of an immense military establishment and a large arms industry is new in the American experience. . . . We recognize the imperative need for this development. Yet we must not fail to comprehend its grave implications. . . . In the councils of government, we must guard against the acquisition of unwarranted influence, whether sought or unsought, by the military-industrial complex. The potential for the disastrous rise of misplaced power exists and will persist.

THE OXFORD DICTIONARY OF MODERN QUOTATIONS 73 (Tony Augarde ed., 1991).

175. On Harrington's anti-army thought see Uviller & Merkel, *The Second Amendment in Context, supra,* note 5 at 448; on Gerry's fear of armies see *id.* at 500–501.

176. *See* WEIGLEY, *supra* note 8, at 509–10, 534–35, 558.

177. *See id.* at 505–06.

178. In addition to the 357,000 National Guard personnel, our citizen defense force includes 1,064,912 army reserves, of whom 395,038 are ready reserves, 684 standby reserves, and 669,190 retired reserves. *See Situation Report* (visited Nov. 11, 2000) <http://www.dtic.mil/soldiers/jan2000/pdfs/sitrep1.pdf>; *U.S. Army Reserve: End Strength* (visited Nov. 11, 2000) <http://www.army.mil/usar/briefings/civilian/sld005.htm>. The regular establishment comprises 491,707 active duty army; 381,203 active duty navy; 363,479 active duty air force; and 172,632 active duty marine personnel. *See* THE WORLD ALMANAC AND BOOK OF FACTS 1999, at 204 (Robert Famighetti et al. eds.).

179. *See Situation Report* (visited Nov. 11, 2000) <http://www.dtic.mil/soldiers/jan2000/pdfs/sitrep1.pdf>; *Situation Report* (visited Nov. 11, 2000) <http://www.dtic.mil/soldiers/jan2000/pdfs/sitrep3.pdf>; *Budget of the United States Government: Fiscal Year 2000,* at 158 (visited Nov. 11, 2000) <http://w3.access.gpo.gov/usbudget/fy2000/pdf/budget.pdf>.

180. Perpich v. Department of Defense, 496 U.S. 334, 351 (1990).

181. In his recent book ARMING AMERICA: THE ORIGINS OF A NATIONAL GUN CULTURE, and elsewhere, see *supra* note 47, Michael A. Bellesiles has argued that early American probate records suggest gun ownership was not at all widespread before 1850, and that fewer than 10 percent of households contained functioning firearms in the early Republic. Northwestern law professor and social scientist James Lindgren has examined the same probate sources and come to very different conclusions. Lindgren and coauthor Justin Lee Heather plan to publish a devastating rebuttal, accusing Bellesiles of incompetence, and maintaining that the very probate records examined by Bellesiles actually indicate guns present in more than half of households inventoried. *See* Lindgren & Heather, *Counting Guns in Early America* (unpublished manuscript, on file with authors at Northwestern). In the interest of fairness, it should perhaps be said that Bellesiles's conclusions in ARMING AMERICA do not depend entirely, or even chiefly, on his analysis of probate data. His argument about the scarcity of guns in early America relies very heavily on letters and reports by colonial, state, crown, and federal officials attesting to the need for weapons with which to arm militia units whose members had no guns of their own. Whether Lindgren's determination of more than 50 percent or Bellesiles's estimate of 10 to 15 percent comes closest to the actual percentage of early Americans who owned or held guns ultimately does not bear on our thesis. For our purposes, what matters is that the Act of 1792 envisioned individual acquisition and maintenance of muskets and rifles to be held ready for militia duty consonant with the Second Amendment, that there was already recognition that this system of private-arming had proved problematic in the past, but that republican values pressed strongly for preservation of the private arming paradigm, that state and federal governments early assumed a role of facilitating and supplementing private acquisition by spending public monies, and that the entire nexus of a universal, individually armed militia had collapsed by 1850.

182. *See id.* at 434.

183. *See* BOORSTIN, THE AMERICANS: THE NATIONAL EXPERIENCE, 31–33 (1966). Whitney executed the contract during the third year of John Adams's presidency and did not make delivery of the last of the 10,000 muskets until Jefferson was preparing to leave office in January 1809. *See id.* at 32–33. Michael Bellesiles insists Whitney's claim that his guns' parts could be interchanged was a hoax designed to dupe the government into awarding him contracts and putting up with his poor performance. *See* ARMING AMERICA at 233–35.

184. The statements concerning modern administrative practice relating to arms issuance in the guard reflect Mr. Merkel's personal experience and observations as a reservist training with the U.S. Army and Maryland National Guard while an ROTC cadet at Johns Hopkins University in the 1980s.

185. *But see* BELLESILES, ARMING AMERICA, *passim,* for evidence and argument that local and central authorities played a determining role in arming the militia from the very beginnings of the Anglo-American experience.

186. *See* David C. Williams, *Civic Republicanism and the Citizen Militia: The Terrifying Second Amendment,* 101 YALE L.J. 551, *passim* (1991), and *The Militia Movement and the Second Amendment Revolution: Conjuring With the People,* 81 CORNELL L. REV. 879, *passim* and esp. 922–24 (1996) for

thoughtful thematic exploration of the disappearance of the republican assumptions concerning civic virtue that informed (indeed defined) debate about the militia and standing armies in the eighteenth century.

187. The ages at which men were required to render militia service varied from time to time, colony to colony, and state to state before 1792, often set between sixteen and forty-five, or even at sixteen until death. *See* Bellesiles, *Origins of Gun Culture, supra* note 47, at 428; Bellesiles, *Gun Laws in Early America: The Regulation of Firearms Ownership, 1607–1794*, 16 LAW & HIST. REV. 567, 582 (1998). Under the Uniform Militia Act of 1792, which remained in force until 1903, men aged eighteen through forty-four were carried on the rolls.

188. Regarding disgraceful performances by the militia during the Revolution, and Washington's reactions thereto, see Uviller & Merkel, *The Second Amendment in Context* accompanying notes 272–75.

189. In 1999, 10 percent of the army allocation went to the guard, which amounted to 2.4 percent of the total defense budget. *See supra* discussion accompanying notes 604–05.

190. *But see* Kates & Barnett, *supra* note 4 at 1228–32 for the argument that today's self-proclaimed militia occupy a constitutional position equivalent to an unorganized, reserved militia from which the militia of the Second Amendment might be drawn. Kates and Barnett argue that defining broad segments of the population (or the entire nonfelonious adult population) as the unorganized militia of a state or county automatically invokes Second Amendment protections as restraints against the application of gun control legislation in that jurisdiction. For counterarguments see Williams, *Conjuring with the People, supra* note 186 at 904–924 and Yassky, *supra* note 111 at **.

7. NATURAL RIGHTS AND THE SECOND AMENDMENT

* Steven J. Heyman is Professor of Law at Chicago-Kent College of Law, Illinois Institute of Technology, where he teaches constitutional law, criminal law, and torts. He is the editor of HATE SPEECH AND THE CONSTITUTION (Garland), as well as the author of many scholarly articles on American constitutional law and the natural rights tradition, including *Righting the Balance: An Inquiry into the Foundations and Limits of Freedom of Expression* (BOSTON UNIVERSITY LAW REVIEW); *The First Duty of Government: Protection, Liberty and the Fourteenth Amendment* (DUKE LAW JOURNAL); and *Foundations of the Duty to Rescue* (VANDERBILT LAW REVIEW), which received Honorable Mention in the 1994 Scholarly papers Competition of the Association of American Law Schools. In 1998, he was elected to the American Law Institute. During the 2000–01 year, he is a visiting professor at Vanderbilt University Law School.

1. JOHN LOCKE, AN ESSAY CONCERNING HUMAN UNDERSTANDING bk. II, ch. XXVIII, § 10, at 353 (Peter H. Nidditch ed., Clarendon Press 1975) (1700).

2. *See, e.g.,* STEPHEN B. HALBROOK, THAT EVERY MAN BE ARMED (1994); JOYCE LEE MALCOLM, TO KEEP AND BEAR ARMS: THE ORIGINS OF AN ANGLO-AMERICAN RIGHT (1994); Randy E. Barnett & Don B. Kates, *Under Fire: The New Consensus on the Second Amendment*, 45 EMORY L.J. 1139 (1996); Don B. Kates, Jr., *Handgun Prohibition and the Original Meaning of the Second Amendment*, 82 MICH. L. REV. 204 (1983) [hereinafter Kates, *Original Meaning*]; Robert E. Shalhope, *The Ideological Origins of the Second Amendment*, J. AM. HIST. 599 (1982); William Van Alstyne, *The Second Amendment and the Personal Right to Bear Arms*, 43 DUKE L.J. 1236 (1994); Symposium, *Gun Control*, 49 L. & CONTEMP. PROBS. 1 (1986); *A Second Amendment Symposium Issue*, 62 TENN. L. REV. 443 (1995). For a more extensive listing of this literature, see 1 LAURENCE H. TRIBE, AMERICAN CONSTITUTIONAL LAW § 5-11, at 897 n.211 (3d ed. 2000). A valuable overview may be found in Glenn Harlan Reynolds, *A Critical Guide to the Second Amendment*, 62 TENN. L. REV. 461 (1995). For some critiques of the individual rights view, see GARRY WILLS, A NECESSARY EVIL: A HISTORY OF AMERICAN DISTRUST OF GOVERNMENT 207–24, 252–60 (1999); Garry Wills, *To Keep and Bear Arms*, N.Y. REV. BOOKS, Sept. 21, 1995, at 62; and the articles that appear in 16 CONST. COMMENTARY 221–81 (1999).

3. In addition to many of the articles in this volume, see, for example, Carl T. Bogus, *The Hidden History of the Second Amendment*, 31 U.C. DAVIS L. REV. 309 (1998); Carl T. Bogus, *Race, Riots, and Guns*, 66 S. CAL. L. REV. 1365 (1993); Lawrence D. Cress, *An Armed Community: The Origins and Meaning of the Right to Bear Arms*, 71 J. AM. HIST. 22 (1984); Keith A. Ehrman & Dennis A. Henigan, *The Second Amendment in the Twentieth Century: Have You Seen Your Militia Lately?*, 15 U. DAYTON

L. REV. 5 (1989); Dennis A. Henigan, *Arms, Anarchy and the Second Amendment,* 26 VAL. U. L. REV. 107 (1991).

4. The Constitution's opening words, "We the People," are clearly applied collectively: only the community is capable of "ordain[ing] and establish[ing]" a constitution for the body politic. U.S. CONST. preamble. The term is also employed collectively in Article I, section 2, clause 1, which provides that the members of the House of Representatives shall be elected by "the People of the several States."

Indeed, the original Constitution never uses "people" in any other sense. When the document refers to individuals, it uses the term "person." *See* U.S. CONST. art. I, § 2, cl. 2 (providing that "no Person shall be a Representative" who shall not have certain specified qualifications); *id.* § 3, cl. 3 (same with respect to Senators); *id.* art. II, § 1, cl. 5 (same with respect to the president); *id.* art. I, § 6, cl. 2 (providing that "no person holding any office under the United States, shall be a member of either House during his Continuance in Office"); *id.* § 7, cl. 2 (providing that, when the House and Senate vote on whether to override the president's veto, "the Names of the Persons voting for and against the Bill shall be entered on the Journal of each House respectively"); *id.* § 9, cl. 1 (barring Congress from prohibiting "[t]he Migration or Importation of such persons as any of the States now existing shall think proper to admit," prior to 1808, but permitting Congress to impose "a Tax or duty . . . on such Importation, not exceeding ten dollars for each Person"); *id.* art. II, § 1, cls. 2–3 (describing the procedure for electing the president); *id.* art. III, § 3, cls. 1–2 (limiting federal power to define and punish treason); *id.* art. IV, § 2, cls. 2–3 (requiring states to deliver up fugitive slaves and fugitives from justice).

In many cases, the Bill of Rights also uses "person," or some other singular term, when referring to individuals. *See id.* amend. III (forbidding the peacetime quartering of soldiers "in any house, without the consent of the Owner"); *id.* amend. IV (requiring that warrants give a particular description of "the persons or things to be seized"); *id.* amend. V (providing that no "person" shall be subjected to certain forms of criminal proceedings, "be deprived of life, liberty, or property, without due process of law," or have property taken for public use without just compensation); *id.* amend. VI (setting forth the rights of "the accused" in criminal prosecutions).

Moreover, the Bill of Rights sometimes uses "the people" in a collective sense. *See id.* amend. X (reserving certain powers to "the States respectively, or to the people"). But not always. It is difficult to deny that the Fourth Amendment's guarantee of "[t]he right of the people to be secure in their persons, houses, papers, and effects, against unreasonable searches and seizures" was intended to protect a right of individuals as such. Other uses of "people" within the Bill of Rights might be interpreted as having either an individual or a collective sense, or perhaps both. For example, while the First Amendment "right of the people peaceably to assemble, and to petition the Government for a redress of grievances" is often said to refer to individuals, assembly involves collective activity (which is one reason why the Stuart monarchy regarded it as a threat to government). Similarly, the Ninth Amendment's reference to "other[rights] retained by the people" is not necessarily limited to individual rights, but may also encompass rights retained by the people as a whole when they establish a government.

In short—contrary to claims often made on both sides of the debate—the Second Amendment's reference to "the people" does not, simply as a textual matter, commit us to either an individual or a collective rights interpretation of the amendment. As I shall show, however, the Second Amendment was largely derived from comparable provisions in the post-Revolutionary state declarations of rights, and the language of these provisions sheds a good deal of light on the problem.

5. The most recent major Supreme Court decision is *United States v. Miller,* 307 U.S. 174 (1939). For a discussion of *Miller* and other cases in the Supreme Court and lower courts, see Michael Dorf, *What Does the Second Amendment Mean Today?,* in this volume.

6. *See, e.g.,* MALCOLM, *supra* note 3; Lois G. Schwoerer, *To Hold and Bear Arms: The English Perspective,* in this volume.

7. *See, e.g.,* Sanford Levinson, *The Embarrassing Second Amendment,* 99 YALE L.J. 637 (1989); David C. Williams, *Civic Republicanism and the Civic Militia: The Terrifying Second Amendment,* 101 YALE L.J. 551 (1991); H. Richard Uviller & William G. Merkel, *Muting the Second Amendment: The Disappearance of the Constitutional Militia,* in this volume.

8. *See, e.g.,* HALBROOK, *supra* note 3; Barnett & Kates, *supra* note 2, at 1176–79; Kates, *Original Mean-*

ing, supra note 2, at 229–30, 254; Don B. Kates, Jr., *The Second Amendment and the Ideology of Self-Protection,* 9 CONST. COMMENTARY 87 (1992) [hereinafter Kates, *Self-Protection*]; Nelson Lund, *The Second Amendment, Political Liberty, and the Right of Self-Preservation,* 39 ALA. L. REV. 103, 118–21 (1987).

9. WILLS, *supra* note 2, at 259.

10. *See* JOHN LOCKE, TWO TREATISES OF GOVERNMENT bk. II, §§ 4–15, 87, 91, 123, 128, 159, 171, 183 (Peter Laslett ed., student ed. 1988) (3d ed. 1698).

11. *See, e.g.,* HALBROOK, *supra* note 2, at 28–29; Kates, *Self-Protection, supra* note 8, at 90; Lund, *supra* note 8, at 119 n.38.

12. *See* Locke, *supra* note 10, §§ 13, 21, 90, 123–27.

13. *Id.* §§ 87–89, 123, 128–30.

14. *Id.* §§ 87–88.

15. *See* JOHN LOCKE, A LETTER CONCERNING TOLERATION 26–28, 46–47 (James Tully ed., Hackett Publishing Co. 1983) (William Popple trans., 1st ed. 1689).

16. For an exploration of Locke's views on freedom of thought, see Steven J. Heyman, "The Liberty of Rational Creatures: Lockean Natural Rights and the Freedom of Speech and Thought" (Nov. 1999) (unpublished manuscript, on file with author).

17. LOCKE, *supra* note 1, bk. II, ch. XXVIII, § 10, at 353. It follows that individual rights scholars are mistaken when they suggest that the natural rights tradition regarded the right to use force for self-preservation as no less fundamental than the rights protected by the First Amendment. *See* Lund, *supra* note 8, at 119 ("In liberal theory, the right to self-defense is the most fundamental of all rights—far more basic than the guarantees of free speech, freedom of religion, jury trial, and due process of law"); *id.* at 123 ("[T]he right of self-defense is more fundamentally rooted in our political traditions than are First Amendment rights").

18. *See* LOCKE, *supra* note 10, §§ 19, 87–88, 171, 207.

19. *Id.* §§ 13, 16, 21, 123–31, 171.

20. *Id.* §§ 3, 88–89, 135–37, 138, 143. For Locke's view that human beings are impelled to pursue their own interests, see LOCKE, *supra* note 1, §§ 41–55, at 258–70.

21. *See* LOCKE, *supra* note 10, at 137.

22. *See, e.g.,* HALBROOK, *supra* note 2, at 28–29.

23. *See* LOCKE, *supra* note 10, §§ 149, 155, 168, 199, 202, 222, 232, 242.

24. *Id.* §§ 88, 168, 203, 208–09, 230, 242.

25. *Id.* §§ 149, 212, 220, 222, 240–43.

26. *Id.* § 168, at 380.

27. *Id.* §§ 20, 22, 87, 90–104, 107, 111, 131, 134–44, 147, 149, 153, 155, 158, 162, 171, 207, 222, 230.

28. *See id.* §§ 13, 92–93; 1 JOHN TRENCHARD & THOMAS GORDON, CATO'S LETTERS NO. 15, at 110 (Ronald Hamowy ed., Liberty Fund 1995) (1755); Steven J. Heyman, *Righting the Balance: An Inquiry into the Foundations and Limits of Freedom of Expression,* 78 B.U. L. REV. 1275, 1283–84 (1998).

29. 1 WILLIAM BLACKSTONE, COMMENTARIES ON THE LAWS OF ENGLAND *144.

30. Kates, *Self-Protection, supra* note 8, at 93; *see also* Lund, *supra* note 8, at 120 (following Kates).

31. MALCOLM, *supra* note 2, at 130 (quoting 1 Blackstone, *supra* note 29, at *144); *see also* Robert T. Cottrol & Raymond C. Diamond, *The Fifth Auxiliary Right,* 104 YALE L.J. 995, 1011 (1995) (describing Blackstone as "[u]ndoubtedly the most important of the eighteenth-century commentators to discuss the right to arms").

32. Bill of Rights, 1 W. & M. stat. 2, ch. 2, § 7 (1689) ("That the subjects which are protestants, may have arms for their defence suitable to their conditions, and as allowed by law").

33. *See* Cottrol & Diamond, *supra* note 31, at 1010 n.65.

34. 1 BLACKSTONE, *supra* note 29, at *143–44.

35. Kates, *Self-Protection, supra* note 8, at 93. Although Kates places quotation marks around the phrase "the absolute rights of individuals at common law," no source for the quotation is identified, and the phrase does not seem to appear in Blackstone.

36. 1 BLACKSTONE, *supra* note 29, at *121, *129, *134, *138, *141.

37. *See id.* at *123–25. For further discussion, see Steven J. Heyman, *The First Duty of Government: Protection, Liberty and the Fourteenth Amendment,* 41 DUKE L.J. 507, 533 (1991).

38. 1 BLACKSTONE, *supra* note 29, at *143–44.

39. Kates, *Self-Protection, supra* note 8, at 93.
40. 1 BLACKSTONE, *supra* note 29, at *140–41, *143–44 (citing Bill of Rights, 1 W. & M. stat. 2, ch. 2 (1689)).
41. 1 *id.* at *125; *id.* at *130–31; 3 *id.* at *4; 4 *id.* at *180–88.
42. *See supra* text following note 18.
43. For a persuasive argument that Article VII of the English Bill of Rights, upon which Blackstone relies, was not concerned with such a right either, see Schwoerer, *supra* note 6.
44. 1 BLACKSTONE, *supra* note 29, at *125; 4 *id.* at *151–53; Heyman, *supra* note 28, at 1285–87.
45. 1 BLACKSTONE, *supra* note 29, at *140–43.
46. *Id.* at *143–44 (emphasis added). That this is Blackstone's meaning is made unmistakably clear in the conclusion to this chapter, where he indicates that the various auxiliary rights, including the right to arms, are intended as protections against "compulsive tyranny and oppression" by the government. *Id.* at *144.
47. *Id.*
48. LOCKE, *supra* note 10, § 149, at 366–67.
49. 1 BLACKSTONE, *supra* note 29, at *141, *143. At least to some extent, the same is true of the second auxiliary right: "[t]he limitation of the king's prerogative" within clearly defined bounds. *Id.*
50. *Id.* at *251. Indeed, as Blackstone makes clear elsewhere, those who take up arms against the Crown under any other circumstances are guilty of treason:

    > For the law does not, neither can it, permit any private man, or set of men, to interfere forcibly [to redress grievances real or pretended]; especially as it has established a sufficient power, for these purposes, in the high court of parliament: neither does the constitution justify any private or particular resistance for private or particular grievances; though in cases of national oppression the nation has very justifiably risen as one man, to vindicate the original contract between the king and his people.

    4 *id.* at *82.
51. 1 *id.* at *211, *233–36; 4 *id.* at *81–82, quoted *supra* note 50.
52. 1 *id.* at *144, *251.
53. *Id.* at *143–44.
54. Blackstone's view is, however, narrower than Locke's in at least two important respects. First, Blackstone denies that private persons have a right even in principle to take arms against the government. *See supra* text accompanying notes 50–53. Second, Blackstone recognizes a popular right of resistance, but not necessarily of revolution. Distancing himself from Locke's theory of revolution, Blackstone writes that

    > however . . . just this [view] may be, in theory, we cannot practically adopt it, nor take any *legal* steps for carrying it into execution, under any dispensation of government at present actually existing. . . . No human laws will . . . suppose a case, which at once must destroy all law, and compel men to build afresh upon a new foundation; nor will they make provision for so desperate an event, as must render all legal provisions ineffectual.

    1 BLACKSTONE, *supra* note 29, at *161–62. It follows that while Blackstone's right to arms allows for popular "resistance and self-preservation," *id.* at *144, it does not necessarily extend to revolution.
55. *See generally* WILLI PAUL ADAMS, THE FIRST STATE CONSTITUTIONS (Rita Kimber and Robert Kimber trans., 1980); GORDON S. WOOD, THE CREATION OF THE AMERICAN REPUBLIC, 1776–1787, at 125–255 (1969). The state constitutions and declarations of rights are collected in WILLIAM SWINDLER, SOURCES AND DOCUMENTS OF U.S. CONSTITUTIONS (1975). All citations to these documents below are to this edition.
56. 1 BERNARD SCHWARTZ, THE BILL OF RIGHTS: A DOCUMENTARY HISTORY 339 (1971).
57. In the following passages, I have marked references to individuals in small capitals, and references to "the people" in italics. For an analysis of the entire document, see Steven J. Heyman, *Natural Rights and the Second Amendment,* 76 CHI.-KENT L. REV. 237, 284–90 (2000) (Appendix).
58. For a similar provision, see N.C. DECLARATION OF RIGHTS of 1776, art. XVII, which opens with the assertion "[t]hat the people have a right to bear arms, for the defence of the State."
59. In addition to the Massachusetts Declaration, see N.C. DECLARATION OF RIGHTS of 1776, art. XVII; PA. CONST. of 1776, DECLARATION OF RIGHTS, art. XIII; VT. CONST. of 1777, ch. I, art. XV. These and other

antecedents of the Second Amendment are collected in THE COMPLETE BILL OF RIGHTS 183–85 (Neil H. Cogan ed., 1997).

60. *See* DEL. DECLARATION OF RIGHTS of 1776, § 18; MD. DECLARATION OF RIGHTS of 1776, art. XXV; N.H. CONST. of 1784, pt. I art. XXIV; N.Y. CONST. of 1777, art. XL; VA. BILL OF RIGHTS of 1776, § 13.

61. *See, e.g.,* LOCKE, *supra* note 10, §§ 87, 132.

62. *See id.* §§ 13, 88–89, 130, 137, 143–44, 218; LOCKE, *supra* note 15, at 26; JOHN LOCKE, A THIRD LETTER FOR TOLERATION, *in* THE WORKS OF JOHN LOCKE 212, 214, 217–18 (12th ed. 1823).

63. *See, e.g.,* VA. BILL OF RIGHTS of 1776, § 13. This principle was accepted not only by radical Whigs but also by conservative Whigs like Blackstone. *See* 1 BLACKSTONE, *supra* note 29, at *408–13 (praising the institution of the citizen militia, and describing it as "the constitutional security, which our laws have provided for the public peace, and for protecting the realm against foreign or domestic violence").

64. For a good summary of this position, which brings out the inseparable connection between the right to bear arms and the militia, see the following statement made during the debate over ratification of the Constitution:

> It is a capital circumstance in favour of our liberty, that the people themselves are the military power of our country. In countries under arbitrary government, the people oppressed and dispirited, neither possess arms nor know how to use them. Tyrants never feel secure, until they have disarmed the people. They can rely upon nothing but standing armies of mercenary troops for the support of their power. But the people of this country have arms in their hands; they are not destitute of military knowledge; every citizen is re-quired by Law to be a soldier; we are all martialed into companies, regiments, and brigades, for the de-fence of our country. This is a circumstance which encreases the power and consequence of the people; and enables them to defend their rights and priveleges against every invader.

"The Republican" to the People, in 1 THE DEBATE ON THE CONSTITUTION 710, 712 (Bernard Bailyn ed., 1993).

65. *See, e.g.,* sources cited *infra* note 193. For a classic statement of the dangers of a standing army, *see* 2 TRENCHARD & GORDON, *supra* note 28, Nos. 94–95, at 669–87.

66. *See* 1 BLACKSTONE, *supra* note 29, at *408; THE FEDERALIST No. 29, at 180 (Alexander Hamilton) (Modern Library ed., n.d.); Williams, *supra* note 7, at 578.

67. *See, e.g.,* THE FEDERALIST NO. 46, *supra* note 66, at 310 (James Madison), *quoted infra* text accompa-nying note 90.

68. *See* LOCKE, *supra* note 10, §§ 149, 243; Williams, *supra* note 7, at 554.

69. Thus, the Virginia Bill of Rights asserted

> [t]hat government is, or ought to be, instituted for the common benefit, protection, and security of the people, nation, or community; of all the various modes and forms of government that is best which is ca-pable of producing the greatest degree of happiness and safety, and is most effectually secured against the danger of mal-administration; and that, when any government shall be found inadequate or contrary to these purposes, a majority of the community hath an indubitable, unalienable, and indefeasible right, to reform, alter, or abolish it, in such manner as shall be judged most conducive to the public weal.

VA. BILL OF RIGHTS of 1776, § 3. For similar provisions, see DEL. DECLARATION OF RIGHTS of 1776, § 5; MASS. CONST. of 1780, pt. I, art. VII; PA. CONST. of 1776, DECLARATION OF RIGHTS, art. V; VT. CONST. of 1777, ch. I, art. VI. "The doctrine of non-resistance, against arbitrary power and oppression," added the Maryland and New Hampshire Declarations, "is absurd, slavish, and destructive of the good and happiness of mankind." MD. DECLARATION OF RIGHTS of 1776, art. IV; N.H. CONST. of 1784, pt. I, art. X. For other assertions of the rights of resistance and revolution in the context of the Revolutionary con-flict, see the preambles of the constitutions of Georgia (1777), New Jersey (1776), New York (1777), Pennsylvania (1776), and Vermont (1777).

70. PA. CONST. of 1776, DECLARATION OF RIGHTS, art. XIII.

71. *See* MALCOLM, *supra* note 2, at 148.

72. The provision as a whole consists of a single sentence, which reads:

> That the people have a right to bear arms for the defence of themselves and the state; and as standing armies in the time of peace are dangerous to liberty, they ought not to be kept up; And that the military should be kept under strict subordination to, and governed by, the civil power.

PA. CONST. of 1776, DECLARATION OF RIGHTS, art. XIII.

73. *Id.,* art. VIII. This interpretation finds further support in a subsequent provision of the Pennsylvania Constitution:

> The freemen of this commonwealth and their sons shall be trained and armed for its defence under such regulations, restrictions, and exceptions as the general assembly shall by law direct, preserving always to the people the right of choosing their colonel and all commissioned officers under that rank, in such manner and as often as by the said laws shall be directed.

PA. CONST. of 1776, PLAN OR FRAME OF GOVERNMENT, § 5. From the language used ("The freemen of this commonwealth . . . shall be trained and armed for its defence"), it seems reasonable to infer that this provision, Article VIII of the Declaration of Rights (on the duty to "yield [one's] personal service" through "bearing arms" for the "protection" of the members of society), and Article XIII of the declaration (on "the people[s'] right to bear arms for the defence of themselves and the state"), are all meant to refer to the same activity—participation in a citizen militia. Similarly, "the people" who have a right to choose their officers under section 5 would appear to be the same "people" who have "a right to bear arms" under Article XIII.

74. *See, e.g.,* GA. CONST. of 1777, art. XXXV (organizing the militia of each county based on the number of men "liable to bear arms"); N.Y. CONST. of 1777, art. XL (exempting Quakers from "the bearing of arms" in defense of the community). For further discussion of the military meaning of "bearing arms," *see* WILLS, *supra* note 2, at 256–59.

75. Apart from Pennsylvania, only Vermont adopted the "defence of themselves" language. See VT. CONST. of 1777, DECLARATION OF RIGHTS, art. XV. Vermont was not recognized as a state of the Union until 1791.

76. The proposals of the state conventions are collected in THE COMPLETE BILL OF RIGHTS, *supra* note 59, at 181–83. The evolution of the Second Amendment is traced in *id.* at 169–81.

77. MALCOLM, *supra* note 2, at 148–49; MASS. CONST. of 1780, pt. I, art. I (emphasis added).

78. As Malcolm observes, *see* MALCOLM, *supra* note 2, at 149, this language was adopted in Massachusetts, *see supra* note 77 and accompanying text, and in Pennsylvania, *see* PA. CONST. of 1776, DECLARATION OF RIGHTS, art. I. Of the original thirteen states, the only other state to recognize a natural right of "defending life" was New Hampshire, which did not describe the right as an inalienable one. See *infra* note 81. Malcolm claims that the "defending life" language also appears in the first section of the Delaware Declaration of Rights. *See* MALCOLM, *supra* note 2, at 149, 215 n.68. In this she is mistaken. Like many other slaveholding states, Delaware chose not to open its declaration of rights with a ringing statement of the natural rights of mankind. *See* DEL. DECLARATION OF RIGHTS of 1776. The language does appear in the Vermont declaration. *See* VT. CONST. of 1777, ch. I, art. I.

79. This is true of Connecticut, Delaware, Maryland, North Carolina, and Virginia. The remaining states—New Jersey, New York, Rhode Island, South Carolina, and Georgia—adopted no bills of rights.

80. LOCKE, *supra* note 10, § 21; *see supra* text following note 18.

81. This is even more clearly true of the New Hampshire declaration, which lists "the enjoying and defending of life and liberty" as a natural right, but adds, "When men enter into a state of society, they surrender up some of their natural rights to that society, in order to insure the protection of others." N.H. CONST. of 1784, pt. I, arts. II–III. While the declaration asserts that other rights, such as those of conscience, "are in their very nature unalienable," it does not say that this is true of the right to use force in self-defense. *Id.* arts. IV–V.

82. MASS. CONST. of 1780, pt. I, art. I.

83. *Id.* art. X. The Pennsylvania Declaration contains substantially similar language. *See* PA. CONST. of 1776, DECLARATION OF RIGHTS, art. VIII; *see also* MASS. CONST. of 1780, preamble (expressing the ideal "that every man may, at all times, find his security in [the laws]").

84. The proposal of the Virginia convention read:

> That there are certain natural rights of which men, when they form a social compact cannot deprive or divest their posterity, among which are the enjoyment of life and liberty, with the means of acquiring, possessing and protecting property, and pursuing and obtaining happiness and safety.

Amendments Proposed by Virginia Convention, Declaration of Rights, first, *in* CREATING THE BILL OF RIGHTS: THE DOCUMENTARY RECORD FROM THE FIRST CONGRESS 17, 17 (Helen E. Veit et al. eds., 1991) [hereinafter CREATING THE BILL OF RIGHTS]. Similar (or identical) proposals were made by the conventions of New York, *see* Amendments Proposed by New York Convention, *in* CREATING THE BILL OF RIGHTS, *supra,* at 21, and North Carolina, *see* Amendments Proposed by North Carolina Convention, Declaration of Rights, art. 1, *in* 4 THE DEBATES IN THE SEVERAL STATE CONVENTIONS ON THE ADOPTION OF THE FEDERAL CONSTITUTION 243, 243 (Jonathan Elliot ed., 2d ed. 1863) [hereinafter ELLIOT'S DEBATES]. For Madison's proposal, see CREATING THE BILL OF RIGHTS, *supra,* at 11.

85. *See, e.g., A Democratic Federalist, in* 1 THE DEBATE ON THE CONSTITUTION, *supra* note 64, at 74–76; *Observations Leading to a Fair Examination of the System of Government Proposed by the Late Convention; And to Several Essential and Necessary Alterations in It. In a Number of Letters from the Federal Farmer to the Republican,* No. 2 [hereinafter *Federal Farmer*], *in* 2 THE COMPLETE ANTI-FEDERALIST 214, 233 (Herbert J. Storing ed., 1981); *Essays of Brutus,* Nos. VIII–X, *in* 2 THE COMPLETE ANTI-FEDERALIST, *supra,* at 358, 405–17; *Dissent of the Minority of the Pennsylvania Convention* [hereinafter *Pennsylvania Minority*], *in* 1 THE DEBATE ON THE CONSTITUTION, *supra* note 64, at 526, 549–50.

86. U.S. CONST. art. I, § 8, cls. 15–16. For some anti-Federalist criticisms, see 2 THE DOCUMENTARY HISTORY OF THE RATIFICATION OF THE CONSTITUTION 508–09 (Merrill Jensen ed., 1976–78) [hereinafter DOCUMENTARY HISTORY] (statement of John Smilie in Pennsylvania's ratifying convention) ("The last resource of a free people is taken away; for Congress are to have the command of the militia"); *Pennsylvania Minority, supra* note 85, at 550–51 (arguing that "under the guidance of an arbitrary [federal] government, [the militia] may be made the unwilling instruments of tyranny").

87. *See, e.g.,* THE FEDERALIST NO. 29, *supra* note 66, at 176–77 (Hamilton); 2 ELLIOT'S DEBATES, *supra* note 84, at 521 (statement of James Wilson in Pennsylvania's ratifying convention); 3 *id.* at 381, 412–14 (statements of James Madison in Virginia convention); *id.* at 392, 428 (statements of George Nicholas); *id.* at 401 (statement of Edmund Randolph).

88. *See, e.g.,* THE FEDERALIST NO. 24, *supra* note 66, at 150–52 (Hamilton); *id.* No. 25, at 156 (Hamilton); *id.* No. 28, at 170–73 (Hamilton); *id.* No. 41, at 261–63 (Madison); 2 ELLIOT'S DEBATES, *supra* note 84, at 520–21 (statement of James Wilson in Pennsylvania's ratifying convention); 3 *id.* at 389–90 (statement of George Nicholas in Virginia convention); *id.* at 401 (statement of Edmund Randolph); *Answers to Mason's "Objections": "Marcus" [James Iredell],* No. IV, *in* 1 DEBATE ON THE CONSTITUTION, *supra* note 64, at 392–94.

89. THE FEDERALIST NO. 46, *supra* note 66, at 310 (Madison). In arguing that a conspiracy to impose military despotism was highly improbable, Madison followed Hamilton, *see id.* No. 26, at 164–65, who concluded that "[i]n reading many of the publications against the Constitution, a man is apt to imagine that he is perusing some ill-written tale or romance":

> There is something so far-fetched and so extravagant in [such objections] that one is at a loss whether to treat [them] with gravity or with raillery; whether to consider [them] as a mere trial of skill, like the paradoxes of rhetoricians; as a disingenuous artifice to instil prejudices at any price; or as the serious offspring of political fanaticism.

Id. No. 29, at 179–80 (Hamilton).

90. THE FEDERALIST NO. 46, *supra* note 66, at 310 (Madison).

91. *See supra* text following note 60.

92. 3 ELLIOT'S DEBATES, *supra* note 84, at 379–80 (statement of George Mason); *id.* at 386 (statement of Patrick Henry); *see also id.* at 418 (statement of William Grayson) (same).

93. *Id.* at 382 (statement of James Madison); *id.* at 380 (statement of George Mason); *id.* at 386–87 (statement of Patrick Henry).

94. Amendments Proposed by the Virginia Convention, Declaration or Bill of Rights, Seventeenth, *in* CREATING THE BILL OF RIGHTS, *supra* note 84, at 19; Amendments Proposed by the New York Convention, *in id.* at 22; Amendments Proposed by North Carolina Convention, Declaration of Rights, No. 17, *in* 4 ELLIOT'S DEBATES, *supra* note 84, at 244. The various state proposals are collected in THE COMPLETE BILL OF RIGHTS, *supra* note 59, at 181–83.

95. Madison Resolution, *in* CREATING THE BILL OF RIGHTS, *supra* note 84, at 12; House Resolution and Articles of Amendment, art. 5, *in id.* at 38; Articles of Amendment, as Agreed to by the Senate, art. 4, *in id.* at 48. The drafting and evolution of the amendment is traced in THE COMPLETE BILL OF RIGHTS, *supra* note 59, at 169–81.

96. *See supra* text following note 60.

97. In explaining the constitutional provision authorizing Congress to provide for calling forth the militia, Madison stated:

> If resistance should be made to the execution of the laws, . . . it ought to be overcome. This could be done only in two ways—either by regular forces or by *the people*. By one or the other it must unquestionably be done. If insurrections should arise, or invasions should take place, *the people* ought unquestionably to be employed, to suppress and repel them, rather than a standing army. The best way to do these things was to put *the militia* on a good and sure footing, and enable the government to make use of their services when necessary.

3 ELLIOT'S DEBATES, *supra* note 84, at 378 (statement of James Madison in Virginia's ratifying convention) (emphasis added). Similarly, in responding to anti-Federalist charges that federal control over the militia might lead to tyranny, Edmund Randolph, the governor of Virginia (who was soon to become the first attorney general of the United States), asked, "Shall we be afraid that the people, this bulwark of freedom [as Patrick Henry had called the militia], will turn instruments of slavery? The officers are to be appointed by the states. Will you admit that they will act so criminally as to turn against their country?" *Id.* at 400 (statement of Edmund Randolph). For another example, see *"The Republican" to the People, supra* note 64, at 712 ("[T]he people themselves are the military power of our country. . . . [E]very citizen is required by Law to be a soldier; we are all martialed into companies, regiments, and brigades, for the defence of our country").

It is likely that this is what the Federalist Noah Webster meant when he wrote (in a passage frequently quoted by supporters of the individualist interpretation of the Second Amendment) that military tyranny is possible only when the government possesses a

> military force . . . superior to any force that exists among the people, or which they can command; for otherwise this force would be annihilated, on the first exercise of acts of oppression. Before a standing army can rule, the people must be disarmed; as they are in almost every kingdom in Europe. The supreme power in America cannot enforce unjust laws by the sword; because the whole body of the people are armed, and constitute a force superior to any band of regular troops that can be, on any pretence, raised in the United States. A military force, at the command of Congress, can execute no laws, but such as the people perceive to be just and constitutional; for they will possess the *power,* and jealousy will instantly inspire the *inclination,* to resist the execution of a law which appears to them unjust and oppressive.

A Citizen of America [Noah Webster], in 1 DEBATE ON THE CONSTITUTION, *supra* note 64, at 129, 155. It seems most unlikely that Webster would have suggested—or would have expected his readers to believe—that unorganized individuals would clearly "constitute a force superior to any band of regular troops that can be . . . raised in the United States." *See infra* note 119 and accompanying text. Instead, when he referred to the superior force that can be exerted when "the whole body of the people are armed," he evidently meant the people acting as an organized, disciplined force, i.e., as a militia.

98. The House debates may be found in CREATING THE BILL OF RIGHTS, *supra* note 84, at 182–85, 198–99, and THE COMPLETE BILL OF RIGHTS, *supra* note 59, at 185–91. At this time, debates in the Senate were not public and went unrecorded.

99. For example, Elbridge Gerry objected to the religious-exemption clause on the ground that it would allow the rulers to "declare who are those religiously scrupulous, and prevent them from bearing arms." CREATING THE BILL OF RIGHTS, *supra* note 84, at 182 (statement of Representative Gerry). This statement makes sense only if "bearing arms" refers to military service, for exclusion from the militia would not prevent individuals from having arms for their own purposes. Similarly, Representative Scott argued that if there were a right to religious exemption, "you can never depend upon your militia. This will lead to the violation of another article in the constitution, which secures to the people the right of keeping arms." *Id.* at 198 (statement of Representative Scott). Again, it is difficult to see how this could be true unless the right in question is to keep arms in the context of the militia.

100. Observing that the Senate rejected a proposal to insert the words "for the common defence" after "bear arms," *see* THE COMPLETE BILL OF RIGHTS, *supra* note 59, at 174–75; Halbrook and Malcolm argue that the amendment must have been intended to recognize an individual right to arms for self-defense, or even for hunting. *See* HALBROOK, *supra* note 2, at 81; MALCOLM, *supra* note 2, at 161. As Wills points out, however, a more likely explanation is that on the national level, the phrase "for the common defence" had come to be used to refer to the defense of the country as a whole. *See* WILLS, *supra* note 12, at 256, 340 n.5. For example, the Articles of Confederation provided that "[a]ll charges

of war, and all other expences that shall be incurred for *the common defence* or general welfare, and allowed by the united states in congress assembled, shall be defrayed out of a common treasury, which shall be supplied by the several states." ARTICLES OF CONFEDERATION, art. VIII (emphasis added); *see also id.* art. VII (prescribing how officers should be appointed "[w]hen land-forces are raised by any state for *the common defence"*) (emphasis added). (The text of the Articles of Confederation may be found in 1 DEBATE ON THE CONSTITUTION, *supra* note 64, at 954–64.) Of course, the phrase bears the same meaning in the original Constitution. *See* U.S. CONST. preamble (declaring that one object of the Constitution is "to provide for the common defence"); *id.* art. I, § 8, cl. 1 (providing that Congress shall have power "[t]o lay and collect Taxes, . . . to pay the Debts and provide for the common Defence and general Welfare of the United States"). Since there was no intention to restrict the militias' right to bear arms to cases in which they were defending the nation as a whole, it would have been inappropriate to add "for the common defence." *See* WILLS, *supra* note 12, at 256.

101. MALCOLM, *supra* note 2, at 162–64.
102. As Elbridge Gerry put it, "the use of a militia" was "to prevent the establishment of a standing army, the bane of liberty." CREATING THE BILL OF RIGHTS, *supra* note 84, at 182 (statement of Rep. Gerry). Yet the Second Amendment did not purport to take away Congress's authority under Article I, section 8, to establish an army. The Federalist George Nicholas expressed the point more clearly in Virginia's ratifying convention when he stated that, by granting Congress this authority while at the same time preserving the institution of the militia, the Constitution had taken the best course:

> Till there be a necessity for an army to be raised, militia will do. And when an army will be raised, the militia will still be employed, which will render a less numerous army sufficient. By these means, there will be a sufficient defence for the country, without having a standing army altogether, or oppressing the people [by relying solely on the militia].

3 ELLIOT'S DEBATES, *supra* note 84, at 389–90 (statement of George Nicholas).
103. Virginia, seconded by North Carolina, proposed the following amendment:

> That Government ought to be instituted for the common benefit, protection and security of the People; and that the doctrine of non-resistance against arbitrary power and oppression is absurd slavish, and destructive of the good and happiness of mankind.

Amendments Proposed by the Virginia Convention, Declaration or Bill of Rights, third, *in* CREATING THE BILL OF RIGHTS, *supra* note 84, at 17; Amendments Proposed by North Carolina Convention, Declaration or Bill of Rights, No. 3, 4 ELLIOT'S DEBATES, *supra* note 84, at 243 (with minor differences in punctuation). New York suggested a declaration "[t]hat the Powers of Government may be reassumed by the People, whensoever it shall become necessary to their Happiness." Amendments Proposed by the New York Convention, *in* CREATING THE BILL OF RIGHTS, *supra* note 84, at 21.
104. Madison Resolution, CREATING THE BILL OF RIGHTS, *supra* note 84, at 11–12.
105. THE FEDERALIST NO. 46, *supra* note 66, at 310 (Madison); *id.* No. 29, at 179 (Hamilton); *see supra* text accompanying note 89.
106. *See, e.g.,* THE FEDERALIST NO. 16, *supra* note 66, at 100 (Hamilton); *id.* No. 27, at 167–68 (Hamilton); *id.* No. 28, at 170–72 (Hamilton); *id.* No. 29, at 181–82 (Hamilton); 3 ELLIOT'S DEBATES, *supra* note 84, at 378, 413-14 (statements of Madison at Virginia's ratifying convention) ("If resistance should be made to the execution of the laws, . . . it ought to be overcome"). For further discussion, see Michael A. Bellesiles, *The Second Amendment in Action,* in this volume; Paul Finkelman, *"A Well Regulated Militia": The Second Amendment in Historical Perspective,* in this volume. As Saul Cornell has shown, fears of insurrection were not limited to Federalists, but were shared by some leading anti-Federalists as well. *See* Saul Cornell, *Commonplace or Anachronism: The Standard Model, the Second Amendment, and the Problem of History in Contemporary Constitutional Theory,* 16 CONST. COMMENTARY 221, 240–45 (1999).
107. *See, e.g.,* THE FEDERALIST, *supra* note 66, No. 26, at 163–64; *id.* No. 28, at 173–75 (Hamilton); *id.* No. 29, at 181 (Hamilton); *id.* No. 46, at 308-11 (Madison).
108. For a similar position, see David C. Williams, *The Constitutional Right to "Conservative" Revolution,* 32 HARV. C.R.-C.L. L. REV. 413, 416 n.9, 426 n.45 (1997) (expressing view that the Second Amendment was intended to "guarantee a right of arms for revolution, but . . . not necessarily . . . the right of revolution itself").

109. *See* Jack N. Rakove, *The Second Amendment: The Highest Stage of Originalism,* in this volume.
110. *See, e.g.,* Barnett & Kates, *supra* note 2, at 1206.
111. On the English militia laws, see 1 BLACKSTONE, *supra* note 29, at *411; MALCOLM, *supra* note 2, at 3–9. On colonial American laws, *see* MALCOLM, *supra* note 2, at 138–41.
112. ARTICLES OF CONFEDERATION art. VI, para. 4. Similarly, New York sought to ensure that its militia should always "be armed and disciplined, and in readiness for service," by ordaining "that a proper magazine of warlike stores, proportionate to the number of inhabitants, be, forever hereafter, at the expense of this State, and by acts of the legislature, established, maintained, and continued in every county of this State." N.Y. CONST. of 1777, art. XL. For further discussion, *see* WILLS, *supra* note 2, at 259 (discussing the common practice of keeping the militia's arms in public arsenals).
113. *See* Bellesiles, *supra* note 106; Michael A. Bellesiles, *The Origins of the Gun Culture in the United States, 1760–1865,* 83 J. AMER. HIST. 425 (1996). As Bellesiles notes, for example, an 1803 government census of firearms found—after more than a decade of intensive federal efforts to promote domestic gun production—that

> [i]n a country with 524,086 official militiamen, . . . [there were only] 183,070 muskets; 39,648 rifles; and 13,113 other firearms, for a total of 235,831 guns. . . . That was enough guns for forty-five percent of the militia, one quarter of the white male population, and just 4.9 percent of the nation's total population. Half of all these guns were in the hands of the federal government, with about one-quarter in state arsenals.

Bellesiles, *supra* note 106. (citing 1 AMERICAN STATE PAPERS: MILITARY AFFAIRS 162, 198–99, 215–17). For a fuller account of Bellesiles's research, *see* MICHAEL A. BELLESILES, ARMING AMERICA: THE ORIGINS OF A NATIONAL GUN CULTURE (2000).
114. *See* Bellesiles, *supra* note 106.
115. *See* Rakove, *supra* note 109. As we have seen, much of the debate over the Constitution and the Second Amendment makes sense only on the assumption that the militia was to be armed by the government itself. *See, e.g., supra* text accompanying notes 92–93 (discussing the objection of George Mason and Patrick Henry that Congress could disarm the state militias simply by failing to arm them); note 99 (discussing remarks of Reps. Gerry and Scott in House debate); *see also* 3 ELLIOT'S DEBATES, *supra* note 84, at 421 (statement of John Marshall) ("If Congress neglect our militia, we can arm them ourselves. Cannot Virginia import arms? Cannot she put them into the hands of her militia-men?").
116. Throughout the debates over the Constitution and the Second Amendment, Federalists argued that constitutional provisions on the militia should contain only general principles, not specifics that were more appropriately left to legislation. *See, e.g.,* 3 ELLIOT'S DEBATES, *supra* note 84, at 421 (statement of John Marshall in Virginia Convention) (rejecting the notion that "a militia law is to be ingrafted on the scheme of government, so as to render it incapable of being changed"); *id.* at 426 (statement of George Nicholas) (stating that the Constitution's militia clauses confer general powers, and that "particular instances must be defined by the legislature"); CREATING THE BILL OF RIGHTS, *supra* note 84, at 184 (statement of Rep. Benson in House debate) (arguing that the Second Amendment should deal only with "fundamentals," and that all other issues "ought to be left to the discretion of the government").
117. It is possible, however, to read Blackstone to implicitly make such a connection. *Compare* 1 BLACKSTONE, *supra* note 29, at *143–44, *and* 4 *id.* at *81–82 (recognizing a limited right to take up arms against the government), *with* 1 *id.* at *408 ("[I]n free states, . . . no man should take up arms, but with a view to defend his country and its laws" through service in the militia.).
118. For the assumption that this is how the right would be exercised within the federal system, *see* THE FEDERALIST NO. 28, *supra* note 66, at 174 (Hamilton); *id.* NO. 46, at 310 (Madison), quoted *supra* text accompanying note 90. As Hamilton explained:

> It may safely be received as an axiom in our political system, that the State governments will, in all possible contingencies, afford complete security against invasions of the public liberty by the national authority. . . . The legislatures will have better means of information [than the people at large]. They can discover the danger at a distance; and possessing all the organs of civil power, and the confidence of the people, they can at once adopt a regular plan of opposition, in which they can combine all the resources of the community. They can readily communicate with each other in the different States, and unite their common forces for the protection of their common liberty.

Id. NO. 28, at 174. Similarly, when Patrick Henry declared, "The great object is, that every man be armed," he was referring to the state militia. 3 ELLIOT'S DEBATES, *supra* note 84, at 386. It was that, and not some form of unorganized resistance, that he regarded as "our ultimate safety." *Id.* at 385; *see also* 2 DOCUMENTARY HISTORY, *supra* note 86, at 508–09 (statement of John Smilie in Pennsylvania's ratifying convention) (describing the militia as "[t]he last resource of a free people").

119. *See, e.g.,* THE FEDERALIST NO. 28, *supra* note 66, at 173–74 (Hamilton); 3 ELLIOT'S DEBATES, *supra* note 84, at 380 (statement of George Mason) ("When, against a regular and disciplined army, yeomanry are the only defence,—yeomanry, unskilful and unarmed,—what chance is there for preserving freedom?"); *id.* at 386–87 (statement of Patrick Henry) (arguing that in the absence of a well-armed and disciplined militia, nothing "will . . . save you, when a strong army of veterans comes upon you").

120. *See supra* text accompanying note 106.

121. 1 BLACKSTONE, *supra* note 29, at *143–44.

122. *See, e.g.,* Reynolds, *supra* note 2, at 487 (suggesting that, if the Second Amendment presupposed a universal civic militia, which no longer exists, the solution is to revive that institution).

8. TO HOLD AND BEAR ARMS: THE ENGLISH PERSPECTIVE

* Lois G. Schwoerer is the Elmer Louis Kayser Professor Emeritus of History at the George Washington University. She is the author of "NO STANDING ARMIES!" THE ANTIARMY IDEOLOGY IN SEVENTEENTH-CENTURY ENGLAND (Johns Hopkins University Press), which won the Berkshire Conference of Women Historians' prize for the best book published by a woman historian in 1974; THE DECLARATION OF RIGHTS, 1689 (Johns Hopkins University Press), which received Honorable Mention in the John Ben Snow Prize competition; as well as LADY RACHEL RUSSELL: "ONE OF THE BEST OF WOMEN" (Johns Hopkins University Press). She edited THE REVOLUTION OF 1688–89: CHANGING PERSPECTIVES (Cambridge University Press) and helped edit THE VARIETIES OF BRITISH POLITICAL THOUGHT 1500–1800 (Cambridge University Press). Her latest book is THE INGENIOUS MR. HENRY CARE: RESTORATION PUBLICIST (Johns Hopkins University Press). Professor Schwoerer has written numerous articles, two of which won awards. POLITICS AND THE POLITICAL IMAGINATION IN LATER STUART BRITAIN is a collection of essays published in her honor. Professor Schwoerer is a Fellow of the Royal Historical Society and is a former president of the North American Conference on British Studies.

I owe thanks to many people. Charlene Bangs Bickford, Kenneth Bowling, Catherine A. Cline, Robert J. Frankle, Eliga Gould, Howard Nenner, John G. A. Pocock, Barbara Taft, and Melinda Zook offered advice and comment, not all of which I followed. Michael Bellesiles, Carl Bogus, Mark Goldie, Janelle Greenberg, and Linda Levy Peck also talked with me about the English perspective on guns. I am also indebted (as always) to the staff at the Folger Shakespeare Library in Washington, D.C., especially to Georgiana Spiegal, and to the staff at the Library of Congress, especially Bruce Martin, and the librarians in the Rare Book Room and the Law Library there. I cheerfully declare that any errors that remain are my own.

1. *See, e.g.,* Lawrence Cress, *An Armed Community: The Origins and Meaning of the Right to Bear Arms,* 71 THE JOURNAL OF AMERICAN HISTORY (1984); STEPHEN P. HALBROOK, THAT EVERY MAN BE ARMED: THE EVOLUTION OF A CONSTITUTIONAL RIGHT (1984); Robert E. Shalhope, *The Ideological Origins of the Second Amendment,* 69 THE JOURNAL OF AMERICAN HISTORY (1982); Roy Weatherup, *Standing Armies and Armed Citizens: An Historical Analysis of the Second Amendment,* 2 HASTINGS CONSTITUTIONAL LAW QUARTERLY 961–1001 (1975). These essays vary in merit. For a measured but critical review, see Joyce Lee Malcolm, *That Every Man Be Armed: The Evolution of a Constitutional Right,* 54 THE GEORGE WASHINGTON LAW REVIEW (1986).

2. JOYCE LEE MALCOLM, TO KEEP AND BEAR ARMS: THE ORIGINS OF AN ANGLO-AMERICAN RIGHT (1994).

3. Of the two printed reviews in English journals, one was an excursus about guns and crime in English society without critical comment on Malcolm's book; the other, by an American in the "Briefly Noted" section of the journal, was a restatement of Malcolm's thesis, again without critical comment. *See* David Wootton, *Disarming the English,* LONDON REVIEW OF BOOKS, (July 21, 1994), at 20; Eliga Gould, *Review,* 111 ENGLISH HISTORICAL REVIEW 1290 (1996).

4. *See* Robert J. Cottrol and Raymond T. Diamond, *The Fifth Auxiliary Right,* 104 THE YALE LAW JOURNAL 995–1026 (1995); David Kopel, *It Isn't About Duck Hunting: The British Origins of the Right to*

Arms, 93 MICHIGAN LAW REVIEW 1333–1362 (1995); Chris Mooney, *The Right to Bear Arms,* LINGUA FRANCA (Feb. 2000), at 27–34.

5. *The Hidden History of the Second Amendment,* AMERICAN RIFLEMAN (April 1994) and WAYNE LAPIERRE, GUNS, CRIME AND FREEDOM (1994) cited in Carl Bogus, *The Hidden History of the Second Amendment,* 31 U.C. DAVIS LAW REVIEW 376, n.318 (1997).

6. Chris Moony, *Liberal Legal Scholars Are Supporting the Right to Bear Arms. But Will Historians Shoot Them Down?* LINGUA FRANCA (Feb. 2000), at 31.

7. Kopel, *supra* note 4, at 1352.

8. Lois G. Schwoerer, *Review,* 61 JOURNAL OF SOUTHERN HISTORY 570–71 (1995); Michael A. Bellesiles, *Review,* 4 LAW AND HISTORY REVIEW 382–84 (1996).

9. Bogus, *supra* note 5, at 311–408; Garry Wills, *To Keep and Bear Arms,* THE NEW YORK REVIEW OF BOOKS, (Sept. 21, 1995), at 62–73.

10. Michael Dorf, *What Does the Second Amendment Mean Today?* in this volume.

11. *See, e.g.,* HERBERT BUTTERFIELD, THE WHIG INTERPRETATION OF HISTORY (1978), a classic study, and many articles by Quentin Skinner, among them *Motives, Intentions and the Interpretation of Texts,* 3 NEW LITERARY HISTORY 393–408 (1972).

12. A copy of the *Declaration of Rights 1689* may be conveniently found in LOIS G. SCHWOERER, THE DECLARATION OF RIGHTS, 1689 (1981), Appendix I.

13. *Id.* at 234.

14. There are three undated prints of the presentation ceremony, none of which is contemporary, in the Print Room of the British Museum.

15. ANCHITELL GREY, 9 DEBATES OF THE HOUSE OF COMMONS, FROM THE YEAR 1667 TO THE YEAR 1694, at 30 (London, 1763).

16. Kenneth R. Bowling, *The Founding Fathers and Adoption of the Federal Bill of Rights,* 8 JOURNAL OF THE EARLY REPUBLIC (1988), reprinted from Virginia Commission on the Bicentennial of the United States Constitution Center for Public Service, University of Virginia. *See* Schwoerer, *supra* note 12, at 185–90. *Also* SAUL CORNELL, OTHER FOUNDERS: ANTI-FEDERALISM AND THE DISSENTING TRADITION IN AMERICA 1788–1828 (1999).

17. *See* Schwoerer, *supra* note 12, at 195–97.

18. Two days later the committee was enlarged to forty members.

19. GREY, *supra* note 15, at 32.

20. *Id. See also* John Somers, *Notes of Debate, January 28, January 29,* in MISCELLANEOUS STATE PAPERS FROM 1501 TO 1726, at 417 (eds., Philip Yorke, Earl of Hardwicke, 2 vols, London, 1778). They may have heard of the complaints of Sir Robert Atkyns, a judge, whose weapons, including the sword with which Charles II had knighted him, were confiscated in 1683. *See* J. R. WESTERN, THE ENGLISH MILITIA IN THE EIGHTEENTH CENTURY: THE STORY OF A POLITICAL ISSUE, 1660–1802 at 4, 69 (1965), referring to *C.S.P.D.,* July to September 1683, pp. 402–403. Professor Malcolm may wish to correct her citation to WESTERN, THE ENGLISH MILITIA IN THE EIGHTEENTH CENTURY at page 92, n.68.

21. GREY, *supra* note 15, at 32. Somers, *supra* note 20, at 416, 417.

22. Somers, *supra* note 20, at 410.

23. GREY, *supra* note 15, at 18.

24. *Id. See also* Lois G. Schwoerer, *A Jornall of the Convention at Westminster Begun the 22 of January 1688/89,* 44 BULLETIN OF THE INSTITUTE OF HISTORICAL RESEARCH 258 (1976).

25. A copy of the Heads of Grievances is in Schwoerer, *supra* note 12, at Appendix II.

26. The committee brought in twenty-three heads; five were added in the debate.

27. THE COMMONWEALTH OF OCEANA, AND A SYSTEM OF POLITICS. JAMES HARRINGTON (John G. A. Pocock, ed., 1992).

28. LOIS G. SCHWOERER, "NO STANDING ARMIES!" THE ANTIARMY IDEOLOGY IN SEVENTEENTH-CENTURY ENGLAND 15–18, 64–67 (1974).

29. J. G. A. POCOCK, THE ANCIENT CONSTITUTION AND THE FEUDAL LAW: A STUDY OF ENGLISH HISTORICAL THOUGHT IN THE SEVENTEENTH CENTURY. A REISSUE WITH A RETROSPECT (1987) is the classic study.

30. P. B. MUNSCHE, GENTLEMEN AND POACHERS THE ENGLISH GAME LAWS 1671–1831 (1981), chap. I: The Game Laws.

31. EDMUND S. MORGAN, INVENTING THE PEOPLE: THE RISE OF POPULAR SOVEREIGNTY IN ENGLAND AND AMERICA 23 (1988).

32. For the terms, *see* 2nd ed. THE STUART CONSTITUTION 457–58 (J. P. Kenyon, ed., 1989). For the reasons, *see* MUNSCHE, *supra* note 30, at 15–19.

33. *See* KEITH WRIGHTSON, ENGLISH SOCIETY 1580–1680 34 (1988); and PETER LASLETT, THE WORLD WE HAVE LOST 36–37 (1972), citing Gregory King's calculations.

34. An original copy of the 1616 Proclamation is at the Folger Shakespeare Library, STC 8539.8.

35. Schwoerer, *supra* note 28, at chap. III.

36. The Levellers' several *Agreements of the People* make no mention of the right to possess arms. That right is not included in *An Agreement of the Free People of England. Tendered as a Peace-Offering to This Distressed Nation.* (1649), described as "the ultimate and full scope of all our desires and intentions." *See* THE WRITINGS OF WILLIAM WALWYN 345 (Jack R. McMichael and Barbara Taft, eds., 1989).

37. *See* B. Behrens, *The Whig Theory of the Constitution in the Reign of Charles II,* 7 CAMBRIDGE HISTORICAL JOURNAL 42–71 (1941); *and* O. W. Furley, *The Whig Exclusionists: Pamphlet Literature in the Exclusion Campaign, 1689–81,* 13 CAMBRIDGE HISTORICAL JOURNAL 19–36 (1957).

38. MELINDA S. ZOOK, RADICAL WHIGS AND CONSPIRATORIAL POLITICS IN LATE STUART ENGLAND (1999).

39. Schwoerer, *supra* note 12, at chap. 8. *See also* Mark Goldie, *The Roots of True Whiggism 1688–94,* 1 JOURNAL OF POLITICAL THOUGHT 195–236 (1980).

40. WESTERN, *supra* note 20, at 83–84.

41. *Maurice Cranston,* WHAT ARE HUMAN RIGHTS? 81 (New York: Taplinger Publishing Co., 1973); Lois G. Schwoerer, *British Lineages and American Choices,* THE BILL OF RIGHTS GOVERNMENT PROSCRIBED 3 (Ronald Hoffman and Peter J. Albert, eds., 1997).

42. OXFORD ENGLISH DICTIONARY (1979 ed.); *cf.* definitions in Garry Wills, *supra* note 9, at 64–65.

43. 10 JOURNALS OF THE HOUSE OF COMMONS 19 [hereinafter H.C.J.]; Robert Frankle, *The Formulation of the Declaration of Rights, 1689,* 17 THE HISTORICAL JOURNAL 268–69, n.25 (1974) stresses the role of the Prince in the amendment process.

44. 10 H.C.J. 22.

45. It is interesting to note that Article VII is the only one in which the verb form "may" occurs.

46. 10 H.C.J. 25.

47. *Id.*

48. Schwoerer, *British Lineages and American Choices,* pp. 4–11.

49. Grey, *supra* note 15, at 27, 34.

50. JOHN MILLER, JAMES II: A STUDY IN KINGSHIP 211–12 (1977); John Miller, *The Militia and the Army in the Reign of James II,* 16 HISTORICAL JOURNAL 659–79 (1973).

51. *See, e.g.,* WRIGHTSON, *supra* note 33, esp. chap I; also the classic study by LASLETT, *supra* note 33 esp. chaps. I, II, VIII.

52. Schwoerer, *supra* note 24, at 252–53.

53. For relationships with peers, see Schwoerer, *supra* note 12, at 39. Five sons of peers were on the committee.

54. William Sachse, *The Mob and the Revolution of 1688,* 4 JOURNAL OF BRITISH STUDIES 23–40 (1964).

55. Cambridge University, Churchill College, Erle Mss. 4/4. The modern edition is Mark Goldie, *Thomas Erle's Instructions for the Revolution Parliament, December 1688,* 14 PARLIAMENTARY HISTORY 337–47 (1995). *See* Schwoerer, *supra* note 12, at 77, 192.

56. *Id.* at 344–45.

57. Bodleian Library, Carte Mss. 81, fol. 766. The terms of the paper are discussed further in Schwoerer, *supra* note 12, at 238–39.

58. Bogus, *supra* note 5, at 383–85.

59. *See* Lois G. Schwoerer, *The Transformation of the Convention into a Parliament, February 1689,* 3 PARLIAMENTARY HISTORY 57–76 (1984).

60. *See* 5 WILLIAM COBBETT, THE PARLIAMENTARY HISTORY OF ENGLAND FROM THE EARLIEST PERIOD TO THE YEAR 1803 at 182–84 (London, 1808–1820).

61. Western, *supra* note 20, at 85–89.

62. *Id.* at 85.

63. Schwoerer, *supra* note 12, at chap. 16.

64. Malcolm gives the date as 1692, using Old Style dating in this instance. The bill moved through the House of Commons in February 1693, New Style. *See* 10 H.C.J. 801, 805, 807, 824.

65. The quotation is from 10 H.C.J. 824, not from THE PARLIAMENTARY DIARY OF NARCISSUS LUTTRELL, 1691–1693 at 444 (Henry Horwitz, ed., 1972), as Malcolm's notes show (p. 209, n. 36).

66. Horwitz identifies the participants in this exchange. *Supra* note 65, at 444. For comment, *see* BASIL DUKE HENNING 3 THE HISTORY OF PARLIAMENT. THE HOUSE OF COMMONS 1660–1690 at 148 (1983). *See also* HENRY HORWITZ, PARLIAMENT, POLICY AND POLITICS IN THE REIGN OF WILLIAM III (1977), Appendix C.

67. 1 HENNING, *supra* note 66, at 696.

68. HORWITZ, *supra* note 65, at p. 444. The other three were: the Hon. Goodwin Wharton (1653–1704), an eccentric, known as an "influential" Whig at this time; Mr. Howe, impossible to identify because one of three "Howes" in the parliament; and Mr. Clarke, probably Sir Gilbert Clarke (c. 1645–1701), a Tory. *See* 3 HENNING, *supra* note 66, at 695–96; 2 HENNING *supra* note 66, at 82.

69. HORWITZ, *supra* note 65, at p. 444.

70. *Id.*

71. Munsche, *supra* note 30, at 32.

72. *Id.* at 80, 81, 82.

73. 1 RICHARD BURN, THE JUSTICE OF THE PEACE, AND PARISH OFFICER: BY RICHARD BURN, CLERK, ONE OF HIS MAJESTY'S JUSTICES OF THE PEACE FOR THE COUNTY OF WESTMORLAND at 442–43 (1755).

74. *Id.*

75. *See* MALCOLM, *supra* note 2, at 129.

76. Malcolm wrote of a "series of court cases" and of "several law cases" but identified only two: pp. 128, 129.

77. *See* MUNSCHE, *supra* note 30, at 80.

78. JOHN SHEBBEARE, A FIFTH LETTER TO THE PEOPLE OF ENGLAND, ON THE SUBVERSION OF THE CONSTITUTION: AND THE NECESSITY OF ITS BEING RESTORED 35 (1757); *cf. id.* 34. The same point was made even more passionately in his A LETTER TO THE PEOPLE OF ENGLAND, ON THE PRESENT SITUATION AND CONDUCT OF NATIONAL AFFAIRS 16 (1755).

79. SHEBBEARE, *supra* note 78, at 49, 57.

80. *See* ELIJAH H. GOULD, THE PERSISTENCE OF EMPIRE BRITISH POLITICAL CULTURE IN THE AGE OF THE AMERICAN REVOLUTION 46, 51, 82 (2000).

81. *Id.* at chapter III, esp. pp. 75, 79, 81, 84, 86, 89.

82. For brief review, see WILLIAM B. WILLCOX AND WALTER L. ARNSTEIN, THE AGE OF ARISTOCRACY 1688 to 1830 182–84 (1966). *See also* THE CONQUEST OF VIOLENCE. ORDER AND LIBERTY IN BRITAIN 81–90 (1970), *and* CHRISTOPHER HIBBERT, KING MOB; THE STORY OF LORD GEORGE GORDON AND THE LONDON RIOTS OF 1780 (1958).

83. 21 COBBETT, *supra* note 60, at 727.

84. 21 COBBETT, *supra* note 60, at 728.

85. For what follows, see GOULD, *supra* note 80, at 174, 176.

86. *See* MALCOLM, *supra* note 2, at 134.

87. GOULD, *supra* note 80, at 173–74, 176.

88. 1 WILLIAM BLACKSTONE, COMMENTARIES ON THE LAWS OF ENGLAND 139 (Stanley N. Katz, ed., 1979).

89. *Id.* at 140.

90. 1 LORD MACAULAY CRITICAL AND HISTORICAL ESSAYS, CONTRIBUTED TO THE EDINBURGH REVIEW 154, 162 (1850).

91. Schwoerer, *supra* note 28, at chapter II.

92. It has been said that with the Magna Charta and the Petition of Right the Bill of Rights formed the "models in hand, or at least in mind" when the colonists drew up their claim. *See* Schwoerer, *supra* note 48, at 2.

93. *See* CREATING THE BILL OF RIGHTS: THE DOCUMENTARY RECORD FROM THE FIRST FEDERAL CONGRESS 4, 12, 17, 19, 22, 30, 38–39n, 48 (Helen E. Veit, Kenneth R. Bowling, and Charlene Bangs Bickford, eds., 1991).

94. MALCOLM, *supra* note 2, at x.

9. DISARMED BY TIME:
THE SECOND AMENDMENT AND THE FAILURE OF ORIGINALISM

* Daniel A. Farber is Associate Dean for Faculty and the Henry J. Fletcher Professor of Law at the University of Minnesota. He clerked for Justice Paul Stevens at the Supreme Court, and taught at the University of Illinois College of Law before joining the Minnesota faculty. He is the author of BEYOND ALL REASON: THE RADICAL ASSAULT ON TRUTH IN AMERICA (Oxford University Press), ECO-PRAGMATISM: MAKING SENSIBLE ENVIRONMENTAL DECISIONS IN AN UNCERTAIN WORLD (University of Chicago Press), and coauthor of leading casebooks in the fields of constitutional and environmental law. Professor Farber has also written more than forty law review articles and numerous book reviews and essays on subjects ranging from free speech to statutory interpretation. He was a founding editor of the journal CONSTITUTIONAL COMMENTARY, and is a member of the editorial board of Foundation Press.

Thanks to Dianne Farber, Gil Grantmore, David McGowan, Katie Moerke, and TK for their helpful comments.

1. A good presentation of this conventional view can be found in Donald W. Dowd, *The Relevance of the Second Amendment to Gun Control Legislation*, 58 MONT. L. REV. 79 (1979). For lively nontechnical introductions to the debate, see AKHIL REED AMAR AND ALAN HIRSCH, FOR THE PEOPLE: WHAT THE CONSTITUTION REALLY SAY ABOUT YOUR RIGHTS 170–80 (1998) (favoring recognition of an individual right to bear arms); GARRY WILLS, A NECESSARY EVIL: A HISTORY OF AMERICAN DISTRUST OF GOVERNMENT 120–22, 207–20, 253–59 (1999) (no such right exists).

2. For extensive citations both to the revisionists and their opponents, see 1 LAURENCE TRIBE, AMERICAN CONSTITUTIONAL LAW 897–98 n.211 (3d ed. 2000). A brief overview of the debate can be found in *Showdown*, LINGUA FRANCA 26 (Feb. 2000). A bibliography appears in Robert J. Spitzer, *Lost and Found: Researching the Second Amendment*, in this volume [appendix]. Tribe himself now seems to be at least flirting with the revisionist view, although the tentativeness of his view may be indicated by the fact that he relegates the point to a somewhat tortuous footnote. *See id.* at 862 n.221. I agree with Tribe's further assertion that acceptance of the revisionist view would be "largely irrelevant to contemporary gun control proposals." *Id.* at 902.

3. Willam Van Alstyne, *The Second Amendment and the Personal Right to Arms*, 43 DUKE L.J. 1236, 1250 (1994).

4. Randy E. Barnett and Don B. Kates, *Under Fire: The New Consensus on the Second Amendment*, 45 EMORY L.J. 1139, 1259 (1996).

5. *See* Michael C. Dorf, *What Does the Second Amendment Mean Today?*, in this volume. A notable exception is L. A. Powe, *Guns, Words, and Constitutional Interpretation*, 38 WILLIAM & MARY L. REV. 1311 (1997). Although it is not my purpose here to explore the full range of arguments regarding the Second Amendment, Dorf makes a strong case against expansively reading the amendment.

6. On the early history of the debate, *see* Murray Dry, *Federalism and the Constitution: The Founders' Design and Contemporary Constitutional Law*, 4 CONST. COMM. 233, 233–34 (1987). A summary of the case for originalism, dating from the same era, can be found in Earl M. Maltz, *The Failure of Attacks on Constitutional Originalism*, 4 CONST. COMM. 43 (1987). For a sample of more recent contributions to the debate, see David McGowan, *Ethos in Law and History: Alexander Hamilton, The Federalist, and the Supreme Court* (forthcoming); Michael J. Klarman, *Antifidelity*, 70 S. CAL. L. REV. 381 (1997); Mark Killenbeck, *The Qualities of Completeness: More? Or Less?*, 87 MICH. L. REV. 1629 (1999) (book review); Michael C. Dorf, *Integrating Normative and Descriptive Constitutional Theory: The Case of Original Meaning*, 85 GEO. L.J. 1765 (1997); Gary Lawson, *On Reading Recipes . . . and Constitutions*, 85 GEO. L.J. 1823 (1997). For a leading historian's perspective, see JACK N. RAKOVE, ORIGINAL MEANINGS: POLITICS AND IDEAS IN THE MAKING OF THE CONSTITUTION 3–22 (1996).

7. I will focus primarily on the Second Amendment itself, rather than the original understanding of the right to bear arms by the framers of the Fourteenth Amendment. Regardless of how the framers of the Fourteenth Amendment viewed the right to bear arms, it seems doubtful that it should apply to the states. In early cases, the Supreme Court refused to do so. The right to own a gun also does not qualify under the Court's current tests, as "implicit in the concept of ordered liberty," Palko v. Connecticut, 302 U.S. 319 (1937), or "fundamental to the American scheme of justice," Duncan v. Louisiana, 391 U.S. 145 (1968).

8. I do not mean to prejudge the policy issues involved in gun control, which are themselves hotly disputed. *See, e.g.,* John R. Lott and David B. Mustard, *Crime, Deterrence, and Right-to-Carry Laws: Contrasting Private and Public Law Enforcement,* 26 J. LEG. STUDIES 1 (1997).

9. The amendment states that, "[a] well regulated Militia, being necessary to the security of a free State, the right of the people to keep and bear Arms, shall not be infringed." U.S. Const., Amend. II.

10. *See* Muscarello v. United States, 118 S. Ct. 1911 (1998).

11. Bailey v. United States, 516 U.S. 137 (1995).

12. Smith v. United States, 508 U.S. 223 (1993).

13. Antonin Scalia, *Originalism: The Lesser Evil,* 57 U. CINN. L. REV. 849, 856–57 (1980).

14. James H. Hutson, *The Creation of the Constitution: The Integrity of the Documentary Record,* 65 TEX. L. REV. 1, 33–35 (1986).

15. *Id.* at 22–24. Rakove reports that there were roughly two thousand actors in the various conventions. RAKOVE, *supra* note 6, at .

16. Hutson, *supra* note 14, at 36.

17. *See* RAKOVE, *supra* note 6, at 133.

18. *See* Larry D. Kramer, *Madison's Audience,* 112 HARV. L. REV. 611 (1999).

19. *See* RAKOVE, *supra* note 6, at 18–21.

20. *See* John C. Yoo, *Clio at War: The Misuse of History in the War Powers Debate,* 70 U. COLO. L. REV. 1169 (1999); Martin S. Flaherty, *History "Lite" in Modern American Constitutionalism,* 95 COLUM. L. REV. 523 (1995); William E. Nelson, *History and Neutrality in Constitutional Adjudication,* 72 VA. L. REV. 1237, 1250–51 (1986).

21. *See* Carlos Manuel Vazquez, *What Is Eleventh Amendment Immunity?,* 106 YALE L.J. 1683, 1694 (1997).

22. Frank H. Easterbrook, *Text, History, and Structure in Statutory Interpretation,* 17 HARV. J.L. & PUB. POLY. 61, 76 (1994).

23. Barnett and Kates, *supra* note 4, at 1139, 1212.

24. WILLS, *supra* note 1, at 215.

25. Barnett and Kates, *supra* note 4, at 1208.

26. Michael A. Bellesiles, *Suicide Pact: New Readings of the Second Amendment,* 16 CONST. COMM. 247, 253–56 (1999). *See also* Don Higginbotham, *The Second Amendment in Historical Context,* 16 CONST. COMM. 263, 267 (1999) (discussing extensive gun regulation by colonial governments).

27. Barnett and Kates, *supra* note 4, at 1214.

28. Robert E. Shalhope, *To Keep and Bear Arms in the Early Republic,* 16 CONST. COMM. 269, 274 (1999).

29. Amar and Hirsch, *supra* note 1, at 170.

30. Carl T. Bogus, *The Hidden History of the Second Amendment,* 31 U.C. DAVIS L. REV. 309, 343 (1997).

31. Saul Cornell, *Commonplace or Anachronism: The Standard Model, the Second Amendment, and the Problem of History in Contemporary Constitutional Theory,* 16 CONST. COMM. 221, 229 (1999).

32. Amar and Hirsch, *supra* note 1, at 175.

33. WILLS, *supra* note 1, at 208–10. Key anti-Federalist leaders were also horrified at the thought of insurrection. *See* Cornell, *supra* note 32, at 240–41.

34. Shalhope, *supra* note 28, at 279–80.

35. WILLS, *supra* note 1, at 259.

36. Originalism should be even less favored by devotees of nonjudicial constitutional interpretation. For those who view elected officials or ordinary citizens as major constitutional interpreters, it should seem even less likely that members of Congress or the average voter would be an astute interpreter of early American history.

37. *See* Lawson, *supra* note 6, at 1823, 1834 ("the Constitution's meaning is its original public meaning").

38. *See* H. Jefferson Powell, *The Original Understanding of Original Intent,* 98 HARV. L. REV. 885, 895–98 (1985).

39. *See* Charles A. Lofgren, *The Original Understanding of Original Intent?,* 5 CONST. COMM. 77 (1988). Rakove argues originalism did not begin as a method of interpretation until some time after the Constitution had gone into effect. *See* RAKOVE, *supra* note 6, at 339–70.

40. For arguments against finding any such limiting effect, *see, e.g.,* Glenn Harlan Reynolds, *A Critical Guide to the Second Amendment,* 62 TENN. L. REV. 461, 466–67 (1995); Van Alstyne, *supra* note 3, at 1236, 1242.

41. Eugene Volokh, *The Commonplace Second Amendment*, 73 NYU L. REV. 793, 805 (1998).

42. William N. Eskridge, *Textualism, the Unknown Ideal?*, 96 MICH. L. REV. 1509, 1523-26 (1998).

43. *Id.* at 1525.

44. *Id.* at 1524. Consider, for instance, the old chestnut about whether someone who murders the testator is entitled to take under the Statute of Wills. See Daniel A. Farber, *Courts, Statutes, and Public Policy: The Case of the Murderous Heir* (forthcoming SMU L. REV.).

45. John F. Manning, *Textualism and the Equity of the Statute*, 101 COLUM. L. REV. 1 (2001). Manning, it should be noted, does not agree that today's federal judges are authorized to engage in equally loose construction, given our current understanding of the separation of powers.

46. *See* Mark D. Greenberg and Harry Litman, *The Meaning of Original Meaning*, 86 GEO. L.J. 569 (1998). For a criticism of Justice Scalia's views on this point, see David Sosa, *The Unintentional Fallacy*, 86 CAL. L. REV. 919, 935-36 (1998).

47. *See* Thomas C. Grey, *Do We Have an Unwritten Constitution?*, 27 STAN. L. REV. 703, 711-14 (1975).

48. Michael McConnell, *Federalism: Evaluating the Founders' Design*, 54 U. CHI. L. REV. 1484, 1490-91 (1987).

49. *See* Robert W. Bennett, *Objectivity in Constitutional Law*, 132 U. PENN. L. REV. 445, 463 (1984).

50. *See* Robert Bork, *The Constitution, Original Intent, and Economic Rights*, 23 SAN DIEGO L. REV. 823, 828 (1986).

51. *See* Jack N. Rakove, *The Second Amendment: The Highest Stage of Originalism*, in this volume.

52. *See* Henry P. Monaghan, *Our Perfect Constitution*, 56 NYU L. REV. 353, 382 (1981). For a more extensive discussion, see Henry Paul Monaghan, *Stare Decisis and Constitutional Adjudication*, 88 COLUM. L. REV. 723 (1988).

53. As examples of novel constitutional rights, he gives: "cases discovering a novel constitutional right against statewide laws denying special protection to homosexuals, a novel constitutional right against excessive jury awards, a novel constitutional right against being excluded from government contracts because of party affiliation, a novel constitutional prohibition of single-sex state schools, and a novel constitutional approval of federal appellate review of jury verdicts." ANTONIN SCALIA, A MATTER OF INTERPRETATION 138-39. His use of these examples is criticized in Jeffrey Rosen, *Originalist Sin: The Achievement of Antonin Scalia, and Its Intellectual Incoherence*, 216 THE NEW REPUBLIC 26 (May 5, 1997). It is very difficult to discern any principled distinction between what Scalia considers a novel right and what he considers merely as novel application of an established one.

54. O'Hare Truck Serv. Inc. v. City of Northlake, 116 S. Ct. 2353 (1996); Board of County Comm'rs v. Umbeher, 116 S. Ct. 2342 (1996).

55. 116 S. Ct. at 2361.

56. 116 S. Ct. 236 (quoting Rutan v. Republican Party, 497 U.S. 62, 95-96 [1980]) (Scalia, J., dissenting).

57. Amar and Hirsch, *supra* note 1, at 180. *See also* Dowd, *supra* note 1, at 83 n.14 (citing consistent line of cases in lower federal courts). For illustrative cases, see United States v. Hale, 978 F.2d 1016, 1018-20 (8th Cir. 1992), cert. denied, 113 S. Ct. 1614 (1993); Farmer v. Higgins, 907 F.2d 10410, 1045 (11th Cir. 1990), cert. denied 498 U.S. 104 (1991); Quilici v. Village of Morton Grove, 695 F.2d 261, 270 (7th Cir. 1982), cert. denied, 464 U.S. 863 (1983). The one exception is the recent district court opinion in United States v. Emerson, 46 F. Supp. 2d 598 (N.D. Texas 1999). A narrow reading of the amendment, however, was adopted at about the same time as *Emerson* by the D.C. Circuit in Fraternal Order of Police v. United States, 173 F.3d 898 (D.C. Cir. 1999).

58. *See* Dorf, *supra* note 5, at 1765, 1772-74 (stare decisis intellectually destabilizes originalism).

59. *See* Justice Scalia's concurrence in Pennsylvania v. Union Gas Co., 491 U.S. 1 (1989).

60. *See* RAKOVE, *supra* note 6, at 9.

61. Edwin Meese, *The Supreme Court of the United States: Bulwark of a Limited Constitution*, 27 S. TEX. L. REV. 455, 464 (1986).

62. JOHN HART ELY, DEMOCRACY AND DISTRUST: A THEORY OF JUDICIAL REVIEW 5-8 (1980).

63. *See* Paul Brest, *The Misconceived Quest for the Original Understanding*, 60 B.U. L. REV. 204, 230 (1980).

64. *See generally* Bogus, *supra* note 30.

65. *Id.* at 372.

66. *Id.* at 339-42.

67. *Id.* at 332-33, 335.

68. *Id.* at 349.
69. It is important to bear in mind that courts are not the only nonmajoritarian institutions in our system of government. Indeed, it is not clear that the Court is radically less "democratic" than the Senate, which is elected from incredibly malapportioned districts. As for accountability, the Court is not the only important national authority lacking direct political accountability: the Federal Reserve is nearly as free from accountability and arguably more important in setting national policy. Most Americans are affected more directly by the inflation and unemployment rates than by whether flag burning is legal or by whether the town hall can display a Christmas tree.

Furthermore, judges are only part of the governance system; they are not our rulers. To assume that the whole system can be legitimate only if each part would be legitimate standing alone is to commit what economists call the fallacy of composition. The attack on judicial review assumes that the idea of democratic legitimacy applies to each particular organ of government or each specific governmental policy considered in isolation, as opposed to the government as a whole. But legitimacy may be better considered a quality that attaches to the entire governance system rather than components. Even markedly nonmajoritarian features, like the United States Senate, do not imperil overall democratic legitimacy, though they may or may not function desirably. For further discussion of these issues, *see* DANIEL FARBER AND SUZANNA SHERRY, DESPERATELY SEEKING CERTAINTY: THE MISGUIDED QUEST FOR CONSTITUTIONAL FOUNDATIONS (forthcoming).
70. *See, e.g.,* Anthony Lester, *The Overseas Trade in the American Bill of Rights,* 88 COLUM. L. REV. 537 (1988). Since Lord Lester wrote, the trend has continued apace.
71. Consider an analogy. One of the core tenets of the American legal system is the importance of the jury. We place particular importance upon the jury in criminal cases but even in civil cases the jury's role is protected by the federal Constitution and many state constitutions. One key function of the jury is to bring community values and judgment to bear on a case, rather than merely the elite opinions of judges. For this reason, as well as for more immediate practical reasons, everyone agrees that judges should not lightly overturn jury verdicts. Still, not infrequently, judges do overturn jury verdicts that they consider unsupported by the evidence. But no one obsesses about the "counterjuritarian" difficulty. No scholar finds it necessary to design a whole theory of civil procedure around the problem of explaining the legitimacy of this practice.
72. *See* Amar and Hirsch, *supra* note 1, at 171.
73. SCALIA, *supra* note 53, at 133.
74. *See* David A. Strauss, *Common Law Constitutional Interpretation,* 63 U. CHI. L. REV. 877 (1996).
75. Michael W. McConnell, *The Importance of Humility in Judicial Review: A Comment on Ronald Dworkin's "Moral Reading" of the Constitution,* 65 FORDHAM L. REV. 1269, 1292 (1997).
76. CASS SUNSTEIN, LEGAL REASONING AND POLITICAL CONFLICT 9 (1996). Sunstein is far from alone in advocating this pragmatic approach. For other prominent examples, *see* RICHARD A. POSNER, THE PROBLEMS OF JURISPRUDENCE (1990); KARL N. LLEWELLYN, JURISPRUDENCE: REALISM IN THEORY AND PRACTICE (1962).
77. SUNSTEIN, *supra* note 76, at 37.
78. *See* Lillian R. BeVier, *The Moment and the Millennium: A Question of Time, or Law?,* 66 GEO. WASH. U. L. REV. 1112, 1117 (1998) (explaining that textualists are "tenaciously devoted to an ideal of legitimacy that requires judicial decision making to be constrained by objective standards and criteria external to the judges themselves").
79. *See* David M. Zlotnick, *Justice Scalia and His Critics: An Exploration of Scalia's Fidelity to His Constitutional Methodology,* 48 EMORY L.J. 1377, 1377–1426 (1999). According to Zlotnick, "Scalia's opinions . . . can be best understood as the product of the three-way tension between a faithful application of his methodology, the ideological motivation for the methodology, and his distinct conservative political values on particular issues." *Id.* at 1425.
80. As Carlos Vazquez has observed, there is a "rare unanimity" among legal scholars that the Eleventh Amendment decisions are unsupported by original understanding. *See* Vazquez, *supra* note 21, at 1694.
81. Missouri v. Holland, 252 U.S. 416, 433 (1920). For modern defenses of this concept, see Barry Friedman and Scott B. Smith, *The Sedimentary Constitution,* 147 U. PENN. L. REV. 1 (1998); Larry Kramer, *Fidelity to History,* 65 FORDHAM L. REV. 1627 (1997). Although the idea of an evolving constitutional regime is often considered liberal, it can also be defended as the truest embodiment of conservatism.

See Ernest Young, *Rediscovering Conservatism: Burkean Political Theory and Constitutional Interpretation*, 72 N.C. L. REV. 621 (1994).

82. See Akhil Amar, *Second Thoughts: What the Right to Bear Arms Really Means*, THE NEW REPUBLIC, July 12, 1999, at 24, 26.

83. See Dorf, *supra* note 5.

84. On the effect of these changed circumstances, see Uviller and Merkel, *The Second Amendment: The Evolution of a Concept*, in this volume; Dorf, supra note [88].

85. See Dorf, *supra* note [5].

86. See JAMES M. MCPHERSON, DRAWN WITH THE SWORD: REFLECTIONS ON THE AMERICAN CIVIL WAR 57 (1996).

87. See DANIEL FARBER AND SUZANNA SHERRY, A HISTORY OF THE AMERICAN CONSTITUTION 301–05 (1990).

88. See Robert Rabin, *Federal Regulation in Historical Perspective*, 38 STAN. L. REV. 1189, 1192 (1986).

89. The reference, of course, is to BRUCE ACKERMAN, WE THE PEOPLE: FOUNDATIONS (1991).

90. For a survey of these developments, see Rabin, *supra* note 88, at 1272–95.

91. See Part II(A) *supra*.

92. See Part II(B) *supra*.

93. See Part II(C) *supra*.

94. See Part II(D) *supra*.

95. See Part III(A) *supra*.

96. See Part III(B) *supra*.

97. See Part III(C) *supra*.

98. See Rakove, *supra* note 51 (discussing use of high-level theoretical constructs by advocates of a broader reading of the Second Amendment).

99. RAKOVE, *supra* note 6, at 14.

100. *Id.* at 15.

10. WHAT DOES THE SECOND AMENDMENT MEAN TODAY?

* Michael C. Dorf is Professor of Law and Vice Dean at Columbia University School of Law, where he teaches courses in constitutional law and civil procedure. Professor Dorf served as a law clerk to Justice Anthony M. Kennedy at the Supreme Court and taught at Rutgers University (Camden) before joining the Columbia faculty. Professor Dorf writes in constitutional law and related subjects. With Laurence H. Tribe, he is the coauthor of ON READING THE CONSTITUTION (Harvard University Press). He has written numerous law review articles, including *The Supreme Court 1997 Term Foreword: The Limits of Socratic Deliberation* (HARVARD LAW REVIEW); *Incidental Burdens on Fundamental Rights* (HARVARD LAW REVIEW); and *Facial Challenges to State and Federal Statutes* (STANFORD LAW REVIEW).

Akhil Amar, Barbara Black, Vincent Blasi, Carl Bogus, Sherry Colb, Christopher Eisgruber, Jeffrey Fagan, Barry Friedman, Kent Greenawalt, Larry Kramer, Sanford Levinson, Henry Monaghan, Gerald Neuman, Lawrence Sager, Robert Spitzer, Mark Tushnet, and Richard Uviller provided helpful comments on earlier drafts and Sarah Stafford provided excellent research assistance.

1. See generally LAURENCE H. TRIBE, AMERICAN CONSTITUTIONAL LAW 897 n.211 (3d ed. 1999).

2. The individual rights scholars sometimes refer to their position as the "standard model," thereby suggesting that other views are idiosyncratic. *See* Michael A. Bellesiles, *Suicide Pact: New Readings of the Second Amendment*, 16 CONST. COMMENTARY 247, 249 (1999) (criticizing the use of such terminology in Randy E. Barnett & Don B. Kates, *Under Fire: The New Consensus on the Second Amendment*, 45 EMORY L.J. 1139, 1141 [1996]; Glenn Harlan Reynolds, *A Critical Guide to the Second Amendment*, 62 TENN. L. REV. 461 [1995]). I use a somewhat more neutral terminology.

3. Sanford Levinson, *The Embarrassing Second Amendment*, 99 YALE L.J. 637 (1989).

4. Eugene Volokh, *The Amazing Vanishing Second Amendment*, 73 N.Y.U. L. REV. 831 (1998).

5. See id. at 840; Eugene Volokh, *The Commonplace Second Amendment*, 73 N.Y.U. L. REV. 793, 805–06 (1998).

6. See, e.g., Brannon P. Denning, *Gun Shy: The Second Amendment as an "Underenforced Constitutional Norm,"* 21 HARV. J.L. & PUB. POL'Y 719 (1998); Dan Polsby, *Treating the Second Amendment Like Normal Constitutional Law*, REASON, Mar. 1996, at 32.

7. *See, e.g.,* JOYCE LEE MALCOLM, TO KEEP AND BEAR ARMS: THE ORIGINS OF AN ANGLO-AMERICAN RIGHT 176 (1994). One notable exception is L. A. Powe, Jr., *Guns, Words, and Constitutional Interpretation,* 38 WM. & MARY L. REV. 1311 (1997).

8. *See* Henry Paul Monaghan, *Stare Decisis and Constitutional Adjudication,* 88 COLUM. L. REV. 723, 727–39 (1988). As two of the other chapters in this book ably demonstrate, the originalist arguments in favor of the individual rights interpretation of the Second Amendment exemplify the problems of originalism. *See* chapter 9, Daniel A. Farber, *Disarmed by Time: The Second Amendment and the Failure of Originalism;* chapter 4, Jack Rakove, *The Second Amendment: The Highest Stage of Originalism.*

9. *See, e.g.,* Keith A. Erhman & Dennis A. Hennigan, *The Second Amendment in the Twentieth Century: Have You Seen Your Militia Lately?,* 15 U. DAYTON L. REV. 5, 57–58 (1989); David C. Williams, *The Militia Movement and Second Amendment Revolution: Conjuring with the People,* 81 CORNELL L. REV. 879, 888–89 (1996).

10. *See* Daniel Abrams, *Ending the Other Arms Race: An Argument for a Ban on Assault Weapons,* 10 YALE L. & POL'Y REV. 488, 504 (1992); Erhman & Hennigan, *supra* note 9, at 57.

11. *See, e.g.,* Camps Newfound/Owatonna, Inc. v. Harrison, 520 U.S. 564, 575 (1997).

12. 92 U.S. 542 (1875).

13. 116 U.S. 252 (1886).

14. *See* Barron v. City of Baltimore 32 U.S. (7 Pet.) 243 (1833).

15. 307 U.S. 174 (1939).

16. *Id.* at 177.

17. Eugene Volokh et al., *The Second Amendment as a Teaching Tool in Constitutional Law Classes,* 48 J. LEGAL EDUC. 591, 595 (1998).

18. *See Miller,* 307 U.S. at 180–82.

19. *See* Erwin Griswold, *Phantom Second Amendment "Rights,"* WASH. POST, Nov. 4, 1990, at C-7; ROBERT J. SPITZER, THE POLITICS OF GUN CONTROL 33 (2d ed. 1998).

20. 445 U.S. 55 (1980).

21. *See* TRIBE, *supra* note 1, at 902–03.

22. *Lewis,* 445 U.S. at 65 n.8.

23. 407 U.S. 143 (1972).

24. *Id.* at 150 (Douglas, J., dissenting).

25. *See also* Burton v. Sills, 394 U.S. 812 (1969); Burton v. Sills, 248 A.2d 521, 527 (N.J. 1968). *But see* United States v. Verdugo-Urquidez, 494 U.S. 259, 265 (1990); Poe v. Ullman, 367 U.S. 497, 543 (1961) (Harlan, J., dissenting).

26. *See* Hickman v. Block, 81 F.3d 98, 101 (9th Cir. 1996); Love v. Pepersack, 47 F.3d 120, 124 (4th Cir. 1995); United States v. Hale, 978 F.2d 1016, 1020 (8th Cir. 1992). The exception is United States v. Emerson, 46 F. Supp. 2d 598 (N.D. Tex. 1999).

27. 347 U.S. 483 (1954).

28. *See id.* at 489–95.

29. *See, e.g.,* Gayle v. Browder, 352 U.S. 903 (1956) (per curiam); Holmes v. City of Atlanta, 350 U.S. 879 (1955) (per curiam); City of Baltimore v. Dawson, 350 U.S. 877 (1955) (per curiam).

30. *See* James Gray Pope, *The First Amendment, the Thirteenth Amendment, and the Right to Organize in the Twenty-first Century,* 51 RUTGERS L. REV. 941, 950–53 (1999).

31. *See, e.g.,* NLRB v. Retail Store Employees Union Local 1001, 447 U.S. 607, 616 (1980).

32. *See* Simon & Schuster, Inc. v. Members of N.Y. State Crime Victims Bd., 502 U.S. 105, 124–27 (1991) (Kennedy, J., concurring).

33. *See, e.g.,* Michael C. Dorf, *The Supreme Court 1997 Term, Foreword: The Limits of Socratic Deliberation,* 112 HARV. L. REV. 4, 60–73 (1998).

34. *See, e.g.,* U.S. Term Limits, Inc. v. Thornton, 514 U.S. 779, 821 n.31 (1995). *See generally* Milton Handler et al., *A Reconsideration of the Relevance and Materiality of the Preamble in Constitutional Interpretation,* 12 CARDOZO L. REV. 117 (1990).

35. *See* Reynolds, *supra* note 2, at 466–67; William Van Alstyne, *The Second Amendment and the Personal Right to Arms,* 43 DUKE L.J. 1236, 1242 (1994).

36. *See* Volokh, *supra* note 5, at 794–95, 814–21.

37. *See id.* at 796.

38. *See id.* at 801–07.
39. *Id.* at 799.
40. *See* MASS. CONST. pt. I, art XXI (1780); N.H. CONST. pt. I, art. XXX (1784); VT. CONST. ch. I, art. XVI (1786).
41. Volokh, *supra* note 5, at 805.
42. *See* David C. Williams, *Response: The Unitary Second Amendment,* 73 N.Y.U. L. REV. 822, 824 (1998).
43. Wayne LaPierre, *NRA Homepage* (visited Jan. 23, 2001) <http.//www.nra.org> (statement of Wayne LaPierre, Executive Vice President).
44. *See* J. M. Balkin, *Agreements with Hell and Other Objects of our Faith,* 65 FORDHAM L. REV. 1703, 1716 n.28 (1997).
45. *See* GARRY WILLS, LINCOLN AT GETTYSBURG (1992).
46. *See* David C. Williams, *Civic Republicanism and the Citizen Militia: The Terrifying Second Amendment,* 101 YALE L.J. 551, 577–78 (1991).
47. *See* BENJAMIN CONSTANT, *The Liberty of the Ancients Compared with That of the Moderns* (1819), *in* BENJAMIN CONSTANT, POLITICAL WRITINGS 297, 307 (Biancamaria Fontana ed. & trans., 1988).
48. *See* AKHIL REED AMAR, THE BILL OF RIGHTS: CREATION AND RECONSTRUCTION 51 (1998); MALCOLM, *supra* note 7, at 162; Volokh, *supra* note 5, at 802.
49. LAURENCE H. TRIBE & MICHAEL C. DORF, ON READING THE CONSTITUTION 25 (1991).
50. George Mason, *Virginia Debates on the Adoption of the Federal Constitution, in* 3 THE DEBATES IN THE SEVERAL STATE CONVENTIONS, ON THE ADOPTION OF THE FEDERAL CONSTITUTION, AS RECOMMENDED BY THE GENERAL CONVENTION AT PHILADELPHIA, *in* 1787, 367, 425 (Jonathan Elliot ed., 2d ed., Philadelphia, J.B. Lippincott Co. 1836). *See, e.g.,* Anthony J. Dennis, *Clearing the Smoke from the Right to Bear Arms and the Second Amendment,* 29 AKRON L. REV. 57, 77 n.91 (1995); Don B. Kates, Jr., *Handgun Prohibition and the Original Meaning of the Second Amendment,* 82 MICH. L. REV. 204, 216 n.51 (1983); Reynolds, *supra,* note 2, at 473.
51. *See* Mason, *supra,* note 50, at 425
52. *See id.* at 410–452
53. This equation is implicit in individual rights scholars' reliance on statements like Mason's; *see* MASON, *supra* note 50, at 425, as he was discussing the term "militia" as it appears in the original Constitution.
54. 496 U.S. 334 (1990).
55. I use the constitutional term "militia" here, as the *Perpich* Court did, to mean what the twentieth-century statutes have called the "reserve" or "unorganized" militia. *See id.* at 342. *See also* SPITZER, *supra* note 19, at 29.
56. *See* 10 U.S.C. § 311(a) (1999); 32 U.S.C. § 313(a) (1999).
57. *See Perpich,* 496 U.S. at 342 n.11 (citing the Dick Act, 32 Stat. 775 [1903]).
58. *See* Martin S. Flaherty, *History "Lite" in Modern American Constitutionalism,* 95 COLUM. L. REV. 523, 527 (1995).
59. *Id.* at 554. *Accord* G. Edward White, *Reflections on the "Republican Revival": Interdisciplinary Scholarship in the Legal Academy,* 6 YALE J.L. & HUMAN. 1 (1994).
60. MALCOLM, *supra* note 7, at 176.
61. *See id.*
62. *See* Daniel Lazare, *Your Constitution Is Killing You,* HARPER'S, Oct. 1999, at 57.
63. James E. Fleming, *Fidelity to Our Imperfect Constitution,* 65 FORDHAM L. REV. 1335, 1344 (1997).
64. Michael C. Dorf, *Integrating Normative and Descriptive Constitutional Theory: The Case of Original Meaning,* 85 GEO. L.J. 1765, 1797–98 (1997).
65. *Id.* at 1801.
66. *Id.*
67. *See id.*
68. *Id.* at 1797–98.
69. For an example of such a study, see MALCOLM, *supra* note 7. For a quite different reading of the English experience, see Michael A. Bellesiles, *Gun Laws in Early America: The Regulation of Firearms Ownership, 1607–1794,* 16 LAW & HIST. REV. 567, 571–73 (1998); chapter 7, Lois Schwoerer, *To Hold and Bear Arms: The English Perspective.*

70. *See* RICHARD H. KOHN, EAGLE AND SWORD: THE FEDERALISTS AND THE CREATION OF THE MILITARY ESTABLISHMENT IN AMERICA, 1783–1802, 3–4 (1975).

71. *Id.* at 4.

72. THE DECLARATION OF INDEPENDENCE, IN CONTEXTS OF THE CONSTITUTION 37, 38 (Neil H. Cogan, ed. 1999).

73. *See* KOHN, *supra* note 70, at 9–10; GARRY WILLS, A NECESSARY EVIL: A HISTORY OF AMERICAN DISTRUST OF GOVERNMENT 31–36 (1999).

74. *See* MALCOLM, *supra* note 7, at 151; KOHN, *supra* note 70, at 86–87.

75. U.S. CONST. art. I, § 8.

76. *See* MALCOLM, *supra* note 7, at 155–56.

77. MICHAEL KAMMEN, THE ORIGINS OF THE AMERICAN CONSTITUTION at vii, xix (Michael Kammen ed., 1986). *See also* Michael C. Dorf, *Incidental Burdens on Fundamental Rights,* 109 HARV. L. REV. 1175, 1187 nn.47–50 (1996) and sources cited therein.

78. The point was not lost on astute anti-Federalists. *See* MALCOLM, *supra* note 7, at 163 (citing *Centinel, Revived,* no. 24, INDEP. GAZETTEER [Sept. 9, 1789]).

79. *See id.* at 156.

80. *See id.* at 164.

81. THE FEDERALIST NO. 46 (James Madison). *Accord* THE FEDERALIST NO. 29 (Alexander Hamilton).

82. THE FEDERALIST NO. 46 (James Madison).

83. *See, e.g.,* David Harmer, *Securing a Free State: Why the Second Amendment Matters,* 1998 BYU L. REV. 55, 83–84; Van Alstyne, *supra* note 35, at 1245.

84. *See* MICHAEL BELLESILES, ARMING AMERICA: THE ORIGINS OF A NATIONAL GUN CULTURE (2000).

85. *See* WILLS, *supra* note 73, at 28–38.

86. *See id.* at 36–37. On the relation between fears of slave revolts and the Second Amendment, see Carl T. Bogus, *The Hidden History of the Second Amendment,* 31 U.C. DAVIS L. REV. 309 (1998) [hereinafter *Hidden History*]; Carl T. Bogus, *Race, Riots, and Guns,* 66 S. CAL. L. REV. 1365 (1993).

87. *See* James Lindgren and Justin Lee Heather, "Counting Guns in Early America" (2001) (unpublished manuscript, on file with the author).

88. Dorf, *supra* note 64, at 1809.

89. *Id.* at 1810.

90. Bogus, *Hidden History, supra* note 86, at 408.

91. AMAR, *supra* note 48, at 51.

92. *See* Garry Wills, *To Keep and Bear Arms,* N.Y. REV. BOOKS, Sept. 21, 1995, at 62, 66. In my view, Wills somewhat overstates his case; *see* Robert E. Shalhope, *To Keep and Bear Arms in the Early Republic,* 16 CONST. COMMENTARY 269, 274–81 (1999), but on this point he is basically correct.

93. The interested reader should visit the Web site <http://memory.locgov/ammem/collections/finder.html>, click on "Political Science and Law," and choose a database.

94. PENN. CONST. of 1776 *in* 8 WILLIAM FINLEY SWINDLER, SOURCES AND DOCUMENTS OF UNITED STATES CONSTITUTIONS 279 (1979).

95. *Amendments Proposed by Pennsylvania Convention Minority* (Dec. 12, 1787), *in* EDWARD DUMBAULD, THE BILL OF RIGHTS AND WHAT IT MEANS TODAY 173, 174 (1957).

96. *See* Stephen P. Halbrook, *What the Framers Intended: A Linguistic Analysis of the Right to "Bear Arms,"* LAW & CONTEMP. PROBS., Winter 1986, at 151, 153.

97. *See* Volokh, *supra* note 5, at 810–12.

98. For a fair rendition of the brief against the Republican Revival from one of its sympathizers, see Nomi Maya Stolzenberg, *A Book of Laughter and Forgetting: Kalman's "Strange Career" and the Marketing of Civic Republicanism,* 111 HARV. L. REV. 1025, 1025–38 (1998) (reviewing LAURA KALMAN, THE STRANGE CAREER OF LEGAL LIBERALISM [1996]).

99. *See* RICHARD A. PRIMUS, THE AMERICAN LANGUAGE OF RIGHTS 85, 87 (1999).

100. *See* Saul Cornell, *Commonplace or Anachronism: The Standard Model, the Second Amendment, and the Problem of History in Contemporary Constitutional Theory,* 16 CONST. COMMENTARY 221, 228–31 (1999).

101. *See* Bellesiles, *supra* note 69, at 574–76; Shalhope, *supra* note 92, at 273.

102. *But see* MALCOLM, *supra* note 7, at ix.

103. 1 WILLIAM BLACKSTONE, COMMENTARIES ON THE LAWS OF ENGLAND 139 (Star ed.). The full quotation is:

The fifth and last auxiliary right of the subject, that I shall at present mention, is that of having arms for their defense, suitable to their condition and degree, and such as are allowed by law. Which is also declared by the same statute, 1 W & M st. 2.c.2. and is indeed a public allowance, under due restrictions, of the natural right of resistance and self-preservation, when the sanctions of society and law are found insufficient to restrain the violence of oppression.

Id.

104. *See, e.g.,* JAMES WILSON, *Of the Natural Rights of Individuals, in* 2 THE WORKS OF JAMES WILSON 307, 335 (J. D. Andrews ed. 1896).

105. *See* PRIMUS, *supra* note 99, at 88. *Compare* Calder v. Bull, 3 U.S. (3 Dall.) 386, 387–88 (1798) (Chase, J.), *with id.* at 399 (Iredell, J., nominally dissenting although actually concurring in the judgment).

106. *See* Stephen P. Halbrook & David B. Kopel, *Tench Coxe and the Right to Keep and Bear Arms, 1787–1823,* 7 WM. & MARY BILL RTS. J. 347 (1999). *But see* Steven J. Heyman, *Natural Rights and the Second Amendment,* chapter 6.

107. *See* WILLS, *supra,* note 73, at 29–31.

108. *See* Ollman v. Evans, 750 F.2d 970, 995 (D.C. Cir. 1984) (en banc) (Bork, J., concurring) ("[I]t is the task of the judge in this generation to discern how the framers' values, defined in the context of the world they knew, apply to the world we know").

109. *See* Michael J. Klarman, *Antifidelity,* 70 S. CAL. L. REV. 381, 402–03 (1997).

110. *Compare* Red Lion Broad. Co. v. FCC, 395 U.S. 367 (1969) *and* National Broad. Co. v. United States, 319 U.S. 190, 216 (1943), *with* Miami Herald Publ'g Co. v. Tornillo, 418 U.S. 241 (1974).

111. Barry Friedman & Scott B. Smith, *The Sedimentary Constitution,* 147 U. PA. L. REV. 1, 5–6 (1998). *See also* Larry Kramer, *Fidelity to History—And Through It,* 65 FORDHAM L. REV. 1627, 1636 (1997).

112. Friedman & Smith, *supra* note 111, at 8.

113. *See* KOHN, *supra* note 70, at 74–75.

114. *See id.* at 157–70.

115. *See* Larry Kramer, *Understanding Federalism,* 47 VAND. L. REV. 1485, 1519 (1994).

116. Akhil Reed Amar, *Some New World Lessons for the Old World,* 58 U. CHI. L. REV. 483, 501 (1991); *accord* Akhil Reed Amar, *Of Sovereignty and Federalism,* 96 YALE L.J. 1425, 1499–1500 (1987).

117. Jo Thomas, *Trial Begins in the Oklahoma City Bombing Case,* N.Y. TIMES, Apr. 25, 1997, at A1.

118. *Id.*

119. *See* Jonathan Schell, *The Unfinished Twentieth Century: What We Have Forgotten About Nuclear Weapons,* HARPER'S, Jan. 2000, at 41.

120. *See* Yates v. United States, 354 U.S. 298 (1957).

121. *Id.* at 318. Although nominally an interpretation of the Smith Act, *Yates* has come to be understood as a constitutional decision. *See* LAURENCE H. TRIBE, AMERICAN CONSTITUTIONAL LAW 847 (2d ed. 1988).

122. John Hart Ely, *Flag Desecration: A Case Study in the Roles of Categorization and Balancing in First Amendment Analysis,* 88 HARV. L. REV. 1482, 1495–96 (1975).

123. *Cf.* AMAR, *supra* note 48, at 49–50.

124. Bellesiles, *supra* note 69, at 581.

125. *See* LAWRENCE M. FRIEDMAN, CRIME AND PUNISHMENT IN AMERICAN HISTORY 67–68 (1993).

126. *See* Carol S. Steiker, *Second Thoughts About First Principles,* 107 HARV. L. REV. 820, 832 (1994) (citing FRIEDMAN, *supra* note 125, at 29, 68, 174, and Pauline Maier, *Popular Uprisings and Civil Authority in Eighteenth-century America,* 27 WM. & MARY Q. 3, 19 [3d ser. 1970]).

127. *See* Bellesiles, *supra* note 69, at 573–74.

128. Andrew Delbanco, *Sunday in the Park with Fred,* N.Y. REV. BOOKS, Jan. 20, 2000, at 55 (reviewing WITOLD RYBCZYNSKI, A CLEARING IN THE DISTANCE: FREDERICK LAW OLMSTED AND AMERICA IN THE NINETEENTH CENTURY [1999]) (citing diary of George Templeton Strong).

129. *See* 2 JOSEPH STORY, COMMENTARIES ON THE CONSTITUTION OF THE UNITED STATES 646 (1833).

130. *See* AMAR, *supra* note 48, at 259.

131. *See id.* at 258–66; *see also* Robert J. Cottrol & Raymond T. Diamond, *The Second Amendment: Toward an Afro-Americanist Reconsideration,* 80 GEO. L.J. 309, 333–49 (1991).

132. AMAR, *supra* note 48, at 221.

133. *See* Akhil Reed Amar, *Second Thoughts: What the Right to Bear Arms Really Means,* NEW REPUBLIC, July 12, 1999, at 24.

134. TRIBE, *supra* note 1, at 902 n.221. *See also* Powe, *supra* note 7, at 1375.

135. AMAR, *supra* note 48, at 243 (discussing the First Amendment).
136. TRIBE, *supra* note 1, at 902 n.221.
137. 347 U.S. 497 (1954).
138. 347 U.S. 483 (1954).
139. *Id.* at 489, 492 ("[W]e cannot turn the clock back to 1868").
140. *Bolling*, 347 U.S. at 500.
141. *See* Akhil Reed Amar, *Intratextualism*, 112 HARV. L. REV. 747, 766–73 (1999); Laurence H. Tribe, *Taking Text and Structure Seriously: Reflections on Free-Form Method in Constitutional Interpretation*, 108 HARV. L. REV. 1221, 1297 n.247 (1995).
142. For an excellent summary, see Herbert Hovenkamp, *The Cultural Crises of the Fuller Court*, 104 YALE L.J. 2309, 2337–43 (1995) (reviewing OWEN M. FISS, TROUBLED BEGINNINGS OF THE MODERN STATE, 1888–1910 [1993]). For a revisionist account, see Michael W. McConnell, *Originalism and the Desegregation Decisions*, 81 VA. L. REV. 947 (1995). For a response, see Michael J. Klarman, *Brown, Originalism, and Constitutional Theory: A Response to Professor McConnell*, 81 VA. L. REV. 1881 (1995).
143. *See* RONALD DWORKIN, FREEDOM'S LAW, THE MORAL READING OF THE AMERICAN CONSTITUTION 271 (1996).
144. TRIBE & DORF, *supra* note 49, at 11.
145. *Id.* at 13.
146. *See* Amar, *supra* note 141, at 754–55.
147. *See* AMAR, *supra* note 48, at 243.
148. *See id.* at 293.
149. TRIBE & DORF, *supra* note 49, at 11.
150. THE DECLARATION OF INDEPENDENCE, *supra* note 72, at 37.
151. For a response to similar, and similarly exaggerated, claims about the power of armed individuals to resist foreign invaders in the context of the experience of the United States in Vietnam, *see* WILLS, *supra* note 73, at 25–26.
152. *See* SWITZ. CONST. art. 7–36 (French version 1999) (visited Jan. 12, 2000) <www.admin.ch/ch/f/rs/101/index.html> (setting forth other fundamental rights).
153. The Violence Policy Center's Web site provides statistics of this sort. <http://www.vpc.org/fact_sht/hgbanfs.htm> (visited Jan. 25, 2000).
154. *See* GARY KLECK, POINT BLANK: GUNS AND VIOLENCE IN AMERICA 304 (1991).
155. *See id.* at 203; JOHN R. LOTT, MORE GUNS, LESS CRIME: UNDERSTANDING CRIME AND GUN-CONTROL LAWS 19 (1998).
156. *See, e.g.*, Otis Dudley Duncan, *Gun Use Surveys: In Numbers We Trust?*, CRIMINOLOGIST Jan./Feb. 2000, at 1, 5.
157. *See* JOHN HART ELY, DEMOCRACY AND DISTRUST: A THEORY OF JUDICIAL REVIEW 21 (1980); United States v. Carolene Products Co., 304 U.S. 144, 153, n.4 (1938); City of Cleburne v. Cleburne Living Center, Inc., 473 U.S. 432, 442 n.10 (1985).
158. *See, e.g.*, Powe, *supra* note 7, at 1392.
159. *See supra* note 100.
160. *See, e.g.*, Martin Killias, *International Correlations Between Gun Ownership and Rates of Homicide and Suicide, reprinted in* 148 CAN. MED. ASSOC. J. 1721 (1993); Catherine F. Sproule & Deborah J. Kennet, *Killing with Guns in the USA and Canada 1977–1983: Further Evidence for the Effectiveness of Gun Control*, 31 CAN. J. CRIM. 245, 249 (1989). *But cf.* Robert J. Mundt, *Gun Control and Rates of Firearms Violence in Canada and the United States*, 32 CAN. J. CRIM. 137, 139 (1990).
161. *See* RONALD DWORKIN, TAKING RIGHTS SERIOUSLY 193.
162. SHELLEY E. TAYLOR, POSITIVE ILLUSIONS: CREATIVE SELF-DECEPTION AND THE HEALTHY MIND 10–11 (1990). *See also* Neil D. Weinstein, *Optimistic Biases About Personal Risks*, 246 CI. 1232 (1989).
163. Halbrook & Kopel, *supra* note 106, at 351.
164. *See* SPITZER, *supra* note 19, at 27.
165. 245 U.S. 366 (1918).
166. *Id.* at 383.
167. *See* United States v. Lopez, 514 U.S. 549, 560 (1995).
168. U.S. CONST. art. I, § 8, cl. 4.
169. U.S. CONST. art. I, § 8, cl. 5.

170. U.S. CONST. art. I, § 8, cl. 6.
171. *See* U.S. CONST. art. I, § 8, cl. 8.
172. 514 U.S. 549 (1995).
173. *See id.* at 587 (Thomas, J., concurring).
174. U.S. CONST. art. I, § 8, cl. 11.
175. *See* BLACK'S LAW DICTIONARY 814 (5th ed. 1979).
176. *See* Employment Div., Dep't. of Human Resources v. Smith, 494 U.S. 872 (1990).
177. For a theory of the Free Exercise Clause that may give it some independent bite notwithstanding *Smith*, *see* Christopher L. Eisgruber & Lawrence G. Sager, *Why the Religious Freedom Restoration Act Is Unconstitutional*, 69 N.Y.U. L. REV. 437 (1994); Christopher L. Eisgruber & Lawrence G. Sager, *The Vulnerability of Conscience: The Constitutional Basis for Protecting Religious Conduct*, 61 U. CHI. L. REV. 1245 (1994).
178. Christopher Eisgruber describes this view as the "aesthetic fallacy." *See* Christopher L. Eisgruber, *The Living Hand of the Past: History and Constitutional Justice*, 65 FORDHAM L. REV. 1611, 1617 (1997).
179. The argument is borrowed, of course, from *McCulloch v. Maryland*, 17 U.S. 316 (1819).
180. *See generally* Debra Livingston, *Police Discretion and the Quality of Life in Public Places: Courts, Communities, and the New Policing*, 97 COLUM. L. REV. 551 (1997).
181. *Cf.* Nelson Lund, *The Second Amendment, Political Liberty, and the Right to Self-Preservation*, 39 ALA. L. REV. 103, 123 (1987).
182. *See* WILLS, *supra* note 73, at 30–31.
183. The ratio of handguns to total guns was reported in 1991. *See How Many Guns?*, ATF NEWS RELEASE FY-91-36. The homicide numbers have been consistent from 1990 through 1998 (the most recent year available), except that in 1990 handguns accounted for slightly less than half of all homicides. *See* Bureau of Justice Statistics, Homicide Trends in the United States (visited Jan. 24, 2001) <http://www.ojp.usdoj.gov/bjs/homicide/weapons.txt>.
184. *See* Amar, *supra* note 133, at 26–27; Balkin, *supra* note 44, at 1718–19; Carl Riehl, *Uncle Sam Has to Want You: The Right of Gay Men and Lesbians (and all Other Americans) to Bear Arms in the Military*, 26 RUTGERS L. J. 343 (1995).
185. AMAR, *supra* note 48, at 48.
186. Plessy v. Ferguson, 163 U.S. 537, 559 (1896) (Harlan, J., dissenting).
187. *See* Romer v. Evans, 517 U.S. 620, 623 (1996) (quoting *Plessy*, 163 U.S. at 559 [Harlan, J., dissenting]).
188. TRIBE, *supra*, note 1, at 902.
189. *See id.* at 903.
190. *See* Laurence H. Tribe & Akhil Reed Amar, *Well-Regulated Militias, and More*, N.Y. TIMES, Oct. 28, 1999, at A31.
191. ALEXANDER BICKEL, THE LEAST DANGEROUS BRANCH: THE SUPREME COURT AT THE BAR OF POLITICS 16 (1962).
192. *See* Griswold v. Connecticut, 381 U.S. 479 (1965).
193. *See* Planned Parenthood v. Casey, 505 U.S. 833 (1992); Roe v. Wade, 410 U.S. 113 (1973).
194. *See* Moore v. East Cleveland, 431 U.S. 494 (1977).
195. 381 U.S. at 484 (1965).
196. *See* DWORKIN, *supra* note 143, at 79–80.

Index